D0458471

with contributions by

THOMAS A. ANDERSON
KARL E. BERGMANN
L. J. FILER, Jr.
CHARLES D. MAY
GUNNAR W. MEEUWISSE
ALEJANDRO M. O'DONNELL
STEPHEN H. Y. WEI
M. K. YOUNOSZAI
EKHARD E. ZIEGLER

SAMUEL J. FOMON, M.D.

Professor of Pediatrics,
College of Medicine,
The University of Iowa,
Iowa City

INFANT NUTRITION

Second Edition

W. B. SAUNDERS COMPANY Philadelphia • London • Toronto

W. B. Saunders Company: West Washington Square
Philadelphia, Pa. 19105

12 Dyott Street
London, WC1A 1DB

833 Oxford Street
Toronto, Ontario M8Z 5T9, Canada

Infant Nutrition ISBN 0-7216-3809-0

Last digit is the print number: 9 8 7 6 5 4 3

To

Betty
Betsy
Rick
Kathy
David
Christopher
Mary
and
*Jennifer**

*Whose picture is on page 37.

CONTRIBUTORS

THOMAS A. ANDERSON, Ph.D., Associate Professor of Pediatrics, College of Medicine, The University of Iowa, Iowa City, Iowa

KARL E. BERGMANN, M.D., J. W. Goethe-Universität, Zentrum der Kinderheilkunde, Allgemeine Pädiatrie I, Entwicklungsphysiologie, Frankfurt/Main, West Germany

L. J. FILER, JR., M.D., Ph.D., Professor of Pediatrics, College of Medicine, The University of Iowa, Iowa City, Iowa

CHARLES D. MAY, M.D., Senior Physician, Department of Pediatric Allergy, National Jewish Hospital and Research Center, Denver, Colorado; and Professor of Pediatrics, University of Colorado, School of Medicine, Denver, Colorado

GUNNAR W. MEEUWISSE, M.D., Assistent Professor, Pediatriska Kliniken, Lunds Universitet, Lund, Sweden

ALEJANDRO M. O'DONNELL, M.D., Unidad Metabólica, Departamento de Pediatría, Hospital Ramón Sarda, Universidad Nacional de Buenos Aires, Buenos Aires, Argentina

STEPHEN H. Y. WEI, B.D.S. (Hons.), M.D.S., M.S., D.D.S., Associate Professor of Pedodontics, College of Dentistry, The University of Iowa, Iowa City, Iowa

M. K. YOUNOSZAI, M.D., Assistant Professor of Pediatrics, College of Medicine, The University of Iowa, Iowa City, Iowa

EKHARD E. ZIEGLER, M.D., Assistant Professor of Pediatrics, College of Medicine, The University of Iowa, Iowa City, Iowa

PREFACE
to the Second Edition

The first edition of this book concerned nutrition and growth of the infant, especially the normal infant, during the first year of life. By some stretching of the word "infant," I have retained the same title for the present edition although now the first 36 rather than the first 12 months of life have been considered. The male reference infant has grown up to be the reference boy.

The difficulty in writing the second edition may have been even greater than in writing the first—although it is easy to forget. The problem with the second edition was twofold: first, I was anxious to include considerably more discussion of clinical problems and, second, I wanted to incorporate much new information from our unit and from other research groups that are concerned with growth, nutrition and feeding of infants and young children. The reader may be especially interested in the discussions of nutritional problems of sick infants and children, but the assembling and interpreting of information on normal growth and nutrition were the harder tasks.

All chapters from the first edition have been rewritten. Mainly through the competence of the contributors, it has been possible to develop in some detail the sections on gastrointestinal development, water and renal solute load, nutritional aspects of dental caries, "beikost," food allergy, diarrhea, congenital heart disease and the low-birth-weight infant. A chapter on evaluation of nutritional status has been included. Three new appendices have been added to provide information on food intake, on the relation between calorie intake and gain in weight, and on nitrogen balance of normal infants.

Since the time of publication of the first edition, the staff of the Pediatric Metabolic Unit of the University of Iowa, with the support of the Bureau of Community Health Services (previously Maternal and Child Health Service, HSMHA), Department of Health, Education and Welfare, has offered a series of intensive courses in pediatric nutrition, each three days or five days in duration. Physicians, nutritionists, dietitians and public health workers attending these courses have contributed many new ideas and have asked hard and important questions. Their contribution to the second edition is considerable.

The authors and coauthors of Chapters 4, 8–11, 13–17 and 19 have been superb in providing relevant material and in persevering good-naturedly through multiple revisions while we attempted to integrate the facts and thoughts of the various chapters, especially as these apply to growth and nutrition of normal subjects. In addition to their contributions to chapters of which they are coauthors, Drs. Filer, Anderson, Ziegler, O'Donnell and Karl Bergmann offered advice and suggestions throughout the book. Dr. Renate Bergmann read the earliest drafts of most chapters, identified additional areas that needed to be covered and was particularly helpful in preparation of Chapter 3. Drs. Ronald J. Carlotti and John S. Small assisted in preparation of Chapters 7 and 14, respectively. Dr. Gilbert B. Forbes provided current information about radionuclides in foods (Chapter 15).

As pointed out in the first edition, it is not possible to separate completely the material of this book from the research effort of the Infant Metabolic Unit, Department of Pediatrics, University of Iowa. The extraordinary capabilities of Mrs. Lora N. Thomas and her nursing staff in the Infant Metabolic Unit have made possible a continuing series of studies of normal infants. Mr. Robert L. Jensen's supervision of the pediatric metabolic laboratory has assured a high degree of quality control in the face of an immense volume of work and considerable diversity of methodology. Mr. Ronald R. Rogers has utilized considerable ingenuity in problem-solving in many areas and has provided general administrative guidance. Mr. Steven E. Nelson has handled capably the biostatistical and computer aspects of the research program and has shared in verification of the tabular and graphic data in the text.

The long, tortuous route from initial rough drafts to final manuscript copy was made possible by the hundreds of complicated jobs carried out by two outstanding secretaries — Ms. Barbara Hudgins and Ms. Jean Drulis. Mr. Robert B. Rowan of the W. B. Saunders Company offered advice, which was sometimes taken, and Ms. Daphne Moo-Young edited the manuscript with competence and dispatch.

SAMUEL J. FOMON, M.D.

CONTENTS

1

RECENT HISTORY AND CURRENT TRENDS

In the early part of the nineteenth century, few infants survived unless they were breastfed. In London at that time, for example, it is estimated that among infants who were not breastfed, seven of eight died (Forsyth, 1911). Because of this high infant mortality, the employment of a wet nurse was relatively common when a mother was unable to breastfeed her infant. Elaborate rules were formulated for selection of a wet nurse (Hamilton, 1793; Underwood, 1818; Dewees, 1825; Eberle, 1845); many of these were reasonable, such as freedom from tuberculosis and other chronic disease, but others were complex and seemingly irrational.

It is clear that only the wealthy would be able to observe the many rules. Even among the wealthy, there was often some reluctance to employ a wet nurse because of widespread belief that the milk of the nurse transmitted the character of the woman. This belief appears to have been perpetuated from antiquity, as delightfully reviewed with a number of examples by Burton in 1651 (Dell and Jordan-Smith, 1927):

> *From a child's nativity, the first ill accident that can likely befall him in this kind (i.e., development of melancholy) is a bad nurse, by whose means alone he may be tainted by this malady from the cradle . . . if a nurse be misshapen, unchaste, unhonest, imprudent, drunk, cruel or the like, the child that sucks upon her breast will so be too. . . . Cato for some such reason would make his servants' children suck upon his wife's breast, because by that means they would love him and his the better . . .*

If a wet nurse must be employed, Burton advises parents

> *. . . that they make choice of a sound woman of good complexion, honest, free from bodily diseases, if it be possible, and all passions and perturbations of the mind, as sorrow, fear, grief, folly, melancholy. For such passions corrupt the milk, and alter the temperature of the child, which now being moist and pliable clay, is easily seasoned and perverted.*

In the southern colonies of the United States, the idea that the characteristics of the nurse were transmitted through the milk to the child was probably strengthened by observations that white children not infrequently displayed some of the accents and mannerisms of their Negro nurses (Spruill, 1938).

Nursing from the udders of goats, cows and asses was attempted but was only rarely successful, presumably because of the practical difficulties as well as the unfavorable curd tension of unaltered fresh milk from these animals.

Although other modes of feeding were attempted, breast feeding was by far the most common until well into the twentieth century. In relation to current custom, weaning was late. A survey of more than 22,000 infants in cities in the United States between 1911 and 1916 demonstrated that 58 per cent were still breastfed at the age of one year (Woodbury, 1925). It may be noted that, in preliterate cultures, weaning from the breast was commonly carried out at two to three years of age (Ford, 1945).

Wide-scale success with bottle feeding became possible through application of newer knowledge in three separate areas: (1) development of safer water supplies and of sanitary standards for handling and storage of milk; (2) development of easily cleansed and sterilized bottles and nipples; and (3) alteration of curd tension of milk. Major advances in each of these areas occurred late in the nineteenth century and during the first two decades of the twentieth century (Fig. 1–1). In addition, increasing awareness of the need for vitamin supplementation of bottle-fed infants during the early part of the twentieth century contributed to success of formula feeding.

Safety of Water and Milk

Chlorination of water was introduced in the United States in the 1880s and, at about the same time, major improvements were made in disposal of garbage (Furnas, 1969). Toward the end of the nineteenth century, advances in general sanitation were stimulated by identification of the colon-bacillus and related organisms and by the demonstration that bloody diarrhea in infants was often caused by organisms

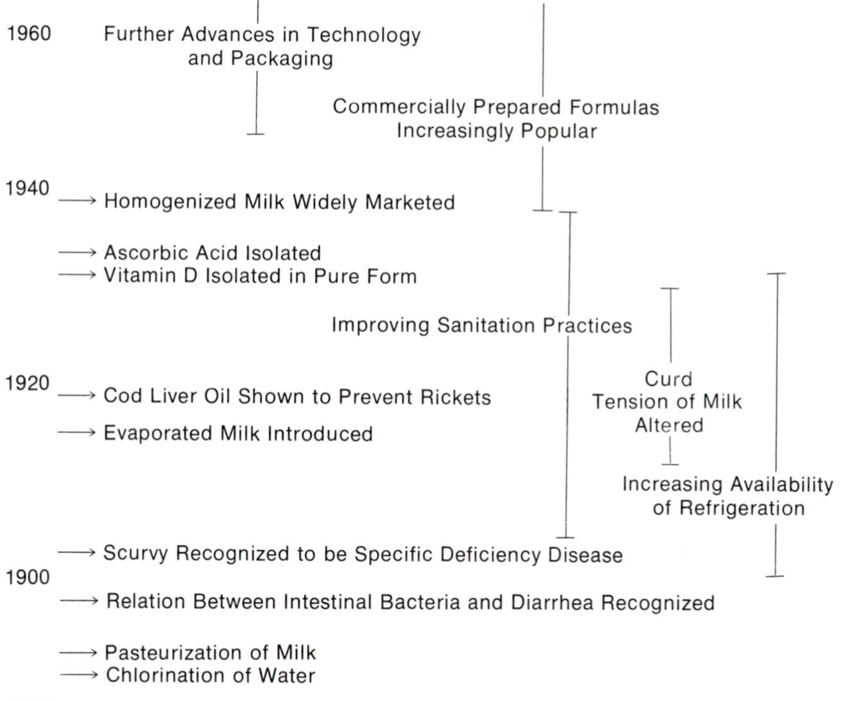

Figure 1–1 Some advances and trends in infant feeding from the late 1800s to the present.

of the dysentery group. Controlled heating of a liquid to eliminate pathogenic bacteria was introduced in Germany in 1882 and in the United States in 1891, although widespread use of pasteurization* was not practiced until considerably later. In any case, purchase of milk on a daily basis was usually not feasible and, therefore, with or without pasteurization, bacterial contamination of milk was a common problem (Davison, 1935). Not until the kitchen icebox became commonplace during the early part of the twentieth century did storage of milk become feasible.

Acidification of milk – one method of reducing the extent of bacterial growth – became popular about 1920 and was believed to exert its beneficial action through reduction of the buffering capacity of cow milk. The high buffering capacity of unacidified cow milk had long been blamed for promotion of bacterial growth, diminution in flow of pancreatic juice and bile and inhibition of gastric digestion (Marriott, 1927). However, the important benefits were probably decreased bacterial growth and reduction in curd tension.

In 1856, Borden was granted a patent for condensing milk with heat but without any additions (Frantz, 1951). However, sugar was

*Now defined as heating to 61°C for 30 minutes.

soon added because it increased keeping properties and prevented bacterial growth. This milk, generally similar to present-day condensed milk, was widely used for infant feeding. It was found to be unsatisfactory, and we may presume that a major reason was the high carbohydrate content, although in some instances high caloric density may have been responsible for inadequate water intake (Chapter 10). The sanitary open-top can allowing clean filling was introduced in the early 1900s, and it was then feasible to market evaporated milk in cans. However, evaporated milk was not widely used in infant feeding until the 1920s.

Feeding Devices

Until the end of the eighteenth century, feeding devices generally consisted of spouted pots made of pottery, pewter or silver. These were difficult to clean and probably were a cumbersome method of transmitting milk to the infant. The advent of glass bottles about 1800 undoubtedly was responsible for more thorough cleaning between feedings.

A tanned heifer's teat was not uncommonly used as a nipple (Dewees, 1825; Judson and Gittings, 1902), a small sponge being placed inside to retard the flow of milk. Other nipples were fashioned of cork, wood or decalcified ivory. A primitive horn fitted with a buckskin nipple was used as late as 1846 in California (Harris, 1932). In 1864 a patent was obtained for a rubber nipple placed at the end of a flexible feeding tube attached to the bottle. Such a feeding tube was a feature of every succeeding patent until 1886 (Drake, 1948). Rubber nipples that could be attached directly to narrow-mouthed glass bottles were in widespread use by the beginning of the twentieth century, and certainly permitted more satisfactory cleaning of bottles and nipples than did previous devices.

Curd Tension

When milk is coagulated, as occurs when it comes in contact with the hydrochloric acid of the stomach, the precipitate (curd) contains most of the casein and calcium of the milk, while the watery portion contains whey proteins and most of the lactose. When fresh, unprocessed cow milk is coagulated, the curd is tough and rubbery and can be demonstrated by standard testing procedures to have high resistance to stirring (i.e., high curd tension). Fresh human milk, on the other hand, contains a relatively small amount of casein and forms a soft, flocculent curd. Processing of cow milk—acidification, dilution, boiling, modification of mineral composition, treatment with enzymes, homogenization—results in a decrease in curd tension, with the result that it is more easily digested by the small infant.

Although a method for homogenization of milk was demonstrated at the World's Fair in Paris in 1900, practical application of the method on a wide scale was not feasible until about 1921, when adequate means were found for sterilizing the equipment (Trout, 1950). Widespread marketing of homogenized milk began about 1940.

The impact on infant feeding of the introduction of evaporated milk in the late 1920s can be appreciated from published comments of some of the leading pediatricians of the time. Marriott and Schoenthal (1929) observed that

> *. . . evaporated milk mixtures were uniformly well digested. . . . There were no cases in which it was found necessary to substitute some other form of milk for the evaporated milk because of untoward symptoms or failure to do well. The results of evaporated milk feedings of newly born infants appear to us to indicate that this form of milk is readily digestible and well utilized by very young infants.*

Brennemann (1929) described his observations as

> *. . . the most startling I have ever encountered in more than twenty-five years of hospital experience in feeding ward babies. The interns had often asked me to show them a normal stool such as I had told them all babies had in private practice and I had had great difficulty in meeting their request. At one swoop I was able to show them normal, yellow, smooth, well formed or thick pasty stools with a perfect putrefactive bouquet in practically every one of these babies.*

The low incidence of gastrointestinal disturbances was commented upon by many observers.

Vitamin Deficiencies

Only two vitamin deficiency diseases are likely to have contributed significantly to lack of success in early attempts at bottle feeding. These are scurvy and rickets.

Scurvy

Although as early as 1734 Bachstrom stated that "... this evil (i.e., scurvy) is solely owing to a total abstinence from fresh vegetable food, and greens; which is alone the true primary cause of the disease" (Stewart and Guthrie, 1953), it was not until 1906 that Hopkins postulated that infantile scurvy was a deficiency disease due to lack of some essential food substance, the exact nature of which was not known. Ascorbic acid was isolated in 1928 by Szent-Györgyi but was not identified as ascorbic acid until 1930. Its structural formula was established in 1933 by Herbert et al.

Lack of understanding of the nature and prevention of scurvy was undoubtedly a major factor in retarding the development of adequate bottle feeding. As late as the second decade of the twentieth century, the American Pediatric Society pointed out that the great majority of 379 cases of scurvy occurred in infants fed sterilized, condensed or pasteurized milk (Friedenwald and Ruhrah, 1915). Reluctance to subject milk to heat treatment because of fear of promoting development of scurvy led to delay in controlling bacterial contamination and in reduction of curd tension.

Rickets

In a series of reports published between 1908 and 1912, the Russian pediatrician, Schabad, demonstrated that cod liver oil was effective in curing and preventing rickets (Holt, 1963). Mellanby (1920) demonstrated that the active substance was a fat-soluble vitamin. Vitamin D was isolated in pure form in 1931.

Although deficiencies of vitamins other than C and D were probably not of major significance in the lack of success of bottle feeding before the twentieth century, the discovery of vitamins and description of their role exerted a major influence on the history of modern infant nutrition. Before the importance of various vitamins was recognized, attention was centered on the harmfulness of having too much of certain foods. In the 1920s, the emphasis shifted to the harmfulness of having too little. Today, the philosophy of avoiding nutritional deficiency is so firmly established that it undoubtedly contributes to our national problem of overnutrition and, once again, it seems necessary to emphasize the possibility that one may ingest too much as well as too little.

Relevance to Developing Countries

The present high mortality and morbidity among nonbreastfed infants in many developing countries result from some of the same conditions which were present in the United States and Western Europe at the end of the nineteenth and beginning of the twentieth centuries. Successful feeding requires the availability of a nutritionally sound food of high digestibility, a water supply free of pathogenic microorganisms, an adequate feeding device (e.g., bottle and nipple), and education regarding formula preparation and feeding. Facilities to permit sterilization of bottles and cool storage are definite assets but are not as critical as the other requirements. Minimal conditions for satisfactory formula preparation are discussed in Chapter 19.

When the requirements for successful bottle feeding cannot be met, all efforts should be directed toward promotion of breast feeding. No amount of education regarding formula preparation will be of much value if a nutritionally sound food and safe water are not available.

TRENDS IN FEEDING BY BREAST AND BOTTLE

Breast Feeding

With the increasing safety and convenience of formula feeding during the past 30 years and the failure of various investigators to provide evidence of definite superiority of breast feeding over formula feeding, most physicians have been unenthusiastic in promotion of breast feeding. Decision to feed by breast or bottle has been left largely to the mother. Information regarding trends in breast feeding in the United States is available from several sources (Bain, 1948; Jackson et al., 1956; Meyer, 1958b, 1968; Salber et al., 1958; Robertson, 1961; Salber and Feinleib, 1966; Rivera, 1971; Fomon and Anderson, 1972; Martinez, 1973).

In the 1940s, approximately 65 per cent of infants in the United States were breastfed during the newborn period (Bain, 1948). By 1958, only 25 per cent of seven-day-old infants were breastfed, and this percentage has remained about the same since that time (Fig. 1–2). Although the number of infants breastfed at age seven days is less than the number breastfed at the time of discharge from the hospital after birth, data at the time of hospital discharge are difficult to interpret because of differences in length of hospital stay. In the 1950s most newborn infants remained in the hospital for five to seven days, whereas it is now customary to discharge infants at two or three days of age.

The data of Martinez (1973) indicate that, by age two months, only 10 or 15 per cent of infants are breastfed (Fig. 1–3) and, by age six months (Fig. 1–4), only about 5 per cent of infants are breastfed. Salber and Feinleib (1966) also reported that only about 5 per cent of infants were breastfed at age six months.

Social class appears to be an important variable influencing breast feeding in the United States and probably in other developed countries. From 1930 until at least the middle of the 1940s in the United States, breast feeding was most common among the lower social

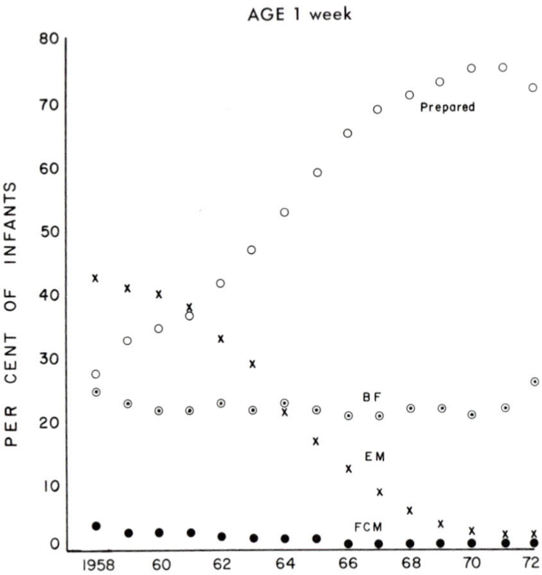

Figure 1–2 Per cent of one-week-old infants in the United States between 1958 and 1972 who were breastfed (BF), fed evaporated milk formulas (EM), commercially prepared formulas (Prepared) or fresh cow milk (FCM). (Data of Martinez, G. A., Ross Laboratories, Columbus, Ohio, 1973.)

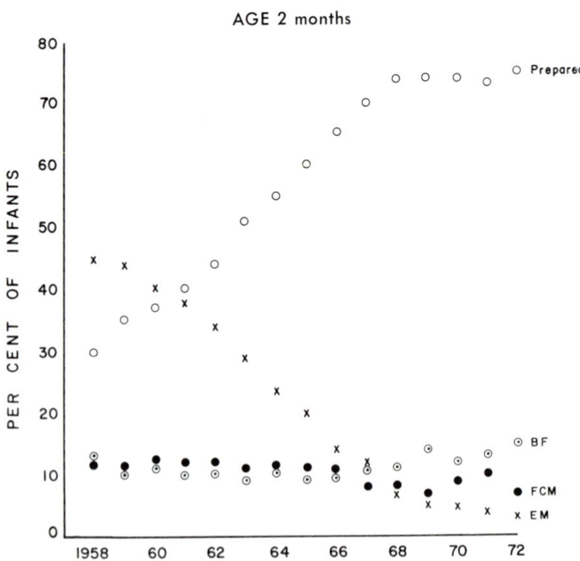

Figure 1–3 Per cent of two-month-old infants in the United States between 1958 and 1972 who were breastfed or received other milks or formulas. Feedings are as in Figure 1–2. (Data of Martinez, G. A., Ross Laboratories, Columbus, Ohio, 1973.)

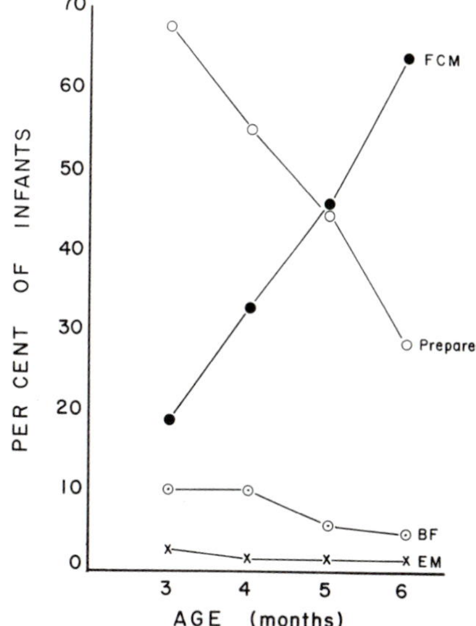

Figure 1–4 Per cent of infants in the United States in 1972 who received various feedings between three and six months of age. Feedings are as in Figure 1–2. (Data of Martinez, G. A., Ross Laboratories, Columbus, Ohio, 1973.)

classes. Since the early 1960s, various studies have suggested that breast feeding is less common among the lower than among the upper social classes in the United States (Salber and Feinleib, 1966; Rivera, 1971; Fomon and Anderson, 1972), in Sweden (Klackenberg and Klackenberg-Larsson, 1968) and in the United Kingdom (Newson and Newson, 1962; Bernal and Richards, 1970). The data of Rivera (1971) concerning infants from low income families in New York City illustrate the infrequency of breast feeding among this group (Fig. 1–5).

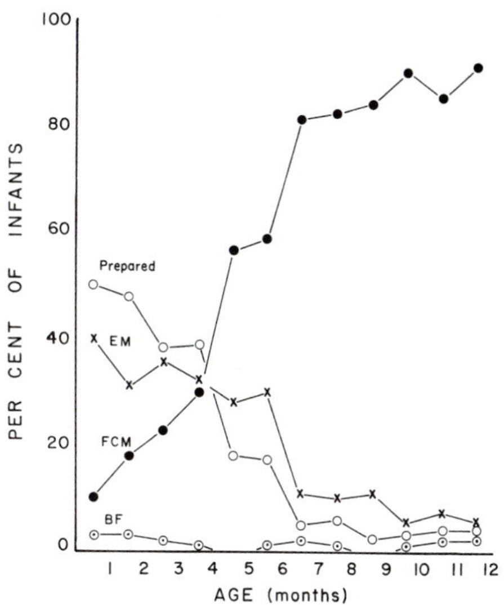

Figure 1–5 Per cent of infants from a low income section of New York City in 1970 who received various feedings during the first year. Feedings are as in Figure 1–2. (Redrawn from Rivera, J.: The frequency of use of various kinds of milk during infancy in middle and lower-income families. Amer. J. Public Health *61*: 277, 1971.)

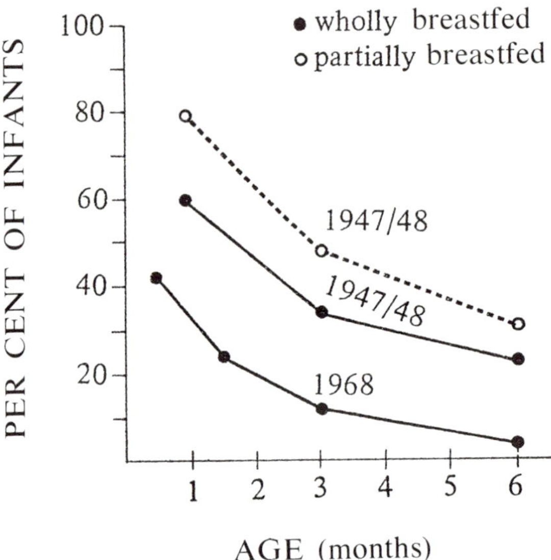

Figure 1–6 Per cent of infants wholly or partially breastfed in United Kingdom in 1947–48 and 1968. (From Vahlquist, B.: Amningssituationen i i- och u-land. Tid för omvärdering. Semper Nutritions Symposium. Naringsforskning *17* (Suppl. 8): 117, 1973.)

Population groups most likely to breastfeed their infants at present are college students (Salber and Feinleib, 1966), physicians (Harris and Chan, 1969) and health food enthusiasts.

The percentage of infants who are breastfed in other countries has also decreased progressively. Figure 1–6 indicates the percentage of wholly breastfed infants in the United Kingdom in 1947/48 and in 1968, and Figure 1–7 indicates the percentage of wholly breastfed infants in Poland in 1937/38, 1959/61 and 1971 (Vahlquist, 1973). There was remarkably little change in the percentage of infants breastfed in Poland between 1959/61 and 1971. The official statistics for breast feeding in Sweden between 1944 and 1970 are presented in Figure 1–8 (Sjölin and Hofvander, 1973). Helsing (1973) has reported a great decrease in percentage of infants breastfed in Norway between 1962 and 1972. In 1962, 66 per cent of two-month-old infants and 44 per cent of four-month-old infants were breastfed. By 1972, only 25 per cent of two-month-old and only 15 per cent of four-month-old infants were breastfed.

Sjölin and Hofvander (1973) studied a random sample of 298 infants, representing 20 per cent of all infants born in Uppsala, Sweden in 1971. As may be seen from Figure 1–9, the great majority of infants were at least partially breastfed during the early weeks of life. At one month of age, more than 50 per cent of infants were partially breastfed and more than 30 per cent totally breastfed. By four months of age,

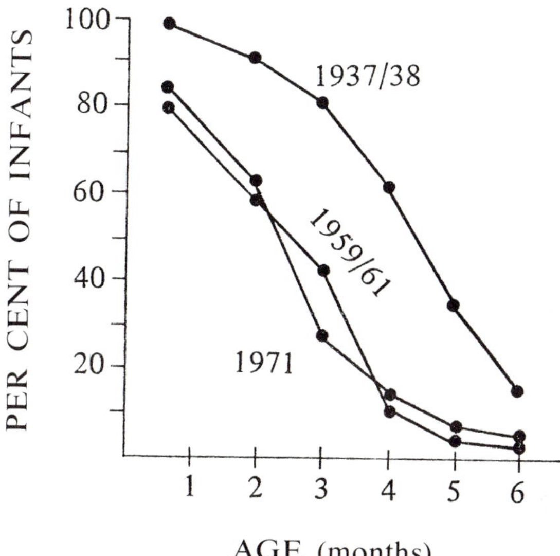

Figure 1–7 Per cent of infants totally breastfed in Poland in 1937–38, 1959–61 and 1971. (From Vahlquist, B.: Amningssituationen i i- och u-land. Tid för omvärdering. Semper Nutritions Symposium. Naringsforskning *17* (Suppl. 8): 117, 1973.)

less than 20 per cent of infants were partially breastfed and less than 10 per cent were totally breastfed.

The percentage of infants wholly or partially breastfed for at least three months in various countries has been summarized by Vahlquist (1973). Belgium and England are generally similar to the United

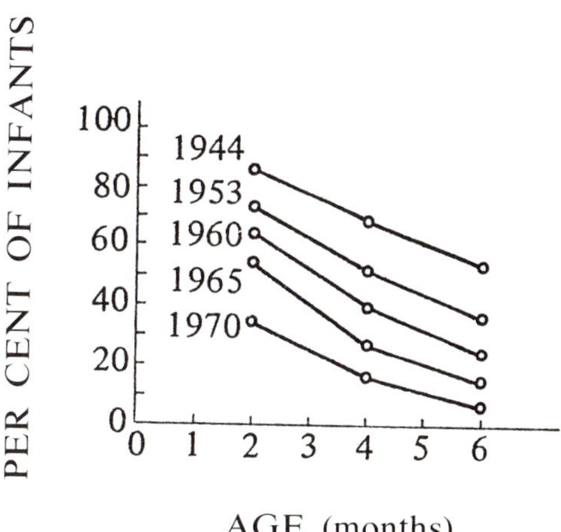

Figure 1–8 Per cent of totally breastfed infants in Sweden from 1944 to 1970 (official statistics). (From Sjölin, S., and Hofvander, Y.: Den laga amningsfrekvensen i Sverige — vad gör vi? Semper Nutritions Symposium. Naringsforskning *17* (Suppl. 8): 103, 1973.)

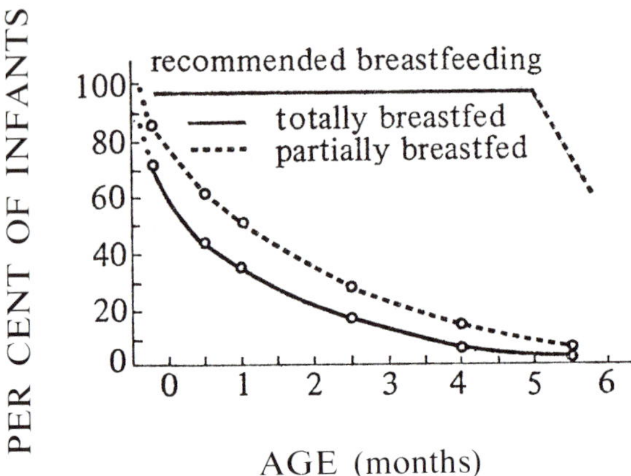

Figure 1–9 Per cent of totally or partially breastfed infants in Uppsala, Sweden, in 1971–72. (From Sjölin, S., and Hofvander, Y.: Den laga amningsfrekvensen i Sverige – vad gör vi? Semper Nutritions Symposium. Naringsforskning *17* (Suppl. 8): 103, 1973.)

States with respect to the rarity of breast feeding after three months of age. In Curico, Chile (Fig. 1–10), Mönckeberg (1970) reported that more than 70 per cent of infants were breastfed between three and six months of age.

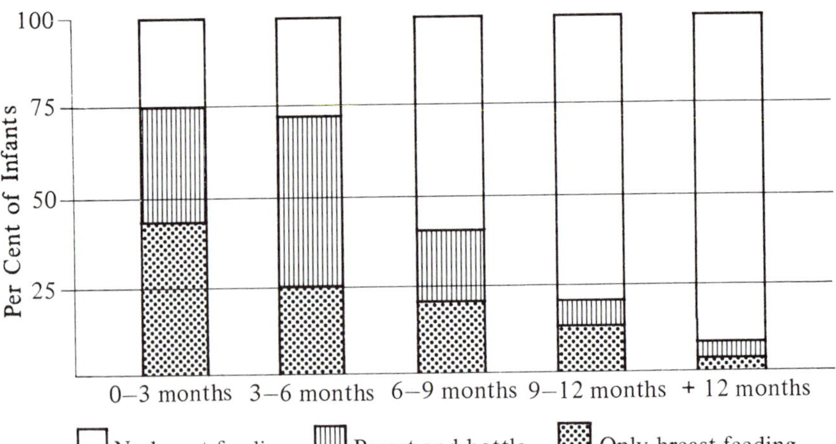

Figure 1–10 Per cent of infants receiving no breast feeding, feeding by breast and bottle or by breast only at various ages in Curico, Chile. (From Mönckeberg, F.: Factors conditioning malnutrition in Latin America, with special reference to Chile. Advices for a volunteers action. *In* Malnutrition Is a Problem of Ecology. Bibl. Nutr. Diet., No. 14, pp. 23–33 [Karger, Basel, 1970.])

Feeding in Hospitals

In the early 1960s, commercial formula services began operating in a number of metropolitan areas in the United States. Such formula services were able to provide a variety of formulas to hospitals, and many hospitals discontinued their own activities in formula preparation (Committee on Nutrition, 1965). By purchasing formulas rather than preparing these intramurally, the hospital was able to use for other purposes the space previously allocated to hospital formula preparation. In some instances, it proved economically beneficial to purchase formulas rather than to maintain and staff a unit for this purpose (Schenkweiler et al., 1960; Howley and Lewis, 1965).

It was evident that a commercial formula service influenced, to some extent, the choice of formula utilized by a hospital. Thus, if an evaporated milk formula was offered at nine cents per bottle while a commercially marketed, prepared formula was offered at 12 cents per bottle (the approximate costs obtaining in the early 1960s), the less expensive formula was likely to be chosen. Manufacturers of various prepared formulas therefore introduced competing feeding systems.

In 1961, the Mead Johnson Company introduced the Beneflex system of feeding in which bulk quantities of any infant formula manufactured by that company could be transferred aseptically to feeders suitable to the needs of individual infants. Later in the 1960s, sterile ready-to-feed formulas began to be supplied to hospitals by a number of manufacturers in disposable bottles with disposable or reusable nipples. Early in 1965, approximately equal numbers of hospitals in the United States used ready-to-feed formulas supplied by manufacturers and formulas supplied by locally operated commercial formula services. By 1970, nearly all hospitals in the United States were using ready-to-feed formulas prepared by the major manufacturers and nearly all the locally based commercial formula services had ceased to exist. Meyer (1958a, 1960, 1965a and b) has discussed types of formulas fed to newborn infants.

Income and Feeding Practices

In all except the lowest income group, more than 70 per cent of infants in the United States receive commercially prepared formulas during the first two months of life (Figs. 1–2 and 1–3). Reports from a number of sources (Fomon and Anderson, 1972) suggest that a substantial percentage of the lowest income families in the United States utilize evaporated milk formulas rather than commercially prepared formulas for infant feeding. As may be seen from Figure 1–3, market research data suggest that in 1971 less than 5 per cent of infants received evaporated milk formulas. The data of Rivera (1971) concerning feeding of infants in low income families attending a New York City clinic indicate that more than 30 per cent of two-month-old infants were fed evaporated milk formulas (Fig. 1–5). It seems likely that the data of Rivera may reflect better than market research data the use of evaporated milk formulas by low income families in the United States. It is evident that market research data will exclude a relatively large percentage of the lowest income families, because these families are least likely to have telephones or to answer their mail. Breast feeding appears to be even less commonly practiced among low income groups in the United States than among higher income groups (Rivera, 1971; Fomon and Anderson, 1972).

Trends in Feeding of Formulas and Milks

In the early 1950s, most commercially prepared formulas were sold in the form of powder. Concentrated liquid formula marketed in 390 ml (13 fl oz) cans became available about 1950 and, within 10 years, had captured a large share of the market. Weight of product sold in various forms, expressed as a percentage of total weight of product sold, is indicated in Figure 1–11 for one of the major infant formulas marketed in the United States. It is apparent that since 1966 little of this product has been sold in the form of powder. Presumably, purchase of powdered formula for use as supplemental bottle feedings for breastfed infants accounts for most sales of this form of the product. It may be noted that sales of ready-to-feed formula have increased rapidly since 1967. The impetus for this increase was, first, the adoption of ready-to-feed formulas by most hospitals and, especially between 1970 and 1972, increased sales of 960 ml (32 fl oz) cans of product for use in the home.

After three months of age, fresh cow milk (whole, "2 per cent" or skim) accounts for increasing percentages of infant feeding in the United States (Fig. 1–4). Market research data such as those presented in Figure 1–4 are generally similar to those reported from observations in various parts of the United States (Harris and Chan, 1969; Fomon and Anderson, 1972).

Late in the 1960s, ready-to-feed formulas in disposable bottles became available for use outside of the hospital. Although of high cost, their convenience was great. Availability of such feedings made possible certain studies of normal infants that could not otherwise have been conducted (Fomon et al., 1971, 1973). In the early 1970s, ready-to-feed formulas were increasingly marketed in 960 ml (1 quart) cans at a price considerably less than that of the same formulas in disposable bottles. Relative costs of various milks and formulas in Iowa City in 1973 are indicated in Table 1–1. Because food intake by

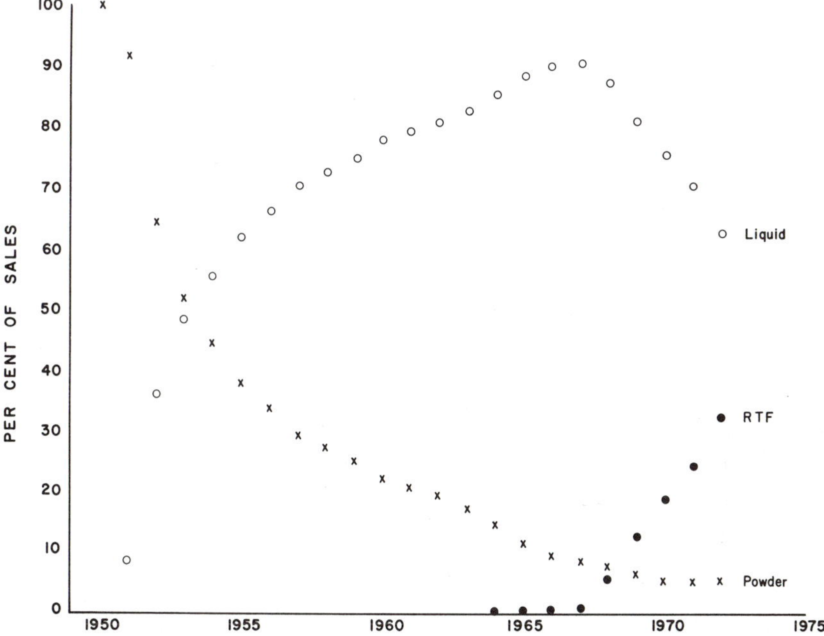

Figure 1–11 Relative popularity of various forms of a commercially prepared formula marketed in the United States between 1950 and 1972 expressed as per cent of sales. The product was marketed as a powder or concentrated liquid (133 kcal/100 ml) in 1950, and in 1964 also became available in (67 kcal/100 ml) ready-to-feed (RTF) form. (Data of Martinez, G. A., Ross Laboratories, Columbus, Ohio, 1973.)

TABLE 1–1 COMPARATIVE COST OF VARIOUS INFANT FOODS*

Item	Cost (¢)	
	100 gm or 100 ml	*100 kcal*
Prepared formula		
Ready-to-feed		
960 ml (32 fl oz) can	6.9	10.3
Concentrated liquid		
385 ml (13 fl oz) can diluted 1:1	4.5	6.8
Fresh fluid milk, 960 ml (32 fl oz)		
Homogenized, vitamin D fortified	3.1	4.7
Low fat (2%)	2.8	4.8
Evaporated milk, 385 ml (13 fl oz)		
137 kcal/100 gm can diluted 1:1	2.7	4.0
Strained foods		
Fruits	7.8	9.2†
Plain vegetables	8.7	19.3†
Soups and dinners	8.7	14.9†

*Supermarket prices, Iowa City, Iowa, November 1973.

†Assuming average caloric density as indicated in Chapter 16 (Table 16–2).

infants fed ad libitum is largely determined by caloric needs (Chapter 2), cost of infant foods per 100 kcal may be of more interest than cost per 100 ml or per 100 gm.

TRENDS IN FEEDING OF BEIKOST*

Until about 1920, solid foods were seldom offered to infants before one year of age (Committee on Nutrition, 1958). The earliest ages recommended for introduction of vegetables as indicated in eleven editions of Holt's *The Diseases of Infancy and Childhood* have been summarized by Adams (1959) (Fig. 1–12). Until 1911 green vegetables were not recommended before 36 months of age and even in 1929 green vegetables were not recommended before nine months of age.

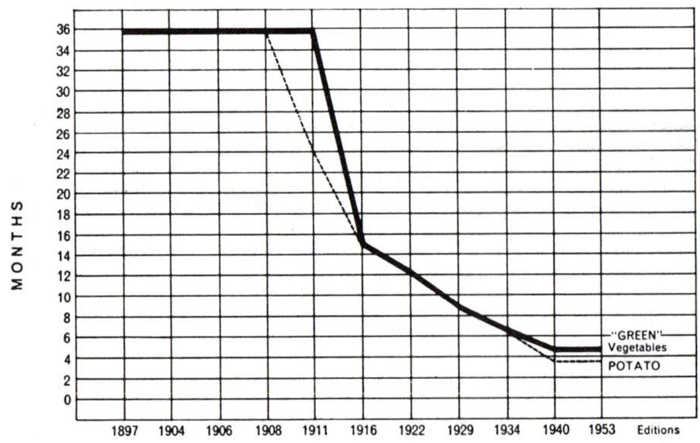

Figure 1–12 Earliest age recommendations for introduction of vegetables, as indicated in 11 editions of Holt's *The Diseases of Infancy and Childhood,* published from 1897 until 1953 (5th edition missing) (150–153). It should be noted that beets are forbidden for ages three to six years until the 6th edition in 1911 ("must be small and fresh"); tomatoes were forbidden until the 8th edition in 1922, and raw vegetables until the 12th edition in 1953. (From Adams, S. F.: Use of vegetables in infant feeding through the ages. J. Amer. Diet. Ass. *35*:362, 1959.)

In 1935, Marriott suggested that six months was the proper age for introduction of solid foods and in 1937 the A.M.A. Council on Foods stated that pediatricians favored feeding of strained fruits and vegetables at about four to six months of age. Beal (1957) demonstrated, in an upper socioeconomic group in Denver, that strained foods were offered to the infant at increasingly early ages during the years 1946 through 1955. Among pediatricians responding to a survey in 1954, feeding of solids was recommended before three months of age by 88 per cent, and before eight weeks of age by 66 per cent (Butler and Wolman, 1954). In 1963, Epps and Jolley reported that approximately

*Foods other than milk or formula (Chapter 16).

83 per cent of infants who were between one and two months of age when seen for a first visit in the Child Health Clinics of the District of Columbia Department of Public Health had already begun to receive solid foods. Similarly, early introduction of solid foods has been reported from other localities in the United States (Harris and Chan, 1969; Fomon and Anderson, 1972) and in Child Welfare Clinics in London (Oates, 1973).

Market research data concerning infants in the United States in 1970 indicated that beikost supplied 31 per cent of calorie intake at age three months, 38 per cent at age six months, 58 per cent at age nine months and 64 per cent at age 12 months (Filer, 1972). Filer and Martinez (1964) had previously reported that approximately one-third of calorie intake was supplied by beikost at age six months.

That extremely early introduction of cereal and strained foods may be tolerated by infants was well demonstrated by Sackett (1956), who began feeding cereal on the second or third day of life, and introduced vegetables at age 10 days, strained meat at age 14 days and fruit at age 17 days. There can no longer be doubt that infants tolerate strained foods early in life, but there is no evidence that such early introduction of beikost is advantageous. One practical disadvantage is cost. As may be seen from Table 1–1, commercially prepared strained foods are considerably more expensive per unit of calories than are most milks and formulas. At least in the case of low income families, there would appear to be a practical economic advantage in avoiding introduction of beikost during the early months of life.

REFERENCES

Adams, S. F.: Use of vegetables in infant feeding through the ages. J. Amer. Diet. Ass. *35*:362, 1959.

A.M.A. Council on Foods: Strained fruits and vegetables in the feeding of infants. J.A.M.A. *108*:1259, 1937.

Bain, K.: The incidence of breastfeeding in hospitals in the United States. Pediatrics *2*:313, 1948.

Beal, V. A.: On the acceptance of solid foods, and other food patterns, of infants and children. Pediatrics *20*:448, 1957.

Bernal, J., and Richards, M. P. M.: The effects of bottle and breast feeding on infant development. J. Psychosom. Res. *14*:247, 1970.

Brennemann, J.: The curd and the buffer in infant feeding. J.A.M.A. *92*:364, 1929.

Butler, A. M., and Wolman, I. J.: Trends in the early feeding of supplementary foods to infants; and analysis and discussion based on a nationwide survey. Quart. Rev. Pediatr. *9*:63, 1954.

Committee on Nutrition, American Academy of Pediatrics: On the feeding of solid foods to infants. Pediatrics *21*:685, 1958.

Committee on Nutrition, American Academy of Pediatrics: Prepared infant formulas and commercial formula services. Pediatrics *36*:282, 1965.

Davison, W.: Elimination of milk-borne disease. Amer. J. Dis. Child. *49*:72, 1935.

Dell, F., and Jordan-Smith, P. (eds.): Burton, R.: The Anatomy of Melancholy. New York, Tudor Publishing Co., 1927, p. 283.

Dewees, W. P.: A Treatise on the Physical and Medical Treatment of Children. Philadelphia, H. C. Carey and I. Lea, 1825.

Drake, T. G. H.: American infant feeding bottles, 1841 to 1946 as disclosed by United States patent specifications. J. Hist. Med. *3*:507, 1948.

Eberle, J.: A Treatise on Diseases and Physical Education of Children. Philadelphia, Grigg & Elliot, 1845.

Epps, R. P., and Jolley, M. P.: Unsupervised early feeding of solids to infants. Med. Ann. District Columbia *32*:493, 1963.

Filer, L. J., Jr.: Citation of unpublished data of Gilbert A. Martinez, Ross Laboratories, 1970. *In* Fomon, S. J., and Anderson, T. A. (eds.): Practices of Low-Income Families in Feeding Infants and Small Children. With Particular Attention to Cultural Subgroups. DHEW/HSMHA Publ. No. 725605. Washington, D.C., Maternal & Child Health Service, 1972.

Filer, L. J., Jr., and Martinez, G. A.: Intake of selected nutrients by infants in the United States. Clin. Pediatr. *3*:633, 1964.

Fomon, S. J., and Anderson, T. A. (eds.): Practices of Low-Income Families in Feeding Infants and Small Children. With Particular Attention to Cultural Subgroups. DHEW/HSMHA Publ. No. 725605. Washington, D.C., Maternal & Child Health Service, 1972.

Fomon, S. J., Thomas, L. N., Filer, L. J., Jr., Anderson, T. A., and Bergmann, K. E.: Requirements for protein and essential amino acids in early infancy. Studies with a soy-isolate formula. Acta Paediatr. Scand. *62*:33, 1973.

Fomon, S. J., Thomas, L. N., Filer, L. J., Jr., Ziegler, E. E., and Leonard, M. T.: Food consumption and growth of normal infants fed milk-based formulas. Acta Paediatr. Scand. (Suppl. 223), 1971.

Ford, C. S.: A Comparative Study of Human Reproduction. New Haven, Yale University Press, 1945.

Forsyth, D.: The history of infant feeding from Elizabethan times. Proc. Soc. Med. *4*:110, 1911.

Frantz, J. B.: Gail Borden, Dairyman to a Nation. Norman, Okla., University of Oklahoma Press, 1951.

Friedenwald, J., and Ruhrah, J.: Diet in Health and Disease. 5th ed. Philadelphia, W. B. Saunders Co., 1915.

Furnas, J. C.: The Americans. A Social History of the United States, 1587–1914. New York, Putnam, 1969.

Hamilton, A.: A Treatise on the Management of Female Complaints, and of Children in Early Infancy. First Worcester ed. Worcester, Mass., Isaiah Thomas, 1793.

Harris, H.: California's Medical Story. San Francisco, J. W. Stacey, Inc., 1932.

Harris, L. E., and Chan, J. C. M.: Infant feeding practices. Amer. J. Dis. Child. *117*:483, 1969.

Helsing, E.: Discussion. Semper Nutritions Symposium. Naringsforskning *17* (Suppl. 8): 137, 1973.

Herbert, R. W., Hirst, E. L., Percival, E. G. V., Reynolds, R. J. W., and Smith, F.: Constitution of ascorbic acid. J. Soc. Chem. Ind. *52*:221, 1933.

Holt, L. E., Jr.: Letter to Editor. Let us give the Russians their due. Pediatrics *32*:462, 1963.

Hopkins, F. G.: The analyst and the medical man. Analyst *31*:385, 1906.

Howley, M. P. F., and Lewis, M. N.: Comparison of hospital-prepared formulas with prebottled infant formulas. Hospitals *39*:97, 1965.

Jackson, E. B., Wilkin, L. C., and Auerbach, H.: Statistical report on incidence and duration of breast feeding in relation to personal-social and hospital maternity factors. Pediatrics *17*:700, 1956.

Judson, C. F., and Gittings, J. C.: The Artificial Feeding of Infants, Including a Critical Review of the Recent Literature of the Subject. Philadelphia, J. B. Lippincott Co., 1902.

Klackenberg, G., and Klackenberg-Larsson, I.: The development of children in a Swedish urban community. A prospective longitudinal study. V. Breast-feeding and weaning: some social-psychological aspects. Acta Paediatr. Scand. (Suppl. 187): 94, 1968.

Marriott, W. M.: Preparation of lactic acid mixtures for infant feeding. J.A.M.A. *89*:862, 1927.

Marriott, W. M.: Infant Nutrition. 2nd ed. St. Louis, C. V. Mosby Co., 1935.

Marriott, W. M., and Schoenthal, L.: An experimental study of use of unsweetened evaporated milk for the preparation of infant feeding formulas. Arch. Pediatr. *46*:135, 1929.

Martinez, G. A.: Personal communication from market research data. Ross Laboratories, Columbus, Ohio, 1973.

Mellanby, E.: Accessory food factors (vitamines) in the feeding of infants. Lancet *1*:856, 1920.

Meyer, H. F.: Infant feeding practices in hospital maternity nurseries. A survey of 1,904 hospitals involving 2,225,000 newborn infants. Pediatrics *21*:288, 1958a.

Meyer, H. F.: Breast feeding in the United States: extent and possible trend. A survey of 1,904 hospitals with two and a quarter million births in 1956. Pediatrics *22*:116, 1958b.

Meyer, H. F.: Infant Foods and Feeding Practice. Springfield, Ill., Charles C Thomas, 1960.

Meyer, H. F.: The new ready-to-feed formulas. Some pertinent considerations. Clin. Pediatr. *4*:376, 1965a.

Meyer, H. F.: Survey of hospital nursery ready-to-feed milk mixtures. Hospitals *39*:60, 1965b.

Meyer, H. F.: Breastfeeding in the United States. Report of a 1966 national survey with comparable 1946 and 1956 data. Clin. Pediatr. *7*:708, 1968.

Mönckeberg, F.: Factors conditioning malnutrition in Latin America, with special reference to Chile. Advice for a volunteers action. *In* György, P., and Kline, O. L. (eds.): Malnutrition is a Problem of Ecology. New York, S. Karger, 1970.

Newson, L. J., and Newson, E.: Breast-feeding in decline. Br. Med. J. *2*:1744, 1962.

Oates, R. K.: Infant-feeding practices. Br. Med. J. *2*:762, 1973.

Rivera, J.: The frequency of use of various kinds of milk during infancy in middle and lower-income families. Amer. J. Public Health *61*:277, 1971.

Robertson, W. O.: Breast feeding practices: some implications of regional variations. Amer. J. Public Health *51*:1035, 1961.

Sackett, W. W., Jr.: Use of solid foods early in infancy. G. P. *14*:98, 1956.

Salber, E. J., and Feinleib, M.: Breast-feeding in Boston. Pediatrics *37*:299, 1966.

Salber, E. J., Stitt, P. G., and Babbott, J. G.: Patterns of breast feeding. I. Factors affecting the frequency of breast feeding in the newborn period. New Eng. J. Med. *259*:707, 1958.

Schenkweiler, L., Hixson, H. H., Paxon, H. H., Clark, J. R., Berke, M., and Hosford, R. F.: Six administrators look at infant formula costs. Hospitals *34*:46, 1960.

Sjölin, S., and Hofvander, Y.: Den laga amningsfrekvensen i Sverige—vad gör vi? Semper Nutritions Symposium. Naringsforskning *17* (Suppl. 8): 103, 1973.

Spruill, J. C.: Women's Life and Work in the Southern Colonies. Chapel Hill, N. C., University of North Carolina Press, 1938.

Stewart, C. P., and Guthrie, P. (eds.): Lind's Treatise on Scurvy. A Reprint of the First Edition of a Treatise of the Scurvy. Edinburgh, University Press, 1953.

Szent-Györgyi, A.: Observations on the function of peroxidase systems and the chemistry of adrenal cortex. Description of new carbohydrate derivative. Biochem. J. *22*:1387, 1928.

Trout, G. M.: Homogenized Milk. A Review and Guide. East Lansing, Michigan State College Press, 1950.

Underwood, M.: A Treatise on the Diseases of Children, with Directions for the Management of Infants from Birth. Notes by a Physician of Philadelphia. From the 6th London ed. Philadelphia, J. Webster and W. Brown, Printer, 1818.

Vahlquist, B.: Amningssituationen i i- och u-land. Tid för omvärdering. Semper Nutritions Symposium. Naringsforskning *17* (Suppl. 8): 117, 1973.

Woodbury, R. M.: Causal Factors in Infant Mortality. Children's Bureau Publication No. 142, Washington, D. C., U. S. Government Printing Office, 1925.

2

VOLUNTARY FOOD INTAKE AND ITS REGULATION

It is apparent from previous reviews (Committee on Nutrition, 1964; Fomon, 1971a, b and c; Fomon and Ziegler, 1971; Fomon, 1972) that we are only beginning to approach an understanding of the interrelationships between the many complex factors influencing food consumption during "ad libitum feeding" of infants. An attempt will be made to summarize current information on this topic, with the expectation that reports of more extensive observations will be likely to appear during the next few years.

Several investigators have speculated (see Chapter 3) that obesity in later childhood and adult life may have its origin in infancy. If this should be the case, preventive measures might need to be introduced during the early weeks of life, and selection of appropriate preventive measures could hardly be made in the absence of knowledge about factors regulating food consumption.

The quantity of food willingly accepted by an infant is determined to a large extent by calorie requirement for maintenance and growth and by the attitudes of the infant's parent or caretaker. In addition, age, sex, size and state of health of the infant and various characteristics of the food are associated directly or indirectly with quantity of food consumed. Among the more important characteristics of the food are caloric density, digestibility, nutritional adequacy, taste and such physical properties as consistency and particle size. Little is as yet known about differences in satiety value of foods of the same caloric density but with different percentages of calories derived from protein, fat and carbohydrate.

In contrast to the situation with most individual nutrients, in the case of calories, mild excess and mild deficiency are likely to be

equally undesirable. A reasonable recommendation for calorie intake should, therefore, provide for the needs of as many infants as possible, while risking overnutrition in as few as possible. At present, insufficient information is available to provide a sound basis for definitive recommendations. However, review of available data concerning presumably normal infants can provide the basis for tentative recommendations.

Attitude of Caretaker

Because infants are dependent individuals, it is apparent that the infant will starve if his parent (or caretaker) refuses to offer feedings, and may become grossly overfed if the person responsible for feeding attempts to feed as much as possible. The attitude of the caretaker is therefore important, and every possible shade of attitude is likely to be represented. Therefore, amounts of food consumed during ad libitum feeding cannot be assumed to reflect only the desires of the infant; rather, they reflect the interaction between infant and caretaker in the feeding situation.

In our studies of normal infants living in a metabolic ward (Fomon et al., 1964), we fed the largest volume of milk or formula that an infant would accept consistently, rather than the least amount that would appear to relieve hunger. In another institutional setting, Brown et al. (1960) offered approximately 165 ml/kg/day of formula, and this volume was not increased unless excessive crying between feedings suggested that the infants were dissatisfied. Median intake in our observations was 189 ml/kg/day, whereas that reported by Brown et al. was 168 ml/kg/day. It seems likely that encouraging infants to consume the largest amounts they are willing to accept may be undesirable.

Whether an infant is fed by breast or bottle, the frequency of feeding will be determined to a large extent by attitudes of the caretaker and by other demands on the caretaker's time and energies. In the belief that an infant "should not be fed too often," the caretaker may attempt to prolong the interval between feedings. Alternatively, the infant may be fed every two or three hours during the day in the belief that he will sleep for longer intervals at night. In either case, the attitudes of the caretaker will influence the frequency of feeding, and few infants are truly fed "on demand."

Breast Versus Formula Feeding

One important advantage of breast feeding may be that the mother does not really know how much milk the infant has taken and, therefore, the amount consumed at a feeding is determined largely by the infant and is modified relatively little by attitudes of the infant's caretaker. When a breastfed baby ceases to suck and swallow, his mother will assume that he is satisfied. The bottle-fed infant, on the other hand, is likely to be subjected to subtle pressures to consume more than would be the case if he were left to follow his natural inclinations. Bottle-fed babies are frequently encouraged to drain the last drop from the bottle so that an artificial end-point is introduced with respect to the amount of food consumed. In this way, bottle feeding may lead to overfeeding.

Although adequate data concerning volume of milk consumed by normal infants fed exclusively at the breast are not available, circumstantial evidence strongly suggests that intake of calories is less by breastfed than by bottle-fed infants. As will be discussed in Chapter 3 (see Fig. 3–8), gain in weight has been demonstrated to be significantly related to calorie intake. In addition, gains in weight by the most rapidly growing bottle-fed infants are greater than those by the most rapidly growing breastfed infants (Chapter 3, Fig. 3–12). Whether the more rapid growth of bottle-fed infants is desirable, undesirable or of no consequence we do not know. Neither do we know whether prolonged encouragement of overeating during infancy will establish undesirable feeding habits that will persist in later life. However, we do know that feeding habits established in young animals are remarkably persistent. Therefore, if it is correct, as we suppose, that formula feeding is more commonly associated with overfeeding than is breast feeding, the latter may to some extent be a prophylactic measure against our national problem of obesity in adult life. Because most infants are bottle-fed rather than breastfed, it seems necessary to educate parents about the undesirability of overfeeding infants.

Frequency of Feeding

Not only the type of food and the amount consumed but also the frequency of eating has important metabolic consequences. Many studies have been carried out with experimental animals on the metabolic consequences of meal-eating as opposed to ad libitum feeding or "nibbling." Some of the more important of these studies have been summarized by Cohn and Joseph (1970), Fábry and Tepperman (1970) and Leveille (1970, 1972).

Meal-eating by the rat—the limitation of access to food to a single, short period daily—appears to cause adaptive changes that permit a more rapid and efficient conversion of carbohydrate to fat. Furthermore, the meal-eating rat is able to gain weight at the same rate as ad libitum-fed animals, while ingesting considerably less food. If forced to consume as much energy as ad libitum-fed animals, the meal-eating rat becomes obese. This apparent increased efficiency of energy metabolism of meal-eating rats is probably explained, at least in part, by reduction in physical activity after meal-eating (Leveille and O'Hea, 1967). Thus, total energy expenditure is less for meal-eating than for ad libitum-fed rats.

Meal-eating animals of various species have been reported to develop hypercholesterolemia, impaired glucose tolerance and ischemic heart disease (Fábry and Tepperman, 1970).

Enormous problems exist with respect to interpreting these studies in terms of the human infant. It is evident that comparisons of the effects of frequent and infrequent meal patterns in animals after weaning may not be relevant to the preweaning period. In rats, an age-related difference in the effects of meal frequency was observed between prepubertal and postpubertal animals (Wardlaw et al., 1969), and one might anticipate even greater differences between results with preweanling and older animals. Data concerning differences between meal-eating and ad libitum-fed preweanling animals are not yet available.

TABLE 2–1 CALORIE INTAKES IN RELATION TO AGE AND WEIGHT BY NORMAL FULLTERM INFANTS FED AD LIBITUM WITH MILK-BASED FORMULA PROVIDING 67 kcal/100 ml*

	Age Interval (days)					
Percentiles	*8–13*	*14–27*	*28–41*	*42–55*	*56–83*	*84–111*
Volume of intake (ml/kg/day)						
Males						
10th	122	142	134	137	123	118
50th	166	181	172	161	148	137
90th	208	214	209	198	178	155
Females						
10th	116	125	128	119	125	116
50th	160	169	159	153	137	133
90th	208	197	195	182	164	156
Calorie intake (kcal/kg/day)						
Males						
10th	82	95	91	91	83	81
50th	111	121	116	108	100	96
90th	142	143	140	133	119	106
Females						
10th	82	86	90	83	87	82
50th	113	117	111	108	97	94
90th	143	136	136	125	114	109

*From Fomon, S. J., et al.: Food consumption and growth of normal infants fed milk-based formulas. Acta Paediatr. Scand. (Suppl. 223), 1971.

TABLE 2–2 DAILY CALORIE INTAKES BY NORMAL INFANTS AND CHILDREN LESS THAN THREE YEARS OF AGE*

AGE RANGE (MONTHS)	NUMBER OF SUBJECTS	CALORIE INTAKE									
		kcal/day							*kcal/kg/day*		
				Percentiles					*Percentiles*		
		Mean	*S.D.*	*10th*	*25th*	*50th*	*75th*	*90th*	*10th*	*50th*	*90th*
					MALES						
0–1	33	405	110	275	315	400	480	580	88	115	150
1–2	39	575	86	465	515	565	635	680	108	131	157
2–3	42	630	107	505	545	625	715	795	93	116	139
3–4	44	655	97	550	590	640	715	785	90	103	124
4–5	46	710	124	550	625	675	810	885	88	101	122
5–6	45	760	138	615	670	740	850	960	81	100	122
6–9	46	845	135	710	760	820	895	1020	82	100	123
9–12	49	985	196	795	845	925	1070	1230	81	101	137
12–15	47	1060	277	745	845	990	1240	1430	71	98	138
15–18	46	1165	276	850	935	1135	1350	1480	78	103	136
18–21	45	1215	271	855	1000	1220	1425	1565	75	102	136
21–24	44	1260	265	895	1050	1255	1415	1560	73	108	127
24–27	45	1320	298	965	1135	1290	1475	1705	75	103	135

27–30	44	1385	294	1055	1205	1375	1560	1840	81	104	136
30–33	45	1420	312	1050	1150	1435	1625	1850	73	102	129
33–36	43	1480	286	1175	1275	1430	1635	1975	78	103	129
					FEMALES						
0–1	23	385	86	290	310	375	440	510	84	115	144
1–2	30	530	105	415	445	510	580	700	100	131	160
2–3	32	565	90	455	510	580	645	675	98	115	133
3–4	34	620	84	515	575	615	665	730	97	111	130
4–5	37	665	85	540	615	675	725	775	89	104	120
5–6	38	715	93	610	635	690	770	840	89	104	127
6–9	41	770	122	620	690	760	825	915	76	97	122
9–12	44	885	149	705	755	890	950	1125	80	97	129
12–15	45	985	216	720	820	980	1095	1245	79	98	136
15–18	45	1080	212	810	880	1075	1250	1355	79	104	139
18–21	44	1140	214	915	970	1080	1290	1430	79	103	135
21–24	45	1195	215	945	1015	1165	1330	1485	78	103	134
24–27	47	1230	248	945	1075	1200	1330	1545	78	99	135
27–30	48	1235	232	945	1070	1210	1375	1515	75	96	131
30–33	46	1245	261	970	1095	1210	1345	1585	74	94	124
33–36	45	1300	296	990	1125	1250	1460	1765	72	93	124

*Data of Beal (1970).

One might speculate (Fomon, 1971c) that, as the human race evolved, the infant was carried by the mother, was probably breastfed at will, suckling frequently throughout the day, and maintaining the concentration of glucose in the blood at a relatively constant level. Food was metered into the body in a rather regular fashion. In association with technologic advances, social pressures have brought about major changes in frequency of feeding and, at the present time, even the breastfed infant is often fed at rather widely spaced intervals. Although a pattern of feeding infants and small children at infrequent intervals is convenient for parents, there is little to suggest that this method of management is nutritionally desirable.

Age, Sex and Size of Infant

The relation between age, sex, volume of intake and calorie intake may be seen in Tables 2–1 and 2–2. Because males are somewhat larger at birth and grow more rapidly during infancy than do females, it is not surprising that calorie intakes are somewhat larger. Calorie intakes expressed per unit of body weight differed little between males and females (Table 2–1).

Volume of intake (ml/day) and calorie intake (kcal/day) increased with increasing age. When expressed per unit of body weight (ml/kg/day or kcal/kg/day), values were greatest in the interval 14 through 27 days of age, and then gradually decreased (Table 2–1). Among infants of the same age and sex, volumes of food consumed and calorie intakes generally increase in relation to body weight (Figure 2–1). Appendix I (p. 522) provides similar graphic data for various age groups. With infants of the same sex and body weight, calorie intake is gener-

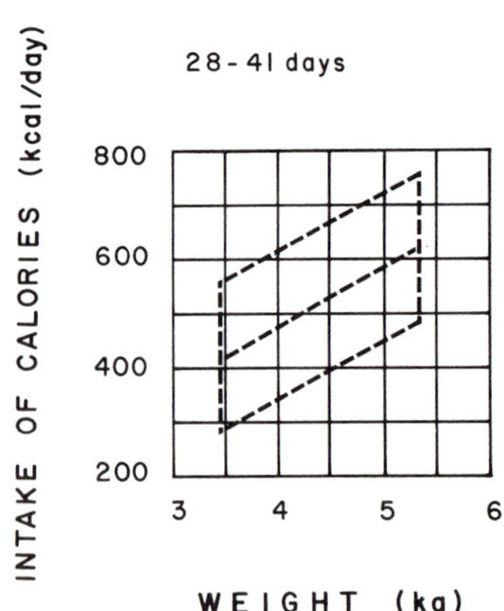

Figure 2–1 Relation of intake of calories to body weight of normal fullterm male infants fed ad libitum during the age interval 28 through 41 days. The regression and 90 per cent confidence intervals are indicated. Data concerning females during this age interval and data for other age intervals for each sex are presented in Appendix I (p. 522). (Data of Fomon et al., 1971.)

ally greater by younger than by older infants. For example, mean calorie intakes by 5 kg male infants fed milk-based formulas (Fomon et al., 1971) averaged 583, 559 and 501 kcal/day, respectively, in the age intervals 28 through 41, 42 through 55 and 56 through 83 days.

The data of Beal (1970) indicate that calorie intakes expressed as kcal/kg/day decrease only slightly between 4 and 12 months of age (Table 2–2). During the second and third years of life, calorie intakes of males averaged 103 kcal/kg/day. Calorie intakes per kilogram were similar by males and females during the second year, but intakes by females were somewhat lower during the third year.

It seems hardly necessary to mention that state of health influences food intake. The seriously ill infant nurses poorly and, even with encouragement, will accept less than his usual amount of food. On the other hand, specific diseases that interfere with absorption of nutrients—e.g., cystic fibrosis of the pancreas—may result in unusually large intakes, presumably in a metabolically regulated attempt to achieve an adequate "net" intake of calories.

COMPOSITION OF THE DIET

Caloric Density of Diet

Performance of normal male infants fed a formula of high caloric density (133 kcal/100 ml) may be compared in Figures 2–2 and 2–3

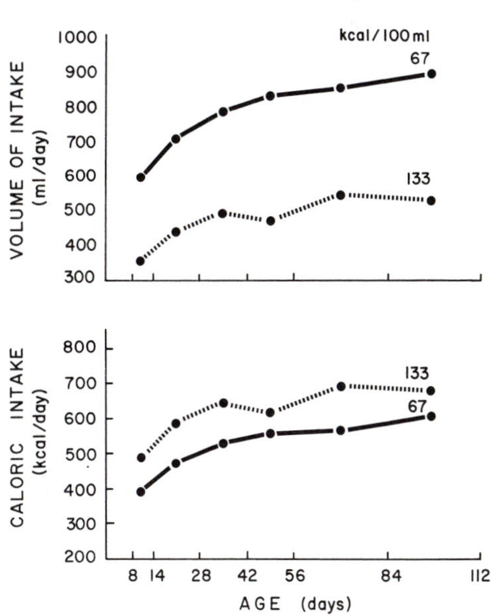

Figure 2–2 Mean volume of intake and caloric intake by normal male infants fed 67 kcal/100 ml or 133 kcal/100 ml milk-based formulas during the age interval 8 through 111 days. (Data concerning 67 kcal/100 ml formulas are from Fomon et al., 1971; data concerning the 133 kcal/100 ml formula are from Fomon et al., 1969.)

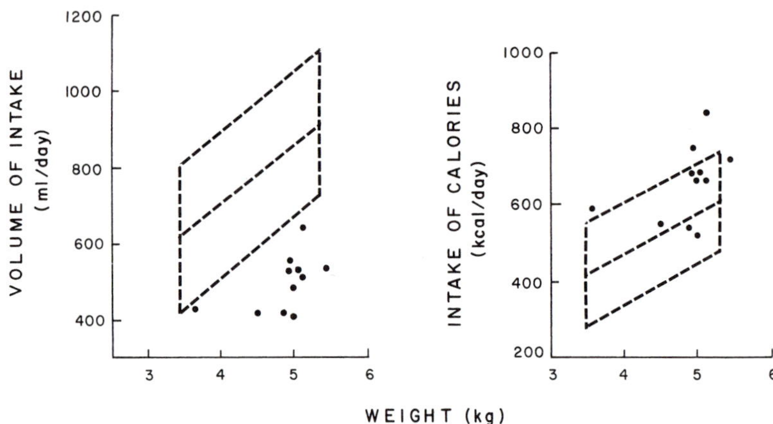

Figure 2–3 Volume of intake and intake of calories by normal male infants fed milk-based formulas during the age interval 28 through 41 days. The outer interrupted lines enclose the 90 per cent confidence intervals for 65 infants fed 67 kcal/100 ml formulas. The regressions are also indicated. Each dot indicates the intake of one infant fed the 133 kcal/100 ml formula. (Sources of data as in Figure 2–2.)

with performance of a larger group of normal male infants fed formulas of conventional caloric density (67 kcal/100 ml). Volumes of intake by infants receiving the calorically concentrated formula were relatively low, but intakes of calories were relatively high. In subsequent studies (Fomon et al., unpublished), two groups of female infants were fed formulas similar except for caloric density—one formula (5018E) providing 100 kcal/100 ml and the other (5018D) providing 53 kcal/100 ml. Results of these observations are presented in Table 2–3 and Figure 2–4. It may be noted that during the first 41 days of life, calorie intake appeared to be correlated with caloric density of the formula. During the interval 42 through 111 days of age, calorie intake per unit of body weight by infants fed the 100 kcal/100 ml formula was nearly identical to intake by those fed 67 kcal/100 ml formulas. During this interval, intakes by infants fed the 53 kcal/100 ml formula were actually slightly greater than those by infants fed 67 kcal/100 ml formulas.

These data suggest that after 41 days of age, infants fed 100 kcal/100 ml or 53 kcal/100 ml formulas are able to regulate their intakes during ad libitum feeding in such a way that calorie consumption is similar to that of infants fed conventional 67 kcal/100 ml formulas. Between 8 and 28 days of age (Fig. 2–4), the lesser caloric intake by infants fed 53 kcal/100 ml formulas than by those fed 67 kcal/100 ml formulas suggests that near maximal volumes of intakes may have been achieved by infants fed 53 kcal/100 ml formulas in this age interval.

TABLE 2–3 FOOD INTAKE AND GROWTH BY NORMAL FEMALE INFANTS FED 100 kcal/100 ml, 53 kcal/100 ml OR VARIOUS MILK-BASED FORMULAS (67 kcal/100 ml)

Formula concentration	100 kcal/100 ml*		53 kcal/100 ml*		67 kcal/100 ml†	
Number of subjects	14		15		77	
	Mean	*S.D.*	*Mean*	*S.D.*	*Mean*	*S.D.*
Volume of intake (ml/kg/day)						
8–41 days	126	17	201	31	164	24
42–111 days	99	10	186	21	141	14
Calorie intake (kcal/kg/day)						
8–41 days	126	18	107	16	110	16
42–111 days	97	9	103	12	95	10
Gain in weight (gm/day)						
8–41 days	41.0	10.4	29.8	4.9	32.9	6.8
42–111 days	24.0	5.3	24.6	4.6	25.0	5.4
Gain in weight (gm/100 kcal)						
8–41 days	7.54	0.86	7.65	1.15	7.48	1.73
42–111 days	4.38	0.79	4.74	0.77	4.76	0.79
Weight gain/length gain (gm/mm)						
8–41 days	36.5	10.5	27.6	6.7	26.4	5.8
42–111 days	31.2	5.9	30.2	12.6	26.4	4.9

*Data from Infant Metabolic Unit, University of Iowa (Formulas 5018E and 5018D) (to be published).

†Data from Fomon et al. (1971).

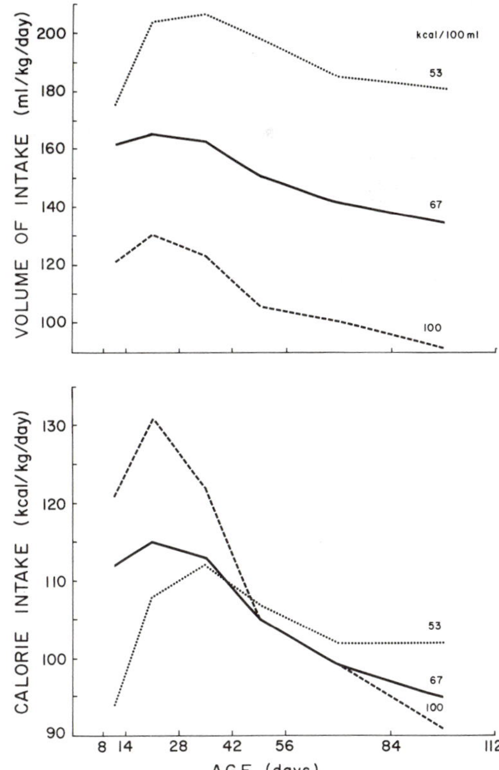

Figure 2–4 Mean volume of intake and intake of calories by normal fullterm female infants fed 100 kcal/100 ml, 67 kcal/100 ml or 53 kcal/100 ml milk-based formulas during the age interval 8 through 111 days. (See Table 2–3.) (Data concerning 67 kcal/100 ml formulas are from Fomon et al., 1971; other data are from Infant Metabolic Unit, University of Iowa, to be published.)

Although infants were able to increase their volumes of intake of a 53 kcal/100 ml formula after 41 days of age to achieve calorie intakes slightly greater than those by infants fed conventional 67 kcal/100 ml formulas, it should not be assumed that infants fed more dilute feedings would be able to consume sufficient formula to achieve calorie intakes equal to those by infants fed 67 kcal/100 ml formulas. Table 2–4 summarizes data on male infants 112 through 167 days of age fed either a 36 kcal/100 ml formula (skim milk with a small amount of added safflower oil) or a conventional formula (Similac, 67 kcal/100 ml). Unrestricted consumption of commercially prepared strained foods was permitted to infants of each group. Greater volume but considerably fewer calories were consumed by infants fed the 36 kcal/100 ml feeding. As discussed in Chapter 3, gain in weight by infants fed skim milk was significantly less than that by infants fed the conventional formula. We assume that the volumes of intake by the infants fed skim milk (Table 2–4) approach maximal values.

From these data we conclude that infants fed dilute feedings will consume relatively large volumes during ad libitum feeding, whereas infants fed calorically concentrated feedings will consume relatively small volumes. The extent to which this adjustment in volume of intake will result in calorie intakes equal to those of infants fed conven-

TABLE 2–4 FOOD CONSUMPTION AND GROWTH OF NORMAL MALE INFANTS FED A 67 kcal/100 ml FORMULA (SIMILAC) OR SKIM MILK (36 kcal/100 ml) DURING THE INTERVAL 112 THROUGH 167 DAYS OF AGE*

	Similac	*Skim Milk*
Number of subjects	15	14
Food consumption		
Milk or formula		
(gm/day)	824 (143)†	1001 (206)
(kcal/day)	552 (96)	361 (74)
Strained foods		
(gm/day)	248 (164)	304 (115)
(kcal/day)	178 (119)	215 (77)
Total		
(gm/day)	1072 (137)	1306 (158)
(kcal/day)	730 (97)	576 (60)
Gain in weight		
(gm/day)	19.1 (3.9)	13.5 (4.3)
(gm/100 kcal)	2.64 (0.61)	2.33 (0.61)
Gain in length		
(mm/day)	0.66 (0.18)	0.72 (0.09)
Weight gain/length gain		
(gm/mm)	35.4 (18.2)	19.2 (6.5)

*Data from Infant Metabolic Unit, University of Iowa (to be published).
†Values in parentheses are standard deviations.

tional 67 kcal/100 ml feedings will depend on caloric density of the feeding and age of the infant. In the case of normal infants, the ability to adjust volume of intake seems considerably greater after 41 days of age. Nevertheless, it is apparent that feedings may be so dilute that, even after 112 days of age, it may not be possible to achieve intakes equal to those by infants fed 67 kcal/100 ml feedings.

Digestibility of the Diet

It has already been mentioned that infants with steatorrhea (e.g., cystic fibrosis of the pancreas) consume greater volumes of food than do normal infants, and that this apparently is done through metabolic regulation in order to achieve an adequate "net" intake of calories. An analogous situation exists with respect to otherwise normal infants fed diets in which some component, most commonly fat, is poorly digested. Infants fed whole cow milk as the sole source of calories are a good example (see Chapter 7, Table 7–3 and Fig. 7–7).

Young infants absorb a considerably smaller percentage of butterfat than of human milk fat or of most vegetable oils. Absorption of butterfat by young infants is particularly poor when intakes of fat are relatively high, as is the case when whole cow milk is the sole source of calories (Fomon, 1961; Fomon et al., 1970). As discussed in Chapter 7, fat excretion by normal infants fed whole cow milk amounted to 23 to 36 per cent of fat intake—equivalent to 12 to 18 per cent of calorie intake. Presumably because of this loss of calories in the feces, infants fed whole cow milk ad libitum as the sole source of calories ingest relatively large volumes of milk.

OTHER INFLUENCES ON FOOD INTAKE

Little is known about the influence on food intake of such factors as taste and consistency of the food. Eckstein (1928) reported inhibition of sucking when premature infants were offered bitter solutions by nipple. Similarly, Jensen (1932) reported that by the second day of life salt solutions inhibited sucking of fullterm infants. In fullterm infants between 1 and 5 days of age, milk feedings appear to stimulate sucking more than does a 5 per cent solution of corn syrup solids or glucose (Kron et al., 1967; Dubignon and Campbell, 1969).

In studies of normal adult rats, Valenstein et al. (1967; Valenstein, 1967) have demonstrated that consumption of drinking water is increased when glucose or saccharin is added to the water. This increase in consumption was considerably greater in the case of females than in the case of males. Somewhat similar observations have been reported by Nisbett and Gurwitz (1970) from study of 42 normal newborn infants (22 males and 20 females). These infants were fed identical formulas except for the added carbohydrate, which was either lactose ("unsweetened formula") or sucrose ("sweetened formula"). Feedings were provided ad libitum in random order at 2 AM and 6 AM daily for one to four days, and the unsweetened formula was fed at all other feeding times. At the 2 AM and 6 AM feedings, female infants consumed 24 per cent more sweetened than unsweetened formula, whereas males consumed only 6 per cent more sweetened than unsweetened formula. In the case of females, the difference was statistically significant.

Nisbett and Gurwitz (1970) also found that the 14 infants (six males and eight females) with birth weights greater than 3540 gm appeared to be more responsive to the difference in taste than were the other infants. The heavy infants consumed 28 per cent more of the sweetened than of the unsweetened formula, whereas the other infants consumed only 8 per cent more of the sweetened than of the unsweetened formula. This difference was also statistically significant. The authors point out that obesity may, to a degree, be genetically determined, that infants with high birth weights are likely to be obese adults (see Chapter 3), and offer "the pessimistic hypothesis" that certain eating behaviors may also be, in part, genetically determined and linked to the individual's weight. Clearly, this area of infant behavior must be further explored.

REFERENCES

Beal, V. A.: Nutritional intake. *In* McCammon, R. W. (ed.): Human Growth and Development. Springfield, Ill., Charles C Thomas, 1970, p. 63.

Brown, G. W., Tuholski, J. M., Sauer, L. W., Minsk, L. D., and Rosenstern, I.: Evaluation of prepared milks for infant nutrition; use of the Latin square technique. J. Pediatr. *56*:391, 1960.

Cohn, C., and Joseph D.: Effects of caloric intake and feeding frequency on carbohydrate metabolism of the rat. J. Nutr. *100*:78, 1970.

Committee on Nutrition, American Academy of Pediatrics: Factors affecting food intake. Pediatrics *33*:135, 1964.

Dubignon, J., and Campbell, D.: Discrimination between nutriments by the human neonate. Psychon. Sci. *16*:186, 1969.

Eckstein, A.: Zur Physiologie der Geschmacksempfindung und des Saugreflexes bei Säuglingen, I. Mitteilung. Z. Kinderheilkd. *45*:1, 1928.

Fábry, P., and Tepperman, J.: Meal frequency—a possible factor in human pathology. Amer. J. Clin. Nutr. *23*:1059, 1970.

Fomon, S. J.: Nitrogen balance studies with normal fullterm infants receiving high intakes of protein. Pediatrics *28*:347, 1961.

Fomon, S. J.: Food intake and growth. Proceedings of the Simposio de Nutrición Infantil, Córdoba, Argentina, 1971a, p. 21.

Fomon, S. J.: L'assunzione di cibo nel lattante a dieta libera. Prospettive in Pediatria *1*:99, 1971b.

Fomon, S. J.: A pediatrician looks at early nutrition. Bull. N. Y. Acad. Med. *47*:569, 1971c.

Fomon, S. J.: Food intake and growth: 1972. Proceedings of the Tenth Panamerican Congress of Pediatrics, Córdoba, Argentina, 1972, p. 1.

Fomon, S. J., Filer, L. J., Jr., Thomas, L. N., Rogers, R. R., and Proksch, A. M.: Relationship between formula concentration and rate of growth of normal infants. J. Nutr. *98*:241, 1969.

Fomon, S. J., Owen, G. M., and Thomas, L. N.: Milk or formula volume ingested by infants fed ad libitum. Amer. J. Dis. Child. *108*:601, 1964.

Fomon, S. J., Thomas, L. N., Filer, L. J., Jr., Ziegler, E. E., and Leonard, M. T.: Food consumption and growth of normal infants fed milk-based formulas. Acta Paediatr. Scand. (Suppl. 223), 1971.

Fomon, S. J., and Ziegler, E.: Spontane Nahrungsaufnahme des Säuglings. *In* Berger, H. (ed.): Moderne Aspekte der künstlichen Säuglingsernährung. Internationales Symposium, Stuttgart, Georg Thieme Verlag, 1971, p. 36.

Fomon, S. J., Ziegler, E. E., Thomas, L. N., Jensen, R. L., and Filer, L. J., Jr.: Excretion of fat by normal fullterm infants fed various milks and formulas. Amer. J. Clin. Nutr. *23*:1299, 1970.

Jensen, K.: Differential reactions to taste and temperature stimuli in newborn infants. Genet. Psychol. Monogr. *12*:361, 1932.

Kron, R. E., Stein, M., Goddard, K. E., and Phoenix, M. D.: Effect of nutrient upon the sucking behavior of newborn infants. Psychosom. Med. *29*:24, 1967.

Leveille, G. A.: Adipose tissue metabolism: influence of periodicity of eating and diet composition. Fed. Proc. *29*:1294, 1970.

Leveille, G. A.: The long-term effects of meal-eating on lipogenesis, enzyme activity, and longevity in the rat. J. Nutr. *102*:549, 1972.

Leveille, G. A., and O'Hea, E. K.: Influence of periodicity of eating on energy metabolism in the rat. J. Nutr. *93*:541, 1967.

Nisbett, R. E., and Gurwitz, S. B.: Weight, sex, and the eating behavior of human newborns. J. Comp. Physiol. Psychol. *73*:215, 1970.

Valenstein, E. S.: Selection of nutritive and non-nutritive solutions under different conditions of need. J. Comp. Physiol. Psychol. *63*:429, 1967.

Valenstein, E. S., Kakolewski, J. W., and Cox, V. C.: Sex differences in taste preference for glucose and saccharin solutions. Science *156*:942, 1967.

Wardlaw, J. M., Hennyey, D. J., and Clarke, R. H.: The effect of decreased feeding frequency on body composition in mature and immature male and female rats. Canad. J. Physiol. Pharmacol *47*:47, 1969.

3

NORMAL GROWTH, FAILURE TO THRIVE AND OBESITY

When an infant who was fullsize at birth weighs only 4 kg at three months of age, the conclusion that he has failed to thrive is justified even if measurement of length has been so inaccurate as to be useless. Thus, in developing countries, it has proved simple and practical to describe grades of malnutrition in terms of the extent to which body weight falls below the average expected weight for age.

Such crude methods of evaluation are of relatively little value to the practitioner in developed countries for, in these, the more frequent problem is one of distinguishing between slow rates of growth that may yet be considered within the normal range and those slightly slower rates of growth that are to be considered abnormal. An attempt will be made in this chapter to define normal rates of growth and failure to thrive. In addition, growth of major body components—water, protein and lipid—will be considered. An estimate will be made concerning the percentage of caloric requirement utilized for growth at various ages, and the problems of failure to thrive and obesity in infancy will be discussed.

METHODS OF MEASUREMENTS

Weight

Body weight should be measured using a beam balance with non-detachable weights which can be read to 10 gm. Calibrated or standard weights should be available to check the accuracy of scales at least two or three times yearly. Measurements of weight of infants are preferably made with subjects unclothed. Toddlers should be unclothed or clothed only in undergarments.

Stature*

Measurements of stature during the first two years of life are not recommended unless satisfactory equipment and two trained examiners are available. In many instances, it will not be practical to measure length routinely. In any case, measurements at birth are particularly difficult, and rarely will conditions be favorable for obtaining accurate data. Measurements made at several days of age are likely to be more satisfactory. Methods of measurement have been described by Falkner (1961) and Owen (1973).

Length. Until age 24 months, stature should be measured with the infant recumbent. Satisfactory measurements of length require adequate equipment and availability of two examiners. One person holds the infant's head with the Frankfort plane† vertical and applies gentle traction to bring the top of the head into contact with the fixed headboard. A second person holds the infant's feet, toes pointing directly upward and, also applying gentle traction, brings the movable footboard to rest firmly against the infant's heels (Fig. 3–1). An examining table, simply and inexpensively modified as described by Falkner (1961), will provide a suitable measuring apparatus. Alternatively, a portable measuring board of the type shown in Figure 3–2 can be utilized.

Height. Children 24 months of age and older may be measured in the standing position. It is strongly recommended that platform scales with movable measuring rods not be used for measuring height of children. Satisfactory equipment can be provided by fixing a measuring stick or tape to a true vertical flat surface, either a wall or a rigid, free-standing measuring device. The child should stand on a horizontal bare floor or platform with his bare heels together, back as straight as possible with the heels, buttocks, shoulders and head touching the wall or vertical surface of the measuring device; the Frankfort plane should be horizontal. A block, squared at right angles against the wall, is then brought to the crown of the head and the measurement noted (Fig. 3–3).

---

*The term "stature" is used throughout this book to include both length (measured recumbent) and height (measured standing).

†This plane, defined in reference to the skeleton, passes through the left porion, right porion and orbitale. In terms of soft tissue, the plane is determined by the most superior point of the left tragion, the most superior point on the right tragion and the most inferior point palpable along the inferior margin of the left orbit. The usual "plane of sight" and Frankfort plane are approximately equivalent.

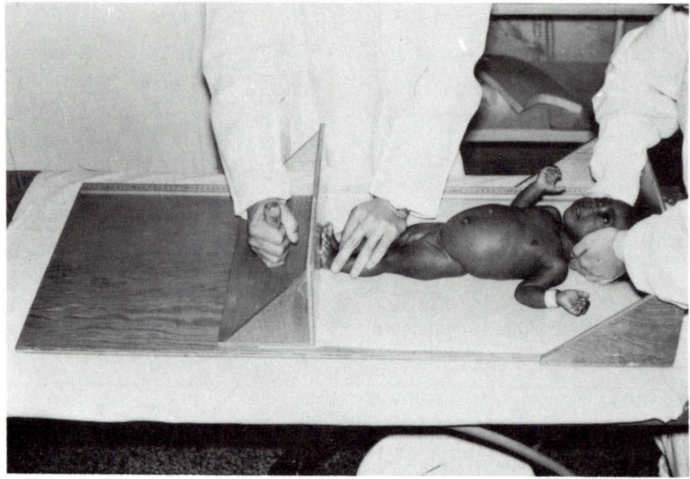

Figure 3–1 Technique of measuring recumbent length. (From Falkner, F.: Office measurement of physical growth. Pediatr. Clin. N. Amer. *8*:15, 1961.)

Head Circumference

For measurement of head circumference, a flexible, narrow steel tape is recommended, because it does not stretch as do cloth and plastic, and because it conforms well to the shape of the head. The tape is applied firmly around the head above the supraorbital ridges,

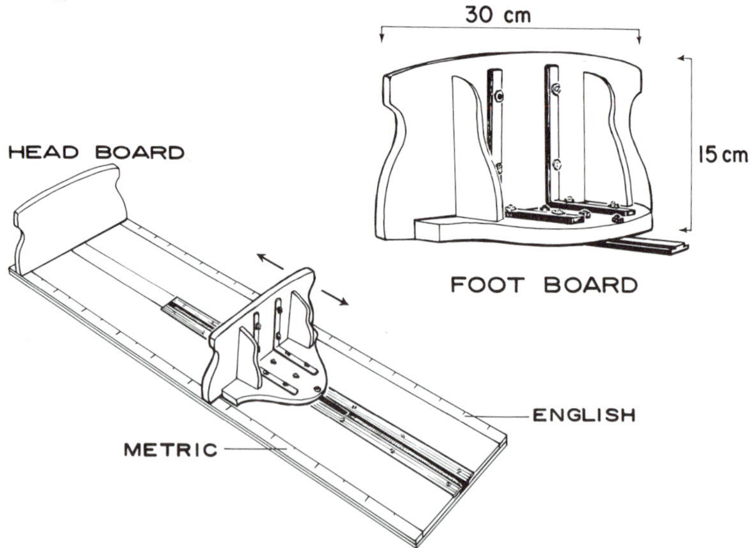

Figure 3–2 Apparatus used for measuring length.

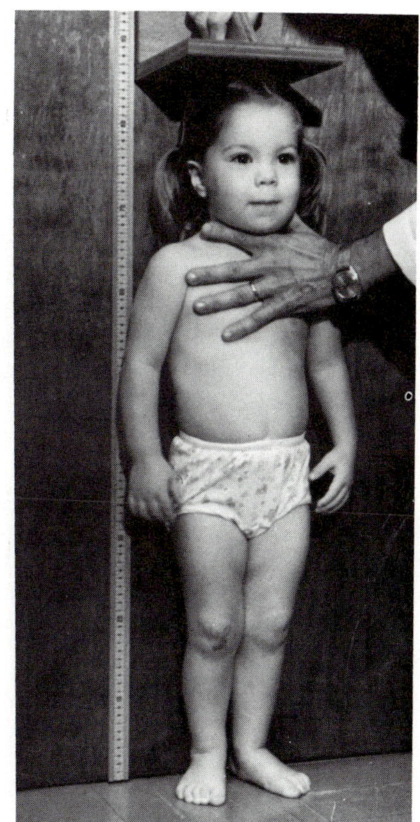

Figure 3–3 Technique of measuring height.

covering the most prominent part of the frontal bulge anteriorly, and over the part of the occiput which gives maximum circumference (Owen, 1973).

Skinfold Thickness

For measurement of skinfold thickness in the first three years of life, the Lange* caliper is preferred. This caliper meets the recommendations of the Committee on Nutritional Anthropometry (1956), and the area included within the jaws (30 mm^2) is small enough to be practical for use with infants. Methods of measurement have been described by Committee on Nutritional Anthropometry (1956) and by Jelliffe (1966). Although other sites may also be useful, those most commonly utilized are triceps and subscapular.

---

*Lange skinfold caliper, Cambridge Scientific Industries, Inc., Cambridge, Md.

Skinfold measurements of infants are difficult and require patience and continuing practice. The infant should be held in the attendant's lap in a semi-upright position, his right side leaning against, and his head turned toward, the attendant. The infant's left hand or forearm should be gently restrained by the attendant so that the infant's left upper extremity will be as relaxed as possible.

For measurement of triceps skinfold thickness, a mark is placed at the left acromium and olecranon. This distance is measured and the midpoint marked. The skinfold is grasped by the examiner 1 cm superior to the previously marked midpoint. For measurement of subscapular skinfold, the fold of skin is grasped by the examiner just inferior to and lateral to the inferior angle of the left scapula in the line of the natural skin cleavage.

The examiner grasps the layer of skin and subcutaneous tissue with the first finger and thumb of one hand, pulling it away from the underlying tissue, and continues to hold it until the measurement is completed. Making certain that the sides of the fold to be compressed by the calipers are parallel, the caliper is applied 1 cm inferior to the point grasped between thumb and forefinger. Readings should be made to 0.5 mm approximately three seconds after application of the caliper.

WEIGHT, STATURE, HEAD CIRCUMFERENCE AND SKINFOLD THICKNESS

Distance Attained

Data concerning distance attained with respect to measurements of weight, stature, head circumference and skinfold thickness are presented in Tables 3–1, 3–2 and 3–3. Incremental data (gain in these measures per unit of time) are presented later in the chapter.

Weight and Stature. Percentile values and the mean ±2 standard deviations for weight and stature at various ages are presented in Table 3–1. With the exception of the values for weight at birth and weight and length at age eight days, the data are those of Karlberg et al. (1968). Stature was determined with the subject recumbent to age three years, and thus the data on stature for 24- to 36-month-old children may exceed, by as much as 1 cm, the corresponding data from measurements made vertically (Boyd, 1929).

Head Circumference. Percentile values and the mean ±2 standard deviations for head circumference at various ages are given in Table 3–2.

Skinfold Thickness. Because subcutaneous tissue is a major depot of total body fat (Keys and Brožek, 1953; Bugyi, 1971), it may be possible to obtain information on relative fat content of the body by measuring one parameter of the subcutaneous tissue size—its thickness. This has been performed directly on cuts through skin (Ogawara, 1933), indirectly with roentgenographs (Brožek and Keys, 1950; Garn, 1957; Maresh, 1961), and by measuring the thickness of a skinfold which includes a double layer of skin proper and tela adiposa. Development of reliable instruments and standardized techniques (Edwards et al., 1955; Tanner, 1959; Committee on Nutritional Anthropometry, 1956; Tanner and Whitehouse, 1962), and selection of suitable body sites (Hammond, 1955; Pařízková, 1961; Seltzer et al., 1965; Seltzer and Mayer, 1967) have made this a useful and practical method for obtaining an estimate of body fat that correlates well with the figures obtained by other anthropometric evaluations (Damon and Goldman, 1964; Bugyi, 1971) and by nonanthropometric methods such as body density (Pařízková, 1961; Seltzer et al., 1965), body-water (Fletcher, 1962; Brook, 1971) and amount of naturally occurring ^{40}K (Barter and Forbes, 1963).

Skinfold thickness for age and sex has been recorded from studies of adults and children in many countries and its usefulness in evaluation of overnutrition (Seltzer et al., 1965; Seltzer and Mayer, 1967; Committee on Nutrition, 1968) and undernutrition (Keet et al., 1970) has been demonstrated. Data concerning infants are relatively few except for newborns (Vincent and Hugon, 1962; Tanner and Whitehouse, 1962; Gampel, 1965; Farr, 1966). The data of Karlberg et al. (1968) from study of Swedish children during the first three years of life (Table 3–3) are particularly valuable. Although the values included in Table 3–3 concern only triceps and subscapular skinfolds, similar data are available for biceps and subiliac skinfolds (Karlberg et al., 1968).

Incremental Data: Fullsize Infants

Weight and Stature. Various percentile values for gain in weight and gain in length between selected ages are indicated in Table 3–4 for young infants and in Table 3–5 for infants and toddlers. In calculating gains in stature between two ages, it is important that both measurements represent length (subject recumbent) or that both measurements represent height (subject standing). The extent of decrease in weight gain with increasing age may be seen from Figure 3–4. The greater gain of males than of females is also evident.

The importance of considering duration of observation in interpreting the 10th or 90th percentiles of gain in weight has been insufficiently emphasized. It was pointed out by Fomon et al. (1970) that

(Text continued on page 54.)

TABLE 3–1 LENGTHS AND WEIGHTS AT VARIOUS AGES*

AGE (MONTHS)	PERCENTILES	S.D.	WEIGHT (KG)		LENGTH (CM)	
			Males	*Females*	*Males*	*Females*
Birth		−2	2.70	2.54		
	10		2.92	2.83		
	25		3.16	3.05		
	50		3.44	3.30		
	75		3.67	3.56		
	90		3.90	3.88		
		+2	4.13	4.12		
1/4		−2	2.72	2.59	48.2	47.6
	10		2.88	2.83	49.1	48.6
	25		3.23	3.12	50.3	49.7
	50		3.48	3.35	51.5	50.8
	75		3.66	3.60	52.4	51.8
	90		3.87	3.88	53.2	52.8
		+2	4.14	4.14	54.4	53.9
1		−2	2.93	3.03	50.3	49.7
	10		3.31	3.34	52.2	51.3
	25		3.60	3.61	53.1	52.3
	50		4.01	3.85	54.5	53.6
	75		4.39	4.10	56.0	55.2
	90		4.68	4.41	57.1	56.2
		+2	5.13	4.67	58.7	57.7
3		−2	4.28	4.59	56.7	56.0
	10		4.88	4.88	58.7	57.5
	25		5.36	5.20	59.7	58.4
	50		5.83	5.60	61.5	60.0
	75		6.37	5.89	62.8	61.3
	90		6.86	6.18	64.0	62.6
		+2	7.52	6.59	65.9	64.0
6		−2	5.95	6.01	63.9	61.9
	10		6.71	6.74	65.6	63.3
	25		7.08	7.09	66.5	65.2
	50		7.72	7.45	67.8	66.3
	75		8.20	7.95	69.2	67.8
	90		8.98	8.37	70.5	69.2
		+2	9.59	8.93	71.9	71.1

TABLE 3–1 LENGTHS AND WEIGHTS AT VARIOUS AGES*
(Continued)

AGE (MONTHS)	PERCENTILES	S.D.	WEIGHT (KG) Males	WEIGHT (KG) Females	LENGTH (CM) Males	LENGTH (CM) Females
9		−2	7.03	7.39	68.3	66.6
	10		7.91	7.94	70.0	68.2
	25		8.33	8.35	70.9	69.5
	50		9.07	8.90	72.3	71.1
	75		9.65	9.43	73.6	73.1
	90		10.69	9.87	75.0	74.0
		+2	11.23	10.39	76.7	75.8
12		−2	7.99	8.16	71.9	70.5
	10		8.84	8.89	73.6	72.5
	25		9.41	9.16	74.7	73.2
	50		10.15	9.85	76.4	75.1
	75		10.85	10.49	78.0	76.9
	90		11.63	11.11	79.3	78.1
		+2	12.47	11.64	81.1	80.1
18		−2	9.14	9.33	78.1	76.7
	10		10.18	10.15	80.0	78.7
	25		10.88	10.54	81.7	80.2
	50		11.61	11.10	83.2	82.0
	75		12.55	11.84	85.3	84.2
	90		13.29	12.70	87.0	86.2
		+2	14.42	13.17	88.9	87.9
24		−2	9.87	10.01	83.0	81.7
	10		10.99	11.00	85.0	84.2
	25		11.89	11.50	87.3	85.8
	50		12.82	12.28	88.8	87.5
	75		13.85	13.14	90.9	90.3
	90		14.48	14.16	92.8	91.9
		+2	15.99	14.85	95.0	94.1
36		−2	11.29	11.44	90.4	89.3
	10		12.90	12.90	93.4	92.1
	25		13.64	13.42	95.3	94.2
	50		14.80	14.33	97.3	96.2
	75		15.70	15.30	100.6	99.0
	90		16.80	17.00	102.6	100.6
		+2	18.61	17.72	105.2	103.7

*Data of Karlberg et al. (1968) except for values at birth and 1/4 month (eight days) which are from Fomon et al. (1970, 1971, 1973).

TABLE 3–2 HEAD CIRCUMFERENCE AT VARIOUS AGES*

Age (months)	Percentiles	S.D.	Head Circumference (cm)	
			Males	*Females*
1		−2	34.4	34.2
	10		35.2	35.0
	25		36.2	35.6
	50		37.0	36.2
	75		37.8	36.7
	90		38.6	37.6
		+2	39.6	38.2
3		−2	37.9	37.3
	10		38.6	37.9
	25		39.5	38.7
	50		40.3	39.5
	75		41.0	39.8
	90		41.7	40.4
		+2	42.3	41.3
6		−2	40.9	40.1
	10		41.9	40.9
	25		42.7	41.5
	50		43.3	42.2
	75		44.0	42.8
	90		44.8	43.4
		+2	45.7	44.1
9		−2	42.8	42.0
	10		43.7	42.7
	25		44.5	43.3
	50		45.0	44.0
	75		45.8	44.5
	90		46.6	45.5
		+2	47.6	46.0

TABLE 3–2 HEAD CIRCUMFERENCE AT VARIOUS AGES*
(Continued)

Age (months)	Percentiles	S.D.	Head Circumference (cm)	
			Males	*Females*
12		−2	44.3	43.3
	10		45.0	44.0
	25		45.8	44.5
	50		46.5	45.3
	75		47.2	45.9
	90		47.7	46.6
		+2	48.7	47.3
18		−2	45.4	44.6
	10		46.4	45.4
	25		47.1	45.9
	50		48.1	46.7
	75		49.0	47.3
	90		49.6	48.2
		+2	50.6	48.6
24		−2	46.4	44.8
	10		47.3	46.4
	25		48.1	46.8
	50		49.0	47.8
	75		49.7	48.3
	90		50.5	49.0
		+2	51.6	50.4
36		−2	47.4	46.5
	10		48.0	47.1
	25		49.3	47.8
	50		50.0	48.8
	75		50.9	49.5
	90		51.7	50.1
		+2	52.6	50.9

*Data of Karlberg et al. (1968).

TABLE 3–3 THICKNESS OF TRICEPS AND SUBSCAPULAR SKINFOLDS AT VARIOUS AGES*

AGE (MONTHS)	PERCENTILES	S.D.	TRICEPS (MM)		SUBSCAPULAR (MM)	
			Males	*Females*	*Males*	*Females*
1		−2	2.9	3.5	3.1	3.8
	10		4.0	4.5	4.2	4.9
	25		4.7	5.2	4.8	5.4
	50		5.3	5.8	5.6	6.2
	75		6.2	6.7	6.5	7.0
	90		7.0	7.6	7.5	7.9
		+2	8.1	8.3	8.3	9.0
3		−2	4.5	5.0	3.5	4.7
	10		6.0	6.2	4.9	5.9
	25		6.8	7.2	5.8	6.9
	50		8.1	8.2	6.9	8.0
	75		9.2	9.2	8.1	8.6
	90		10.3	10.5	9.0	9.4
		+2	11.7	11.8	10.7	11.1
6		−2	6.3	6.7	3.8	4.0
	10		7.8	8.2	5.5	5.9
	25		8.6	9.0	6.2	6.9
	50		9.7	10.4	7.1	8.1
	75		11.1	11.3	8.4	8.9
	90		11.8	12.7	10.1	10.3
		+2	13.5	13.9	11.0	12.4
9		−2	6.0	6.7	3.4	4.7
	10		7.5	7.9	5.3	6.0
	25		8.7	8.8	6.0	6.7
	50		9.9	10.1	7.1	7.6
	75		11.2	11.3	8.5	8.8
	90		12.5	12.5	9.7	10.1
		+2	14.0	13.5	11.4	11.1

TABLE 3–3 THICKNESS OF TRICEPS AND SUBSCAPULAR SKINFOLDS AT VARIOUS AGES* *(Continued)*

Age (months)	Percentiles	S.D.	Triceps (mm)		Subscapular (mm)	
			Males	*Females*	*Males*	*Females*
12		−2	6.2	6.4	3.8	4.5
	10		7.8	7.6	5.3	6.0
	25		8.6	8.7	6.0	6.5
	50		9.8	9.8	7.2	7.5
	75		11.1	11.2	8.6	8.7
	90		12.2	12.2	9.6	9.8
		+2	13.8	13.6	11.0	10.9
18		−2	6.4	6.8	3.9	4.2
	10		7.7	7.9	5.3	5.7
	25		8.6	8.9	6.0	6.2
	50		9.9	10.3	6.8	7.1
	75		11.4	11.3	7.9	8.0
	90		12.2	12.3	9.3	9.0
		+2	13.6	13.6	10.3	10.2
24		−2	5.8	6.5	3.0	3.9
	10		7.4	8.3	4.6	5.3
	25		8.5	8.9	5.4	5.6
	50		9.8	10.1	6.5	6.5
	75		11.6	11.6	7.4	7.3
	90		13.1	12.8	8.3	8.4
		+2	14.2	14.1	10.2	9.5
36		−2	6.6	6.4	2.9	2.6
	10		7.8	8.2	4.5	4.7
	25		9.0	9.4	5.0	5.2
	50		9.8	10.3	5.5	6.1
	75		11.0	11.5	6.4	7.2
	90		12.2	12.5	7.1	8.6
		+2	13.4	14.4	8.9	10.6

*Data of Karlberg et al. (1968).

TABLE 3–4 DAILY CHANGES IN WEIGHT AND LENGTH BETWEEN SELECTED AGES*

Age (days)	Percentiles	S.D.	8 days	14 days	28 days	42 days	56 days	84 days	112 days
			Change in Weight (gm/day), Males						
Birth		−2	−36	−9	9	16	18	19	18
	10		−18	0	16	22	23	24	23
	25		−10	7	22	27	28	27	26
	50		2	16	29	32	32	31	29
	75		15	23	33	38	38	35	32
	90		23	28	39	41	43	39	38
		+2	39	40	48	48	47	44	41
8		−2		1	18	22	22	21	20
	10			13	28	29	29	26	24
	25			22	32	33	32	30	28
	50			34	38	38	36	33	32
	75			44	46	46	44	37	35
	90			55	52	50	48	44	41
		+2		66	60	56	54	48	44
14		−2			19	23	22	21	19
	10				28	29	29	26	24
	25				35	34	33	30	27
	50				41	40	38	34	31
	75				49	46	44	38	35
	90				56	51	49	44	40
		+2			64	57	54	48	44
28		−2				20	19	18	17
	10					28	26	24	22
	25					33	31	27	25
	50					38	36	32	29
	75					45	42	37	34
	90					52	50	43	39
		+2				59	55	48	43

42		−2						11	14	14
	10							20	21	20
	25							26	24	23
	50							35	30	27
	75							40	35	32
	90							50	41	37
		+2						58	47	42
56		−2							12	13
	10								19	19
	25								22	22
	50								28	26
	75								34	31
	90								40	35
		+2							45	40
84		−2								9
	10									14
	25									19
	50									25
	75									30
	90									34
		+2								40
Change in Weight (gm/day), Females										
Birth		−2	−29	− 7	10	15	16	16	16	
	10		−19	0	16	20	20	20	19	
	25		− 7	7	21	23	23	23	22	
	50		5	16	26	27	28	27	25	
	75		18	25	31	32	32	30	28	
	90		26	31	35	35	35	33	32	
		+2	39	38	41	40	39	37	35	

TABLE 3–4 DAILY CHANGES IN WEIGHT AND LENGTH BETWEEN SELECTED AGES* (*Continued*)

AGE (DAYS)	PERCENTILES	S.D.	8 DAYS	14 DAYS	28 DAYS	42 DAYS	56 DAYS	84 DAYS	112 DAYS
			Change in Weight (gm/day), Females						
8		−2		2	17	19	18	18	17
	10			13	23	24	23	21	20
	25			21	28	28	27	25	24
	50			32	33	33	32	29	27
	75			43	40	38	36	33	30
	90			48	46	42	39	36	33
		+2		59	51	47	44	40	37
14		−2			18	19	18	18	17
	10				24	25	24	21	20
	25				29	29	27	25	24
	50				35	33	32	29	26
	75				41	38	36	33	30
	90				48	42	39	35	33
		+2			53	48	44	40	37
28		−2				14	15	15	15
	10					19	20	20	18
	25					26	25	23	22
	50					31	29	27	25
	75					37	34	30	28
	90					41	39	36	32
		+2				48	43	39	36
42		−2					10	14	13
	10						16	18	17
	25						22	21	20
	50						27	26	24
	75						34	30	27
	90						39	35	31
		+2					45	38	35

56		−2					12	12
	10						16	16
	25						20	20
	50						25	23
	75						29	26
	90						34	30
		+2					38	34
84		−2						7
	10							14
	25							18
	50							20
	75							24
	90							30
		+2						35
Change in Length (mm/day), Males								
8		−2	0.1	0.8	0.9	0.9	0.9	0.9
	10		0.6	1.0	1.0	1.0	1.0	1.0
	25		1.1	1.2	1.2	1.2	1.1	1.0
	50		1.7	1.4	1.4	1.3	1.2	1.1
	75		2.3	1.6	1.5	1.4	1.2	1.2
	90		2.8	1.7	1.6	1.5	1.3	1.2
		+2	3.2	1.9	1.7	1.6	1.4	1.3
14		−2		0.6	0.8	0.9	0.9	0.9
	10			0.8	1.0	1.0	1.0	1.0
	25			1.0	1.1	1.1	1.0	1.0
	50			1.3	1.3	1.2	1.1	1.1
	75			1.5	1.5	1.3	1.2	1.1
	90			1.7	1.6	1.4	1.3	1.2
		+2		1.9	1.7	1.5	1.4	1.3
28		−2			0.6	0.7	0.8	0.8
	10				0.8	0.9	0.9	0.9
	25				1.1	1.1	1.0	1.0
	50				1.3	1.2	1.1	1.0
	75				1.6	1.3	1.2	1.1
	90				1.8	1.5	1.3	1.2
		+2			2.0	1.6	1.4	1.3

TABLE 3–4 DAILY CHANGES IN WEIGHT AND LENGTH BETWEEN SELECTED AGES* *(Continued)*

AGE (DAYS)	PERCENTILES	S.D.	8 DAYS	14 DAYS	28 DAYS	42 DAYS	56 DAYS	84 DAYS	112 DAYS
			Change in Length (mm/day), Males						
42		−2					0.4	0.7	0.7
	10						0.6	0.8	0.9
	25						0.9	0.9	0.9
	50						1.1	1.0	1.0
	75						1.2	1.1	1.1
	90						1.5	1.3	1.1
		+2					1.7	1.4	1.2
56		−2						0.6	0.7
	10							0.8	0.8
	25							0.9	0.9
	50							1.0	1.0
	75							1.2	1.1
	90							1.3	1.2
		+2						1.4	1.2
84		−2							0.4
	10								0.6
	25								0.8
	50								0.9
	75								1.1
	90								1.2
		+2							1.4
			Change in Length (mm/day), Females						
8		−2		0.0	0.8	0.9	0.9	0.9	0.8
	10			0.7	1.0	1.0	1.0	0.9	0.9
	25			1.1	1.1	1.1	1.1	1.0	1.0
	50			1.6	1.4	1.3	1.2	1.1	1.0
	75			2.2	1.6	1.4	1.3	1.2	1.1
	90			2.6	1.8	1.5	1.4	1.3	1.2
		+2		3.3	2.0	1.7	1.5	1.3	1.2

14		−2	0.5	0.8	0.8	0.8	0.8
	10		0.7	0.9	0.9	0.9	0.9
	25		1.0	1.0	1.1	1.0	0.9
	50		1.3	1.2	1.1	1.1	1.0
	75		1.5	1.3	1.2	1.1	1.1
	90		1.7	1.4	1.4	1.2	1.1
		+2	2.1	1.6	1.4	1.3	1.2
28		−2		0.3	0.6	0.7	0.7
	10			0.5	0.8	0.8	0.8
	25			0.9	0.9	0.9	0.9
	50			1.1	1.1	1.0	1.0
	75			1.3	1.2	1.1	1.0
	90			1.6	1.4	1.2	1.1
		+2		1.9	1.5	1.3	1.2
42		−2			0.3	0.7	0.7
	10				0.5	0.8	0.8
	25				0.8	0.9	0.9
	50				1.1	1.0	0.9
	75				1.3	1.1	1.0
	90				1.5	1.2	1.1
		+2			1.7	1.3	1.2
56		−2				0.5	0.6
	10					0.7	0.7
	25					0.8	0.8
	50					0.9	0.9
	75					1.1	1.0
	90					1.2	1.1
		+2				1.4	1.2
84		−2					0.4
	10						0.5
	25						0.7
	50						0.9
	75						1.0
	90						1.1
		+2					1.3

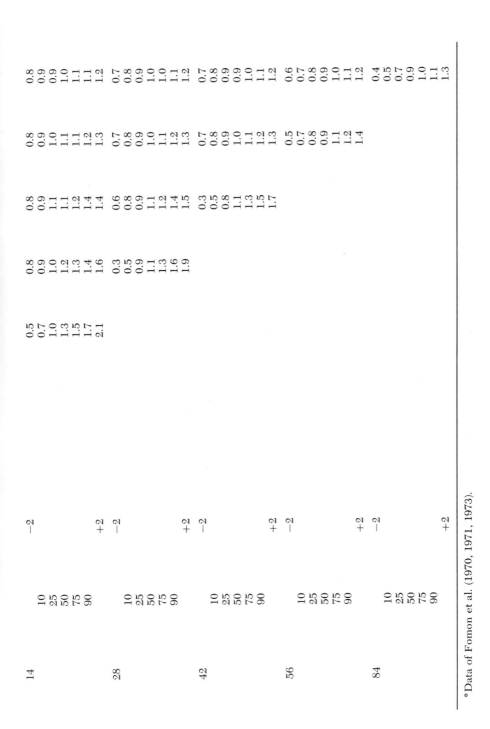

*Data of Fomon et al. (1970, 1971, 1973).

TABLE 3–5 DAILY CHANGES IN WEIGHT AND LENGTH BETWEEN SELECTED AGES*

Age Interval (months)	Percentiles	S.D.	Gain in Weight (gm/day)		Gain in Length (mm/day)	
			Males	*Females*	*Males*	*Females*
3–6		−2	8.9	9.3	0.4	0.4
	10		14.1	15.4	0.5	0.5
	25		16.6	18.1	0.6	0.6
	50		19.5	20.7	0.7	0.7
	75		24.4	23.6	0.8	0.8
	90		28.2	25.8	1.0	0.9
		+2	32.5	31.7	1.1	1.0
6–9		−2	5.4	4.6	0.2	0.3
	10		9.0	10.3	0.4	0.4
	25		11.3	12.3	0.4	0.5
	50		14.7	14.7	0.5	0.5
	75		18.3	17.9	0.5	0.6
	90		21.3	21.0	0.6	0.7
		+2	24.6	27.0	0.8	0.8
9–12		−2	−0.2	3.1	0.2	0.2
	10		5.7	5.9	0.3	0.3
	25		8.3	8.6	0.4	0.4
	50		11.7	10.9	0.4	0.4
	75		14.9	13.7	0.5	0.5
	90		18.6	15.6	0.6	0.6
		+2	24.3	18.8	0.7	0.7
12–18		−2	2.2	2.1	0.2	0.3
	10		4.9	5.0	0.3	0.3
	25		6.4	5.8	0.3	0.4
	50		8.2	7.2	0.4	0.4
	75		10.4	8.8	0.4	0.4
	90		12.0	10.4	0.5	0.5
		+2	14.9	13.1	0.6	0.5
18–24		−2	0.1	1.0	0.2	0.2
	10		2.2	2.9	0.2	0.2
	25		3.7	4.0	0.3	0.3
	50		6.0	6.5	0.3	0.3
	75		8.1	8.3	0.4	0.4
	90		10.1	10.6	0.4	0.4
		+2	12.3	12.0	0.4	0.5
24–36		−2	1.8	2.1	0.2	0.2
	10		3.6	3.6	0.2	0.2
	25		4.2	4.5	0.2	0.2
	50		5.4	5.8	0.2	0.2
	75		6.0	6.9	0.3	0.3
	90		7.3	7.9	0.3	0.3
		+2	9.0	9.7	0.3	0.3

*Data of Karlberg et al. (1968).

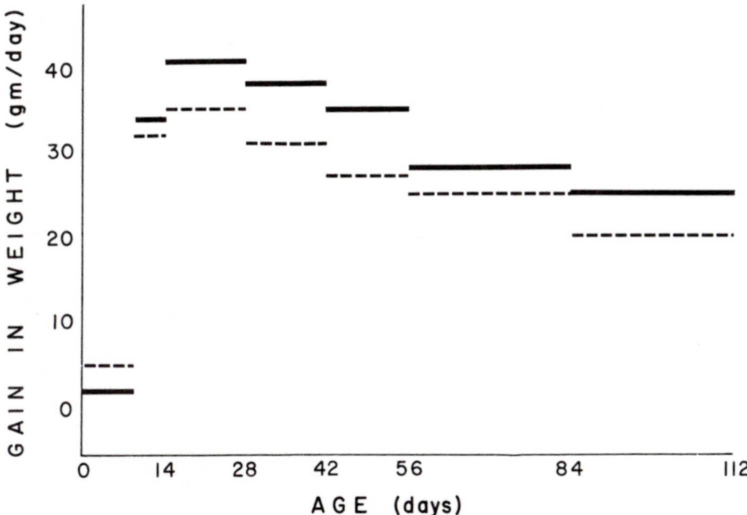

Figure 3–4 Gain in weight during various age intervals. Solid lines pertain to gains of males, interrupted lines to gains of females. (Data are 50th percentile values from Table 3–4.)

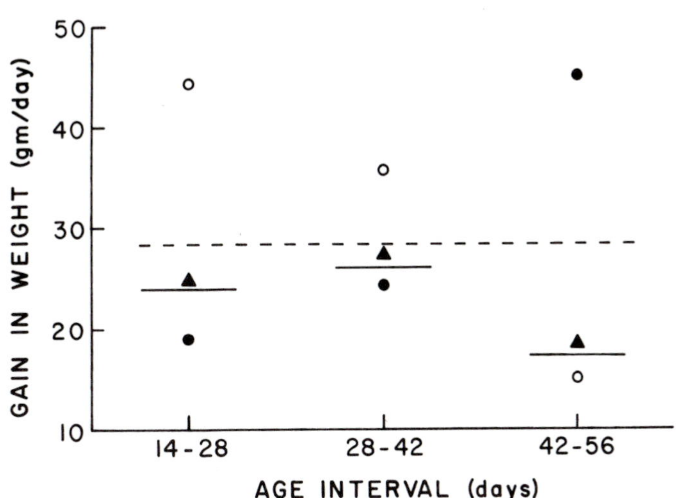

Figure 3–5 Patterns of weight gain of three individual infants in relation to 10th percentile values for 58 male breastfed infants. The three solid horizontal lines indicate the 10th percentile gains for the designated 14-day intervals; the interrupted horizontal line indicates the 10th percentile rate of gain for the entire 42-day interval from 14 to 56 days of age. Each symbol refers to the performance of one infant. (From Fomon, S. J., et al.: Growth and serum chemical values of normal breastfed infants. Acta Paediatr. Scand. [Suppl. 202], 1970.)

the 10th percentile values for gain in weight by male breastfed infants during three consecutive 14-day intervals (14 to 28, 28 to 42 and 42 to 56 days) were 24.0, 26.0 and 17.3 gm/day, respectively. However, the 10th percentile value for the entire interval, 14 to 56 days of age, was 28.2 gm/day, a value larger than that of any of the component 14-day intervals. This apparent paradox is explained by the fact that the infants who gained weight most slowly during one 14-day interval were not, in many instances, the ones who gained most slowly in the next 14-day interval. Several examples are presented in Figure 3–5.

In Table 3–4, it may be seen that the 90th percentile gains in weight for male infants during the successive 14-day intervals 14 to 28, 28 to 42 and 42 to 56 days, were 56, 52 and 50 gm/day, respec-

TABLE 3–6 INCREMENT IN HEAD CIRCUMFERENCE IN VARIOUS AGE INTERVALS*

Age Interval (months)	Percentiles	S.D.	Increment in Head Circumference (cm)	
			Males	*Females*
0–1		−2	1.0	0.8
	10		2.0	1.5
	25		2.5	2.6
	50		3.6	3.3
	75		4.3	4.0
	90		5.3	4.7
		+2	6.2	5.6
1–3		−2	1.9	1.9
	10		2.4	2.5
	25		2.8	2.6
	50		3.3	3.1
	75		3.7	3.4
	90		4.2	3.8
		+2	4.7	4.3
3–6		−2	1.7	1.8
	10		2.2	2.3
	25		2.6	2.5
	50		3.0	2.9
	75		3.3	3.2
	90		4.0	3.4
		+2	4.5	3.8
6–9		−2	1.1	0.9
	10		1.3	1.4
	25		1.6	1.6
	50		1.9	1.9
	75		2.1	2.2
	90		2.3	2.5
		+2	2.7	2.9

tively. The 90th percentile gain for the same infants during the entire 42-day interval, 14 to 56 days of age, was 49 gm/day. From these examples, it is apparent that duration of observation is an important determinant of the 10th and 90th percentile values for gain in weight.

Head Circumference. In Table 3–6, a marked deceleration in rate of increase in head circumference is apparent. In the successive age intervals birth to one month, 1 to 3, 3 to 6, 6 to 9, 9 to 12 and 12 to 18 months, the 50th percentile values for males are 3.6, 3.3, 3.0, 1.9, 1.3 and 1.6 cm, respectively—equivalent to 3.6, 1.65, 1.0, 0.63, 0.43 and 0.27 cm/month.

Skinfold Thickness. Data on increments (or decrements) in triceps and subscapular skinfold thickness are presented in Table 3–7. It is of interest that between 6 and 36 months of age, skinfold

TABLE 3–6 INCREMENT IN HEAD CIRCUMFERENCE IN VARIOUS AGE INTERVALS* *(Continued)*

Age Interval (Months)	Percentiles	S.D.	Increment in Head Circumference (cm)	
			Males	*Females*
9–12		−2	0.5	0.4
	10		0.8	0.8
	25		1.0	1.0
	50		1.3	1.2
	75		1.6	1.6
	90		1.8	1.7
		+2	2.1	2.0
12–18		−2	0.6	0.4
	10		1.0	0.7
	25		1.3	1.1
	50		1.6	1.5
	75		1.8	1.7
	90		2.1	1.9
		+2	2.6	2.4
18–24		−2	0.0	0.0
	10		0.2	0.5
	25		0.6	0.7
	50		0.9	0.9
	75		1.3	1.2
	90		1.7	1.5
		+2	2.0	2.0
24–36		−2	0.0	−0.5
	10		0.5	0.5
	25		0.7	0.8
	50		1.0	1.1
	75		1.3	1.3
	90		1.5	1.6
		+2	2.0	2.7

*Data of Karlberg et al. (1968).

TABLE 3–7 INCREMENTS IN SKINFOLD THICKNESS IN VARIOUS AGE INTERVALS*

Age Interval (months)	Percentiles	S.D.	Triceps (mm)		Subscapular (mm)	
			Males	*Females*	*Males*	*Females*
1–3		−2	−0.6	−0.9	−1.8	−1.4
	10		0.7	0.1	−0.5	−0.7
	25		1.5	1.4	0.2	0.5
	50		2.5	2.5	1.4	1.6
	75		3.6	3.4	2.2	2.6
	90		4.7	4.4	3.1	3.4
		+2	5.8	5.9	4.6	4.6
3–6		−2	−1.5	−1.7	−3.3	−2.3
	10		−0.1	−0.1	−1.5	−1.2
	25		0.8	0.7	−0.7	−0.6
	50		1.8	2.1	0.2	0.2
	75		2.8	3.3	1.2	1.1
	90		3.6	4.4	2.3	2.0
		+2	5.3	5.9	3.9	2.9
6–9		−2	−3.0	−3.5	−2.9	−3.3
	10		−1.7	−2.2	−1.5	−2.0
	25		−0.7	−1.1	−0.8	−1.1
	50		0.2	−0.2	0.0	−0.2
	75		1.4	0.8	0.8	0.5
	90		2.6	1.6	1.9	1.2
		+2	3.8	3.3	3.1	2.7
9–12		−2	−3.7	−3.6	−3.2	−2.5
	10		−2.4	−2.4	−1.4	−1.6
	25		−1.5	−1.4	−0.6	−1.0
	50		0.0	−0.2	0.0	−0.3
	75		1.2	1.0	0.7	0.4
	90		2.4	2.1	1.8	1.1
		+2	3.5	3.2	3.2	1.9
12–18		−2	−3.2	−3.0	−3.3	−3.1
	10		−2.0	−2.2	−2.1	−2.1
	25		−1.0	−0.9	−1.0	−1.3
	50		−0.1	0.2	−0.4	−0.6
	75		1.4	1.3	0.4	0.2
	90		2.3	2.1	1.3	1.5
		+2	3.6	3.4	2.7	2.1
18–24		−2	−3.4	−3.0	−3.2	−2.7
	10		−2.0	−2.0	−1.7	−1.6
	25		−1.3	−0.8	−1.2	−1.1
	50		0.0	0.1	−0.5	−0.6
	75		1.2	1.2	0.2	0.2
	90		2.4	2.5	0.9	0.9
		+2	3.4	3.4	2.4	1.7
24–36		−2	−3.5	−4.2	−2.9	−3.5
	10		−2.3	−2.7	−1.9	−1.8
	25		−1.2	−1.2	−1.2	−0.9
	50		−0.2	0.3	−0.6	−0.4
	75		1.2	1.3	0.0	0.3
	90		2.3	2.3	0.4	1.2
		+2	3.3	4.2	1.5	3.3

*Data of Karlberg et al. (1968).

thickness actually decreases in a large percentage of children. This agrees with clinical observations that the obese-appearing six-month-old commonly becomes a relatively slim three-year-old.

Secular Change in Weight and Stature

Data from the Fels Institute indicate similarity in mean stature of like-sexed children in Yellow Springs, Ohio, whether they were born before (77 males and 83 females) or after (112 males and 101 females) November 1942 (Garn, 1967). At age three years, mean stature was 96.5 and 95.3 cm, respectively, for earlier born males and females. Corresponding values for the later born children were 97.2 and 95.9 cm. Similarly, Maresh (1972) reported no secular changes toward larger size or earlier adolescence between earlier-born and later-born children during 45 years of data collection in the Child Research Council study in Denver. Thus, it seems likely that in economically and educationally favored populations, the secular change toward larger size may have reached a plateau.

Genetic Influences

Garn and Rohmann (1966) have demonstrated that, at equal ages, body lengths of siblings during infancy are more similar than are body lengths of nonsiblings. Furthermore, regression of length of male infants on midparental height is 0.196 at birth ($r=0.56$) and 0.305 at age one year ($r=0.61$). Although of value in assessing size of groups of infants, these correlations have relatively slight predictive value when applied to individuals. Parent-specific data for rate of gain in length and weight of infants are not yet available.

Growth of Low-Birth-Weight Infants

Perinatal Growth Potential. McKeown and Record (1953) observed that between 30 and 36 weeks of gestation and again between birth and 13 weeks of age, gains in weight averaged approximately 31.5 gm/day (Fig. 3–6). These authors also demonstrated that during the early part of gestation, single and multiple fetuses gain at similar rates (McKeown and Record, 1952). By 28 weeks of gestation, quadruplet fetuses are smaller than triplets, twins or singletons; by 30 weeks of gestation, triplets are smaller than twins or singletons and, by 32 weeks of gestation, twins are smaller than singletons (Fig. 3–7). These observations are consistent with the hypothesis that the decreased

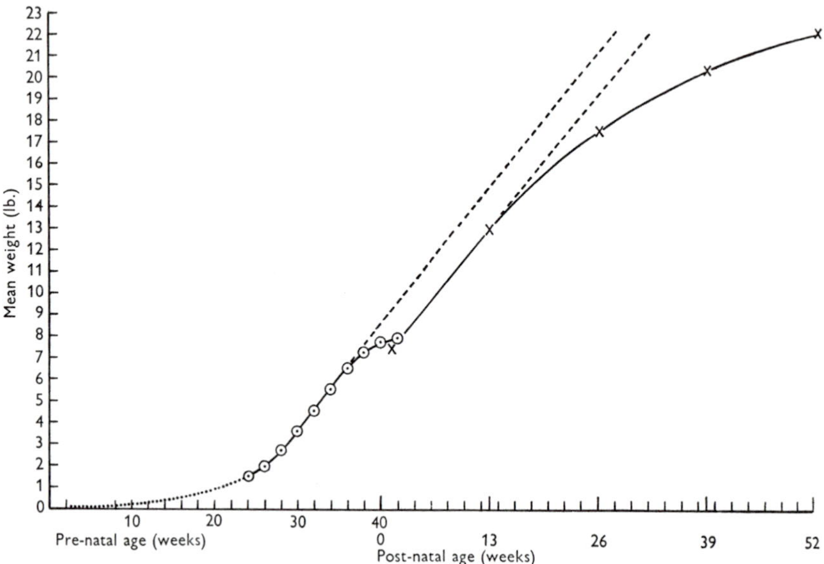

Figure 3–6 Prenatal and postnatal growth rates of singletons. (From McKeown, T., and Record, R. G.: The influence of placental size on fetal growth in man, with special reference to multiple pregnancy. J. Endocr. *9*:418, 1953.)

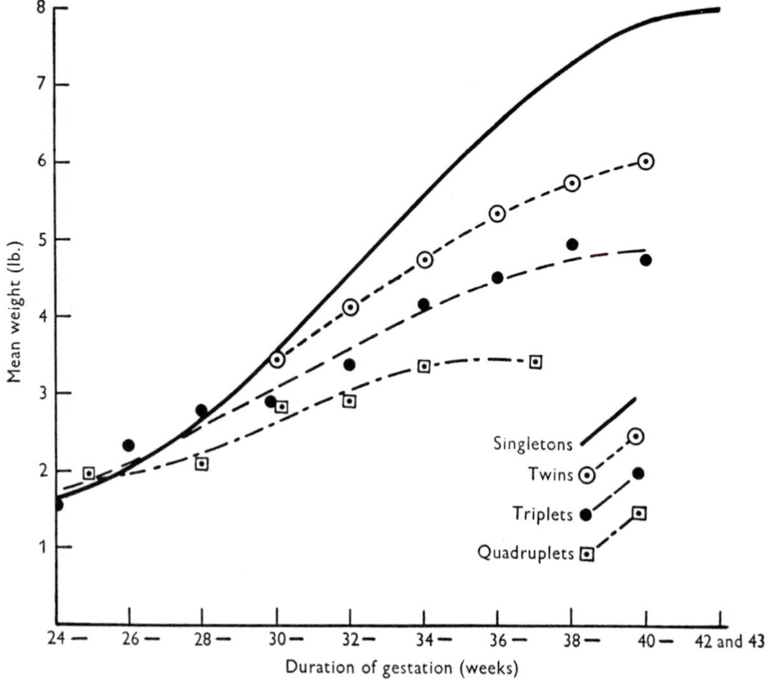

Figure 3–7 Mean birth weight of single and multiple fetuses related to duration of gestation. Cubic curves fitted by method of least squares. (From McKeown, T., and Record, R. G.: Observations on foetal growth in multiple pregnancy in man. J. Endocr. *8*:386, 1952.)

rate of growth of fetuses toward the end of gestation reflects environmental factors (presumably, relative placental insufficiency), and that the true growth potential during the latter part of gestation is approximately 31 or 32 gm/day. This hypothesis has implications with respect to management of the premature infant (Chapter 19).

Increments in Stature and Weight. Data on increments in stature and weight of low-birth-weight infants are available from several sources (Babson, 1970; Fitzhardinge and Steven, 1972; Cruise, 1973). The data of Cruise (1973) are summarized in Table 3–8.

RELATION OF GAIN IN WEIGHT TO CALORIE INTAKE

Although Rose and Mayer (1968) failed to demonstrate a statistically significant relation between calorie intake and rate of gain in weight by normal fullterm infants, Ashworth et al. (1968; Ashworth, 1969) have demonstrated a statistically significant relation between calorie intake and rate of growth of infants recovering from marasmus, and Fomon et al. (1969, 1971) have demonstrated such a relation for normal infants fed milk-based formulas between 8 and 112 days of age.

Means and standard deviations for gain in weight, expressed as grams gained per 100 kcal consumed, are presented for various ages in Table 3–9. An example of the relation between weight gain and calorie intake in one short age interval (28 through 41 days) is presented in Figure 3–8. Similar relations for other age intervals are included in Appendix II (p. 535).

As discussed in Chapter 7, diets of poor digestibility result in relatively low gain in weight per unit of calorie intake (Fig. 7–7). Similarly, infants with steatorrhea or carbohydrate intolerance may be expected to demonstrate low gains in weight per unit of calorie intake. We do not yet know whether deficiencies of specific essential nutrients may yield abnormally low values for weight gain per unit of calorie intake.

CATCH-UP GROWTH

The phenomenon of catch-up growth after illness is well recognized (Prader et al., 1963). As has been stated by Barr et al. (1972), the extent of recovery probably depends on many factors, such as the effects of adverse environment or disease before, during and after the period of malnutrition, and the timing, degree and duration of the malnutrition itself. Follow-up studies of malnutrition during infancy have

TABLE 3–8 CHANGES IN WEIGHT AND LENGTH BY LOW-BIRTH-WEIGHT AND FULLSIZE INFANTS DURING THE FIRST THREE YEARS OF LIFE

AGE INTERVAL (MONTHS)	SIZE APPROPRIATE FOR GESTATIONAL AGE (GA)									SIZE SMALL FOR GA		
	GA 28–32 Weeks			*GA 33–36 Weeks*			*GA 37–42 Weeks**			*GA 37–42 Weeks*		
	N	*Mean*	*S.D.*	*N*	*Mean*	*S.D.*	*N*	*Mean*	*S.D.*	*N*	*Mean*	*S.D.*
	Males – Change in Weight (kg)											
0–3	17	2.9	0.6	28	2.9	0.6	123	2.8	0.6	22	2.9	0.5
3–6	17	2.3	0.6	25	2.2	0.5	104	1.9	0.5	19	2.1	0.7
6–9	17	1.4	0.5	26	1.5	0.5	106	1.4	0.4	17	1.3	0.4
9–12	17	1.1	0.4	28	1.0	0.4	121	1.1	0.6	17	0.8	0.3
12–24	16	2.2	0.5	34	2.1	0.6	–	–	–	23	2.1	0.9
24–36	13	2.0	0.5	32	1.8	0.6	114	2.0	0.7	21	2.0	1.2
	Males – Change in Length (cm)											
0–3	17	12.4	1.7	28	12.2	1.6	123	10.6	1.1	22	11.0	1.3
3–6	17	9.7	1.5	25	8.6	1.3	104	6.6	1.6	19	7.5	2.3
6–9	17	6.4	0.9	26	5.6	1.4	106	4.5	1.3	17	5.7	1.3
9–12	17	4.1	1.4	28	4.5	1.1	121	4.0	1.0	17	4.0	1.0

12–24	16	11.9	1.9	34	11.9	1.7	—	—	—	23	11.6	2.1
24–36	13	8.3	1.5	32	7.7	1.7	114	8.7	1.5	21	8.1	1.2
Females—Change in Weight (kg)												
0–3	22	2.4	0.5	34	2.7	0.5	136	2.4	0.5	32	2.5	0.6
3–6	18	2.1	0.4	34	2.1	0.6	78	1.9	0.5	28	1.8	0.4
6–9	16	1.4	0.3	32	1.4	0.3	78	1.4	0.5	26	1.2	0.4
9–12	18	1.2	0.4	28	0.9	0.4	86	1.0	0.4	27	1.0	0.4
12–24	21	2.6	0.6	34	2.4	0.7	—	—	—	35	2.1	0.6
24–36	21	2.2	0.9	29	2.0	0.7	79	2.2	0.7	35	1.9	0.9
Females—Change in Length (cm)												
0–3	22	11.7	1.8	34	11.0	1.1	136	10.0	1.1	32	10.9	1.4
3–6	18	9.1	1.5	34	7.9	1.4	78	6.5	1.4	28	6.9	1.3
6–9	16	5.9	1.5	32	4.9	1.0	78	4.8	1.2	26	4.9	0.5
9–12	18	4.6	1.0	28	4.8	1.4	86	4.1	1.0	27	3.8	1.0
12–24	21	12.8	2.1	34	12.3	1.7	—	—	—	35	11.8	1.7
24–36	21	8.8	1.9	29	8.5	1.6	79	8.5	1.2	35	7.9	1.5

*Data of Fomon et al. (1970, 1971, 1973) for the interval 0 to 3 months and of Karlberg et al. (1968) for subsequent age intervals; all other data are those of Cruise (1973).

TABLE 3–9 GAIN IN WEIGHT PER UNIT OF CALORIE INTAKE*

Age Interval (days)	Gain in Weight (gm/100 kcal)			
	Males		*Females*	
	Mean	*S.D.*	*Mean*	*S.D.*
8–13	8.0	3.7	8.3	3.7
14–27	8.9	1.7	8.1	1.8
28–41	7.6	1.7	6.3	1.5
42–55	6.3	1.7	5.8	1.2
56–83	5.2	1.0	4.8	1.0
84–111	4.2	1.0	3.9	1.2
8–55	7.5	1.1	6.8	1.0
56–111	4.7	0.8	4.4	0.8
8–111	5.9	0.7	5.4	0.8

*Data of Fomon et al. (1971).

been reported by some investigators (Suckling and Campbell, 1957; MacWilliam and Dean, 1965; Stoch and Smythe, 1967; Graham, 1968; Krueger, 1969) to demonstrate incomplete catch-up growth, whereas other investigators (Hansen, 1965; Cabak and Najdanvic, 1965; Garrow and Pike, 1967; Keet et al., 1971) have reported that catch-up growth occurred at least to the extent of achieving size equal to that of siblings or local standards. Satgé et al. (1970) reported incomplete recovery after three to four years but nearly complete recovery by puberty.

Studies of catch-up growth in developing countries are difficult to evaluate because of the unfavorable environmental circumstances usually present. As pointed out by Graham et al. (1969), "We need to define more precisely the effects of severe malnutrition in infancy and early childhood, particularly reversibility or permanence. Having

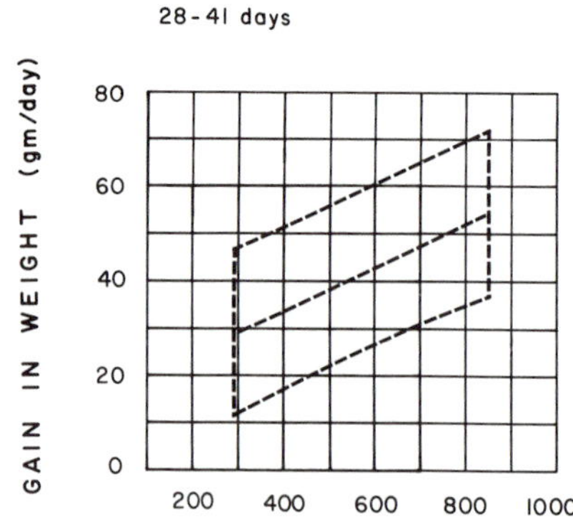

Figure 3–8 Relation of gain in weight to intake of calories by male infants from 28 through 41 days of age. The regression and 90 per cent confidence ranges are indicated. (Modified from Fomon, S. J., et al.: Food consumption and growth of normal infants fed milk-based formulas. Acta Paediatr. Scand. [Suppl. 223], 1971.)

defined these, we need to know if it is possible to prevent or ameliorate the apparently inevitable after-effects."

A number of investigators (Shmerling et al., 1968; Rey et al., 1971; Barr et al., 1972) have employed celiac disease as a model for study of catch-up growth. Children with celiac disease develop growth retardation in infancy because of malabsorption. They are not exposed to intrauterine or early infantile malnutrition and have a well defined period of malnutrition caused by a specific disease process that can be completely reversed by a gluten-free diet; the entire course of their illness and subsequent rehabilitation take place in satisfactory environmental conditions (Barr et al., 1972). These studies of catch-up growth of patients with celiac disease have demonstrated complete recovery.

In the study reported by Barr et al. (1972), 13 girls between 9 and 15 months of age were followed for a period of at least three years while strictly adhering to a gluten-free diet. Symptoms of malabsorption had been demonstrated for a mean of 4.8 months (range two to eight months) before the diagnosis of celiac disease was made. At the time of initiation of treatment, body weight with one exception was between 60 and 80 per cent of the expected mean weight for age. Complete recovery in weight, height, bone age and metacarpal cortical thickness occurred during the three-year period of rehabilitation.

These observations concerning catch-up growth by infants adequately treated for celiac disease cannot be considered predictive of the catch-up growth of infants recovering from protein-calorie malnutrition. Age of onset, severity and duration of malnutrition are all likely to influence the eventual outcome in relation to physical and mental development. Malnutrition in infancy and subsequent mental development are discussed in Chapter 19.

Data concerning catch-up growth of older children have been derived from studies of hyperactive children treated with amphetamines during the school year but not during summer vacations. Growth in weight and height was suppressed during the school year and catch-up growth was demonstrated during the summer (Safer et al., 1972; Safer and Allen, 1973).

BODY COMPOSITION DURING INFANCY

Owen and Brožek (1966) summarized data on chemical composition from whole body chemical analyses of the fetus and infant. Whole body chemical analyses of malnourished infants were reported by Garrow et al. (1965) and Halliday (1967). Subsequently, these data and data of other investigators concerning normal and malnourished infants were summarized by Garrow et al. (1968).

Methods for Estimating Composition of Living Subjects

Because of the paucity of data from whole body chemical analyses of normal infants, much of our information about chemical growth has been obtained by indirect approaches. The more important indirect methods concern estimations of total body water and chloride (or exchangeable bromide), total body potassium, urinary excretion of endogenous creatinine and hydroxyproline, and oxygen consumption.

Total Body Water and Bromide Space. Body weight may be considered to consist of a lipid and a lipid-free compartment. Water accounts for an appreciable percentage of the "fat-free body mass"—approximately 84.3 per cent in the newborn and 72.4 per cent in the adult (Fomon, 1967). During the course of chemical maturation of fat-free body mass between birth and adult life, much of the decrease in percentage of water is related to the decrease in percentage of extracellular fluid. Although other methods are available (Cheek, 1968), estimation of the body content of water and bromide space can be made as described by Owen et al. (1962).

It is apparent that if one can make a reasonable estimate of the water content of fat-free body mass and if water content of the body is determined, the quantity of fat-free body may be estimated and, by subtraction of that quantity from total body weight, the mass of lipid in the body can be estimated. Bromide space is probably proportional to volume of extracellular fluid and thus can offer important clues regarding changes in volume of extracellular fluid with increasing age. Determinations of total body water and bromide space are of considerable importance in estimating chemical growth of the male reference infant (Fomon, 1967).

Total Body Potassium. In normal individuals of a specified age, potassium concentration of fat-free body mass is remarkably constant. Therefore, if body content of potassium can be determined and if a reasonable estimate of potassium concentration of fat-free body mass can be made for the age in question, calculation of fat-free body mass is possible. By subtracting fat-free body mass from whole body weight, the fat content of the body can be determined.

Because the naturally occurring radioisotope ^{40}K exists in fixed proportion to total potassium, whole body counting for ^{40}K has been useful in study of body composition of adults and older children (Forbes, 1962; Owen and Brožek, 1966; Novak et al., 1970). Methods suitable for ^{40}K counting of adults and older children appear to be unsatisfactory with infants, because of rapid changes in geometry. However, the 4 π counter described by Garrow (1965a) has proved adequate for measurement of total body potassium of malnourished infants (Garrow, 1965b; Alleyne, 1968, 1970; Alleyne et al., 1970). A 4 π counter has been employed by Romahn and Burmeister (1970) in study of normal infants. Normal infants have been studied by Novak et al. (1970) at age one month and by Novak (1973) serially through the first year of life, using 10 plastic scintillators arranged in two banks.

As additional data on total body potassium become available, major advances will occur in our understanding of chemical growth of infants and preschool children.

Urinary Excretion of Endogenous Creatinine. Approximately 98 per cent of creatine in the body exists in muscle and about 2 per cent of total body creatine is converted to creatinine each day and excreted in the urine (Borsook and Dubnoff, 1947). A high correlation between urinary excretion of endogenous creatinine and muscle mass or fat-free body mass has been demonstrated in the rat (Kumar et al., 1959; Chinn, 1966) and in sheep carcasses (Van Niekerk et al., 1963), and indirect evidence suggests that urinary excretion of endogenous creatinine also reflects muscle mass of the human adult, child and infant. It is generally assumed that urinary excretion of 1 mg of endogenous creatinine per day corresponds to 20 gm of muscle (Waterlow and Alleyne, 1971). Many reports of urinary excretion of creatinine by infants have been published (e.g., Catherwood and Stearns, 1937; Standard et al., 1959; Cheek, 1968; Alleyne et al., 1970) but, in nearly every instance, the infants were receiving milk-based diets, which provide an exogenous source of creatine and creatinine. The importance of a creatine- and creatinine-free diet in achieving endogenous excretion of creatinine has been well demonstrated by Bleiler and Schedl (1962) in studies of adults.

The extent to which dietary intake of creatine and creatinine influences urinary excretion of creatinine is not generally appreciated. Table 3–10 summarizes data concerning six infants fed milk-based formulas (but no other source of creatine or creatinine) during various intervals of the first six months of life and soy-based formulas free of creatine and creatinine during other intervals. Mean urinary excretion of creatinine by these infants was slightly more than 14 per cent greater when receiving milk-based than when receiving soy-based formulas. Meat-containing diets would presumably give rise to greater urinary excretion of exogenous creatinine than is observed with milk-based diets free of meat.

Table 3–11 presents data on urinary excretion of endogenous creatinine by normal infants studied during the first 12 months of life. Excretion per unit of body weight by males was greater than by females. In the case of both males and females, excretion was greater between birth and four months than between 4 and 12 months. Unfortunately, data are not available to indicate whether urinary excretion

TABLE 3–10 URINARY EXCRETION OF CREATININE BY NORMAL INFANTS FED MILK-BASED OR SOY-BASED FORMULA*

		Milk-Based Formula				Soy-Based Formula			
				Excretion of Creatinine (mg/kg/day)				*Excretion of Creatinine (mg/kg/day)*	
Subject	Sex	*Age (days)*	*N*†	*Mean*	*Range*	*Age (days)*	*N*†	*Mean*	*Range*
1	M	43–71	2	13.8	13.6–14.0	57	1	12.7	
2	F	50–78	2	12.8	12.7–12.8	64	1	12.1	
3	M	52–151	4	12.3	11.8–12.9	67–165	3	10.7	10.4–10.9
4	M	63–161	5	12.2	11.4–13.4	77–119	2	11.0	10.6–11.4
5	F	101–157	3	10.8	10.1–11.3	115–178	2	8.2	8.0–8.4
6	M	103–131	2	13.7	13.1–14.3	117	1	11.6	

*Unpublished data.
†Number of three-day urinary collections.

TABLE 3–11 URINARY EXCRETION OF ENDOGENOUS CREATININE*

AGE (MONTHS)	SEX	NUMBER OF SUBJECTS	NUMBER OF STUDIES	EXCRETION OF CREATININE (MG/KG/DAY)	
				Mean	*S.D.*
0–4	Males	12	81	11.54	1.55
	Females	7	36	10.48	1.11
4–12	Males	25	119	10.90	1.70
	Females	17	80	10.12	1.72

*Unpublished data. Each study is based on a 72-hour urine collection. All infants were receiving soy-based formulas and the diet was free of creatine and creatinine.

of endogenous creatinine per unit of muscle mass is similar during early and later infancy, or, in fact, for males and females of the same age. The data in Table 3–11 are useful in indicating excretions of endogenous creatinine by normal infants but cannot yet be adequately interpreted in relation to changes in body composition with growth.

Urinary Excretion of Hydroxyproline. Collagen accounts for about 25 per cent of total body proteins of adult man (Widdowson and Dickerson, 1960), but may account for as much as 48 per cent of total body proteins of the infant with severe malnutrition (Picou et al., 1966). It is found primarily in skin, tendons, cartilage, blood vessels, connective tissue, organ capsules and bone matrix. Nearly all the hydroxyproline in vertebrates is found in collagen (Prockop, 1964), and endogenous hydroxyproline excreted in urine almost certainly reflects degradation of collagen or, possibly, its precursors. Newly formed collagen is soluble in neutral salt solutions and is metabolically quite active; mature collagen is insoluble and metabolically inert. Increased rates of urinary excretion of endogenous hydroxyproline (primarily in the form of peptides) are observed during periods of rapid synthesis of collagen, as occurs during normal growth in early infancy and during periods of rapid degradation of collagen, as in individuals with severe burns (Smiley and Ziff, 1964). Decreased rates of excretion are characteristic of growth failure resulting from nutritional deficiency (Whitehead, 1965; Picou et al., 1965) or from pituitary dwarfism or hypothyroidism.

When growing subjects receive a collagen-free diet and are not affected by those few specific abnormalities that result in excessive rates of degradation of collagen, rates of urinary excretion probably reflect rates of collagen synthesis in the body. Serial studies of urinary excretion of endogenous hydroxyproline in normal infants may, therefore, aid in defining the pattern of growth of this body component during early life. In addition, establishment of a range of values for urinary excretion of endogenous hydroxyproline by normal infants of various ages may be useful in interpreting results obtained with infants who fail to thrive or are suspected of various disorders of collagen metabolism.

Younoszai et al. (1967) reported results of serial studies of urinary excretion of hydroxyproline by nine male infants between 20 and 120 days of age. Three-day urinary excretions of hydroxyproline were determined on five to seven occasions with each infant. When the mean urinary excretion of hydroxyproline for each infant was plotted against the rate of gain in body length of that infant, a high degree of correlation was demonstrated ($r = 0.78$). Correlation between mean rate of urinary excretion of hydroxyproline and gain in weight was much less ($r = 0.26$). Since much of the growth of collagen during early life is accounted for by growth of long bones, it is not surprising that rate of urinary excretion of hydroxyproline and rate of growth in length should be related.

Oxygen Consumption. Rate of consumption of oxygen by infants in the resting thermoneutral state probably reflects body mass of actively metabolizing tissue and is, therefore, of interest in relation to body composition, even though "actively metabolizing tissue" cannot be anatomically defined. Relatively high rates of oxygen comsumption per unit of body weight have been observed in infants with low birth weight in relation to gestational age (Sinclair and Silverman, 1966) and in at least some infants with severe congenital heart disease (Pittman and Cohen, 1964; Lees et al., 1965; Stocker et al., 1972).

Male Reference Infant

On the basis of data from a variety of sources, the body composition of a male reference infant was estimated from birth to age one year (Fomon, 1967). This hypothetic infant was assumed to weigh 3.5 kg at birth, 7.0 kg at age four months and 10.5 kg at age one year.

The estimated body composition of the male reference boy during the first year of life, as presented in Table 3–12, differs slightly from that presented in 1967. In addition, chemical composition of the body has been estimated for age two years and age three years on the assumption that these values must be intermediate between those applicable at age one year (Fomon, 1967) and those of the adult. Chemical maturity of the fat-free body mass is probably achieved by age four years (Moulton, 1923).

The actual values selected for water and protein as percentage of fat-free mass at age two and three years were chosen to conform, so far

TABLE 3–12 BODY COMPOSITION OF REFERENCE BOY BETWEEN BIRTH AND THREE YEARS OF AGE

Age	Body Weight (kg)	Fat-Free Body Mass (gm/100 gm)			Whole Body (gm/100 gm)			
		Water	*Protein*	*Other*	*Water*	*Protein*	*Lipid*	*Other*
Birth	3.5	84.3	12.8	2.9	75.1	11.4	11.0	2.5
4 months	7.0	81.7	15.4	2.9	60.2	11.4	26.3	2.1
12 months	10.5	77.5	19.2	3.3	59.0	14.6	23.9	2.5
24 months	13.0	76.8	19.8	3.4	61.0	15.7	20.6	2.7
36 months	15.0	75.9	20.0	4.1	62.0	16.4	18.3	3.3
Adult		72.4	20.5	7.1				

as possible, to data on composition of individual organs and tissues as summarized by Widdowson and Dickerson (1964). It has been assumed that the water content of the fat-free body mass decreases from 77.5 per cent at age one year to 76.8 per cent at age two years and 75.9 per cent at age three years (Table 3–12), and that protein content of the fat-free body mass correspondingly increases from 19.2 per cent at age one year to 19.8 per cent at age two years and 20.0 per cent at age three years (compared with 20.5 per cent for the adult).

Unfortunately, data on total body water of healthy living subjects between one and three years of age are meager. On the basis of data summarized by Forbes (1962), together with the data of Cheek (1968) and our own unpublished data, we have assumed mean values for total body water to be 61.0 and 62.0 per cent of body weight at two and three years of age, respectively (Table 3–12). Lipid content of the body may therefore be calculated to be 20.6 and 18.3 per cent of body weight at ages two and three years.

The estimated chemical composition of the gains between birth and four months, 4 and 12 months, one and two years and two and three years may be seen in Table 3–13 and Figure 3–9. It will be noted that the gain of lipid between one and three years of age is extremely small.

An accurate estimate of the composition of the reference infant (and reference child) at various ages is of considerable importance, and it is unfortunate that better data are not presently available to serve as a basis for estimating body composition. Conclusions about the calorie requirement for growth at various ages (discussed later in this chapter), the percentage of protein requirement accounted for by the increment in body protein (Chapter 6, Fig. 6–7), and the requirements for various major minerals (Chapter 11) are based on the estimated composition of the gain in body weight between various intervals. As knowledge of body composition increases, the results of such calculations will provide increasingly reliable predictions.

CELL NUMBER AND CELL SIZE

Deoxyribonucleic acid (DNA) is located almost entirely within the cell nucleus, and the amount of DNA per diploid nucleus of a species is constant (6.0 pg for the human). With few exceptions (Winick et al., 1972), the cells of the human body are diploid and there is only one nucleus per cell. Thus, the content of DNA per gram of the organ or tissue in question may be divided by the DNA content per nucleus of that species to give the number of nuclei per gram of organ weight. Once the number of cells is determined, the average weight per cell, protein content per cell or lipid content per cell can be estimated by

TABLE 3–13 GAIN IN BODY COMPONENTS OF REFERENCE BOY AT VARIOUS INTERVALS BETWEEN BIRTH AND THREE YEARS

Age Interval (months)	Gain in Weight (kg)	Composition of Gain (gm/100 gm)				Gain in FFBM*	
		Water	*Protein*	*Lipid*	*Other*	*(kg)*	*(gm/day)*
0–4	3.5	45.3	11.4	41.6	1.7	2.04	17.0
4–12	3.5	56.6	21.0	19.1	3.3	2.83	11.6
12–24	2.5	69.4	20.3	6.8	3.5	2.33	6.4
24–36	2.0	68.5	20.9	3.4	7.2	1.93	5.5

*Fat-free body mass.

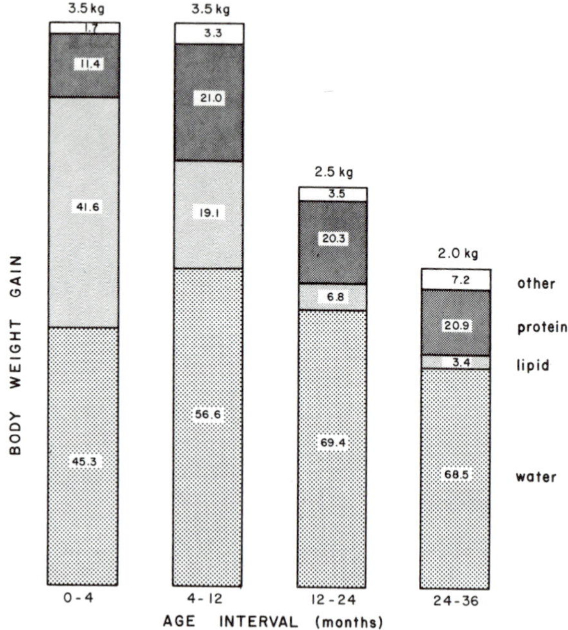

Figure 3–9 Composition of weight gain of the male reference infant during the first three years of life. The amount of gain in each age interval is indicated at the top of the column. The percentage of weight gain accounted for by water, lipid and protein is indicated.

determining the amount of the component and dividing by the number of cells.

Patterns of increase in cell number and cell size in various organs during normal growth have been studied extensively in the rat and less extensively in several other animals and in the human (Winick et al., 1972). During prenatal and early postnatal development of the rat, all organs appear to grow by cell division alone (hyperplasia). Gradually there is a shift to a pattern of increasing cell size (hypertrophy) as the major component of growth. This shift occurs first in brain and lung, and last in skeletal muscle.

Caloric restriction during the period of cellular hyperplasia in rats results in decreased ultimate body size, decreased size of individual organs and reduction in cell number in these organs without major change in cell size (Winick and Noble, 1966). Conversely, overfeeding during the period of cellular hyperplasia results in greater ultimate stature with larger numbers of cells in the various organs (Winick and Noble, 1967). When growth failure results from malnutrition imposed on the individual after the neonatal period, cell size rather than cell number is reduced (Waterlow and Weisz, 1956; Mendes and Waterlow, 1958).

It seems possible that knowledge of cell number and cell size in one or more organs or tissues of infants who are small for their age may provide considerable insight into the nature of growth failure (Cheek and Cooke, 1964) and might be of predictive value in relation to results of therapeutic measures. For example, muscle cells of certain children who have congenital heart disease and failure to thrive have been shown to be decreased in number but normal or somewhat increased in size (Cheek et al., 1966). One may speculate that such children are unlikely to attain normal ultimate stature even if the congenital heart disease is corrected.

ADIPOSE TISSUE

Method of Measurement

Methods suitable for estimating cell number and cell size of the entire body or of most organs and tissues are not suitable for estimating the number of adipocytes (i. e., those cells of adipose tissue that are capable of storing fat). Much of the DNA content of adipose tissue is present in connective tissue, blood vessels and other nonadipocytes. The method of Hirsch and Gallian (1968) has been used most extensively for estimation of adipocyte number and size (Sims et al., 1968; Hirsch and Knittle, 1970; Salans et al., 1971; Knittle, 1972; Salans et al., 1973). This method requires that a sample of adipose tissue, usually obtained by needle biopsy, be divided into two portions, one for counting cell number and another for determination of fat content. Cell number is estimated by separating the cells, staining them with osmium and counting in a Coulter counter. From the number of cells and quantity of fat per gram of adipose tissue, cell size is calculated in terms of fat content per cell.

The method suffers from the obvious problem that the aspirated sample of adipose tissue obtained at one site may not be representative of any larger mass of adipose tissue. Perhaps even more serious is the fact that adipocytes must contain sufficient fat to be stained to an extent that will permit counting. A generally similar objection applies to the method of Björntorp and Sjöström (1971) for counting adipocytes. In the case of obese adults who have not experienced weight reduction, it is likely that virtually every adipocyte will contain sufficient fat to be stained and recognized as an adipocyte. In the case of infants (or adults after weight reduction), many adipocytes may contain insufficient fat to permit counting. Thus, conclusions reached from estimations of adipocyte number and size in infants must be considered suspect.

Growth of Adipose Tissue

Adipose tissue accounts for a relatively large proportion of body weight of the infant after the first month or two of life. Some appreciation of the size of the adipose tissue mass is therefore desirable. On the basis of three assumptions, the adipose tissue mass of the male reference infant at age four months may be calculated: (1) fat accounts for 26.3 per cent of body weight at age four months (Table 3–12); (2) 90 per cent of the body content of fat is located in adipose tissue; (3) at age four months, as appears to be the case at age six months (Dju, 1953; Dju et al., 1958; Baker, 1969), fat accounts for approximately 47 per cent of weight of adipose tissue. From the first two assumptions, the fat content of adipose tissue of the male reference infant at age four months is found to be 23.7 per cent of body weight. Utilizing the third assumption, it is then found that at age four months adipose tissue accounts for 50.4 per cent of body weight.

Because fat comprises a smaller percentage of body weight at age one year than at age four months, and because the fat content of adipose tissue is greater at age one year, it is evident that adipose tissue accounts for a smaller percentage of body weight at age one year than at age four months. At ages two and three years, adipose tissue accounts for an even smaller percentage of body weight than at age one year.

SEX-RELATED DIFFERENCES

Commonly employed charts for plotting length and weight indicate that infant boys are somewhat larger than infant girls. These differences are probably gonadal in origin, but the mechanism is unknown. In lambs, prenatal growth of a twin is influenced not only by its own sex, but by the sex of its co-twin (Donald and Purser, 1956). Among lambs, birth weight superiority of males over females is twice as great in mixed-sex twins as in like-sex twins. In human twins, birth weight of a male is significantly greater when the co-twin is a female than when the co-twin is another male (Karn, 1952, 1953). However, sex of the co-twin does not appear to exert a significant influence on weight of a female twin. Not only are boys slightly larger than girls at birth, but rates of gain in length and weight are greater during the early months of life. The extent of the difference in rates of gain in weight may be seen from Tables 3–4 and 3–5 and from Figure 3–4. Skinfold thickness is generally greater in females than in males (Table 3–3).

Gain in weight per unit of gain in length between 8 and 112 days of age appears to be slightly greater for breastfed male than for

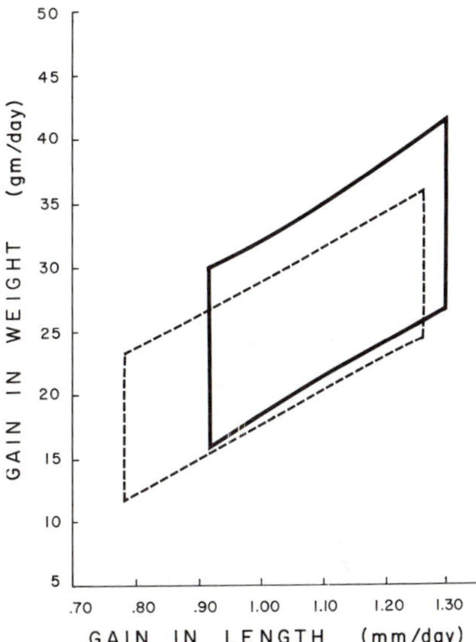

Figure 3–10 Relation of gain in weight to gain in length of normal breastfed infants during the interval 8 to 112 days of age. The 90 per cent confidence ranges for males (*solid lines*) and females (*interrupted lines*) are indicated. (Data of Fomon et al., 1970.)

breastfed female infants (Fig. 3–10). Because incremental data on skinfold thickness (Table 3–7) do not suggest greater gain in adipose tissue by male than by female infants, it seems likely that a greater mass of bone and muscle is included in the weight gained by males.

Evidence of sex-related differences in body composition during infancy was summarized by Owen et al. (1966). Possibly the factors responsible for these differences in body composition are similar to those responsible for the larger mean weight and length of male than of female infants at birth and the more rapid rates of gain in weight of male than of female infants during early life. In any case, the existence of a sex-related difference in body composition during infancy strongly suggests that fundamental physiologic processes differ between infant males and females.

Not only do size, growth and body composition demonstrate sex-related differences during infancy, but several biochemical parameters in serum also differ. Alkaline phosphatase activity is greater and concentration of cholesterol is less in serum of male than of female breastfed infants (Chaper 19, Table 19–1).

Sex-related differences in physiologic functions during infancy may have implications of far greater importance than differences in body composition. Definite sex-related differences in susceptibility to certain infectious diseases (Thompson et al., 1963; Washburn et al., 1965) and the well recognized sex-related differences in incidence of such disorders as hypertrophic pyloric stenosis suggest the need for intensified investigation of other sex-related differences during infancy.

CALORIE REQUIREMENT FOR GROWTH

At least during the period of infancy and early childhood, requirement for protein is probably best expressed as grams of protein per 100 kcal consumed (Chapter 6). It may be desirable to express certain other nutrient requirements in similar terms. Because requirements for many nutrients for growth and for maintenance are different, it is of interest to speculate about the calorie requirement for growth at various ages.

Although it is readily apparent that some fraction of calorie intake of a normal infant or child must be utilized for growth while the remainder is allocated to other energy needs, quantitative aspects of this partitioning of energy between growth and nongrowth have received relatively little attention. In order to arrive at a tentative estimate of such energy partitioning, one may utilize calculations based on assumed rates of gain in weight, composition of the gain, energy costs of synthesis of the newly formed tissue and total calorie intake of a hypothetic infant during the first three years of life.

Studies of experimental animals by a number of investigators (Kielanowski, 1969; Ørskov and McDonald, 1970; Thorbek, 1970) have provided data on the energy costs of synthesis of protein and fat by growing animals. The data of Kielanowski (1969) concerning growing pigs seem likely to be most relevant to energy costs of tissue synthesis by young infants, and it is therefore concluded, tentatively, that 7.5 kcal are required for synthesis of 1 gm of protein, and 11.6 kcal are required for synthesis of 1 gm of fat. Somewhat similar calculations have been applied to energy costs of growth by Payne and Waterlow (1971) over a wider range of ages and by Ashworth et al. (1968) in a study of Jamaican infants during recovery from malnutrition.

Data from a study of infants fed milk-based formulas (Fomon et al., 1971) suggest that the male reference infant will consume 61,000 kcal during the first four months of life. This hypothetic infant might consume 180,000 kcal between 4 and 12 months of age, 365,000 kcal between 12 and 24 months of age and 400,000 kcal between 24 and 36 months of age. Utilizing the energy costs of tissue synthesis already mentioned (7.5 kcal for synthesis of 1 gm of protein and 11.6 kcal for synthesis of 1 gm of fat), it will be found (Fig. 3–11) that the percentage of calorie intake required for growth is 32.8 per cent between birth and four months, 7.4 per cent between 4 and 12 months, 1.6 per cent between 12 and 24 months and 1.0 per cent between 24 and 36 months. Thus, in his allocation of calorie intake between growth and nongrowth, the one- to two-year-old infant appears to be more similar to the adult than to the small, rapidly growing infant.

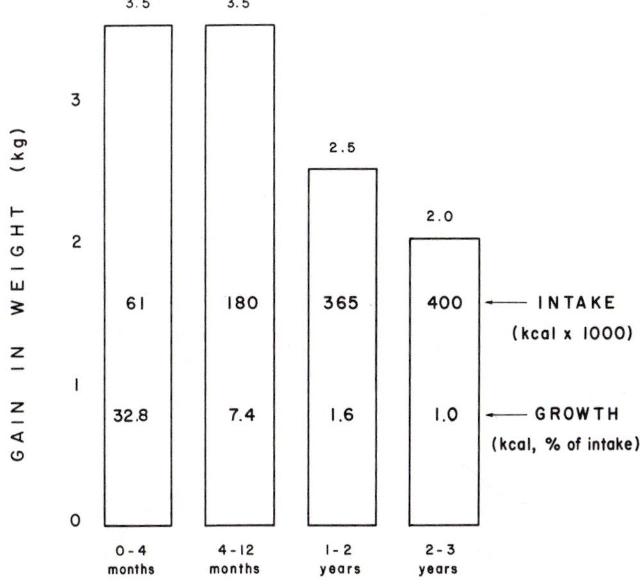

Figure 3–11 Gain in weight, intake of calories and estimated percentage of calories utilized for growth at various ages.

EFFECT OF MODE OF FEEDING AND DIETARY COMPOSITION ON GROWTH AND BODY COMPOSITION DURING EARLY INFANCY

Breastfed Versus Bottle-Fed Infants

Bottle-fed infants gain more rapidly in weight and length during the first 112 days of life than do breastfed infants (Fomon et al., 1971). As may be seen from Figure 3–12, a longitudinal study of breastfed and bottle-fed infants during the first few months of life demonstrated that the 10th and 90th percentile values for weight and length of the two groups were similar at birth, and that the 10th percentile values of the two groups were similar at age 112 days. The 90th percentile values at 112 days were substantially greater for the bottle-fed infants. As discussed in Chapter 2, it seems likely that these differences are explained primarily by difference in calorie intake rather than by difference in composition of the diet.

The greater gain by bottle-fed than by breastfed infants in the study by Fomon et al. (1971) is similar to that reported earlier by

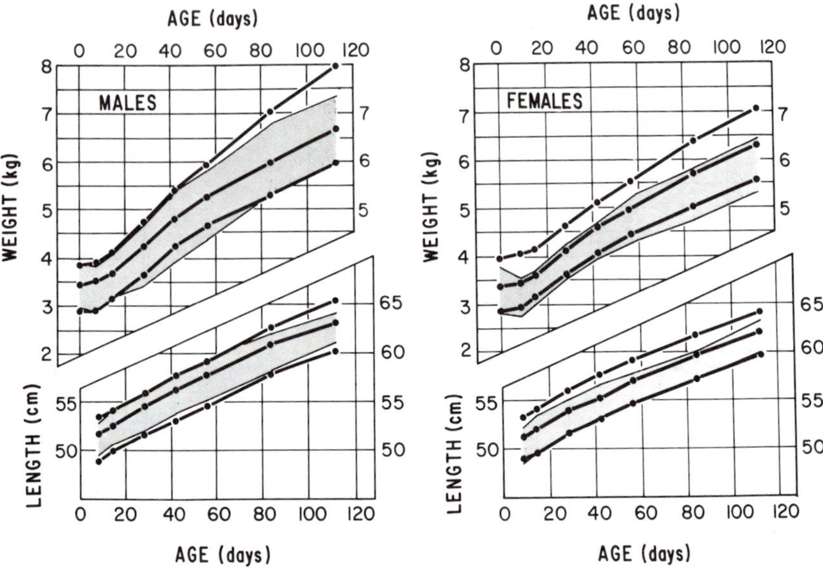

Figure 3–12 Weights and lengths of formula-fed and breastfed infants between birth and 112 days of age. The heavy lines indicate the 10th, 50th and 90th percentile values for formula-fed infants. The shaded areas include the 10th to 90th percentile values for weight and length of breastfed infants. (From Fomon, S. J., et al.: Food consumption and growth of normal infants fed milk-based formulas. Acta Paediatr. Scand. (Suppl. 223), 1971.)

Stewart and Westropp (1953) in England and by Mellander et al. (1959) in Sweden. During the first six months of life, weight gains of infants studied by Stewart and Westropp (1953) averaged 4.48 kg for 142 fully bottle-fed infants and 4.09 kg for 235 breastfed infants. In the Swedish study (Mellander et al., 1959), infants predominantly breastfed during the first four and one-half months of life gained less weight than did bottle-fed infants; mean gain was 3.34 kg for 162 breastfed infants and 3.53 kg for 143 bottle-fed infants.

On the other hand, Jackson et al. (1964) reported a study of 599 infants, including 215 infants who were breastfed for four to six months. No difference in weight gain between breastfed and bottle-fed infants was noted during the first four months of life, although gain in length and weight were somewhat less rapid in the breastfed than in the bottle-fed infants between four and six months of age. Recent studies by other investigators have generally included relatively few breastfed infants. Hooper (1965) and Hooper and Alexander (1971) reported mean gains in weight between birth and six months to be less for "breastfed" than for "bottle-fed" infants. However, many of the "bottle-fed" infants had originally been breastfed and the results are therefore difficult to interpret.

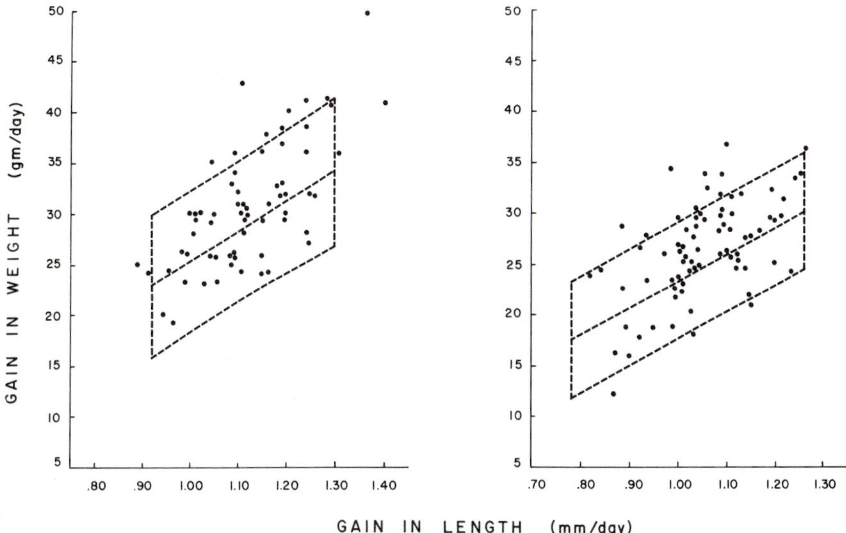

Figure 3–13 Gain in weight in relation to gain in length by normal male (*left panel*) and female (*right panel*) infants during the interval 8 to 112 days of age. The regression and 90 per cent confidence ranges for breastfed infants (Fomon et al., 1970) are indicated by interrupted lines. Each dot applies to one infant fed a milk-based formula (Fomon et al., 1971).

In the studies by Fomon et al. (1970, 1971), not only were gains in weight and length greater by bottle-fed than by breastfed infants, but the relation between gain in weight and gain in length was different (Fig. 3–13). Bottle-fed infants generally gained more weight for a specified gain in length than did breastfed infants.

As discussed in Chapter 2, it seems possible that the greater gains in weight by bottle-fed than by breastfed infants reflect the effects of overfeeding of the bottle-fed infants. Such overfeeding might contribute to subsequent obesity because of development of an abnormally large population of adipocytes or because of establishment of a habit of overeating. In this regard, it is of some interest that Eid (1970) did not find a statistically significant difference in percentage of "obese" or "overweight" six- to eight-year-old children in relation to whether they had been breastfed (55 infants) or bottle-fed (83 infants). Unfortunately, the definition of "breastfed" was not given in this study.

Calorically Concentrated Feedings

As discussed in Chapter 2, ad libitum feeding of a calorically concentrated formula results in greater caloric intakes during the first six weeks of life than are observed in infants fed formulas of conventional caloric concentration (Fig. 2–2, 2–3 and 2–4). After six weeks of age, the infant demonstrates considerable ability to adjust his intake of a calorically concentrated feeding to the point at which calorie intake expressed per unit of body weight is no greater than that of infants fed conventional formulas. The greater intakes of calories during the early weeks of life by infants fed a calorically concentrated formula (133 kcal/100 ml) were associated with greater gains in weight than gains by infants fed a more dilute (67 kcal/100 ml) but otherwise similar formula (Fomon et al., 1969). Between 8 and 42 days of age, gains in weight and length averaged 51 gm/day and 1.56 mm/day by male infants fed the 133 kcal/100 ml formula and 29 gm/day and 0.99 mm/day by male infants fed the 67 kcal/100 ml formula. Gains in weight and length were nearly identical for the two groups of infants between 42 and 112 days of age.

Skim Milk

Verbal reports from physicians and nutritionists in various parts of the United States indicate that skim milk is not infrequently fed to infants, beginning at four to six months of age. The probable motivations for this practice are the desire to treat real or imagined obesity, to prevent obesity and/or to prevent atherosclerosis.

To examine the effects of feeding skim milk to young infants, a study was conducted in the Pediatric Metabolic Unit of the University of Iowa (Fomon et al., 1974). Two groups of male infants were observed from 112 through 167 days of age while fed either a conventional formula or skim milk with a small amount of added safflower oil (to provide linoleic acid). Fat-soluble vitamins and iron were also given. The formula or skim milk was fed ad libitum and the parents were permitted to offer unlimited quantities of commercially prepared strained foods. As discussed in Chapter 2 (Table 2–4), caloric intake was considerably less by infants fed the skim milk. Gain in weight was somewhat less and gain in length was slightly but not significantly greater by infants fed skim milk. Although this result may seem desirable for infants thought to be obese, consideration of the probable energy balance of the infants offers some cause for concern.

If one assumes that 7.4 per cent of calorie intake by the formula-fed infants was utilized for growth (Fig. 3–11), approximately 55 kcal/day were utilized for growth (7.4 per cent × 730 kcal, Table 2–4) and, therefore, energy expenditures for purposes other than growth amounted to 675 kcal/day. Assuming that the infants fed skim milk had similar energy needs for purposes other than growth, with additional calories necessary to permit weight gain of 13.5 gm/day (Table

2–4), it is apparent that the observed energy intake of 576 kcal/day was inadequate. It seems likely that the infants fed skim milk were utilizing body stores of fat to fulfill energy requirements. By utilizing fat stores and synthesizing fat-free tissue, an infant could, for an extended period, maintain the appearance of satisfactory state of health and nutrition. Nevertheless, once fat stores have become depleted, it seems likely that any illness which interfered to a major extent with food intake could prove life-threatening. Possibly, the deaths from measles and other acute illnesses known to occur in malnourished children are explained as much by lack of energy reserves as by failure of immune responses.

Infants receiving a major percentage of caloric intake from skim milk will receive exceedingly high intakes of protein and low intakes of fat (Chapter 19, Table 19–3) and may receive inadequate intakes of essential fatty acids (Chapter 7).

FAILURE TO THRIVE

Definition

The term "failure to thrive" has often been used uncritically to indicate growth failure, with no delineation of the boundary between normal and abnormal rates of growth. It is proposed that failure to thrive be defined as a rate of gain in length and/or weight less than the value corresponding to two standard deviations below the mean during an interval of at least 56 days for infants less than five months of age and during an interval of at least three months for older infants. Values two standard deviations below the mean in gains in length and weight for various age intervals are presented in Tables 3–4 and 3–5. The longer the interval of observation, the more conclusive the diagnosis. It is suggested that infants gaining in length or weight at rates less than the 10th percentile values be regarded as suspect. Such infants deserve more careful and more frequent medical evaluation than do other infants.

Suggested Approach to Diagnosis

History, physical examination and simple laboratory studies may provide clues that suggest avenues of approach to diagnosis in infants who fail to thrive. Obviously, if the history indicates the occurrence of persistent vomiting or diarrhea, causes of these manifestations should be investigated before focusing attention on the broader and less well defined category of failure to thrive. Similarly, when history, physical examination, simple laboratory tests (leukocyte count, erythrocyte sedimentation rate, urinalysis) or roentgenograms suggest infection, other inflammatory disease or abnormality of some organ system (e.g., renal, cardiovascular, gastrointestinal, endocrine), attempts should be made to arrive at a definitive diagnosis and to establish appropriate treatment before pursuing further the question of growth failure. Clues of the sort just mentioned will often not be available, and it is then desirable to follow a stepwise, methodical approach that may permit classifying the disorder in terms of energy balance.

From this point of view, one must distinguish first between infants who do or do not receive a net calorie intake adequate to permit satisfactory gain in weight by normal infants of the specified size. By "net" calorie intake is meant total calorie intake minus amounts lost through regurgitation or vomiting. "Adequate" calorie intake may be judged in relation to the data in Appendix I (p. 522). Among infants receiving net calorie intakes inadequate to promote normal rates of growth by normal infants, one must distinguish between those to whom an adequate intake was offered but was not accepted by the infant (refusal) or was accepted but lost through vomiting or regurgitation, and those to whom an adequate calorie intake was not offered. The latter group include infants fed infrequently, fed small quantities at each feeding and/or fed diets of low caloric density. Among infants receiving net calorie intakes adequate to promote normal rates of growth by most normal infants, failure to thrive is explained by excessive fecal loss of nutrients or by unusually high energy requirements.

When there is no obvious cause of failure to thrive, such as vomiting or severe congenital heart disease, it will generally be found that the calorie intake is well below the intakes of normal infants (Chapter 2, Tables 2–1 and 2–2; Appendix I, p. 522). It is important to recognize that parents will seldom admit that they feed an infant infrequently or that they restrict severely the amount offered at each feeding. History is therefore frequently unreliable and should be interpreted with caution. For this reason, when history, physical examination and simple laboratory tests fail to yield clues that seem likely to explain the failure to thrive, admission to the hospital will generally be desirable. Direct observation will permit a conclusion about whether an infant offered an adequate diet and fed by experienced personnel will gain weight at a normal rate.

Most infants designated as failing to thrive are the size, if not the age, of normal infants less than six months of age. For most such infants, a period of 10 to 14 days of direct observation of the infant, usually in the hospital, will permit classification of the disorder in terms of energy balance. During the interval of observation, an adequate and readily digestible diet should be offered to the infant by ex-

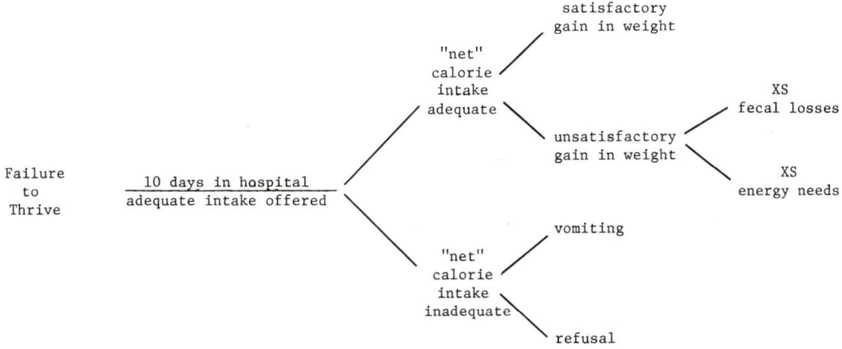

Figure 3–14 Schema for classifying infants with failure to thrive.

perienced personnel at least five times daily. Time and energy should be devoted to the feeding; accurate records of food intake and feeding behavior should be maintained. Studies that interfere with food intake, such as glucose tolerance tests and roentgenography of the gastrointestinal tract after administration of barium, should be deferred.

By the end of 10 or 14 days of observation (often in less time), it will usually be possible to distinguish between infants with adequate and those with inadequate net calorie intake (Fig. 3–14). In the majority of instances, "net" calorie intake will be adequate and satisfactory weight gain will occur. Detailed instructions about the diet and about frequency and technique of feeding should then be given to the parents, and the infant should be returned to parental care for a period of approximately three weeks. If adequate weight gain continues during this interval, further observation on an outpatient basis is indicated. If weight gain at home is inadequate, the infant should again be admitted to the hospital for observation.

With the exception of the infants just discussed—those who accept an adequate calorie intake and demonstrate satisfactory gain in weight—the largest group of infants admitted to the hospital for failure to thrive will be those who refuse to consume an adequate calorie intake. Infants who refuse to consume adequate calorie intakes can be identified after only a few days of observation, and it is then reasonable to proceed with tests aimed at determining the cause of refusal of feedings. Included in this group are infants with central nervous system disease, various neuromuscular or endocrine diseases, many chronic illnesses and congenital or acquired abnormalities. Partial intestinal obstruction is not uncommon among infants who refuse adequate calorie intake, and this possibility should be explored by appropriate roentgenographic studies.

As indicated in Figure 3–14, an infant who consumes an adequate net intake of calories and yet fails to gain weight normally will probably have steatorrhea or unusually high energy requirements. Only in this group are metabolic balance studies (Appendix IV, p. 549) indicated. As discussed in Chapter 7, steatorrhea is considered to exist when fecal losses of fat are at least 2 gm/kg/day.

Little information is available concerning failure to thrive because of unusually high energy requirements. It seems reasonable to assume that infants with muscular hypertonia or spastic cerebral palsy may have high energy requirements because of constant muscular contractions. Similarly, infants with congenital heart disease and tachypnea may, in fact, be constantly exercising and may demonstrate markedly elevated energy requirements. Rates of oxygen consumption per unit of body weight have been shown to be high in infants with severe congenital heart disease (Pittman and Cohen, 1964; Lees et al., 1965; Stocker et al., 1972) and in those whose birth weights are low in relation to gestational age (Sinclair and Silverman, 1966). Management of such infants often requires use of calorically concentrated formulas.

In terms of energy balance, more than one cause of failure to thrive may exist at the same time. An infant with severe hypertonia might be unable to consume an adequate calorie intake (i.e., refusal) because of neuromuscular disease and may simultaneously demonstrate greater than normal energy requirements because of increased muscular tone. An infant with hepatitis might refuse an adequate calorie intake because of the anorexia associated with the disease and, at the same time, have steatorrhea. As discussed in Chapters 10 and 19, infants with severe congenital heart disease may be unable to consume an adequate calorie intake and may also demonstrate increased energy expenditures and steatorrhea.

OBESITY

Definition

A truly satisfactory definition of obesity at any age would presumably be based on the percentage of body weight accounted for by fat. It might be possible, at some future time, to demonstrate that adverse consequences result when fat comprises a percentage of body weight greater than some specified value. Much additional study will be necessary to reach this goal. Any definition developed at present will be arbitrary, but even an arbitrary definition may offer a considerable advantage over "clinical impressions." It is proposed that values greater than the +2 standard deviation value for triceps and subscapular skinfold thickness (Table 3–3) be considered evidence of obesity.

TABLE 3–14 TENTATIVE DEFINITION OF OBESITY*

AGE (MONTHS)	MALES Length (cm) Less than	Weight (kg) More than	FEMALES Length (cm) Less than	Weight (kg) More than
1	51.8	4.2	51.5	4.0
	53.0	4.5	52.2	4.3
	54.2	4.7	53.5	4.6
	55.2	5.1	54.6	4.8
3	58.0	6.0	57.1	5.6
	59.2	6.4	58.0	5.9
	60.2	6.9	59.2	6.2
	61.5	7.3	60.2	6.6
6	65.6	7.7	63.3	7.5
	66.5	8.2	65.2	8.0
	67.8	9.0	66.3	8.4
	69.2	9.6	67.8	8.9
9	70.0	9.1	68.2	8.9
	70.9	9.7	69.5	9.4
	72.3	10.7	71.1	9.9
	73.6	11.2	73.1	10.4
12	73.6	10.2	72.5	9.9
	74.7	10.9	73.2	10.5
	76.4	11.6	75.1	11.1
	78.0	12.5	76.9	11.6
18	80.0	11.6	78.7	11.1
	81.7	12.6	80.2	11.8
	83.2	13.3	82.0	12.7
	85.3	14.4	84.2	13.2
24	85.0	12.8	84.2	12.3
	87.3	13.9	85.8	13.1
	88.8	14.5	87.5	14.2
	90.9	16.0	90.3	14.9
36	93.4	14.8	92.1	14.3
	95.3	15.7	94.2	15.3
	97.3	16.8	96.2	17.0
	100.6	18.6	99.0	17.7

*The table is based on data of Fomon et al. (1970, 1971, 1973) for ages one and three months, and on the data of Karlberg et al. (1968) for subsequent ages. At each age, the values for length for each sex are the 10th, 25th, 50th and 75th percentiles, while the values for weight are the 50th, 75th and 90th percentiles, and the mean plus two standard deviations.

Because of the difficulty in measuring skinfold thickness at any age and, especially, during infancy, an alternate (and less satisfactory) approach to identification of obesity is also offered. As may be seen from Table 3–14, this approach is based on the relation of body weight and stature. Some infants with heavy bone structure and musculature and without an excessive fat content of the body may appear to be obese by this definition. In addition, by basing the evaluation on the relation between weight and stature, some subjects with excessive fat content of the body may fail to be identified. Nevertheless, the simplicity of the approach may make it preferable to skinfold thickness for most purposes.

Do Obese Infants Become Obese Adults?

Many reports concerning obesity in adult subjects include statements indicating that a substantial percentage of the patients became obese during childhood. According to Mossberg (1948), the extent of obesity frequently decreases during adolescence but then once again increases. Mullins (1958) reported that approximately one-third of a group of 373 obese patients had been obese since childhood. Of 98 obese children studied by Lloyd et al. (1961), only one-fourth had achieved normal weight at the time of an eight-year follow-up evaluation. Abraham and Nordsieck (1960), in a 20-year follow-up of 120 obese and nonobese children 10 to 13 years of age, found that the majority of obese children became obese adults. Although such studies are somewhat difficult to evaluate, there is reason to believe that obesity in school-age children and adolescents predisposes to obesity in adult life.

Whether obesity in infancy predisposes to obesity in the school-age child or in the adult is even more difficult to ascertain than is the relation between adolescent and adult obesity. Although Meredith (1965) has reported low correlations for interage relationships of the size-size, size-gain and gain-gain varieties during infancy and childhood, his analyses do not apply specifically to early infancy. The possibility that food intake and growth during early infancy may have predictive value with respect to subsequent obesity has not been adequately explored.

Several retrospective studies have suggested that a substantial percentage of obese adolescents or children had been obese during infancy. However, even the better studies of this type (e.g., Heald and Hollander, 1965; Asher, 1966) are quite inconclusive and leave a number of questions unanswered.

Eid (1970) reported a follow-up study of 224 infants classified as rapid, moderate or slow gainers on the basis of weight gain during the first six weeks, three months and/or six months of life. When reexamined at six to eight years of age, a greater prevalence of obesity (defined on the basis of the relation of weight to height) was found in the rapid gainers than in the other two groups combined. The difference was statistically significant. Unfortunately, in the majority of the tables, only derived data were presented and it is therefore impossible to evaluate the results adequately.

The rapid gaining group included a predominance of males (more than 2:1), whereas the other groups included a predominance of females (more than 2:1). Because the definitions of obesity were not developed on a sex-specific basis, the different sex distribution might have exerted an important influence on the result. At six to eight years of age, 20.3 per cent of the rapid gainers and only 6.9 per cent of the other groups were classified as overweight. Yet, the data on skinfold thickness are nearly identical for the rapid gainers and the less rapid gainers. It is apparent that use of a definition of obesity based on skinfold thickness would have led to the conclusion that infants who gained rapidly during infancy were not more prone than other infants to subsequent development of obesity.

Thus, the question of whether obese infants become obese adults cannot yet be answered. Until an answer to this question is available, it seems desirable to avoid obesity during infancy and childhood. Prevention of obesity is clearly preferable to treatment and should be approached by educating parents with respect to feeding practices during infancy (Chapter 2). When treatment is undertaken, it should be carried out with caution. It is apparent that in the adult the ratio of weight of fat to total body weight can be decreased little if any by increase in the nonfat component. Therefore, management of obesity in the adult needs to be focused on decrease in the mass of fat. In the infant, on the other hand, the ratio of fat to nonfat can be decreased by decreasing the mass of fat, by increasing the mass of nonfat, or by altering both components simultaneously. In our ignorance of the consequences of major reduction in fat stores during infancy, it seems desirable to decrease the ratio of fat to nonfat predominantly through the mechanism of increase in the weight of the nonfat portion of the body.

APPETITE STIMULANTS

The problem of "poor appetite" in apparently normal children has long been of concern to parents and, consequently, to physicians. Vitamin preparations were commonly prescribed as "tonics" for preschool children in the United States in the 1940s and 1950s. In particular, there was lively debate over the possible appetite-stimulating effects of vitamin B_{12} (Committee on Nutrition, 1958; Howe, 1958a and b). Subsequent failure to obtain convincing evidence of an appetite-stimulating effect of vitamin supplements for children in developed countries implies lack of such effect.

Although not effective, vitamin supplements given as appetite stimulants were probably harmless. The physician is now faced with the question of use of a drug that appears to increase appetite and cannot be assumed to be harmless. Administration of cyproheptadine (Periactin) has been demonstrated to result in increased food intake and weight gain in children with bronchial asthma (Lavenstein et al., 1962; Bergen, 1964; Drash et al., 1966), in normal adults (Drash et al., 1966; Noble, 1969; Stiel et al., 1970) and in children and/or adults with pulmonary tuberculosis, brain damage and other abnormalities (Drash et al., 1966; Shah, 1968; Schreier and Krach, 1969).

Decreased physical activity of individuals taking the drug may contribute to positive energy balance and weight gain (Stiel et al., 1970), but it seems probable that the most important cause of weight gain is increased food intake, presumably through stimulation of appetite. The mechanism by which cyproheptadine affects appetite remains unknown, and no data are available concerning possible long-term adverse consequences of its administration. If appetite were to remain relatively great and weight gain were to continue at an excessive rate after discontinuation of treatment, the resulting obesity might prove to be a more serious problem than that for which the cyproheptadine had originally been prescribed. However, decreased rate of gain in weight has been noted on termination of therapy with cyproheptadine (Bergen, 1964; Stiel et al., 1970) – a phenomenon that we have designated "catch-down" growth. The possibility that completely unsuspected physical, biochemical or behavioral abnormalities might arise during the course of therapy must also be considered. Such abnormalities might be quite subtle or late in demonstrating themselves and, therefore, might be difficult to associate with administration of the drug.

As is so often true in medicine, the unknown risks of therapy must be weighed against the presumed risks presented by the disorder under consideration. "Poor appetite" is a symptom common to a variety of disorders and is a rather frequent complaint of parents concerning their normal children. When anorexia is sufficiently severe to represent a major hazard to health, the cause of the anorexia should be sought and, if possible, corrected. In rare instances, treatment with cyproheptadine may be warranted. In most cases, the complaint of "poor appetite" in children will not represent a sufficient threat to health to justify acceptance of unknown risk, and physicians will need to resist the pressures of parents who besiege them to prescribe a "tonic" to correct the "poor appetites" of their children.

REFERENCES

Abraham, S., and Nordsieck, M.: Relationship of excess weight in children and adults. Public Health Reports *75*:263, 1960.

Alleyne, G. A. O.: Studies on total body potassium in infantile malnutrition: the relation to body fluid spaces and urinary creatinine. Clin. Sci. *34*:199, 1968.

Alleyne, G. A. O.: Studies on total body potassium in malnourished infants. Factors affecting potassium repletion. Br. J. Nutr. *24*:205, 1970.
Alleyne, G. A. O., Viteri, F., and Alvarado, J.: Indices of body composition in infantile malnutrition: total body potassium and urinary creatinine. Amer. J. Clin. Nutr. *23*:875, 1970.
Asher, P.: Fat babies and fat children. The prognosis of obesity in the very young. Arch. Dis. Child. *41*:672, 1966.
Ashworth, A.: Growth rates in children recovering from protein-calorie malnutrition. Br. J. Nutr. *23*:835, 1969.
Ashworth, A., Bell, R., James, W. P. T., and Waterlow, J. C.: Calorie requirements of children recovering from protein-calorie malnutrition. Lancet *2*:600, 1968.
Babson, S. G.: Growth of low-birth-weight infants. J. Pediatr. *77*:11, 1970.
Baker, G. L.: Human adipose tissue composition. Amer. J. Clin. Nutr. *22*:829, 1969.
Barr, D. G. D., Shmerling, D. H., and Prader, A.: Catch-up growth in malnutrition, studied in celiac disease after institution of gluten-free diet. Pediatr. Res. *6*:521, 1972.
Barter, J., and Forbes, G. B.: Correlation of potassium-40 data with anthropometric measurements. Ann. N. Y. Acad. Sci. *110*:264, 1963.
Bergen, S. S., Jr.: Appetite stimulating properties of cyproheptadine. Amer. J. Dis. Child. *108*:270, 1964.
Björntorp, P., and Sjöström, L.: Number and size of adipose tissue fat cells in relation to metabolism in human obesity. Metabolism *20*:703, 1971.
Bleiler, R. E., and Schedl, H. P.: Creatinine excretion: variability and relationships to diet and body size. J. Lab. Clin. Med. *59*:945, 1962.
Borsook, H., and Dubnoff, J. W.: The hydrolysis of phosphocreatine and the origin of urinary creatinine. J. Biol. Chem. *168*:493, 1947.
Boyd, E.: The experimental error inherent in measuring the growing human body. Amer. J. Phys. Anthrop. *13*:389, 1929.
Brook, C. G. D.: Determination of body composition of children from skinfold measurements. Arch. Dis. Child. *46*:182, 1971.
Brožek, J., and Keys, A.: Evaluation of leanness-fatness in man: a survey of methods. Nutr. Absts. Revs. *20*:247, 1950.
Bugyi, B.: Vergleiche einiger Methoden zur Bestimmung des Körperfettes und des Magergewichtes bei Jugendlichen. Z. Ernährungswiss. *10*:364, 1971.
Cabak, V., and Najdanvic, R.: Effect of undernutrition in early life on physical and mental development. Arch. Dis. Child. *40*:532, 1965.
Catherwood, R., and Stearns, G.: Creatine and creatinine excretion in infancy. J. Biol. Chem. *119*:201, 1937.
Cheek, D. B., (ed.): Human Growth. Body Composition, Cell Growth, Energy and Intelligence. Philadelphia, Lea & Febiger, 1968.
Cheek, D. B., and Cooke, R. E.: Growth and growth retardation. Ann. Rev. Med. *15*:357, 1964.
Cheek, D. B., Graystone, J., and Mehrizi, A.: The importance of muscle cell number in children with congenital heart disease. Bull. Johns Hopkins Hosp. *118*:140, 1966.
Chinn, K. S. K.: Potassium and creatinine as indexes of muscle and nonmuscle protein in rats. J. Nutr. *90*:323, 1966.
Committee on Nutrition, American Academy of Pediatrics: Appraisal of the use of vitamins B_1 and B_{12} as supplements promoted for the stimulation of growth and appetite in children. Pediatrics *21*:860, 1958.
Committee on Nutrition, American Academy of Pediatrics: Measurement of skinfold-thickness in childhood. Pediatrics *42*:538, 1968.
Committee on Nutritional Anthropometry of the Food and Nutrition Board of the National Research Council. Keys, A.: Recommendations concerning body measurements for the characterization of nutritional status. Human Biol. *28*:11, 1956.
Cruise, M. O.: A longitudinal study of the growth of low birth weight infants. I. Velocity and distance growth, birth to 3 years. Pediatrics *51*:620, 1973.
Damon, A., and Goldman, R. F.: Predicting fat from body measurements: densitometric validation of ten anthropometric equations. Human Biol. *36*:31, 1964.
Dju, M. Y.: Tocopherol content of human tissues from conception to old age. Doctoral thesis, University of Rochester, 1953.

Dju, M. Y., Mason, K. E., and Filer, L. J., Jr.: Vitamin E (Tocopherol) in human tissues from birth to old age. Amer. J. Clin. Nutr. *6*:50, 1958.

Donald, H. P., and Purser, A. F.: Competition in utero between twin lambs. J. Agric. Sci. *48*:245, 1956.

Drash, A., Elliott, J., Laugs, H., Lavenstein, A. I., and Cooke, R. E.: The effect of cyproheptadine on carbohydrate metabolism. Clin. Pharm. Therap. *7*:340, 1966.

Edwards, D. A. W., Hammond, W. H., Healy, M. J. R., Tanner, J. M., and Whitehouse, R. H.: Design and accuracy of calipers for measuring subcutaneous tissue thickness. Br. J. Nutr. *9*:133, 1955.

Eid, E. E.: Follow-up study of physical growth of children who had excessive weight gain in first six months of life. Br. Med. J. *2*:74, 1970.

Falkner, F.: Office measurement of physical growth. Pediatr. Clin. N. Amer. *8*:13, 1961.

Farr, V.: Skinfold thickness as an indication of maturity of the newborn. Arch. Dis. Child. *41*:301, 1966.

Fitzhardinge, P. M., and Steven, E. M.: The small-for-date infant. 1. Later growth patterns. Pediatrics *49*:671, 1972.

Fletcher, R. F.: The measurement of total body fat with skinfold calipers. Clin. Sci. *22*:333, 1962.

Fomon, S. J.: Body composition of the male reference infant during the first year of life. Borden Award Address, October 1966. Pediatrics *40*:863, 1967.

Fomon, S. J., Filer, L. J., Jr., Thomas, L. N., and Rogers, R. R.: Growth and serum chemical values of normal breastfed infants. Acta Paediatr. Scand. (Suppl. 202), 1970.

Fomon, S. J., Filer, L. J., Jr., Thomas, L. N., Rogers, R. R., and Proksch, A. M.: Relationship between formula concentration and rate of growth of normal infants. J. Nutr. *98*:241, 1969.

Fomon, S. J., Thomas, L. N., and Filer, L. J., Jr.: Calorie intake by normal infants fed skim milk ad libitum between four and six months of age. To be published, 1974.

Fomon, S. J., Thomas, L. N., Filer, L. J., Jr., Anderson, T. A., and Bergmann, K. E.: Requirements for protein and essential amino acids in early infancy. Acta Paediatr. Scand. *62*:33, 1973.

Fomon, S. J., Thomas, L. N., Filer, L. J., Jr., Ziegler, E. E., and Leonard, M. T.: Food consumption and growth of normal infants fed milk-based formulas. Acta Paediatr. Scand. (Suppl. 223), 1971.

Forbes, G. B.: Methods for determining composition of the human body. With a note on the effect of diet on body composition. Pediatrics *29*:477, 1962.

Gampel, B.: The relation of skinfold thickness in the neonate to sex, length of gestation, size at birth and maternal skinfold. Human Biol. *37*:29, 1965.

Garn, S. M.: Roentgenogrammetric determinations of body composition. Human Biol. *29*:337, 1957.

Garn, S. M.: Personal communication, 1967.

Garn, S. M., and Rohmann, C. G.: Interaction of nutrition and genetics in the timing of growth and development. Pediatr. Clin. N. Amer. *13*:353, 1966.

Garrow, J. S.: The use and calibration of a small whole body counter for the measurement of total body potassium in malnourished infants. W. Indian Med. J. *14*:73, 1965a.

Garrow, J. S.: Total body-potassium in kwashiorkor and marasmus. Lancet *2*:455, 1965b.

Garrow, J. S., Fletcher, K., and Halliday, D.: Body composition in severe infantile malnutrition. J. Clin. Invest. *44*:417, 1965.

Garrow, J. S., and Pike, M. C.: The long-term prognosis of severe infantile malnutrition. Lancet *1*:1, 1967.

Garrow, J. S., Smith, R., and Ward, E. E.: Electrolyte Metabolism in Severe Infantile Malnutrition. Oxford, Pergamon Press, 1968.

Graham, G. G.: The later growth of malnourished infants: Effects of age, severity and subsequent diet. *In* McCance, R. A., and Widdowson, E. M. (eds.): Calorie Deficiencies and Protein Deficiencies. London, Churchill, 1968.

Graham, G. G., Cordano, A., Blizzard, R. M., and Cheek, D. B.: Infantile malnutrition: changes in body composition during rehabilitation. Pediatr. Res. *3*:579, 1969.

Halliday, D.: Chemical composition of the whole body and individual tissues of two Jamaican children whose death resulted primarily from malnutrition. Clin. Sci. *33*:365, 1967.

Hammond, W. H.: Measurement and interpretation of subcutaneous fat, with norms for children and young adult males. Br. J. Prev. Soc. Med. *9*:201, 1955.

Hansen, J. D. L.: Body composition and appraisal of nutriture, Part II. *In* Brožek, J. (ed.): Human Body Composition: Approaches and Applications. Symposium of the Society for the Study of Human Biology. Vol. VII. Oxford, Pergamon, 1965, p. 255.

Heald, F. P., and Hollander, R. J.: The relationship between obesity in adolescence and early growth. J. Pediatr. *67*:35, 1965.

Hirsch, J., and Gallian, E.: Methods for the determination of adipose cell size in man and animals. J. Lipid Res. *9*:110, 1968.

Hirsch, J., and Knittle, J. L.: Cellularity of obese and nonobese human adipose tissue. Fed. Proc. *29*:1516, 1970.

Hooper, P. D.: Infant feeding and its relationship to weight gain and illness. Practitioner *194*:391, 1965.

Hooper, P. D., and Alexander, E. L.: Infant morbidity and obesity. A survey of 151 infants from general practice. Practitioner *207*:221, 1971.

Howe, E. E.: Effect of vitamin B_{12} on growth-retarded children: a review. Amer. J. Clin. Nutr. *6*:818, 1958a.

Howe, E. E.: (Letter to Editor.) Vitamin B_{12} supplementation. Pediatrics *22*:1202, 1958b.

Jackson, R. L., Westerfeld, R., Flynn, M. A., Kimball, E. R., and Lewis, R. B.: Growth of "well-born" American infants fed human and cow's milk. Pediatrics *33*:642, 1964.

Jelliffe, D. B.: The assessment of the nutritional status of the community. W. H. O. Monograph Series, No. 53. Geneva, 1966, p. 72.

Karlberg, P., Engström, I., Lichtenstein, H., and Svennberg, I.: The development of children in a Swedish urban community. A prospective longitudinal study. III. Physical growth during the first three years of life. Acta Paediatr. Scand. (Suppl. 187): 48, 1968.

Karn, M. N.: Birth weight and length of gestation of twins, together with maternal age, parity and survival rate. Ann. Eugenics *16*:365, 1952.

Karn, M. N.: Twin data: a further study of birth weight, gestation time, maternal age, order of birth, and survival. Ann. Eugenics *17*:233, 1953.

Keet, M. P., Hansen, J. D. L., and Truswell, A. S.: Are skinfold measurements of value in the assessment of suboptimal nutrition in young children? Pediatrics *45*:965, 1970.

Keet, M. P., Moodie, A. D., Wittmann, W., and Hansen, J. D. L.: Kwashiorkor: a prospective ten-year follow-up study. S. Afr. Med. J. *45*:1427, 1971.

Keys, A., and Brožek, J.: Body fat in adult man. Physiol. Rev. *33*:245, 1953.

Kielanowski, J.: Estimates of the energy cost of protein deposition in growing animals. *In* Blaxter, K. L. (ed.): Proceedings of Third Symposium on Energy Metabolism. New York, Academic Press, 1969, p. 13.

Knittle, J. L.: Obesity in childhood: a problem in adipose tissue cellular development. J. Pediatr. *81*:1048, 1972.

Krueger, R. H.: Some long-term effects of severe malnutrition in early life. Lancet *2*:514, 1969.

Kumar, I., Land, D. G., and Boyne, A. W.: The determination of body composition of living animals. The daily endogenous creatinine excretion as a measure of body composition in rats. Br. J. Nutr. *13*:320, 1959.

Lavenstein, A. F., Dacaney, E. P., Lasagna, L., and Van Metre, T. E.: Effect of cyproheptadine on asthmatic children: study of appetite, weight gain and linear growth. J. A. M. A. *180*:912, 1962.

Lees, M. H., Bristow, J. D., Griswold, H. E., and Olmsted, R. W.: Relative hypermetabolism in infants with congenital heart disease and undernutrition. Pediatrics *36*:183, 1965.

Lloyd, J. K., Wolff, O. H., and Whelen, W. S.: Childhood obesity. A long-term study of height and weight. Br. Med. J. *2*:145, 1961.

MacWilliam, K. M., and Dean, R. F. A.: The growth of malnourished children after hospital treatment. East Afr. Med. J. *42*:297, 1965.

Maresh, M. M.: Bone, muscle and fat measurements. Pediatrics *28*:971, 1961.

Maresh, M. M.: A forty-five year investigation for secular changes in physical maturation. Amer. J. Phys. Anthrop. *36*:103, 1972.

McKeown, T., and Record, R. G.: Observations on foetal growth in multiple pregnancy in man. J. Endocr. *8*:386, 1952.
McKeown, T., and Record, R. G.: The influence of placental size on foetal growth in man, with special reference to multiple pregnancy. J. Endocr. 9:418, 1953.
Mellander, O., Vahlquist, B., Mellbin, T., and collaborators: Breast feeding and artificial feeding: a clinical, serological, and biochemical study of 402 infants, with a survey of the literature. The Norbotten study. Acta Paediatr. Scand. *48*:(Suppl. 116), 1959.
Mendes, C. B., and Waterlow, J. C.: The effect of a low protein diet, and of refeeding on the composition of liver and muscle in the weanling rat. Br. J. Nutr. *12*:74, 1958.
Meredith, H. V.: Selected anatomic variables analyzed for interage relationships of the size-size, size-gain, and gain-gain varieties. *In* Lipsitt, L. P., and Spiker, C. C., (eds.): Advances in Child Development and Behavior. Vol. 2. New York, Academic Press, 1965, p. 221.
Mossberg, H.-O.: Obesity in children. A clinical-prognostical investigation. Acta Paediatr. Scand. *35*(Suppl. 2): 1948.
Moulton, C. R.: Age and chemical development in mammals. J. Biol. Chem. *57*:79, 1923.
Mullins, A. G.: The prognosis in juvenile obesity. Arch. Dis. Child. *33*:307, 1958.
Noble, R. E.: Effect of cyproheptadine on appetite and weight gain in children. J.A.M.A. *209*:2054, 1969.
Novak, L. P.: Total-body potassium during the first year of life determined by whole-body counting of ^{40}K. J. Nucl. Med. *14*:550, 1973.
Novak, L. P., Hamamoto, K., Orvis, A. L., and Burke, E. C.: Total body potassium in infants. Determination by whole-body counting of radioactive potassium (^{40}K). Amer. J. Dis Child. *119*:419, 1970.
Ogawara, S.: Über die Fettgewebsverteilung an der Körperoberfläche des Kindes. Konstitutionslehre *17*:90, 1933.
Ørskov, E. R., and McDonald, I.: The utilization of dietary energy for maintenance and for fat and protein deposition in young growing sheep. *In* 5th Symposium on Energy Metabolism of Farm Animals. European Association for Animal Production, Publ. 13. Zürich, Juris, 1970, p. 121.
Owen, G. M.: The assessment and recording of measurements of growth of children: report of a small conference. Pediatrics *51*:461, 1973.
Owen, G. M., and Brožek, J.: Influence of age, sex and nutrition on body composition during childhood and adolescence. *In* Falkner, F. (ed.): Human Development. Philadelphia, W. B. Saunders Co., 1966, p. 222.
Owen, G. M., Filer, L. J., Jr., Maresh, M., and Fomon, S. J.: Body composition of the infant. Part II. Sex-related differences in body composition in infancy. *In* Falkner, F. (ed.): Human Development. Philadelphia, W. B. Saunders Co., 1966, p. 246.
Owen, G. M., Jensen, R. L., and Fomon, S. J.: Sex-related difference in total body water and exchangeable chloride during infancy. J. Pediatr. *60*:858, 1962.
Pařízková, J.: Total body fat and skinfold thickness in children. Metabolism *10*:794, 1961.
Payne, P. R., and Waterlow, J. C.: Relative energy requirements for maintenance, growth, and physical activity. Lancet *2*:210, 1971.
Picou, D., Alleyne, G. A. O., and Seakins, A.: Hydroxyproline and creatine excretion in infantile protein malnutrition. Clin. Sci. *29*:517, 1965.
Picou, D., Halliday, D., and Garrow, J. S.: Total body protein, collagen and noncollagen protein in infantile malnutrition. Clin. Sci. *30*:345, 1966.
Pittman, G. J., and Cohen, P.: The pathogenesis of cardiac cachexia. N. Eng. J. Med. *271*:403 and 453, 1964.
Prader, A., Tanner, J. M., and von Harnack, G. A.: Catch-up growth following illness or starvation. An example of developmental canalization in man. J. Pediatr. *62*:646, 1963.
Prockop, D. J.: Isotopic studies on collagen degradation and the urine excretion of hydroxyproline. J. Clin. Invest. *43*:453, 1964.
Rey, J., Rey, F., Jos, J., and Amusquivar, L. S.: Etude de la croissance dans 50 cas de maladie coeliaque de l'enfant. l. Effets du regime sans gluten. Arch. Fr. Pédiatr. *28*:37, 1971.

Romahn, A., and Burmeister, W.: Gesamtkaliumbestimmung bei Säuglingen und Kleinkindern mit einem Babycounter. Arch. Kinderh. *180*:239, 1970.

Rose, H. E., and Mayer, J.: Activity, calorie intake, fat storage, and the energy balance of infants. Pediatrics *41*:18, 1968.

Safer, D. J., and Allen, R. P.: Factors influencing the suppressant effects of two stimulant drugs on the growth of hyperactive children. Pediatrics *51*:660, 1973.

Safer, D., Allen, R., and Barr, E.: Depression of growth in hyperactive children on stimulant drugs. N. Eng. J. Med. *287*:217, 1972.

Salans, L. B., Cushman, S. W., and Weismann, R. E.: Studies of human adipose tissue. Adipose cell size and number in nonobese and obese patients. J. Clin. Invest. *52*: 929, 1973.

Salans, L. B., Horton, E. S., and Sims, E. A. H.: Experimental obesity in man: cellular character of the adipose tissue. J. Clin. Invest. *50*:1005, 1971.

Satgé, P., Matei, J. F., and Dan, V.: Avenir somatique des enfants atteints de kwashiorkor. Ann. Pediatr. (Paris) *17*:368, 1970.

Schreier, K., and Krach, V.: The effect of cyproheptadine on appetite in children. Med. Ernähr. *10*:164, 1969.

Seltzer, C. C., Goldman, R. F., and Mayer, J.: The triceps skinfold as a predictive measure of body density and body fat in obese adolescent girls Pediatrics *36*:212, 1965.

Seltzer, C. C., and Mayer, J.: Greater reliability of the triceps skin fold over the subscapular skin fold as an index of obesity. Amer. J. Clin. Nutr. *20*:950, 1967.

Shah, N. M.: A double-blind study on appetite stimulation and weight gain with cyproheptadine as adjunct to specific therapy in pulmonary tuberculosis. Curr. Med. Pract. *12*:861, 1968.

Shmerling, D. H., Prader, A., and Zachmann, M.: The effect of dietary treatment on growth in coeliac disease. *In* McCance, R. A., and Widdowson, E. M. (eds.): Calorie Deficiencies and Protein Deficiencies. London, Churchill, 1968, p. 159.

Sims, E. A. H., Goldman, R. F., Gluck, C. M., Horton, E. S., Kelleher, P. C., and Rowe, D. W.: Experimental obesity in man. Trans. Ass. Amer. Phys. *81*:153, 1968.

Sinclair, J. C., and Silverman, W. A.: Intrauterine growth in active tissue mass of the human fetus, with particular reference to the undergrown baby. Pediatrics *38*:48, 1966.

Smiley, J. D., and Ziff, M.: Urinary hydroxyproline excretion and growth. Physiol. Rev. *44*:31, 1964.

Standard, K. L., Wills, U. G., and Waterlow, J. C.: Indirect indicators of muscle mass in malnourished children. Amer. J. Clin. Nutr. *7*:271, 1959.

Stewart, A., and Westropp, C.: Breast feeding in the Oxford child health survey. Part II. Comparison of bottle- and breast-fed babies. Br. Med. J. *2*:305, 1953.

Stiel, J. N., Liddle, G. W., and Lacy, W. W.: Studies of mechanism of cyproheptadine-induced weight gain in human subjects. Metabolism *19*:192, 1970.

Stoch, M. B., and Smythe, P. M.: The effect of undernutrition during infancy on subsequent brain growth and intellectual development. S. Afr. Med. J. *41*:1027, 1967.

Stocker, F. P., Wilkoff, W., Miettinen, O. S., and Nadas, A. S.: Oxygen consumption in infants with heart disease. J. Pediatr. *80*:43, 1972.

Suckling, P. V., and Campbell, J. A. H.: A five year follow-up of coloured children with kwashiorkor in Cape Town. J. Trop. Pediatr. *2*:173, 1957.

Tanner, J. M.: The measurement of body fat in man. Proc. Nutr. Soc. *18*:148, 1959.

Tanner, J. M., and Whitehouse, R. H.: Standards for subcutaneous fat in British children. Br. Med. J. *1*:446, 1962.

Thompson, D. J., Gezon, H. M., Hatch, T. F., Rycheck, R. R., and Rogers, K. D.: Sex distribution of Staphylococcus aureus colonization and disease in newborn infants. N. Eng. J. Med. *269*:337, 1963.

Thorbek, G.: The utilization of metabolizable energy for protein and fat gain in growing pigs. *In* 5th Symposium on Energy Metabolism of Farm Animals. European Association for Animal Production, Publ. 13. Zürich, Juris, 1970, p. 129.

Van Niekerk, B. D. H., Reid, J. T., Bensadoun, A., and Paladines, O. L.: Urinary creatinine as an index of body composition. J. Nutr. *79*:463, 1963.

Vincent, M., and Hugon, J.: Relationships between various criteria of maturity at birth. Biol. Neonat. *4*:223, 1962.

Washburn, T. C., Medearis, D. N., Jr., and Childs, B.: Sex differences in susceptibility to infections. Pediatrics *35*:57, 1965.

Waterlow, J. C., and Alleyne, G. A. O.: Protein malnutrition in children: advances in knowledge in the last ten years. *In* Advances in Protein Chemistry. Vol. 25. New York, Academic Press, 1971, p. 117.

Waterlow, J. C., and Weisz, T.: The fat, protein and nucleic acid content of the liver in malnourished human infants. J. Clin. Invest. *35*:346, 1956.

Whitehead, R. G.: Hydroxyproline creatinine ratio as an index of nutritional status and rate of growth. Lancet *2*:567, 1965.

Widdowson, E. M., and Dickerson, J. W. T.: The effect of growth and function on the chemical composition of soft tissues. Biochem. J. *77*:30, 1960.

Widdowson, E. M., and Dickerson, J. W. T.: Chemical composition of the body. *In* Comar, C. L., and Bronner, F. (eds.): Mineral Metabolism. Vol. 2. Part A. New York, Academic Press, 1964, p. 1.

Winick, M., Brasel, J. A., and Rosso, P.: Nutrition and cell growth. *In* Winick, M. (ed.): Nutrition and Development. New York, J. Wiley & Sons, 1972, p. 49.

Winick, M., and Noble, A.: Cellular response in rats during malnutrition at various ages. J. Nutr. *89*:300, 1966.

Winick, M., and Noble, A.: Cellular response with increased feeding in neonatal rats. J. Nutr. *91*:179, 1967.

Younoszai, M. K., Andersen, D. W., Filer, L. J., Jr., and Fomon, S. J.: Urinary excretion of hydroxyproline by normal infants during the first six months of life. Pediatr. Res. *1*:266, 1967.

4

GASTROINTESTINAL FUNCTION DURING INFANCY

M. K. Younoszai

Although information regarding functional development of the gastrointestinal tract in the human being is limited, it is apparent that several aspects of gastrointestinal function are less well developed during early infancy than in the older child or adult (Deren, 1968; Koldovsky, 1969, 1970, 1972). Normal processes involved in the digestion of protein, fat and carbohydrate are discussed in Chapters 6, 7 and 8, respectively. The present chapter will attempt to summarize information regarding the development of these processes during early infancy.

Function of Salivary Glands and Tongue

Saliva arises mainly from the secretions of the parotid, submandibular and submaxillary glands. It aids in moistening the food in the mouth and in lubricating (with mucus) the bolus of food before the latter is swallowed. Of the various components of saliva, amylase may be of some significance for the digestive process. At the nearly neutral pH of the mouth, it can hydrolyze starch (Davenport, 1968), but the food remains in the mouth and esophagus so briefly that little starch is actually likely to be hydrolyzed. Because of low gastric acidity of young infants, salivary amylase may be responsible for some hydrolysis of starch in the stomach. After the first few months of life, when gastric acidity increases, it is unlikely that salivary amylase is active in the stomach.

On the basis of earlier studies of cattle and a more recent study by Hamosh and Scow (1973) in rats, the possibility that lingual lipase may contribute to digestion of fat by human subjects must be considered.

Gastric Function

The lumen of the stomach serves as a temporary reservoir in which food is subjected to the actions of gastric secretions.

Protein Digestion. Pepsin initiates hydrolysis of protein, and hydrochloric acid establishes the acid condition in which pepsin is active. Gastric digestion of protein is optimal in the pH ranges of 1.8 to 2.2 and 3.5 to 3.6 (Taylor, 1959).

Immediately after birth, the pH of the stomach is relatively high—generally about pH 6—presumably because of the presence of slightly alkaline amniotic fluid. Twenty-four hours later, the pH has generally decreased to about 2.5 (Avery et al., 1966). The high acidity of gastric juice a few hours after birth may reflect transplacental passage of maternal gastrin, stimulating gastric mucosa of the infant in utero. The gastric parietal cell mass of the fullterm newborn is relatively well developed (Polacek and Ellison, 1966). Werner (1948) showed that infants under 2500 gm show no, or only extremely few, pepsinogen granules in their chief cells. In the fullterm infant over 3000 gm, pepsinogen was found in all chief cells, although in variable amounts. Cells containing granules were confined to the basal parts of the gastric glands, whereas in the adult they occupy three-fourths of the gland. Peptic activity of gastric tissue correlates well with the histologic pattern.

During the first week after birth, gastric acidity decreases (Miller, 1941). In spite of the relatively well developed gastric parietal cell mass and low gastric pH at birth, the data of Agunod et al. (1969) suggest that secretion of hydrochloric acid and pepsin per unit of body weight is less for the infant than for the adult. When one considers the greater intake of protein per unit of body weight of infants than of adults, it would seem that gastric digestion of protein is relatively unimportant during infancy. This is consistent with the observation that protein digestion is not impaired despite substantial buffering capacity of the cow milk (Mason, 1962) that serves as a major source of protein for most infants in developed countries.

The observations of Agunod et al. (1969) concerning gastric secretion of hydrochloric acid and pepsin after injection of Histalog (an analog of histamine) are presented in Figures 4–1 and 4–2. It may be seen that secretion of hydrochloric acid and pepsin per unit of body weight remained low during the first month of life. Although few data are available for infants beyond one month of age, it would appear that rates of secretion of pepsin continue to be relatively low.

Gastric juice of premature infants appears to be less acidic than that of fullterm infants (Ames, 1966; Avery et al., 1966). Secretion of gastric acid may be lower in premature than in fullterm infants after a meal or after histamine stimulation (Miller, 1941). Proteolytic activity

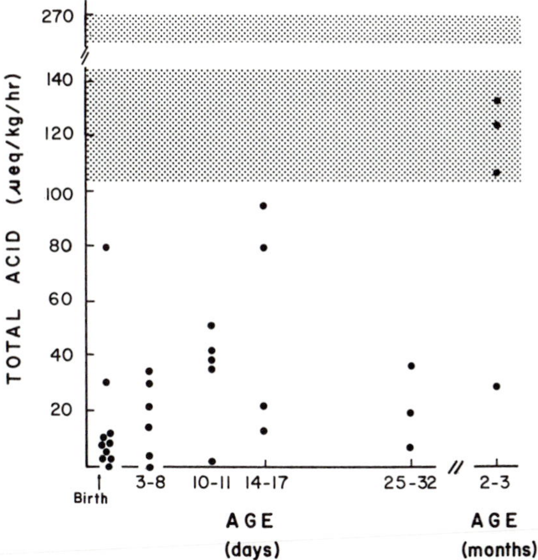

Figure 4–1 Rate of gastric secretion of hydrochloric acid in relation to age. Each dot indicates the result of study of one infant. The shaded area refers to the normal range for adult subjects. (Modified from Agunod, M., et al.: Correlative study of hydrochloric acid, pepsin and intrinsic factor secretion in newborns and infants. Amer. J. Dig. Dis. *14*:400, 1969.)

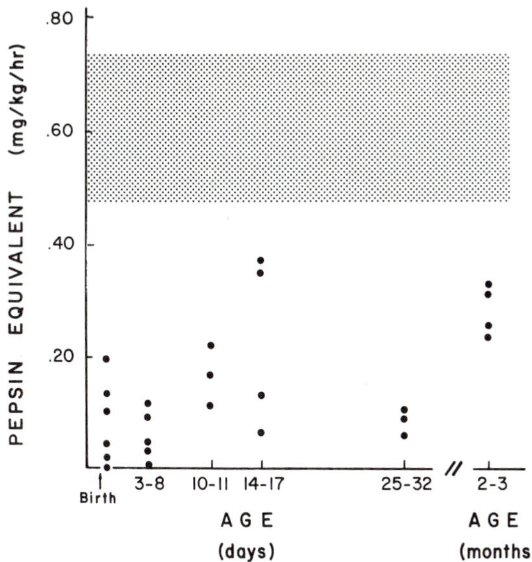

Figure 4–2 Rate of gastric secretion of pepsin equivalent (i.e., peptic activity) in relation to age. Symbols and shaded area as in Figure 4–1. (Modified from Agunod, M., et al.: Correlative study of hydrochloric acid, pepsin and intrinsic factor secretion in newborns and infants. Amer. J. Dig. Dis. *14*:400, 1969.)

of the stomach in the premature also seems to be lower than in the fullterm infant (Werner, 1948).

Fat Digestion. Infant gastric juice has lipolytic activity (Cohen et al., 1971; Olivecrona et al., 1973). Properties of this lipase differ from those of pancreatic lipase. Lipolytic activity of gastric juice is stable at pH 2 and demonstrates optimal activity between pH 4 and 8. Gastric lipase splits long-chain triglycerides more slowly than medium-chain triglycerides. Bile acids are not essential for hydrolysis of milk particle triglyceride by gastric juice. Gastric lipase could be important in infants and in patients in whom medium-chain triglycerides are a major calorie source. It may contribute to fat digestion in infants with congenital absence of pancreatic lipase (Sheldon, 1964). Lipolytic properties of gastric juice obtained from infants and adults appear identical in vitro (Cohen et al., 1971).

Gastric Emptying. Emptying of gastric contents into the duodenum is thought to be under the control of osmoreceptors in the duodenum (Hunt, 1961). These osmoreceptors seem to function within the first few days of life (Husband et al., 1970). Gastric contents appear to empty into the duodenum in small amounts over several hours, the rate of gastric emptying depending on size and composition of the meal (Hunt, 1960). In normal newborn infants, a test meal containing 10 per cent starch emptied at a faster rate than a test meal containing 10 per cent glucose (Husband et al., 1970). A 5 per cent glucose solution emptied at a faster rate than a 10 per cent glucose solution (Husband and Husband, 1969). This is contrary to the finding in adults, in whom isocaloric solutions of starch and glucose empty at the same rate (Hunt, 1960). The significance of curd formation with respect to protein digestion and gastric emptying is not fully understood (Platt, 1961).

Small Intestinal Function

Secretion of pancreatic juice and bile is stimulated by entry of food into the duodenum. Although absorption of some protein, fat and glucose occurs in the duodenum, the greater part of the absorption of these substances occurs more distally in the small intestine, particularly in the upper jejunum. Fat is absorbed more rapidly than glucose, and glucose more rapidly than protein (Borgström et al., 1960, 1961).

Protein Digestion. A summary of sequential steps involved in digestion of protein is presented in Chapter 6. More than 30 years ago, Andersen (1942) provided evidence that tryptic activity of duodenal fluid is less in infants than in older children (Fig. 4–3).

When the pancreas is stimulated with secretin and pancreozymin, rate of secretion of duodenal fluid and activity of trypsin and chymo-

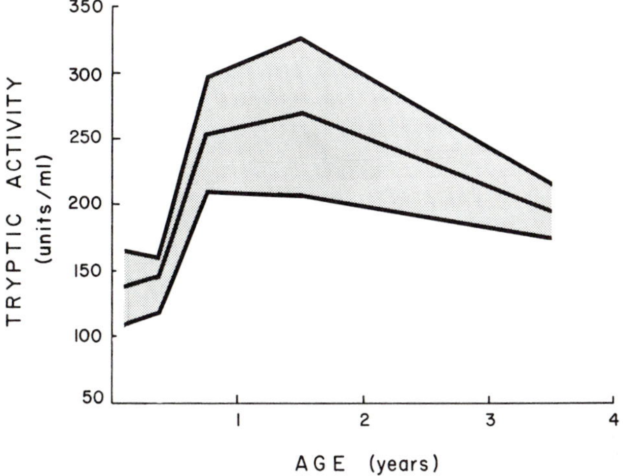

Figure 4–3 Tryptic activity of duodenal juice in relation to age. The 10th, 50th and 90th percentiles are indicated. (Modified from Andersen, D. H.: Pancreatic enzymes in the duodenal juice in the celiac syndrome. Amer. J. Dis. Child. *63*:643, 1942.)

trypsin of the fluid are less in infants than in older individuals; in children weighing less than 12 kg, rate of secretion and proteolytic activity are positively correlated with age and body weight (Delachaume-Salem and Sarles, 1970). However, Hadorn et al. (1968; Hadorn, 1971) found that, per kilogram of body weight, rate of secretion of chymotrypsin was similar at all ages.

Borgström et al. (1960) demonstrated that tryptic activity of duodenal juice of the premature infant is even less than that of the fullterm infant. Furthermore, although entrance of food into the duodenum of the fullterm infant appears to increase tryptic activity, such increase does not occur in the case of the premature infant. Zoppi et al. (1972) found that exocrine pancreatic function in premature (2.0 to 2.4 kg) infants was fairly well developed but lower than that of fullterm neonates. One week after birth, pancreatic function was higher in premature than in fullterm neonates. These investigators also found that feeding a high protein diet stimulated production of trypsin. Werner (1948) found that the proteolytic activity of pancreatic tissue was much greater in fullterm than in premature infants. Zymogen granules were absent or present in only small numbers in the parenchymal cells of the pancreas of the low-birth-weight infant. In the fullterm infant, zymogen granules were present in adequate numbers, the histologic appearance almost resembling that in adults. Regardless of these findings, neither Borgström et al. (1960) nor other investigators have demonstrated differences of practical significance in protein digestion between fullterm and premature infants or between infants and older individuals.

Enterokinase, which converts trypsinogen to trypsin, is found in the intestine of fetuses weighing 1500 gm or more (Lieberman, 1966). Intestinal mucosal peptidase activities are also well developed as early as 11 weeks of gestational age and remain highly active postnatally (Lindberg, 1966; 1971).

Mechanisms necessary for active absorption of amino acids in the intestine develop early in intrauterine life and attain adult levels before the third trimester of pregnancy (Koldovsky, 1969). Total fecal nitrogen in healthy infants and children is usually less than 1 gm/day (Shmerling et al., 1970), probably representing less than 5 per cent of the total amount of protein traversing the intestinal lumen.

It is possible that, during the first few days of life, immunoglobulins from maternal milk may enter the body of the infant through the intestinal tract (Leissring et al., 1962; Iyengar and Selvaraj, 1972). Although such absorption undoubtedly occurs in many animals, the evidence for its occurrence in the human infant is poorly documented and the extent of entry may be quite limited (Lecce, 1966; Morris, 1968; Brambell, 1970).

Fat Digestion. The steps involved in the digestion of fats are discussed in Chapter 7. As already mentioned, some lipids may be hydrolyzed in the stomach through the action of gastric lipase. However, gastric lipase entering the duodenum is inactivated by trypsin, and further hydrolysis will therefore be dependent on pancreatic lipase. In addition, the presence of bile acids is important in the dispersal of lipids and their hydrolytic products in the aqueous phase of the intestinal contents.

Pancreatic Lipase. Although Andersen (1942) reported that lipase activity, expressed as units per milliliter of duodenal fluid, was greater in normal infants between six months and one year of age than in two- to three-year-old children (Fig. 4–4), the more recent studies of Hadorn et al. (1968) indicate that lipase output per unit of body weight is independent of age during infancy and childhood. After stimulation with secretin and pancreozymin, rate of secretion of pancreatic lipase increases with age (Delachaume-Salem and Sarles, 1970). At birth, lipase activity after stimulation is less in premature than in fullterm infants but, at age one week, activity is higher in premature than in fullterm infants. Feeding a diet with high protein content stimulated production of lipase, while feeding of high fat diet alone had no effect on pancreatic lipase secretion in these infants (Zoppi et al., 1972).

Bile Acids. As discussed in Chapter 7, bile acids are important in promoting formation of micelles. It is from micelles that fatty acids and 2-monoglycerides are primarily absorbed. It is generally stated that a concentration of approximately 2 mmoles of bile salts per liter of duodenal juice is essential for formation of micelles (Holt, 1972). The

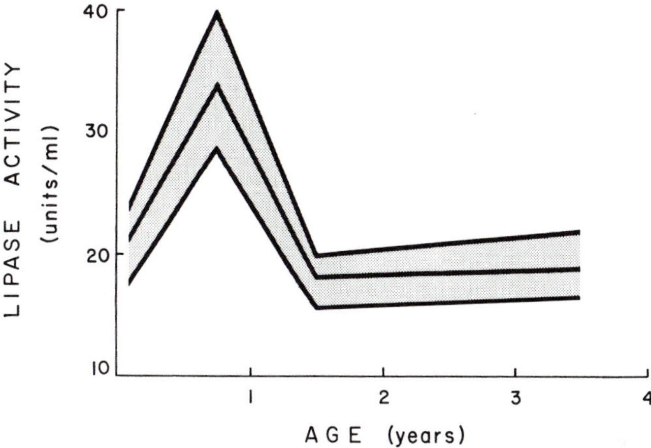

Figure 4–4 Lipase activity of duodenal juice in relation to age. The 10th, 50th and 90th percentiles are indicated. (Modified from Andersen, D. H.: Pancreatic enzymes in the duodenal juice in the celiac syndrome. Amer. J. Dis. Child. *63*:643, 1942.)

"critical micellar concentration" for a mixture of bile salts depends on many factors such as pH, temperature, proportions of the various bile salts and concentration of lecithin (Small, 1971). The critical micellar concentration of bile salts in duodenal juice is therefore likely to be different from individual to individual. The bile salt concentration of duodenal aspirates of adults is usually greater than 2 mmoles/liter.

Although bile salts have been found in the gallbladder of human fetuses (Poley et al., 1964), several studies suggest that concentrations of bile acids in duodenal juice of small infants may be low (Bongiovanni, 1965). Thus, Norman et al. (1972) found concentrations of only 0.4 to 1.5 mmoles/liter in duodenal aspirates of 3- to 15-day-old infants who had been fed 40 to 90 ml of human milk. These low concentrations persisted for four hours after the feeding. In low-birth-weight infants, Lavy et al. (1971) have reported relatively low concentrations of bile acids (less than 2 mmoles/liter) in duodenal contents aspirated two to three hours after a feeding. Duodenal fluid aspirated from fasting older infants and children appears to demonstrate concentrations of bile salts similar to those of adults.

Unfortunately, our knowledge of bile salt synthesis in infancy is meager. In relation to body weight, the size of the bile salt pool and rate of synthesis of bile salts may be lower in newborn infants than in adults (Watkins et al., 1973). The details of the enterohepatic circulation of bile salts in the infant and child have not been worked out. A significant correlation between amounts of bile salts and of fat excreted in the feces has been reported (Weber et al., 1971), and it therefore seems likely that loss of bile salts in the feces may be relatively greater during the early months of life than later in childhood.

TABLE 4–1 BILE SALTS IN DUODENAL FLUID OF YOUNG INFANTS AND ADULTS

	Young Infants	Adults
Total bile salts (mmole/liter)	<2	>2
Deoxycholate	Absent	Present
Glycine conjugates: taurine conjugates	<2:1	>2:1

The lesser ability of the infant than of the adult to absorb fats may be due more to differences in bile salt composition than to differences in quantity of bile salts. At birth, the concentration of taurine conjugates predominates; between the second week and seventh month, the concentration of glycine conjugates increases threefold (Poley et al., 1964). By one year of age, the proportion of glycine to taurine conjugates approaches that found in adults. Deoxycholates appear to be absent from bile of infants (Encrantz and Sjövall, 1959; Poley et al., 1964; Bongiovanni, 1965; Norman et al., 1972). The major differences between infants and adults in concentration and composition of bile salts are summarized in Table 4–1. Because deoxycholates are secondary bile salts formed from cholates by intestinal bacteria, it is possible that the specific composition of the intestinal bacterial flora of infants may be responsible for the absence of deoxycholates from bile of infants (Gustafsson and Werner, 1968). However, other explanations may be more attractive. For example, the infant might be less able than the adult to absorb deoxycholates synthesized by bacteria.

Fat Absorption. Fatty acids and monoglycerides diffuse through the mucosal epithelial membrane and are reesterified to triglycerides inside the epithelial cells. These triglycerides as components of chylomicrons are released into the submucosal tissues of the intestinal wall and enter the intestinal lymphatic system. Data regarding absorption of monoglycerides and fatty acids during infancy are discussed in detail in Chapter 7. The efficiency with which infants, especially premature infants, reesterify fatty acids and form chylomicrons is unknown. No chylomicrons could be observed in peripheral venous blood during the first four to five days of life. A postprandial increase in esterified fatty acids was found in children older than one week (Melichar et al., 1962). Balance studies suggest that long-chain, saturated fatty acids in particular are less well absorbed by infants than by older individuals. The maximum rise in blood concentrations of triglycerides and vitamin A after feeding of a test meal is positively related to age of infants up to age 20 months (Norman et al., 1971).

Carbohydrate Digestion. That α-amylase activity is low in duodenal fluid of young infants has been reported by several investigators (Andersen, 1942; Auricchio et al., 1967; Hadorn et al., 1968) and, in fact, Borgström et al. (1960) have suggested that much of the amylase found in duodenal fluid of infants may arise from saliva. Duodenal aspirates obtained from infants and children show increasing α-amylase activity with increasing age (Andersen, 1942; Borgström et al., 1960, 1961; Auricchio et al., 1967, 1968, 1971; Hadorn et al., 1968). The rise in activity is slow and, even by the sixth month of life, activity is much lower than that of older children (Fig. 4–5). When stimulated by secretin and pancreozymin, secretion of pancreatic α-amylase increases with increasing age (Delachaume-Salem and Sarles, 1970). At birth, stimulated α-amylase activity is lower in premature than in fullterm infants. Feeding small amounts of starch to infants stimulated pancreatic α-amylase production (Zoppi et al., 1972). As discussed in Chapter 8, capacity to hydrolyze starch may be less in infants than in children. An alternate pathway of starch digestion by way of glucamylase activity of the intestinal mucosa may play a role in starch hydrolysis during infancy (Alpers and Solin, 1970).

Lactase, sucrase and maltase activity can be demonstrated in the mucosa of the small intestine of the fetus by the third lunar month of gestation (Semenza and Auricchio, 1962; Dahlqvist, 1964). As indicated in Figure 4–6, sucrase and maltase attain maximal activity by the eighth lunar month of gestation, whereas the increase in lactase activity occurs closer to term. Activities of sucrase and maltase are greater than activity of lactase (Lindberg, 1966; Koldovsky, 1969; Eggermont, 1969).

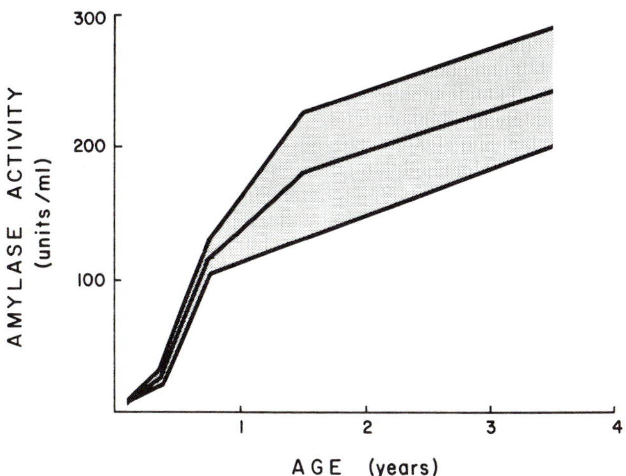

Figure 4–5 Amylase activity of duodenal juice in relation to age. The 10th, 50th and 90th percentiles are indicated. (Modified from Andersen, D. H.: Pancreatic enzymes in the duodenal juice in the celiac syndrome. Amer. J. Dis. Child. *63*:643, 1942.)

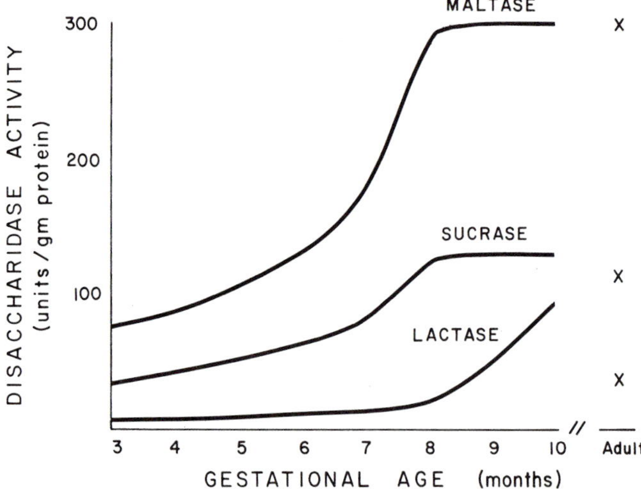

Figure 4–6 Disaccharidase activity of jejunal mucosa of human fetus in relation to lunar months of gestational age. (Modified from Auricchio, S., et al.: Intestinal glycosidase activities in the human embryo, fetus and newborn. Pediatrics *35*:944, 1965.)

The capacity of the small intestinal mucosa of the human infant to hydrolyze disaccharides has been studied in vitro by Auricchio et al. (1965). On the basis of these studies, estimates have been made of amounts of various carbohydrates that might be hydrolyzed by the entire small intestine assuming maximum rates of hydrolysis. It was estimated that, after the first day of life, infants born during the eighth and ninth lunar months of gestation may be able to hydrolyze only about one-third the quantity of lactose hydrolyzed by fullterm infants. Abdo-Bassols et al. (1971) have summarized data (Auricchio et al., 1965; Boellner et al., 1965; Dahlqvist and Lindberg, 1966) indicating that otherwise healthy premature infants are relatively deficient in intestinal lactase activity.

Lactase activity of the small intestinal mucosa of fullterm infants is high at birth and remains high throughout infancy. Even in populations in which the adults demonstrate a high prevalence of lactose intolerance, infants nearly always tolerate lactose well. After infancy, increasing numbers of children in these populations exhibit lactose intolerance as age increases. By about eight years of age, the prevalence of intolerance is the same as in the adult (Bolin et al., 1970; Kretchmer, 1971; Kretchmer et al., 1971; Yamashita et al., 1971; Paige et al., 1972). Approximately 2 to 6 per cent of Caucasians of North America and Western Europe are lactose intolerant (Gudmand-Höyer et al., 1969; Sahi et al., 1972).

Carbohydrate Absorption. In the intestine, the mechanisms for absorbing hydrolytic products of the disaccharides—glucose, galac-

TABLE 4–2 GLUCOSE ABSORPTION MEASURED DURING PERFUSION OF THE PROXIMAL SMALL INTESTINE IN HUMAN INFANTS AND ADULTS*

	Length of Intestine Perfused (cm)	Total Load Perfused (gm/hr)	Absorption Rate (gm/hr/cm)	Per Cent Absorption
Infant				
Torres-Pinedo et al.	25	5.9	0.15	64
(1966)	25	11.3	0.14	30
James (1970)	40	2.3	0.04	77
	40	4.5	0.09	78
	40	9.0	0.15	67
Adult				
Holdsworth and Dawson	30	6.0	0.16	80
(1964)	30	12.0	0.28	70
Malawer et al.	30	2.8	0.07	71
(1965)	30	5.4	0.12	69
Gray and Ingelfinger	30	4.8	0.13	83
(1966)	30	11.7	0.26	67

*A smaller percentage of the perfused load was absorbed in infants than in adults. Absorption seemed to be at maximal rates in infants but not in adults, where an increase in the load perfused was associated with higher rates of absorption (Fordtran and Ingelfinger, 1968).

tose and fructose – develop early in utero (Koldovsky, 1969, 1972), and one would not expect preterm infants to have difficulty in absorbing hexoses. However, absorption seems to proceed at a slower rate in premature babies than in term newborns (Borgström et al., 1960).

Results of studies in adults (Fordtran and Ingelfinger, 1968) and infants (Torres-Pinedo et al., 1966; James, 1968, 1970), in which similar amounts of glucose were perfused through similar lengths of the proximal intestine, suggest that rate of glucose absorption may be less in infants than in adults (Table 4–2).

Colonic Function

The large bowel functions as a temporary receptacle for the fluids delivered to it by the small intestine. Composition of the intestinal contents is altered during passage through the colon. Water, sodium and chloride are absorbed and, under usual conditions, potassium and bicarbonate are secreted into the lumen. There seems to be a proximal to distal gradient in the absorptive functions of the colon. Very little water is absorbed from the semi-solid contents in the rectum (Giller and Phillips, 1972). In young children, aldosterone may to some extent affect the homeostatic function of the colon (Rubens and Lambert, 1971). However, the homeostatic functions of the colon seem to be limited, as evidenced by the large losses of fluid and electrolytes that occur in gastroenteritis in the absence of colonic pathology.

REFERENCES

Abdo-Bassols, F., Lifshitz, F., and Del Castillo, E. D.: Transient lactose intolerance in premature infants. Pediatrics *48*:816, 1971.

Agunod, M., Yamaguchi, N., Lopez, R., Luhby, A. L., and Glass, G. B. J.: Correlative study of hydrochloric acid, pepsin and intrinsic factor secretion in newborns and infants. Amer. J. Dig. Dis. *14*:400, 1969.

Alpers, D. H., and Solin, M.: The characterization of rat intestinal amylase. Gastroenterology *58*:833, 1970.

Ames, M. D.: Gastric acidity in the first ten days of life of the prematurely born baby. Amer. J. Dis. Child. *100*:122, 1966.

Andersen, D. H.: Pancreatic enzymes in the duodenal juice in the celiac syndrome. Amer. J. Dis. Child. *63*:643, 1942.

Auricchio, S., Ciccimarra, F., and De Vizia, B.: Starch malabsorption. *In* XIIIth International Congress of Pediatrics. Vol. II. Nutrition and Gastroenterology. Vienna Academy of Medicine, 1971, p. 139.

Auricchio, S., Ciccimarra, F., Rubino, A., and Prader, A.: Studies of intestinal hydrolysis of starch in man. III. The absorption coefficient of starch in infants and children. Enzym. Biol. Clin. 9:321, 1968.

Auricchio, S., Pietra, D., and Vegnente, A.: Studies on intestinal digestion of starch in man. II. Intestinal hydrolysis of amylopectin in infants and children. Pediatrics *39*:853, 1967.

Auricchio, S., Rubino, A., and Murset, G.: Intestinal glycosidase activities in the human embryo, fetus and newborn. Pediatrics *35*:944, 1965.

Avery, G. B., Randolph, J. G., and Weaver, T.: Gastric acidity in the first day of life. Pediatrics *37*:1005, 1966.

Boellner, S. W., Beard, A. G., Panos, T. C., and Ross, A.: Impairment of intestinal hydrolysis of lactose in newborn infants. Pediatrics *36*:542, 1965.

Bolin, T. D., Morrison, R. M., and Steel, J. E.: Lactose intolerance in Australia. Med. J. Aust. *1*:1289, 1970.

Bongiovanni, A. M.: Bile acid content of gallbladder of infants, children and adults. J. Clin. Endocr. *25*:678, 1965.

Borgström, B., Lindquist, B., and Lundh, G.: Enzyme concentration and absorption of protein and glucose in duodenum of premature infants. Amer. J. Dis. Child. *99*:338, 1960.

Borgström, B., Lindquist, B., and Lundh, G.: Digestive studies in children. Amer. J. Dis. Child. *101*:454, 1961.

Brambell, F. W. R.: The transmission of passive immunity from mother to young. Amsterdam-New York, North Holland-American Elsevier, 1970.

Cohen, M., Morgan, R. G. H., and Hoffman, A. F.: Lipolytic activity of human gastric and duodenal juice against medium and long chain triglycerides. Gastroenterology *60*:1, 1971.

Dahlqvist, A.: Intestinal Disaccharidases. *In* Durand, P. (ed.): Disorders due to Intestinal Defective Carbohydrate Digestion and Absorption. New York, Grune & Stratton, 1964, p. 5.

Dahlqvist, A., and Lindberg, T.: Fetal development of the small-intestinal disaccharidase and alkaline phosphatase activities in the human. Biol. Neonate 9:24, 1966.

Davenport, H. W.: Salivary Secretion. *In* Davenport, H. W. (ed.): Physiology of the Digestive Tract. Chicago, Year Book Medical Publishers, 1968, p. 83.

Delachaume-Salem, E., and Sarles, H.: Évolution en fonction de l'age de la sécrétion pancréatique humaine normale. Biol. Gastro-Enterol. *2*:135, 1970.

Deren, J. J.: Development of intestinal structure and function. *In* Handbook of Physiology. Sec. 6. Vol. III. Washington D.C., American Physiological Society, 1968, p. 1099.

Eggermont, E.: The hydrolysis of the naturally occurring alphaglucosides by the human intestinal mucosa. Europ. J. Biochem. 9:483, 1969.

Encrantz, J. C., and Sjövall, J.: On the bile acids in duodenal contents of infants and children. Clin. Chim. Acta *4*:793, 1959.

Fordtran, J. S., and Ingelfinger, F. J.: Absorption of water, electrolytes and sugars from the human gut. *In* Handbook of Physiology. Sect. 6. Alimentary Canal. Vol. III. Washington, D.C., American Physiological Society, 1968, p. 1457.

Giller, J., and Phillips, S. F.: Electrolyte absorption and secretion in the human colon. Amer. J. Dig. Dis. *17*:1003, 1972.

Gray, G. M., and Ingelfinger, F. J.: Intestinal absorption of sucrose in man: interrelation of hydrolysis and monosaccharide product absorption. J. Clin. Invest. *45*:388, 1966.

Gudmand-Höyer, E., Dahlqvist, A., and Jarnum, S.: Specific small-intestinal lactase deficiency in adults. Scand. J. Gastroent. *4*:377, 1969.

Gustafsson, J. A., and Werner, B.: Fecal sterols in infants. (Bile acids and steroids 194.) Acta Physiol. Scand. *73*:305, 1968.

Hadorn, B.: Some aspects of the development of pancreatic enzymes in animals and in man. *In* XIIIth International Congress of Pediatrics. Vol. VII. Metabolism. Vienna, Academy of Medicine, 1971, p. 109.

Hadorn, B., Zoppi, G., Shmerling, D. H., Prader, A., McIntyre, I., and Anderson, C. M.: Quantitative assessment of exocrine pancreatic function in infants and children. J. Pediatr. *73*:39, 1968.

Hamosh, M., and Scow, R. O.: Lingual lipase and its role in the digestion of dietary lipid. J. Clin. Invest. *52*:88, 1973.

Holdsworth, C. D., and Dawson, A. M.: Absorption of monosaccharides in man. Clin. Sci. 27:379, 1964.

Holt, P. R.: The roles of bile acids during the process of normal fat and cholesterol absorption. Arch. Intern. Med. *130*:574, 1972.

Hunt, J. N.: The site of receptors slowing gastric emptying in response to starch in test meals. J. Physiol. *154*:270, 1960.

Hunt, J. N.: The osmotic control of gastric emptying. Gastroenterology *41*:49, 1961.

Husband, J., and Husband, P.: Gastric emptying of water and glucose solutions in the newborn. Lancet *2*:409, 1969.

Husband, J., Husband, P., and Mallinson, C. N.: Gastric emptying of starch meals in the newborn. Lancet *2*:290, 1970.

Iyengar, L., and Selvaraj, R. J.: Intestinal absorption of immunoglobulins by newborn infants. Arch. Dis. Child. *47*:411, 1972.

James, W. P. T.: Intestinal absorption in protein-calorie malnutrition, Lancet *1*:333, 1968.

James, W. P. T.: Sugar absorption and intestinal motility in children when malnourished and after treatment. Clin. Sci. *39*:305, 1970.

Koldovsky, O.: Development of functions of the small intestine in mammals and man. Basel, New York, S. Karger, 1969.

Koldovsky, O.: Digestion and absorption during development. *In* Stave, U. (ed.): Physiology of the Perinatal Period. New York, Appleton-Century-Crofts, 1970.

Koldovsky, O.: Hormonal and dietary factors in the development of digestion and absorption. *In* Winick, M. (ed.): Nutrition and Development. New York, J. Wiley & Sons, 1972.

Kretchmer, N.: Memorial lecture: lactose and lactase—a historical perspective. Gastroenterology *61*:805, 1971.

Kretchmer, N., Ransome-Kuti, O., Hurwitz, R., Dungy, C., and Alakija, W.: Intestinal absorption of lactose in Nigerian ethnic groups. Lancet *2*:392, 1971.

Lavy, U., Silverberg, M., and Davidson, M.: Role of bile acids in fat absorption in low birth weight infants. Pediatr. Res. *5*:387, 1971.

Lecce, J. G.: Absorption of macromolecules by neonatal intestine. Biol. Neonate *9*:50, 1966.

Leissring, J. C., Anderson, J. W., and Smith, D. W.: Uptake of antibodies by the intestine of the newborn infant. Amer. J. Dis. Child. *103*:160, 1962.

Lieberman, J.: Proteolytic enzyme activity in fetal pancreas and meconium. Gastroenterology *50*:183, 1966.

Lindberg, T.: Intestinal dipeptidases: characterization, development and distribution of intestinal dipeptidases of the human foetus. Clin. Sci. *30*:505, 1966.

Lindberg, T.: The development of intestinal dipeptidases. *In* XIIIth International Congress of Pediatrics. Vol. VII. Metabolism. Vienna Academy of Medicine, 1971, p. 127.

Malawer, S. J., Ewton, M., Fordtran, J. S., and Ingelfinger, F. J.: Interrelation between jejunal absorption of sodium, glucose, and water in man. J. Clin. Invest. *44*:1072, 1965.

Mason, S.: Some aspects of gastric function in the newborn. Arch. Dis. Child. *37*:387, 1962.

Melichar, V., Novák, M., Hahn, P., Koldovsky, O., and Zeman. L.: Changes in the blood levels of lipid metabolites and glucose following a fatty meal in infants. Acta Paediatr. Scand. *51*:481, 1962.

Miller, R. A.: Observations on the gastric acidity during the first month of life. Arch. Dis. Child. *16*:22, 1941.

Morris, I. G.: Gamma globulin absorption in the newborn. *In* Handbook of Physiology. Sect. 6. Alimentary Canal, Vol. III. Washington, D.C., American Physiological Society, 1968, p. 1491.

Norman, A., Strandvik, B., and Ojamäe, O.: Bile acids and pancreatic enzymes during absorption in the newborn. Acta Paediatr. Scand. *61*:571, 1972.

Norman, A., Strandvik, B., and Zetterström, R.: Test-meal in the diagnosis of malabsorption in infancy. Acta Paediatr. Scand. *60*:165, 1971.

Olivecrona, T., Billström, A., Fredrikson, B., Johnson, O., and Samuelson, G.: Gastric lipolysis of human milk lipids in infants with pyloric stenosis. Acta Paediatr. Scand. *62*:520, 1973.

Paige, D. M., Leonardo, E., Cordano, A., Nakashima, J., Adrianzen, T., and Graham, G. G.: Lactose intolerance in Peruvian children: effect of age and early nutrition. Amer. J. Clin. Nutr. *25*:297, 1972.

Platt, B. S.: Digestion in infancy. Fed. Proc. *20* (Suppl. 7): 188, 1961.

Polacek, M. A., and Ellison, E. H.: Gastric acid secretion and parietal cell mass in the stomach of a newborn infant. Amer. J. Surg. *111*:777, 1966.

Poley, J. R., Dower, J. C., Owen, C. A., Jr., and Stickler, G. B.: Bile acids in infants and children. J. Lab. Clin. Med. *63*:838, 1964.

Rubens, R. D., and Lambert, H. P.: The homeostatic function of the colon in acute gastroenteritis. Pediatrics *48*:816, 1971.

Sahi, T., Isokoski, M., Jussila, J., and Launiala, K.: Lactose malabsorption in Finnish children of school age. Acta Paediatr. Scand. *61*:11, 1972.

Semenza, G., and Auricchio, S.: Chromatographic separation of human intestinal disaccharidases. Biochim. Biophys. Acta *65*:172, 1962.

Sheldon, W.: Congenital pancreatic lipase deficiency. Arch. Dis. Child. *39*:268, 1964.

Shmerling, D. H., Forrer, J. C. W., and Prader, A.: Fecal fat and nitrogen in healthy children and in children with malabsorption or maldigestion. Pediatrics *46*:690, 1970.

Small, D.: The physical chemistry of cholanic acids. *In* Nair, P. P., and Kritchevsky, D. (eds.): The Bile Acids. Vol. 1. New York, Plenum Press, 1971, p. 302.

Taylor, W. H.: Studies on gastric proteolysis. 1. The proteolytic activity of human gastric juice and pig and calf gastric mucosal extracts below pH 5. Biochem. J. *71*:73, 1959.

Torres-Pinedo, R., Rivera, C. L., and Fernandez, S.: Studies on infant diarrhea. II. Absorption of glucose and net fluxes of water and sodium chloride in a segment of the jejunum. J. Clin. Invest. *45*:1916, 1966.

Watkins, J. B., Ingall, D., Szczepanik, P., Klein, P. D., and Lester, R.: Bile-salt metabolism in the newborn. Measurement of pool size and synthesis by stable isotope technic. New Eng. J. Med. *288*:431, 1973.

Weber, A., Ste-Marie, N., Doyon, G., Chartrand, L., and Roy, C.: The influence of fecal fat content on the intestinal reabsorption of bile salts. (Abstract) Clin. Res. *19*:781, 1971.

Werner, B.: Peptic and tryptic capacity of the digestive glands in newborns. Acta Paediatr. Scand. *35* (Suppl. 6), 1948.

Yamashita, F., Shibuya, S., and Funatsu, T.: Developmental activity of lactase in Japanese children. *In* XIIIth Internationsl Congress of Pediatrics. Vol. II. Nutrition and Gastroenterology. Vienna Academy of Medicine, 1971, p. 207.

Zoppi, G., Andreotti, G., Pajno-Ferrara, F., Njai, D. M., and Gaburro, D.: Exocrine pancreas function in premature and full term neonates. Pediatr. Res. *6*:880, 1972.

5

ESTIMATED REQUIREMENTS AND ADVISABLE INTAKES

Chapters 6 to 14 include estimates of requirements and recommendations regarding intakes of various nutrients. The present brief chapter, included as an introduction to these later chapters, will attempt to define the term "requirement" and to review the major approaches available for estimating the requirement for specific nutrients and the limitations of these approaches. Examples will be included to indicate the manner in which the estimated requirement of a nutrient is utilized to arrive at a recommendation. The specific recommendations presented in this chapter are referred to as "advisable intakes" to distinguish them from other recommendations, such as the "Recommended Dietary Allowances" of the National Academy of Sciences (Food and Nutrition Board, 1974).

ESTIMATED REQUIREMENT

Meaning of "Requirement"

The *requirement* of an individual for a specific nutrient may be defined as the least amount of that nutrient that will promote an optimal state of health. The meanings of the terms "requirement" and "minimal requirement" for an individual are identical, and the latter term should be avoided in reference to requirements of individuals. As knowledge of nutrition increases, we may expect to achieve a more enlightened definition of "optimal state of health" with respect to individual nutrients. At present, the requirement is necessarily determined primarily on the basis of freedom from all evidences of undernutrition attributable to deficiency of that particular nutrient.

If the requirement for a particular nutrient were the same under all conditions of diet, activity, environmental temperature and rates of growth, if all individuals in an age group had exactly the same requirement, and if optimal health with respect to that nutrient could be accurately defined, the advisable intake of a nutrient would be identical to the requirement. None of these conditions is true, and therefore our estimates of requirements include a considerable element of uncertainty, and advisable intakes are set at values greater than the estimated requirements.

Although knowledge of requirements for specific nutrients may be of less immediate practical value than the recommendations for intakes of these nutrients by some committee of experts, all recommendations must ultimately be based on data concerning requirements. Without appreciation of the degree of confidence one may have in the stated value for requirement and without some knowledge of the philosophy which the committee or individual has employed in converting data on requirements into recommendations, any table of nutrient requirements or recommended intakes will be difficult to interpret.

The requirement for a specified nutrient is clearly not an absolute value independent of other variables. In fact, the estimated requirement has direct application only to those exact circumstances under which it was determined.

Unfortunately, the designation "daily requirement" may imply that deficiency will develop rather rapidly if this intake is not regularly achieved each day. Actually, for most vitamins and for certain other nutrients, an intake twice the daily requirement on one day will obviate the need for any intake of that nutrient on the next day. For example, sufficient amounts of most of the fat-soluble vitamins can be stored in the body to protect the individual for months against evidences of deficiency.

Methods of Estimating Requirements

A method suitable for estimating the requirement for one nutrient may be inapplicable or impractical for estimating the requirement of another. Five major approaches are utilized, sometimes in combination: (1) analogy with breastfed infant, (2) direct experimental evidence, (3) extrapolation from experimental evidence relating to human adults or to infant or adult animals, (4) reports of intakes by individuals who developed evidence of deficiency (indicating inadequate intake) and reports of intakes by healthy individuals, and (5) theoretically based calculations. A brief comment about each of the five approaches will be presented here, and additional discussion of some of the approaches will be included in subsequent chapters.

Analogy with Breastfed Infant. When a young infant is breastfed by a healthy, well nourished mother and receives an adequate caloric intake from this source, requirements for most specific nutrients appear to be fulfilled. The exceptions are iron, fluoride and vitamin D.

Although caloric intakes by breastfed infants (which have not been reliably determined) may be slightly less than those by bottle-fed infants (Chapter 2), the difference is not great. It is therefore possible to utilize the 50th percentile value for caloric intake in Table 2–1 in conjunction with data on nutrient concentrations in human milk (Chapter 15, Tables 15–1 and 15–2) to obtain an estimate of the intake of a specified nutrient by the breastfed infant. This estimate would presumably indicate the average or 50th percentile intake of the nutrient in question, and one could assume that the average requirement for breastfed infants is *no greater than* that amount. How much less than that amount the average requirement might be cannot be estimated.

For some nutrients, it is reasonable to assume that the requirement for infants fed formulas based on cow milk will be no greater than the requirement of the breastfed infant. Thiamin is an example. The requirement for thiamin is related to the carbohydrate content of the diet and both human milk and many infant formulas provide approximately 40 to 50 per cent of the calories from carbohydrate. Thiamin is well absorbed and presumably the requirement for the formula-fed infant is similar to that for the breastfed infant. On the other hand, as discussed in Chapter 9, the requirement for vitamin B_6 is more closely related to protein than to caloric intake and may be expected to be greater for formula-fed infants (who generally receive relatively large intakes of protein) than for breastfed infants.

The approach to estimation of requirement by analogy with the breastfed infant is seriously limited by the variability in volume of milk consumed by different infants and, especially, by the great differences in composition of human milk from one woman to another and from one stage of lactation to another (Chapter 15).

Direct Experimental Evidence. It is, of course, unacceptable to induce evidences of nutrient deficiency in infants in order to establish requirements. However, by feeding a diet that will provide intakes of a specific nutrient only slightly above the estimated requirement, it is possible to confirm estimates made by less direct approaches. One may then state with some confidence that the requirement for the nutrient in question is no greater than the amounts consumed by the infants under observation. Under such conditions, precise data on intakes of the nutrient in question will be possible and the adequacy of the diet for each individual under study may be assessed.

This approach has been utilized by Fomon et al. (1973) in estimating requirements for protein and certain essential amino acids (Chapter 6) and by Snyderman, Holt and co-workers (summarized by Holt and Snyderman, 1961, 1967, and by Fomon and Filer, 1967) in estimating requirements of essential amino acids.

Most such studies involve relatively few experimental subjects and, in some cases, the periods of observation have been undesirably short. In addition, experimental conditions may be quite different from conditions obtaining generally in management of infants. For example, the estimates of requirements for essential amino acids by Snyderman, Holt and co-workers are based on studies of mixtures of 18 L-amino acids. Such studies may have considerable relevance to the amino acid requirements of infants with inborn errors of amino acid metabolism who are fed mixtures of amino acids. The relevance of these estimates of requirement to management of infants fed usual diets containing whole proteins has been questioned (Fomon and Filer, 1967; Fomon et al., 1973). Similarly, the estimates of requirements for methionine and isoleucine determined by Fomon et al. (1973) in studies of infants fed diets providing 1.6 gm protein/100 kcal are likely to be less than those that would apply to infants receiving greater intakes of protein. As mentioned previously, the estimated requirement actually has direct application only to the exact circumstances under which it was determined.

Extrapolation from Studies of Human Adults or of Infant or Adult Animals. In some instances, estimates of requirements for a specific nutrient have been obtained by experimental production of deficiency in adult volunteers. For example, as discussed in Chapter 9, the requirement for ascorbic acid has been determined by two groups of investigators (Bartley et al., 1953; Hodges et al., 1969). Because ascorbic acid functions primarily in maintaining the integrity of collagen, requirement is probably related primarily to body content of collagen. In view of the much smaller body content of collagen of the infant and toddler than of the adult, it seems likely that the requirement for ascorbic acid of the infant must be substantially less than that of the adult. Exactly how much less remains a matter for speculation.

In the case of thiamin, studies of adult humans and of experimental animals have suggested that the requirement is approximately 0.2 mg/1000 kcal (Chapter 9). Because this vitamin functions in carbohydrate metabolism, presumably in a generally similar manner for the infant and the adult and for the human and the experimental animal, 0.2 mg/1000 kcal is also utilized as an estimate of requirement for the infant.

Data on Intakes by Healthy Individuals. As will be discussed in Chapter 12, concentrations of hemoglobin in low income groups in the United States are frequently low during the end of the first year and the beginning of the second year of life; however, the prevalence of low concentrations of hemoglobin decreases remarkably thereafter, and relatively few children between 24 and 36 months of age and even fewer children between 36 and 48 months of age demonstrate low concentrations of hemoglobin. Data on intakes of iron by infants and toddlers from low income families are available from surveys (Chapter 12), and one may assume that intakes observed between 12 and 24 months and 24 and 36 months—a time when the percentage of children with low concentrations of hemoglobin is decreasing—are generally greater than the requirement.

A somewhat similar approach applies to consideration of the requirement for fluoride in prevention of dental caries (Chapter 14).

Theoretically Based Calculations. The "factorial method" of estimating the requirement of infants for protein was originally proposed by Hegsted (1957) and subsequently was widely adopted by official groups. As discussed in Chapter 6, it seems unlikely that calculations of this type will be of major assistance in establishing requirements for protein at various ages during infancy and early childhood. Nevertheless, theoretically based calculations may be of considerable value in relation to certain other nutrients. Nutrients most suitable for this approach are those for which reasonable estimates are available with respect to (1) body increment of the nutrient per unit of time (i.e., requirement for growth), (2) losses from skin and (3) apparent retention (intake minus urinary and fecal excretion). Requirements for major minerals have been estimated in this manner (Chapter 11).

Nutrient Interactions

Not only does requirement frequently vary with age, size, rate of growth and level of activity, but relationships between various nutrients are of major importance. For example, requirements for individual amino acids probably increase when total protein content of the diet increases and requirement for one essential amino acid is related to intakes of others. As discussed in Chapter 6, deficiency symptoms arising from inadequate intake of two essential amino acids may be aggravated by supplementing the diet with only one of these essential amino acids.

Requirements for various vitamins depend on intake of total calories, protein, fat, carbohydrate, specific amino acids and other vitamins. For example, because thiamin functions as an essential coenzyme in decarboxylation of pyruvic acid, its requirement is related to the carbohydrate content of the diet; tryptophan, a niacin precursor, can substitute for part of the requirement for niacin.

Interrelations between minerals and other dietary components and between one mineral and another are particularly complex. The reason for the frequent association of steatorrhea with abnormal mineral absorption is poorly understood. Presence of large amounts of phytates in the diet interferes with absorption of a number of minerals, but we do not know the extent to which mineral absorption is altered by lesser amounts of phytates—a point of some interest in relation to infants fed soy isolate-based formulas in the United States and in relation to toddlers fed predominantly vegetable-based diets in many developing countries. Absorption and metabolism of calcium, phosphorus, magnesium and zinc are highly interrelated, and excessive intake of one of these minerals adversely affects absorption of the others. A number of trace minerals also appear to be involved in these interactions.

From these examples, it is apparent that the value for requirement of a nutrient established under one set of conditions may not apply to other conditions. Caution in use of values for estimated requirements is therefore necessary.

Advisable Intakes

Because of the uncertainty of our estimates of requirements for various nutrients, it seems desirable to recommend intakes somewhat in excess of the estimated requirement. The margin between estimated requirement and advisable intake will be determined, at least in part, by the degree of confidence in the value assigned as the estimated requirement and by the likelihood of hazard from an excess intake of the nutrient. In the case of fluoride, for which the margin of safety between beneficial and detrimental effects is small, the advisable intake has been set in an attempt to achieve maximum protection against dental caries with minimal risk of dental fluorosis. However, for most nutrients, intakes somewhat in excess of the requirement present no known hazard and are to be preferred to long-continued ingestion of a diet providing a slight deficiency of the nutrient.

When considerable confidence can be placed in an estimate of requirement, the advisable intake may be set at a value only slightly greater than the estimated requirement. Thus, the advisable intakes for protein and for calcium are set just 20 per cent above the estimated requirement. When there is less confidence in the estimated requirement but there is reason to suspect that the estimate is generous—e.g., vitamin C (Chapter 9)—the estimated requirement is doubled to give an advisable intake. When the estimate of requirement is highly uncertain, as in the case of sodium, the estimated requirement has been multiplied by three to give a value for advisable intake.

From these examples, it will be evident that a large element of personal judgment enters into setting a value for advisable intake. This is true because of the unsatisfactory state of current knowledge regarding nutrient requirements. Recommendations of official groups (FAO/WHO, Food and Nutrition Board, etc.) are also based on inadequate information and, for this reason, recommendations for intakes of specific nutrients not uncommonly undergo substantial changes from one edition of an official publication to the next. As more adequate information about requirements becomes available, it seems likely that greater consistency will be found regarding recommendations by various official groups and also by various individual authors.

Other Recommendations

Official groups in a number of countries publish recommendations for intakes of specific nutrients. These recommendations have been summarized by the Food and Nutrition Board (1974). Each official group approaches its recommendations with a slightly different philosophy. For example, in the initial publication of the Recommended Dietary Allowances by the Food and Nutrition Board in 1943 and in each of its seven revisions, the focus has been on groups of individuals. The following advice was offered by Goldsmith (1953) in relation to the third revision of the publication:

> *In interpreting the Recommended Dietary Allowances, it should be understood that they indicate levels of nutrient intake which appear to be desirable goals toward which to strive in planning diets and food supplies. The allowances are high enough "to cover substantially all individual variations in the requirements of normal people" and include a margin of safety above the critical or minimal level of each nutrient to "permit additional benefits." The nutritive intakes recommended are, in general, higher than the average requirements and lower than the amounts needed in pathologic states or rehabilitation following depletion.*

A similar philosophy was expressed 20 years later in the eighth edition (Food and Nutrition Board, 1974):

> *From their original function of serving as a guide for advising "on nutrition problems in connection with national defense," RDA have come to serve generally as a guide: for planning and procuring food supplies for population groups; for interpreting food consumption records; for establishing standards for public assistance programs; for evaluating the adequacy of food*

supplies in meeting national nutritional needs; for the development of nutrition education programs; for the development of new products by industry; and for establishing guidelines for nutritional labeling of foods. As our concept of health is broadened and the uses of RDA continue to expand, it becomes ever more critical that their meaning and limitations be clearly understood.

The recommended dietary allowances are the levels of intake of essential nutrients considered, in the judgment of the Food and Nutrition Board on the basis of available scientific knowledge, to be adequate to meet the known nutritional needs of almost every healthy person.

In somewhat similar manner, the several reports of the Joint FAO/WHO Expert Groups (1962, 1967, 1970, 1973) concern "levels of intake recommended . . . to ensure the health of large groups of people, and are not necessarily applicable to individuals" (Joint FAO/WHO Expert Group, 1970).

Group Versus Individuals

In the chapters that follow, the approach is oriented toward requirements of, and recommendations (advisable intakes) for, *individual* infants and toddlers. It must be recognized that the state of knowledge about requirements by infants and toddlers for most nutrients has not yet reached the point where a clear distinction can be made with respect to recommendations for groups and for individuals. Nevertheless, it seems important to maintain a definite philosophy of approach. In the case of requirement for protein, for example, it is apparent (Chapter 6) that requirements for individual infants during the early months of life are better expressed in relation to calorie intake than to body weight. In dealing with groups of individuals, it may not be considered feasible to individualize, to this extent, the estimate of requirement or the recommended intake.

REFERENCES

Bartley, W., Krebs, H. A., and O'Brien, J. R. P.: Vitamin C requirement of human adults. Report by Vitamin C Subcommittee of Accessory Food Factors Committee. Med. Res. Coun., Spec. Rep. Ser. 280, 1953.

Fomon, S. J., and Filer, L. J., Jr.: Amino acid requirements for normal growth. *In* Nyhan, W. L. (ed.): Amino Acid Metabolism and Genetic Variation. New York, McGraw-Hill Book Co., 1967, p. 391.

Fomon, S. J., Thomas, L. N., Filer, L. J., Jr., Anderson, T. A., and Bergmann, K. E.: Requirements for protein and essential amino acids in early infancy. Studies with a soy-isolate formula. Acta Paediatr. Scand. 62:33, 1973.

Food and Nutrition Board: Recommended Dietary Allowances. 8th ed. Washington, D.C., National Academy of Sciences-National Research Council, Publication 2216, 1974.

Goldsmith, G. A.: Human nutritive requirements and recommended dietary allowances. J. Amer. Dietet. Ass. 29:109, 1953.

Hegsted, D. M.: Theoretical estimates of the protein requirements of children. J. Amer. Dietet. Ass. *33*:225, 1957.

Hodges, R. E., Baker, E. M., Hood, J., Sauberlich, H. E., and March, S. C.: Experimental scurvy in man. Amer. J. Clin. Nutr. *22*:535, 1969.

Holt, L. E., Jr., and Snyderman, S. E.: The amino acid requirement of infants. J.A.M.A. *175*:100, 1961.

Holt, L. E., Jr., and Snyderman, S. E.: The amino acid requirements of children. *In* Nyhan, W. L. (ed.): Amino Acid Metabolism and Genetic Variation. New York, McGraw-Hill Book Co., 1967, p. 381.

Joint FAO/WHO Expert Group: Calcium Requirements. WHO Technical Report Series, No. 230. Rome, FAO and WHO, 1962.

Joint FAO/WHO Expert Group: Requirements of Vitamin A, Thiamine, Riboflavine and Niacin. WHO Technical Report Series, No. 362. Rome, FAO and WHO, 1967.

Joint FAO/WHO Expert Group: Requirements of Ascorbic Acid, Vitamin D, Vitamin B_{12}, Folate and Iron. WHO Technical Report Series, No. 452. Rome, FAO and WHO, 1970.

Joint FAO/WHO Expert Group: Protein Requirements. WHO Technical Report Series, No. 522. Rome, FAO and WHO, 1973.

6

PROTEIN

In developing countries, infants and young children frequently receive intakes of protein or various essential amino acids that are inadequate to promote normal growth and health. In developed countries, on the other hand, diets generally provide abundant amounts of high quality protein, and problems of protein or amino acid deficiency are rarely encountered.

Nevertheless, an understanding of protein needs, both quantitatively and qualitatively, is essential in evaluation of new infant formulas that continue to appear on the market, in management of infants who are unwilling or unable to accept usual diets and in management of those with exceptional requirements, as in phenylketonuria and other disorders characterized by specific defects in amino acid metabolism. The present chapter emphasizes aspects of protein nutrition believed of most interest in relation to infant nutrition.

PROTEIN DIGESTION

A number of enzymes are involved sequentially in splitting of dietary proteins so that the amino acids or, in some cases, smaller peptides can be absorbed. An excellent review of this topic has been prepared by Gray and Cooper (1971), and much of the material that follows has been summarized from that source. The enzymes (proteases) involved in splitting of proteins include trypsin, chymotrypsin, elastase and the carboxypeptidases. Trypsin, chymotrypsin and elastase are referred to as endopeptidases (Fig. 6–1), because they attack the interior CO-NH bond connecting adjacent amino acids within the peptide. They differ functionally from one another in their specificity for particular groups of amino acids. The carboxypeptidases act on terminal peptide bonds at the carboxyl ends of the peptide

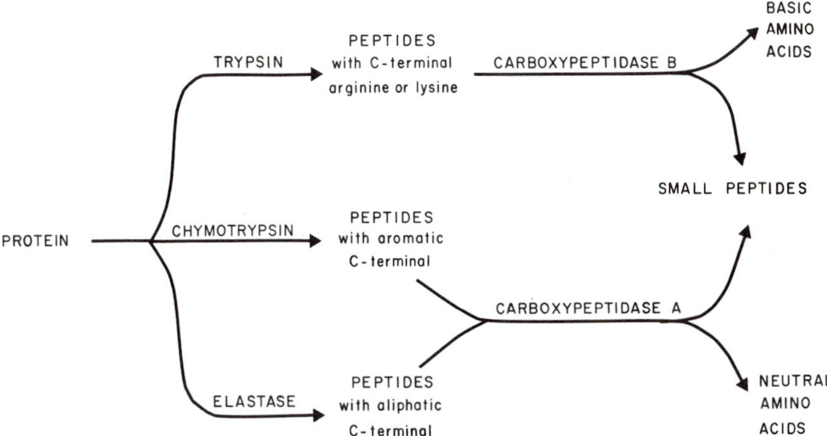

Figure 6–1 Intraduodenal sequential action of pancreatic endopeptidases and exopeptidases on dietary protein. The final products at the right are the substrates that must be handled by the intestinal cell. (Modified slightly from Gray, G. M., and Cooper, H. L.: Protein digestion and absorption. Gastroenterology *61*:535, 1971.)

chains and are therefore referred to as exopeptidases. As may be seen from Figure 6–1, carboxypeptidase A and carboxypeptidase B attack different groups of amino acids.

The proteases are synthesized in the pancreatic acinar cells as inactive proenzymes (or zymogens) and secreted into the proximal portion of the duodenal lumen where initial activation of the proenzyme, trypsinogen, is catalyzed by enterokinase. Enterokinase, an enzyme located on the surface of the duodenal mucosa, splits a fragment from trypsinogen, thereby converting it to the active trypsin. Trypsin then acts autocatalytically to convert the bulk of trypsinogen to trypsin and similarly activates the other precursor peptidases—chymotrypsinogen, proelastase and procarboxypeptidases.

With the exception of elastase, which has the ability to split the peptide molecule at a variety of sites, the endopeptidases are quite specific in their site of activity. Trypsin is active only at the locations of the basic amino acids, arginine and lysine (Fig. 6–1), thus yielding peptides with one of these amino acids on the carboxyl terminal end of the molecule. Chymotrypsin, on the other hand, acts interiorly at aromatic amino acid sites to produce peptides with a C-terminal phenylalanine, tyrosine or tryptophan. The carboxypeptidases then split the terminal amino acids from the peptides.

The initial stage of digestion of dietary protein is therefore accomplished by sequential action of activated pancreatic proteases within the intestinal lumen. This sequential action yields about 30 per cent neutral and basic amino acids and 70 per cent small peptides.

Protein is secreted into the intestinal lumen during digestion, and it has been estimated (Nixon and Mawer, 1970a and b) that 10 to 35 per cent of postprandial intraintestinal protein or protein-digestion products is of endogenous origin.

As is true of the disaccharidases, enzymes hydrolyzing small peptides are present in the intestinal epithelial cell rather than in the pancreatic or intestinal secretions. Ten to 20 per cent of intestinal dipeptidase activity is present in the brush border, the remainder being attributable to intracellular (soluble) peptidases. Both the brush border and the intracellular peptidases appear to be quite specific.

It seems probable that only the neutral and basic amino acids are normally transported into the cell in the form of amino acids. Dietary proline, hydroxyproline, glycine, glutamic acid and aspartic acid appear to enter the cell primarily as constituents of small peptides that are then hydrolyzed by specific intracellular peptidases. Current concepts of the type of transport of various amino acids (Table 6–1) have been summarized by Gray and Cooper (1971).

TABLE 6–1 INTESTINAL AMINO ACID TRANSPORT MECHANISMS*

Type of Amino Acid	Type of Transport	Relative Rate
Neutral (monoaminomonocarboxylic): Aromatic: tyrosine, tryptophan, phenylalanine Aliphatic: glycine†, alanine, serine, threonine, valine, leucine, isoleucine Other neutral: methionine, histidine, glutamine, asparagine, cysteine	Active, sodium dependent	Very rapid
Basic (diamino): lysine, arginine, ornithine, cystine	Active, partially sodium dependent	Rapid (10% rate of neutral)
Acidic (dicarboxylic): glutamic acid, aspartic acid	Carrier-mediated, active, partially sodium dependent	Rapid
Imino acids and glycine: proline, hydroxyproline, glycine†	Active, ? sodium dependent	Slow

*Modified slightly from Gray, G. M., and Cooper, H. L.: Protein digestion and absorption. Gastroenterology, *61*:535, 1971. © 1971 The Williams & Wilkins Company, Baltimore.

†Glycine shares both the neutral and imino mechanism with low affinity for the neutral.

AMINO ACIDS

Essential Amino Acids

In growing rats, Rose (1938) defined essential amino acids as those that "cannot be synthesized by the animal body from materials readily available at a speed commensurate with the demands for normal growth." For the human adult, essential amino acids have been defined as those necessary for avoidance of negative nitrogen balance. These are isoleucine, leucine, lysine, methionine, phenylalanine, threonine, tryptophan and valine. In the case of the human infant, it seems reasonable to define essential amino acids as those necessary (1) to promote growth equal to that of breastfed infants, (2) to maintain serum concentrations of albumin equal to those of breastfed infants and (3) to permit positive nitrogen balance with a relation between retention of nitrogen and intake of nitrogen equivalent to that by infants fed fresh or processed human milk. On the basis of these criteria, it seems likely that those amino acids essential for the adult are essential for the infant. In addition, histidine appears essential for the fullsize infant (Snyderman et al., 1963); tyrosine (Snyderman, 1971) and cystine (Gaull et al., 1972) as well as histidine may be essential for the premature infant.

Because cystine can be formed by the human body only from methionine, and tyrosine can be formed only from phenylalanine, the requirements for methionine and phenylalanine are modified by the amounts of cystine and tyrosine in the diet. Conversely, cystine can substitute for a major portion of the requirement for methionine. When patients with phenylketonuria are fed a diet low in content of phenylalanine, tyrosine becomes an essential amino acid and must be included in the diet in adequate amounts. In addition, since tryptophan functions as a precursor of niacin, dietary intake of niacin is important in modifying the requirement for tryptophan.

Amino Acid Imbalance and Amino Acid Toxicity

Whereas amino acid deficiency results from an inadequate intake of an essential amino acid, amino acid imbalance results from surpluses of essential amino acids (Harper et al., 1970). Amino acid imbalance has been caused in experimental animals fed low protein diets that provide adequate calories and adequate quantities of all non-nitrogenous essential nutrients. When such animals are fed supplementary amino acid-deficient proteins or nutritionally incomplete mixtures of amino acids, further growth depression results from amino

TABLE 6–2 EFFECTS OF AMINO ACID IMBALANCE ON WEIGHT GAIN OF RATS*

Group	Diet	Weight Gain in 2 Weeks (gm)
1	6% casein	18
2	6% casein, amino acid mixture	10
3	6% casein, amino acid mixture, threonine	21

*Data of Harper et al. (1964).

acid imbalance and can be readily prevented by feeding a small supplement of the growth-limiting amino acid (Harper et al., 1966).

An example of amino acid imbalance is presented in Table 6–2. Rats in group 1 received a diet deficient in threonine while those in group 2 received a diet equally deficient in threonine but supplemented with other essential amino acids. This amino acid supplementation resulted in further depression of growth rate, which was overcome (group 3) by administering a supplement of threonine.

Until recently, human infants in technically advanced countries have been breastfed or fed milk-based formulas or various formulas based on soy or on casein hydrolysates. Under these conditions, the possibility of amino acid imbalance was remote. Currently, as metabolic abnormalities of amino acid metabolism are identified with increasing frequency each year, more and more special diets are being devised. These diets commonly provide nitrogen either from a mixture of amino acids or from protein hydrolysates subjected to chromatographic procedures to remove specific amino acids. Such diets have not yet been adequately evaluated for the possibility of amino acid imbalance.

"UNESSENTIAL" NITROGEN

There is now abundant evidence that small amounts of urea or ammonium salts can be utilized by nonruminant mammals. The inclusion of urea or ammonium salts in diets otherwise deficient in nitrogen has been demonstrated to restore positive nitrogen balance and rate of growth in protein-deficient rats (Rose et al., 1949) and malnourished children (Snyderman et al., 1962). Studies with labeled urea have demonstrated that urea is hydrolyzed to ammonia in the gastrointestinal tract, particularly in the colon, as a result of bacterial action. These studies have been reviewed by Picou and Phillips

(1972). Ammonia enters the portal vein and presumably mixes with and shares the fate of the metabolic pool of nitrogen. Thus, it may be utilized for protein synthesis or it may be reconverted to urea and excreted. The general order of magnitude of the potential contribution of urea or ammonium salts to protein synthesis is probably in the neighborhood of 10 per cent of total protein synthesis (Picou and Phillips, 1972). It seems likely that nonamino acid nitrogen is able to replace part of the protein requirement only when the diet provides sufficient glucose for synthesis of nonessential amino acids (Gallina and Dominguez, 1971).

CALCULATED PROTEIN INTAKE

The protein content of a food is generally estimated on the basis of analysis of the food for nitrogen, together with a calculation based on the assumption that nitrogen accounts for approximately 16 per cent by weight of protein. A factor of 6.25 ($100 \div 16 = 6.25$) is therefore commonly used for conversion of dietary nitrogen to protein; use of this factor will rarely result in an important error when dietary protein is of high quality. In the case of some proteins, the factor 6.25 may not be appropriate, since the assortment of amino acids varies from protein to protein and each amino acid has its own ratio of nitrogen to total weight. McCance and Widdowson (1960) have suggested factors of 5.5 for gelatin and 5.7 for cereals. Although certain foods contain significant amounts of nonprotein nitrogen (e.g., 15 per cent of the nitrogen in human milk), a portion of the nonprotein nitrogen may consist of free amino acids that are utilized by the body in nearly the same manner as protein; some of the remainder, as has already been mentioned, can probably also be utilized for protein synthesis.

EVALUATION OF PROTEIN QUALITY

In technically developed countries, amounts of protein consumed by normal infants are generally well in excess of the requirement. Under these conditions of feeding, small differences in protein quality are unlikely to be nutritionally significant. However, in countries in which protein intakes are frequently at or below the required amounts, consideration of protein quality is of extreme importance. Such consideration will also be relevant to management of infants with renal insufficiency, inborn errors of amino acid metabolism or other disorders that warrant restriction of protein intake.

Although animal studies of protein quality and comparisons of protein chemical scores are unquestionably useful in providing a preliminary evaluation of protein quality, it is obvious that these evaluations will not necessarily predict the relative adequacy of proteins for the human infant. Caution is therefore necessary in interpreting studies of protein quality. This point will be considered further in relation to the relative nutritive value of whey protein and casein for the human infant.

Tests with Animals

The quality of a protein depends on its ability to supply essential amino acids in sufficient amounts to fulfill all the requirements for maintenance and growth. Terms most widely employed in discussions of protein quality are protein efficiency ratio (PER), biologic value (BV), true digestibility (D), net protein utilization (NPU), chemical score and nitrogen balance. These are defined in the Chapter Appendix (page 145).

Ideally, proteins to be used for feeding human infants should be evaluated in the normal human infant. However, the difficulty in devising sound experiments is exceptionally great, and practical considerations make it essential that all initial studies be done with experimental animals. A number of tests of protein quality have been developed with the weanling rat as the assay animal. The method most widely used for determining quality of protein is the PER, which relates gain in weight of weanling rats to amount of protein consumed under standardized conditions (see Chapter Appendix). Concentration of protein in the diet is less than that required for maximal growth rates of the animals.

Although a number of criticisms have been raised concerning the method (Mitchell, 1944; Bender and Doell, 1957), only three seem to be of major significance with respect to evaluation of protein quality for the human infant or child. First, since PER varies with dietary level of protein, results of the standardized assay with rats may not be predictive of the relative values of these proteins under the conditions obtaining when they are fed to the human infant. Second, it seems likely that the weanling rat requires proportionately less of its protein intake for maintenance and more for growth than does the human infant. Quality of a protein for growth may not be identical to quality for maintenance. Third, requirements of growing rats for certain essential amino acids are different from those of the human infant; for example, the growing rat probably requires proportionately more of the sulfur-containing amino acids than does the human infant.

In spite of these limitations, the PER may be assumed to provide a generally useful index of the amount of the limiting essential amino acid in the diet. Among its major advantages are simplicity, convenience and the widespread use of a standardized method.

Chemical Score

Since a protein of high quality is one that supplies all essential amino acids in relation to their need for maintenance and growth, the relation between amounts of various amino acids in the protein has been employed as the basis for several scoring systems. Such systems have compared the concentration of a limiting essential amino acid in a test protein to its concentration in a reference protein. The reference protein has generally been whole egg or a hypothetic protein in which ratios between concentrations of amino acids are identical to the supposed requirement ratios. In general, the higher the protein score, the higher the biologic value. It is worth noting, however, that proteins such as zein and maize, each devoid of one essential amino acid, have some biologic value in spite of a protein score of zero.

Three major limitations of chemical scoring should be noted: (1) Protein quality may be altered without change in content of specific amino acids. For example, the influence of moist heat in the processing of soy protein is beneficial, since it inactivates a trypsin inhibitor that otherwise interferes with digestion. Thus, protein quality is improved without change in protein score. Conversely, as discussed in the next section of this chapter, various amino acids may become unavailable to the organism because of the Maillard reaction in which amino acids combine with sugars in the presence of heat. (2) Requirement for nitrogen may, in some circumstances, be limiting even though requirements for all essential amino acids are met (Snyderman et al., 1962). Such nitrogen could be supplied as essential or nonessential amino acids and, as already mentioned, a small amount may be supplied in forms other than amino acids (for example, urea, ammonia). (3) The chosen reference protein may not, in fact, reflect the amino acid requirements of the individual for the purpose intended. Because requirements probably differ for growth and for maintenance, a reference protein reflecting requirements of the human adult may not be completely satisfactory as an indication of the needs of the rapidly growing human infant.

Maillard Reaction

Heat treatment of proteins in the presence of reducing sugars causes browning and decrease in nutritive value as a result of the Maillard reaction between amino acids and the sugars (Evans and Butts, 1949; Ellis, 1959; Donoso et al., 1962; Rios-Iriarte and Barnes, 1966). In vitro, it is found that proteins which have undergone the Maillard reaction are not completely digested by digestive enzymes (Ford and Salter, 1966), and nutritional value as measured by growth studies in animals or by net protein utilization studies is also reduced. However, little excretion of Maillard products has been found in feces (Henry and Kon, 1950). Nesheim and Carpenter (1967) have suggested that gastrointestinal bacterial flora may degrade the heat-damaged amino acids so that they are not excreted in feces. However, Valle-Riestra and Barnes (1970) and Pronczuk et al. (1973) have provided evidence that the heat-damaged amino acids are at least partially absorbed and subsequently excreted in the urine. Short-term studies of growth and nitrogen balance of normal fullterm infants fed an overheated milk-based formula failed to provide evidence of nutritional impairment of the protein (Fomon and Owen, 1962b).

Tests with Human Infants

Although there can be no question about the desirability of testing protein adequacy of a diet in human subjects, certain limitations will necessarily be imposed in such testing. The PER test in rats is sensitive because it is conducted at an inadequate intake of protein. It is obviously unacceptable to provide infants with diets known to be inadequate in an essential nutrient. Thus, in studies of human infants, two proteins are commonly fed to comparable groups of subjects under similar conditions of study. Protein intake will be identical in both groups and the quantity of protein provided will be at or only slightly above the estimated requirement. This approach has been used particularly in evaluation of various proteins in management of the recovery phase of protein-calorie malnutrition. Various parameters relating to the improvement or maintenance of protein nutritional status are employed. In many respects, this approach is similar to that utilized in establishing the requirement for protein during early infancy. Evaluation of protein nutritional status and requirements for protein during infancy are discussed subsequently in this chapter.

Protein Nutritional Status

Measures useful in evaluation of protein nutritional status of infants are rate of growth, serum concentration of albumin and transferrin, and urinary excretion of endogenous creatinine. Growth in weight and length will not progress normally if the diet is deficient in any essential nutrient, including protein. Therefore, the demonstration of normal gains in weight and length over a sufficient period of observation (Chapter 3) is strong evidence in favor of the adequacy of protein intake.

Available data suggest that serum concentration of albumin is a relatively sensitive index of protein nutritional status in infancy, and recent reports have indicated that serum concentration of transferrin may also be a useful measure. As discussed in Chapter 3, urinary excretion of endogenous creatinine is a potentially useful measure of protein nutritional status, but rarely will it prove practical to utilize this index.

Serum Concentration of Albumin

Data concerning serum concentrations of proteins must be interpreted in relation to the methods employed. Electrophoresis on cellulose acetate is recommended for determining the relative percentages of major protein fractions (Chapter 18). Absolute values for protein fractions are therefore dependent on accuracy of determination of concentration of total protein. Although the commonly employed biuret method, performed in the customary manner without a serum blank, appears to be satisfactory for analysis of serum obtained from fasting individuals, lipemia leads to falsely high values (Fomon et al., 1970). Rarely is it feasible to obtain blood from infants in the fasting state, and it is therefore important to include a serum blank. Values presented in Table 6–3 represent determinations performed with serum of normal breastfed infants by an automated method employing a serum blank. Our published (Fomon et al., 1973) and un-

TABLE 6–3 SERUM CONCENTRATIONS OF PROTEINS OF NORMAL BREASTFED INFANTS*

		Concentration (gm/100 ml)					
				Globulins			
Age (days)	Number of Infants	*Total Protein*	*Albumin*	*alpha₁*	*alpha₂*	*beta*	*gamma*
28	41	5.42 (0.38)†	3.69 (0.32)	0.15 (0.08)	0.46 (0.09)	0.58 (0.11)	0.54 (0.16)
56	36	5.46 (0.51)	3.75 (0.42)	0.16 (0.04)	0.56 (0.12)	0.57 (0.12)	0.41 (0.12)
84	49	5.56 (0.53)	3.85 (0.48)	0.16 (0.03)	0.61 (0.12)	0.60 (0.13)	0.33 (0.10)
112	43	5.84 (0.52)	4.05 (0.45)	0.17 (0.04)	0.66 (0.11)	0.61 (0.13)	0.35 (0.14)

*Published (Fomon et al., 1973) and unpublished data from Pediatric Metabolic Unit, University of Iowa.

†Values in parentheses are standard deviations.

published observations indicate that breastfed infants and those fed milk-based or L-methionine-fortified soy isolate-based formulas demonstrate similar concentrations of albumin.

There appears to be little question that serum concentrations of albumin reflect protein nutritional status. Schendel et al. (1962) demonstrated that when children were fed a poor quality diet, in which protein was supplied from corn, the serum concentration of albumin decreased appreciably in several weeks. In malnourished children, Wittman and Hansen (1965) demonstrated a significant correlation between deficit in body weight and extent of hypoalbuminemia. In addition, Wittmann et al. (1967) have reported small but statistically significant differences in average serum concentrations of albumin between apparently healthy children from different socioeconomic classes in South Africa. On the basis of such data, Waterlow and Alleyne (1971) have concluded that a moderate decrease in serum concentration of albumin may be interpreted as a sign of long-continued, though not necessarily severe, protein deficiency. However, at least under some circumstances of inadequate protein nutrition, serum concentrations of albumin may decrease in children exhibiting adequate rates of growth (Whitehead et al., 1971). Our own unpublished observations are in agreement with those of Whitehead et al. (1971). Tentatively, we conclude that groups of infants and children receiving adequate intakes of calories will demonstrate slight but statistically significant decreases in serum concentrations of albumin as an early index of unsatisfactory protein nutritional status.

Serum Concentration of Transferrin

Serum concentrations of transferrin are known to be abnormally low in patients with kwashiorkor (Scrimshaw and Behar, 1961; Antia et al., 1968; McFarlane et al., 1969, 1970; Gabr et al., 1971) and it has been suggested that serum concentrations of this protein may be useful as an index of severity of protein nutritional status (Antia et al., 1968; McFarlane et al., 1969, 1970; Gabr et al., 1971). Further study of this measure is certainly indicated.

MEASUREMENTS REFLECTING RECENT DIETARY INTAKE OF PROTEIN OR AMINO ACIDS

During infancy, the quantity of nitrogen in the diet is reflected by the serum concentration of urea nitrogen and by urinary excretion of nitrogen and urea. Serum concentrations of amino acids or the ratios between serum concentrations of various individual amino acids or groups of amino acids have been utilized to indicate adequacy of nitrogen intake with respect both to quantity and quality.

Urinary Excretion of Nitrogen and/or Urea

The predictability of the relation between intakes of nitrogen and urinary excretion of nitrogen has been established by a number of investigators under various experimental conditions. In our own studies of normal infants, for example, the relation between intake and urinary excretion of nitrogen during various age intervals may be seen from Figures 6–2 and 6–3. However, it is apparent that urinary collection during periods of 72 hours or 24 hours will rarely be practical with infants. It is doubtful that the ratio of urinary excretion of nitrogen (or of urea) to that of creatinine will give more reliable data concerning protein intake than can be obtained from serum concentration of urea.

Waterlow and Alleyne (1971) have pointed out that the smaller the intake of nitrogen, the smaller is the percentage contribution of urea to nitrogen excretion. They report that urinary excretion of urea accounts for approximately 80 per cent of total urinary excretion of nitrogen by subjects receiving "normal" intakes of protein, but for only about 50 per cent of the total by subjects receiving low intakes of pro-

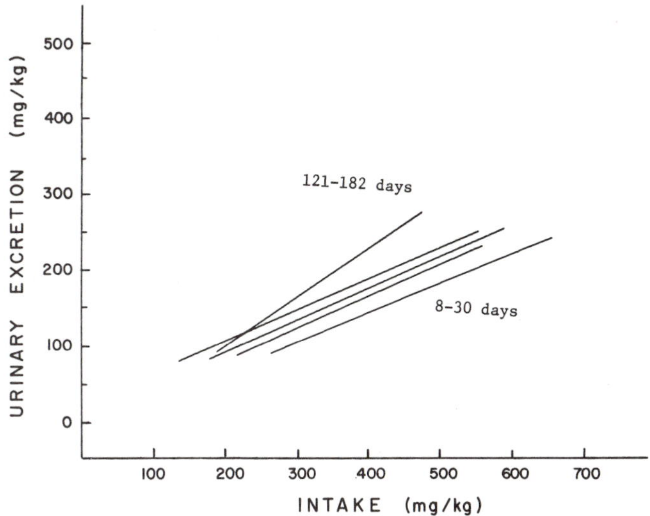

Figure 6–2 Influence of age on relation between urinary excretion of nitrogen and intake of nitrogen by normal fullsize infants fed human milk or milk-based formulas. The regressions apply (in sequence from bottom to top) to ages 8 to 30, 31 to 60, 61 to 90, 91 to 120 and 121 to 182 days. Sources of the data and equations of the regression lines are included in Appendix III (p. 542).

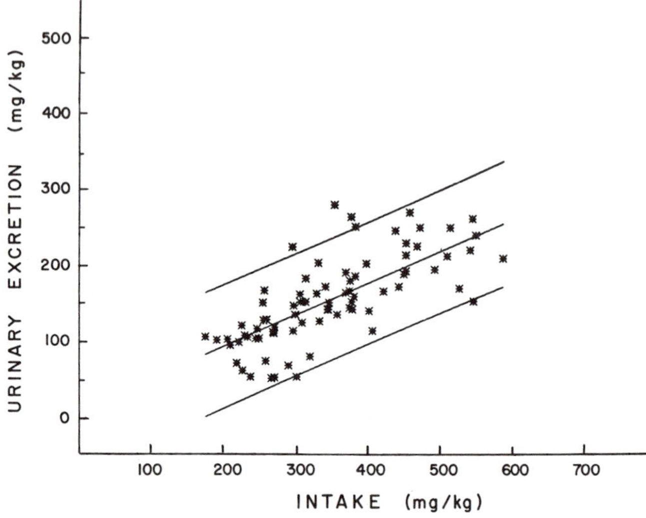

Figure 6–3 Relation between urinary excretion of nitrogen and intake of nitrogen by normal fullsize infants fed human milk or milk-based formulas between 61 and 90 days of age. The regression and 90 per cent confidence interval are indicated. Sources of the data and similar relations for other age intervals are included in Appendix III (p. 542).

tein. Possibly, the ratio of concentration of urea to that of total nitrogen in urine may prove useful as an indicator of recent dietary intake of protein.

Serum Concentration of Urea Nitrogen

As may be seen from Table 6–4, serum concentrations of urea nitrogen of normal infants fed ad libitum reflect the percentage of dietary calories provided from protein. Analysis of 611 determinations of concentrations of urea nitrogen in serum of 170 normal breastfed infants between 15 and 126 days of age has demonstrated that less than 4 per cent of the values were less than 3.5 mg/100 ml. It seems reasonable to conclude that concentrations less than 3.5 mg/100 ml reflect low recent dietary intake of nitrogen. However, greater serum concentrations of urea nitrogen, especially in the case of infants receiving inadequate calorie intakes or those with various degrees of dehydration, may be encountered in infants receiving inadequate protein intakes.

Without knowledge of the intake of protein, it is impossible to state a normal range of concentration of urea nitrogen in serum. As may be calculated from Table 6–4, few healthy breastfed infants (6 to 7 per cent of calories from protein) demonstrated serum concentrations of urea nitrogen greater than 12 mg/100 ml (mean plus two stand-

TABLE 6–4 CONCENTRATION IN SERUM OF UREA NITROGEN (mg/100 ml)*

Protein Intake (% of Calories)	Age														
	15–42 days			*43–70 days*			*71–98 days*			*99–126 days*			*127–182 days*		
	N	*Mean*	*S.D.*	*N*	*Mean*	*S.D.*	*N*	*Mean*	*S.D.*	*N*	*Mean*	*S.D.*	*N*	*Mean*	*S.D.*
26	8	32.5	2.2	4	24.3	8.6	4	24.0	3.0	4	20.4	3.3			
20	7	26.7	5.4	8	26.2	4.1	8	21.8	2.2	6	18.6	4.4			
9–11	98	12.4	3.4	91	11.1	2.6	94	10.1	2.5	88	9.5	2.1			
6–7†	146	8.1	2.6	146	6.6	2.1	157	6.6	2.2	162	6.8	3.7			
1–2‡													13	2.8	1.6

*Published (Fomon, 1961; Fomon et al., 1965, 1970, 1973) and unpublished data from Pediatric Metabolic Unit, University of Iowa.

†Breastfed infants (Fomon et al., 1970, and unpublished).

‡Infants received this diet for only four to six days. All other diets were fed for weeks or months.

ard deviations.) On the other hand, most infants receiving 20 per cent of calories from protein demonstrated serum concentrations greater than 12 mg/100 ml. Thus, in the breastfed infant, a concentration of urea nitrogen of 14 mg/100 ml is suggestive of abnormality—most likely renal disease or inadequate intake of fluid. This same concentration of urea nitrogen would fall at about the *lower* limit of the normal range for infants fed homogenized whole cow milk without added carbohydrate—i.e., 20 per cent of calories from protein.

Several investigators (Omans et al., 1961; Williams, 1963; Davidson et al., 1967) have demonstrated that quite high concentrations of urea nitrogen may be found in sera of infants of low birth weight when feedings provide 20 per cent or more of the calories from protein.

Serum or Plasma Concentrations of Amino Acids

Data on concentrations of amino acids in serum or plasma of premature and fullterm infants, children and adults have been summarized by Scriver and Rosenberg (1973). Representative values are presented in Table 6–5.

The data of Snyderman et al. (1968) indicate that the plasma aminogram responds promptly to alterations in protein intake. Low intakes of protein result in markedly decreased plasma concentrations of the branched-chain amino acids and of lysine and tyrosine, and less marked decreases in plasma concentrations of most other amino acids, whereas concentrations of glycine and serine become moderately elevated. High intakes of milk protein (9 gm/kg/day) result in increased plasma concentrations of most amino acids, especially the branched-chain amino acids, proline and methionine and decreased concentration of glycine.

Concentrations of amino acids in plasma of infants and children with overt or marginal states of protein-calorie malnutrition have been reported by a number of investigators. These studies have been reviewed in detail by Waterlow and Alleyne (1971) and by Alleyne et al. (1972). In children with kwashiorkor, the total amount of amino acids in plasma is decreased to about half the normal value (Arroyave et al., 1962). As in the case of normal infants fed low intakes of protein (Snyderman et al., 1968), plasma concentrations of malnourished infants demonstrate marked decrease in most essential amino acids and tyrosine and little change or some increase in nonessential amino acids (Holt et al., 1963).

Although increase in the ratio of concentrations of nonessential to essential amino acids in plasma (based, for simplicity, on selected amino acids) was at one time proposed as an index of abnormal protein nutritional status (Whitehead and Dean, 1964; Whitehead and

Harland, 1966), this ratio almost certainly reflects recent dietary intake of protein rather than nutritional status. During recovery from kwashiorkor, plasma concentrations of amino acids return to normal long before clinical evidence of recovery is present (Saunders et al., 1967). Furthermore, when normal adults are fed a diet low in protein, alterations of plasma amino acid concentrations similar to those seen in kwashiorkor occur in 1 to 15 days (Swendseid et al., 1966; Young and Scrimshaw, 1968; Weller et al., 1969).

As concluded by Waterlow and Alleyne (1971), an increased ratio of nonessential to essential amino acids and, in particular, a decrease in the concentration of branched-chain amino acids (valine, leucine and isoleucine) in the plasma are fairly sensitive indications of low recent protein intake.

WHEY PROTEIN VERSUS CASEIN

Proteins of human milk and cow milk are classified into two major categories: casein (the protein in the curd) and whey. Because whey is the predominant protein of human milk while casein is the predominant protein of cow milk, a comparison of nutritive value of these proteins for the human infant is of some importance.

It has been known since 1915 (Osborne and Mendel, 1915) that the addition of methionine to casein improves nitrogen utilization by the rat. As indicated in studies reviewed by Mueller and Cox (1947a and b), casein and lactalbumin are nutritively different when measured by the growth of rats, dogs, mice and chicks. In the protein-depleted dog, whey proteins are more effective than casein in promoting regeneration of serum albumin (Weech, 1942; Chow et al., 1948). The protein of SMA, with a whey protein to casein ratio similar to that of human milk, has a higher biologic value for rats than does cow milk protein (Tomarelli and Bernhart, 1962). However, with a liberal intake of protein, casein and lactalbumin have been shown to be equally effective in maintaining nitrogen balance in man (Mueller and Cox, 1947a and b). Furthermore, addition of small amounts of methionine, although improving the nutritive value of casein for the rat and dog to a value equivalent to that of lactalbumin, did not alter the nutritive value of casein for man (Cox et al., 1947). The greater requirement of fur-bearing animals than of man for sulfur-containing amino acids is presumably related to the relatively high concentration of cystine in hair.

Earlier work by Gordon et al. (1937) demonstrated that the protein of cow milk was as effective as that of human milk in promoting nitrogen retention by infants of low birth weight. This work has been confirmed more recently in studies with fullsize infants (Barness et

TABLE 6–5 AMINO ACID CONCENTRATION IN PLASMA OR SERUM[a, b] (μmole/liter)

Amino Acid	"Prematures"[c]		Neonates[d]		Infants[e]		Children[f]		Children[g]		Adults[h, i]	
	Mean	*S.D.*	*Mean*	*S.D.*	*Mean*	*S.D.*	*Mean*	*Range*	*Mean*	*Range*	*Mean*	*Range*
Taurine	180	75	141	40			49	19–91	80	57–115	66	27–168
Hydroxyproline	40	40	32						25			
Aspartic acid	10	10	8	4	19	2	2	0–9	10	4–20	16	0–24
Threonine	215	60	217	21	177	36	60	33–128	76	42–95	162	79–246
Serine	270[j]	75	163	34	131	27[j]	92	24–172	94	79–112	112	67–193
Asp (NH_2) + Glu (NH_2)[k]	905[l]	250	759	136			135	46–290	295	57–467	603	413–690
Proline	230	75	183	32	193	52	115	51–185	106	68–148	233	100–442
Glutamic acid	65	35	52	25					110	23–250	58	14–192
Glycine	460	275	343	69	213	35	170	56–308	166	117–223	231	120–553
Alanine	375	50	329	55	292	53	219	99–313	234	137–305	344	209–659
Valine	130	50	136	39	161	38	127	57–262	162	128–283	169	116–315
Half Cystine	65	10	62	13	42	9			60	45–77	74	48–141
Methionine	35	5	29	8	18	3	21	3–29	14	11–16	21	6–39
Isoleucine	40	20	39	8	39	8	44	26–94	43	28–84	54	35–97
Leucine	70	25	72	17	77	21	75	45–155	85	56–178	100	71–175

Tyrosine	120	100	69	16	54	21	45	11–122	43	31–71	50	21–87
Phenylalanine	90	20	78	14	55	10	40	23–69	42	26–61	57	37–115
Ornithine	90	20	91	25	50	11	40	10–107	33	27–86	69	29–125
Lysine	190	60	200	46	135	28	87	45–144	111	71–151	173	82–236
Histidine	50	20	77	16	78	14	64	24–112	55	24–85	79	31–106
Arginine	50	20	54	17	62	9	31	11–65	53	23–86	81	21–137
Tryptophan	30	15	32	17								
β-alanine			14.5									25–73

[a]Modified from Scriver, C. R., and Rosenberg, L. E.: Amino Acid Metabolism and Its Disorders. Philadelphia, W. B. Saunders Co., 1973, p. 42.

[b]All data obtained by elution chromatography on ion exchange resin columns.

[c]Adapted from Dickinson et al., 1970. Data for the first day of life from 10 premature infants with birth weights less than 2500 grams. Some of these infants may have been small-for-gestational-age rather than prematurely born.

[d]Recalculated from Dickinson et al., 1965; 25 infants (more than 2500 grams) studied before first feeding.

[e]Recalculated from Brodehl and Gellissen, 1968; 12 infants, 16 days to 4 months of age, studied after 6- to 8-hour fast.

[f]Soupart, 1962; 20 children, 9 months to 2 years of age, studied after overnight fast.

[g]Scriver and Davies, 1965; 9 children, 3 to 10 years of age, studied after overnight fast.

[h]Recalculated from Dickinson et al., 1965; 8 adults.

[i]Data on 76 adults compiled from nine sources by Dickinson et al., 1965; includes variation recorded by Soupart, 1962.

[j]Includes asparagine.

[k]Asparagine and glutamine as combined amounts.

[l]Glutamine alone.

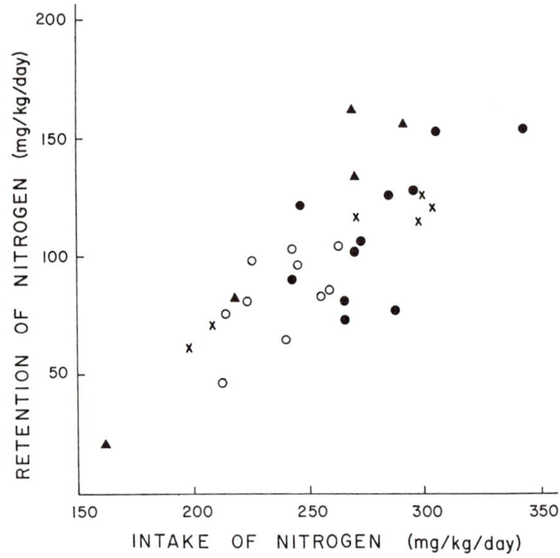

Figure 6–4 Retention of nitrogen versus intake of nitrogen by normal infants between 90 and 120 days of age. Each point refers to results of one three-day metabolic balance study with the symbols distinguishing the feeding: x, a soy-isolate formula (Formula 5224A) (Fomon et al., 1973); triangles, milk-based Formula 29B (Fomon and Filer, 1967); open circles, fresh human milk (Fomon et al., 1958); solid dots, processed human milk (Fomon and May, 1958). (From Fomon, S. J., et al.: Requirements for protein and essential amino acids in early infancy. Studies with a soy-isolate formula. Acta Paediatr. Scand. *62*: 33, 1973.)

al., 1957; Fomon and May, 1958; Fomon, 1960; Fomon and Owen, 1962b; Fomon and Filer, 1967). Rates of gain in length and weight by fullsize infants receiving 6 to 7 per cent of calories from cow milk protein or soy protein have been found to be similar to those by breastfed infants (Fomon, 1959; Fomon and Filer, 1967; Fomon et al., 1969, 1973). The relation between retention of nitrogen and intake of nitrogen is also the same (Fig. 6–4).

As discussed in Chapter 15, some commercially available formulas provide a ratio of whey protein to casein similar to that of human milk. A study in which one group of premature infants was fed such a formula and another group was fed a formula containing cow milk protein failed to demonstrate a difference between the two groups in rate of growth, nitrogen balance or food efficiency (Barness et al., 1963).

Because whey proteins are relatively low in content of phenylalanine, Hambraeus et al. (1970) have suggested that whey protein-containing formulas be used to supplement a phenylalanine-free or phenylalanine-low diet in management of infants with phenylketonuria. More recently, Forsum and Hambraeus (1972) have isolated a specific whey fraction with remarkably low content of phenylalanine. Such a product would seem to be a distinct asset in management of patients with phenylketonuria.

NITROGEN BALANCE STUDIES

Nitrogen balance is affected by many factors, including age, state of health, nitrogen content of diet, amino acid deficiency or imbalance, deficiency of other essential dietary factors, and calorie intake. Failure to control these variables has often led to misinterpretation of data from nitrogen balance studies. In addition, rate of synthesis of body protein may be overestimated if based on calculations involving nitrogen balance studies (Wallace, 1959; Fomon and Owen, 1962a).

Requirements for satisfactory studies with infants are as follows: (1) Groups of infants should be matched with respect to age, size and state of health. Lack of general availability of normal fullsize infants for such studies means that infants of low birth weight or infants recovering from disease are generally utilized, and the difficulty in matching groups of such subjects is great. The practice of studying two diets alternately with the same subject, although possibly desirable in studies of infants more than six months of age, is of little value

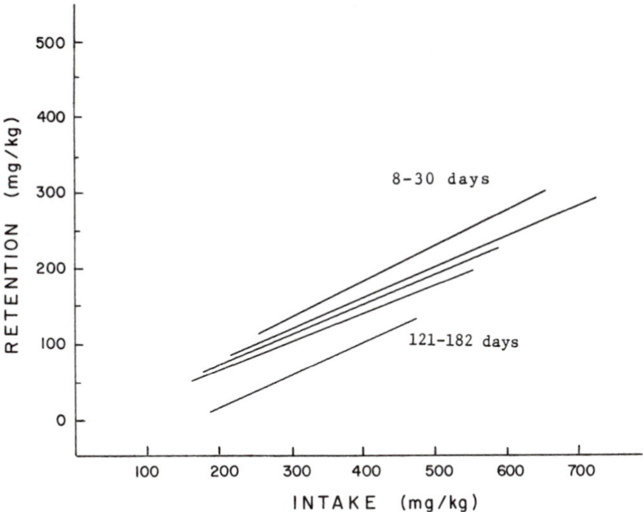

Figure 6–5 Influence of age on relation between retention of nitrogen and intake of nitrogen by normal fullsize infants fed human milk or milk-based formulas. The regressions apply (in sequence from top to bottom) to ages 8 to 30, 31 to 60, 61 to 90, 91 to 120 and 121 to 182 days. Sources of the data and equations of the regression lines are included in Appendix III (p. 542).

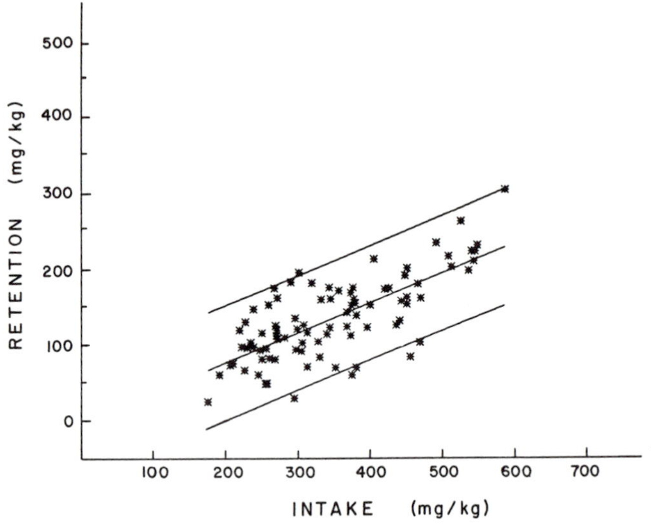

Figure 6–6 Relation between retention of nitrogen and intake of nitrogen by normal fullsize infants fed human milk or milk-based formulas between 61 and 90 days of age. The regression and 90 per cent confidence interval are indicated. Sources of the data and similar relations for other age intervals are included in Appendix III (p. 542).

with small infants. Differences in nitrogen balance among carefully matched infants of the same age are likely to be less than differences in nitrogen balance recorded with the same infant at different ages. (2) Diets should be identical in protein concentration and, as nearly as possible, in other constituents. Comparisons of protein quality are more sensitive when performed at an intake of protein approximating the requirement than when intake is considerably in excess of the requirement. Ad libitum feeding is more practical than pair feeding. (3) In analyzing the data, both age and nitrogen intake must be considered. With identical intakes per kilogram of body weight, retention of nitrogen per kilogram will be greater for younger than for older infants (Fig. 6–5).

In prolonged feeding studies of normal fullsize infants, nitrogen balance appears to be less sensitive than serum concentration of albumin as an index of nutritional adequacy of the diet. However, in studies of infants recovering from protein-calorie malnutrition, nitrogen balance studies may be of considerable value in comparison of nutritional quality of feedings (Scrimshaw et al., 1958; Bressani et al., 1960; Hansen and Freesemann, 1960; Rice et al., 1960; Waterlow and Wills, 1960; Scrimshaw et al., 1961; Graham et al., 1966, 1969a and b, 1972; Graham and Placko, 1970).

REQUIREMENTS FOR PROTEIN AND ESSENTIAL AMINO ACIDS

Studies of requirements for protein and amino acids by individuals of all ages have been reviewed by Irwin and Hegsted (1971a and b). Waterlow and Alleyne (1971) have reviewed studies concerning protein requirements of infants and children.

Protein Requirement in Infancy

Although requirements for protein have in the past generally been estimated by the "factorial method" (Waterlow and Alleyne, 1971; Joint FAO/WHO Expert Group, 1973; Food and Nutrition Board, 1974), this method depends on a satisfactory estimate of obligatory losses of nitrogen. Obligatory excretions of nitrogen in urine and feces are dependent both on current and on prior dietary intake (Fomon et al., 1965) and, thus, the obligatory losses determined with infants consuming a protein-deficient diet have little relevance to the situation in which an adequate intake of protein is fed. As pointed out by Waterlow and Alleyne (1971), when the factorial approach is utilized to arrive at an estimate of protein requirement of 9- to 12-month-old infants, the value obtained is so low that normal gain in weight would not occur.

As an alternate approach to estimating protein requirements during infancy, we have fed relatively low intakes of protein to normal infants during the first few months of life. In studies with a milk-based formula (Fomon and Filer, 1967; Fomon et al., 1969, 1971) and an L-methionine-fortified soy isolate-based formula (Fomon et al., 1973), 1.6 gm of protein/100 kcal appeared adequate to support normal growth, maintain normal concentrations of albumin in serum and promote nitrogen balance similar to that of infants fed human milk. On the basis of these findings, it was assumed that the requirements for protein and amino acids were no greater than the amounts consumed.

In considering the infant's requirement for protein, it is useful to think separately about needs for growth and for nongrowth. In the case of the normal adult, the entire protein requirement will consist of the requirement for uses other than growth, a requirement related to body size and therefore reasonably expressed per unit of body weight. As may be seen from Figure 6–7, the situation with the small, rapidly growing infant is quite different. Although this figure is based on a number of assumptions, there can be little doubt that normal fullsize infants and, especially, low-birth-weight infants during their period of most rapid postnatal growth utilize an extremely high proportion of protein intake for growth. By contrast, children beyond infancy utilize a relatively small proportion of their protein intake for growth.

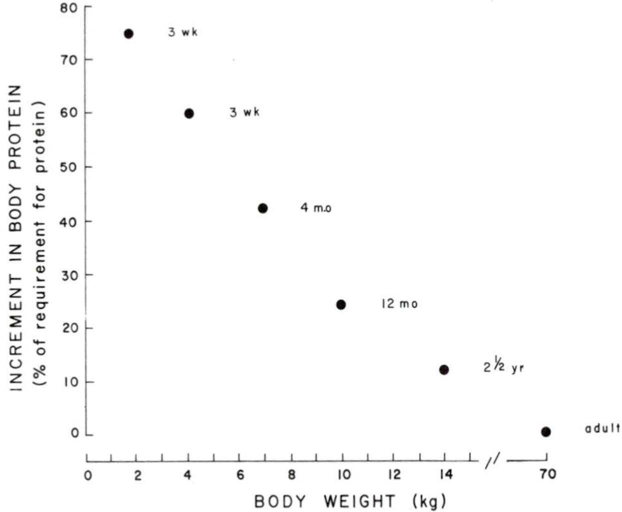

Figure 6–7 Increment in body protein, expressed as percentage of protein requirement, in relation to body weight of hypothetic infants of various weights. In the case of a rapidly growing low-birth-weight infant (1.7 kg), more than 70 per cent of protein intake might be accounted for by the increment in body protein. On the other hand, only about 12 per cent of the protein requirement for a two-and-a-half-year-old child and none of the adult's protein requirement can be accounted for by increment in body protein.

Because protein requirement during early infancy is highly correlated both with body size and with rate of gain in weight and because calorie intake during ad libitum feeding is generally correlated with these same variables, it is reasonable to express protein requirement per unit of calorie intake. If the requirement is 1.6 gm/100 kcal during the first six weeks of life, we estimate that it is approximately 1.4 gm/100 kcal during the remainder of the first year (Fomon et al., 1973).

These estimates of requirement for protein per unit of calorie intake do not differ remarkably from the protein to calorie ratio of human milk. An impressive clinical experience over several thousand years suggests that an infant receives an adequate intake of protein when his entire calorie intake is obtained by feeding at the breast of a well nourished woman. Assuming that human milk averages 1.1 gm of protein and 75 kcal/100 ml (Chapter 15, Table 15–1), the ratio of protein to calories is 1.5 gm/100 kcal.

In rare instances, energy requirements may be so great that expressing protein requirement per unit of calorie intake may be misleading. The infant with muscular hypertonia, athetosis or other hyperactivity may require an extremely large energy intake without concomitant increase in protein requirement. This situation would be somewhat analogous to the lower protein requirement per unit of calorie intake demonstrated for rats raised in a cold environment (and therefore having high energy expenditures) (Andik et al., 1963).

TABLE 6–6 ESTIMATED REQUIREMENTS AND ADVISABLE INTAKES FOR PROTEIN FOR NORMAL FULLSIZE INFANTS AND CHILDREN

AGE	REQUIREMENT	ADVISABLE INTAKE
Birth to 4 months (gm/100 kcal)	1.6	1.9
4 to 12 months (gm/100 kcal)	1.4	1.7
12 to 36 months (gm/kg/day)	1.2	1.4

Between one and three years of age, requirement for protein is determined so predominantly by size rather than by rate of growth that it is completely acceptable to express requirement per unit of body weight rather than per unit of calorie intake. Chan and Waterlow (1966) have suggested a value of 1.2 gm/kg/day for older infants and, tentatively, this value may be utilized for the interval one to three years of age. Table 6–6 indicates the estimated requirements for protein at various ages.

Advisable Intakes of Protein

Although there can be little question that the ratio of protein to calories in human milk is adequate for the breastfed infant, experience in feeding infants this ratio of protein to calories from other protein sources is severely limited. Thus, it seems desirable that advisable intakes be set at values somewhat greater than the estimates of requirement: 1.9 gm/100 kcal during the first four months of life, 1.7 gm/100 kcal from age four months to one year, and 1.4 gm/kg/day thereafter (Table 6–6). These advisable intakes are approximately 20 per cent greater than our estimates of requirement.

Amino Acid Requirements in Infancy

Requirements for essential amino acids must be considered in much the same way as requirements for protein. Per unit of nitrogen, requirements for individual amino acids for growth are not likely to be identical to those for nongrowth. It is well recognized that certain protein-containing tissues turn over relatively rapidly (e.g., intestinal epithelial cells), while other body components (e.g., collagen) turn over quite slowly. In growing individuals, it is therefore reasonable to attempt to distinguish between requirements for essential amino acids for growth and for maintenance. Requirements for growth will be related to rate of synthesis of various tissues and to the amino acid composition of those tissues. Amino acid requirements for maintenance will depend on (1) the rate of turnover of various body tissues, (2) the amino acid composition of those tissues and (3) the extent to which various amino acids released at the time of cell death can be recycled into anabolic processes. Because of probable differences between amino acid requirements for growth and for maintenance, it is not surprising that requirements for essential amino acids might be different for rapidly growing infants than for older children or adults.

Care is necessary in evaluating various estimates of requirements for essential amino acids both in adults and in infants. Most studies of amino acid requirements have utilized semi-synthetic diets containing mixtures of amino acids rather than whole proteins. Snyderman and co-workers, in a series of reports published between 1955 and 1964, provided estimates of requirements for individual essential amino acids based on studies in which mixtures of amino acids were fed to human infants. These studies have been summarized by Holt and Snyderman (1961, 1967) and by Fomon and Filer (1967). We have questioned the extent of relevance of such studies to requirements of infants fed whole proteins (Fomon et al., 1964; Fomon and Filer, 1967; Fomon et al., 1973). In addition, we have pointed out that in the studies of Snyderman and co-workers, nitrogen intakes were rather high (equivalent to protein intakes of approximately 3 gm/kg/day), attempts to estimate the requirements for a particular amino acid were carried out with relatively few infants, observations at a specified amino acid intake were of short duration, and conclusions about adequacy of amino acid intake were based on short-term rates of gain in weight and on nitrogen balance, which may not be the most sensitive criteria.

Data accumulated in our studies (Fomon and Filer, 1967; Fomon et al., 1973) suggest that, at least in the case of infants, requirements may be different when amino acids are supplied as mixtures of amino acids than when they are supplied in the form of whole proteins.

The preliminary estimates of requirements based on these studies are presented in Table 6–7. They are believed applicable when the diet is adequate in total calories and non-nitrogenous essential nutrients, when nitrogen is provided primarily in the form of whole proteins of high biologic value and when protein intakes do not greatly exceed the requirement. The approach is, of course, likely to yield estimates of requirements for some amino acids that are substantially greater than the true requirements. Nevertheless, our estimates of requirements for isoleucine and methionine are distinctly less than those reported by Holt and Snyderman (1961, 1967). We conclude that the estimates of Holt and Snyderman from studies of infants fed mixtures of amino acids are less relevant than are the estimates of Fomon et al. (1973) to circumstances in which whole proteins are fed in amounts that do not greatly exceed the requirement for protein.

TABLE 6–7 PRELIMINARY ESTIMATES OF REQUIREMENTS FOR AMINO ACIDS BY INFANTS*

Amino Acid	Estimate (mg/100 kcal)†
Histidine	26
Isoleucine	66
Leucine	132
Lysine	101
Phenylalanine	57
Methionine	24
Cystine	23
Threonine	59
Tryptophan	16
Valine	83

*Data of Fomon et al. (1973).

†Because of the manner in which these estimates were made, the true requirement for several of the amino acids is likely to be substantially less than the preliminary estimate given here.

Food Choice in Relation to Advisable Intake of Protein in Infancy

The ratio of protein to calories in various foods commonly fed to infants may be seen from Table 6–8. It is apparent that per unit of calories, amounts of protein provided by commercially prepared formulas are in excess (probably harmlessly in excess) of the advisable intakes. Most commercially prepared strained and junior fruits, desserts and puddings provide less than 1.4 gm of protein/100 kcal, whereas most other foods provide more than 1.7 gm/100 kcal.

As previously mentioned, the solely breastfed infant will receive an adequate intake of protein. However, some caution is required in nutritional management of the infant who receives a portion of his calorie intake from human milk and the remainder from other foods. As

TABLE 6–8 CONCENTRATION OF PROTEIN PER UNIT OF CALORIES IN VARIOUS FOODS COMMONLY FED TO INFANTS

Foods	Protein (gm/100 kcal)
Human milk	1.6*
Commercially prepared formulas	
Milk-based	2.2–2.7
Soy isolate-based	2.7–3.3
Whole cow milk	5.0
Commercially prepared strained and junior foods	
Most fruits, desserts, puddings	<1.4
Most other foods	>1.7

*Although the infant receiving his entire calorie intake from human milk receives an adequate intake of protein, the advisable intake for other infants is 1.9 gm/100 kcal during the first four months of life and 1.7 gm/100 kcal thereafter.

TABLE 6–9 INFLUENCE OF LOW-PROTEIN COMMERCIALLY PREPARED STRAINED FOODS ON PROTEIN INTAKE BY INFANTS RECEIVING VARIOUS MILKS OR FORMULAS

MILK OR FORMULA	PROTEIN INTAKE (GM/100 KCAL)	
	Milk or Formula Only	*75% Milk or Formula 25% Low-Protein Foods**
Human milk	1.6	1.4
Commercially prepared formula		
Milk-based, 1.5 gm protein/100 ml	2.2	1.9
Soy isolate-based, 2.3 gm protein /100 ml	3.4	2.8
Whole cow milk	5.2	4.1

*Most fruits and desserts (see text). Protein intake calculated on the assumption that the average protein concentration of fruits and desserts is 0.8 gm/100 kcal.

will be apparent from the example presented in Table 6–9, the breastfed infant who receives a substantial portion of his calorie intake from other foods will need to receive additional protein from these foods. If a breastfed infant should receive a relatively large portion of his diet in the form of foods of low protein content, intake of protein might be inadequate. Conversely, when commercially prepared formulas (or whole cow milk) provide a high percentage of calorie intake, there is no reason to supply other protein-rich foods. In fact, if as much as one-third of calorie intake is supplied by whole cow milk, the advisable intake of protein will be met and other foods may be selected with attention to supplying an adequate intake of calories and essential nutrients other than protein.

INTAKES OF PROTEIN BY CHILDREN 12 TO 36 MONTHS OF AGE IN THE UNITED STATES

Several surveys (Fryer et al., 1971; Eagles and Steele, 1972; Center for Disease Control, 1972; Owen et al., 1974) have included data on protein intakes by children between 12 and 36 months of age. As may be seen from Table 6–10, less than 4 per cent of children were reported to receive intakes of protein less than 20 gm/day. Some of the children receiving 10 to 20 gm of protein/day (Table 6–10) were undoubtedly receiving more than the estimated 1.2 gm/kg/day requirement of this age group (Table 6–6).

Data on serum concentrations of albumin from two surveys (Center for Disease Control, 1972; Owen et al., 1974) also suggest that

TABLE 6–10 INTAKES OF PROTEIN BY CHILDREN 12 TO 36 MONTHS OF AGE IN THE UNITED STATES
Report of Various Surveys

AGE (MONTHS)	SURVEY*	NUMBER OF CHILDREN	INTAKE OF PROTEIN (GM/DAY) <10	10–19	20–29	>29
			(Per Cent of Children)			
12–24	10-State	693	<1	3	9	88
	PNS	632	0	2	14	84
	USDA	93	0	1	9	90
	NCRS	497				>90
24–36	10-State	708	<1	3	9	87
	PNS	681	0	1	7	92
	USDA	105	0	4	6	90
	NCRS	551				>90

*10-State is Ten-State Nutrition Survey, 1968–1970 (Center for Disease Control, 1972); PNS is Preschool Nutrition Survey (Owen et al., 1974); USDA is U.S. Department of Agriculture Survey of low income families (Eagles and Steele, 1972); and NCRS is North Central Regional Survey (Fryer et al., 1971).

protein deficiency is uncommon among small children in the United States. Of 633 children less than six years of age in the Ten-State Nutrition Survey (Center for Disease Control, 1972), concentrations of albumin were less than 3.0 gm/100 ml in 2.4 per cent, and concentrations were greater than 3.5 gm/100 ml in 90 per cent. Of 678 children between 12 and 36 months of age in the Preschool Nutrition Survey (Owen et al., 1974), only one child was found to have serum concentration of albumin less than 3.1 gm/100 ml and only 2 per cent demonstrated concentrations less than 3.4 gm/100 ml.

Appendix

Terms Employed in Discussion of Protein Quality

Protein Efficiency Ratio (PER)

Formula: $\dfrac{\text{weight gain (gm)}}{\text{protein consumed (gm)}}$

Among the factors known to influence rate of growth of rats are amount of food consumed, level of protein in the diet, age, sex, strain of rat and length of assay period. Methods most commonly employed (Chapman et al., 1959; Horwitz, 1970) utilize 21-day-old male rats fed ad libitum a diet containing 9 to 10 per cent protein by weight for a period of four weeks. The test is standardized by use of rats fed casein as a control protein. See text for comment about limitations of the method.

Because the weanling rat uses lactose poorly (DeGrott and Engel, 1956) and demonstrates relatively slow growth when fed milk-based formulas low in content of protein and high in content of lactose (Tomarelli et al., 1953), PER studies comparing milk-based formulas should be conducted with products adjusted to the same concentrations of protein, fat and carbohydrate (including identical concentrations of lactose). The casein control should be similarly adjusted, including content of lactose (Sarett, 1973). Liquid formulas will, of course, need to be lyophilized.

Biologic Value (BV)

$$\text{Formula: } \frac{\text{retained N} \times 100}{\text{absorbed N}}$$

$$= \frac{(\text{food N} - \text{urine N} - \text{fecal N} + \text{endogenous N}) \times 100}{\text{food N} - \text{fecal N} + \text{fecal endogenous N}}$$

where endogenous N is the amount of nitrogen excreted in urine and feces by animals receiving a protein-free diet.

True Digestibility (D)

$$\text{Formula: } \frac{\text{absorbed N} \times 100}{\text{food N}}$$

$$= \frac{(\text{food N} - \text{fecal N} + \text{fecal endogenous N}) \times 100}{\text{food N}}$$

Net Protein Utilization (NPU)

$$\text{Formula: BV} \times \text{D}$$

$$= \frac{\text{retained N} \times 100}{\text{food N}}$$

$$= \frac{(C_p - C_0) \times 100}{\text{food N}}$$

where C_p is the amount of nitrogen in the carcass of an animal fed the protein-containing diet and C_0 is the amount of nitrogen in the carcass of an animal fed the protein-free diet. NPU is defined as the difference in carcass content of nitrogen* between animals receiving

*Since the ratio of nitrogen to water in the carcass has been found to be fairly constant at a specified age, dry weight rather than nitrogen content of the carcass may be utilized (Miller and Bender, 1955).

the protein-containing test diet and those receiving a protein-free control diet, divided by the amount of nitrogen consumed by the test animals (Miller and Bender, 1955). It is assumed that nitrogen content of the carcass of animals fed the protein-free diet decreases during the course of the assay in proportion to the requirements of the animal for maintenance, and therefore the result is interpreted in relation to requirements of the test animals for growth plus maintenance rather than for growth. However, body turnover of proteins is almost certainly less for animals receiving a protein-free diet than for animals receiving appreciable amounts of protein. The major advantage of NPU over PER is that the former takes into account an aspect of body composition while the latter merely concerns change in weight.

Chemical Score

$$\text{Formula: } \frac{\%\ \text{limiting amino acid} \times 100}{\%\ \text{of that amino acid in egg}}$$

Nitrogen Balance

Formula: $I - U - F$

where I is nitrogen in ingested food, U is nitrogen excreted in urine and F is nitrogen in feces. True accretion of nitrogen by the subject will always be less than the apparent nitrogen retention estimated by this formula (see Appendix IV, p. 549).

REFERENCES

Alleyne, G. A. O., Flores, H., Picou, D. I. M., and Waterlow, J. C.: Metabolic changes in children with protein-calorie malnutrition. *In* Winick, M. (ed.): Nutrition and Development, New York, J. Wiley & Sons, 1972, p. 201.

Andik, I., Donhoffer, S., Farkas, M., and Schmidt, P.: Ambient temperature and survival on a protein-deficient diet. Br. J. Nutr. *17*:257, 1963.

Antia, A. U., McFarlane, H., and Soothill, J. F.: Serum siderophilin in kwashiorkor. Arch. Dis. Child. *43*:459, 1968.

Arroyave, G., Wilson, D., De Funes, C., and Béhar, M.: The free amino acids in blood plasma of children with kwashiorkor and marasmus. Amer. J. Clin. Nutr. *11*:517, 1962.

Barness, L. A., Baker, D., Guilbert, P., Torres, F. E., and György, P.: Nitrogen metabolism of infants fed human and cow's milk. J. Pediatr. *51*:29, 1957.

Barness, L. A., Omans, W. B., Rose, C. S., and György, P.: Progress of premature infants fed a formula containing demineralized whey. Pediatrics *32*:52, 1963.

Bender, A. E., and Doell, B. H.: Biological evaluation of proteins: a new aspect. Br. J. Nutr. *11*:140, 1957.

Bressani, R., Wilson, D. L., Béhar, M., and Scrimshaw, N. S.: Supplementation of cereal proteins with amino acids. III. Effect of amino acid supplementation of wheat flour as measured by nitrogen retention of young children. J. Nutr. *70*:176, 1960.

Brodehl, J., and Gellissen, K.: Endogenous renal transport of free amino acids in infancy and childhood. Pediatrics *42*:395, 1968.

Center for Disease Control: Ten-State Nutrition Survey, 1968–70. DHEW Publication No. (HSM) 72-8130, 72-8131, 72-8132, 72-8133. Atlanta, Georgia, Center for Disease Control, 1972.

Chan, H., and Waterlow, J. C.: The protein requirement of infants at the age of about 1 year. Br. J. Nutr. *20*:775, 1966.

Chapman, D. G., Castrillo, R., and Campbell, J. A.: Evaluation of protein in foods. I. A method for the determination of protein efficiency ratios. Canad. J. Biochem. *37*:679, 1959.

Chow, B. F., Alper, C., and DeBiase, S.: The effects of oral administration of different proteins on the plasma proteins of protein-depleted dogs. J. Nutr. *36*:785, 1948.

Cox, W. M., Jr., Mueller, A. J., Elman, R., Albanese, A. A., Kemmerer, K. S., Barton, R. W., and Holt, L. E., Jr.: Nitrogen retention studies on rats, dogs and man: the effect of adding methionine to an enzymic casein hydrolysate. J. Nutr. *33*:437, 1947.

Davidson, M., Levine, S. Z., Bauer, C. H., and Dann, M.: Feeding studies in low-birth-weight infants. I. Relationships of dietary protein, fat, and electrolyte to rates of weight gain, clinical courses, and serum chemical concentrations. J. Pediatr. *70*:695, 1967.

DeGrott, A. P., and Engel, C.: The harmful effect of lactose. I. Experiments with growing rats. Voeding *17*:325, 1956.

Dickinson, J. C., Rosenblum, H., and Hamilton, P. B.: Ion exchange chromatography of the free amino acids in the plasma of the newborn infant. Pediatrics *36*:2, 1965.

Dickinson, J. C., Rosenblum, H., and Hamilton, P. B.: Ion exchange chromatography of the free amino acids in the plasma of infants under 2,500 gm at birth. Pediatrics *45*:606, 1970.

Donoso, G., Lewis, O. A. M., Miller, D. S., and Payne, P. R.: Effect of heat treatment on the nutritive value of protein. J. Sci. Food Agric. *13*:192, 1962.

Eagles, J. A., and Steele, P. D.: Food and nutrient intake of children from birth to four years of age. *In* Fomon, S. J., and Anderson, T. A. (eds.): Practices of Low-Income Families in Feeding Infants and Small Children. With Particular Attention to Cultural Subgroups. DHEW/HSMHA Publ. No. 725605. Maternal and Child Health Service, 1972, p. 19.

Ellis, G. P.: The Maillard reaction. *In* Wolfrom, M. L. (ed.): Advances in Carbohydrate Chemistry. Vol. 14. New York and London, Academic Press, 1959, p. 63.

Evans, R. J., and Butts, H. A.: Inactivation of amino acids by autoclaving. Science *109*:569, 1949.

Fomon, S. J.: Comparative study of human milk and a soya bean formula in promoting growth and nitrogen retention by infants. Pediatrics *24*:577, 1959.

Fomon, S. J.: Comparative study of adequacy of protein from human milk and cow's milk in promoting nitrogen retention by normal full-term infants. Pediatrics *26*:51, 1960.

Fomon, S. J.: Nitrogen balance studies with normal full-term infants receiving high intakes of protein. Comparisons with previous studies employing lower intakes of protein. Pediatrics *28*:347, 1961.

Fomon, S. J., DeMaeyer, E. M., and Owen, G. M.: Urinary and fecal excretion of endogenous nitrogen by infants and children. J. Nutr. *85*:235, 1965.

Fomon, S. J., and Filer, L. J., Jr.: Amino acid requirements for normal growth. *In* Nyhan, W. L. (ed.): Amino Acid Metabolism and Genetic Variation. New York, McGraw-Hill Book Co., 1967, p. 391.

Fomon, S. J., Filer, L. J., Jr., Thomas, L. N., and Rogers, R. R.: Growth and serum chemical values of normal breastfed infants. Acta Paediatr. Scand. (Suppl. 202), 1970.

Fomon, S. J., Filer, L. J., Jr., Thomas, L. N., Rogers, R. R., and Proksch, A. M.: Relationship between formula concentration and rate of growth of normal infants. J. Nutr. *98*:241, 1969.

Fomon, S. J., and May, C. D.: Metabolic studies of normal full-term infants fed pasteurized human milk. Pediatrics *22*:101, 1958.

Fomon, S. J., and Owen, G. M.: Comment on metabolic balance studies as a method of estimating body composition of infants. Pediatrics *29*:495, 1962a.

Fomon, S. J., and Owen, G. M.: Retention of nitrogen by normal full-term infants receiving an autoclaved formula. Pediatrics *29*:1005, 1962b.

Fomon, S. J., Owen, G. M., and Thomas, L. N.: Methionine, valine and isoleucine. Requirements during infancy: growth and nitrogen balance studies with normal fullterm infants receiving soybean protein. Amer. J. Dis. Child. *108*:487, 1964.

Fomon, S. J., Thomas, L. N., Filer, L. J., Jr., Anderson, T. A., and Bergmann, K. E.:

Requirements for protein and essential amino acids in early infancy. Studies with a soy-isolate formula. Acta Paediatr. Scand. *62*:33, 1973.

Fomon, S. J., Thomas, L. N., and May C. D.: Equivalence of pasteurized and fresh human milk in promoting nitrogen retention by normal full-term infants. Pediatrics *22*:935, 1958.

Fomon, S. J., Ziegler, E. E., Thomas, L. N., and Filer, L. J., Jr.: Protein requirement of normal infants between 8 and 56 days of age. *In* Jonxis, J. H. P., Visser, H. K. A., and Troelstra, J. A. (eds.): Nutricia Symposium: Metabolic Processes in the Foetus and Newborn Infant, Leiden, Stenfert Kroese., 1971, p. 144.

Food and Nutrition Board: Recommended Dietary Allowances. 8th ed. Washington, D.C., National Academy of Sciences, Publ. No. 2216, 1974.

Ford, J. E., and Salter, D. N.: Analysis of enzymatically digested food proteins by Sephadex-gel filtration. Br. J. Nutr. *20*:843, 1966.

Forsum, E., and Hambraeus, L.: Biological evaluation of a whey protein fraction, with special reference to its use as a phenylalanine-low protein source in the dietary treatment of PKU. Nutr. Metab. *14*:48, 1972.

Fryer, B. A., Lamkin, G. H., Vivian, V. M., Eppright, E. S., and Fox, H. M.: Diets of preschool children in the north central region. J. Amer. Diet. Ass. *59*:228, 1971.

Gabr, M., El-Hawary, M. F. S., and El-Dali, M.: Serum transferrin in kwashiorkor. J. Trop. Med. Hyg. *74*:216, 1971.

Gallina, D. L., and Dominguez, J. M.: Human utilization of urea nitrogen in low calorie diets. J. Nutr. *101*:1029, 1971.

Gaull, G., Sturman, J. A., and Räihä, N. C. R.: Development of mammalian sulfur metabolism: absence of cystathionase in human fetal tissues. Pediatr. Res. *6*:538, 1972.

Gordon, H. H., Levine, S. Z., Wheatley, M. A., and Marples, E.: Respiratory metabolism in infancy and in childhood. XX. The nitrogen metabolism in premature infants—comparative studies of human milk and cow's milk. Amer. J. Dis. Child. *54*:1030, 1937.

Graham, G. G., Baertl, J. M., and Cordano, A.: Studies of infantile malnutrition. V. The effect of dietary protein source on serum proteins. Amer. J. Clin. Nutr. *18*:16, 1966.

Graham, G. G., Baertl, J. M., Placko, R. P., and Cordano, A.: Dietary protein quality in infants and children. VIII. Wheat- or oat-soy mixtures. Amer. J. Clin. Nutr. *25*:875, 1972.

Graham, G. G., Morales, E., Acevedo, G., Baertl, J. M., and Cordano, A.: Dietary protein quality in infants and children. II. Metabolic studies with cottonseed flour. Amer. J. Clin. Nutr. *22*:577, 1969a.

Graham, G. G., and Placko, R. P.: Fasting plasma free amino acids of infants on milk protein diets. Johns Hopkins Med. J. *126*:19, 1970.

Graham, G. G., Placko, R. P., Acevedo, G., Morales, E., and Cordano, A.: Lysine enrichment of wheat flour: evaluation in infants. Amer. J. Clin. Nutr. *22*:1459, 1969b.

Gray, G. M., and Cooper, H. L.: Protein digestion and absorption. Gastroenterology *61*:535, 1971.

Hambraeus, L., Wranne, L., and Lorentsson, R.: Whey protein formulas in the treatment of phenylketonuria in infants. Nutr. Metab. *12*:152, 1970.

Hansen, J. D. L., and Freesemann, C.: The use of the nitrogen balance technique in the assessment of the nutritive value of proteins for children. Proc. Nutr. Soc. (S. Afr.) *1*:47, 1960.

Harper, A. E., Becker, R. V., and Stucki, W. P.: Some effects of excessive intakes of indispensable amino acids. Proc. Soc. Exp. Biol. Med. *121*:695, 1966.

Harper, A. E., Benevenga, N. J., and Wahlhueter, R. M.: Effects of ingestion of disproportionate amounts of amino acids. Physiol Rev. *50*:428, 1970.

Harper, A. E., Leung, P., Yoshida, A., and Rogers, Q. R.: Some new thoughts on amino acid imbalance. Fed. Proc. *23*:1087, 1964.

Henry, K. M., and Kon, S. K.: Effect of reaction with glucose on the nutritive value of casein. Biochem. Biophys. Acta *5*:455, 1950.

Holt, L. E., Jr., and Snyderman, S. E.: The amino acid requirements of infants. J.A.M.A. *175*:100, 1961.

Holt, L. E., Jr., and Snyderman, S. E.: The amino acid requirements of children. *In* Nyhan, W. L. (ed.): Amino Acid Metabolism and Genetic Variation. New York, McGraw-Hill Book Co., 1967, p. 381.

Holt, L. E., Jr., Snyderman, S. E., Norton, P. H., Roitman, E., and Finch, J.: The plasma aminogram in kwashiorkor. Lancet *2*:1343, 1963.

Horwitz, W. (ed).: Official Methods of Analysis of the Association of Official Analytical Chemists. 11th ed. Washington, D.C. Association of Official Analytical Chemists, 1970, p. 800.

Irwin, M. I., and Hegsted, D. M.: A conspectus of research on protein requirements of man. J. Nutr. *101*:385, 1971a.

Irwin, M. I., and Hegsted, D. M.: A conspectus of research on amino acid requirements of man. J. Nutr. *101*:539, 1971b.

Joint FAO/WHO Expert Group: Energy and Protein Requirements. WHO Tech. Rept. Series No. 522, Geneva, World Health Organization, 1973.

McCance, R. A., and Widdowson, E. M.: The composition of foods. Med. Res. Counc., Spec. Rep. Ser. 296, 1960.

McFarlane, H., Ogbeide, M. I., Reddy, S., Adcock, K. J., Adeshina, H., Gurney, J. M., Cooke, A., Taylor, G. O., and Mordie, J. A.: Biochemical assessment of protein-calorie malnutrition. Lancet *1*:392, 1969.

McFarlane, H., Reddy, S., Adcock, K. J., Adeshina, H., Cooke, A. R., and Akene, J.: Immunity, transferrin, and survival in kwashiorkor. Br. Med. J. *4*:268, 1970.

Miller, D. S., and Bender, A. E.: The determination of the net utilization of proteins by a shortened method. Br. J. Nutr. *9*:382, 1955.

Mitchell, H. H.: Determination of the nutritive value of the proteins of food products. Ind. Eng. Chem., Anal. Ed. *16*:696, 1944.

Mueller, A. J., and Cox, W. M., Jr.: Comparative nutritive value of casein and lactalbumin for man. J. Nutr. *34*:285, 1947a.

Mueller, A. J., and Cox, W. M., Jr.: Comparative nutritive value of casein and lactalbumin for man. Science *105*:580, 1947b.

Nesheim, M. C., and Carpenter, K. J.: The digestion of heat-damaged protein. Br. J. Nutr. *21*:399, 1967.

Nixon, S. E., and Mawer, G. E.: The digestion and absorption of protein in man. I. The site of absorption. Br. J. Nutr. *24*:227, 1970a.

Nixon, S. E., and Mawer, G. E.: The digestion and absorption of protein in man. II. The form in which digested protein is absorbed. Br. J. Nutr. *24*:241, 1970b.

Omans, W. B., Barness, L. A., Rose, C. S., and György, P.: Prolonged feeding studies in premature infants. J. Pediatr. *59*:951, 1961.

Osborne, T. B., and Mendel, L. B.: The comparative nutritive value of certain proteins in growth and the problem of the protein minimum. J. Biol. Chem. *20*:351, 1915.

Owen, G. M., Kram, K. M., Garry, P. J., Lowe, J. E., Jr., and Lubin, A. H.: A study of nutritional status of preschool children in the United States, 1968–1970. Pediatrics *53*:597, 1974.

Perry, T. L., and Hansen, S.: Technical pitfalls leading to errors in the quantitation of plasma amino acids. Clin. Chim. Acta *25*:53, 1969.

Picou, D., and Phillips, M.: Urea metabolism in malnourished and recovered children receiving a high or low protein diet. Amer. J. Clin. Nutr. *25*:1261, 1972.

Pronczuk, A., Pawlowska, D., and Bartnik, J.: Effect of heat treatment on the digestibility and utilization of protein. Nutr. Metab. *15*:171, 1973.

Rice, H. L., Flodin, N. W., and Shuman, A. C.: Nitrogen balance response of young men to changes in quality of dietary protein. Fed. Proc. *19*:13, 1960.

Rios-Iriarte, B. J., and Barnes, R. H.: The effect of overheating on certain nutritional properties of the protein of soybeans. Food Technol. *20*:131, 1966.

Rose, W. C.: The nutritive significance of the amino acids. Physiol. Rev. *18*:109, 1938.

Rose, W. C., Smith, L. C., Womack, M., and Shane, M.: The utilization of the nitrogen of ammonium salts, urea and certain other compounds in the synthesis of non-essential amino acids in vivo. J. Biol. Chem. *181*:307, 1949.

Sarett, H. P.: Nutritional value of commercially produced foods for infants. Bibliotheca Nutr. Diet. Vol. 18. Basel, Karger, 1973, p. 246.

Saunders, S. J., Truswell, A. S., Barbezat, G. O., Wittman, W., and Hansen, J. D. L.: Plasma free amino acid pattern in protein-calorie malnutrition. Lancet *2*:795, 1967.

Schendel, H. E., Hansen, J. D. L., and Brock, J. F.: The biochemical assessment of protein nutritional status. 1. Marginal hypoalbuminaemia. 2. Serum cholinesterase. S. Afr. J. Lab. Clin. Med. *8*:23, 1962.

Scrimshaw, N. S., and Béhar, M.: Protein malnutrition in young children. Science *133*: 2039, 1961.

Scrimshaw, N. S., Béhar, M., Wilson, D., Viteri, F., Arroyave, G., and Bressani, R.: All-vegetable protein mixtures for human feeding. V. Clinical trials with INCAP mixtures 8 and 9 and with corn and beans. Amer. J. Clin. 9:196, 1961.

Scrimshaw, N. S., Bressani, R., Béhar, M., and Viteri, F.: Supplementation of cereal proteins with amino acids. I. Effect of amino acid supplementation of corn-masa at high levels of protein intake on the nitrogen retention of young children. J. Nutr. *66*:485, 1958.

Scriver, C. R., and Davies, E.: Endogenous renal clearance rates of free amino acids in pre-pubertal children. (Employing an accelerated procedure for elution chromatography of basic amino acids on ion exchange resin). Pediatrics *36*:592, 1965.

Scriver, C. R., and Rosenberg, L. E.: Amino Acid Metabolism and its Disorders. Philadelphia, W. B. Saunders Co., 1973.

Snyderman, S. E.: The protein and amino acid requirements of the premature infant. *In* Jonxis, J. H. P., Visser, H. K. A., and Troelstra, J. A. (eds.): Nutricia Symposium: Metabolic Processes in the Foetus and Newborn Infant. Leiden, Stenfert Korese, 1971, p. 128.

Snyderman, S. E., Boyer, A., Roitman, E., Holt, L. E., Jr., and Prose, P. H.: The histidine requirement of the infant. Pediatrics *31*:786, 1963.

Snyderman, S. E., Holt, L. E., Jr., Dancis, J., Roitman, E., Boyer, A., and Balis, M. E.: "Unessential" nitrogen: a limiting factor for human growth. J. Nutr. *78*:57, 1962.

Snyderman, S. E., Holt, L. E., Jr., Norton, P. M., Roitman, E., and Phansalkar, S. V.: The plasma aminogram. I. Influence of the level of protein intake and a comparison of whole protein and amino acid diets. Pediatr. Res. 2:131, 1968.

Soupart, P.: Free amino acids of blood and urine in the human. *In* Holden, J. T. (ed.): Amino Acid Pools. Amsterdam, Elsevier, 1962, p. 220.

Swendseid, M. E., Tuttle, S. G., Figueroa, W. S., Mulcare, D., Clark, A. J., and Massey, F. J.: Plasma amino acid levels of men fed diets differing in protein content. Some observations with valine-deficient diets. J. Nutr. *88*:239, 1966.

Tomarelli, R. M., and Bernhart, F. W.: Biological assay of milk and whey protein compositions for infant feeding. J. Nutr. *78*:44, 1962.

Tomarelli, R. M., Linden, E., Durbin, G. T., and Bernhart, F. W.: The effect of mucin on the growth of rats fed simulated human milk. J. Nutr. *51*:251, 1953.

Valle-Riestra, J., and Barnes, R. H.: Digestion of heat-damaged egg albumen by the rat. J. Nutr. *100*:873, 1970.

Wallace, W. M.: Nitrogen content of the body and its relation to retention and loss of nitrogen. Fed. Proc. *18*:1125, 1959.

Waterlow, J. C., and Alleyne, G. A. O.: Protein malnutrition in children: advances in knowledge in the last ten years. *In* Anfinsen, C. B., Jr., Edsall, J. T., and Richards, F. M. (eds.): Advances in Protein Chemistry. Vol. 25. New York and London, Academic Press, 1971, p. 117.

Waterlow, J. C., and Wills, V. G.: Balance studies in malnourished Jamaican infants. I. Absorption and retention of nitrogen and phosphorus. Br. J. Nutr. *14*:183, 1960.

Weech, A. A.: Dietary protein and the regeneration of serum albumin: IV. The potency values of dried beef serum, whole egg, cow's milk, cow's colostrum, lactalbumin, and wheat gluten. Johns Hopkins Med. J. *70*:157, 1942.

Weller, L. A., Margen, S., and Calloway, D. H.: Variation in fasting and postprandial amino acids of men fed adequate or protein-free diets. Amer. J. Clin. Nutr. *22*:1577, 1969.

Whitehead, R. G., and Dean, R. F. A.: Serum amino acids in kwashiorkor. I. Relationship to clinical condition. Amer. J. Clin. Nutr. *14*:313, 1964.

Whitehead, R. G., Frood, J. D. L., and Poskitt, E. M. E.: Value of serum-albumin measurements in nutritional surveys. A reappraisal. Lancet *1*:287, 1971.

Whitehead, R. G., and Harland, P. S. E. G.: Blood glucose, lactate and pyruvate in kwashiorkor. Br. J. Nutr. *20*:825, 1966.

Williams, C. M.: Effect of different feeding on blood urea levels in prematurity. Med. J. Aust. 2:698, 1963.

Wittmann, W., and Hansen, J. D. L.: Gastroenteritis and malnutrition. S. Afr. Med. J. *39*:223, 1965.

Wittmann, W., Moodie, A. D., Fellingham, S. A., and Hansen, J. D. L.: An evaluation of the relationship between nutritional status and infection by means of a field study. S. Afr. Med J. *41*:664, 1967.

Young, V. R., and Scrimshaw, N. S.: Endogenous nitrogen metabolism and plasma free amino acids in young adults given a "protein-free" diet. Br. J. Nutr. *22*:9, 1968.

7

FAT

During the past 20 years, a number of separate considerations have increased the interest of physicians and nutritionists in the amount and type of fat in the diets of infants and children. Various questions remain unanswered or answered only in part: Why is the fat of human milk so much better absorbed by the infant than is the fat of cow milk? What is the desirable range of energy intakes in the form of fat? What is the desirable intake of essential fatty acids? Because human milk and the milks of most other mammals are relatively rich sources of cholesterol, is it possible that cholesterol is an essential nutrient for the human infant? If so, what adverse consequences might result from current practices of feeding cholesterol-free formulas? Should attempts to prevent atherosclerosis begin during infancy? What methods of screening and management are desirable in relation to familial hypercholesterolemia?

The present chapter will review information relative to these questions.

TERMINOLOGY AND CHEMISTRY

Fats (or lipids) include an array of rather dissimilar organic compounds that have been grouped together on the basis of their solubility in such "fat solvents" as chloroform, ether, benzene and acetone. Most separated (visible) natural fats are made up of about 98 to 99 per cent triglycerides. The remaining 1 or 2 per cent includes phospholipids, free fatty acids, monoglycerides, diglycerides, cholesterol and other nonsaponifiable matter.

Triglycerides

The triglyceride molecule consists of about 95 per cent (by weight) fatty acids and 5 per cent glycerol (Fig. 7–1). Triglycerides usually contain at least two and commonly three different fatty acids. Ordinarily, both saturated and unsaturated fatty acids are included in food fats, and most fats contain at least eight fatty acids attached in various positions to the glyceride molecule. These positions are numbered 1 (terminal) and 2 (interior)—a point of some importance because, as will be discussed subsequently, palmitic acid is well absorbed from the 2-position but poorly absorbed from the 1-position. Data on the positions of fatty acids in triglycerides of various food fats have been summarized by Coleman (1963) and Hilditch and Williams (1964), but much additional information on this point is needed.

Trace amounts of the mono- and diglycerides and of free fatty acids are present in natural fats; within the body, these lipids are found during digestion and absorption and are present in the circulating lipids of the plasma.

Phospholipids

Although visible fat contains only a small amount of phospholipids, these compounds are essential components of cell membranes

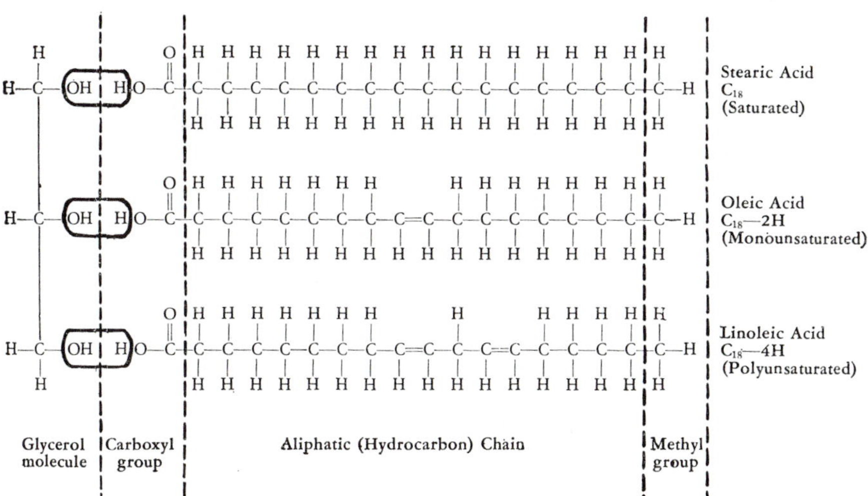

Figure 7–1 Structure of a mixed triglyceride. (From Coons, C. M.: Fats and fatty acids. *In* Stefferud, A. (ed.): Food. The Yearbook of Agriculture, 1959. Washington, D.C., U.S. Government Printing Office, 1959, pp. 74–87.)

and of various other cellular components. They form a large percentage of lipids of serum, and are important in absorption and transport of fatty acids. Phospholipids contain phosphoric acid esterified with glycerol or sphingosine. The most prevalent compounds of this group in animal tissues are the lecithins, composed of glycerol, two fatty acids in ester linkage, phosphoric acid and choline.

Nonsaponifiable Lipids

When lipids are treated with alkali, fatty acids and phosphoric acid are split from the glycerol molecule—a process known as saponification. Sterols and a few compounds of relatively little nutritional interest may then be separated from the saponified components and are termed "nonsaponifiable lipids." The nonsaponifiable fraction makes up only about 1 per cent of dietary fat but may comprise a considerably higher percentage of fecal fat.

Fatty Acids

Naturally occurring fatty acids may contain from four to about 24 carbon atoms in a molecule; most prevalent are long-chain fatty acids, which contain 12 or more carbon atoms; of these, fatty acids with 16 or 18 carbon atoms predominate. About 51 per cent of the fatty acids of human milk and 43 per cent of the fatty acids of cow milk have 18 carbons in the chain. Triglycerides with long-chain fatty acids yield approximately 9 kcal/gm on combustion. Medium-chain triglycerides, containing 8 to 12 carbon atoms in the chains, yield 8.3 kcal/gm and, although not prevalent in food fats, are of considerable interest because they are more readily absorbed than triglycerides of longer chain fatty acids. Short-chain triglycerides, containing four to six carbon atoms in the chains, are not abundant in food fats; they yield only 5.3 kcal/gm.

Fatty acids are classified according to the number of reactive (unsaturated or "double-bond") linkages between the carbon atoms. Saturated fatty acids, those devoid of double bonds, are rather stable chemically and account for much of the firmness of fats at room temperature. The most common saturated fatty acids in natural fats are palmitic (16 carbon atoms) and stearic (18 carbon atoms).

Monounsaturated fatty acids (monoenoic) are those with one reactive, unsaturated ("double-bond") linkage—i.e., two hydrogen atoms missing. Oleic acid, with one double-bond linkage and 18 carbon atoms, furnishes approximately one-third of all the fatty acids in human milk and cow milk (Table 7–1). Polyunsaturated fatty acids are

TABLE 7–1 FATTY ACID COMPOSITION OF SELECTED ANIMAL AND VEGETABLE FATS*

	Saturated							Unsaturated					
	4:0–8:0	*10:0*	*12:0*	*14:0*	*16:0*	*18:0*	*20:0†*	*16:1*	*18:1*	*18:2*	*18:3*	*20:4*	Reference
Human milk		1.5	7.0	8.5	21.0	7.0	1.0	2.5	36.0	7.0	1.0	0.5	Food and Nutrition Board (1966)
Cow milk	5.5	3.0	3.5	12.0	28.0	13.0		3.0	28.5	1.0			Food and Nutrition Board (1966)
Goat milk‡	8.2	8.4	3.3	10.3	24.6	12.5		2.2	28.5	2.2			Glass et al. (1967)
Lard				1.5	27.0	13.5		3.0	43.5	10.5	0.5		Food and Nutrition Board (1966)
Chicken			2.0	7.0	25.0	6.0		8.0	36.0	14.0			Food and Nutrition Board (1966)
Egg					25.0	10.0			50.0	10.0	2.0	3.0	Food and Nutrition Board (1966)
Beef				3.0	29.0	21.0	0.5	3.0	41.0	2.0	0.5	0.5	Food and Nutrition Board (1966)
Oleo oils			0.2	3.3	26.0	20.0			45.5	3.0	0.5		Silverio (1973)
Corn					13.0	4.0	trace		29.0	54.0			Fedeli and Jacini (1971)
Coconut	7.0	6.0	49.5	19.5	8.5	2.0	trace		6.0	1.5			Food and Nutrition Board (1966)
Soy				trace	11.0	4.0	trace		25.0	51.0	9.0		Fedeli and Jacini (1971)
Cotton				1.0	29.0	4.0	trace	2.0	24.0	40.0			Fedeli and Jacini (1971)
Peanut				trace	6.0	5.0	6.0	trace	61.0	22.0			Fedeli and Jacini (1971)
Olive				trace	14.0	2.0	trace	2.0	64.0	16.0			Fedeli and Jacini (1971)
Palm				1.0	48.0	4.0			38.0	9.0			Fedeli and Jacini (1971)
Sunflower					11.0	6.0			29.0	52.0			Fedeli and Jacini (1971)
Sesame					10.0	5.0			40.0	45.0			Fedeli and Jacini (1971)
Safflower				trace	8.0	3.0	trace		13.0	75.0	1.0		Fedeli and Jacini (1971)
Safflower ("high oleic")		0.1	0.8	0.4	6.0	2.0	0.2	0.1	75.8	15.0	0.2		Silverio (1973)

*Composition is given in percentage by weight as determined by gas chromatography. Values are considered representative; however, considerable variation is to be anticipated from sample to sample.

†Includes small amounts of longer chain saturated fatty acids.

‡Also small amounts of other fatty acids.

classed as dienoic, trienoic and tetraenoic, depending on the number of double-bond linkages. Of greatest interest are linoleic acid (18 carbon atoms, two double bonds), arachidonic (20 carbon atoms, four double bonds) and linolenic (18 carbon atoms, three double bonds).

The position of unsaturation influences the point of breakup of the chain in metabolism and the ability of the body to modify the molecule and to metabolize the remaining fragments. In addition, the shape of the molecule is of nutritional significance. As polyunsaturated fatty acids normally occur in unprocessed foods, the fatty acid molecule is folded upon itself at each of the double bonds (called the cis configuration). During the course of processing, the cis form may be converted to the trans (unfolded) form, thereby acquiring different nutritional properties. For example, when linoleic acid is converted from the cis to the trans form, it becomes ineffective as an essential fatty acid. Positions of the carbon atoms in fatty acids are numbered successively beginning at the carboxyl (acid) end of the chain, which attaches to the glycerol (Fig. 7–1). The position of the double bond carries the number of the first of the two carbons that it joins. Most common fatty acids with a single unsaturated linkage, including oleic, have this double bond in the 9-position, that is, between the ninth and tenth carbons. Unsaturated linkages of linoleic acid are in the 9 and 12 positions.

As indicated in Table 7–1, the fatty acid composition of common food fats is extremely variable. Most vegetable fats are rich in polyunsaturated fatty acids, although coconut oil consists primarily of medium- and short-chain saturated fatty acids. Palm oil contains a high percentage of palmitic acid (saturated, C-16) and is a poor source of polyunsaturated fatty acids. Genetic differences may account for variations in fatty acid composition of vegetable oils. Examples of a conventional safflower oil and a "high-oleic" safflower oil are given in Table 7–1. Most animal fats are rather poor sources of polyunsaturated fatty acids, although poultry is a relatively good source of linoleic acid. The fatty acid composition of fat in nonruminant animals is markedly influenced by diet; linoleic acid content of lard, for example, varies from a few per cent to more than 30 per cent of total fatty acids. Fish oils are rich in polyunsaturated fatty acids but are poor sources of essential fatty acids.

DIGESTION AND ABSORPTION

By far the largest proportion of the dietary fat consumed both by adults and by infants is in the form of triglycerides of long-chain fatty acids (referred to as long-chain triglycerides). Triglycerides of medium-chain fatty acids, although present in exceedingly small amounts in normal diets, are of considerable importance in managing specific disorders. The digestion and absorption of long-chain and medium-chain triglycerides differ and will be considered separately.

Long-Chain Triglycerides

With few exceptions, several steps are necessary before long-chain triglycerides of the diet can enter the cells of the intestinal mucosa: The fat must be emulsified and hydrolyzed and the products of hydrolysis made soluble in the aqueous phase of the intestinal contents (Senior, 1964; Simmonds, 1969; Holt, 1972). Emulsification consists of converting large fat globules into small, stable droplets—a process presumably depending on the mechanical energy provided by gastrointestinal motility and reduced surface tension that occurs in the presence of bile acids, monoglycerides, fatty acids and lecithin. The hydrolysis of the ester bonds in the 1-position of long-chain triglycerides results in the formation of 2-monoglycerides and fatty acids. Although pancreatic juice contains a lipase capable of hydrolyzing 2-monoglycerides, little hydrolysis of 2-monoglycerides ordinarily occurs (Simmonds, 1969; Hofman, 1973). Absorption therefore primarily concerns fatty acids and 2-monoglycerides.

It is generally believed that the major role of the bile salts resides in their capacity for solubilizing fatty acids, monoglycerides, cholesterol and various fat-soluble vitamins, including D and K (Schiff and Dietschy, 1969; Hofman, 1973). Because one portion of a bile salt molecule is relatively water soluble while another portion is relatively lipid soluble, they are able to perform as surface-active agents, forming macromolecular aggregates called micelles. From these micelles, fatty acids and monoglycerides are transferred into the intestinal mucosal cell (Figs. 7–2 and 7–3). The bile acids themselves continue distally in the small intestine and the majority are eventually reabsorbed, sometimes after chemical alteration by intestinal bacteria (Schiff and Dietschy, 1969). They are then transported to the liver and eventually reappear in the bile.

Among the long-chain fatty acids, unsaturated fatty acids undergo absorption more readily than do saturated fatty acids. Stearic acid is particularly poorly absorbed by the infant. In the case of palmitic acid, the position of the fatty acid on the triglyceride molecule is of great importance with respect to absorption (Renner and Hill, 1961; Mattson and Volpenhein, 1962; Tomarelli et al., 1968; Filer et al., 1969). The 2-monoglyceride of palmitic acid is well absorbed, whereas free palmitic acid is poorly absorbed (Mattson and Volpenhein, 1962). The extent to which the position of palmitic acid in the triglyceride may influence fat absorption by human infants may be seen from an experi-

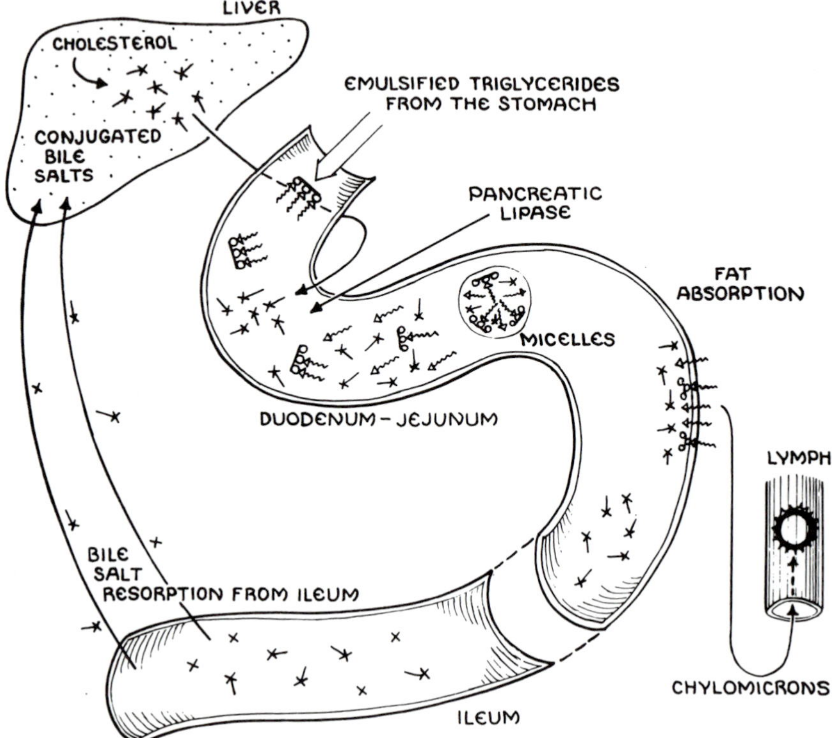

Figure 7–2 A scheme of intraluminal micelle formation, fat and bile salt absorption: ✕—, conjugated bile salt; x, unconjugated bile salt; ◁~~, free fatty acid; ooo, free glycerol. (From Senior, J. R.: Intestinal absorption of fats. J. Lipid Res. *5*:495, 1964.)

ment by Filer et al. (1969), in which young infants were fed formulas of identical composition except for the arrangement of fatty acids in the triglycerides. Results of this study are presented in Figure 7–4.

One formula contained natural lard (84 per cent of the palmitic acid esterified in the 2-position of the triglyceride molecule) and the other contained "randomized lard." Randomized lard is transesterified so that the palmitic acid is equally distributed between the three sites of esterification in the triglyceride molecule. It is apparent that after hydrolysis of these fats by pancreatic lipase, most of the palmitic acid of natural lard would be the readily absorbable 2-monopalmitin, whereas most of the palmitic acid of randomized lard would exist as the poorly absorbed free fatty acid. As may be seen from Figure 7–4, natural lard was much better absorbed than was randomized lard.

Presumably, the location of palmitic acid in the triglyceride molecule explains, in part, the better absorption of human milk fat than of butterfat. This will be discussed later in the chapter.

Once having entered the mucosal cell, the long-chain fatty acids

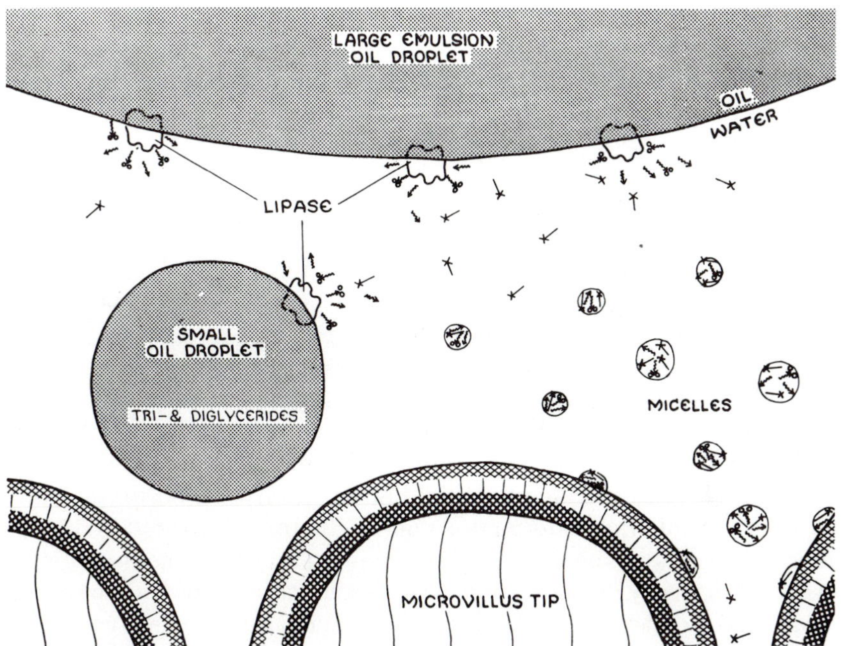

Figure 7–3 Microvillus' eye view of fat absorption. The comparative "appearance" of oil droplets versus micelles. Symbols as in Figure 7–2. (From Senior, J. R.: Intestinal absorption of fats. J. Lipid Res. *5*:495, 1964.)

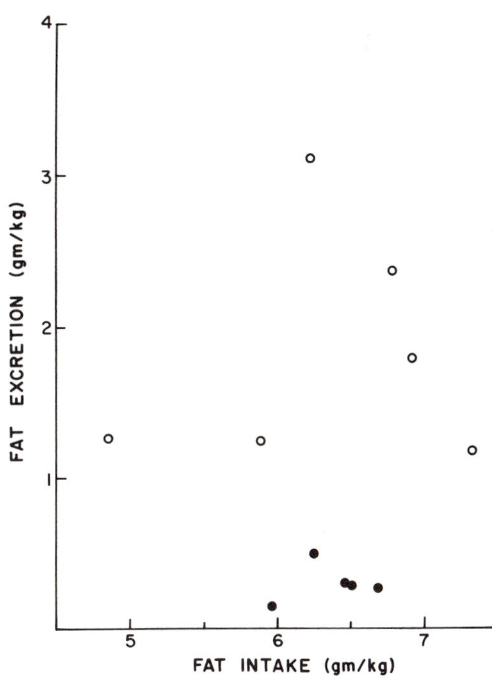

Figure 7–4 Excretion of fat in relation to intake of fat by normal fullterm infants between 4 and 10 days of age. Each symbol indicates the result of one three-day metabolic balance study by an infant fed an experimental formula with fat supplied as natural lard (*black dots*) or randomized lard (*open circles*). (Data of Filer et al., 1969.)

and monoglycerides are reesterified into triglycerides, then combined with protein, phospholipid and cholesterol into chylomicrons or very low density lipoproteins. In this form, they enter the intestinal lymphatics, thoracic duct and peripheral circulation.

Medium-Chain Triglycerides

For several reasons, triglycerides of medium-chain fatty acids are more readily digested and absorbed than are triglycerides of long-chain fatty acids. Pancreatic lipase is more active in hydrolyzing the 1-ester bonds of medium-chain than of long-chain triglycerides (Desnuelle and Savary, 1963) and, in addition, there may be a gastric lipase effective in hydrolyzing medium-chain triglycerides (Holt, 1968). Because of the relatively good solubility of medium-chain fatty acids in the aqueous phase of the intestinal lumen, absorption occurs without the necessity of micelle formation and can therefore proceed in the absence of bile salts and 2-monoglycerides. In addition, medium-chain triglycerides may be absorbed into the mucosal cell without prior lipolysis (Isselbacher, 1968; Clark, 1968), and it has been estimated by Holt (1968) that the extent of such absorption could be sufficient to account for the efficacy of therapy with medium-chain triglycerides in pancreatic disease. However, most patients with pancreatic disease maintain some intraluminal lipolytic activity, and the rapid rate of hydrolysis of medium-chain triglycerides may, in most instances, be more important than absorption of intact medium-chain triglycerides.

Medium-chain fatty acids are bound to albumin and transported from the mucosal cell directly into the portal blood; therefore, reesterification within the mucosal cell is not required. Neither is the formation of chylomicrons required. On the basis of one or more of the characteristics mentioned, medium-chain triglycerides have been found useful in a variety of pancreatic, hepatic, biliary and intestinal disorders (Senior, 1968). They are readily absorbed by fullterm newborn (Ziegler et al., 1972) and by premature (Tantibhedhyangkul and Hashim, 1971) infants.

Short-Chain Triglycerides

Triglycerides of short-chain fatty acids have been shown by Snyderman et al. (1955) to be well absorbed by infants. However, because of their chemical instability and their low caloric density (5.3 kcal/gm), they are of less practical value than medium-chain triglycerides.

DESIRABLE INTAKES OF FAT

Although it may prove possible to manage infants satisfactorily with diets providing 1 per cent of calories from linoleic acid and no other fat, little is known about such diets. Diets extremely low in content of fat may be excessive in content of carbohydrate and/or protein. They may also be of low satiety value. If the carbohydrate consists primarily of small molecules (disaccharides and monosaccharides), the osmolality of the feeding will be high and diarrhea may result. Alternatively, diets extremely high in fat and low in carbohydrate content may give rise to ketosis. Wide clinical experience relates primarily to diets providing 30 to 55 per cent of calories from fat. Diets deviating markedly from this range of fat intake should be employed with caution (see Chapter 19).

When skim milk or "2 per cent milk" is fed to infants, the diet will almost certainly be undesirably high in content of protein and carbohydrate and undesirably low in content of fat. Another and probably more important objection to feeding of skim milk to infants is that it results in a deficient intake of calories (see Chapter 2).

EXTENT OF ABSORPTION OF VARIOUS FATS

The extent of absorption of fat from human milk, from cow milk and from various formulas containing butterfat or vegetable oils has been studied by a number of investigators with normal fullterm infants and with low-birth-weight infants. The difficulty in assembling homogeneous groups of low-birth-weight infants is substantial. Studies of fullterm newborn infants are likely to offer less between-subject variability.

Fullterm Newborn Infants

Digestibility of various fats has been studied in 4- to 10-day-old infants by a number of investigators (Guilbert et al., 1955; Welsch et al., 1965; Widdowson, 1965; Southgate et al., 1969; Filer et al., 1969; Williams et al., 1970; Hanna et al., 1970). Fat is generally less well absorbed by newborn infants than by older infants, but it is not entirely clear why this is so (Chapter 4). With the exception of Williams et al. (1970), who reported somewhat lower absorption (possibly because pooled human milk was frozen and subsequently thawed and autoclaved), it has generally been found that newborn infants absorb 85 to 90 per cent of human milk fat. Our own observations of newborn infants fed milk-based formulas (Ziegler et al., 1972) indicate that butterfat is poorly absorbed, whereas mixtures of corn and coconut oils with or without soy oil or medium-chain triglycerides are absorbed nearly to the same extent as the fat of human milk. Corn and coconut oils or soy oil are well absorbed from some soy-based formulas and poorly absorbed from others. Thus, presumably, different methods of processing (or minor differences in other components of the formula) influence absorption of fats.

The infant formula, SMA (Wyeth Laboratories), includes oleo oils (destearinated beef fat) as a part of the mixture of fats. This was true also of an earlier formulation of Enfamil (Mead Johnson Company). Data from metabolic balance studies by various investigators appear to give inconsistent results with these formulas. Widdowson (1965) and Southgate et al. (1969) reported lower absorptions of a mixture of oleo and vegetable oils (a fat mixture used in SMA in the 1960s) than those observed by Williams et al. (1970). The most recent formulation of SMA includes safflower oil with high oleic acid content (Table 7–1), oleo oils, corn and coconut oils. Fat of this formula has been reported by Williams et al. (1970) to be well absorbed, and our unpublished observations confirm these results. Because stearic and palmitic acids (mainly contributed by the oleo oils) contribute 8.4 and 13.5 per cent by weight of the fatty acids, respectively, of this formula, and because most of the palmitic acid is in the 1-position of the triglyceride, it is not clear why this fat is relatively well absorbed. The high oleic acid content (39.5 per cent by weight of the fatty acids) may be involved in this unexpectedly good absorption.

Infants Beyond the Newborn Period

Results of metabolic balance studies with normal fullterm infants between 8 and 180 days of age are summarized in Figures 7–5 and 7–6 and in Tables 7–2 and 7–3. It is apparent that human milk and most vegetable oils are well absorbed, whereas butterfat is relatively poorly absorbed.

The better absorption of human milk fat than of butterfat appears to be explained more by triglyceride arrangement of the fatty acids than by percentages of fat accounted for by individual fatty acids. Palmitic acid accounts for a substantial percentage of the weight of total fatty acids of each of these fats (Table 7–1) but, in butterfat, is nearly equally distributed among the three positions of the triglyceride molecule, whereas the palmitic acid in human milk is primarily esterified in the 2-position (Freeman et al., 1965).

If 50 per cent of calorie intake is derived from butterfat, as in the case of infants whose entire calorie intake is obtained from whole cow milk, fecal losses of fat will generally be sufficiently great to result in

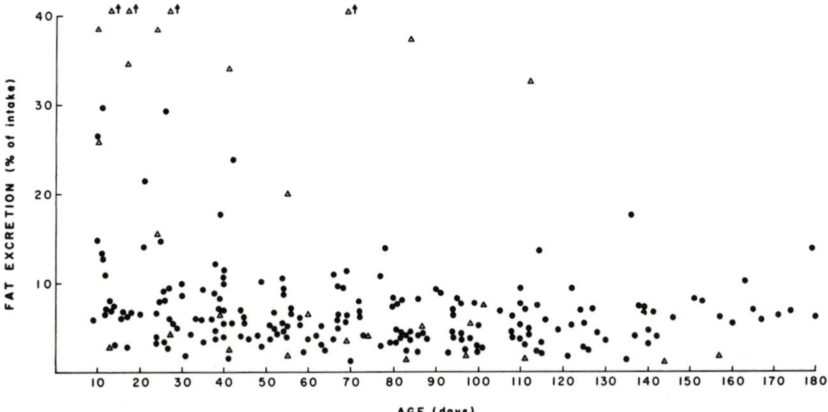

Figure 7–5 Fat excretion (per cent of intake) in relation to age of infants fed formulas in which the fat consisted of vegetable oils. Each point indicates the result of one three-day metabolic balance study. Each triangle refers to excretion by an infant fed Formula 29A (an experimental soy isolate-based formula with a mixture of corn and coconut oils); each black dot refers to excretion by an infant fed one of six other formulas. Arrow next to symbol indicates that the value is greater than that shown on the ordinate. (From Fomon, S. J., et al.: Excretion of fat by normal full-term infants fed various milks and formulas. Amer. J. Clin. Nutr. *23*:1299, 1970.)

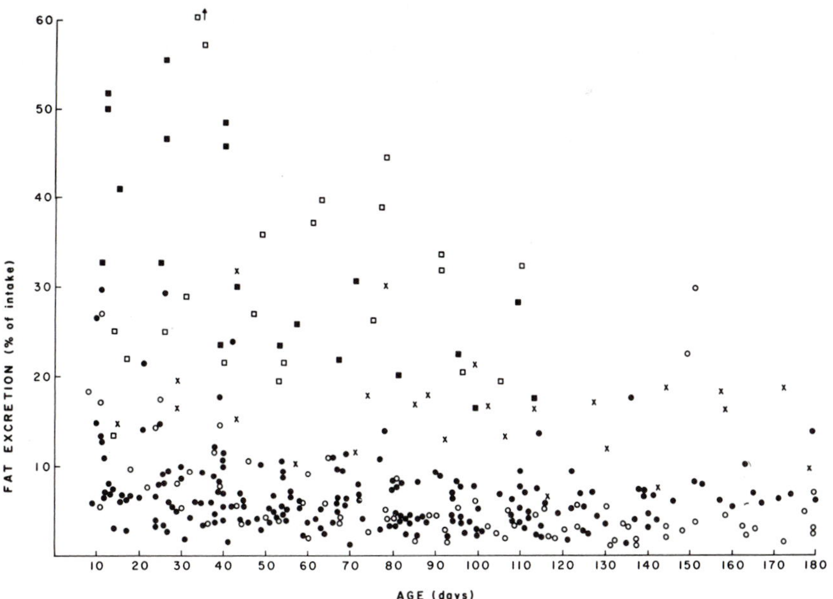

Figure 7–6 Fat excretion (per cent of intake) in relation to age of infants fed various milks and formulas. Each point indicates the result of one three-day metabolic balance study. Symbols distinguish between the different milks or formulas: *open circles,* processed human milk; *open squares,* homogenized milk; *x,* evaporated milk; *black squares,* a formula with butterfat; *black dots,* formulas (except Formula 29A) in which fat consisted of vegetable oils. Arrow next to a symbol indicates that value is greater than that shown on the ordinate. (From Fomon, S. J., et al.: Excretion of fat by normal full-term infants fed various milks and formulas. Amer. J. Clin. Nutr. *23*:1299, 1970.)

TABLE 7–2 DAILY EXCRETIONS OF FAT BY NORMAL FULLTERM INFANTS BETWEEN 8 AND 180 DAYS OF AGE

Selected Reports from Literature*

Number of Infants	Number of Studies	Age Range (days)	Weight Range (gm)	Intake of Fat (gm/kg)	Excretion of Fat (gm/kg)	Excretion of Fat (% of Intake)	Comments	References
				Human Milk				
1	2	70–77	4300–4350	6.78 (6.26–7.30)†	0.45 (0.35-0.55)	6.6 (5.7–7.5)		Lindberg (1917)
5	7	21–120				5.5 (0.8–9.7)		Holt et al. (1919a)
2	2	105–111	5310–5330	6.25 (5.87–6.63)	0.19 (0.15–0.23)	3.0 (2.5–3.5)		Malmberg (1922–1923)
4	5	50–120	4210–6100	5.73 (4.78–6.94)	0.18 (0.14–0.28)	3.3 (2.6–4.0)		Muhl (1924)
4	4	115–150	4150–6650	4.23 (3.67–5.42)	0.19 (0.10–0.27)	4.8 (2.5–7.1)		Holt et al. (1935)
3	4	19–69	4170–5130	5.58 (3.34–7.44)	0.41 (0.12–0.85)	7.5 (2.3–12.7)		Guilbert et al. (1955)
2	2	28–42	3500–3950	5.82 (3.59–7.07)	0.23 (0.11–0.44)	4.0 (1.6–6.2)	Weight range applies to birth	Widdowson (1965)
10	10	11–17	3120–4190	6.72 (5.18–8.26)	0.37 (0.15–0.59)	5.5 (1.9–9.1)	Values in parentheses are ± 2 S.D.	Southgate and Barrett (1966)
				Fresh Fluid Cow Milk, Water and Added Carbohydrate				
5	5	60–180	3450–6860	3.82 (2.31–5.65)	0.47 (0.10–0.78)	15.6 (4.3–16.5)		Holt et al. (1919b)

3	4	22–180	3430–4400	5.91 (5.42–6.37)	0.82 (0.65–1.02)	14.0 (10.2–17.6)	Unhomogenized milk	Holt et al. (1935)
12	16	30–175	3550–6650	5.13 (3.59–6.52)	0.64 (0.33–1.00)	12.4 (8.7–17.3)	Homogenized milk	Holt et al. (1935)
11		8–80		(2.00–3.10)		(19.0–27.0)	Continuous balances	Droese and Stolley (1961)
Dried Cow Milk and Added Carbohydrate								
2	2	120	3662–5055	3.39 (3.11–3.66)	0.46 (0.34–0.57)	13.2 (11.0–15.4)		Holt et al. (1919b)
6	6	13–70	3520–4080	4.85 (4.30–5.20)	1.20 (0.60–2.00)	24.7 (14.0–30.0)		Gordon and McNamara (1941)
6	6	35–63	3200–4670	7.42 (6.50–8.44)	0.43 (0.31–0.59)	5.7 (4.8–8.3)		Joppich et al. (1959)
10	10	11–22	2910–4060	5.01 (4.09–5.93)	0.73 (0.35–1.11)	14.6 (10.2–17.6)	Values in parentheses are ± 2 S.D.	Southgate and Barrett (1966)
Evaporated Cow Milk, Water and Added Carbohydrate								
11		8–80		(3.10–5.10)		(11.0–18.0)	Continuous balances	Droese and Stolley (1961)
Pelargon								
12	129	14–180		(3.80–4.20)		16.0		Huber and Scheibl (1965)

*Modified slightly from Fomon, S. J., et al.: Excretion of fat by normal fullterm infants fed various milks and formulas. Amer. J. Clin. Nutr. *23*:1299, 1970.

†Values in parentheses indicate range except as noted in Comments column.

TABLE 7–3 DAILY INTAKES AND EXCRETIONS OF FAT BY NORMAL INFANTS FED WHOLE COW MILK*

Subject	Sex	Age Range (days)	Weight Range (kg)	Number of Balance Studies	Intake of Fat (gm/kg)	Excretion of Fat (% of intake)
AH	Male	14–105	3.4–6.2	7	7.76	36
TW	Male	26–54	3.6–4.4	3	6.71	23
KA	Female	14–91	2.9–4.9	3	6.36	30
JA	Female	17–53	2.8–3.8	3	7.24	23
RD	Female	33–110	3.8–6.0	6	7.78	35

*Modified from Fomon, S. J., et al.: Excretion of fat by normal fullterm infants fed various milks and formulas. Amer. J. Clin. Nutr. 23:1299, 1970.

large, bulky, foul-smelling stools and the need for increased food intake to compensate for fecal losses of calories in the form of fat. The extent of fecal losses of fat by five normal infants fed whole cow milk as the sole source of calories may be seen from Table 7–3. Average excretion of fat by individual infants amounted to 23 to 36 per cent of intake of fat—approximately 12 to 18 per cent of calorie intake. The extent to which such fecal losses of fat influenced the quantity of milk consumed and, hence, calorie intake is indicated in Figure 7–7.

If 35 per cent or less of calorie intake is derived from butterfat, excretion of fat will be relatively small. In practical terms, this means that if an infant receives approximately four-fifths of his calorie intake from cow milk and one-fifth from added carbohydrate (e.g., the once widely used formula containing 390 ml (13 oz) evaporated milk, 570 ml (19 oz) water and 45 ml (1½ oz) of corn syrup), fecal loss of calories will not be excessive. However, fecal loss of calories is likely to be undesirably great when whole milk or evaporated milk without added carbohydrate is fed. It is recommended that a change in diet from formula to whole milk be delayed at least until the infant is receiving approximately two jars of commercially prepared strained foods or the equivalent in mashed table foods. Most such foods are rich sources of carbohydrate (Chapter 16).

We have suggested (Fomon et al., 1970b) that excretions of fat greater than 2 gm/kg/day (18 kcal/kg/day) be considered clinically significant. Such excretions will account for more than 15 per cent of calorie intake of most infants. Although it may be anticipated that most normal infants fed ad libitum will compensate for large fecal losses of fat by increasing intake (Fig. 7–7), under these conditions, feces will be large, foul and greasy.

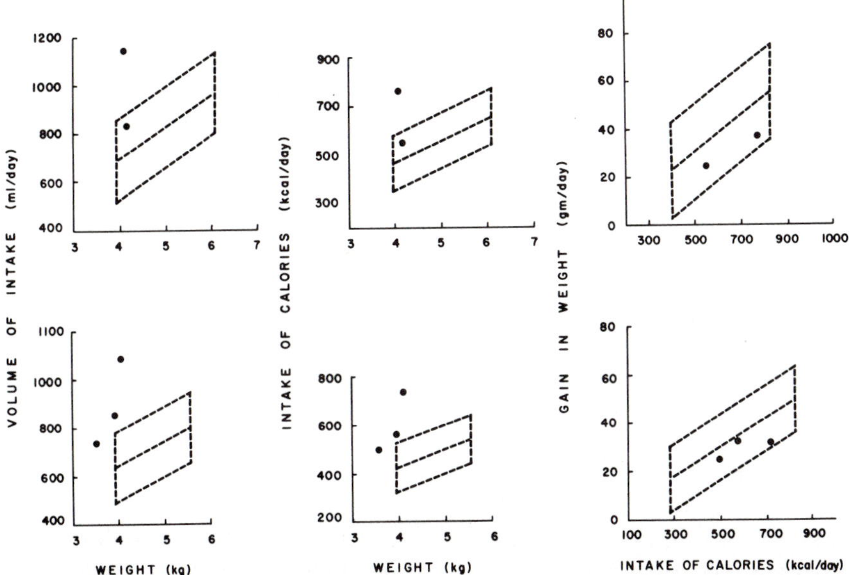

Figure 7–7 Volume of intake and intake of calories in relation to body weight, and gain in weight in relation to intake of calories by normal male (upper series of panels) and female (lower series of panels) infants fed whole cow milk as the sole source of calories during the interval 42 through 55 days of age. The regression lines and 90 per cent confidence limits refer to infants fed milk-based formulas (Fomon et al., 1971).

When adequate calorie intakes are provided from diets that offer no more than 40 per cent of calories from butterfat or no more than 50 per cent of calories from vegetable oils (or vegetable and oleo oils), excretions of fat greater than 2 gm/kg/day may be considered diagnostic of fat malabsorption (Fomon et al., 1970b). When fat malabsorption is demonstrated, especially in the presence of failure to thrive, studies should be undertaken to detect such abnormalities as cystic fibrosis of the pancreas, celiac disease, chronic liver disease or exudative enteropathy.

Low-Birth-Weight Infants

Per unit of body weight, with similar intakes of fat, fecal excretions of fat are greater by low-birth-weight than by fullsize infants. This is true for fats of poor digestibility, such as butterfat, and for readily digestible fats such as human milk fat and soy oil (Tidwell et al., 1935). The relative inability of the low-birth-weight infant to digest fat has been substantiated by a number of investigators (Gordon and Mc-

Namara, 1941; Morales et al., 1950; Davidson and Bauer, 1960; Zoula et al., 1966; Tantibhedhyangkul and Hashim, 1971; Senterre and Lambrechts, 1972; Barltrop and Oppé, 1973). Digestion of fat seems to be about equally impaired in low-birth-weight infants whether small size is the result of prematurity or of intrauterine growth retardation (Barltrop and Oppé, 1973).

TESTS FOR FAT ABSORPTION

When conditions permit, it seems desirable to determine the extent of fat absorption by metabolic balance studies as described in Appendix IV (p. 549). In arriving at a quantitative estimation of fat absorption, such an approach is believed to be preferable to various other absorption tests. However, other absorption tests have the obvious advantages of speed (hours rather than days to complete the test) and more simple methodology.

The Lipiodol test described by Jones and di Sant 'Agnese (1963) is simple and appears to yield useful information, although it does not invariably correspond with results of fecal fat analyses (Hunter et al., 1967). The Lipiodol test described by Neerhout et al. (1964) also appears useful but lacks the simplicity of the test described by Jones and di Sant 'Agnese. Measurement of turbidity of serum after administration of a standardized quantity of butterfat (Goldbloom et al., 1964) may also be of value. When performed under carefully standardized conditions, results obtained with the vitamin A absorption test (Chesney and McCord, 1934) correlate well with those of the butterfat absorption test (Kahan, 1970). However, it is doubtful that either of these tests is more informative than the Lipiodol test.

ESSENTIAL FATTY ACIDS

More than 40 years ago, Burr and Burr (1929) provided evidence of the requirement for fat in the diet of rats. It was subsequently demonstrated that small amounts of linoleic or arachidonic acids were able to correct the deficiency manifestations – scaliness of the skin, loss of hair, emaciation, impairment of growth and of reproductive capacity, increase in intake of food and water, increase in metabolic rate, and death at a relatively early age (Aaes-Jorgensen, 1961) – in rats and other mammals. These two fatty acids were therefore considered to be the essential fatty acids, although it was recognized that some of the manifestations of fatty acid deficiency, notably the skin changes, could be relieved by administration of linolenic acid.*

---

*Only gamma-linolenic acid (double bonds at 6, 9 and 12 positions) is effective in this regard.

More recently, it has been shown that four fatty acids with odd-numbered carbon chain lengths can function as essential fatty acids in rats, correcting or preventing the growth retardation and other symptoms of essential fatty acid deficiency (Schlenk, 1972). These newly recognized essential fatty acids have chain lengths of 19 or 21 carbons and double bonds in positions 8, 11 and 14 or 5, 8, 11 and 14. They, as well as linoleic and arachidonic acids, function as precursors of prostaglandins. It is, in fact, likely that at least some of the manifestations of essential fatty acid deficiency result from impaired ability to synthesize prostaglandins.

Requirement for Essential Fatty Acids

Hansen et al. (1962) demonstrated that evidences of essential fatty acid deficiency can be produced experimentally in the human infant when linoleic acid accounts for less than 0.1 per cent of total caloric intake. In these studies, there was no explanation for the more rapid development of skin manifestations by infants receiving diets nearly devoid of fat than by those receiving a diet equally deficient in linoleic acid but supplying 18 per cent of calories from fat. The possibility that the fat contained small amounts of other essential fatty acids not at that time recognized must be considered.

When linoleic acid comprises about 1 per cent of caloric intake of normal infants, skin manifestations of essential fatty acid deficiency do not appear, and rates of growth are as rapid as those of infants receiving higher intakes of linoleic acid. Although it has been reported (Hansen et al., 1962) that infants receiving 1 per cent of the calories from linoleic acid voluntarily ingest more calories than do infants receiving 4 to 5 per cent of the calories from linoleic acid, the significance of this observation is unknown. It is important to note that studies have not been carried out to indicate whether growth and dermal integrity are different when 0.5 or 0.7 per cent of the calories are supplied as linoleic acid than when 1 per cent of the calories are so supplied.

Triene-Tetraene Ratio

The ratio of concentration of triene to that of tetraene fatty acids in heart muscle, liver and serum of experimental animals has been demonstrated by Holman and co-workers (Holman, 1960; Hill et al., 1961; Caster et al., 1962, 1963) to correlate well with manifestations of essential fatty acid deficiency. This ratio is high in essential fatty acid deficiency and low in normal animals. Holman et al. (1964) demonstrated that in two- to four-month-old infants who had been fed a formula providing less than 0.1 per cent of calories from linoleic acid for one month or more, the triene-tetraene ratio of serum averaged more than 1.5. Infants of the same age fed 1.3 per cent of the calories or more from linoleic acid demonstrated triene-tetraene ratios generally less than 0.4. Utilizing a curve-fitting procedure proposed by Caster et al. (1962), it was concluded that the requirement for linoleic acid by the human infant is approximately 1 per cent of calorie intake.

Whether serum ratios of these fatty acids reflect tissue ratios under all conditions is uncertain. At present, it seems reasonable to conclude that serum concentrations reflect recent dietary intake and not necessarily nutritional status with respect to essential fatty acids.

Atopic Eczema

The suggestion that atopic eczema in infancy may be related to deficiency of essential fatty acids is based on several reports, published more than 20 years ago, which stated that this condition is more common in infants fed formulas of cow milk than in breastfed infants, and on the observation that concentrations of polyunsaturated fatty acids are lower in sera of infants with eczema than in sera of normal infants (Hansen et al., 1962). However, more recent studies have failed to demonstrate a greater incidence of infantile eczema in the formula-fed than in the breastfed infant; furthermore, administration of linoleic acid has not regularly resulted in improvement of eczema. It seems unlikely that atopic eczema is related to deficiency of essential fatty acids.

PROSTAGLANDINS

Prostaglandins are cyclic, hydroxy fatty acids containing 20 carbon atoms. As already mentioned, they are formed from essential fatty acids, and at least some of the manifestations of essential fatty acid deficiency may be the result of inadequate synthesis of prostaglandins. The chemistry and metabolic functions of prostaglandins have been reviewed by Hinman (1972).

Prostaglandins appear to function mainly on the vascular system, increasing blood flow to various organs when the organs are active and decreasing blood flow when they are inactive. Prostaglandins probably are important also in mediating the inflammatory response and may function in regulation of synaptic pathways within the brain. Prostaglandins appear to be intimately related to cyclic adenosine monophosphate (cAMP), both being involved in modulation of hormonal control and in transport of water and electrolytes across epithelial membranes.

FATTY ACID COMPOSITION OF DIET AND OF ADIPOSE TISSUE

It is well recognized that the fatty acid composition of an animal's depot fat can be modified by dietary means (e.g., Brooks, 1971). The suggestion has been made that the extent of adherence to a diet high in content of polyunsaturated fat can be determined in adults (Dayton et al., 1967) and children (Albutt and Chance, 1969) by analysis of adipose tissue biopsy material. Sweeney et al. (1963), from study of fullterm infants, and Ballabriga et al. (1972), from study of premature infants, demonstrated that by six to eight weeks of age the fatty acid composition of serum and adipose tissue resembled, to some extent, the lipid content of the diet. The medical significance of these observations is unknown.

Hashim and Asfour (1968) have reported serial studies of fatty acid composition of adipose tissue of six infants fed a formula with fat from cottonseed oil, five infants fed evaporated milk formulas and four breastfed infants. Results are presented in Table 7–4. The most impressive differences in fatty acid composition of adipose tissue were in content of linoleic acid. At age one month, linoleic acid ac-

TABLE 7–4 FATTY ACID COMPOSITION OF ADIPOSE TISSUE OF BREASTFED INFANTS AND INFANTS FED FORMULAS WITH COTTONSEED OIL OR EVAPORATED MILK*

	Breastfed				Cottonseed Oil Formula				Evaporated Milk Formula			
	Age (months)				Age (months)				Age (months)			
Fatty Acid	*Birth*	*1*	*2*	*3*	*Birth*	*1*	*2*	*3*	*Birth*	*1*	*2*	*3*
14:0	2.7 (0.1)†	2.8 (0.5)	4.3 (1.3)	5.0 (0.5)	3.4 (0.3)	1.3 (0.4)	1.4 (0.3)	1.6 (2.8)	3.6 (0.2)	6.1 (1.7)	6.5 (1.2)	6.8 (0.9)
14:1	0.6 (0.3)	0.5 (0.2)	0.4 (0.2)	0.4 (0.2)	0.6 (0.6)	0.3 (0.1)	0.1 (0.1)	0.2 (0.1)	0.2 (0.1)	0.5 (0.3)	1.9 (0.8)	1.6 (0.2)
16:0	49.7 (1.1)	44.6 (1.2)	37.3 (4.6)	30.3 (8.4)	53.2 (5.3)	43.1 (12.3)	36.8 (4.5)	27.3 (0.5)	53.0 (4.0)	44.1 (7.5)	37.9 (9.8)	33.4 (3.2)
16:1	9.4 (1.2)	7.3 (1.5)	6.4 (2.3)	4.5 (1.0)	9.6 (0.9)	7.1 (0.9)	5.4 (0.3)	5.2 (0.5)	9.3 (1.1)	8.9 (1.1)	9.8 (0.9)	9.1 (0.4)
18:0	3.7 (0.4)	3.9 (0.9)	3.7 (0.8)	2.5 (1.2)	4.3 (1.3)	3.2 (1.3)	2.4 (0.9)	2.2 (0.7)	4.4 (0.6)	2.7 (1.8)	3.2 (0.3)	4.3 (2.4)
18:1	28.4 (1.2)	32.4 (1.4)	41.6 (6.0)	47.3 (1.9)	26.6 (3.3)	24.5 (1.7)	23.3 (4.4)	26.0 (4.5)	24.4 (1.2)	32.6 (2.6)	37.8 (6.5)	41.9 (6.1)
18:2	1.1 (0.9)	4.0 (0.2)	4.6 (2.1)	6.1 (1.1)	0.7 (0.6)	19.7 (9.0)	30.1 (5.6)	39.3 (2.8)	0.7 (0.5)	1.3 (0.7)	1.4 (0.3)	1.1 (0.6)

*Data of Hashim and Asfour (1968).
†Values in parentheses are standard deviations.

counted for 19.7, 1.3 and 4.0 per cent, respectively, of fatty acids in adipose tissue of infants fed the cottonseed oil formula, the evaporated milk formula and in those who were breastfed. By age three months, corresponding values were 39.3, 1.1 and 6.1 per cent.

SERUM CONCENTRATION OF CHOLESTEROL

Concentration of cholesterol in plasma or serum of the infant's cord blood is almost invariably lower than that of maternal blood (Glueck et al., 1971; Barnes et al., 1972). A small but statistically significant sex-related difference (concentration of cholesterol greater in plasma of females) has been demonstrated (Table 7–5). It has been suggested that concentration of cholesterol greater than 100 mg/100 ml (Glueck et al., 1971) or greater than 115 mg/100 ml (Barnes et al., 1972) in plasma or serum of cord blood be considered abnormal. The value of routine screening of newborn infants by determining cholesterol content of cord blood as a means of detecting type II hyperlipoproteinemia (familial hypercholesterolemia) has not yet been demonstrated. Among infants examined by Darmady et al. (1972), concentrations of cholesterol greater than 100 mg/100 ml in cord blood had relatively little predictive value with respect to serum concentrations at age one year.

Serum concentrations of cholesterol increase after birth and, as may be seen from Tables 7–6 and 7–7, the extent of the increase is related to type of feeding. Among breastfed infants, serum concentrations of cholesterol were found to be greater in females than in males (Chapter 19, Table 19–1). A similar sex-related difference has been observed in infant sow-reared pigs (Filer et al., 1973). Feeding of formulas with the fat in the form of butterfat results in serum concen-

TABLE 7–5 PLASMA CONCENTRATION OF CHOLESTEROL OF UMBILICAL CORD BLOOD*

		Cholesterol (mg/100 ml)	
Sex	Number of Infants	*Mean*	*S.D.*
Male	368	73.6	18.2
Female	379	78.5	20.4

*Modified slightly from Barnes, K., et al.: Neonatal plasma lipids. Med. J. Aust. 2:1002, 1972. The sex-related difference is statistically significant ($p<0.001$).

TABLE 7–6 SERUM CONCENTRATION OF CHOLESTEROL OF SIX-WEEK-OLD INFANTS IN RELATION TO FEEDING*

Feeding	Fat	Number of Infants	Cholesterol (mg/100 ml)	
			Mean	*S.D.*
Human milk	Human milk	24	175	29
Cow milk formula	Butterfat	148	158	26
SMA	Vegetable and oleo oils	19	129	27

*Data of Darmady et al. (1972).

trations of cholesterol nearly equal to those of breastfed infants, whereas feeding of formulas with fat in the form of vegetable oils or of a mixture of vegetable and oleo oils results in much lower concentrations.

That serum concentrations of cholesterol may be high in preschool children is apparent from the data of Owen et al. (1974). Of 667 children 12 to 36 months of age, serum concentrations of cholesterol were greater than 189 mg/100 ml in 13 per cent and greater than 204 mg/100 ml in 4 per cent. Of 1277 children 36 to 71 months of age, serum concentrations of cholesterol were greater than 204 mg/100 ml in 6.5 per cent.

TABLE 7–7 SERUM CONCENTRATION OF CHOLESTEROL OF MALE INFANTS AT AGES 56 AND 112 DAYS

Nature of Feeding	Age 56 Days			Age 112 Days		
	N	*Mean*	*S.D.*	*N*	*Mean*	*S.D.*
Breastfed*	24	125	20	23	133	26
Milk-based formulas†	41	102	25	47	113	29
Soy-based formulas	23	110	19	23	121	32

*Breastfed infants were managed as described by Fomon et al. (1970a). Concentrations of cholesterol are greater in breastfed females (Table 19–1).

†Data concerning infants fed milk-based and soy-based formulas are unpublished values from Pediatric Metabolic Unit, University of Iowa. Management of infants fed milk-based formulas has been described (Fomon et al., 1971). Infants fed soy-based formulas were managed in the same manner.

Is Cholesterol an Essential Nutrient for the Newborn Infant?

There is no question that the newborn infant can synthesize cholesterol. In the brain of the human fetus, synthesis of cholesterol (a component of myelin) appears to occur in situ from glucose (Plotz et al., 1968), and one presumes that after birth exogenous cholesterol is also of little importance in myelination.

Whether the infant is able to synthesize cholesterol sufficiently rapidly to meet his other needs for cholesterol is uncertain. Most mammalian milks are rich sources of cholesterol, and animals receiving these milks obtain a generous exogenous supply of cholesterol that could supplement limited endogenous production. It is conceivable that absence of an exogenous supply of cholesterol during early infancy might limit the ability of the infant to synthesize steroid hormones and bile acids. With respect to formation of bile acids, Wilson (1962) has shown that increase in dietary intake of cholesterol by the rat is accompanied by increase in formation of bile acids.

Dietary Management During Early Infancy and Subsequent Serum Concentration of Cholesterol

As discussed subsequently in this chapter, elevated serum concentration of cholesterol during adult life has been identified as a major risk factor with respect to atherosclerosis. Therefore, the influence of dietary management during early infancy on subsequent serum concentration of cholesterol is of interest. Several authors (Hahn and Koldovsky, 1966; Fomon, 1971; Reiser and Sidelman, 1972) have suggested that an exogenous source of cholesterol may be desirable for the human infant. It is conceivable that dietary cholesterol is necessary during early infancy to induce enzyme systems responsible for normal functioning of the feedback mechanism regulating biosynthesis and catabolism of cholesterol. Such an adaptive change occurring during early postnatal life would not be unprecedented. Hahn and Koldovsky (1966) have provided several examples of adaptive changes in infant animals. Two recent studies are of interest with respect to the possibility of such an adaptive change in cholesterol metabolism.

Reiser and Sidelman (1972) have reported a study of rats in which milk of the dams was altered by dietary means to provide mean concentrations of cholesterol of approximately 40 to 50, 30 and 23 mg/100 ml. Pups were weaned at 30 days of age and then given a semi-synthetic diet low in content of cholesterol until age eight months. At that time, serum concentrations of cholesterol of male (but not of female) rats were found to vary inversely with the cholesterol content of the

TABLE 7–8 SERUM CONCENTRATION OF CHOLESTEROL OF MALE RATS WEANED AT 15 OR 30 DAYS OF AGE AND THEN FED A STOCK DIET*

	Cholesterol (mg/100 ml)					
	Weaned at 15 Days			*Weaned at 30 Days*		
Age (days)	*Number*	*Mean*	*S.E.*†	*Number*	*Mean*	*S.E.*
30	4	76	7.3	4	81	1.2
57	4	62	8.2	4	76	7.3
215	5	107	6.3	5	67	5.3

*Modified from Hahn, P., and Kirby, L.: Immediate and late effects of premature weaning and of feeding a high fat or high carbohydrate diet to weanling rats. J. Nutr. *103*:690, 1973.

†Standard error of mean.

milk they had received as infants. Male rats that had received milk with 40 to 50, 30 and 23 mg of cholesterol/100 ml were found, at age eight months, to have serum concentrations of cholesterol of 150, 215 and 250 mg/100 ml, respectively.

Another study suggesting that early management may influence subsequent serum concentration of cholesterol has been reported by Hahn and Kirby (1973). Male rats were weaned at 15 or 30 days of age, then fed a cholesterol-free stock diet. As may be seen from Table 7–8, concentrations of cholesterol in serum of these two groups of rats were similar at ages 30 and 57 days, but concentrations at 215 days of age were significantly greater in the early-weaned rats. In a general manner, these results seem to confirm the earlier and less well documented observations of Kubát (Hahn and Koldovksy, 1966). The data of Reiser and Sidelman (1972), Hahn and Kirby (1973) and Kubát are compatible with the hypothesis that moderate rather than low intakes of cholesterol during infancy are conducive to development of satisfactory regulatory mechanisms for cholesterol metabolism in the adult. Because most infants in the United States and many in other countries are fed formulas free of cholesterol, this area of investigation should be pursued further.

ATHEROSCLEROSIS AS A PEDIATRIC PROBLEM

Although it has been some years since Holman (1961) called attention to atherosclerosis as a pediatric problem, the number of reports and commentaries on this topic since 1970 suggests that atherosclerosis is now of general interest to pediatricians. The report of Inter-Society Commission for Heart Disease Resources (1970), the report by the Committee on Nutrition, American Academy of Pediatrics (1972) and statements by various authors (Mitchell et al., 1972; Fredrickson, 1972; Kannel and Dawber, 1972; Lowe, 1972; Drash, 1972) have helped to put the problem in perspective.

Current knowledge on the topic has been well presented by Kannel and Dawber (1972) and may be summarized as follows: Some evidence of coronary artery atherosclerosis has been reported in at least 45 per cent of young men less than 30 years of age killed in wartime (Rigal et al., 1960; Mason, 1963; McNamara et al., 1971). Thus, although coronary heart disease does not manifest itself clinically until later in adult life, its origins must be in childhood.

The earliest grossly visible lesion is the "fatty streak," representing accumulation of lipid, predominantly cholesterol, in the intima of medium-sized and large arteries. These lipid deposits are chemically similar to lipids of the blood and presumably arise from the blood. Fatty streaks are commonly seen in arteries of preschool children. In some individuals, fatty streaks may spontaneously regress and, under experimental conditions, early lesions may regress almost completely. More advanced lesions include cellular proliferation with resulting fibrous plaques. These become ulcerated, calcified and vascularized so that subsequent regression could, at best, be only partial. Circumstantial evidence is strong that gradual progression ordinarily occurs at least from middle or late childhood through adult life. Aortas of children who have died from cystic fibrosis of the pancreas are relatively free of atherosclerotic changes, presumably because of their lifelong steatorrhea (Holman et al., 1959).

Of the various risk factors, the serum concentration of cholesterol is generally believed to be the most reliable predictor of coronary heart disease (Kannel et al., 1971; Council on Foods and Nutrition, 1972; Connor and Connor, 1972; Drash, 1972). The Committee on Nutrition of the American Academy of Pediatrics (1972) has summarized the evidence relating dietary intake of cholesterol to coronary heart disease as follows: (1) Some inborn and acquired diseases with hypercholesterolemia are associated with premature atherosclerosis. (2) Serum concentrations of cholesterol are frequently relatively high in persons with coronary heart disease. (3) In prospective studies, persons with high serum concentrations of cholesterol are more prone to develop coronary heart disease than are those with lower serum concentrations. (4) The mortality rate from coronary heart disease in different countries varies in relation to average serum concentrations of cholesterol. (5) Experimentally induced hypercholesterolemia in animals is associated with development of atherosclerotic deposits. (6) Atherosclerotic plaques contain lipids similar to those in the blood. To this evidence, one might add that serum concentration of cholesterol is unequivocally related to diet, especially cholesterol content of the diet (Council on Foods and Nutrition, 1972; Connor and Connor, 1972), and some regression of experimentally induced atherosclerotic changes has been reported in rhesus monkeys fed cholesterol-free diets (Armstrong et al., 1970).

It is worth pointing out that none of the statements mentioned previously in relation to atherosclerosis as a pediatric problem have included the recommendation that dietary intervention be imposed on normal infants. In the present state of uncertainty of the later consequences of dietary intervention in infancy, it seems unreasonable to recommend major departure from the model of the breastfed infant. Although breast feeding in developed countries is rarely continued beyond the first few months of life, the "preweaning period" for the human infant may be thought of as extending until 18 to 24 months of age. As already discussed, it is possible that limitation of dietary intake of cholesterol during this period may be harmful.

With respect to adults and adolescents, the circumstantial evidence suggesting harm from long-continued, high intakes of cholesterol seems sufficient to warrant the recommendation to limit dietary intake of cholesterol. No basis has been suggested for believing that such dietary restriction will have a detrimental effect on health. The recommendation for children between infancy (when restriction of cholesterol intake may be unwise) and adolescence (when such restriction is almost certainly desirable) is currently a matter of considerable controversy. Moderate restriction of cholesterol intake of all children beyond infancy seems reasonable. Education regarding the desirable diet during adolescence and adult life must begin in childhood, preferably in early childhood. Screening activities with reference to serum lipid values should be increased, and children with serum concentrations of cholesterol greater than 200 mg/100 ml should remain under medical supervision.

TYPE II HYPERLIPOPROTEINEMIA (FAMILIAL HYPERCHOLESTEROLEMIA)

Of the five types of hyperlipoproteinemia (Fredrickson and Levy, 1972; Levy et al., 1972), only type II (familial hypercholesterolemia) is likely to be diagnosed in infancy. Concentration of cholesterol in serum will be greater than 230 mg/100 ml and electrophoretic analysis of plasma will demonstrate increased concentration of beta lipoproteins. Currently available evidence suggests that type II hyperlipoproteinemia is associated with premature vascular disease, and it has been demonstrated that diets low in concentration of cholesterol and saturated fats and high in polyunsaturated fats will result in moderate decrease in serum concentrations of cholesterol (Fredrickson and Levy, 1972; Levy et al., 1972). In the case of this life-threatening disease, it seems reasonable to begin dietary intervention even in infancy. In doing so, it is worth noting that the diet to be recommended is similar to that fed to the majority of small infants in the United States – that is, commercially prepared formulas with fats from vegetable oils.

REFERENCES

Aaes-Jorgensen, E.: Essential fatty acids. Physiol. Rev. *41*:1, 1961.

Albutt, E. C., and Chance, G. W.: Plasma and adipose tissue fatty acids of diabetic children on long-term corn oil diets. J. Clin. Invest. *48*:139, 1969.

Armstrong, M. L., Warner, E. D., and Connor, W. E.: Regression of coronary atheromatosis in rhesus monkeys. Circ. Res. *27*:59, 1970.

Ballabriga, A., Martinez, A., and Gallart-Catala, A.: Composition of subcutaneous fat depot in prematures in relationship with fat intake. Helv. Paediatr. Acta *27*:91, 1972.

Barltrop, D., and Oppé, T. E.: Absorption of fat and calcium by low birthweight infants from milks containing butterfat and olive oil. Arch. Dis. Child. *48*:496, 1973.

Barnes, K., Nestel, P. J., Pryke, E. S., and Whyte, H. M.: Neonatal plasma lipids. Med. J. Aust. *2*:1002, 1972.

Brooks, C. C.: Fatty acid composition of pork lipids as affected by basal diet, fat source and fat level. J. Anim. Sci. *33*:1224, 1971.

Burr, G. O., and Burr, M. M.: A new deficiency disease produced by the rigid exclusion of fat from the diet. J. Biol. Chem. *82*:345, 1929.

Caster, W. O., Ahn, P., Hill, E. G., Mohrhauer, H., and Holman, R. T.: Determination of linoleate requirement of swine by a new method of estimating nutritional requirement. J. Nutr. *78*:147, 1962.

Caster, W. O., Hill, E. G., and Holman, R. T.: Estimation of essential fatty acid intake in swine. J. Anim. Sci. *22*:389, 1963.

Chesney, J., and McCord, A. B.: Vitamin A of serum following administration of haliver oil in normal children and in chronic steatorrhea. Proc. Soc. Exp. Biol. *31*:887, 1934.

Clark, S. B.: Limiting factors in maximal steady state absorption of medium chain triglycerides. *In* Senior, J. R. (ed.): Medium Chain Triglycerides. Philadelphia, University of Pennsylvania Press, 1968, p. 69.

Coleman, M. H.: The structural investigation of natural fats. *In* Paoletti, R., and Kritchevsky, D. (eds.): Advances in Lipid Research. Vol. 1. New York, Academic Press, 1963, p. 1.

Committee on Nutrition, American Academy of Pediatrics: Childhood diet and coronary heart disease. Pediatrics *49*:305, 1972.

Connor, W. E., and Connor, S. L.: The key role of nutritional factors in the prevention of coronary heart disease. Prevent. Med. *1*:49, 1972.

Coons, C. M.: Fats and fatty acids. *In* Stefferud, A. (ed.): Food. The Yearbook of Agriculture 1959. Washington, D.C., U.S. Government Printing Office, 1959, pp. 74–87.

Council on Foods and Nutrition: Diet and coronary heart disease. J.A.M.A. *222*:1647, 1972.

Darmady, J. M., Fosbrooke, A. S., and Lloyd, J. K.: Prospective study of serum cholesterol levels during first year of life. Br. Med. J. *2*:685, 1972.

Davidson, M., and Bauer, C. H.: Patterns of fat excretion in feces of premature infants fed various preparations of milk. Pediatrics *25*:375, 1960.

Dayton, S., Hashimoto, S., and Pearce, M. L.: Adipose tissue linoleic acid as a criterion of adherence to a modified diet. J. Lipid Res. *8*:508, 1967.

Desnuelle, P., and Savary, P.: Specificities of lipases. J. Lipid Res. *4*:369, 1963.

Drash, A.: Atherosclerosis, cholesterol and the pediatrician. J. Pediatr. *80*:693, 1972.

Droese, W., and Stolley, H.: Kuhmilchfett und pflanzliches Fett in der Ernährung des jungen, gesunden Säuglings. Dtsch. Med. Wochenschr. *86*:855, 1961.
Fedeli, E., and Jacini, G.: Lipid composition of vegetable oils. *In* Paoletti, R., and Kritchevsky, D. (eds.): Advances in Lipid Research. Vol. 9. New York, Academic Press, 1971, p. 335.
Filer, L. J., Jr., Fomon, S. J., Anderson, T. A., Andersen, D. W., Rogers, R. R., and Jensen, R. L.: Growth, serum chemical values and carcass composition of Pitman-Moore miniature pigs during the first eight weeks of life. J. Nutr. *103*:425, 1973.
Filer, L. J., Jr., Mattson, F. H., and Fomon, S. J.: Triglyceride configuration and fat absorption by the human infant. J. Nutr. *99*:293, 1969.
Fomon, S. J.: A pediatrician looks at early nutrition. Bull. N.Y. Acad. Med. *47*:569, 1971.
Fomon, S. J., Filer, L. J., Jr., Thomas, L. N., and Rogers, R. R.: Growth and serum chemical values of normal breastfed infants. Acta Paediatr. Scand. (Suppl. 202), 1970a.
Fomon, S. J., Thomas, L. N., Filer, L. J., Jr., Ziegler, E. E., and Leonard, M. T.: Food consumption and growth of normal infants fed milk-based formulas. Acta Paediatr. Scand. (Suppl. 223), 1971.
Fomon, S. J., Ziegler, E. E., Thomas, L. N., Jensen, R. L., and Filer, L. J., Jr.: Excretion of fat by normal full-term infants fed various milks and formulas. Amer. J. Clin. Nutr. *23*:1299, 1970b.
Food and Nutrition Board: Dietary Fat and Human Health. Washington, D.C., National Academy of Sciences-National Research Council, Publ. 1147, 1966.
Fredrickson, D. S.: Introduction. Symposium: Factors in childhood that influence the development of atherosclerosis and hypertension. Amer. J. Clin. Nutr. *25*:221, 1972.
Fredrickson, D. S., and Levy, R. I.: Familial hyperlipoproteinemia. *In* Stanbury, J. B., Wyngaarden, J. B., and Fredrickson, D. S. (eds.): The Metabolic Basis of Inherited Disease. 3rd ed. New York, McGraw-Hill Book Co., 1972, p. 545.
Freeman, C. P., Jack, E. L., and Smith, L. M.: Intramolecular fatty acid distribution in the milk fat triglycerides of several species. J. Dairy Sci. *48*:853, 1965.
Glass, R. L., Troolin, H. A., and Jenness, R.: Comparative biochemical studies of milks. IV. Constituent fatty acids of milk fats. Comp. Biochem. Physiol. *22*:415, 1967.
Glueck, C. J., Heckman, F., Schoenfeld, M., Steiner, P., and Pearce, W.: Neonatal familial Type II hyperlipoproteinemia: cord blood cholesterol in 1,800 births. Metabolism *20*:597, 1971.
Goldbloom, R. B., Blake, R. M., and Cameron, D.: Assessment of three methods for measuring intestinal fat absorption in infants and children. Pediatrics *34*:814, 1964.
Gordon, H. H., and McNamara, H.: Fat excretion of premature infants. I. Effect on fecal fat of decreasing fat intake. Amer. J. Dis. Child. *62*:328, 1941.
Guilbert, P., Baker, D., and Barness, L. A.: Fat retention in infants fed breast milk and humanized cow's milk. J. Pediatr. *47*:683, 1955.
Hahn, P., and Kirby, L.: Immediate and late effects of premature weaning and of feeding a high fat or high carbohydrate diet to weanling rats. J. Nutr. *103*:690, 1973.
Hahn, P., and Koldovsky, O.: Utilization of Nutrients During Postnatal Development. New York, Pergamon, 1966.
Hanna, F. M., Navarrete, D. A., and Hsu, F. A.: Calcium-fatty acid absorption in term infants fed human milk and prepared formulas simulating human milk. Pediatrics *45*:216, 1970.
Hansen, A. E., Stewart, R. A., Hughes, G., and Söderhjelm, L.: The relation of linoleic acid to infant feeding. Acta Paediatr. Scand. *51*:(Suppl. 137), 1962.
Hashim, S. A., and Asfour, R. H.: Tocopherol in infants fed diets rich in polyunsaturated fatty acids. Amer. J. Clin. Nutr. *21*:75, 1968.
Hilditch, T. P., and Williams, P. N.: The Chemical Constitution of Natural Fats. 4th ed. New York, J. Wiley & Sons, 1964.
Hill, E. G., Warmanen, E. L., Silbernick, C. L., and Holman, R. T.: Essential fatty acid nutrition in swine. I. Linoleate requirement estimated from triene:tetraene ratio of tissue lipids. J. Nutr. *74*:335, 1961.
Hinman, J. W.: Prostaglandins. Ann. Rev. Biochem. *41*:161, 1972.
Hofman, A. F.: The chemistry of intraluminal digestion. Mayo Clin. Proc. *48*:617, 1973.
Holman, R. L.: Atherosclerosis: a pediatric nutrition problem? Amer. J. Clin. Nutr. *9*:565, 1961.

Holman, R. L., Blanc, W. A., and Andersen, D.: Decreased aortic atherosclerosis in cystic fibrosis of the pancreas. Pediatrics *24*:34, 1959.

Holman, R. T.: The ratio of trienoic:tetraenoic acids in tissue lipids as a measure of essential fatty acid requirement. J. Nutr. *70*:405, 1960.

Holman, R. T., Caster, W. O., and Wiese, H. F.: The essential fatty acid requirement of infants and the assessment of their dietary intake of linoleate by serum fatty acid analysis. Amer. J. Clin. Nutr. *14*:70, 1964.

Holt, L. E., Courtney, A. M., and Fales, H. L.: A study of the fat metabolism of infants and young children. I. Fat in the stools of breast fed infants. Amer. J. Dis. Child. *17*:241, 1919a.

Holt, L. E., Courtney, A. M., and Fales, H. L.: Fat metabolism of infants and young children. II. Fat in the stools of infants fed on modifications of cow's milk. Amer. J. Dis. Child. *17*:423, 1919b.

Holt, L. E., Jr., Tidwell, H. C., Kirk, C. M., Cross, D. M., and Neale, S.: Studies in fat metabolism. I. Fat absorption in normal infants. J. Pediatr. *6*:427, 1935.

Holt, P. R.: Studies of medium chain triglycerides in patients with differing mechanisms for fat malabsorption. *In* Senior, J. R. (ed.): Medium Chain Triglycerides. Philadelphia, University of Pennsylvania Press, 1968, p. 97.

Holt, P. R.: The roles of bile acids during the process of normal fat and cholesterol absorption. Arch. Intern. Med. *130*:574, 1972.

Huber, E. G., and Scheibl, F.: Die Entwicklung der Fettresorptionsfähigkeit. *In* Linneweh, F. (ed.): Fortschritte der Pädologie. Berlin, Springer-Verlag, 1965, p. 87.

Hunter, J. L. P., Johnstone, J. M., and Kemp, J. H.: An evaluation of the lipiodol test for the detection of steatorrhea. Arch. Dis. Child. *42*:97, 1967.

Inter-Society Commission for Heart Disease Resources: Primary prevention of the atherosclerotic diseases. Circulation *42*:A–55, 1970.

Isselbacher, K. J.: Mechanisms of absorption of long and medium chain triglycerides. *In* Senior, J. R. (ed.): Medium Chain Triglycerides. Philadelphia, University of Pennsylvania Press, 1968, p. 21.

Jones, W. O., and di Sant 'Agnese, P. A.: Laboratory aids in the diagnosis of malabsorption in pediatrics. I. Lipiodol absorption as a simple test for steatorrhea. J. Pediatr. *62*:44, 1963.

Joppich, G., Löhr, H., and Wolf, H.: Fettbilanzstudien mit fettausgetauschter Milch. Z. Kinderheilkd. *82*:7, 1959.

Kahan, J.: The vitamin A absorption test. II. Studies on children and adults with disorders in the alimentary tract. Scand. J. Gastroent. *5*:5, 1970.

Kannel, W. B., Castelli, W. P., Gordon, T., and McNamara, P. M.: Serum cholesterol, lipoproteins and the risk of coronary heart disease. Ann. Intern. Med. *74*:1, 1971.

Kannel, W. B., and Dawber, T. R.: Atherosclerosis as a pediatric problem. J. Pediatr. *80*:544, 1972.

Levy, R. I., Fredrickson, D. S., Shulman, R., Bilheimer, D. W., Breslow, J. L., Stone, N. J., Lux, S. E., Sloan, H. R., Krauss, R. M., and Herbert, P. N.: Dietary and drug treatment of primary hyperlipoproteinemia. Ann. Intern. Med. *77*:267, 1972.

Lindberg, G.: Über den Stoffwechsel des gesunden, natürlich ernährten Säuglings und dessen Beeinflussung durch Frauenmilchfett. Z. Kinderheilkd. *16*:90, 1917.

Lowe, C. U.: Research in infant nutrition: the untapped well. Amer. J. Clin. Nutr. *25*:245, 1972.

McNamara, J. J., Molot, M. A., Stremple, J. F., and Cutting, R. T.: Coronary artery disease in combat casualties in Vietnam. J.A.M.A. *216*:1185, 1971.

Malmberg, N.: Über den Stoffwechsel des gesunden, natürlich ernährten Säuglings und dessen Beeinflussung durch parenterale Infektion und Intoxikation. Acta Paediatr. Scand. *2*:209, 1922–23.

Mason, J. K.: Asymptomatic disease of coronary arteries in young men. Br. Med. J. *2*:1234, 1963.

Mattson, F. H., and Volpenhein, R. A.: Rearrangement of glyceride fatty acids during digestion and absorption. J. Biol. Chem. *237*:53, 1962.

Mitchell, S., Blount, S. G., Jr., Blumenthal, S., Jesse, M. J., and Weidman, W.: The pediatrician and atherosclerosis. Pediatrics *49*:165, 1972.

Morales, S., Chung, A. W., Lewis, J. M., Messina, A., and Holt, L. E., Jr.: Absorption of fat and vitamin A in premature infants. I. Effect of different levels of fat intake on the retention of fat and vitamin A. Pediatrics *6*:86, 1950.

Muhl, G.: Über den Stoffwechsel des gesunden, natürlich ernährten Säuglings und dessen Beeinflussung durch Fettreduktion der Nahrung. Acta Paediatr. Scand. *2* (Suppl. 1), 1924.

Neerhout, R. C., Lanzkowsky, P., Kimmel, J. R., Lloyd, E. A., Wilson, J. F., and Lahey, M. E.: A new test for fat absorption which employs an iodinated triglyceride. J. Pediatr. *65*:701, 1964.

Owen, G. M., Kram, K. M., Garry, P. J., Lowe, J. E., Jr., and Lubin, A. H.: A study of nutritional status of preschool children in the United States, 1968–1970. Pediatrics *53*:597, 1974.

Plotz, E. J., Kabara, J. J., Davis, M. E., LeRoy, G. V., and Gould, R. G.: Studies on the synthesis of cholesterol in the brain of the human fetus. Amer. J. Obstet. Gynecol. *101*:534, 1968.

Reiser, R., and Sidelman, Z.: Control of serum cholesterol homeostasis by cholesterol in milk of the suckling rat. J. Nutr. *102*:1009, 1972.

Renner, R., and Hill, F. W.: Factors affecting the absorbability of saturated fatty acids in the chick. J. Nutr. *74*:254, 1961.

Rigal, R. D., Lovell, F. W., and Townsend, F. M.: Pathologic findings in the cardiovascular systems of military flying personnel. Amer. J. Cardiol. *6*:19, 1960.

Schiff, E. R., and Dietschy, J. M.: Current concepts of bile acid absorption. Amer. J. Clin. Nutr. *22*:273, 1969.

Schlenk, H.: Odd numbered and new essential fatty acids. Fed. Proc. *31*:1430, 1972.

Senior, J. R.: Intestinal absorption of fats. J. Lipid Res. *5*:495, 1964.

Senior, J. R. (ed.): Medium Chain Triglycerides. Philadelphia, University of Pennsylvania Press, 1968.

Senterre, J., and Lambrechts, A.: Nitrogen, fat and minerals' balances in premature infants fed acidified or nonacidified half-skimmed cow milk. Biol. Neonate *20*:107, 1972.

Silverio, J.: Personal communication, Wyeth Laboratories, Radnor, Pennsylvania, 1973.

Simmonds, W. J.: Effect of bile salts on the rate of fat absorption. Amer. J. Clin. Nutr. *22*:266, 1969.

Snyderman, S. E., Morales, S., and Holt, L. E., Jr.: The absorption of short-chain fats by premature infants. Arch. Dis. Child. *30*:83, 1955.

Southgate, D. A. T., and Barrett, I. M.: The intake and excretion of calorific constituents of milk by babies. Br. J. Nutr. *20*:363, 1966.

Southgate, D. A. T., Widdowson, E. M., Smits, B. J., Cooke, W. T., Walker, C. H. M., and Mathers, N. P.: Absorption and excretion of calcium and fat by young infants. Lancet *1*:487, 1969.

Sweeney, M. J., Etteldorf, J. N., Throop, L. J., Timma, D. L., and Wrenn, E. L.: Diet and fatty acid distribution in subcutaneous fat and in the cholesterol-triglyceride fraction of serum of young infants. J. Clin. Invest. *42*:1, 1963.

Tantibhedhyangkul, P., and Hashim, S. A.: Clinical and physiologic aspects of medium-chain triglycerides: alleviation of steatorrhea in premature infants. Bull. N.Y. Acad. Med. *47*:17, 1971.

Tidwell, H. C., Holt, L. E., Jr., Farrow, H. L., and Neale, S.: Studies of fat metabolism. II. Fat absorption in premature infants and twins. J. Pediatr. *6*:481, 1935.

Tomarelli, R. M., Meyer, B. J., Weaber, J. R., and Bernhart, F. W.: Effect of positional distribution on the absorption of the fatty acids of human milk and infant formulas. J. Nutr. *95*:583, 1968.

Welsch, H., Heinz, F., Lagally, G., and Stuhlfauth, K.: Fettresorption aus Frauenmilch bei Neugeborenen. Klin. Wochenschr. *43*:60, 1965.

Widdowson, E. M.: Absorption and excretion of fat, nitrogen, and minerals from "filled" milks by babies one week old. Lancet *2*:1099, 1965.

Williams, M. L., Rose, C. S., Morrow, G., III, Sloan, S. E., and Barness, L. A.: Calcium and fat absorption in neonatal period. Amer. J. Clin. Nutr. *23*:1322, 1970.

Wilson, J. D.: Relation between dietary cholesterol and bile acid excretion in the rat. Amer. J. Physiol. *203*:1029, 1962.

Ziegler, E. E., Fomon, S. J., Filer, L. J., Jr., and Thomas, L. N.: Absorption of various fats by newborn infants. (Abstract.) Proc. Internat. Symp.: Dietary Lipids and Postnatal Development. Milan, Italy, 1972.

Zoula, J., Melichar, M., Novak, M., Hahn, P., and Koldovsky, O.: Nitrogen and fat retention in premature infants fed breast milk, "humanized" cow's milk or half skimmed cow's milk. Acta Paediatr. Scand. *55*:26, 1966.

8

CARBOHYDRATE

Thomas A. Anderson,
Gunnar W. Meeuwisse
and
Samuel J. Fomon

Carbohydrate accounts for the greatest percentage of calorie intake in the diets of most adults. The "average" adult in the Western World ingests about 350 gm of carbohydrate daily, of which 60 per cent is starch, 30 per cent sucrose and nearly 10 per cent lactose (Greaves and Hollingsworth, 1964). During early infancy, when the diet consists primarily of milk or formula, carbohydrate usually supplies 35 to 55 per cent of calorie intake and lactose generally accounts for a significant portion of this. For the breastfed infant and for infants receiving various commercially prepared formulas, lactose may be the only carbohydrate consumed. However, as cereals and other beikost (Chapter 16) are introduced into the infant's diet—in the United States, commonly before four weeks of age—consumption of complex carbohydrates and of sucrose rapidly increases.

In recent years, the metabolism of various carbohydrates has received increasing attention. Evidence has accumulated to demonstrate that secondary lactose intolerance develops not infrequently during diarrheal and other diseases of infancy. The relation of sucrose consumption to development of dental caries has been widely discussed (Chapter 14). The ability of the infant to digest starches, especially modified food starches, has been questioned.

DIGESTION AND ABSORPTION

Digestion of carbohydrate begins in the mouth with the action of salivary amylase on starch. In the adult, and presumably even in the small infant, gastric acidity rapidly inactivates salivary amylase. In the adult and to a lesser extent in the small infant, digestion of starch continues within the lumen of the small intestine by the action of pancreatic α-amylase.

Amylose consists of a straight chain of glucose molecules in which the fourth carbon of one glucose molecule is attached to the first carbon of its neighbor via an oxygen bridge with α-linkage (Fig. 8–1). Salivary and pancreatic α-amylases attack the interior α-1,4 linkages but are relatively ineffective against those near the ends of the molecule. The final products of α-amylolysis are maltose and maltotriose (see Chapter Appendix).

Amylopectin is a large, branched starch molecule consisting of straight chains of about 25 glucose units with α-1,4 bonds linked at branching points by α-1,6 bonds (Fig. 8–1). Alpha-amylase is inactive against the α-1,6 linkages in amylopectin and relatively inactive with respect to the α-1,4 links adjacent to the branch points. Final intraluminal digestion of the branched-chain amylopectin molecule yields maltose, maltotriose and α-dextrins averaging eight glucose molecules (Gray, 1970). The smallest α-dextrin is estimated to be a pentasac-

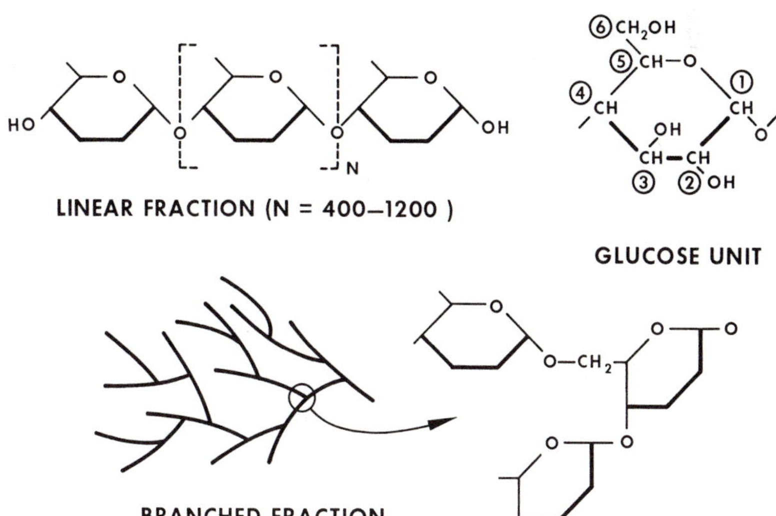

Figure 8–1 Diagrammatic representation of linear fraction (amylose) and branched fraction (amylopectin) of starch molecule. (From Schoch, T. J.: *In* Schultz, H. W., Cain, R. F., and Wrolstad, R. W. (eds.): Carbohydrates and Their Roles. Westport, Conn., AVI Publishing Co., Inc., 1969, p. 395.)

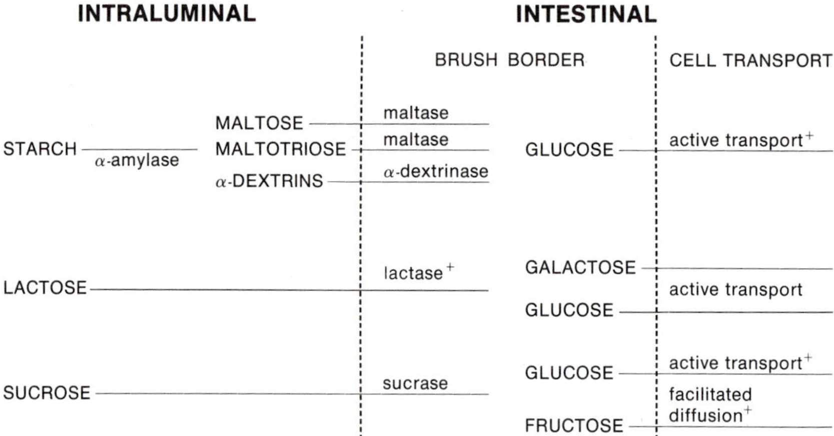

Figure 8–2 Schematic presentation of digestion and absorption of starch, lactose and sucrose. Rate-limiting steps are indicated by $^+$. (Adapted from Gray, G. M.: Carbohydrate digestion and absorption. Gastroenterology *58*:96, 1970.)

charide. It has been postulated (Ugolev, 1965) that α-amylase is bound to the surface of the intestinal mucosa and is active primarily at that site. Some "membrane digestion" of starch may occur; however, the concentration of α-amylase free in the intestinal fluid is more than sufficient to account for the rapid intraluminal hydrolysis of starch in the adult.

The various enzymes responsible for the further digestion of smaller polysaccharides and disaccharides are indicated in Figure 8–2. The type of transport involved in absorption of the resulting monosaccharides is also indicated. Whereas the concentration of glucose in the blood is commonly elevated after ingestion of carbohydrate, concentrations of fructose and galactose are rarely detectable in the peripheral blood because of efficient hepatic conversion of these monosaccharides to glucose and glycogen.

The entry of glucose and galactose into the intestinal cells is facilitated by an active transport mechanism known to involve the binding of these monosaccharides to Na^+ and a carrier. The absorption of fructose occurs by facilitated, or carrier-mediated, diffusion (Gray, 1970); however, some active transport also occurs (Gracey et al., 1972).

A key intermediate for a variety of metabolic pathways is glucose-6-phosphate, a substance that can be formed from glucose by all the tissues of the body. Energy requirements of the cell, availability of other substrates, and concentrations of oxygen and certain hormones determine whether glucose-6-phosphate is then converted to glycogen for storage, metabolized by way of the glycolytic pathway to provide glycerol for fat synthesis and high energy phosphates (ATP), or oxidized by way of the pentose phosphate cycle to provide reduced cofactors (NADPH) for synthesis of fatty acids and pentoses.

QUANTITATIVE ASPECTS OF CARBOHYDRATE METABOLISM IN THE INFANT

Carbohydrate Tolerance

The pattern and magnitude of the rise in glucose concentration of the blood after oral administration of a carbohydrate load depends upon a number of factors, including size of the load, type of carbohydrate and age of the individual being tested. Although there is much individual variation in response, a number of workers (Jarrett and Holman, 1966; Pedersen, 1967; Pildes et al., 1969; Anderson et al., 1972) have reported the peak rise in glucose concentration of the blood of young infants to occur 60 minutes after oral administration of a carbohydrate load (Fig. 8–3). The peak rise in glucose concentration of the blood was also observed to occur 60 minutes after oral adminis-

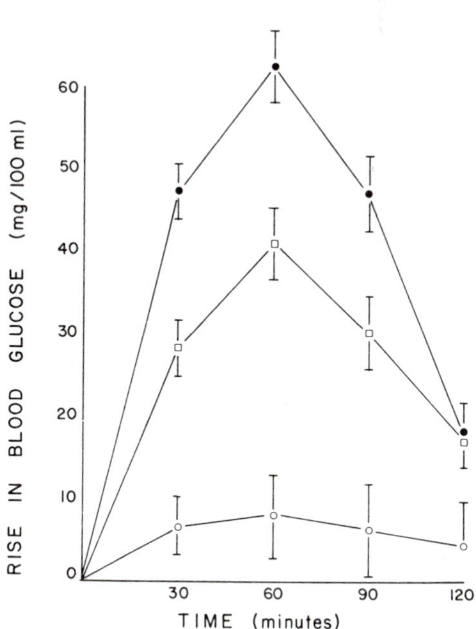

Figure 8–3 Increase in concentration of glucose in the blood of three-day-old infants after feeding of various carbohydrates in aqueous solution: ● glucose, □ maltose and two cornstarch hydrolysates, and ○ starch. The mean and standard error of the mean are presented. (Modified from Anderson, T. A., Fomon, S. J., and Filer, L. J., Jr.: Carbohydrate tolerance studies with 3-day-old infants. J. Lab. Clin. Med. *79*:31, 1972.)

tration of a glucose load to obese children (Court et al., 1971) and elderly adults (Lauvaux and Staquet, 1970). However, oral glucose tolerance studies of normal children (Pickens et al., 1967; Cole, 1972) and adults (Hales and Randle, 1963; Swan et al., 1966; Boyns et al., 1969; Castro et al., 1970; Förster et al., 1970) have demonstrated that the maximum rise in glucose concentration occurs at 30 minutes. This age-related difference in response to oral administration of glucose may be the result of differences in gastric emptying time, rate of absorption, intestinal motility and/or other factors (such as insulin secretion) influencing removal of glucose at the cellular level.

Lactose Metabolism

The rather frequent, loose stools with acid pH characteristic of the young breastfed infant may reflect lactose intake somewhat greater than can be split by the lactase of the intestinal mucosa. By age four to six weeks, stools of breastfed infants are commonly observed to be of a pasty consistency rather than loose, suggesting that by this age the normal infant is able to digest the considerable amounts of lactose in his diet.

Approximately 10 per cent of infants in the United States (350,000 infants per year) receive commercially prepared soy-based formulas, presumably because of concern about milk allergy or milk intolerance. Strained and junior fruits, plain vegetables, meats and most high-meat dinners are lactose-free and therefore suitable for infants suspected of lactose intolerance.

Starch Digestion

As discussed in Chapter 4, activity of pancreatic α-amylase is low in the small intestine of the very young infant and increases gradually with increasing age. Although Auricchio et al. (1967) fed a diet containing rice starch and macaroni to a group of four- to seven-month-old infants and failed to find even 1 per cent of the starch in the feces, there is reason to doubt that starch is well digested by infants. Only minimal rises in glucose concentrations in the blood have been observed after feeding of cooked starch to young infants by gavage (Husband et al., 1970) or by nipple (Anderson et al., 1972) (Fig. 8–3). These findings suggest slow hydrolysis and/or absorption of the starch since Husband et al. (1970) have shown that starch empties from the stomach more rapidly than does an equal weight of glucose.

The modest increase in glucose concentration of the blood in the absence of starch in the feces could be explained by bacterial digestion of starch within the colon (Bond and Levitt, 1972) as well as in feces after passage from the colon. In vitro studies in our laboratory (Bergmann, unpublished) have demonstrated that rapid degradation of starch occurs in the presence of fecal bacteria. Therefore, for determining the extent of digestion of starch by the infant, we believe that the increase in glucose concentration of the blood after feeding starch is more reliable than are determinations of fecal excretion of starch. Thus far, starch tolerance tests carried out with infants have been predominantly restricted to the first few weeks of life. Studies of older infants are needed.

Salivary amylase is not essential for the digestion of polysaccharides, and diseases with impaired salivary secretion are rare, especially in children. Deficient production of pancreatic α-amylase has not been described as a pure selective disorder. Impaired digestion of starch is therefore always combined with reduced production of other pancreatic enzymes, as in congenital hypoplasia of the exocrine pancreas (Bodian et al., 1964), cystic fibrosis of the pancreas and kwashiorkor. Temporary pancreatic insufficiency may result from starvation.

There appears to be little reason to question the ability of the infant to digest corn starch hydrolysates. As shown in Figure 8–3, feedings of two hydrolysates – Dextri-Maltose (DE 37)* and a DE 11 hydrolysate – were followed by increases in glucose concentrations of the blood similar to those observed after feeding maltose – that is, not quite as great as after feeding glucose but considerably greater than after feeding starch.

CARBOHYDRATE CONTENT OF INFANT FOODS

Milks and Formulas

Human milk provides 37 per cent of calories from carbohydrate, and cow milk 29 per cent of calories from this dietary component (Table 8–1). Commercially prepared formulas most widely marketed in the United States provide approximately 42 per cent of calories from carbohydrate (Chapter 15). The types of carbohydrate currently used in commercially prepared formulas are listed in Table 8–2. A detailed classification of carbohydrates is given in the Chapter Appendix.

---

*Dextrose Equivalent (DE) – a chemical method for determining the amount of reducing sugar in a starch hydrolysate. The reducing power is compared with that produced by anhydrous dextrose (dextrose = 100), hence the term Dextrose Equivalent. A DE 20 corn syrup would contain one reducing group in approximately 5 anhydroglucose units.

TABLE 8–1 AVERAGE CARBOHYDRATE CONTENT OF SEVERAL FOODS FOR INFANTS

Food	Carbohydrate (% of Calories)
Human milk	37
Cow milk	29
Commercially prepared formula*	42
Strained meat	1
Strained fruits	96
Strained desserts	89
Strained vegetables	80
Strained soups and dinners	56
Strained high-meat dinners	29
"Typical" strained food†	80

*Chapter 15, Table 15–7.
†Weighted according to sales by product category.

The carbohydrate composition of corn syrup solids and dextrins-maltose-dextrose (from corn) depends upon the degree to which the corn starch has been hydrolyzed. As shown in Figure 8–4, an acid-hydrolyzed corn syrup, DE 25, contains approximately 20 per cent as much dextrose as a corn syrup with a DE of 60. As the DE increases, the concentration of higher saccharides in an acid-hydrolyzed corn starch decreases proportionately to the increase in dextrose content.

The various starches used in infant formulas act as thickeners and aid in the suspension of the added minerals which may not be soluble. Tapioca starch is obtained from the root of the cassava or manioc plant, and arrowroot starch from the maranta plant. The "modified" food starches commonly employed in infant foods have been chemically treated to give properties desirable in food processing (see Chapter Appendix).

TABLE 8–2 TYPES OF CARBOHYDRATE USED IN COMMERCIALLY PREPARED INFANT FORMULAS

Lactose
Corn syrup solids
Sucrose
Dextrose
Dextrins-maltose-dextrose (from corn)
Arrowroot starch
Cornstarch
Modified cornstarch
Modified tapioca starch
Banana powder
Carrageenan

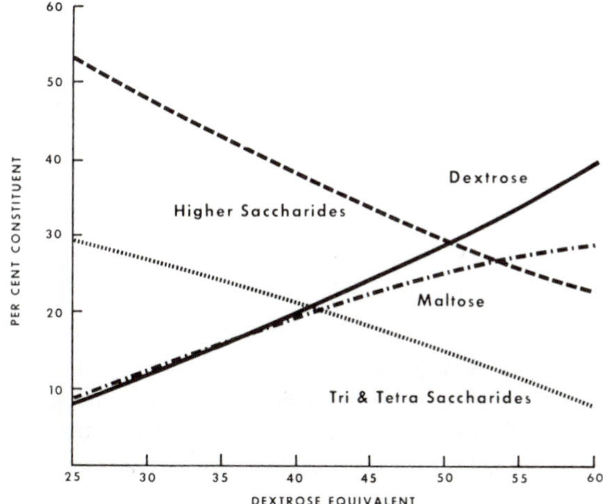

Figure 8–4 Percentage of higher saccharides, tri- and tetrasaccharides, maltose and glucose in acid hydrolyzed corn syrup with dextrose equivalency from 25 to 60. (From Newton, J. M.: Corn syrups. *In* Symposium Proceedings. Washington, D.C., Corn Refiners Association, Inc., 1970, p. IV–13.)

Carrageenan, a substance obtained from the red seaweed, is a sulfated polysaccharide with a high proportion of galactose groups. It is an effective emulsifier used to disperse and stabilize the vegetable oils in infant formulas; it is not digested.

Formulas containing sucrose or mixtures of sucrose and corn syrup solids are markedly sweeter to the taste than are those containing only lactose (Table 8–3). We know little of the long-term consequences, if any, associated with the feeding of sweeter formulas. On the basis of quantity of formula consumed, Nisbett and Gurwitz (1970) concluded that newborn infants with birth weights greater

TABLE 8–3 RELATIVE SWEETNESS OF SUGARS*

SUGAR	SUCROSE = 100
Lactose	16
Galactose	32
Maltose	32
Glucose	74
Sucrose	100
Invert sugar†	130
Fructose	173

*Adapted from Oser, B. L. (ed.): Hawks Physiological Chemistry. 14th ed. New York, The Blakiston Division, McGraw-Hill Book Co., 1965, p. 62.

†Mixture of glucose and fructose (1:1).

than 3540 gm were more responsive than were lighter infants to sweet taste of formula and that female infants were more responsive to sweet taste than were male infants.

Beikost

The percentage of calories supplied by carbohydrate (Table 8–1) varies widely among foods other than milk or formula (i.e., beikost, Chapter 16). With the exception of strained meats and high-meat dinners, most commercially prepared strained foods provide a higher percentage of calories from carbohydrate than does milk or formula.

The content of free sugars in some foods commonly consumed by infants and small children is presented in Table 8–4.

EFFECTS OF SUGARS ON ABSORPTION OF CALCIUM, MAGNESIUM AND STRONTIUM

The stimulating effect of dietary lactose on absorption of calcium has been known for many years and has been shown to occur in rats, parathyroidectomized dogs, dairy calves and chicks (Lengemann et

TABLE 8–4 FREE SUGARS IN FOODS CONSUMED BY INFANTS*

Foods	Total Solids (%)	Sugar Content of Food (Per Cent of Weight)					
		Glucose	*Fructose*	*Sucrose*	*Maltose*	*Raffinose*	*Stachyose*
Fruits							
Apple	15.96	1.17	6.04	3.78	trace		
Apricot	14.44	1.73	1.28	5.84			
Peach	12.79	0.91	1.18	6.92	0.12		
Pear	13.58	0.95	6.77	1.61	0.31		
Plum	17.97	3.49	1.53	4.94	0.15		
Vegetables							
Beet	11.19	0.18	0.16	6.11			
Carrot	12.00	0.85	0.85	4.24			
Potato (stored)		1.04	1.15	1.69			
Sweet corn	22.69	0.34	0.31	3.03			
Squash (winter)	13.08	0.96	1.16	1.61			
Sweet potato	22.53	0.33	0.30	3.37			
Legumes							
Lima bean	26.74	0.04	0.08	2.59		0.66	0.59
Snap bean	7.79	1.08	1.20	0.25		0.11	0.19
Pea (Alaska)	25.54		0.08	3.00		0.06	0.06

*Adapted from Shallenberger, R. S.: Occurrence of various sugars in foods, Sugars in Nutrition, An International Conference, Vanderbilt University, Nashville, Tenn., 1972. New York, Academic Press, 1974.

al., 1959). Interpretation of animal studies is difficult, because of differences in species, in the age of animals, in the amounts of lactose given and in the experimental procedures. Wasserman and Comar (1959) have demonstrated that absorption of calcium by rats is not enhanced by administration of sugars that are rapidly absorbed from the intestinal tract (glucose, fructose, galactose and sucrose), whereas carbohydrates that are more slowly absorbed (lactose, cellobiose and several others) do enhance calcium absorption. Studies of isolated intestinal loops have demonstrated that, in the rat, many sugars promote absorption of calcium in the lower end of the gut (Vaughan and Filer, 1960). Although the mechanism is unknown, the favorable effect of lactose may be related to its relatively slow absorption, thus providing amounts of sugar in the lower intestinal tract which promote calcium absorption. Absorption of magnesium and strontium is probably influenced by factors similar to those influencing absorption of calcium.

Although lactose may exert a favorable effect on absorption of minerals in human subjects, little evidence on this point is available. Condon et al. (1970) demonstrated decreased fecal and urinary excretion of calcium when lactose was added to the diets of normal adults. However, increase in intestinal absorption of calcium was not demonstrated by other investigators in studies of adults (Greenwald et al., 1963), children (Mills et al., 1940) or low-birth-weight infants (Stephan et al., 1962). Decreased urinary excretion was reported by Mills et al. (1940). Further studies of the relation of dietary lactose to absorption of minerals are desirable.

Lactosuria and Lactulosuria

Presence of lactose in urine in small amounts (less than 100 mg/100 ml) was found by Gryboski and Boehm (1965) in 4 of 26 infants fed evaporated milk, 19 of 88 infants fed Similac and two of seven breastfed infants. Lactulose, a synthetic disaccharide containing fructose and galactose, is formed during heat processing of milk by converting the glucose portion of the lactose molecule to fructose. This sugar, for which no disaccharidase is present in the human, was not excreted in urine of breastfed infants but was present to the extent of 50 to 200 mg/100 ml in urine of 4 of 26 infants fed evaporated milk and 34 of 88 infants fed Similac (Gryboski and Boehm, 1965).

HYPOGLYCEMIA OF THE NEWBORN

Hypoglycemia in the fullsize newborn infant is defined as concentration of glucose in blood less than 30 mg/100 ml between birth and 72 hours of age or concentration less than 40 mg/100 ml thereafter (Cornblath and Schwartz, 1966). In the infant of low birth weight, hypoglycemia is defined as concentration of glucose in the blood less than 20 mg/100 ml. The finding of low concentration of glucose should be confirmed by repeating the determination with a second specimen of the infant's blood, although it will usually be wise to begin therapy before the report of the second specimen is received. With this definition, hypoglycemia will be found in one to three per 1000 newborns; however, the incidence is much higher among certain high risk groups of infants.

Pildes et al. (1967) reported that 5.7 per cent of low-birth-weight infants had concentrations of glucose in the blood less than 20 mg/100 ml. Hypoglycemia within 48 hours after birth has been reported by Haworth and Vidyasagar (1971) in 18 per cent of 33 fullterm infants with birthweights less than two standard deviations below the mean for gestational age. Haworth and Vidyasagar (1971) cite an incidence of hypoglycemia of 60 to 80 per cent among infants born of diabetic mothers, with 10 to 25 per cent of the infants symptomatic. Severe and prolonged hypoglycemia has been reported in infants born of mothers treated with oral hypoglycemic agents during pregnancy (Zucker and Simon, 1968). Hypoglycemia also occurs in erythroblastosis fetalis (Haworth and Vidyasagar, 1971; Milner, 1972; Greenberg and Christiansen, 1972), and in a number of other conditions (Greenberg and Christiansen, 1972).

The two major causes of hypoglycemia of the newborn are deficient hepatic glucose production and hyperinsulinism (Haworth and Vidyasagar, 1971; Milner, 1972; Greenberg and Christiansen, 1972). A detailed classification of causes of hypoglycemia has been presented by Greenberg and Christiansen (1972). Among low-birth-weight infants, hypoglycemia probably develops because of deficient hepatic gluconeogenesis from lipids and amino acids, from lack of delivery of substrate, particularly lipid, to the liver, or from a combination of these two causes (Adam, 1971). The hypoglycemia of infants born to women with diabetes mellitus is the result of hyperinsulinism, and the frequency and severity of symptomatic hypoglycemia in these infants appears related to the quality of maternal diabetic control (Milner, 1972). The second most common cause of hyperinsulinism in the newborn is probably erythroblastosis fetalis (Milner, 1971, 1972).

Clinical findings associated with hypoglycemia are tremors, cyanosis, convulsions, apnea, apathy, high-pitched or weak cry, refusal to feed, eye-rolling and irregular respirations. Differential diagnosis of neonatal hypoglycemia has been discussed in detail by Cornblath and Schwartz (1966).

Studies of infants of low birth weight have demonstrated that concentrations of glucose in the blood are correlated significantly with the age at which feedings are instituted. In general, the earlier a group of infants is fed, the greater will be the mean concentration of glucose in the blood during the early days of life. Studies currently in progress in several centers concern the relation between the age of initiation of feedings, the concentrations of glucose in the blood and mortality.

The age at which feedings are instituted is clearly only one feature of management requiring study. Equally important are caloric intake and composition of the diet.

When a diagnosis of symptomatic hypoglycemia is made, Cornblath and Schwartz (1966) have recommended rapid intravenous administration of 1 to 2 ml/kg of a solution of glucose in water (50 gm/100 ml), followed by continuous infusion, 75 to 110 ml/kg/day, of a 15 gm/100 ml solution of glucose in water. Oral feedings are instituted as soon as clinical manifestations subside, but the intravenous infusion is continued for 48 hours after concentration of glucose returns to normal. To avoid postinfusion hypoglycemia, concentration of glucose in the infusion solution should be reduced to 10 and then 5 gm/100 ml before being discontinued. Haworth and Vidyasagar (1971) state that the prognosis of symptomatic hypoglycemia is poor. In a follow-up study, 15 of 25 infants with symptomatic neonatal hypoglycemia, as compared with only 4 of 24 infants with asymptomatic hypoglycemia, demonstrated abnormality of the central nervous system.

Choice of feeding in management of hypoglycemia of the newborn has not been a subject of study. Whether a 15 gm/100 ml solution of glucose or a milk-based formula is to be preferred is unknown but, at least after 48 hours of age, a milk-based formula seems preferable because of its provision of various nutrients other than carbohydrate. Frequent small feedings are probably preferable to larger feedings at greater intervals, but the residual stomach content must be monitored closely. Feedings by gavage at intervals of two to three hours will generally be found to be practical.

QUANTITATIVE ASPECTS OF DISACCHARIDE HYDROLYSIS IN NEWBORN INFANTS

Capacity of the infant to split disaccharides is presumably related to disaccharidase activity per unit of small intestinal mucosa and to the length of the small intestine. In studies of three fullterm newborn infants who died after one day of age, Auricchio et al. (1965) estimated the maximal velocities of hydrolysis of various disaccharides in vitro. The maximal rate of hydrolysis of lactose, ranging from 57 to 67 gm in 24 hours, probably exceeds by a considerable margin the actual in vivo capacity of the intestinal mucosa to split lactose. It may be noted, for example, that the rate of passage of a carmine marker from time of feeding to appearance of carmine in the stool may be only three to four hours (Chapter 15, Fig. 15–1). Presumably, the greater portion of the feeding reaches the small intestine in a relatively short period of time, and carbohydrate either is hydrolyzed and absorbed or passes into the colon.

When disaccharides are not hydrolyzed and absorbed, their presence in the colon exerts an osmotic effect that leads to passage of frequent, loose stools. In the case of lactase deficiency, the presence of lactose in the ileocecal region leads to fermentation of the carbohydrate by intestinal bacteria with resultant production of carbon dioxide and of lactic and other organic acids. These products of bacterial activity exert osmotic and irritative effects on the colon, further aggravating the diarrhea and being responsible for the acid pH of the stools. As concluded by Haemmerli et al. (1965), it seems likely that the relatively large quantities of lactose ingested by the breastfed infant may exceed the capacity of the small intestinal mucosa for hydrolysis. Several formulas commercially prepared for infants contain lactose as the only carbohydrate in concentration similar to that of human milk. Infants receiving these feedings during the early weeks of life have frequent, rather loose stools of acid pH, thus resembling breastfed infants in stool pattern (Barbero et al., 1952; Pratt and Read, 1955). Because of the relatively late development of lactase activity in fetal life, preterm infants are particularly prone to demonstrate signs of impaired lactose tolerance during the first weeks of life.

Much additional information will be required for a full understanding of the relation between the load of disaccharide ingested and the ability to hydrolyze the load. It seems probable that the most efficient hydrolysis of disaccharides would result from ingestion of relatively small amounts of milk or formula in equally spaced feedings throughout the 24-hour period.

MALABSORPTION OF SUGARS

Regardless of the nature of the disorder, the consequences of malabsorption of sugars are much the same—meteorism, diarrhea, dehydration, acidosis and hypoglycemia (Launiala, 1968). Because the human intestine cannot produce hypertonic stools (Metcalfe-Gibson et al., 1967; Devroede and Phillips, 1969), failure to absorb solutes causes osmotic diarrhea (Lindquist and Meeuwisse, 1962), which may lead to dehydration. The stools are isosmotic, with carbohydrates accounting for a considerable portion of the intestinal solute load (Launiala, 1968; Meeuwisse and Melin, 1969). Increased serum osmolality has been reported in infants with acute enteritis after consumption of milk (Torres-Pinedo et al., 1966) and in several patients with glucose-galactose malabsorption (Meeuwisse and Melin, 1969).

Carbohydrate starvation may to some extent explain the metabolic acidosis in disaccharide intolerance and glucose-galactose malabsorption, but the fecal loss of cations trapped by organic acids produced by bacteria from unabsorbed carbohydrates seems to be of greater importance (Torres-Pinedo et al., 1966; Meeuwisse and Melin, 1969).

Disaccharidase Deficiency – General Considerations

Before they can be absorbed, dietary disaccharides and small oligosaccharides arising from cleavage of starch by α-amylase must be hydrolyzed to monosaccharides by the membrane-bound disaccharidases of the small-intestinal mucosal cells. Because disaccharidase deficiency results in clinical findings only when the diet contains significant amounts of the relevant disaccharide, knowledge of the carbohydrate composition of foods consumed by the child is of considerable importance.

Disaccharidase deficiency is diagnosed most reliably by direct assay of disaccharidase activities of small-intestinal mucosal specimens obtained by peroral intestinal biopsy (Shmerling, 1970). However, valuable information may also be obtained by comparing the increase in glucose concentration of the blood after oral administration of a disaccharide load with the increase obtained after oral administration of an equal load of the constituent monosaccharides (Dahlqvist et al., 1968). Determinations of fecal content of organic acids, reducing substances and fecal pH may also be of value in diagnosis.

If disaccharidase deficiency is diagnosed on the basis of results of intestinal mucosal biopsy and disaccharide intolerance is diagnosed on the basis of clinical response to ingestion of the disaccharide, it is evident that the two conditions will not always coincide. The disparity of symptoms in individuals with equally low disaccharidase activities may be explained by differences in intestinal transit time and bacterial ecology. Furthermore, it may be noted that disaccharidase activities are usually measured in the mucosa from a single site of the small gut (e.g., proximal jejunum), whereas testing disaccharide tolerance involves a varying, but longer, length of gut. This distinction is especially relevant in states of secondary disaccharidase deficiency – e.g., celiac disease.

Lactase Deficiency

In contrast to the low intestinal lactase activity reported in a high proportion of older children and adults of certain ethnic groups, only a few cases have been reported in which deficiency of lactase was demonstrated shortly after birth and thus could be assumed to be congenital (Launiala et al., 1966). Lactose intolerance resulting from diminishing activity of intestinal lactase after weaning is a common feature in almost all mammals. Many white Europeans and their offspring in other continents seem to be exceptions to this rule, retaining high lactase activities throughout life. Suppression of intestinal lactase synthesis is thought to be genetically determined, but the time at which this occurs is not uniform. Low intestinal lactase activity develops gradually during school age in about 15 per cent of the Finnish population (Jussila et al., 1970), whereas in Thai children lactase activity decreases to low values before school age (Flatz et al., 1969). Although a number of investigators have reported that loss of intestinal lactase activity occurs as a consequence of enteric infections or malnutrition, it is possible that in many instances the low lactase activity reflects a physiologic change rather than the result of disease.

It seems likely that the "severe lactose intolerance" described by Holzel et al. (1962) may be unrelated to intestinal lactase deficiency. The case reported by Durand (1958) appears to have been similar, and a somewhat milder case has been described by Berg et al. (1969). The infants are critically ill, demonstrate lactosuria, signs of renal tubular dysfunction (generalized aminoaciduria) and impairment of liver function. If lactose is excluded from the diet, the infant may recover and subsequently be tolerant to lactose.

Sucrase-Isomaltase Deficiency

Congenital deficiency of intestinal sucrase (invertase) is always combined with deficiency of isomaltase, although the α-glucosidases are different. The first cases of this inherited disorder were described by Weijers et al. (1961) and soon after by Prader et al. (1961). The mode of inheritance is autosomal recessive, and asymptomatic parents have been shown to have α-glucosidase activities intermediate between those demonstrated by symptomatic offspring and normal individuals (Kerry and Townley, 1965).

Infants with this type of sugar intolerance remain well as long as they are mainly breastfed or given formulas containing lactose, dextrose or invert sugar as carbohydrate components. When sucrose is introduced, as in a formula or in strained fruits or syrups, the infant reacts with osmotic diarrhea. Older children are likely to develop an aversion to sweet food items and then become asymptomatic.

Symptoms usually subside when the sugar content of the diet is reduced, but a starch meal may cause distress (Weijers et al., 1961). There are two reasons why consumption of starch may provoke symptoms in some patients with hereditary sucrase-isomaltase deficiency.

The α-1,6 glycosidic linkage in isomaltotriose remaining after α-amylase hydrolysis of starch cannot be further hydrolyzed if isomaltase is lacking. However, only a minority of the glycosidic linkages in starch are of the α-1,6 type (less than 5 per cent in amylopectin). Dahlqvist (1962) calculated that, in healthy individuals, sucrase and isomaltase account for approximately 75 per cent of small intestinal maltase activity. Therefore, another reason for starch intolerance is that, in the absence of sucrase and isomaltase, the remaining maltase activity is too low for optimum hydrolysis of α-1,4 linkages of maltose and small oligosaccharides.

If reduction of dietary sucrose has insufficient therapeutic effect, enzyme substitution with glucamylase* in doses of 200 to 500 mg before the major meals can be beneficial (Meeuwisse and Jodl, unpublished).

Secondary Deficiency of Disaccharidases

It is obvious that the activities of disaccharidases are reduced in gastrointestinal disorders with structural abnormalities of the small-intestinal mucosa, especially in the presence of villous atrophy (Lubos et al., 1967; Bayless and Huang, 1969; Dahlqvist et al., 1970). In such conditions, including celiac disease, cystic fibrosis of pancreas, kwashiorkor, *Giardia lamblia* infestation and infectious diarrhea, activity of all disaccharidases may be decreased.

Therapy consists primarily of treating the underlying disease, but temporary limitation of the amount of dietary disaccharides may be effective in reducing the number of watery stools (Burke and Danks, 1966; Torres-Pinedo et al., 1966; Prinsloo et al., 1969).

Malabsorption of Monosaccharides

Disturbed absorption of monosaccharides exists as a primary, genetic disorder as well as secondary to other diseases. The small-intestinal mucosa has separate, specific pathways for absorption of glucose, galactose (Crane, 1968) and fructose (Gracey et al., 1972). Monosaccharide malabsorption may be a consequence of a congenital defect in absorption, deconjugation of bile acids or mucosal damage. So far, only glucose-galactose malabsorption has been described as a primary congenital disturbance.

---

*Bi-myconase, which contains glucamylase and invertase from molds, is manufactured by Gist-Brocades, Delft, Netherlands.

Glucose-Galactose Malabsorption

This recessively inherited congenital disorder has been recognized since 1962 (Meeuwisse and Melin, 1969). Diarrhea (with glucose in the stools), failure to thrive, metabolic acidosis and slight renal glucosuria begin after the first feedings. Partial improvement is obtained with diets containing sucrose as the carbohydrate component, but normal stools are not produced until almost all carbohydrates have been replaced by fructose. The infant may then develop normally; although the reduced transport of glucose and galactose continues, increasing amounts of starch and milk can be tolerated if taken in divided feedings throughout the day. The renal glucosuria suggests that there is some disturbance of tubular glucose transport as well.

Malabsorption Caused by Bacterial Deconjugation of Bile Salts

Severe intolerance to all dietary carbohydrates has been reported in newborn infants after abdominal surgery (Burke and Danks, 1966). In surviving infants, the disorder was transient and it is now well established that the causative factor is bacterial multiplication within the lumen of the proximal segment of the small intestine. The "stagnant loop syndrome" or "contaminated bowel syndrome" is thus a variant of the already well-known "blind-loop syndrome," although the consequences in infants are different from those in adults.

Anatomic abnormalities or reduced peristalsis after severe neonatal illness favors bacterial multiplication (Gracey et al., 1969). Some anaerobic species, mainly bacteroides and lactobacilli, can deconjugate the taurine and glycine conjugates of bile acids, producing a reversible inhibition of the transport of monosaccharides into the intestinal mucosa (Gracey et al., 1971).

Treatment consists of a diet containing no carbohydrate. Glucose can be given by parenteral infusion. This regimen has to be continued for some weeks and the carbohydrate content of the diet is then gradually increased. Administration of antibiotics may be beneficial but is not without risk because of the possibility that further derangement of the intestinal flora will result.

Malabsorption Due to Mucosal Damage

The same conditions that cause secondary deficiency of disaccharidases may also impair the transport of monosaccharides; hence, replacement of starch and disaccharides by monosaccharides in the diet of such patients may be of little benefit. Slow absorption of glucose in acute diarrhea was demonstrated by Torres-Pinedo et al. (1966), and in protein-calorie malnutrition by James (1968). In celiac disease, the absorption of all nutrients, including carbohydrates, is impaired. Xylose and glucose tolerance tests have frequently been used to test the absorptive capacity of individuals with suspected disease of the small-intestinal mucosa.

INBORN ERRORS OF FRUCTOSE METABOLISM

Two relatively rare autosomal recessive inborn errors involving the metabolism of fructose have been reported. The first, essential fructosuria, is a benign disorder, whereas the second, hereditary fructose intolerance, may be life-threatening if proper diet is not instituted early in the course of the disease. An excellent review of these two disorders has been prepared by Froesch (1972).

Essential Fructosuria

This asymptomatic, benign disorder was estimated by Lasker (1941) to occur in approximately 1 in 130,000 individuals in the general population; however, Froesch (1972) suggests that the incidence may have been underestimated because the disorder is harmless, asymptomatic and may not come to medical attention.

It has been found that essential fructosuria results from a primary lack of the enzyme, hepatic fructokinase, which is involved in the phosphorylation of fructose to fructose-1-phosphate. Fructosuria occurs only after ingestion of fructose as the monosaccharide or in the form of sucrose. Metabolism of other monosaccharides is normal.

Hereditary Fructose Intolerance

Infants inheriting this disorder are healthy and free of symptoms as long as they continue to consume a diet free of fructose. The inclusion of fructose in the diet results in symptoms of failure to thrive, vomiting, hypoglycemia, hepatosplenomegaly, jaundice, albuminuria and aminoaciduria (Froesch, 1972). This disease is caused by a lack of fructose-1-phosphate aldolase, the enzyme which splits fructose-1-phosphate to D-glyceraldehyde and dihydroxyacetone phosphate. The fructose-induced hypoglycemia, which frequently occurs in patients with hereditary fructose intolerance, is not due to hyperinsulinism (Froesch et al., 1959) but is thought to result from a block in glucose release from the liver. The hypoglycemic attacks after ingestion of fructose do not appear to cause serious brain damage, since intelligence of older children and adults has been found to be normal (Cornblath et al., 1963; Levin et al., 1963, 1968; Froesch et al., 1963). One beneficial aspect of the disease is that the teeth of patients with this disorder appear to be relatively free of caries (Marthaler and Froesch, 1967; Newbrun, 1969; Scherp, 1971). The aversion developed for sweets and fruits eliminates much of the substrate for growth of caries-producing bacteria in the mouth. Treatment of hereditary fructose intolerance involves the virtual elimination of fructose-(and, of course, sucrose-) containing foods from the diet.

INBORN ERRORS OF GALACTOSE METABOLISM

Segal (1972) has pointed out that the term "galactosemia" has become inadequate to describe the several known disorders in the metabolism of galactose. Isselbacher et al. (1956) described a disturbance in the normal metabolism of galactose caused by deficiency of galactose-1-phosphate uridyl transferase, an enzyme which participates in the reaction of galactose-1-phosphate with uridine diphosphate glucose. Deficiency of the enzyme in the untreated infant will result in failure to thrive, liver disease, cataracts and mental retardation. Prevalence of the disorder has been reported to be 1 in 18,000 births (Hansen et al., 1964). Gitzelmann (1967) has reported another inherited syndrome of elevated plasma galactose concentration, galactosuria and juvenile cataracts, which appears to be caused by a deficiency of galactokinase, the enzyme involved in the phosphorylation of galactose to galactose-1-phosphate.

Segal (1972) has classified these two disorders as transferase-deficiency galactosemia and galactokinase-deficiency galactosemia. He speculates that inborn errors involving the other enzymes concerned with conversion of galactose to glucose-1-phosphate may exist. Both of the known forms of galactosemia are inherited as autosomal recessive traits.

Because glucose can be converted by the body to galactose in sufficient quantities to fulfill the requirements for galactose, dietary management can be based on the goal of eliminating galactose from the diet. All symptoms and signs of the disorder can be prevented by elimination of galactose from the diet. Even when manifestations of galactosemia are advanced, much improvement may result from consumption of a galactose-free diet.

The toxic effects of galactose in the lens appear to be related to the reduction of galactose by aldose reductase to the polyol, galactitol. The development of cataracts in both forms of galactosemia is closely associated with imbibition of water by the lens as an accumulation of galactitol occurs (Kinoshita and Merola, 1964; Sippel, 1966). Galactitol is found in the liver, kidney and brain of galactosemic patients; however, the severity of the involvement of these organs appears to be greatest with the transferase deficiency. The mental retardation resulting from the toxicity of galactose and its metabolites appears to be irreversible. Although an age-related tolerance to galactose has been postulated, Segal et al. (1965) cite data suggesting that individuals with transferase deficiency galactosemia do not develop the ability to metabolize galactose as they grow older.

In infancy, it is relatively easy to provide a galactose-free diet since parental control of food intake is almost absolute. A galactose-free diet consists of a milk substitute and avoidance of all foods containing physiologically available galactose.

Soy-based formulas contain appreciable amounts of the α-galactosides, stachyose and raffinose, which contain galactose. Gitzelmann and Auricchio (1965) have calculated that a protein intake of 3 gm/kg/day from soy would provide a daily intake of stachyose and raffinose of 0.32 and 0.07 gm/kg/day, respectively, equivalent to 0.18 gm/kg/day of galactose. If this quantity of galactose could be released from the stachyose and raffinose, it would surely be harmful, and several authors have warned against use of soy-based formulas for management of infants with galactosemia (Schwarz, 1966; Cornblath and Schwartz, 1966). However, clinical observations indicate that soy-based formulas are satisfactory in management of galactosemia (Gitzelmann and Auricchio, 1965; Gitzelmann, 1966).

Gitzelmann and Auricchio (1965) point out that ingestion of α-galactosides could be hazardous for a galactosemic patient by three possible mechanisms: they could be hydrolyzed by intestinal mucosal cells with absorption of galactose; they could be absorbed as α-galactosides and transported to other tissues where hydrolysis might occur; they could be acted upon by intestinal bacteria with liberation of galactose, which might then be absorbed. It has now been shown that α-galactosidases are absent in the human intestinal mucosa (Gitzelmann and Auricchio, 1965). Small amounts of raffinose do appear in the urine after feeding of this sugar, indicating that it can be absorbed, but erythrocyte content of galactose-1-phosphate does not increase, and evidence of hydrolysis in various body tissues is therefore lacking. During diarrhea, hydrolysis of α-galactosides occurs as demonstrated by the finding of free hexoses in the stools. However, absorption from the colon appears to be extremely limited. It therefore appears safe to utilize soy-based formulas for treatment of galactosemia.

Nutramigen (Mead) contains approximately 16 mg of lactose (equivalent to 8 mg of galactose) in 67 kcal (Committee on Nutrition, 1963), but this amount appears to be too small to constitute a hazard, and the formula has been used successfully in management of galactosemia (Isselbacher, 1959; Donnell et al., 1961).

A list of foods permitted in the diet of galactosemic patients has been published by Koch et al. (1965).

Appendix

Classification of Carbohydrates Important in Infant Feeding

MONOSACCHARIDES

Glucose is found as a simple sugar in honey and in certain fruits and vegetables. This sugar, commonly referred to as dextrose, is produced commercially by the action of the bacterial enzyme glucoamylase on cornstarch. Dextrose is not used in commercially prepared liquid formulas for infants, because of the nonenzymatic browning reaction which occurs when dextrose and certain amino acids (e.g., lysine) are heated together.

Fructose also occurs as a simple sugar in honey and in certain fruits and vegetables. Fructose, upon ingestion, is rapidly converted to glucose, the primary carbohydrate utilized by body tissues.

OLIGOSACCHARIDES

Disaccharides

Lactose is the primary carbohydrate of milks (with the exception of that of the California sea lion). Lactose is a reducing sugar which is hydrolyzed by acids and the enzyme lactase to its constituent monosaccharides, glucose and galactose. It is the primary carbohydrate used in commercially prepared formulas for infants and is probably the most abundant carbohydrate in the diet of infants up to six months of age.

Sucrose occurs in the juices of plants such as sugar beets, sugar cane and ripe fruits. A nonreducing sugar, sucrose, upon hydrolysis by dilute acid or the enzyme sucrase, produces one molecule each of glucose and fructose. This disaccharide is widely used in the formulation of strained and junior foods and is substituted for lactose in certain hypoallergenic formulas. The cariogenicity of sucrose is believed to be higher than that of any other carbohydrate.

Maltose is a reducing sugar composed of two glucose units joined in an α-1,4-glucosidic linkage and is formed by the action of amylase on starch. The enzyme maltase hydrolyzes maltose to two molecules of glucose. Maltose is an intermediate product of starch hydrolysis and consequently is an important constituent of corn syrups.

Isomaltose is not found free in nature but exists as a disaccharide in glycogen and amylopectin. The enzyme oligo-1,6-α-glucosidase (isomaltase or α-dextrinase) hydrolyzes the α-1,6-glucosidic linkage of isomaltose to yield two molecules of glucose.

Lactulose is a synthetic disaccharide composed of one molecule each of galactose and fructose. It does not occur in nature and cannot be metabolized by the infant. It is formed in the commercial processing of cow milk by the alkaline enolization of the glucose moiety of lactose to fructose. Adachi and Patton (1961) have reported that the lactulose content of commercial evaporated milk may be as high as 940 mg/100 ml. This disaccharide has recently been suggested by Bush (1970) to be an ideal laxative for children.

Trisaccharides

Raffinose, the most important of the naturally occurring trisaccharides, occurs in sugar beets and is concentrated in sugar beet molasses. When hydrolyzed completely, raffinose yields one molecule each of fructose, glucose and galactose. It may be partially hydrolyzed by maltase or sucrase.

Maltotriose is an intermediate hydrolysis product in the α-amylolysis of starch and consists of 3 glucose units joined by α-1,4-glucosidic linkages.

POLYSACCHARIDES

Corn syrup solids are hydrolysates produced by the action of acid and/or enzymes on cornstarch. They contain varying amounts of dextrose, maltose, tri- and higher saccharides, depending upon the DE, which may range from 20 to more than 95 (Fig. 8–4). Corn syrup solids used in commercially prepared formulas for infants have DEs in the range of 30–42.

Malto-dextrins are saccharides obtained from starch and have a DE less than 20.

Starch occurs in two forms (Fig. 8–1). Most starches contain 16 to 24 per cent amylose and 76 to 84 per cent amylopectin. The waxy varieties of starch are composed almost entirely of amylopectin.

Modified food starches are starches which have been chemically cross-linked and/or stabilized to provide special properties which are desirable in food processing. Modified food starches are more resistant to syneresis, have higher viscosity, are more stable in acid foods and have a different "mouth-feel" than unmodified starches. Use of modified food starches in infant foods has been discussed in an NAS-NRC report (Filer, 1971).

Glycogen has a structure similar to that of amylopectin, except that it is more highly branched (i.e., the degree of branching in glycogen is about 0.09 versus 0.04 in amylopectin). Glycogen is the storage form of glucose in animals and, depending upon diet, the content in adult skeletal muscle may range as high as 5 gm/100 gm tissue (Consolazio and Johnson, 1972). An excellent review by Åstrand (1967) discusses how endurance during strenuous physical activity may be enhanced by changes in the carbohydrate content of the diet.

REFERENCES

Adachi, S., and Patton, S.: Presence and significance of lactulose in milk products: a review. J. Dairy Sci. *44*:1375, 1961.

Adam, P. A. J.: Control of glucose metabolism in the human fetus and newborn infant. *In* Levine, R., and Luft, R. (eds.): Advances in Metabolic Disorders. Vol. 5. New York and London, Academic Press, 1971, p. 183.

Anderson, T. A., Fomon, S. J., and Filer, L. J., Jr.: Carbohydrate tolerance studies with 3-day-old infants. J. Lab. Clin. Med. *79*:31, 1972.

Åstrand, P.-O.: Diet and athletic performance. Fed. Proc. *26*:1772, 1967.

Auricchio, S., Della Pietra, D., and Vegnente, A.: Studies on intestinal digestion of starch in man. II. Intestinal hydrolysis of amylopectin in infants and children. Pediatrics *39*:853, 1967.

Auricchio, S., Rubino, A., and Mürset, G.: Intestinal glycosidase activities in the human embryo, fetus, and newborn. Pediatrics *35*:944, 1965.

Barbero, G. J., Runge, G., Fischer, D., Crawford, M. N., Torres, F. E., and György, P.: Investigations on the bacterial flora, pH, and sugar content in the intestinal tract of infants. J. Pediatr. *40*:152, 1952.

Bayless, T. M., and Huang, S.: Inadequate intestinal digestion of lactose. Amer. J. Clin. Nutr. *22*:250, 1969.

Berg, N. O., Dahlqvist, A., Lindberg, T., and Studnitz, W. v.: Severe familial lactose intolerance—a gastrogen disorder? Acta Paediatr. Scand. *58*:525, 1969.

Bergmann, K. E.: Unpublished observations.

Bodian, M., Sheldon, W., and Lightwood, R.: Congenital hypoplasia of the exocrine pancreas. Acta Paediatr. Scand. *53*:282, 1964.

Bond, J. H., and Levitt, M. D.: Use of pulmonary hydrogen (H_2) measurements to quantitate carbohydrate absorption. J. Clin. Invest. *51*:1219, 1972.

Boyns, D. R., Crossley, J. N., Abrams, M. E., Jarrett, R. J., and Keens, H.: Oral glucose tolerance and related factors in a normal population sample. I. Blood sugar, plasma insulin, glyceride, and cholesterol measurements and the effects of age and sex. Br. Med. J. *1*:595, 1969.

Burke, V., and Danks, D. M.: Monosaccharide malabsorption in young infants. Lancet *1*:1177, 1966.

Bush, R. T.: Lactulose: an ideal laxative for children. New Zeal. Med. J. *71*:364, 1970.

Castro, A., Scott, J. P., Grettie, D. P., Macfarlane, D., and Bailey, R. E.: Plasma insulin and glucose responses of healthy subjects to varying glucose loads during three-hour oral glucose tolerance tests. Diabetes *19*:842, 1970.

Cole, H. S.: Low response to orally administered glucose in children. Amer. J. Dis. Child. *123*:572, 1972.

Committee on Nutrition, American Academy of Pediatrics: Appraisal of nutritional adequacy of infant formulas used as cow milk substitutes. Pediatrics *31*:329, 1963.

Condon, J. R., Nassim, J. R., Millard, F. J. C., Hilbe, A., and Stainthorpe, E. M.: Calcium and phosphorus metabolism in relation to lactose tolerance. Lancet *1*:1027, 1970.

Consolazio, C. F., and Johnson, H. L.: Dietary carbohydrate and work capacity. Amer. J. Clin. Nutr. *25*:85, 1972.

Cornblath, M., Rosenthal, I. M., Reisner, S. H., Wybregt, S. H., and Crane, R. K.: Hereditary fructose intolerance. New Eng. J. Med. *269*:1271, 1963.

Cornblath, M., and Schwartz, R.: Disorders of Carbohydrate Metabolism in Infancy. Philadelphia, W. B. Saunders Co., 1966.

Court, J. M., Dunlop, M., Leonard, I., and Leonard, R. F.: Five-hour oral glucose tolerance test in obese children. Arch. Dis. Child. *46*:791, 1971.

Crane, R. K.: Absorption of sugars. *In* Handbook of Physiology. Sec. 6. Alimentary Canal. Vol. III. Washington, D.C., American Physiological Society, 1968, p. 1323.

Dahlqvist, A.: Specificity of the human intestinal disaccharidases and implications for hereditary disaccharide intolerance. J. Clin. Invest. *41*:463, 1962.

Dahlqvist, A., Hammond, J. B., Crane, R. K., Dunphy, J. V., and Littman, A.: Intestinal lactase deficiency and lactose intolerance in adults. Gastroenterology *54*:807, 1968.

Dahlqvist, A., Lindberg, T., Meeuwisse, G., and Akerman, M.: Intestinal dipeptidases and disaccharidases in children with malabsorption. Acta Paediatr. Scand. *59*:621, 1970.

Devroede, G. J., and Phillips, S. F.: Conservation of sodium, chloride, and water by the human colon. Gastroenterology *56*:101, 1969.

Donnell, G. N., Collado, M., and Koch, R.: Growth and development of children with galactosemia. J. Pediatr. *58*:836, 1961.

Durand, P.: Lattosuria idiopatica in un paziente con diarrea cronica ed acidosi. Min. Pediatr. *10*:706, 1958.

Filer, L. J., Jr.: Modified food starches for use in infant foods. Nutr. Rev. *29*:55, 1971.

Flatz, G., Saengudom, C., and Sanguanbhokhai, T.: Lactose intolerance in Thailand. Nature *221*:758, 1969.

Förster, H., Haslbeck, M., Geser, C.-A., and Mehnert, H.: Blood glucose and serum insulin after oral loading with glucose and starch syrup in varying doses. Diabetologia *6*:482, 1970.

Froesch, E. R.: Essential fructosuria and hereditary fructose intolerance. *In* Stanbury, J. B., Wyngaarden, J. B., and Fredrickson, D. S. (eds.): The Metabolic Basis of Inherited Disease. New York, McGraw-Hill Book Co., 1972, p. 131.

Froesch, E. R., Prader, A., Wolf, H. P., and Labhart, A.: Die hereditäre Fructoseintoleranz. Helv. Paediatr. Acta *14*:99, 1959.

Froesch, E. R., Wolf, H. P., Baitsch, H., Prader, A., and Labhart, A.: Hereditary fructose intolerance: an inborn defect of hepatic fructose-1-phosphate splitting aldolase. Amer. J. Med. *34*:151, 1963.

Gitzelmann, R.: (Letter to the Editor.) The handling of soya α-galactosides by a normal and a galactosemic child. Pediatrics *37*:531, 1966.

Gitzelmann, R.: Hereditary galactokinase deficiency, a newly recognized cause of juvenile cataracts. Pediatr. Res. *1*:14, 1967.

Gitzelmann, R., and Auricchio, S.: The handling of soya alpha-galactosides by a normal and a galactosemic child. Pediatrics *36*:231, 1965.

Gracey, M., Burke, V., and Anderson, C. M.: Association of monosaccharide malabsorption with abnormal small-intestinal flora. Lancet *2*:384, 1969.

Gracey, M., Burke, V., and Oshin, A.: Reversible inhibition of intestinal active sugar transport by deconjugated bile salt in vitro. Biochim. Biophys. Acta *225*:308, 1971.

Gracey, M., Burke, V., and Oshin, A.: Active intestinal transport of D-fructose. Biochim. Biophys. Acta *266*:397, 1972.
Gray, G. M.: Carbohydrate digestion and absorption. Gastroenterology *58*:96, 1970.
Greaves, J. P., and Hollingsworth, D. F.: Changes in the pattern of carbohydrate consumption in Britain. Proc. Nutr. Soc. *23*:136, 1964.
Greenberg, R. E., and Christiansen, R. O.: Hypoglycemia. *In* Smith, C. A. (ed.): The Critically Ill Child. Philadelphia, W. B. Saunders Co., 1972, p. 180.
Greenwald, E., Samachson, J., and Spencer, H.: Effect of lactose on calcium metabolism in man. J. Nutr. *79*:531, 1963.
Gryboski, J. D., and Boehm, J. J.: Lactulosuria in the neonate: a preliminary report. Pediatrics *35*:340, 1965.
Haemmerli, U. P., Kistler, H., Ammann, R., Marthaler, T., Semenza, G., Auricchio, S., and Prader, A.: Acquired milk intolerance in the adult caused by lactose malabsorption due to a selective deficiency of intestinal lactase activity. Amer. J. Med. *38*:7, 1965.
Hales, C. N., and Randle, P. J.: Effects of low-carbohydrate diet and diabetes mellitus on plasma concentrations of glucose, non-esterified fatty acid, and insulin during oral glucose-tolerance tests. Lancet *1*:790, 1963.
Hansen, R. G., Bretthauer, R. K., Mayes, J., and Nordin, J. H.: Estimation of frequency of occurrence of galactosemia in the population. Proc. Soc. Exp. Biol. Med. *115*:560, 1964.
Haworth, J. C., and Vidyasagar, D.: Hypoglycemia in the newborn. Clin. Obstet. Gynecol. *14*:821, 1971.
Holzel, A., Mereu, T., and Thomson, M. L.: Severe lactose intolerance in infancy. Lancet *2*:1346, 1962.
Husband, J., Husband, P., and Mallinson, C. N.: Gastric emptying of starch meals in the newborn. Lancet *2*:290, 1970.
Isselbacher, K. J.: Galactose metabolism and galactosemia. Amer. J. Med. *26*:715, 1959.
Isselbacher, K. J., Anderson, E. P., Kurahashi, K., and Kalckar, H. M.: Congenital galactosemia, a single enzymatic block in galactose metabolism. Science *123*:635, 1956.
James, W. P. T.: Intestinal absorption in protein-calorie malnutrition. Lancet *1*:333, 1968.
Jarrett, E. C., and Holman, G. H.: Lactose absorption in the premature infant. Arch. Dis. Child. *41*:525, 1966.
Jussila, J., Isokoski, M., and Launiala, K.: Prevalence of lactose malabsorption in a Finnish rural population. Scand. J. Gastroent. *5*:49, 1970.
Kerry, K. R., and Townley, R. R. W.: Genetic aspects of intestinal sucrase-isomaltase deficiency. Aust. Paediatr. J. *1*:223, 1965.
Kinoshita, J. H., and Merola, L. O.: Hydration of the lens during the development of galactose cataract. Invest. Ophthal. *3*:577, 1964.
Koch, R., Acosta, P., Donnell, G., and Lieberman, E.: Nutritional therapy of galactosemia. Clin. Pediatr. *4*:571, 1965.
Lasker, M.: Essential fructosuria. Hum. Biol. *13*:51, 1941.
Launiala, K.: The mechanism of diarrhoea in congenital disaccharide malabsorption. Acta Paediatr. Scand. *57*:425, 1968.
Launiala, K., Kuitunen, P., and Visakorpi, J. K.: Disaccharidases and histology of duodenal mucosa in congenital lactose malabsorption. Acta Paediatr. Scand. *55*:257, 1966.
Lauvaux, J. P., and Staquet, M.: The oral glucose tolerance test: a study of the influence of age on the response to the standard oral 50 g glucose load. Diabetologia *6*:414, 1970.
Lengemann, F. W., Wasserman, R. H., and Comar, C. L.: Studies on the enhancement of radiocalcium and radiostrontium absorption by lactose in the rat. J. Nutr. *68*:443, 1959.
Levin, B., Oberholzer, V. G., Snodgrass, G. J. A. I., Stimmler, L., and Wilmers, M. J.: Fructosaemia: an inborn error of fructose metabolism. Arch. Dis. Child. *38*:220, 1963.
Levin, B., Snodgrass, G. J. A. I., Oberholzer, V. G., Burgess, E. A., and Dobbs, R. H.: Fructosaemia: observations on seven cases. Amer. J. Med. *45*:826, 1968.
Lindquist, B., and Meeuwisse, G. W.: Chronic diarrhoea caused by monosaccharide malabsorption. Acta Paediatr. Scand. *51*:674, 1962.

Lubos, M. C., Gerrard, J. W., and Buchan, D. J.: Disaccharidase activities in milk-sensitive and celiac patients. J. Pediatr. *70*:325, 1967.
Marthaler, T. M., and Froesch, E. R.: Hereditary fructose intolerance. Dental status of eight patients. Br. Dent. J. *123*:597, 1967.
Meeuwisse, G. W., and Jodl, J.: Unpublished observation.
Meeuwisse, G. W., and Melin, K.: Glucose-galactose malabsorption. Acta Paediatr. Scand. (Suppl. 188), 1969.
Metcalfe-Gibson, A., Ing, T. S., Kuiper, J. J., Richards, P., Ward, E. E., and Wrong, O. M.: In vivo dialysis of faeces as a method of stool analysis. II. The influence of diet. Clin. Sci. *33*:89, 1967.
Mills, R., Breiter, H., Kempster, E., McKey, B., Pickens, M., and Outhouse, J.: The influence of lactose on calcium retention in children. J. Nutr. *20*:467, 1940.
Milner, R. D. G.: The development of insulin secretion in man. *In* Jonxis, J. H. P., Visser, H. K. A., and Troelstra, J. A. (eds.): Metabolic Processes in the Foetus and Newborn Infant. Leiden, Stenfert Kroese, 1971, p. 193.
Milner, R. D. G.: Neonatal hypoglycaemia—a critical reappraisal. Arch. Dis. Child. *47*:679, 1972.
Newbrun, E.: Sucrose, the arch-criminal of dental caries. J. Dent. Child. *36*:239, 1969.
Newton, J. M.: Corn syrups. *In* Symposium Proceedings. Washington, D.C., Corn Refiners Association, Inc., 1970, p. IV–13.
Nisbett, R. E., and Gurwitz, S. B.: Weight, sex, and the eating behavior of human newborns. J. Comp. Physiol. Psychol. *73*:245, 1970.
Oser, B. L. (ed.): Hawks Physiological Chemistry. 14th ed. New York, The Blakiston Division, McGraw-Hill Book Co., 1965, p. 62.
Pedersen, J.: The Pregnant Diabetic and Her Newborn. Problems and Management. Scandinavian University Books, Copenhagen, Ejnar Forlay, Munksgaards, 1967, p. 80.
Pickens, J. M., Burkeholder, J. N., and Womack, W. N.: Oral glucose tolerance test in normal children. Diabetes *16*:11, 1967.
Pildes, R., Forbes, A. E., O'Connor, S. M., and Cornblath, M.: The incidence of neonatal hypoglycemia—a completed survey. J. Pediatr. *70*:76, 1967.
Pildes, R. S., Hart, R. J., Warrner, R., and Cornblath, M.: Plasma insulin response during oral glucose tolerance tests in newborns of normal and gestational diabetic mothers. Pediatrics *44*:76, 1969.
Prader, V. A., Auricchio, S., and Mürset, G.: Durchfall infolge hereditären Mangels an intestinaler Saccharaseaktivität (Saccharoseintoleranz). Schweiz. Med. Wochenschr. *91*:465, 1961.
Pratt, A. G., and Read, W. T., Jr.: Influence of type of feeding on pH of stool, pH of skin, and incidence of perianal dermatitis in the newborn infant. J. Pediatr. *46*:539, 1955.
Prinsloo, J. G., Wittmann, W., Pretorius, P. J., Kruger, H., and Fellingham, S. A.: Effect of different sugars on diarrhoea of acute kwashiorkor. Arch. Dis. Child. *44*:593, 1969.
Scherp, H. W.: Dental caries: prospects for prevention. Science *173*:1199, 1971.
Schoch, T. J.: Starches in foods. *In* Schultz, H. W., Cain, R. F., and Wrolstad, R. W. (eds.): Symposium on Foods: Carbohydrates and Their Roles. Westport, Conn., AVI Publishing, 1969, p. 395.
Schwarz, V.: (Letter to the Editor.) The handling of soya α-galactosides by a normal and a galactosemic child. Pediatrics *37*:531, 1966.
Segal, S.: Disorders of galactose metabolism. *In* Stanbury, J. B., Wyngaarden, J. B., and Fredrickson, D. S. (eds): The Metabolic Basis of Inherited Disease. New York, McGraw-Hill Book Co., 1972, p. 174.
Segal, S., Blair, A., and Roth, H.: The metabolism of galactose by patients with congenital galactosemia. Amer. J. Med. *38*:62, 1965.
Shallenberger, R. S.: Occurrence of various sugars in foods. Sugars in Nutrition, An International Conference. Nashville, Tenn., Vanderbilt University, 1972.
Shmerling, D. H.: Peroral intestinal mucosal biopsies in infants and children. Helv. Paediatr. Acta (Suppl. 22), 1970.
Sippel, T. O.: Changes in the water, protein and glutathione contents of the lens in the course of galactose cataract development in rats. Invest. Ophthal. *5*:568, 1966.
Stephan, U., Hövels, O., and Thilenius, O. G.: Untersuchungen zum Calcium- und Phosphatstoffwechsel Frühgeborener. Z. Kinderheilkd. *86*:447, 1962.

Swan, D. C., Davidson, P., and Albrink, M. J.: Effect of simple and complex carbohydrates on plasma non-esterified fatty acids, plasma-sugar, and plasma-insulin during oral carbohydrate tolerance tests. Lancet *1*:60, 1966.

Torres-Pinedo, R., Lavastida, M., Rivera, C. L., Rodriguez, H., and Ortiz, A.: Studies on infant diarrhea. I. A comparison of the effects of milk feeding and intravenous therapy upon the composition and volume of the stool and urine. J. Clin. Invest. *45*:469, 1966.

Ugolev, A. M.: Membrane (contact) digestion. Physiol. Rev. *45*:555, 1965.

Vaughan, O. W., and Filer, L. J., Jr.: The enhancing action of certain carbohydrates on the intestinal absorption of calcium in the rat. J. Nutr. *71*:10, 1960.

Wasserman, R. H., and Comar, C. L.: Carbohydrates and gastrointestinal absorption of radiostrontium and radiocalcium in the rat. Proc. Soc. Exp. Biol. Med. *101*:314, 1959.

Weijers, H. A., Van De Kamer, J. H., Dicke, W. K., and Ijsseling, J.: Diarrhoea caused by deficiency of sugar splitting enzymes. Acta Paediatr. Scand. *50*:55, 1961.

Zucker, P., and Simon, G.: Prolonged symptomatic neonatal hypoglycemia associated with maternal chlorpropamide therapy. Pediatrics *42*:824, 1968.

9

VITAMINS

Thomas A. Anderson
and
Samuel J. Fomon

In technically advanced countries, vitamin deficiency diseases in infancy are relatively uncommon. For example, in the United States during the past 25 years, vitamin A deficiency has been reported only in infants with steatorrhea or in those receiving milk-free diets (or diets based on skim milk) not fortified with vitamin A; thiamin* deficiency has been reported in only two infants, both of whom had received a soy-based formula which was not fortified with thiamin; deficiencies of riboflavin and niacin in infancy have not been reported. During this period, reports of vitamin A intoxication outnumbered reports of deficiency, suggesting the need for reappraisal of current practices in infant feeding. Publicity during the early 1960s about a possible causal relation between mild overdosage of vitamin D and infantile hypercalcemia has called attention to the need for caution in vitamin administration to infants, although the number of children potentially at risk from such mild overdosage is undoubtedly small.

Deficiency diseases related to certain other vitamins have by no means been eliminated in the United States. Mild deficiency of vitamin K is relatively common in the newborn and deficiency in older infants with steatorrhea is well recognized. Rickets due to vitamin D deficiency continues to occur sporadically, and scurvy occurs in certain geographic areas. Because iron-deficiency anemia may mask

*The generic descriptors and trivial names for vitamins and related compounds used in the following discussion are those recommended for adoption by the IUNS Committee on Nomenclature (1971).

manifestations of folacin deficiency, the prevalence of folacin deficiency in infancy may be considerably higher than is now appreciated.

As discussed previously (Chapter 5), requirements for essential nutrients vary considerably with the circumstances of their determination. Nowhere is this more evident than with respect to the vitamins (Gershoff, 1964). As the carbohydrate content of the diet increases, the requirement for thiamin increases. As protein content of the diet increases, requirement for vitamin B_6 increases and requirements for niacin and pantothenic acid decrease. Increased dietary intake of polyunsaturated fatty acids results in increased requirement for vitamin E. Methionine may have a sparing effect with respect to requirement for folacin and vitamin B_{12}. Tryptophan can replace part of the dietary requirement for niacin. Abundant evidence indicates that composition of the diet influences synthesis of B vitamins by microorganisms of the gastrointestinal tract, but whether in the human these vitamins are then absorbed to a sufficient extent to be of practical value is uncertain.

Chemistry and physiologic functions have been well summarized for the fat-soluble vitamins by DeLuca and Suttie (1970); Wasserman and Corradino (1971); Wasserman and Taylor (1972); and Nair and Kayden (1972); and for various of the water-soluble vitamins by Fasella (1967); Chaykin (1967); Ariaey-Nejad et al. (1970); Knappe (1970); Rivlin (1970) and Barker (1972).

FAT-SOLUBLE VITAMINS

Vitamin A

Vitamin A (retinol) occurs only in tissues and fluids (e.g., milk) of animals, being present in high concentrations in livers of fish and of most land vertebrates, and in eggs, meat and dairy products. At least 10 different carotenoids exhibit provitamin A activity but only α-, β- and γ-carotene and cryptoxanthin are of importance in human nutrition (Dam and Søndergaard, 1964).

One international unit of vitamin A activity is equivalent to 0.30 μg of all-trans vitamin A_1 alcohol (retinol), 0.344 μg of retinyl acetate and 0.60 μg of all-trans β-carotene.

Deficiency

Vitamin A deficiency is among the most prevalent of nutritional deficiency diseases in most developing countries of the world.

In developed countries, this deficiency is rare for three main reasons: first, intake of dairy products and meat is relatively large; second, carotenes, the precursors of vitamin A, are present in many commonly ingested foods, particularly yellow and green vegetables; third, the amount of fat in the diet is sufficient to assure adequate absorption of vitamin A and carotenes. By contrast, in countries in which vitamin A deficiency is prevalent, animal fats are rarely consumed and total dietary intake of fat is so low that, even if carotenes are present in moderate amounts in the diet, they are poorly absorbed. In addition, diets are often deficient in protein, resulting in decreased intestinal absorption of retinol (Arroyave et al., 1959; Mahadevan et al., 1965; Wasserman and Corradino, 1971) and impairment of its transport in the blood (Moore, 1960; Arroyave, 1969).

In vitamin A deficiency, young animals cease to grow and, especially in prolonged deficiency, nearly all organs are affected. Impaired dark adaptation, the first clinical sign of vitamin A deficiency (Roels, 1970), is difficult to measure in the infant and young child. The more severely vitamin A-deficient human infant manifests failure to thrive, apathy, mental retardation, dry and scaly skin and corneal changes that may progress to a stage of ulceration (Jolly, 1967a and b). Cartilage and bone are often involved in addition to other epithelial and connective tissues. Serum concentrations of vitamin A less than 10 μg/100 ml suggest deficiency, and values less than 20 μg/100 ml suggest low stores (Maternal and Child Health Service, 1971). Bulging anterior fontanelle and intracranial hypertension—findings commonly encountered in vitamin A toxicity—have been reported in two cases of vitamin A deficiency in four-month-old infants with cystic fibrosis of the pancreas (Keating and Feigin, 1970).

Estimated Requirement and Advisable Intake

An extensive review of the literature by Rodriguez and Irwin (1972) has cited studies indicating that normal weight gain and dark adaptation are achieved by infants receiving 25 to 35 I.U. of vitamin A per kilogram of body weight per day. Several studies suggested that carotene is utilized less efficiently than retinol by infants and young children. Rønne (1941), using hepatic storage of vitamin A as a criterion, estimated the requirement for vitamin A to be between 20 and 40 I.U./kg/day. Thus, there appears to be reasonable agreement that the requirement for vitamin A during infancy is approximately 30 I.U./kg/day. This is the value selected for inclusion in Table 9–1, the assumption being made that the average weight between birth and 12 months is approximately 8 kg and between 12 and 36 months is approximately 13 kg.

TABLE 9–1 ESTIMATED REQUIREMENTS FOR VITAMINS

Vitamin	Age	
	Birth to 12 Months	*12 to 36 Months*
A	250 I.U./day	400 I.U./day
D	100–200 I.U./day	100–200 I.U./day
E	0.4 mg/gm PUFA*	0.4 mg/gm PUFA
K	5 μg/day	5 μg/day
C	10 mg/day	10 mg/day
Thiamin	0.2 mg/1000 kcal	0.2 mg/1000 kcal
Riboflavin	<0.5 mg/1000 kcal	<0.5 mg/1000 kcal
Niacin†	4.4 mg/1000 kcal	4.4 mg/1000 kcal
B_6	9 μg/gm protein	9 μg/gm protein
Folacin	<50 μg/day	<50 μg/day

*Polyunsaturated fatty acid.
†Including nicotinamide equivalents (60 mg tryptophan = 1 mg niacin).

The advisable intake is tentatively set as twice the estimated requirement—500 I.U. daily between birth and one year and 800 I.U. daily between one and three years of age (Table 9–2). Little is known about the requirement for vitamin A of low-birth-weight infants. It therefore seems reasonable, in spite of smaller size of low-birth-weight infants, to recommend the same intake (500 I.U. daily) for infants weighing less than 2500 gm as for larger infants.

TABLE 9–2 ADVISABLE INTAKES OF VITAMINS

Vitamin	Age	
	Birth to 12 Months Daily Intake	*12 to 36 Months Daily Intake*
A	500 I.U.	800 I.U.
D	400 I.U.	400 I.U.
E	4 I.U.*	4 I.U.
K	15 μg	15 μg
C	20 mg	20 mg
Thiamin	0.2 mg	0.3 mg
Riboflavin	0.4 mg	0.6 mg
Niacin†	5 mg	5 mg
B_6	0.4 mg	0.5 mg
Folacin	50 μg	60 μg

*Greater intakes may be desirable for infants receiving formulas supplying more than 15 per cent of calories from polyunsaturated fatty acids (e.g., formulas in which approximately one-half of the fat is supplied from corn oil or soy oil).
†Including nicotinamide equivalents (60 mg tryptophan = 1 mg niacin).

Sources of Vitamin A

As discussed in Chapter 15 (Tables 15–1 and 15–7), human milk, cow milk and commercially prepared infant formulas are relatively rich sources of vitamin A. In addition, many strained or chopped foods commercially prepared for infants (Chapter 16, Table 16–2) and many table foods commonly fed to infants supply abundant amounts of carotene. Therefore, supplementation of the diet of normal infants and toddlers is rarely necessary.

Infants with chronic steatorrhea and those receiving low fat diets should receive a daily supplement of a water-miscible preparation of vitamin A, preferably about 2000 I.U. daily. Water-miscible preparations of vitamin A are better absorbed than oily preparations.

Intakes by Children in the United States

Intakes of vitamin A by children between 12 and 36 months of age have been recorded in several surveys in the United States. Data from three of these surveys are presented in Table 9–3. Relatively few children were receiving less vitamin A than the advisable intake (Table 9–2) at the time of the survey.

Comparison of dietary intake data with biochemical data is possible for children in the Preschool Nutrition Survey (Owen et al., 1974). Serum concentrations of vitamin A were less than 20 μg/100 ml in only 1 per cent of 507 determinations. Concentrations less than 20 μg/100 ml have generally been accepted as evidence of low body stores (Maternal and Child Health Service, 1971; Owen et al., 1971;

TABLE 9–3 PERCENTAGE OF CHILDREN 12 TO 36 MONTHS OF AGE RECEIVING VARIOUS INTAKES OF VITAMIN A

		Intake of Vitamin A (I.U./day)		
Survey*	Number of Subjects	*<1000*	*1000–1999*	*>1999*
			(Per Cent of Children)	
PNS				
Unsupplemented	600	7	26	67
Supplemented	713	<0.05	2	98
USDA	198	16	24	61
10-State	1401	9	29	62

*PNS is Preschool Nutrition Survey (Owen et al., 1974) with intakes listed separately for infants reported to be receiving or not to be receiving vitamin supplements; USDA is U.S. Department of Agriculture survey of low-income families (Eagles and Steele, 1972); 10-State is Ten-State Nutrition Survey, 1968–70 (Center for Disease Control, 1972).

Center for Disease Control, 1972). Thus, both dietary intake data and serum concentrations of vitamin A suggest that intakes of most children in this age range are not only adequate but generous.

Toxicity

For the reasons mentioned, it seems unlikely that any normal infant in the United States receiving an otherwise adequate diet will benefit from supplementary administration of vitamin A. American physicians have unfortunately not heeded the thoughtful warnings of several writers about overdosage of vitamin A. These warnings were aptly summarized by Caffey (1950): "The hazards of vitamin A poisoning from the routine prophylactic feeding of vitamin concentrates A and D to healthy infants and children on good diets are considerably greater than the hazards of vitamin A deficiency in healthy infants and children not fed vitamin concentrates."

Manifestations of vitamin A toxicity include anorexia, irritability, increased intracranial pressure, desquamation of the skin, roentgenographically demonstrable changes in the long bones and increased concentration of vitamin A in serum. Until the 1960s, chronic vitamin A poisoning had been reported only in the case of prolonged gross overdosage (e.g., ingestion of teaspoonful amounts of a vitamin preparation containing the recommended daily allowance in a fraction of a milliliter). Generally, the individual had received 75,000 to 500,000 I.U. daily for 3 to 12 months before overt signs of toxicity were recognized (Caffey, 1950). Since aqueous suspensions of vitamin A have become commercially available, the dosage of vitamin A and the time required to produce manifestations of toxicity seem to have been markedly reduced. Persson et al. (1965) reported five cases of vitamin A toxicity developing in infants less than six months of age. In one instance, 18,500 I.U. of vitamin A daily for three months and, in three instances, 22,500 I.U. of vitamin A daily for one to one and one-half months resulted in manifestations of toxicity.

Presumably, the greater ease of absorption of vitamin A in aqueous suspension than in an oily medium (Kramer et al., 1947; Lewis et al., 1947) results in greater toxicity. We must now consider that daily ingestion of 20,000 I.U. of vitamin A for one or two months is likely to be toxic. In discussing vitamin A toxicity, it is necessary to distinguish between ingestion of retinol or retinyl esters and ingestion of carotenes. Although carotenes can fulfill the requirement for vitamin A, excessive ingestion of carotenes results in the benign disorder, carotenemia, and not in hypervitaminosis A.

A joint committee statement on the use and abuse of vitamin A has been issued by the Committee on Drugs and the Committee on Nutrition of the American Academy of Pediatrics (1971). These committees have advised against the use of preparations providing more than 6000 I.U./dose. A statement on use and abuse of vitamin A prepared by the Nutrition Committee of the Canadian Paediatric Society (1971) recommends that physicians do not prescribe vitamin A supplements containing more than 2500 I.U./dose.

Vitamin D

Recent research on the metabolism of vitamin D, the generic descriptor for a group of steroid alcohols promoting absorption of calcium and phosphorus, casts doubt upon its role as a true vitamin (DeLuca and Suttie, 1970). With adequate exposure to sunlight, there is no dietary requirement for vitamin D. Furthermore, both vitamins D_2 (ergocalciferol) and D_3 (cholecalciferol), under strong feedback control, must be further modified, first to 25-hydroxycholecalciferol by the liver, then to 1,25-dihydroxycholecalciferol by the kidney, before activity is achieved. These facts suggest that vitamin D functions more as a hormone than as a vitamin (Holick et al., 1972).

Although both ergocalciferol (D_2) and cholecalciferol (D_3), together with ergosterol and 7-dehydrocholesterol, must now be thought of as precursors of the active compound, the international unit of vitamin D continues to be expressed as equivalents of 0.025 μg of cholecalciferol.

Deficiency

Vitamin D deficiency of infants is manifested by clinical, biochemical (especially decreased concentration of inorganic phosphorus and increased activity of alkaline phosphatase in the serum) and roentgenographic evidence of rickets. During the years 1956 to 1960, 843 cases of rickets were recognized among approximately 2,350,000 infants and children admitted to 226 teaching hospitals in the United States (Committee on Nutrition, 1962). Because some cases of rickets were probably not recognized, because not all children with rickets were admitted to hospitals, and because the survey mentioned was limited to relatively few hospitals, it seems likely that nutritional rickets was not uncommon at that time in the United States, and there is little reason to believe that the prevalence of rickets has changed since then.

Until 1968, vitamin D fortification of cow milk was less widespread in Canada than in the United States. It is worth noting that more than 400 cases of rickets per year were reported in 1967 and 1968 by three pediatric hospitals in Montreal and Toronto (Canadian Council on Nutrition, 1968). Presently, in Ontario approximately 90 per cent of homogenized milk, and of 2 per cent milk and 75 per cent of skim milk are fortified with vitamin D (Murray, 1973). A survey conducted by the British Paediatric Association (1964) indicated approximately 50 reported cases of vitamin D-deficiency rickets during a 17-month period in 1960–61. Most of the affected infants were either breastfed or fed fresh cow milk, which is unfortified in Great Britain, and were not receiving vitamin supplements containing vitamin D. Richards et al. (1968) reported the incidence of vitamin D-deficiency rickets in Glasgow to be higher in 1967 than in 1957. Results of two surveys suggested that between one-fourth and one-third of Scottish infants received less than 100 I.U./day from dietary sources (Richards et al., 1968).

Estimated Requirement and Advisable Intake

The daily requirement for vitamin D during infancy is probably between 100 and 200 I.U. (Committee on Nutrition, 1963a). Because little storage of vitamin D occurs, regular ingestion of the advisable intake is important. An intake of 400 I.U. represents at least twice the requirement and is suggested as the advisable daily intake. From a practical viewpoint, this means that breastfed infants and low-birth-weight infants will need to receive a daily supplement of vitamin D. Human milk provides only about 22 I.U. of vitamin D/liter (Chapter 15, Table 15–1). Although the requirement may be less for breastfed infants than for other infants, little is known about relative requirements and it seems desirable to provide 400 I.U. daily. Similarly, we do not know whether vitamin D requirements of low-birth-weight infants differ from those of fullsize infants. We have therefore assumed that the advisable intake is similar and recommend daily supplementation. The relatively small quantities of formula consumed by low-birth-weight infants will generally not include 400 I.U. of vitamin D.

Although casual exposure to sunlight will ordinarily fulfill the need for vitamin D after one year of age, it seems reasonable to ignore the contribution of sunlight during the first year of life and to provide the advisable intake of 400 I.U. of vitamin D daily from foods and, when necessary, a vitamin supplement. Administration of a supplement of vitamin D is inadvisable when dietary sources provide 400 I.U. daily.

Sources of Vitamin D

In the United States, evaporated milk, most commercially prepared formulas for infants and most fresh whole milk sold by dairies are fortified with vitamin D so as to provide at least 400 I.U./U.S. quart.

With the exception of milk, few foods commonly consumed by infants are fortified with vitamin D. Among commercially available strained foods for infants, egg yolk provides approximately 200 I.U. of vitamin D/100 gm, but amounts of vitamin D in other strained foods are extremely low. Therefore, when an infant's average daily intake of vitamin D from milk or formula remains below 400 I.U., it is reasonable to administer a supplement sufficient to raise the daily intake to 400 I.U.

Toxicity and Hypersensitivity

Concern regarding excessive intakes of vitamin D arises primarily from the possible but unproven etiologic role of vitamin D in producing infantile idiopathic hypercalcemia. The severe form of this disorder is characterized by failure to thrive, vomiting, mental retardation, bony changes, elevated concentration of calcium in serum and, in some cases, aortic stenosis and/or progressive renal failure and hypertension. The facies have been described as elflike.

In 1953 and 1954, approximately 100 new cases of idiopathic hypercalcemia were diagnosed annually in Great Britain, and an extensive survey of infant feeding practices revealed that many infants were receiving 3000 to 4000 I.U. of vitamin D daily (British Paediatric Association, 1956). Major sources of vitamin D in infants' diets were powdered milks, cereals and vitamin supplements. On the basis of recommendations made in 1956 and 1957, the extent of fortification of foods with vitamin D in Great Britain was reduced to the degree that relatively few infants received as much as 1500 I.U. daily. The incidence of idiopathic hypercalcemia in infants in Great Britain then decreased. However, the decrease did not occur immediately but only after several years, and thus the sequence of events does not offer strong support for the conclusion that the generous intakes of vitamin D were etiologically related to infantile hypercalcemia (British Paediatric Association, 1964).

When the extent of vitamin D fortification of foods for infants was reduced in Great Britain in 1957, there was some concern that this measure, undertaken for the benefit of relatively few infants, would result in an increased incidence of rickets. Thus, the overall effect of reduction in intake of vitamin D by the infant population would prove to be detrimental rather than beneficial. This concern seems to have been ill founded, because no increase in incidence of rickets was noted (Editorial, 1964; British Paediatric Association, 1964; Bransby et al., 1964).

Although the relation between intake of vitamin D and infantile hypercalcemia is still poorly understood, there appears to be no hazard and some possible benefit from maintaining intakes of vitamin D at about 400 I.U. daily. Intakes greater than 1000 I.U./day should be avoided. Vitamin D supplements should provide 400 I.U./daily dose and should not be prescribed for infants whose intakes from other sources amount to 400 I.U. daily.

The practice of administering relatively large ("Stoss") oral doses of vitamin D at infrequent intervals was introduced in Germany in the 1930s (Harnapp, 1939) and proved to be an effective prophylactic measure against rickets. At present, this method of prophylaxis continues in some parts of East and West Germany, with doses of 5 to 15 mg (200,000 to 600,000 I.U.) given at intervals of approximately three months. However, most German authorities do not approve of the practice (Hövels and Reis, 1965; Wolf, 1970; Palitzsch, 1971; Wolf et al., 1972; Gladel, 1972). It is of some interest that idiopathic hypercalcemia has not been demonstrated to be more common among infants receiving "Stoss" prophylaxis than among those receiving other prophylaxis.

It appears that biosynthesis of the active compound, 1,25-dihydroxycholecalciferol, occurs only in the kidney. This synthesis is impaired in uremia, giving rise to the vitamin D-resistant rickets not infrequently encountered in uremia. Brickman et al. (1972) administered small doses (100 I.U. or 2.7 μg) of 1,25-dihydroxycholecalciferol to uremic patients who had not responded to as much as 40,000 I.U. (1 mg) of cholecalciferol daily. Impressive increases in serum concentrations of calcium were observed and, in one patient, manifestations of toxicity developed. It is evident that this form of vitamin D must be used with caution.

Vitamin E

Vitamin E represents a group of fat-soluble compounds required by many species for normal reproduction, muscle integrity, resistance of erythrocytes to hemolysis and a series of other biochemical and physiologic functions (Nair and Kayden, 1972; Gallo-Torres, 1972). There is no longer reason for doubt that this vitamin is essential for the human infant, although its precise function in nutrition of the adult remains uncertain. Vitamin E has recently been shown to play a role in the biosynthesis of porphyrin and heme (Nair et al., 1971, 1972).

Four chemically related compounds (α-, β-, γ-, δ-tocopherol) and four corresponding unsaturated derivatives (α-, β-, γ-, δ-tocotrienol) exert vitamin E activity. Of these, α-tocopherol promotes the greatest tissue retention relative to the other compounds (Witting, 1972a). An international unit of vitamin E is equal to 1.0 mg of synthetic DL-α-tocopheryl acetate, 0.91 mg of the free alcohol DL-α-tocopherol, 0.74 mg of the natural form D-α-tocopheryl acetate or 0.67 mg of D-α-

TABLE 9–4 CONCENTRATION OF α-TOCOPHEROL IN MILKS AND FORMULAS*

Milk or Formula	Concentration of α-Tocopherol (μg/gm lipid) Mean	Concentration of α-Tocopherol (μg/gm lipid) Range	Concentration of α-Tocopherol (mg/liter)† Mean
Human milk	40	20–64	1.8
Cow			
Colostrum	78	29–142	3.7
Milk	11	7–18	0.4
Evaporated milk			
Purchased in April	10	5–16	0.4
Purchased in October	25	9–46	1.0
Commercially prepared formula (concentrated liquid)‡			
Milk-based	142	103–201	5.0
Soy-based	154	85–224	5.4

*Adapted from Herting, D. O., and Drury, E.-J. E.: Vitamin E content of milk, milk products, and simulated milks: relevance to infant nutrition. Amer. J. Clin. Nutr. 22:147, 1969.

†Assuming mean lipid concentrations of milks to be those indicated in Tables 15–1 and 15–2 and mean lipid concentration of formulas to be 3.5 gm/100 ml.

‡Diluted to 67 kcal/100 ml (1:1).

tocopherol. The natural tocopherols are found in greatest concentration in oil seeds. The amount found in fruits and vegetables is comparatively small (Slover, 1971). Tocopherols are important natural antioxidants in foods and tissues (Green, 1972) and are especially effective in preventing peroxidation of lipids (Witting, 1965; Tappel, 1972).

Tocopherol content of biologic fluids, tissues and foods may be measured by several chromatographic techniques, including paper, thin-layer, column and gas-liquid chromatography. New procedures now make it possible to separate and quantitate all of the tocopherols and, unlike the older methods of analysis, do not detect nontocopherol reducing substances (Bunnell, 1971). Hence, values obtained with the latest techniques are generally somewhat lower than values reported in the older literature and differentiate between α-, β-, γ-, δ-tocopherol and the tocotrienols. Concentrations of α-tocopherol in human milk, cow milk and several infant formulas are indicated in Table 9–4.

Deficiency

Human infants who receive low intakes of vitamin E and children who fail to absorb vitamin E because of steatorrhea, especially those with cystic fibrosis of the pancreas (Underwood and Denning, 1972; Underwood et al., 1972) or biliary atresia, demonstrate biochemical and pathologic findings similar to those seen in experimentally produced vitamin E deficiency in animals. Children with chronic steatorrhea, infants of low birth weight (Clausen and Friis-Hansen, 1971) and, occasionally, fullsize infants whose intakes of tocopherol have been low demonstrate low concentrations of tocopherol in plasma, excessive creatinuria and increased hemolysis of erythrocytes in dilute solutions of hydrogen peroxide. All these findings are reversed by administration of α-tocopherol (Nitowsky et al., 1962a; Oski and Barness, 1967; Lo et al., 1973). In addition, the creatine content of muscle of patients with cystic fibrosis of the pancreas increases after administration of α-tocopherol (Nitowsky et al., 1962b).

Pathologic manifestations, including focal necrosis of skeletal muscle (Oppenheimer, 1956; Weinberg et al., 1958) and deposition of ceroid pigment in smooth muscle (Blanc et al., 1958; Kerner and Goldbloom, 1960), have been demonstrated in patients with cystic fibrosis of the pancreas or biliary atresia. It seems likely that these manifestations are, in part, evidences of vitamin E deficiency. Hemolytic anemia has been reported in premature infants with low serum concentrations of vitamin E and in vitro hemolysis (Melhorn and Gross, 1971a). Administration of therapeutic doses of iron to these infants was followed by increased hemolysis; the investigators suggested that oral administration of iron may interfere with intestinal absorption of vitamin E, but destruction of vitamin E by the iron is also a possibility. A direct relationship appeared to exist between gestational age of the premature infant and his ability to maintain satisfactory vitamin E nutritional status during the first three months of life (Melhorn and Gross, 1971b, Gross and Melhorn, 1972).

Estimated Requirement and Advisable Intake

The requirement for vitamin E in body tissues is related to the polyunsaturated fatty acid (PUFA) content of cellular structures, and this is dependent on dietary fat (Witting, 1972b). Satisfactory concentrations of α-tocopherol in plasma—i.e., approximately 1 mg/100 ml (Lewis, 1969)—are maintained by infants fed a formula with vitamin E to PUFA ratio of 0.4 mg/gm.

There is a direct relationship between the plasma concentration of α-tocopherol in the infant at birth and that of the mother (Leonard et al., 1972). Although serum concentrations of vitamin E are relatively low at birth (<1.0 mg/100 ml) (Clausen and Friis-Hansen, 1971; Underwood et al., 1972), they rise rapidly in the breastfed infant but may remain low for many months when milk-based formulas are fed (Gordon et al., 1958). Because the fat added to most commercially prepared formulas in the United States is considerably more unsaturated than is the fat of human milk, it would seem advisable to attempt to maintain the same plasma concentrations of vitamin E in formula-fed infants as in breastfed infants.

With the exception of infants fed formulas in which all of the fat is supplied by a highly unsaturated vegetable oil (e.g., corn oil or soy oil), few infants or small children are likely to receive more than 7.5 gm of polyunsaturated fatty acids per day. Thus, a vitamin E intake of 4 I.U. daily (see Table 9–2) will provide the desired dietary vitamin E to PUFA ratio of 0.4 mg/gm. In the United States, formulas providing a particularly high percentage of calories from polyunsaturated fatty acids are adequately fortified with vitamin E.

Body stores of tocopherol at birth are less for the premature than for the fullterm infant (Dju et al., 1952), and the hemolytic anemia previously mentioned provides at least a suggestion that tocopherol deficiency exists (Oski and Barness, 1967; Melhorn and Gross, 1971b; Lo et al., 1973). Dyggve and Probst (1963) demonstrated that average serum concentrations of bilirubin were less and concentrations of hemoglobin in blood were greater in premature infants who had received 100 mg of α-tocopherol intramuscularly at birth than in those who had not received α-tocopherol. Presumably, the premature infant is somewhat handicapped in achieving normal concentrations of α-tocopherol in plasma and tissues because of relatively low body stores at birth, relatively rapid rate of gain in weight and diminished ability to absorb fat. For these reasons, it seems desirable to accept the recommendation of several authors (Mackenzie, 1954; Nitowsky et al., 1956, 1962a and b; Goldbloom, 1963; Committee on Nutrition, 1963b) that a supplement of vitamin E be given to premature infants. A daily supplement of α-tocopherol of 0.5 mg/kg would seem to be a reasonable recommendation (Nitowsky et al., 1962b).

Patients with intestinal malabsorption associated with chronic steatorrhea should receive daily supplementation with a water-miscible preparation of α-tocopherol. Harries and Muller (1971) have suggested that patients with cystic fibrosis of the pancreas should receive 1 mg/kg/day, and it seems reasonable to utilize this dosage generally for patients with chronic steatorrhea.

Vitamin K

Vitamin K is the generic descriptor for a group of fat-soluble methylnaphthoquinone derivatives required for biosynthesis of several factors necessary for normal clotting of the blood. Vitamin K_1 (phytylmenaquinone) is present in green plants, and a series of substances referred to as vitamin K_2 (multiprenylmenaquinones) are synthesized by bacteria. Synthetic as well as natural compounds have vitamin K activity. Water-soluble analogues of menaquinone (menadione) are available (Hykinone [Abbott], Synkayvite [Roche]) and may be safely used in treatment or prophylaxis of individuals beyond the first few months of age. As will be discussed, these products are not recommended for use in the newborn period.

Laboratory confirmation of vitamin K deficiency and of its correction after treatment is readily obtained by determining one-stage prothrombin time (Suttie, 1969; Wasserman and Taylor, 1972). This test is sensitive to four of the vitamin K-dependent clotting factors – II, V, VII and X.

Estimated Requirement and Advisable Intake

The requirement of the infant for vitamin K is estimated to be no greater than 5 μg daily (Committee on Nutrition, 1961). Human milk contains approximately 15 μg and cow milk 60 μg of vitamin K per liter (Dam et al., 1952). Fifteen micrograms daily is suggested as the advisable intake between one week and three years of age.

Vitamin K status during the first few days of life requires special attention. Many infants, particularly those who are breastfed, develop a mild deficiency of vitamin K two to three days after birth (Aballí et al., 1957; Vietti et al., 1960; Committee on Nutrition, 1961; Keenan et al., 1971). In approximately 1 in 400 infants, the deficiency is associated with clinical manifestations of bleeding and is then termed "hemorrhagic disease of the newborn" (Smith, 1972). The coagulation abnormality can be corrected by administration of compounds with vitamin K activity (Aballí et al., 1957; Vietti et al., 1960; Keenan et al., 1971). Until the early 1960s, water-soluble analogues of menaquinone (menadione) were used extensively for the treatment and prophylaxis of hemorrhagic disease of the newborn. These vitamin K compounds could be administered by subcutaneous or intramuscular routes, whereas the available preparations of vitamin K_1 (phytylmenaquinone) could be administered only by the oral or intravenous routes. However, administration of large doses of water-soluble analogues of menaquinone to the woman in labor or to the newborn infant may be followed by hemolytic anemia, hyperbilirubinemia, kernicterus and death to the infant (Committee on Nutrition, 1961).

Water-miscible preparations of phytylmenaquinone now available (AquaMEPHYTON [Merck], Konakion [Roche]) may be administered orally, intramuscularly, subcutaneously or intravenously. Since the margin of safety with phytylmenaquinone is great, it seems unwise to administer water-soluble vitamin K preparations (Hykinone

[Abbott], Synkayvite [Roche]) known to have a small margin of safety during the newborn period. The Committee on Nutrition (1971) has strongly reaffirmed its earlier recommendation (Committee on Nutrition, 1961) that every newborn infant should receive a single parenteral dose of 0.5 to 1.0 mg of phytylmenaquinone soon after birth.

Because human milk provides less vitamin K than does cow milk, and because breastfed infants generally consume less milk during the first few days of life than do formula-fed infants, vitamin K deficiency in the newborn period is much more common in breastfed than in formula-fed infants (Sutherland et al., 1967; Keenan et al., 1971). The desirability of parenteral administration of vitamin K to the newborn soon after birth is therefore particularly great in the case of breastfed infants.

Infants born to women who have been receiving coumarin drugs in anticoagulant therapy may demonstrate severe clotting defects (Gordon and Dean, 1955) and require repeated doses of vitamin K.

It is obvious that no program of vitamin K administration begun after birth will protect the infant from bleeding at the time of birth. Owen et al. (1967) demonstrated that oral administration of 5 mg of phytylmenaquinone daily to women for several days before delivery resulted in significant improvement in prothrombin time of the newborn infant. Whether this improvement in prothrombin time is associated with decrease in morbidity (e.g., from intracranial hemorrhage at the time of birth) is unknown.

For normal infants receiving milk-based formulas or milk-free formulas supplemented with vitamin K, it is unnecessary to supplement the diet with vitamin K after the newborn period. Infants with cystic fibrosis of the pancreas require supplemental vitamin K (Torstenson et al., 1970; Walters and Koch, 1972). The Committee on Nutrition (1971) has recommended that subcutaneous or intramuscular injection of the phytylmenaquinone be utilized for prophylaxis in infants with malabsorption. However, oral administration of a water-miscible preparation of phytylmenaquinone should be adequate and, for infants more than a few months of age, water-soluble vitamin K preparations (Synkayvite [Roche], Hykinone [Abbott]) are satisfactory (Chapter 19).

Infants beyond the newborn period may be at risk of developing vitamin K deficiency if fed milk-free formulas unsupplemented with vitamin K (Committee on Nutrition, 1971). Although normal infants demonstrated no increase in prothrombin time when fed a formula containing 27 μg of vitamin K per liter for three months (Williams et al., 1970), reports of vitamin K deficiency among infants fed soy-isolate formulas unsupplemented with vitamin K have appeared (Moss, 1969; Morgan, 1969). These formulas have now been fortified with vitamin K.

WATER-SOLUBLE VITAMINS

Vitamin C

Vitamin C is the generic descriptor for all compounds exhibiting qualitatively the biologic activity of L-ascorbic acid. The two principal forms of the vitamin are L-ascorbic acid and its oxidized form, dehydroascorbic acid. It has been shown that dehydroascorbic acid is partially reduced to L-ascorbic acid in man, but apparently only reduced L-ascorbic acid and not its oxidized forms is incorporated into the body ascorbate pool (Baker et al., 1966; Baker, 1967). Baker et al. (1966) have described a reversible oxidation-reduction system consisting of dehydro-, monodehydro- and ascorbic acids. Ascorbic acid is important for the normal development of fibroblasts, osteoblasts and odontoblasts, although the mechanism of its action is poorly understood. In addition, it functions in intermediary metabolism of a number of substances, including hydroxylation of proline to hydroxyproline in collagen synthesis, the 5-hydroxylation of tryptophan and the oxidation of tyrosine. It may also be important in formation of adrenal steroids.

Deficiency

Hodges et al. (1971) found petechial hemorrhages to be the earliest clinical evidences of vitamin C deficiency. As the illness progresses, fatigue and irritability increase, tenderness of the lower extremities is prominent and swelling of the joints and gums develops. Kinsman and Hood (1971) reported changes in measures of personality, psychomotor performance and physical fitness to occur in vitamin C-deficient adult volunteers. Iron-deficiency anemia is a frequent accompaniment. Serum concentrations of ascorbic acid are less than 0.1 mg/100 ml and roentgenograms demonstrate characteristic changes at the cartilage-shaft junctions of the long bones, especially the distal end of the femur.

A state of relative deficiency may exist in premature infants with transient neonatal tyrosinemia. The biochemical basis for this condition has been reviewed by Scriver and Rosenberg (1973). In the immature infant, the activity of p-hydroxyphenylpyruvic acid oxidase may be inhibited by a relative deficiency of ascorbic acid and/or a buildup of enzyme substrate formed when large quantities of protein and, therefore, tyrosine, are present in the diet. Reduction of protein intake to 2 to 3 gm/kg/day and dosages of 50 to 100 mg/day of ascorbic acid will reduce the tyrosinemia in most infants. When protein

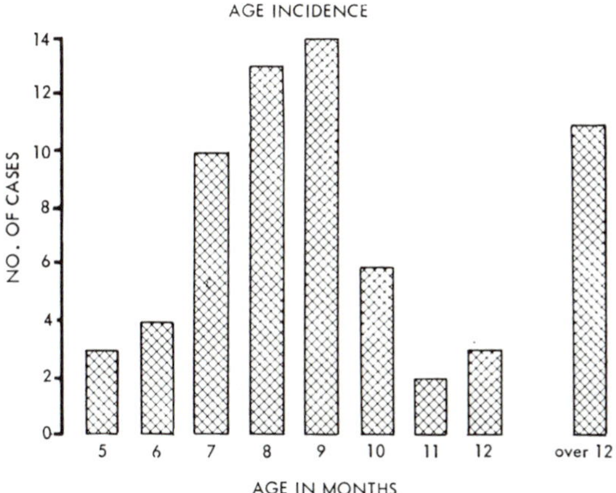

Figure 9–1 Age incidence of scurvy. (From Grewar, D.: Infantile scurvy. Clin. Pediatr. *4*:82, 1965.)

intake is high and the diet is unsupplemented with ascorbic acid, neonatal tyrosinemia may persist for several weeks after birth (Avery et al., 1967; Levy et al., 1969). This transient tyrosinemia is a benign disorder and should not be confused with hereditary tyrosinemia or tyrosinosis—disorders which do not respond to ascorbic acid supplementation (La Du and Gjessing, 1972).

In the five-year period, 1956–60, 226 teaching hospitals in the United States reported admission of 713 infants and children with scurvy (Committee on Nutrition, 1962). The percentage of hospital admissions accounted for by scurvy was greatest in the southeastern portion of the country despite the ready availability of citrus fruits in much of that area. Among an estimated 58,400 infants and children admitted to hospitals in Louisiana during the five-year period, 128 cases of scurvy were identified, or one case of scurvy in every 460 infants and children admitted. Reports of scurvy in Canada in 1958 and 1959 (Whelan et al., 1958; Grewar, 1958, 1959) were of sufficient concern to result in legislation permitting the addition of ascorbic acid to evaporated milk.

The age of occurrence of infantile scurvy may be seen in Figure 9–1. Caffey (1967) has stated that neither clinical nor roentgenographic evidence of scurvy has been verified in infants younger than three months of age. Roentgenographic manifestations of congenital syphilis have occasionally been interpreted as those of scurvy. Grewar (1965) found that infants over 12 months of age developed scurvy only in instances of severe feeding difficulties, as in those associated with mental retardation.

Estimated Requirement and Advisable Intake

Capillary fragility, bony abnormalities and other early manifestations of scurvy are prevented by daily ingestion of much smaller doses than those required for tissue saturation. Until some advantage of tissue saturation is demonstrated, it seems unreasonable to assume that maximal concentration of ascorbic acid in tissues indicates optimal nutritional status.

Concentrations of ascorbic acid in serum reflect dietary intake during the preceding weeks or few months. Tissue concentrations (e.g., concentrations in leukocytes) reflect more remote intake. Concentrations of ascorbic acid both in serum and in leukocytes of breastfed infants may average 0.6 mg/100 ml (or 100 gm). If the infant is then given a diet free of ascorbic acid, by analogy with experimental data from studies of adults, one might assume that serum concentration would decrease to about 0.1 mg/100 ml in two to three months and to undetectable levels thereafter. Concentrations in leukocytes will remain at detectable levels for a month or so longer than in serum. Evidence of scurvy develops only when concentrations in leukocytes are no longer detectable. Thus, concentrations of 0.2 to 0.3 mg/100 ml in serum of the adult would seem to indicate a considerable margin of safety with respect to prevention of scurvy. Such serum concentrations can be maintained in adults by intakes of 10 mg of ascorbic acid daily (Bartley et al., 1953).

A supplement of 10 mg/day was found by Hodges et al. (1969) to cure or prevent clinical scurvy in adult volunteers, and Woodruff (1964) estimated the requirement for the infant for prevention of scurvy to range between 5 and 10 mg daily. Hamil et al. (1938) found that 10 mg daily was sufficient to prevent the earliest roentgenographic evidences of disease. This value has therefore been listed as the estimated requirement (Table 9–1) and twice this value as the advisable intake (Table 9–2).

Intakes by Children in the United States

As may be seen in Table 9–5, nearly one-third of the 12- to 36-month-old children in the USDA Survey (Eagles and Steele, 1972) and Ten-State Nutrition Survey (Center for Disease Control, 1972) received intakes of vitamin C less than 15 mg/day. Although not shown in the table, among the lowest income group in the Preschool Nutrition Survey (Owen et al., 1974), 18 per cent of children between 12 and 36 months of age were found to have intakes of vitamin C less than 15 mg/day. Thus, it would appear that the advisable intakes (Table 9–2) were not met in a relatively high percentage of cases.

TABLE 9–5 PERCENTAGE OF CHILDREN 12 TO 36 MONTHS OF AGE RECEIVING VARIOUS INTAKES OF VITAMIN C

Survey*	Number of Subjects	Intake of Vitamin C (mg/day)		
		<15.0	*15.0–29.9*	*>29.9*
		(Per Cent of Children)		
PNS				
Unsupplemented	599	14	27	59
Supplemented	713	1	3	96
USDA	198	39	25	36
10-State	1401	31	21	48

*PNS, USDA and 10-State as in Table 9–3.

It is of some interest to compare records of dietary intake of vitamin C by groups of individuals with concentrations of vitamin C found in serum of these same groups. This is possible, to some extent, with infants from birth to 24 months of age from "low income ratio states" (Kentucky, Louisiana, South Carolina, Texas, West Virginia) in the Ten-State Nutrition Survey. Dietary survey of 534 infants demonstrated that intakes of vitamin C were less than 5 mg/day in 12.7 per cent, less than 10 mg/day in 29.4 per cent, and less than 15 mg/day in 39.5 per cent. Concentrations of vitamin C were determined in sera of 107 infants and found to be less than 0.10 mg/100 ml in 2.8 per cent, less than 0.20 mg/100 ml in 10.3 per cent and less than 0.30 mg/100 ml in 29.0 per cent. Thus, both dietary intakes and serum chemical values in this population of infants suggest low recent dietary intakes of ascorbic acid. In all probability, some of the infants reported to have had low dietary intakes of vitamin C at the time of the survey had considerably higher intakes in the weeks before the survey, explaining the relatively high concentrations in serum.

As indicated in Table 9–5, intakes of vitamin C were recorded in the Preschool Nutrition Survey (Owen et al., 1974) for 599 children 12 to 36 months of age who were not receiving vitamin supplements. Intakes of vitamin C less than 15 mg/day were reported for 14 per cent of these children. Concentrations of ascorbic acid in serum were determined in 633 children in this age group who were not receiving vitamin supplements and were found to be less than 0.30 mg/100 ml in approximately 6 per cent.

Ascorbic Acid Content of Foods

As indicated in Chapter 15, human milk is a rich source of ascorbic acid, but cow milk in any form, unless it has been fortified, is a poor source by the time it reaches the consumer. Although most commercially prepared formulas marketed in the United States are now fortified with ascorbic acid, this is not uniformly the case in other countries. The physician must be aware of the vitamin content of infant formulas he prescribes.

Processing of strained foods commercially prepared for infants results in appreciable loss of ascorbic acid so that few such foods provide adequate amounts unless they have been fortified. As discussed in Chapter 16, fruit juices commercially prepared for infants are fortified with ascorbic acid. There is a wide range in ascorbic acid content of strained fruits. Some varieties are fortified with the vitamin while others are not (Table 16–2). Scurvy has been reported in a mentally retarded child whose diet for the preceding year had consisted almost entirely of chopped ("junior") vegetables with meat (LoPresti et al., 1964).

Thiamin

Metabolism of carbohydrate, with eventual liberation of carbon dioxide and water, requires the presence of decarboxylating enzymes, usually consisting of thiamin pyrophosphate and magnesium linked to a substrate-specific protein. Participation of thiamin in human metabolism has been discussed in detail by Ariaey-Nejad et al. (1970). Because of its key role in carbohydrate metabolism, requirements for thiamin are considered to be proportional to carbohydrate content of the diet.

Deficiency

As already mentioned, in the United States and Canada thiamin deficiency has been reported in only two infants during the past 25 years (Davis and Wolf, 1958; Cochrane et al., 1961). Soy-based formulas not supplemented with thiamin had served as the major source of calories for these infants for prolonged periods. The infrequency of thiamin deficiency in developed countries strongly suggests that milks and formulas generally provide an adequate intake of thiamin.

Estimated Requirements and Advisable Intakes

On the basis of both human and animal studies, the requirement for thiamin has been estimated to be 0.2 mg/1000 kcal. Human milk provides approximately 0.16 mg of thiamin per liter or about 0.22 mg/1000 kcal. Assuming that consumption of calories by breastfed infants differs only slightly from consumption by infants fed other milks or formulas, average thiamin intake by breastfed infants may be estimated to be 0.12 mg daily at age one month and 0.16 mg daily at age six months. Because these intakes clearly meet the requirements, an advisable intake of 0.2 mg daily seems reasonable for the first year of life and 0.3 mg daily for children from one to three years of age (Table 9–2).

Intakes by Children in the United States

Intakes of thiamin by children between 12 and 36 months of age in two surveys are presented in Table 9–6. It may be seen that intakes less than the advisable intakes (Table 9–2) were reported in a relatively small percentage of children.

Biochemical data on urinary excretion of thiamin are generally consistent with those concerning dietary intakes. Urinary excretions less than about 125 μg/gm of creatinine are considered evidence that intakes have been inadequate (Maternal and Child Health Service, 1971; Center for Disease Control, 1972), and excretions less than 175 μg/gm of creatinine have been considered "low" (Center for Disease Control, 1972). Of 348 determinations of urinary excretion of thiamin by children 12 to 36 months of age in the Preschool Nutrition Survey (Owen et al., 1974), only 2 (0.6 per cent) demonstrated urinary excretions less than 250 μg/gm of creatinine.

Riboflavin

The metabolic role of riboflavin occurs mainly after its conversion to the coenzymes flavin mononucleotide and flavin adenine dinucleotide. Amino acid oxidases, succinic dehydrogenase, xanthine and aldehyde oxidases and a number of other enzymes important in cellular oxidation reactions require riboflavin as a part of their struc-

TABLE 9–6 PERCENTAGE OF CHILDREN 12 TO 36 MONTHS OF AGE RECEIVING VARIOUS INTAKES OF THIAMIN

		INTAKE OF THIAMIN (MG/DAY)		
SURVEY*	NUMBER OF SUBJECTS	*<0.30*	*0.30–0.49* (*Per Cent of Children*)	*>0.49*
PNS				
Unsupplemented	600	3	22	75
Supplemented	713	<0.05	3	97
10-State	1401	6	18	76

*PNS and 10-State as in Table 9–3.

ture. An excellent review of riboflavin metabolism has been prepared by Rivlin (1970).

Requirement for riboflavin is closely dependent on energy metabolism (Bro-Rasmussen, 1958). The average concentration of riboflavin in human milk is 0.36 mg/liter (Chapter 15) or approximately 0.5 mg/1000 kcal.

By the utilization of data from Chapter 2 (as described for calculations of intakes of thiamin), 50th percentile values for riboflavin intakes by breastfed infants can be estimated to be approximately 0.27 and 0.34 mg/day at ages one and six months, respectively. A value of 0.40 mg/day is therefore suggested as the advisable intake from birth to one year, and a value of 0.60 mg/day is suggested as the advisable intake for one- to three-year-old children (Table 9–2).

Rich sources of riboflavin are meats, milk, eggs, green leafy vegetables, legumes and whole grains. Since several of these are likely to be included in an infant's diet in the United States, the absence of riboflavin deficiency is not surprising.

Intakes by Children in the United States

As may be seen in Table 9–7, intakes of riboflavin by children between 12 and 36 months of age in the United States were found in two surveys to be generally well above the advisable intakes (Table 9–2). Urinary excretions of riboflavin also suggest that most children in this age group received adequate or generous intakes of riboflavin. The Center for Disease Control (1972) considers urinary excretions less than 150 μg/gm of creatinine to be evidence of deficient intakes, and excretions less than 500 μg/gm of creatinine to be "low." Maternal and Child Health Service (1971) has specified values less than 250 μg/gm of creatinine in urine to be evidence of low recent dietary intake. In this regard it is of interest that of 445 determinations in

TABLE 9–7 PERCENTAGE OF CHILDREN 12 TO 36 MONTHS OF AGE RECEIVING VARIOUS INTAKES OF RIBOFLAVIN

Survey*	Number of Subjects	Intake of Riboflavin (mg/day) <0.50	0.50–0.79 (Per Cent of Children)	>0.79
PNS				
Unsupplemented	600	4	13	83
Supplemented	713	<0.05	2	98
10-State	1401	4	8	88

*PNS and 10-State as in Table 9–3.

children between 12 and 36 months of age in the Preschool Nutrition Survey (Owen et al., 1974), only 2 (0.4 per cent) demonstrated excretions less than 250 μg/gm of creatinine and only 4 per cent demonstrated excretions less than 500 μg/gm of creatinine.

Niacin

Niacin or one of its derivatives is an essential component of coenzyme I (nicotinamide adenine dinucleotide) and coenzyme II (nicotinamide adenine dinucleotide phosphate), which are involved in glycolysis, protein and amino acid metabolism, pentose biosynthesis, lipid metabolism and the process by which high-energy phosphate bonds are synthesized (Chaykin, 1967). As is true of thiamin and riboflavin, requirement is related to energy metabolism.

Under suitable conditions, including an adequate dietary intake of vitamin B_6, niacin can be synthesized from tryptophan in mammalian tissues; hence, niacin requirement is also influenced by the amount and quality of dietary protein. Approximately 60 mg of tryptophan are required for synthesis of 1 mg of niacin. The minimum amount of niacin* that will prevent pellagra in the adult is 4.4 mg/1000 kcal, or at least 9 mg daily when calorie intake is less than 2000 kcal (Food and Nutrition Board, 1974). Human milk provides approximately 4.4 mg of niacin per liter, and one may estimate the 50th percentile intakes of the breastfed infant to be 3.3 mg/day at age one month and 4.1 mg/day at age six months. Advisable intake of niacin from birth to three years has been set at 5.0 mg/day (Table 9–2).

Niacin deficiency is most likely to occur in patients with cirrhosis of the liver, chronic diarrheal diseases, diabetes mellitus, neoplasia, prolonged febrile illnesses and after parenteral feeding without niacin supplements (Goldsmith, 1964).

Vitamin B_6

Vitamin B_6 is the generic descriptor for three chemically related compounds—pyridoxine, pyridoxal and pyridoxamine. These substances are readily phosphorylated and converted from one form to another in the body. The physiologically active form, pyridoxal-5′-phosphate, is important in protein, carbohydrate and lipid metabolism, serving as a coenzyme for nearly all enzymatic reactions involv-

*Niacin, as used here, includes the preformed vitamin plus 1 mg of nicotinamide equivalent for each 60 mg of tryptophan.

ing nonoxidative degradation and interconversion of amino acids. It forms one component of the phosphorylase responsible for breakdown of glycogen to glucose-1-phosphate, and serves in lipid metabolism, including conversion of linoleic to arachidonic acid. In vitamin B_6 deficiency, Axelrod (1971) has demonstrated a marked decrease in production of antibody-forming cells after antigenic stimulation.

In 1953 and 1954, several investigators reported convulsive seizures in infants receiving a commercially prepared formula subjected to a new type of heat processing (Committee on Nutrition, 1966). The findings were similar to those previously described in an infant in whom vitamin B_6 deficiency had been produced experimentally (Snyderman et al., 1950). The seizures observed in 1953 and 1954 and the other manifestations suggesting vitamin B_6 deficiency (abnormal electroencephalogram, abnormal tryptophan load test) disappeared after administration of pyridoxine. Most of the vitamin B_6 in milk and other products of animal origin is in the form of pyridoxal or pyridoxamine, both of which are quite sensitive to heat, and it was shown that the formula contained only 60 μg of vitamin B_6 compounds. Subsequently, it has been demonstrated that a physiologically inactive disulfide of pyridoxal phosphate may also be formed on exposure to heat (Wendt and Bernhart, 1960). Commercially prepared formulas marketed at present commonly are fortified with the relatively heat-stable pyridoxine hydrochloride. Concentrations of vitamin B_6 in various strained and junior foods are presented in Chapter 16 (Table 16–2).

Estimated Requirement and Advisable Intake

Requirement for pyridoxine is probably related more to protein content than to caloric content of the diet. Breastfed infants rarely develop clinical manifestations of vitamin B_6 deficiency, although excretion of xanthurenic acid may be high after administration of tryptophan (i.e., "abnormal" result of tryptophan load test). Thus, the average concentration of vitamin B_6 in mature human milk (100 μg/1000 ml) is presumably adequate for handling the relatively small protein load (1.1 gm/100 ml) presented by this feeding, and an intake of 9 μg/gm of protein may be utilized as an approximation of the requirement. Bessey et al. (1957) have reported that infants receiving human milk containing less than 100 μg of vitamin B_6 per liter developed convulsions. The ratio of vitamin B_6 to protein in cow milk is approximately 19 μg/gm and is thus considerably greater than the ratio in human milk. Because some infants and small children will receive 20 per cent of calorie intakes from protein, the advisable intakes of vitamin B_6 (Table 9–2) are generous and are not necessary for infants receiving lesser intakes of protein.

Because administration of isoniazid increases the requirement for vitamin B_6, it is recommended that infants receiving isoniazid be given 10 to 25 mg of pyridoxine daily. Other infants who may benefit from large daily doses of pyridoxine are those with myoclonic epilepsy (100 to 200 mg daily), phenylketonuria and congenital or acquired vitamin B_6 dependency (Committee on Nutrition, 1966). The extent to which administration of pyridoxine may benefit patients with phenylketonuria remains to be determined (Loo and Ritman, 1964; Heeley, 1965; Editorial, 1966).

Folacin

Folacin is the generic descriptor for folic acid (pteroylmonoglutamic acid) and related compounds exhibiting qualitatively the biologic activity of folic acid. The physiologically active forms of the vitamin are reduction products (tetrahydrofolic acids) conjugated with glutamic acid. Pteroylmonoglutamic acid is absorbed more efficiently than the heptaglutamate (Rosenberg and Godwin, 1971). Folacin functions as a coenzyme in such reactions as methylation of homocysteine to methionine, conversion of glycine to serine and the formation of creatine, thymine deoxyriboside, ribose nucleic acids and porphyrin compounds. From a clinical standpoint, the most important activity of folacin is the role it plays in the synthesis of the purine and pyrimidine compounds which are utilized for the formation of nucleoproteins. In the absence of an adequate supply of nucleoproteins, normal maturation of primordial erythrocytes fails to occur and hematopoiesis is arrested at the megaloblastic stage. Nutritional deficiency of folacin is thought to be a far more common cause of megaloblastic anemia in developing countries than deficiency of vitamin B_{12} (Herbert, 1970).

Not only folic acid but several other compounds in foods exhibit folacin activity. Unfortunately, folacin available to the microorganisms used in assay procedures may differ considerably from folacin available to the human subject (Ghitis, 1966). Thus, only a human assay is valid for determining the available folacin in food for man. However, the commonly employed L. casei assay provides information on the apparent folacin content and, as our information increases, we may anticipate that for specified foods it will be possible to relate apparent folacin content to folacin activity for man.

Major sources of folacin are meats and leafy green vegetables. Megaloblastic anemia responsive to folacin has been reported in in-

TABLE 9–8 FOLIC ACID ACTIVITY IN MILK*

MILK	FOLIC ACID (μG/LITER)	
	Mean	*Range*
Human milk (22 samples)	52	31–81
Cow milk (bulked herd milk; 16 samples)	55	37–72
Pasteurized cow milk (8 samples)	51	40–65
Goat milk (17 samples)	6	2–11

*Adapted from Ford, J. E., and Scott, K. J.: The folic acid activity of some milk foods for babies. J. Dairy Res. 35:85, 1968.

fants of low birth weight fed formulas of cow milk, suggesting that the amounts of folacin provided by these formulas, although presumably adequate for most fullsize infants, may be inadequate for low-birth-weight infants (Strelling et al., 1966).

Concentrations of folates in goat milk are less than those in cow milk (Table 9–8), and megaloblastic anemia is likely to develop in infants fed goat milk unless other sources of folates are provided (Naiman and Oski, 1964; Sullivan et al., 1966; Becroft and Holland, 1966; Braude, 1972).

The free and total folate activity in 40 Canadian strained baby foods has been analyzed by Hoppner (1971).

The requirement for folacin for the adult has been estimated to be about 50 μg/day (Herbert, 1962). Requirements for infants and children have been estimated by Velez et al. (1963) to be 5 to 20 μg/day and by Sullivan et al. (1966) to be 20 to 50 μg/day. These data suggest that the requirement for folacin in infancy is less (and probably substantially less) than 50 μg/day. Because no precise estimate seems possible at this time, we have listed the estimated requirement as less than 50 μg/day (Table 9–1) and the advisable intake as 50 μg/day during the first year and slightly greater amounts thereafter (Table 9–2).

Greater doses of folacin may be required for treatment than for prophylaxis. Kamel et al. (1972) and Waslien et al. (1972) have estimated that 11.2 μg of total free dietary folacin per kilogram of body weight per day would be sufficient to promote recovery from folacin deficiency in most children recovering from protein-calorie malnutrition. These authors indicated, however, that 18.8 μg/kg/day of folacin was insufficient for maximal therapeutic response.

Herbert (1973) has discussed an etiologic classification of vitamin B_{12} and folacin deficiency in man. The interference of anticonvulsant drugs with folacin metabolism has been described by Gordon (1968). Infants and children with cardiac disease appear to be particularly susceptible to folacin deficiency (Rook et al., 1973).

Vitamin B_{12}

Vitamin B_{12} (cyanocobalamin) functions in such transmethylations as synthesis of choline from methionine, serine from glycine and methionine from homocysteine. It is also involved in pyrimidine and purine metabolism and in the synthesis of the deoxyriboside moiety of deoxyribonucleic acid (Stadtman, 1971). Vitamin B_{12} affects, directly or indirectly, the metabolism of folacin and may be essential in certain reactions in which folacin serves as a coenzyme (Nixon and Bertino, 1970). The manner in which the vitamin is involved in metabolism of nervous tissue is unknown. The most commonly detected manifestation of vitamin B_{12} deficiency is megaloblastic anemia. Vitamin B_{12} occurs almost exclusively in animal tissue, bound to protein; very little is present in vegetables. Vitamin B_{12} deficiency does not occur in infants or children receiving adequate intakes of calories and animal protein.

In the 1950s, there was considerable controversy about the effect of vitamin B_{12} deficiency on appetite and growth retardation in childhood (Committee on Nutrition, 1958; Howe, 1958a and b). As discussed in Chapter 3, the possibility that vitamin B_{12} or other vitamins can act as effective "tonics" or appetite stimulants in otherwise normal children has not been supported by additional evidence.

Little evidence is available concerning the requirement of the infant or preschool child for vitamin B_{12}. The breastfed infant probably receives approximately 0.3 μg of vitamin B_{12} daily (Joint FAO/WHO Expert Group, 1970) and the requirement for the infant is almost certainly less than that amount. Daily intakes of vitamin B_{12} recommended by the Joint FAO/WHO Expert Group (1970) are 0.3 μg for infants during the first year of life and 0.9 μg for one- to three-year-old children. No explanation is offered for the much larger intake recommended for children after one year of age.

VITAMIN-RESPONSIVE INBORN ERRORS OF METABOLISM

Several vitamin dependency states with genetic etiology have been recognized. These rare inborn errors of metabolism are usually, but not always, transmitted as autosomal recessive traits. Abnormalities of vitamin metabolism may impair intestinal absorption of a particular vitamin or may inhibit the biochemical reaction(s) required in the normal metabolism of the vitamin. Vitamin-responsive inborn errors usually require pharmacologic doses of the particular vitamin to alleviate the abnormality.

TABLE 9–9 THE VITAMIN-RESPONSIVE DISORDERS OF AMINO ACID METABOLISM*

Vitamin	Disorder	Therapeutic Dose	Biochemical Basis	References
Thiamine (B_1)	Lacticacidosis	5–20 mg	Pyruvate carboxylase deficiency	Brunette et al. (1972)
	Branched-chain aminoacidopathy (MSUD variant)	5–20 mg	Branched-chain ketoacid decarboxylase deficiency	Scriver et al. (1971)
Pyridoxine (B_6)	Infantile convulsions	10–50 mg	Glutamic acid decarboxylase deficiency	Hunt et al. (1954); Scriver and Whelan (1969); Yoshida et al. (1971)
	Hypochromic anemia	>10 mg	Unknown	Horrigan and Harris (1964)
	Cystathioninuria	100–500 mg	Cystathionase deficiency	Frimpter et al. (1963); Frimpter (1965)
	Xanthurenicaciduria	5–10 mg	Kynureninase deficiency	Knapp (1960); Tada et al. (1968)
	Homocystinuria	25–500 mg	Cystathionine synthase deficiency	Barber and Spaeth (1967); Mudd et al. (1970); Seashore et al. (1972)
	Hyperoxaluria	100–500 mg	Glyoxylate:α-ketoglutarate carboligase deficiency	Smith and Williams (1967)
Cobalamin (B_{12})	Juvenile pernicious anemia	<5 μg	IF deficiency or defective ileal transport	Mohamed et al. (1966); Katz et al. (1972)
	Transcobalamin II deficiency	>100 μg	Deficiency of transcobalamin II	Hakami et al. (1971)
	Methylmalonicaciduria	>250 μg	Defective synthesis of Ad–B_{12} coenzyme	Rosenberg et al. (1968, 1969); Mahoney et al. (1971)
	Methylmalonicaciduria, homocystinuria and hypomethioninemia	>500 μg	Defective synthesis of Ad–B_{12} and CH_3–B_{12} coenzymes	Mudd et al. (1969, 1970); Goodman et al. (1970); Mahoney et al. (1971)
Folic acid	Megaloblastic anemia	<0.05 mg	Defective intestinal absorption of folate	Luhby et al. (1961); Lanzkowsky (1970)
	Formiminotransferase deficiency	>5 mg	Formiminotransferase deficiency	Arakawa et al. (1963); Arakawa (1970)
	Homocystinuria and hypomethioninemia	>10 mg	N^5, N^{10}-methylenetetrahydrofolate reductase deficiency	Mudd et al. (1972); Shih et al. (1972); Freeman et al. (1972)
	Congenital megaloblastic anemia	>0.1 mg	Dihydrofolate reductase deficiency	Walters (1967)
Biotin	Propionicacidemia	10 mg	Propionyl-CoA carboxylase deficiency	Barnes et al. (1970)
Niacin	Hartnup disease	40–200 mg	Defective intestinal and renal transport of tryptophan and other "neutral" amino acids	Jepson (1972)

*From Scriver, C. R., and Rosenberg, L. E.: Amino Acid Metabolism and Its Disorders. Philadelphia, W. B. Saunders Co., 1973, p. 472.

The biochemical role of most of the vitamins is associated with their coenzyme function. Rosenberg (1969, 1970) has presented a scheme of sites at which mutations could interfere with vitamin-catalyzed reactions. This interference may result in defective transport of the vitamin either across the cell membrane or within the cell itself. Other mutations may impair the conversion of the vitamin to the coenzyme or the association of the coenzyme with the apoenzyme to form the holoenzyme.

Inborn Errors of Vitamin D Metabolism

Several diseases characterized by symptoms of vitamin D deficiency respond to administration of high doses of vitamin D—100 to 200 times the advisable intakes for normal individuals. These diseases may result from an abnormality in conversion of vitamin D to one of its biologically active metabolites (DeLuca et al., 1967; Arnaud et al., 1970). Familial (hereditary) vitamin D-resistant rickets with hypophosphatemia is inherited as an X-linked dominant trait (Williams and Winters, 1972) and vitamin D-dependent rickets is transmitted as an autosomal recessive trait (Arnaud et al., 1970).

Vitamin-Responsive Aminoacidopathies

Inborn errors involving the metabolism of various of the amino acids comprise the largest category of metabolic defects which may be treated by massive vitamin dosages. Scriver and Rosenberg (1973) have summarized the current state of knowledge in this rapidly developing field. The presently known disorders in amino acid metabolism which respond to administration of vitamins have been tabulated by Scriver and Rosenberg (1973), and the presumed biochemical basis underlying each disorder has been specified (Table 9–9).

REFERENCES

Aballí, A. J., Banús, V. L., de Lamerens, S., and Rozengvaig, S.: Coagulation studies in the newborn period. Alterations of thromboplastin generation and effects of vitamin K in full-term and premature infants. Amer. J. Dis. Child. *94*:589, 1957.

Arakawa, T.: Congenital defects in folate utilization. Amer. J. Med. *48*:594, 1970.

Arakawa, T., Ohara, K., Kudo, Z., Tada, K., Hayashi, T., and Mizuno, T.: Hyperfolic-acidemia with formiminoglutamic-aciduria following histidine loading. Tohoku J. Exp. Med. *80*:370, 1963.

Ariaey-Nejad, M. R., Balaghi, M., Baker, E. M., and Sauberlich, H. E.: Thiamin metabolism in man. Amer. J. Clin. Nutr. *23*:764, 1970.

Arnaud, C., Maijer, R., Reade, T., Scriver, C. R., and Whelan, D. T.: Vitamin D dependency: an inherited postnatal syndrome with secondary hyperparathyroidism. Pediatrics *46*:871, 1970.

Arroyave, G.: Interrelations between protein and vitamin A and metabolism. Amer. J. Clin. Nutr. *22*:1119, 1969.

Arroyave, G., Viteri, F., Béhar, M., and Scrimshaw, N. S.: Impairment of intestinal absorption of vitamin A palmitate in severe protein malnutrition (kwashiorkor). Amer. J. Clin. Nutr. *7*:185, 1959.

Avery, M. E., Clow, C. L., Menkes, J. H., Ramos, A., Scriver, C. R., Stern, L., and Wasserman, B. P.: Transient tyrosinemia of the newborn: dietary and clinical aspects. Pediatrics *39*:378, 1967.

Axelrod, A. E.: Immune processes in vitamin deficiency states. Amer. J. Clin. Nutr. *24*:265, 1971.

Baker, E. M.: Vitamin C requirements in stress. Amer. J. Clin. Nutr. *20*:583, 1967.

Baker, E. M., Saari, J. C., and Tolbert, B. M.: Ascorbic acid metabolism in man. Amer. J. Clin. Nutr. *19*:371, 1966.

Barber, G. W., and Spaeth, G. L.: Pyridoxine therapy in homocystinuria. Lancet *1*:337, 1967.

Barker, H. A.: Corrinoid-dependent enzymic reactions. Ann. Rev. Biochem. *41*:55, 1972.

Barnes, N. D., Hull, D., Balgobin, L., and Gompertz, D.: Biotin-responsive propionicacidaemia. Lancet *2*:244, 1970.

Bartley, W., Krebs, H. A., and O'Brien, J. R. P.: Vitamin C requirement of human adults. Report by Vitamin C Subcommittee of Accessory Food Factors Committee. Med. Res. Coun., Spec. Rep. Ser. 280, 1953.

Becroft, D.M.O., and Holland, J. T.: Goat's milk and megaloblastic anaemia of infancy: a report of three cases and a survey of the folic acid activity of some New Zealand milks. New Zeal. Med. J. *65*:303, 1966.

Bessey, O. A., Adam, D. J. D., and Hansen, A. E.: Intake of vitamin B_6 and infantile convulsions: a first approximation of requirements of pyridoxine in infants. Pediatrics *20*:33, 1957.

Blanc, W. A., Reid, J. D., and Andersen, D. H.: Avitaminosis E in cystic fibrosis of the pancreas. Pediatrics *22*:494, 1958.

Bransby, E. R., Berry, W. T. C., and Taylor, D. M.: Study of vitamin-D intakes of infants in 1960. Br. Med. J. *1*:1661, 1964.

Braude, H.: Megaloblastic anaemia in an infant fed on goat's milk. S. Afr. Med. J. *46*:1288, 1972.

Brickman, A. S., Coburn, J. W., and Norman, A. W.: Action of 1,25-dihydroxycholecalciferol, a potent, kidney-produced metabolite of vitamin D_3, in uremic man. New Eng. J. Med. *287*:891, 1972.

British Paediatric Association, Committee on Hypercalcaemia: Hypercalcaemia in infants and vitamin D. Br. Med. J. *2*:149, 1956.

British Paediatric Association: Infantile hypercalcaemia, nutritional rickets, and infantile scurvy in Great Britain. Br. Med. J. *1*:1659, 1964.

Bro-Rasmussen, F.: The riboflavin requirement of animals and man and associated metabolic relations. Nutr. Abst. Rev. *28*:369, 1958.

Brunette, M. G., Delvin, E., Hazel, B., and Scriver, C. R.: Thiamine-responsive lactic acidosis in a patient with deficient low-Km pyruvate carboxylase activity in liver. Pediatrics *50*:702, 1972.

Bunnell, R. H.: Modern procedures for the analysis of tocopherols. Lipids *6*:245, 1971.

Caffey, J.: Chronic poisoning due to excess of vitamin A. Pediatrics *5*:672, 1950.

Caffey, J.: Pediatric X-ray Diagnosis. 5th ed. Chicago, Year Book Medical Publishers, 1967, p. 987.

Canadian Council on Nutrition: Vitamin D deficiency in Canada. Canad. Nutr. Notes *24*:85, 1968.

Center for Disease Control: Ten-State Nutrition Survey 1968–70. Vol. V. Dietary. Atlanta, Georgia, DHEW Publ. No. (HSM) 72–8133, 1972.

Chaykin, S.: Nicotinamide coenzymes. Ann. Rev. Biochem. *36*:149, 1967.

Clausen, J., and Friis-Hansen, B.: Studies on changes in vitamin-E and fatty acids of neonatal serum. Z. Ernährungswiss. *10*:264, 1971.

Cochrane, W. A., Collins-Williams, C., and Donohue, W. L.: Superior hemorrhagic polioencephalitis (Wernicke's disease) occurring in an infant—probably due to thiamin deficiency from use of a soya bean product. Pediatrics *28*:771, 1961.

Committee on Drugs and Committee on Nutrition, American Academy of Pediatrics: The use and abuse of vitamin A. Pediatrics *48*:655, 1971.

Committee on Nutrition, American Academy of Pediatrics: Appraisal of the use of vitamins B_1 and B_{12} as supplements promoted for the stimulation of growth and appetite in children. Pediatrics *21*:860, 1958.
Committee on Nutrition, American Academy of Pediatrics: Vitamin K compounds and the water-soluble analogues. Pediatrics *28*:501, 1961.
Committee on Nutrition, American Academy of Pediatrics: Infantile scurvy and nutritional rickets in the United States. Pediatrics *29*:646, 1962.
Committee on Nutrition, American Academy of Pediatrics: The prophylactic requirement and the toxicity of vitamin D. Pediatrics *31*:512, 1963a.
Committee on Nutrition, American Academy of Pediatrics: Vitamin E in human nutrition. Pediatrics *31*:324, 1963b.
Committee on Nutrition, American Academy of Pediatrics: Vitamin B_6 requirements in man. Pediatrics *38*:1068, 1966.
Committee on Nutrition, American Academy of Pediatrics: Vitamin K supplementation for infants receiving milk substitute infant formulas and for those with fat malabsorption. Pediatrics *48*:483, 1971.
Dam, H., Dyggve, H., Larsen, H., and Plum, P.: The relation of vitamin K deficiency to hemorrhagic disease of the newborn. Advances Pediatr. *5*:129, 1952.
Dam, H., and Søndergaard, E.: Fat-soluble vitamins. *In* Beaton, G. H., and McHenry, E. W. (eds.): Nutrition. Vol. II. New York, Academic Press, 1964, p. 1.
Davis, R. A., and Wolf, A.: Infantile beriberi associated with Wernicke's encephalopathy. Pediatrics *21*:409, 1958.
DeLuca, H. F., Lund, J., Rosenbloom, A., and Lobeck, C. C.: Metabolism of tritiated vitamin D_3 in familial vitamin D-resistant rickets with hypophosphatemia. J. Pediatr. *70*:828, 1967.
DeLuca, H. F., and Suttie, J. W. (eds.): The Fat-Soluble Vitamins. Madison, Wisc., University of Wisconsin Press, 1970.
Dju, M. Y., Mason, K. E., and Filer, L. J., Jr.: Vitamin E (tocopherol) in human fetuses and placentae. Etud. Neonat. *1*:49, 1952.
Dyggve, H. V., and Probst, J. H.: Vitamin E to premature infants. Acta Paediatr. Scand. *48* (Suppl. 146), 1963.
Eagles, J. A., and Steele, P. D.: Food and nutrient intake of children from birth to four years of age. *In* Fomon, S. J., and Anderson, T. A. (eds.): Practices of Low-Income Families in Feeding Infants and Small Children. With Particular Attention to Cultural Subgroups. DHEW Publ. No. (HSM) 72–5605. Washington, D.C., U.S. Government Printing Office, 1972, p. 19.
Editorial: Vitamin D as a public health problem. Br. Med. J. *1*:1654, 1964.
Editorial: Pyridoxine and phenylketonuria. J.A.M.A. *196*:361, 1966.
Fasella, P.: Pyridoxal phosphate. Ann. Rev. Biochem. *36*:185, 1967.
Food and Nutrition Board: Recommended Dietary Allowances. 8th ed. Washington, D. C., National Academy of Sciences—National Research Council. Publ. No. 2216, 1974.
Ford, J. E., and Scott, K. J.: The folic acid activity of some milk foods for babies. J. Dairy Res. *35*:85, 1968.
Freeman, J. M., Finkelstein, J. D., Mudd, S. H., and Uhlendorf, B. W.: Homocystinuria presenting as reversible "schizophrenia." A new defect in methionine metabolism with reduced methylene-tetrahydrofolate-reductase activity (Abstract). Pediatr. Res. *6*:423, 1972.
Frimpter, G. W.: Cystathioninuria: nature of the defect. Science *149*:1095, 1965.
Frimpter, G. W., Haymovitz, A., and Horwith, M.: Cystathioninuria. New Eng. J. Med. *268*:333, 1963.
Gallo-Torres, H. E.: Vitamin E in animal nutrition. Int. J. Vit. Nutr. Res. *42*:312, 1972.
Gershoff, S. N.: Effects of dietary levels of macronutrients on vitamin requirements. Fed. Proc. *23*:1077, 1964.
Ghitis, J.: The labile folate of milk. Amer. J. Clin. Nutr. *18*:452, 1966.
Gladel, W.: Rachitisprophylaxe, Münch. Med. Wschr. *114*:398, 1972.
Goldsmith, G. A.: The B vitamins: thiamine, riboflavin, niacin. *In* Beaton, G. H., and McHenry, E. W. (eds.): Nutrition. Vol. II. New York, Academic Press, 1964, p. 109.
Goodman, S. I., Moe, P. G., Hammond, K. B., Mudd, S. H., and Uhlendorf, B. W.: Homocystinuria with methylmalonic aciduria: two cases in a sibship. Biochem. Med. *4*:500, 1970.

Gordon, H. H., Nitowsky, H. M., Tildon, J. T., and Levin, S.: Studies of tocopherol deficiency in infants and children. V. An interim summary. Pediatrics *21*:673, 1958.
Gordon, N.: Folic acid deficiency from anticonvulsant therapy. Develop. Med. Child. Neurol. *10*:497, 1968.
Gordon, R. R., and Dean, T.: Foetal deaths from antenatal anticoagulant therapy. Br. Med. J. *2*:719, 1955.
Green, J.: Vitamin E and the biological antioxidant theory. Ann. N.Y. Acad. Sci. *203*:29, 1972.
Grewar, D.: Infantile scurvy in Manitoba. Canad. Med. Ass. J. *78*:675, 1958.
Grewar, D.: Scurvy and its prevention by vitamin C fortified evaporated milk. Canad. Med. Ass. J. *80*:977, 1959.
Grewar, D.: Infantile scurvy. Clin. Pediatr. *4*:82, 1965.
Gross, S., and Melhorn, D. K.: Vitamin E, red cell lipids and red cell stability in prematurity. Ann N.Y. Acad. Sci. *203*:141, 1972.
Hakami, N., Neiman, P. E., Canellos, G. P., and Lazerson, J.: Neonatal megaloblastic anemia due to inherited transcobalamin II deficiency in two siblings. New Eng. J. Med. *285*:1163, 1971.
Hamil, B. M., Reynolds, L., Poole, M. W., and Macy, I. G.: Minimal vitamin C requirement of artificially fed infants. Amer. J. Dis. Child. *55*:561, 1938.
Harnapp, G. O.: Zur Stosstherapie und Stossprophylaxe der Rachitis. Dtsch. Med. Wschr. *65*:1414, 1939.
Harries, J. T., and Muller, D. P. R.: Absorption of different doses of fat soluble and water miscible preparations of vitamin E in children with cystic fibrosis. Arch. Dis. Child. *46*:341, 1971.
Heeley, A. F.: The effect of pyridoxine on tryptophan metabolism in phenylketonuria. Clin. Sci. *29*:465, 1965.
Herbert, V.: Minimal daily adult folate requirement. Arch. Intern. Med. *110*:649, 1962.
Herbert, V.: Introduction: symposium on folic acid deficiency. Amer. J. Clin. Nutr. *23*:841, 1970.
Herbert, V.: The five possible causes of all nutrient deficiency: illustrated by deficiencies of vitamin B_{12} and folic acid. Amer. J. Clin. Nutr. *26*:77, 1973.
Herting, D. C., and Drury, E.-J. E.: Vitamin E content of milk, milk products, and simulated milks: relevance to infant nutrition. Amer. J. Clin. Nutr. *22*:147, 1969.
Hodges, R. E., Baker, E. M., Hood, J., Sauberlich, H. E., and March, S. C.: Experimental scurvy in man. Amer. J. Clin. Nutr. *22*:535, 1969.
Hodges, R. E., Hood, J., Canham, J. E., Sauberlich, H. E., and Baker, E. M.: Clinical manifestations of ascorbic acid deficiency in man. Amer. J. Clin. Nutr. *24*:432, 1971.
Holick, M. F., Garabedian, M., and DeLuca, H. F.: 1,25-dihydroxycholecalciferol: metabolite of vitamin D_3 active on bone in anephric rats. Science *176*:1146, 1972.
Hoppner, K.: Free and total folate activity in strained baby foods. J. Inst. Canad. Technol. Aliment. *4*:51, 1971.
Horrigan, D. L., and Harris, J. W.: Pyridoxine-responsive anemia: analysis of 62 cases. Advances Intern. Med. *12*:103, 1964.
Hövels, O., and Reis, D.: Die Vitamin D-Mangelrachitis. *In* Opitz, H., and Schmid, F. (eds): Handbuch der Kinderheilkunde. Berlin, Springer, 1965, p. 434.
Howe, E. E.: Effect of vitamin B_{12} on growth-retarded children: a review. Amer. J. Clin. Nutr. *6*:18, 1958a.
Howe, E. E.: (Letter to Editor.) Vitamin B_{12} supplementation. Pediatrics *22*:1202, 1958b.
Hunt, A. D., Jr., Stokes, J., Jr., McCrory, W. W., and Stroud, H. H.: Pyridoxine dependency: report of a case of intractable convulsions in an infant controlled by pyridoxine. Pediatrics *13*:140, 1954.
IUNS Committee on Nomenclature: Tentative rules for generic descriptors and trivial names for vitamins and related compounds. J. Nutr. *101*:133, 1971.
Jepson, J. B.: Hartnup disease. *In* Stanbury, J. B., Wyngaarden, J. B., and Fredrickson, D. S. (eds.): The Metabolic Basis of Inherited Disease. 3rd ed. New York, McGraw-Hill Book Co., 1972, p. 1486.
Joint FAO/WHO Expert Group: Requirements of Ascorbic Acid, Vitamin D, Vitamin B_{12}, Folate, and Iron. WHO Techn. Rep. Ser. No. 452. Geneva, FAO and WHO, 1970.
Jolly, M.: Vitamin A deficiency: a review. I. J. Oral Therap. Pharmacol. *3*:364, 1967a.
Jolly, M.: Vitamin A deficiency: a review. II. J. Oral Therap. Pharmacol. *3*:439, 1967b.

Kamel, K., Waslien, C. I., El-Ramly, Z., Guindy, S., Mourad, K. A., Khattab, A.-K., Hashem, N., Patwardhan, V. N., and Darby, W. J.: Folate requirements of children. II. Response of children recovering from protein-calorie malnutrition to graded doses of parenterally administered folic acid. Amer. J. Clin. Nutr. *25*:152, 1972.

Katz, M., Lee, S. K., and Cooper, B. A.: Vitamin B_{12} malabsorption due to a biologically inert intrinsic factor. New Eng. J. Med. *287*:425, 1972.

Keating, J. P., and Feigin, R. D.: Increased intracranial pressure associated with probable vitamin A deficiency in cystic fibrosis. Pediatrics *46*:41, 1970.

Keenan, W. J., Jewett, T., and Glueck, H. I.: Role of feeding and vitamin K in hypoprothrombinemia of the newborn. Amer. J. Dis. Child. *121*:271, 1971.

Kerner, I., and Goldbloom, R. B.: Investigations of tocopherol deficiency in infancy and childhood. Amer. J. Dis. Child. *99*:597, 1960.

Kinsman, R. A., and Hood, J.: Some behavioral effects of ascorbic acid deficiency. Amer. J. Clin. Nutr. *24*:455, 1971.

Knapp, A.: Über eine neue, hereditäre, von Vitamin-B_6 abhängige Störung im Tryptophan-Stoffwechsel. Clin. Chim. Acta *5*:6, 1960.

Knappe, J.: Mechanism of biotin action. Ann. Rev. Biochem. *39*:757, 1970.

Kramer, B., Sobel, A. E., and Gottfried, S. P.: Serum levels of vitamin A in children: a comparison following the oral and intramuscular administration of vitamin A in oily and aqueous mediums. Amer. J. Dis. Child. *73*:543, 1947.

La Du, B. N., and Gjessing, L. R.: Tyrosinosis and tyrosinemia. *In* Stanbury, J. B., Wyngaarden, J. B., and Frederickson, D. S. (eds.): The Metabolic Basis of Inherited Disease. 3rd ed. New York, McGraw Hill Book Co., 1972, p. 296.

Lanzkowsky, P.: Congenital malabsorption of folate. Amer. J. Med. *48*:580, 1970.

Leonard, P. J., Doyle, E., and Harrington, W.: Levels of vitamin E in the plasma of newborn infants and of the mothers. Amer. J. Clin. Nutr. *25*:480, 1972.

Levy, H. L., Shih, V. E., Madigan, P. M., and MacCready, R. A.: Transient tyrosinemia in full-term infants. J.A.M.A. *209*:249, 1969.

Lewis, J. M., Bodansky, O., Birmingham, J., and Cohlan, S. Q.: Comparative absorption, excretion, and storage of oily and aqueous preparations of vitamin A. J. Pediatr. *31*:496, 1947.

Lewis, J. S.: An E/PUFA ratio of 0.4 maintains normal plasma tocopherol levels in growing children. Fed. Proc. *28*:758, 1969.

Lo, S. S., Frank, D., and Hitzig, W. H.: Vitamin E and haemolytic anaemia in premature infants. Arch. Dis. Child. *48*:360, 1973.

Loo, Y. H., and Ritman, P.: New metabolites of phenylalanine. Nature *203*:1237, 1964.

LoPresti, J. M., Gutelius, M. F., and Lefkowicz, L.: Grand rounds: scurvy. Clin. Proc. Child. Hosp. Dist. Columbia *20*:119, 1964.

Luhby, A. L., Eagle, F. J., Roth, E., and Cooperman, J. M.: Relapsing megaloblastic anemia in an infant due to a specific defect in gastrointestinal absorption of folic acid. Amer. J. Dis. Child. *102*:482, 1961.

Mackenzie, J. B.: Relations between serum tocopherol and hemolysis in hydrogen peroxide of erythrocytes in premature infants. Pediatrics *13*:346, 1954.

Mahadevan, S., Malathi, P., and Ganguly, J.: Influence of proteins on absorption and metabolism of vitamin A. World Rev. Nutr. Diet. *5*:209, 1965.

Mahoney, M. J., Rosenberg, L. E., Mudd, S. H., and Uhlendorf, B. W.: Defective metabolism of vitamin B_{12} in fibroblasts from children with methylmalonicaciduria. Biochem. Biophys. Res. Commun. *44*:375, 1971.

Maternal and Child Health Service: Screening Children for Nutritional Status: Suggestions for Child Health Programs. DHEW Publ. No. (HSM) 72-5603. Washington, D.C., U.S. Government Printing Office, 1971.

Melhorn, D. K., and Gross, S.: Vitamin E-dependent anemia in the premature infant. I. Effects of large doses of medicinal iron. J. Pediatr. *79*:569, 1971a.

Melhorn, D. K., and Gross, S.: Vitamin E-dependent anemia in the premature infant. II. Relationships between gestational age and absorption of vitamin E. J. Pediatr. *79*:581, 1971b.

Mohamed, S. D., McKay, E., and Galloway, W. H.: Juvenile familial megaloblastic anaemia due to selective malabsorption of vitamin B_{12}. Quart. J. Med. *35*:433, 1966.

Moore, T.: Vitamin A and proteins. Vitamins Hormones *18*:431, 1960.

Morgan, S. K.: Vitamin K in bleeding infants. J. S. Carolina Med. Ass. *65*:5, 1969.

Moss, M. H.: Hypoprothrombinemic bleeding in a young infant. Amer. J. Dis. Child *117*:540, 1969.

Mudd, S. H., Edwards, W. A., Loeb, P. M., Brown, M. S., and Laster, L.: Homocystinuria due to cystathionine synthase deficiency: the effect of pyridoxine. J. Clin. Invest. *49*:1762, 1970.

Mudd, S. H., Levy, H. L., and Abeles, R. H.: A derangement in B_{12} metabolism leading to homocystinemia, cystathioninemia and methylmalonic aciduria. Biochem. Biophys. Res. Commun. *35*:121, 1969.

Mudd, S. H., Uhlendorf, B. W., Freeman, J. M., Finkelstein, J. D., and Shih, V. E.: Homocystinuria associated with decreased methylenetetrahydrofolate reductase activity. Biochem. Biophys. Res. Commun. *46*:905, 1972.

Murray, T. K.: Personal communication, 1973.

Naiman, J. L., and Oski, F. A.: The folic acid content of milk: revised figures based on an improved assay method. Pediatrics *34*:274, 1964.

Nair, P. P., and Kayden, H. J. (eds): International conference on vitamin E and its role in cellular metabolism. Ann. N.Y. Acad. Sci. *203*:1, 1972.

Nair, P. P., Mezey, E., Murty, H. S., Quartner, J., and Mendeloff, A. I.: Vitamin E and porphyrin metabolism in man. Arch. Intern. Med. *128*:411, 1971.

Nair, P. P., Murty, H. S., Caasi, P. I., Brooks, S. K., and Quartner, J.: Vitamin E. Regulation of the biosynthesis of porphyrins and heme. J. Agr. Food Chem. *20*:476, 1972.

Nitowsky, H. M., Gordon, H. H., and Tildon, J. T.: Studies of tocopherol deficiency in infants and children. IV. The effect of alpha tocopherol on creatinuria in patients with cystic fibrosis of the pancreas and biliary atresia. Bull. Johns Hopkins Hosp. *98*:361, 1956.

Nitowsky, H. M., Hsu, K. S., and Gordon, H. H.: Vitamin E requirements of human infants. Vitamins Hormones *20*:559, 1962a.

Nitowsky, H. M., Tildon, J. T., Levin, S., and Gordon, H. H.: Studies of tocopherol deficiency in infants and children. VII. The effect of tocopherol on urinary, plasma and muscle creatine. Amer. J. Clin. Nutr. *10*:368, 1962b.

Nixon, P. F., and Bertino, J. R.: Interrelationships of vitamin B_{12} and folate in man. Amer. J. Med. *48*:555, 1970.

Nutrition Committee, Canadian Paediatric Society: The use and abuse of vitamin A. Canad. Med. Ass. J. *104*:521, 1971.

Oppenheimer, E. H.: Focal necrosis of striated muscle in an infant with cystic fibrosis of the pancreas and evidence of lack of absorption of fat-soluble vitamins. Bull. Johns Hopkins Hosp. *98*:353, 1956.

Oski, F. A., and Barness, L. A.: Vitamin E deficiency: a previously unrecognized cause of hemolytic anemia in the premature infant. J. Pediat. *70*:211, 1967.

Owen, G. M., Garry, P. J., Lubin, A. H., and Kram, K. M.: Nutritional status of preschool children: plasma vitamin A. J. Pediatr. *78*:1042, 1971.

Owen, G. M., Kram, K. M., Garry, P. J., Lowe, J. E., Jr., and Lubin, A. H.: A study of nutritional status of preschool children in the U.S., 1968–70. Pediatrics *53*:597, 1974.

Owen, G. M., Nelsen, C. E., Baker, G. L., Connor, W. E., and Jacobs, J. P.: Use of vitamin K_1 in pregnancy. Amer. J. Obstet. Gynec. *99*:368, 1967.

Palitzsch, D.: Rachitisprophylaxe. Münch. Med. Wschr. *113*:1516, 1971.

Persson, B., Tunell, R., and Ekengren, K.: Chronic vitamin A intoxication during the first half year of life: description of 5 cases. Acta Paediatr. Scand. *54*:49, 1965.

Richards, I. D. G., Sweet, E. M., and Arneil, G. C.: Infantile rickets persists in Glasgow. Lancet *1*:803, 1968.

Rivlin, R. S.: Riboflavin metabolism. New Eng. J. Med. *283*:463, 1970.

Rodriquez, M. S., and Irwin, M. I.: A conspectus of research on vitamin A requirements of man. J. Nutr. *102*:909, 1972.

Roels, O. A.: Vitamin A physiology. J.A.M.A. *214*:1097, 1970.

Rønne, G.: A-vitaminbehov hos nyfødte og spaede. Ugeskr. Laeger. *103*:1432, 1941. *Cited in* Nutr. Rev. *12*:(abstr. no. 2631), 1943.

Rook, G. D., Lopez, R., Shimizu, N., and Cooperman, J. M: Folic acid deficiency in infants and children with heart disease. Br. Heart J. *35*:87, 1973.

Rosenberg, I. H., and Godwin, H. A.: The digestion and absorption of dietary folate. Gastroenterology *60*:445, 1971.

Rosenberg, L. E.: Inherited aminoacidopathies demonstrating vitamin dependency. New Eng. J. Med. *281*:145, 1969.

Rosenberg, L. E.: Vitamin-dependent genetic disease. Hosp. Prac. *5*:59, 1970.

Rosenberg, L. E., Lilljeqvist, A.-Ch., and Hsia, Y. E.: Methylmalonic aciduria. Metabolic block localization and vitamin B_{12} dependency. Science *162*:805, 1968.

Rosenberg, L. E., Lilljeqvist, A.-Ch., Hsia, Y. E., and Rosenbloom, F. M.: Vitamin B_{12} dependent methylmalonicaciduria: defective B_{12} metabolism in cultured fibroblasts. Biochem. Biophys. Res. Commun. *37*:607, 1969.

Scriver, C. R., Mackenzie, S., Clow, C. L., and Delvin, E.: Thiamine-responsive maple-syrup-urine disease. Lancet *1*:310, 1971.

Scriver, C. R., and Rosenberg, L. E.: Amino Acid Metabolism and its Disorders. Philadelphia, W. B. Saunders Co., 1973.

Scriver, C. R., and Whelan, D. T.: Glutamic acid decarboxylase (GAD) in mammalian tissue outside the central nervous system, and its possible relevance to hereditary vitamin B_6 dependency with seizures. Ann. N.Y. Acad. Sci. *166*:83, 1969.

Seashore, M. R., Durant, J. L., and Rosenberg, L. E.: Studies of the mechanism of pyridoxine-responsive homocystinuria. Pediatr. Res. *6*:187, 1972.

Shih, V. E., Salam, M. Z., Mudd, S. H., Uhlendorf, B. W., and Adams, R. D.: A new form of homocystinuria due to $N^{5,10}$-methylenetetrahydrofolate reductase deficiency. (Abstract) Pediatr. Res. *6*:395, 1972.

Slover, H. T.: Tocopherols in foods and fats. Lipids *6*:291, 1971.

Smith, C. H.: Blood Diseases of Infancy and Childhood. 3rd ed. St. Louis, C. V. Mosby Co., 1972, p. 717.

Smith, L. H., Jr., and Williams, H. E.: Treatment of primary hyperoxaluria. Mod. Treatm. *4*:522, 1967.

Snyderman, S. E., Carretero, R., and Holt, L. E., Jr.: Pyridoxine deficiency in the human being. Fed. Proc. *9*:371, 1950.

Stadtman, T. C.: Vitamin B_{12}. Science *171*:859, 1971.

Strelling, M. K., Blackledge, G. D., Goodall, H. B., and Walker, C. H. M.: Megaloblastic anaemia and whole-blood folate levels in premature infants. Lancet *1*:898, 1966.

Sullivan, L. W., Luhby, A. L., and Streiff, R. R.: Studies of the daily requirement for folic acid in infants and the etiology of folate deficiency in goat's milk megaloblastic anemia. Amer. J. Clin. Nutr. *18*:311, 1966.

Sutherland, J. M., Glueck, H. I., and Gleser, G.: Hemorrhagic disease of the newborn. Amer. J. Dis. Child. *113*:524, 1967.

Suttie, J. W.: Control of clotting factor biosynthesis by vitamin K. Fed. Proc. *28*:1696, 1969.

Tada, K., Yokoyama, Y., Nakagawa, H., and Arakawa, T.: Vitamin B_6 dependent xanthurenic aciduria (the second report). Tohoku J. Exp. Med. *95*:107, 1968.

Tappel, A. L.: Vitamin E and free radical peroxidation of lipids. Ann. N.Y. Acad. Sci. *203*:12, 1972.

Torstenson, O. L., Humphrey, G. B., Edson, J. R., and Warwick, W. J.: Cystic fibrosis presenting with severe hemorrhage due to vitamin K malabsorption: a report of three cases. Pediatrics *45*:857, 1970.

Underwood, B. A., and Denning, C. R.: Blood and liver concentrations of vitamins A and E in children with cystic fibrosis of the pancreas. Pediatr. Res. *6*:26, 1972.

Underwood, B. A., Denning, C. R., and Navab, M.: Polyunsaturated fatty acids and tocopherol levels in patients with cystic fibrosis. Ann. N.Y. Acad. Sci. *203*:237, 1972.

Velez, H., Ghitis, J., Pradilla, A., and Vitale, J. J.: Cali-Harvard nutrition project. I. Megaloblastic anemia in kwashiorkor. Amer. J. Clin. Nutr. *12*:54, 1963.

Vietti, T. J., Murphy, T. P., James, J. A., and Pritchard, J. A.: Observations on the prophylactic use of vitamin K in the newborn infant. J. Pediatr. *56*:343, 1960.

Walters, T. R.: Congenital megaloblastic anemia responsive to N^5-formyl tetrahydrofolic acid administration. J. Pediatr. *70*:686, 1967.

Walters, T. R., and Koch, H. F.: Hemorrhagic diathesis and cystic fibrosis in infancy. Amer. J. Dis. Child. *124*:641, 1972.

Waslien, C. I., Kamel, K., El-Ramly, Z., Carter, J. P., Mourad, K. A., Khattab, A.-K., and Darby, W. J.: Folate requirements of children. I. A formula diet low in folic acid for study of folate deficiency in protein-calorie malnutrition. Amer. J. Clin. Nutr. *25*:147, 1972.

Wasserman, R. H., and Corradino, R. A.: Metabolic role of vitamins A and D. Ann. Rev. Biochem. *40*:501, 1971.

Wasserman, R. H., and Taylor, A. N.: Metabolic roles of fat-soluble vitamins, D, E, and K. Ann. Rev. Biochem. *41*:179, 1972.

Weinberg, T., Gordon, H. H., Oppenheimer, E. H., and Nitowsky, H. M.: Myopathy in association with tocopherol deficiency in cases of congenital biliary atresia and cystic fibrosis of the pancreas. Amer. J. Path. *34*:565, 1958.

Wendt, G., and Bernhart, F. W.: The structure of a sulfur-containing compound with vitamin B_6 activity. Arch. Biochem. Biophys. *88*:270, 1960.

Whelan, W. S., Fraser, D., Robertson, E. C., and Tomczak, H.: The rising incidence of scurvy in infants. Canad. Med. Ass. J.: *78*:177, 1958.

Williams, T. E., Arango, L., Donaldson, M. H., and Shepard, F. M.: Vitamin K requirement of normal infants on soy protein formula. Clin. Pediatr. *9*:79, 1970.

Williams, T. F., and Winters, R. W.: Familial (hereditary) vitamin D-resistant rickets with hypophosphatemia. *In* Stanbury, J. B., Wyngaarden, J. B., and Fredrickson, D. S. (eds.): The Metabolic Basis of Inherited Disease. 3rd ed. New York, McGraw Hill Book Co., 1972, p. 1465.

Witting, L. A.: Lipid peroxidation in vivo. J. Amer. Oil. Chem. Soc. *42*:908, 1965.

Witting, L. A.: Recommended dietary allowance for vitamin E. Amer. J. Clin. Nutr. *25*:257, 1972a.

Witting, L. A.: The role of polyunsaturated fatty acids in determining vitamin E requirement. Ann. N.Y. Acad. Sci. *203*:192, 1972b.

Wolf, H.: Rachitisprophylaxe beim Säugling. Dtsch. Med. Wschr. *95*:1530, 1970.

Wolf, H., Kerstan, J., und Kreutz, F.-H.: Kontinuierliche Rachitisprophylaxe – schon beim Neugeborenen? Mschr. Kinderheilkd. *120*:329, 1972.

Woodruff, C. W.: Ascorbic acid. *In* Beaton, G. H., and McHenry, E. W. (eds.): Nutrition. Vol. II. New York, Academic Press, 1964, p. 265.

Yoshida, T., Tada, K., and Arakawa, T.: Vitamin B_6-dependency of glutamic acid decarboxylase in the kidney from a patient with vitamin B_6 dependent convulsion. Tohoku J. Exp. Med. *104*:195, 1971.

10

WATER AND RENAL SOLUTE LOAD

Karl E. Bergmann,
Ekhard E. Ziegler
and
Samuel J. Fomon

Water requirement may be subdivided into renal and extrarenal categories. Water required for renal excretion is determined predominantly by the magnitude of the renal solute load and this, in turn, is largely dependent on the diet. In the case of healthy infants receiving commonly employed diets, renal solute load will ordinarily be low in relation to the amount of water available for its excretion. However, in the case of infants with various illnesses, unusual diets, adverse environmental conditions or combinations of these factors, understanding of the relation between renal solute load, renal concentrating ability and water balance may be essential in preserving the health of the infant. The present chapter will consider these relationships.

WATER

Water is required by the human infant to replace loss of water from skin and lungs and losses in feces and urine. In addition, a small amount of water is needed for growth. As a general formulation, one may consider that the requirement for water is the sum of four components: evaporative water losses (i.e., losses from skin and lungs), fecal water losses, water required for renal excretion of solutes and water

TABLE 10–1 ESTIMATED WATER EXPENDITURES OF NORMAL SUBJECTS OF VARIOUS AGES (CIRCUMSTANCES IN WHICH WATER REQUIREMENTS ARE MINIMAL)*

	WATER REQUIREMENT (ML/DAY)			
SOURCES OF WATER LOSS	*Age 1 Mo 4.2 kg*	*Age 4 Mo 7.0 kg*	*Age 12 Mo 10.5 kg*	*Age 36 Mo 15 kg*
Growth	18 (6)†	9 (2)	6 (1)	5 (1)
Losses from skin and lungs	210 (64)	350 (66)	500 (63)	600 (63)
Fecal losses	42 (13)	70 (13)	105 (13)	140 (15)
Urine	56 (17)	105 (19)	182 (23)	203 (21)

*Assumes average rate of growth (see text), thermoneutral environment, diet of low renal solute load (approximately equivalent to that of human milk) and ability to concentrate the urine to 1000 mosmol/liter.

†Values in parentheses indicate percentage of total water requirement.

required for growth. Under all conditions, water for growth accounts for a relatively small percentage of total requirement for water (Table 10–1). Therefore, for practical purposes, water requirement may be considered to consist of the amount needed for replacement of evaporative, fecal and urinary losses.

Water Intake

Preformed water is consumed either in the form of water or as a component of food. Cow milk and infant formulas of conventional caloric density (67 kcal/100 ml) provide approximately 90 ml of preformed water in each 100 ml of milk or formula consumed. Most commercially prepared strained and junior foods provide only slightly less water per unit of volume than do milk and formula (Chapter 16, Tables 16–2 and 16–3). In addition to preformed water, foods yield water of oxidation—0.41, 1.07 and 0.55 ml, respectively—from the complete combustion of 1 gm each of protein, fat and carbohydrate (Maxwell and Kleeman, 1962). Because some amino acids and fatty acids must be utilized in tissue synthesis, it is apparent that complete combustion of all foods does not occur. Therefore, calculation of the sum of preformed water and water of oxidation for each food would be likely to be misleading. With a variety of commonly consumed infant foods, our calculations suggest that preformed water plus water of oxidation amounts to about 95 per cent of the volume of the food. However, when caloric density of a formula approaches 100 kcal/100 ml, preformed water plus water of oxidation will amount to only 90 per cent of the volume of the food.

Water Losses

Evaporative Water Loss. Loss of water from skin and lungs accounts for the greatest part of water requirement, generally ranging from 30 to 70 ml/kg/day in healthy fullterm infants not exposed to extreme environmental conditions (Levine et al., 1929; Pratt et al., 1948; Cooke et al., 1950; Darrow et al., 1954; Heeley and Talbot, 1955; Drescher et al., 1962). Estimates of evaporative water losses by normal subjects under thermoneutral conditions are summarized in Table 10–1.

When infants are exposed to elevated environmental temperatures, water losses from skin and lungs may increase by 50 to 100 per cent (Levine et al., 1929; Cooke et al., 1950; Darrow et al., 1954). Although it is commonly assumed (Committee on Nutrition, 1957) that evaporative water losses increase approximately 10 per cent for each degree centigrade rise in body temperature, documentation of this value does not appear to be available.

From Table 10–1 it may be seen that evaporative water losses (i.e., those from skin and lungs) account for approximately two-thirds of the total water requirement during the first three years of life. Because evaporative water losses are closely related to energy expenditures, water requirement is sometimes expressed per unit of energy production, and Winters (1973) has suggested the convenient ratio of 1 ml/kcal. However, it is apparent that the ratio of water requirement to energy production will increase when extrarenal losses are unusually high (e.g., elevated environmental temperature) or when renal water loss is great (e.g., high renal solute load, especially in the presence of decreased renal concentrating ability).

Fecal Water Loss. Fecal water losses of normal infants generally average about 10 ml/kg/day (Pratt et al., 1948; Cooke et al., 1950; Darrow et al., 1954), thus amounting to about 13 per cent of total water requirement (Table 10–1). In infants with diarrhea, fecal water losses may easily be five or six times normal (Holt et al., 1915; Chung, 1948; Darrow et al., 1949).

Urinary Water Loss. When intake of water approaches requirement, the amount of water excreted in the urine will be determined by the renal solute load and renal concentrating ability. When intake of water is greater than the requirement, the excess water will ordinarily be excreted in the urine. There is no evidence that increases in water intake above the requirement influence the water utilized for growth or water losses through skin, lungs and gastrointestinal tract. In the case of healthy infants receiving usual diets, intakes of water are greatly in excess of requirement. For example, the estimated water requirement of a one-month-old infant is 326 ml/day under conditions in which water requirements are minimal (Table 10–1). As may be seen from data presented in Chapter 2, actual intake of formula by such an infant might be 700 ml, equivalent to approximately 665 ml of water (i.e., preformed water plus water of oxidation—see Water Intake). Therefore, water available for renal excretion will be several times the quantity required. It is for this reason that normal infants ordinarily excrete dilute urine and that problems of water balance rarely develop in healthy infants fed usual diets.

RENAL SOLUTE LOAD

Solutes that must be excreted by the kidney are spoken of collectively as the renal solute load. Most commonly, the urinary excretion of renal solutes is expressed in milliosmols per day, and the concentration of the urine in milliosmols per liter. The renal solute load consists primarily of nonmetabolizable dietary components, especially electrolytes, ingested in excess of body needs, and metabolic end products. The latter consist mainly of nitrogenous compounds resulting from digestion and metabolism of protein.

Consideration of renal solute load in infant feeding is particularly important in the following circumstances: (1) low fluid intake, including the feeding of calorically highly concentrated diets (Chapter 2); (2) abnormally high extrarenal water losses, as in fever, elevated environmental temperature, hyperventilation and diarrhea; and (3) impaired renal concentrating ability, as in renal disease, protein-calorie malnutrition (Alleyne, 1967) and diabetes insipidus. Ability to concentrate the urine appears to be relatively low in the case of some otherwise normal fullterm infants (Winberg, 1959; Edelmann et al., 1960; Pólaček et al., 1965) and, presumably, such limitation of concentrating ability may be even more frequent in the case of premature infants. Thus, it is apparent that the importance of renal solute load must be kept in mind in a variety of circumstances.

Unfortunately, the solute concentration of a feeding is of little value in predicting its renal solute load. In most infant formulas, a high percentage of solutes will consist of disaccharides and polysaccharides of relatively small molecular weight. These will normally be metabolized and will yield few solutes for renal excretion. Protein, on the other hand, will contribute little to the solute concentration of the formula, but the metabolic end products of protein metabolism will comprise an important part of the renal solute load.

An estimate of renal solute load may be obtained by subtracting from the potential renal solute load resulting from ingestion of the diet that portion of the potential renal solute load excreted through extrarenal routes (mainly gastrointestinal tract and skin), and that portion of the potential renal solute load utilized for growth. In the great majority of instances, however, a sufficiently accurate prediction of renal solute load may be made by the simplified approach of Ziegler and Fomon (1971). This approach will be utilized in the examples that follow. A more general (and more complicated) formula necessary for special circumstances, especially management of the low-birth-weight infant, is presented later in the chapter.

Simplified Prediction of Renal Solute Load

A simple estimate of renal solute load may be based on dietary intake of nitrogen and of three minerals—sodium, potassium and chloride. For reasons discussed by Ziegler and Fomon (1971), each gram of dietary protein is considered to yield 4 mosmol of renal solute load (assumed to be all urea), and each milliequivalent of sodium, potassium and chloride is assumed to contribute 1 mosmol.

This estimate of renal solute load was developed primarily from data pertaining to infants fed whole cow milk or other feedings that yield relatively high renal solute loads. Under these circumstances, the fraction of dietary nitrogen and various electrolytes incorporated into newly synthesized body tissue or lost through skin is relatively small.

When diets provide lesser amounts of protein and electrolytes, retention for growth and losses through skin constitute a larger fraction of the intake, and the proposed calculation will overestimate the renal solute load. However, problems arising from overestimating the size of the renal solute load are of less clinical importance than are problems arising from underestimating it. In addition, knowledge of the size of the renal solute load is more important when the renal solute load is large than when it is small.

FULLSIZE INFANTS WITHOUT CHRONIC DISEASE

The examples presented in Figures 10–1 to 10–4 concern fluid intake, renal solute load, extrarenal losses and osmolar concentration of the urine of a hypothetic four- or five-month-old infant weighing 7 kg. Each example concerns intake and excretion during a 24-hour interval.

Volume of Intake and Evaporative Water Losses

In Figure 10–1, the example concerns an infant fed either 1000 or 750 ml of whole cow milk; extrarenal losses of fluid are assumed to be

TABLE 10–2 DIETARY INTAKE OF PROTEIN, SODIUM, CHLORIDE AND POTASSIUM AND ESTIMATED RENAL SOLUTE LOAD FROM VARIOUS FEEDINGS

FEEDINGS	CALORIC DENSITY (KCAL/100 ML)†	DIETARY INTAKE					ESTIMATED RENAL SOLUTE LOAD*		
		Quantity (ml)†	*Protein (gm)*	*Na (meq)*	*Cl (meq)*	*K (meq)*	*Urea (mosmol)‡*	*Na+Cl+K (mosmol)*	*Total (mosmol)*
Milks									
Whole cow milk	67	1000	33	25	29	35	132	89	221
Boiled skim milk	33	1000	46	35	40	49	184	124	308
Human milk	67	1000	12	7	11	13	48	31	79
Formulas									
SMA	100	1000	22	10	18	21	90	49	139
Similac	100	1000	24	17	24	28	97	69	166
Strained foods									
Pears	69	100	0.3	0.2	0.2	1.6	1	2	3
Applesauce	84	100	0.2	0.3	0.2	2.6	1	3	4
Beef with vegetables	104	100	6.5	13.3	10.6	3.7	26	28	54
Chicken with vegetables	100	100	7.2	5.7	4.6	1.8	29	12	41

*This simplified estimate of renal solute load is appropriate for use with respect to fullsize but not low-birth-weight infants (see text).

†For strained foods, 100 gm rather than 100 ml.

‡Assumed to account for 70 per cent of nitrogen intake (Ziegler and Fomon, 1971).

Figure 10–1 Relation between volume consumed, extrarenal losses and solute concentration of urine of hypothetic 7 kg infant fed 1000 ml (a and b) or 750 ml (c and d) of whole cow milk per day. The upper stippled area of each column indicates the volume of losses from skin and lungs. The central, more densely stippled area indicates the volume of fecal loss (assumed in each instance to be 50 ml). The unstippled lower segment of each column indicates the volume of water available for urinary excretion and the urine concentration that would result from excretion of the renal solute load in that volume of urine. (From Ziegler, E. E., and Fomon, S. J.: Fluid intake, renal solute load, and water balance in infancy. J. Pediatr. *78*: 561, 1971.)

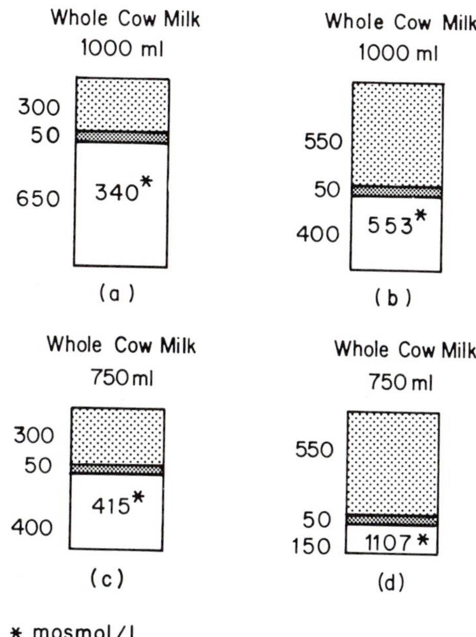

350 ml (300 ml from skin and lungs* and 50 ml in feces) when exposed to normal environmental temperature (Fig. 10–1a and c), and 600 ml (550 ml from skin and lungs and 50 ml in feces†) when exposed to elevated environmental temperature (Fig. 10–1b and d). As may be seen from Table 10–2, estimated renal solute load arising from 1000 ml of whole cow milk is 221 mosmol. At normal environmental temperature (Fig. 10–1a), this hypothetic infant consuming 1000 ml of milk has 650 ml of water available for renal excretion of these solutes, and urinary concentration is 340 mosmol/liter. At elevated environmental temperature (Fig. 10–1b), only 400 ml of water are available for renal excretion, and urine concentration is 553 mosmol/liter. Since nearly all normal infants will be able to concentrate the urine to more than 553 mosmol/liter (Winberg, 1959; Edelmann et al., 1960; Pólacek et al., 1965), there is no threat to water balance.

It should be noted that the assumed value (550 ml) for losses of water from skin and lungs at elevated environmental temperature is by no means extreme. Several reports (Cooke et al., 1950; Darrow et al., 1949, 1954) have documented situations in which water losses

*The examples in Figures 10–1 to 10–4, reproduced from the report by Ziegler and Fomon (1971), employ a slightly lesser evaporative water loss for a 7 kg infant than the value given in Table 10–1 (300 versus 350 ml/day).

†Increased fecal losses will be considered separately (see Diarrhea).

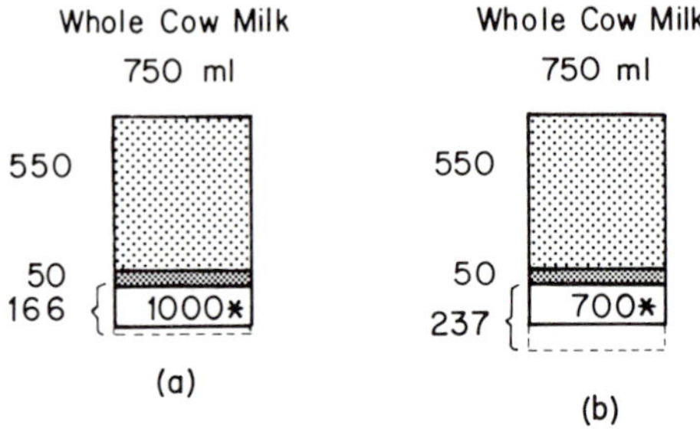

Figure 10–2 Influence of renal concentrating ability of 1000 mosmol/liter (a) or 700 mosmol/liter (b) on water balance of hypothetic infant with extrarenal losses of 600 ml and dietary intake of 750 ml of whole cow milk. Various areas of the columns have the same significance as in Figure 10–1. The segment of the column outlined by interrupted lines indicates the extent of negative water balance. (From Ziegler, E. E., and Fomon, S. J.: Fluid intake, renal solute load, and water balance in infancy. J. Pediatr. *78*:561, 1971.)

through skin and lungs were greater.* Fever increases water losses through skin and lungs, probably to a lesser extent than does elevated environmental temperature; however, the literature provides little basis for quantitative estimation of the effect of fever. Using the commonly employed estimate of a 10 per cent rise in evaporative water loss per degree centigrade rise in body temperature, evaporative losses by the hypothetic 7 kg infant may be assumed to be 420 ml/day for an elevation of body temperature of 4° C.

If intake of cow milk is decreased to 750 ml, renal solute load will be decreased proportionately (221 mosmol/liter × 0.75 liter = 166 mosmol). Since extrarenal water losses will be unchanged, at normal environmental temperature 166 mosmol will be excreted in 400 ml of available water (Fig. 10–1c), resulting in urine concentration of 415 mosmol/liter. It is apparent that decrease in the amount of intake of a specified diet will ordinarily lead to increased concentration of the urine (until the maximal concentrating ability has been reached).

If 750 ml of cow milk are consumed in the presence of extrarenal losses of 600 ml (Fig. 10–1d), urine concentration would need to be 1107 mosmol/liter to maintain water balance. Many infants will be able to achieve this urine concentration, particularly when the ratio of urea to nonurea solutes in the urine is high (Winberg, 1959; Drescher et al., 1962). However, it is apparent from the literature (Winberg, 1959; Edelmann et al., 1960; Pólaček et al., 1965) that some otherwise normal infants are unable to concentrate the urine above 600 or 700 mosmol/liter. With a specified diet (and therefore specified renal solute load), it is apparent that in this situation renal concentrating

*For the sake of simplicity, we have chosen to ignore observations (Cooke et al., 1950; Darrow et al., 1954) suggesting that during heat stress there may be some tendency toward retention of electrolytes.

ability will determine how closely extrarenal losses may approach water intake before water balance will become negative.

Renal Concentrating Ability

Figure 10–2 concerns a hypothetic infant consuming 750 ml of whole cow milk and with extrarenal losses of 600 ml. The examples chosen are similar to those in Figure 10–1d, except that concentrating ability is limited to 1000 mosmol/liter or to 700 mosmol/liter. Because of the limitation of renal concentrating ability, excretion of the renal solute load of 166 mosmol cannot be accomplished in the 150 ml of water available from the diet. Negative water balance will therefore result. The extent of the negative water balance will be small (16 ml) when renal concentrating ability is 1000 mosmol/liter (Fig. 10–2a) and moderate (87 ml) when renal concentrating ability is 700 mosmol/liter (Fig. 10–2b). If renal concentrating ability of the infant in the example were severely limited (e.g., inability to concentrate urine above 300 mosmol/liter), it is apparent from Figure 10–1a that, even with an intake of 1000 ml of whole cow milk, water balance would be negative.

Feeding Choice and Renal Solute Load

In the case of high extrarenal water losses, low fluid intake or severe limitation of renal concentrating ability, the choice of feeding may be a critical factor in water balance. For example, the infant just mentioned with inability to concentrate the urine above 300 mosmol/liter was calculated to be in negative water balance when receiving 1000 ml of whole cow milk. However, if this infant received 1000 ml of human milk instead of 1000 ml of whole cow milk, it would be necessary for him to excrete only 79 instead of 221 mosmol (Table 10–2) in 650 ml of water, and water balance would be easily maintained. Even if extrarenal losses were high, as in Figure 10–3a, water balance would not be jeopardized.

Figures 10–3c and d concern the water balance of the same hypothetic infant with high extrarenal fluid losses when food intake, instead of consisting of 1000 ml of human milk or of whole cow milk, consists of 730 ml of cow milk and two jars (135 gm each) of commercially prepared strained food—one (pears) yielding a low renal solute load and one (beef and vegetables) yielding a high renal solute load. The renal solute load from 730 ml of whole cow milk is 161 mosmol (221 mosmol/liter × 0.730 liter). Renal solute load from 270 gm of strained pears (Table 10–2) is only 8 mosmol. Thus, renal solute load arising from the combination of cow milk and pears would be 169

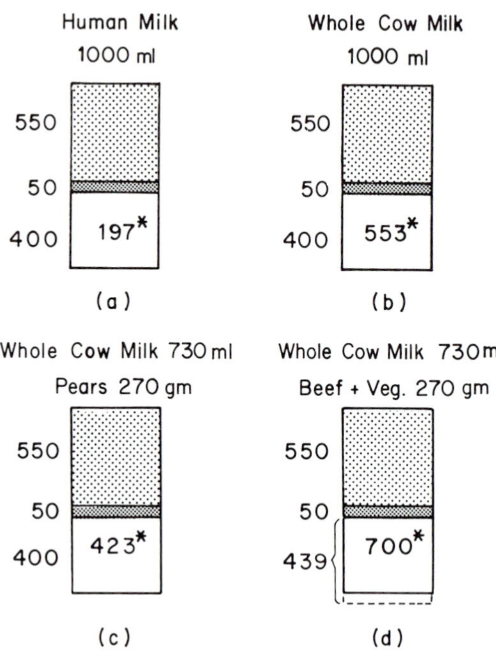

Figure 10–3 Influence of various diets on urine concentration and water balance of hypothetic infant with extrarenal losses of 600 ml. Various areas of the columns have the same significance as in Figures 10–1 and 10–2. (From Ziegler, E. E., and Fomon, S. J.: Fluid intake, renal solute load, and water balance in infancy. J. Pediatr. *78*:561, 1971.)

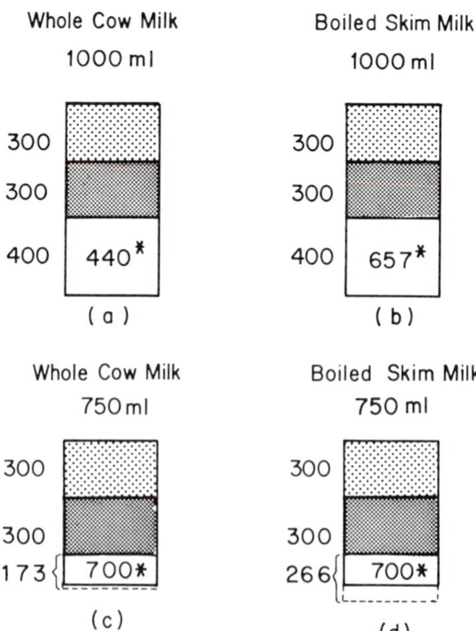

Figure 10–4 Urine concentration and water balance of hypothetic infant with diarrhea fed 1000 ml or 750 ml of whole cow milk or boiled skim milk. Various areas of the columns have the same significance as in Figures 10–1 and 10–2. (From Ziegler, E. E., and Fomon, S. J.: Fluid intake, renal solute load, and water balance in infancy. J. Pediatr. *78*:561, 1971.)

mosmol, a lesser load than that presented by an approximately similar total volume of intake from cow milk alone.

If, however, protein and electrolyte content of the strained food were high, total renal solute load might be substantially greater than that depicted in Figure 10–3b. In Figure 10–3d, it is assumed that 270 gm of strained beef and vegetables are fed, presenting a renal solute load of 146 mosmol. Total renal solute of strained food plus milk would be 307 mosmol and, with renal concentrating ability limited to 700 mosmol/liter, 439 ml of urine would be required for excretion. With extrarenal water losses of 600 ml, the infant would be in negative water balance.

Most commercially prepared formulas as well as cow milk with added carbohydrate and water will yield renal solute loads that are considerably less than that from whole cow milk, though greater than the renal solute load presented by human milk (Table 10–2). The greater margin of safety provided by these feedings will be of little significance under most circumstances, but may be of considerable value during illness or under adverse environmental conditions.

DIARRHEA

When fecal losses of fluid are increased because of diarrhea, fecal losses of solutes are also increased. Although the actual solute concentration of diarrheal fluid may be somewhat greater, loss of solutes that would otherwise require excretion in the urine amounts to approximately 150 mosmol/liter (Holt et al., 1915; Chung, 1948; Darrow et al., 1949; Finberg et al., 1960; Kooh and Metcoff, 1963; Bruck et al., 1968). Figure 10–4 indicates the renal solute load and fluid balance of a hypothetic infant who is assumed to lose 300 ml of diarrheal fluid (Holt et al., 1915; Chung, 1948; Darrow et al., 1949) containing 45 mosmol of substances that would, if absorbed, contribute to renal solute load. Therefore, the renal solute load, as calculated in the earlier examples would, in the presence of diarrhea, be decreased by 45 mosmol.

When 1000 ml of whole cow milk are consumed by the hypothetic infant (Fig. 10–4a), 176 mosmol ($221 - 45 = 176$) will be excreted in a urine volume of 400 ml, resulting in urine concentration of 440 mosmol/liter. Because boiled skim milk is still recommended by some physicians in management of diarrhea, Figure 10–4b has been included for comparison with Figure 10–4a. It is important to recognize that, per unit of volume, skim milk provides a slightly greater renal solute load than does whole milk, and solute concentration is further increased by loss of water during boiling. We have assumed that skim milk, after gentle boiling for five minutes, will yield a renal solute load of 308 mosmol/1000 ml (Table 10–2). With an intake of 1000 ml of boiled skim milk (Fig. 10–4b) and fecal loss in diarrheal fluid of 45 mosmol of potential renal solute load, there will remain 263 mosmol to be excreted in 400 ml of urine, resulting in urine concentration of 657 mosmol/liter.

The inadvisability of using boiled skim milk in treatment of diarrhea can be demonstrated more dramatically by considering a hypothetic infant with moderately decreased volume of intake (750 ml) and renal concentrating ability limited to 700 mosmol/liter. Volumes of intake by infants with diarrhea are, in fact, often low (Bruck et al., 1968). Renal concentrating ability of such infants does not appear to be less than that of healthy infants (Bruck et al., 1968) but, as already mentioned, renal concentrating ability of some otherwise normal infants is limited to 700 mosmol/liter.

Under these circumstances, feeding of whole cow milk (Fig. 10–4c) will yield a renal solute load of 121 mosmol (166 mosmol of potential renal solute load provided by diet minus 45 mosmol assumed to be lost in diarrheal fluid) and will require 173 ml of urine for excretion, resulting in slightly negative water balance. Feeding of 750 ml of boiled skim milk (Fig. 10–4d) will yield a renal solute load of 186 mosmol (231 mosmol of potential renal solute load provided by diet minus 45 mosmol assumed to be lost in diarrheal fluid) and require 266 ml of urine for excretion. The magnitude of the negative water balance will therefore be considerably greater when boiled skim milk is fed than when whole cow milk is fed.

FEEDING CALORICALLY CONCENTRATED DIETS TO FULLSIZE INFANTS

Infants with severe congenital heart disease, with various neuromuscular disorders and with certain other chronic diseases may have difficulty in consuming sufficient volume of conventional feedings to promote adequate growth. Under these circumstances, it is reasonable to utilize more concentrated feedings. With adequate monitoring of water balance, it is usually feasible to feed commercially prepared formulas diluted to a concentration of 100 kcal/100 ml instead of to the conventional concentration of 67 kcal/100 ml. The discussion that follows applies to water balance and renal solute load of fullsize infants fed calorically concentrated formulas. Other aspects of nutritional management of fullsize infants with chronic disease are considered in Chapter 19. Water balance and renal solute load in feeding of low-birth-weight infants are considered later in this chapter.

As has already been mentioned, the simplified approach to prediction of renal solute load utilized in Table 10–2 is primarily applicable to diets consisting of whole cow milk or other feedings yielding relatively high renal solute loads. Under these circumstances, the fraction of dietary nitrogen and of various electrolytes incorporated into newly synthesized body tissue or lost through the skin is relatively small. When the ratio of protein and electrolytes to calories in the diet is relatively low, as will be the case in those diets proposed for infants who are to be fed calorically concentrated diets, retention of nitrogen and minerals for growth and losses through the skin may constitute a larger fraction of the intake, and the proposed calculation is likely to overestimate the renal solute load. For these reasons, the safety of feeding formulas concentrated to 100 kcal/100 ml is probably greater than the calculations would suggest.

As will be discussed below, urinary osmolality should be determined at frequent intervals and dietary adjustment should be made as necessary. Calculations are useful for the purpose of comparing the renal solute load of various foods in relation to their contribution of calories and essential nutrients, but these calculations should be used only as a rough guide. The safety of the diet will be much better evaluated by repeated determinations of urinary osmolality.

Milk and Formula

For purposes of illustrating the importance of the renal solute load in the nutritional management of infants with severe congenital heart disease, Fomon and Ziegler (1972) have considered a hypothetic nine-month-old boy weighing 7 kg and unable to consume more than 750 ml of food daily. If such an infant were fed whole cow milk or formula providing 67 kcal/100 ml, his intake would amount to only 72 kcal/kg/day, and his rate of growth would at best be extremely slow. If he were fed a formula providing 100 kcal/100 ml, 750 ml would provide 107 kcal/kg/day, and satisfactory growth would be more likely.

That formulas providing 100 kcal/100 ml do not necessarily yield excessive renal solute loads may be seen from the examples presented in Figure 10–5. Assuming extrarenal expenditures of water at normal environmental temperature to be 400 ml (350 ml from skin and lungs* and 50 ml in feces), 350 ml of water will be available for renal excretion. Examples included in Figure 10–5 are (1) SMA, a partially demineralized formula, at a concentration of 100 kcal/100 ml; (2)

*Because water losses from the skin and lungs of infants with congenital heart disease are often greater than those of normal infants (Morgan and Nadas, 1963; Elliott and Cooke, 1968; Puyau, 1969; Stocker et al., 1972), losses of 350 ml/day were assumed for the examples in Figures 10–5 and 10–6 rather than the 300 ml/day assumed for normal infants (Figs. 10–1 to 10–4).

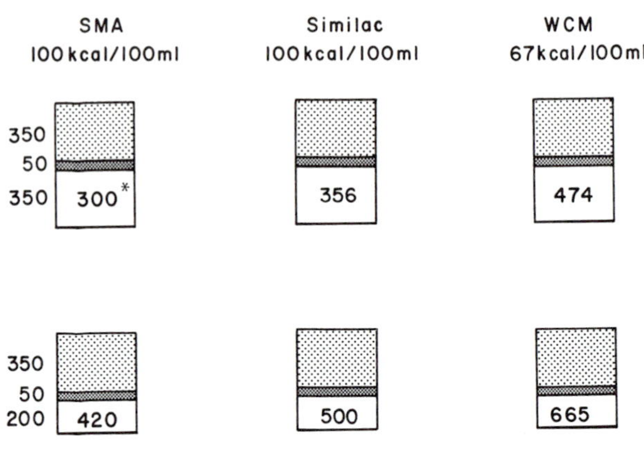

*mosmol/l

Figure 10–5 Water balance of hypothetic nine-month-old infant with congenital heart disease and daily food consumption limited to 750 ml (upper set of bar graphs) or to 600 ml (lower set of bar graphs). It is assumed that the entire calorie intake is provided by 100 kcal/100 ml of formula or by whole cow milk. Various areas of the columns have the same significance as in Figure 10–1.

Similac at a concentration of 100 kcal/100 ml; and (3) whole cow milk. Estimated renal solute load from consumption of each of these feedings is presented in Table 10–2.

Consumption of 1000 ml of SMA at a caloric density of 100 kcal/100 ml may be seen to yield an estimated renal solute load of 139 mosmol (Table 10–2). The estimated renal solute load from 750 ml of 100 kcal/100 ml SMA is therefore 105 mosmol; excretion of 105 mosmol in 350 ml of urine (Fig. 10–5, upper set of bar graphs) results in urine concentration of 300 mosmol/liter. Similarly, 750 ml of Similac would yield a renal solute load of 125 mosmol. Excretion of 125 mosmol in 350 ml of urine water would be accomplished with a urine concentration of 356 mosmol per liter. As may be seen from Table 10–2, whole cow milk (67 kcal/100 ml) provides a greater renal solute load than do the other feedings at 100 kcal/100 ml. The estimated renal solute load from 750 ml of whole cow milk is 166 mosmol; yet, 750 ml of whole cow milk would provide only 503 kcal compared with 750 kcal from an equal volume of 100 kcal/100 ml SMA or Similac.

If the hypothetic infants just discussed were to receive only 600 ml of formula daily instead of 750 ml, the calculated renal solute loads would be decreased to 84, 100 and 133 mosmol/day, respectively. These renal solute loads would need to be excreted in only 200 ml of urine (Fig. 10–5, lower set of bar graphs), with resultant urine concentrations of 420, 500 and 665 mosmol/liter. Because most normal infants (and probably most infants with congenital heart disease) can achieve urinary concentrations of at least 700 mosmol/liter, the water balance would probably be maintained in all the examples presented in Figure 10–5.

Assuming that extrarenal losses of fluid by these hypothetic infants remain at a level of 400 ml/day, one can readily calculate the effect of further decreases in fluid intake. With intakes of 500 ml/day, the infant fed whole cow milk would be in negative water balance unless he were able to concentrate the urine to 1105 mosmol/liter; the infant fed 100 kcal/100 ml Similac would be in negative water balance unless he were able to concentrate the urine to 830 mosmol/liter.

Similarly, one may calculate the influence of increased losses of water through the skin and lungs, as might occur with moderate increases in environmental temperature or with fever. An infant consuming 750 ml/day of 100 kcal/100 ml SMA and losing 650 ml/day through extrarenal routes would almost surely be in negative water balance.

Liquid Versus Powdered Formulas. When calorically concentrated formulas are to be fed, accuracy in dilution is of great importance. For this reason, commercially prepared liquid products are preferred to products supplied in powdered form. Three parts of commercially prepared concentrated liquid product (133 kcal/100 ml) mixed with one part of water will yield 100 kcal/100 ml.

Foods Other Than Formula

For some infants with chronic disease associated with decreased ability to consume usual amounts of food, bottle feeding may be extremely difficult and a greater quantity of food may be consumed if a portion of the food is fed by spoon. If foods other than formula are to be fed, they should be selected with attention to caloric density, digestibility, sodium content and renal solute load as discussed in Chapter 19. With the exception of most fruits and a few desserts and puddings, commercially prepared strained foods with caloric densities approaching 100 kcal/100 gm generally present unduly high renal solute loads (Table 10–3). The ratio of protein to calories in strained fruits is low, and it is therefore recommended that no more than 20 per cent of calorie intake be supplied from this source.

The importance of proper choice of strained foods may be seen from the examples presented in Figure 10–6. The calculated renal solute load resulting from the consumption of 100 gm of strained applesauce or 100 gm of strained chicken with vegetables is indicated in Table 10–2.

TABLE 10–3 ESTIMATED RENAL SOLUTE LOAD FROM COMMERCIALLY PREPARED STRAINED AND JUNIOR FOODS*

	Estimated Renal Solute Load (mosmol)†			
	Per 100 gm		*Per 100 kcal*	
Product Category	*Mean*	*S.D.*‡	*Mean*	*S.D.*
Strained				
Juices	5	1.7	8	2.9
Fruits	10	7.2	12	7.9
Vegetables				
Plain	56	13.1	135	44.5
Creamed	51	9.1	91	42.6
Dinners and soups	67	18.5	118	23.9
High-meat dinners	135	22.9	164	31.7
Meats	187	30.4	179	25.9
Egg yolks	102	22.8	53	13.0
Desserts	27	21.3	28	20.6
Junior				
Fruits	10	8.2	12	9.7
Vegetables				
Plain	56	6.8	134	38.7
Creamed	56	48.7	96	82.3
Dinners and soups	64	22.4	108	33.5
High-meat dinners	151	40.3	183	60.9
Meats	194	21.3	190	20.1
Meat sticks	419	75.9	265	102.4
Desserts	26	20.9	30	23.0

*Average of foods included in Table 16–2.
†Calculated according to the method of Ziegler and Fomon (1971).
‡Standard deviation.

Means of Assuring Safety

Means of evaluating the diet with respect to maintenance of adequate water balance will be discussed in this section. More general considerations of dietary management and evaluation of the progress of growth of infants with congenital heart disease will be discussed in Chapter 19.

Parents of infants receiving calorically concentrated feedings should be instructed in formula preparation and in maintaining accurate records of the infant's fluid intake. They should observe the frequency of urination (number of wet diapers) and the color of the urine. At the time of each clinic visit, osmolality of a sample of recently prepared formula should be determined as well as that of several randomly voided specimens of urine. Major inaccuracies in formula dilution may be detected by determining formula osmolality. We suggest that osmolality of the urine (average osmolality of two or three consecutively voided specimens) be maintained below 400 mosmol/liter.

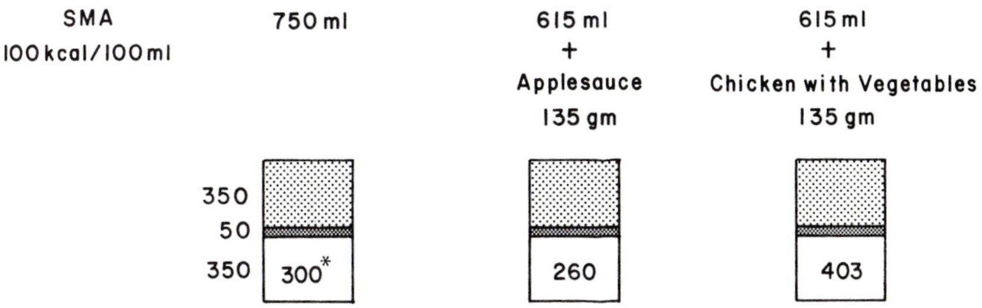

Figure 10–6 Effect of substituting commercially prepared strained foods for an equal quantity of 100 kcal/100 ml formula. Various areas of the columns have the same significance as in Figure 10–1.

When growth progress is not satisfactory and urinary concentration is consistently less than 300 mosmol/liter, use of a diet of greater caloric density is indicated. When urinary concentration approximates 400 mosmol/liter and growth is unsatisfactory, the renal solute load should be reduced. By increasing the percentage of calories supplied from carbohydrate and fat, it will ordinarily be possible to reduce the renal solute load without decreasing calorie intake. As discussed in Chapter 19, metabolic balance studies may be desirable to obtain a quantitative estimation of amount of fat excreted in the feces.

When the infant is exposed to elevated environmental temperatures, additional water should be provided. During illness or at other times when the volume of intake is less than that usually consumed, a more dilute feeding is likely to be required. The need for use of a diet of lesser caloric density may be determined by measuring the osmolality of the urine. Through careful monitoring of water balance, it will be possible to avoid most of the hazards of feeding a concentrated diet.

FEEDING CALORICALLY CONCENTRATED DIETS TO LOW-BIRTH-WEIGHT INFANTS

It has been recognized for some time that weight gain by low-birth-weight infants is more rapid when they are fed calorically concentrated formulas than when they are fed conventional formulas providing 67 kcal/100 ml (Snyderman and Holt, 1961; Falkner et al., 1962). Perhaps because of limited stomach capacity, low-birth-weight infants—especially those with weights less than 1500 gm—seem unable to consume a sufficient volume of 67 kcal/100 ml formula to promote rapid growth. However, rapid growth may occur when calorically concentrated formulas (e.g., 100 kcal/100 ml) are given. Under these circumstances, attention must be paid to maintenance of water balance.

The simplified estimate of renal solute load thus far discussed was developed on the basis of observations of fullsize infants receiving diets that provided relatively generous intakes of protein and minerals. The estimate is not appropriate for management of low-birth-weight infants. As already mentioned, problems of renal solute load and water balance rarely occur in healthy, fullsize infants who are growing rapidly. Because small infants grow rapidly in relation to body size, a relatively large percentage of the "potential renal solute load" may be utilized for growth and therefore will not require renal excretion.

The designation "potential renal solute load" is utilized to include all of the solutes of dietary origin that would need to be excreted in the urine if none were diverted into synthesis of new tissue and none were lost through nonrenal routes. (In fact, loss through nonrenal routes is small and may be ignored). Thus, the potential renal solute load consists of minerals absorbed from the diet and solutes derived from metabolism of dietary protein. For the sake of clarity, we prefer to express this model by means of an equation.

Urinary osmolar concentration ($\mathbf{C}_{urine}$, expressed as mosmol/liter) may be written as

$$\mathbf{C}_{urine} = \frac{\mathbf{S}_{food} - \mathbf{S}_{growth}}{\mathbf{W}_{food} - \mathbf{W}_{extrarenal}},$$

where $\mathbf{S}_{food}$ denotes total potential renal solute load derived from food consumed, expressed as mosmol/day. Table 10–4 shows how potential renal solute load may be derived from composition of food consumed. $\mathbf{S}_{food}$ may be computed as potential renal solute load (mosmol/kcal) × food intake (kcal/day).

$\mathbf{S}_{growth}$ denotes amount of potential renal solute load utilized for synthesis of new tissue, expressed as mosmol/day. One gram of weight gain is assumed to contain 0.9 mosmol of potential renal solute load (calculations based on data of Widdowson and Dickerson, 1964).

$\mathbf{W}_{food}$ denotes amount of water available from dietary sources (i.e., preformed water plus water of oxidation, expressed as liters/day) and is assumed to be 0.90 liter of water per liter of concentrated (e.g., 100 kcal/100 ml) formula and 0.95 liter of water per liter of standard (67 kcal/100 ml) formula consumed (see Water Losses).

$\mathbf{W}_{extrarenal}$ denotes extrarenal water losses—i.e., losses from skin, lungs and intestines, expressed as liters/day. Although extrarenal, especially insensible, losses of water are extremely variable

TABLE 10–4 POTENTIAL RENAL SOLUTE LOAD OF THREE INFANT FORMULAS (UTILIZED IN CALCULATIONS RELATING TO LOW-BIRTH-WEIGHT INFANTS)

FORMULAS	DIETARY INTAKE/100 KCAL					POTENTIAL RENAL SOLUTE LOAD/100 KCAL*			
	Protein (gm)	*Na (meq)*	*Cl (meq)*	*K (meq)*	*P (mg)*	*Urea (mosmol)*	*Na+Cl+K (mosmol)*	*P (mosmol)*	*Total (mosmol)*
Similac	2.40	1.75	2.41	2.78	65.4	13.7	6.94	2.21	22.9
Enfamil	2.24	1.64	1.79	2.84	67.9	12.8	6.27	2.19	21.3
SMA	2.24	1.05	1.70	2.09	49.3	12.8	4.84	1.59	19.2

*The estimate ignores the contribution of organic acids, sulfate, calcium, magnesium and other lesser urinary solutes. The combined contribution of these to renal solute load is considered insignificant in relation to that of protein, sodium, chloride, potassium and phosphorus.

in low-birth-weight infants, we have utilized a value of 0.07 liter/kg/day (Fanaroff et al., 1972).

As already discussed, extrarenal losses of potential renal solute load and the amount of water required for formation of new tissue are small. Therefore, these factors have been omitted from the equation.

If a 1.5 kg infant consumes 225 kcal of Similac in a volume of 225 ml (i.e., 100 kcal/100 ml) and gains 30 gm/day, the predicted value for urine concentration will be 250 mosmol/liter. If this infant were given 225 kcal of Similac in a volume of 170 ml (i.e., 133 kcal/100 ml), the predicted value for urine concentration would be 510 mosmol/liter. This predicted value can serve as a useful guide in the planning of feeding but is likely to differ from the observed value because of wide variations in extrarenal water losses. Therefore, for the low-birth-weight infant, as for the infant with congenital heart disease, urine concentration should be monitored at frequent intervals and should be maintained at values less than 400 mosmol/liter.

ERRORS IN FORMULA DILUTION

Inaccuracies or gross errors in dilution of milk or formula may result in a formula of low caloric density, with eventual development of undernutrition, or in a formula of high caloric density, with a threat to maintaining normal hydration. When formulas of high caloric density are fed, infants accept small volumes of intake so that renal solute load is high in relation to water available for renal excretion.

Although errors may occur in the dilution of concentrated liquid products, such errors are much more common and often more serious in use of powdered products. Many individuals who prepare formulas from powdered product and water appear to add the powder rather generously, using, for example, a heaping rather than a level scoop as a measure. Taitz and Byers (1972) found that sodium concentrations exceeded anticipated values in 21 of 32 formulas prepared from powdered product in the home. In one instance, the concentration of sodium was two and one-half times the expected value.

Gross errors in formula preparation have been reported as causes of serious illness and even death. Formulas providing 133 kcal/100 ml have been fed because of failure to dilute concentrated liquid product (Colle et al., 1958; Roloff and Stern, 1971) or because of the assumption that a tablespoonful of water was equal to 1 ounce (Simpson and O'Duffy, 1967). More commonly, instructions meant to be applied to dilution of concentrated liquid products have been applied to dilution of powder (Skinner, 1967; Jung and Done, 1969; Coodin et al., 1971). Such mixture of one part of powder with one part of water yields a formula of approximately 266 kcal/100 ml. Feeding of these highly concentrated formulas results in exceedingly low volumes of intake, weight loss, oliguria, fever, irritability and cyanosis. Eventually, hypernatremia may occur with convulsions and coma. Although appropriate treatment will usually prevent death, brain damage is a possible sequela (Macaulay and Watson, 1967).

A different type of error occurred in 1962 when, in a hospital formula room, salt was used instead of sugar in preparing infant formulas. Of 14 infants receiving the formula, 11 developed symptoms of hypernatremic dehydration and six died (Finberg et al., 1963).

REFERENCES

Alleyne, G. A. O.: The effect of severe protein calorie malnutrition on the renal function of Jamaican children. Pediatrics *39*:400, 1967.

Bruck, E., Abal, G., and Aceto, T., Jr.: Pathogenesis and pathophysiology of hypertonic dehydration with diarrhea. Amer. J. Dis. Child. *115*:122, 1968.

Chung, A. W.: The effect of oral feeding at different levels on the absorption of foodstuffs in infantile diarrhea. J. Pediatr. *33*:1, 1948.

Colle, E., Ayoub, E., and Raile, R.: Hypertonic dehydration (hypernatremia): the role of feedings high in solutes. Pediatrics *22*:5, 1958.

Committee on Nutrition, American Academy of Pediatrics: Water requirement in relation to osmolar load as it applies to infant feeding. Pediatrics *19*:339, 1957.

Coodin, F. J., Gabrielson, I. W., and Addiego, J. E.: Formula fatality. Pediatrics *47*:438, 1971.

Cooke, R. E., Pratt, E. L., and Darrow, D. C.: The metabolic response of infants to heat stress. Yale J. Biol. Med. *22*:227, 1950.

Darrow, D. C., Cooke, R. E., and Segar, W. E.: Water and electrolyte metabolism in infants fed cow's milk mixtures during heat stress. Pediatrics *14*:602, 1954.

Darrow, D. C., Pratt, E. L., Flett, J., Jr., Gamble, A. H., and Wiese, H. F.: Disturbances of water and electrolytes in infantile diarrhea. Pediatrics *3*:129, 1949.

Drescher, A. N., Barnett, H. L., and Troupkou, V.: Water balance in infants during water deprivation. Amer. J. Dis. Child. *104*:366, 1962.

Edelmann, C. M., Jr., Barnett, H. L., and Troupkou, V.: Renal concentrating mechanisms in newborn infants. Effect of dietary protein and water content, role of urea, and responsiveness to antidiuretic hormone. J. Clin. Invest. *39*:1062, 1960.

Elliott, D. A., and Cooke, R. E.: Insensible weight loss in normal children and cardiacs. *In* Cheek, D. B. (ed.): Human Growth: Body Composition, Cell Growth, Energy, and Intelligence. Philadelphia, Lea & Febiger, 1968, p. 494.

Falkner, F., Steigman, A. J., and Cruise, M. O.: The physical development of the premature infant. I. Some standards and certain relationships to caloric intake. J. Pediatr. *60*:895, 1962.

Fanaroff, A. A., Wald, M., Gruber, H. S., and Klaus, M. H.: Insensible water loss in low birth weight infants. Pediatrics *50*:236, 1972.

Finberg, L., Cheung, C.-S., and Fleishman, E.: The significance of the concentrations of electrolytes in stool water during infantile diarrhea. Amer. J. Dis. Child. *100*:809, 1960.

Finberg, L., Kiley, J., and Luttrell, C. N.: Mass accidental salt poisoning in infancy. J.A.M.A. *184*:121, 1963.

Fomon, S. J., and Ziegler, E. E.: Nutritional management of infants with congenital heart disease. Amer. Heart J. *83*:581, 1972.

Heeley, A. M., and Talbot, N. B.: Insensible water losses per day by hospitalized infants and children. Amer. J. Dis. Child. *90*:251, 1955.

Holt, L. E., Courtney, A. M., and Fales, H. L.: The chemical composition of diarrheal as compared with normal stools in infants. Amer. J. Dis. Child. 9:213, 1915.

Jung, A. L., and Done, A. K.: Extreme hyperosmolality and "transient diabetes" due to inappropriately diluted infant formula. Amer. J. Dis. Child. *118*:859, 1969.

Kooh, S. W., and Metcoff, J.: Physiologic considerations in fluid and electrolyte therapy with particular reference to diarrheal dehydration in children. J. Pediatr. *62*:107, 1963.

Levine, S. Z., Wilson, J. R., and Kelley, M.: The insensible perspiration in infancy and in childhood. I. Its constancy in infants under standard conditions and the effect of various physiologic factors. Amer. J. Dis. Child. *37*:791, 1929.

Macaulay, D., and Watson, M.: Hypernatraemia in infants as a cause of brain damage. Arch. Dis. Child. *42*:485, 1967.

Maxwell, W. H., and Kleeman, C. R. (eds.): Clinical Disorders of Fluid and Electrolyte Metabolism. New York, McGraw-Hill Book Co., 1962.

Morgan, C. L., and Nadas, A. S.: Sweating and congestive heart failure. New Eng. J. Med. *268*:580, 1963.

Pólaček, E., Vocel, J., Neugebauerová, L., Šebková, M., and Věchetová, E.: The osmotic concentrating ability in healthy infants and children. Arch. Dis. Child. *40*:291, 1965.

Pratt, E. L., Bienvenu, B., and Whyte, M. M.: Concentration of urine solutes by young infants. Pediatrics *1*:181, 1948.

Puyau, F. A.: Evaporative heat losses of infants with congenital heart disease. Amer. J. Clin. Nutr. *22*:1435, 1969.

Roloff, D. W., and Stern, L.: Hypertonic dehydration due to improperly prepared infant formula: a potential hazard. Canad. Med. Ass. J. *105*:1311, 1971.

Simpson, H., and O'Duffy, J.: Need for clarity in infant feeding instructions. Br. Med. J. *3*:536, 1967.

Skinner, A. L.: Water depletion associated with improperly constituted powdered milk formulas. Letter to the editor. Pediatrics *39*:625, 1967.

Snyderman, S. E., and Holt, L. E., Jr.: The effect of high caloric feeding on the growth of premature infants. J. Pediatr. *58*:237, 1961.

Stocker, F. P., Wilkoff, W., Miettinen, O. S., and Nadas, A. S.: Oxygen consumption in infants with heart disease. J. Pediatr. *80*:43, 1972.

Taitz, L. S., and Byers, H. D.: High calorie/osmolar feeding and hypertonic dehydration. Arch. Dis. Child. *47*:257, 1972.

Widdowson, E. M., and Dickerson, J. W. T.: Chemical composition of the body. *In* Comar, C. L., and Bronner, F. (eds.): Mineral Metabolism. Vol. II, Part A. New York, Academic Press, 1964, p. 1.

Winberg, J.: Determination of renal concentration capacity in infants and children without renal disease. Acta Paediatr. Scand. *48*:318, 1959.

Winters, R. W. (ed.): The Body Fluids in Pediatrics. Boston, Little, Brown & Co., 1973.

Ziegler, E. E., and Fomon, S. J.: Fluid intake, renal solute load, and water balance in infancy. J. Pediatr. *78*:561, 1971.

11

MAJOR MINERALS

Ekhard E. Ziegler
and
Samuel J. Fomon

Because of their relative abundance in the human body, the major minerals are considered to be sodium, chloride, potassium, calcium, phosphorus, magnesium and sulfur.* This chapter will review some aspects of these minerals as they relate to growth and health of the infant and toddler. Estimated requirements, advisable intakes, the extent of absorption and urinary excretion, and data on usual intakes in the United States will be considered. In addition, we shall consider concentrations of calcium, phosphorus and magnesium in serum in health and disease and the possible implications of amounts of salt consumed by normal infants.

ESTIMATED REQUIREMENTS AND ADVISABLE INTAKES

As is discussed in Chapter 5, the requirement for any nutrient strictly applies only to the exact circumstances under which it was determined. With respect to requirements for certain of the minerals, it is particularly important to recognize factors known to affect intestinal absorption of the mineral under consideration—the chemical form of the mineral, amounts of other nutrients, including other major minerals, in the diet, and the presence or absence of substances that inter-

*Sulfur is unique among the major minerals in that it probably functions as a trace element except for the appreciable requirement for sulfur-containing amino acids.

fere with absorption. Calcium seems to be more affected by these influences than is phosphorus or magnesium. Absorption of sodium, chloride and potassium is much less importantly affected by other dietary components.

Although estimates of requirements are to be applied only with great caution, it is nevertheless necessary that some estimate of requirement be available. If used properly, even crude estimates may be extremely valuable in situations where it is imperative that excessive intakes be avoided. Such a situation exists, for example, with respect to intake of sodium by the infant with congenital heart disease and congestive failure. Sodium intake needs to be reduced drastically and yet must not fail to provide amounts of sodium required for growth and replacement of losses (Chapter 19).

Approach to Estimate of Requirement

Requirement for a major mineral consists of the amount needed for formation of new tissue and the amount required to replace inevitable losses, notably those from skin and in urine and feces. Metabolic balance studies are useful in providing a preliminary estimate of losses in urine and feces under various conditions of study. If the estimated tissue increment (i.e., requirement for growth) for a specified mineral were 2 mg daily and estimated dermal losses were 1 mg daily, the apparent retention (dietary intake minus excretion in urine and feces) would need to be 3 mg daily. If the apparent retention of this mineral averaged 25 per cent of intake, daily requirement would be estimated to be 12 mg.

Details of the manner of calculating requirements for growth are presented in the Chapter Appendix and the estimated requirements for various minerals are summarized in Table 11–1.

Sodium, Chloride and Potassium

Estimated Requirement. Significant amounts of sodium, chloride and potassium are lost through the skin. High intakes of these minerals result in slightly higher skin losses than do lower intakes (Darrow et al., 1954). When losses of water through skin are increased as a result of increased environmental temperature (or, presumably, with fever), dermal losses of sodium, chloride and potassium also increase and may become several times greater than those occurring at more usual environmental temperatures (Darrow et al., 1954). As an estimate of the extent of dermal loss of these minerals, we have utilized the data of Cooke et al. (1950).

TABLE 11–1 ESTIMATED DAILY TISSUE INCREMENTS, DERMAL LOSSES, ESTIMATED REQUIREMENTS AND ADVISABLE INTAKES OF MAJOR MINERALS IN VARIOUS AGE INTERVALS

Age Interval (months)	Minerals	Tissue Increment	Dermal Loss*	Estimated Requirement†	Advisable Intake‡
Birth to 4	Sodium (meq)	1.4	1.0	2.5	8
	Chloride (meq)	0.8	1.4	2.3	7
	Potassium (meq)	1.2	1.1	2.4	7
	Calcium (mg)	155.0	–	388.0	450
	Phosphorus (mg)	79.0	–	132.0	160
	Magnesium (mg)	3.3	–	16.5	25
4 to 12	Sodium (meq)	1.0	1.0	2.1	6
	Chloride (meq)	0.6	1.4	2.1	6
	Potassium (meq)	0.8	1.1	2.0	6
	Calcium (mg)	130.0	–	289.0	350
	Phosphorus (mg)	66.0	–	110.0	130
	Magnesium (mg)	2.7	–	13.5	20
12 to 24	Sodium (meq)	0.5	1.5	2.1	6
	Chloride (meq)	0.3	2.1	2.5	7
	Potassium (meq)	0.4	1.6	2.1	6
	Calcium (mg)	139.0	–	309.0	370
	Phosphorus (mg)	71.0	–	118.0	140
	Magnesium (mg)	2.9	–	14.5	22
24 to 36	Sodium (meq)	0.5	2.0	2.6	8
	Chloride (meq)	0.3	2.8	3.3	10
	Potassium (meq)	0.4	2.2	2.7	8
	Calcium (mg)	115.0	–	256.0	300
	Phosphorus (mg)	59.0	–	98.0	120
	Magnesium (mg)	2.4	–	12.0	18

*Data of Cooke et al. (1950) for the first year of life. Losses between 12 and 24 months of age assumed to be 50 per cent greater than during the first year; losses between 24 and 36 months of age assumed to be twice those during the first year.

†Assuming 95 per cent retention of dietary sodium, chloride and potassium; 40 per cent retention of dietary calcium from birth to age four months and 45 per cent retention thereafter; 60 per cent retention of phosphorus and 20 per cent retention of magnesium.

‡Advisable intake is tentatively set as approximately three times the estimated requirement for sodium, chloride and potassium, as 20 per cent above estimated requirement for calcium and phosphorus and 50 per cent above the estimated requirement for magnesium.

When intakes of sodium, chloride and potassium are at or below the requirement, urinary and fecal losses are quite low and we have assumed an apparent retention (intake minus losses in urine and feces) of 95 per cent in arriving at the value for estimated requirement (Table 11–1).

Advisable Intakes. Because of the variability in losses of these minerals through skin and because obligatory losses in urine and feces may in some instances be greater than the assumed value (5 per cent of intake), the estimate of requirement is considered to be quite uncertain and possibly somewhat low. For this reason, advisable intakes have been set at approximately three times the estimated requirement.

Calcium, Phosphorus and Magnesium

During the first three years of life, dermal losses of calcium, phosphorus and magnesium are small in relation to the requirement for growth. Therefore, the estimated daily increment in body content of these minerals divided by the apparent retention provides a reasonable estimate of requirement. For purposes of these calculations, an average value for retention has been assumed on the basis of metabolic balance studies with infants fed human milk or formulas based on demineralized whey (Fomon et al., 1963 and unpublished).

In view of the more satisfactory estimate of requirement for calcium, phosphorus and magnesium than for sodium, chloride and potassium, a lesser factor is utilized in converting the estimated requirement to an advisable intake.

Calcium. The increment in body content of calcium between birth and age four months, calculated as described in the Chapter Appendix, is 155 mg/day. This value agrees quite well with the observed retention of calcium reported from metabolic balance studies with infants fed human milk (Fomon et al., 1963). Mean retention of calcium in balance studies during the first four months of life averaged approximately 28 mg/kg/day. Assuming an average body weight of 5.3 kg for the male reference infant between birth and age four months, the average retention may be calculated to be 148 mg daily. Because the apparent retention in metabolic balance studies is likely to be somewhat greater than the true retention, it is likely that the estimate of increment in body calcium provided in the Chapter Appendix is somewhat generous for the interval birth to age four months.

The values set as advisable intakes for calcium are approximately 20 per cent greater than the estimated requirements. The modest difference between estimated requirements and advisable intakes reflects the belief that the estimated requirements may be generous. However, it should be noted that the advisable intakes pertain to circumstances in which calcium is relatively well absorbed, as is the case with human milk and at least several of the formulas based on demineralized whey. With vegetable-based diets, greater intakes of calcium are probably desirable.

Phosphorus. The increment in body content of phosphorus has been calculated in a manner similar to that for calcium. The daily increment in body content of phosphorus between birth and age four months has been estimated in the Chapter Appendix to be 79 mg. This is somewhat greater than the increment calculated from metabolic balance studies with infants fed human milk. Such studies (Fomon et al., 1963) yielded a mean retention of 12.4 mg/kg/day during the first four months of life. Assuming an average weight of 5.3 kg for the male reference infant in this age interval, retention would average 66 mg daily.

As in the case of calcium, values for advisable intakes of phosphorus have been set 20 per cent above the estimated requirements. These advisable intakes, however, apply to circumstances in which absorption of phosphorus is equivalent to that from human milk. Particular care is necessary in the case of diets based on soy or other vegetables in which some of the phosphorus is in the form of phytate and is not readily available for absorption.

Magnesium. The increment in body content of magnesium has been calculated in a manner similar to that employed in the case of calcium and phosphorus. Values for apparent retention are less extensive than for calcium and phosphorus. The advisable intake has been set at a value 50 per cent greater than the estimated requirement, reflecting the greater uncertainty of the estimate in the case of magnesium than in the case of calcium or phosphorus.

Sulfur

Although sulfur has been shown to activate glucose dehydrogenase in microsomes of rat liver (Horne and Nordlie, 1971) and may be important in activation of other enzymes, its importance is mainly as a component of methionine and cystine. Because the requirements for methionine and cystine during the first four months of life may be in the neighborhood of 24 and 23 mg/100 kcal, respectively (Chapter 6), and because sulfur accounts for 21.5 and 26.7 per cent, respectively, of the weights of these amino acids, requirements for sulfur at this age may be as much as 11 to 12 mg/100 kcal. The extent to which inorganic sulfur may reduce the requirement for sulfur-containing amino acids in human nutrition has not been studied.

METABOLIC BALANCE STUDIES

CALCIUM, PHOSPHORUS AND MAGNESIUM

As was discussed in relation to nitrogen balance studies (Chapter 6), balance studies are of limited value as a means of estimating changes in body composition during growth. Errors inherent in metabolic balance studies are likely to lead to overestimation of true retention (Fomon and Owen, 1962). From Table 11–2, it may be seen that retentions of calcium and phosphorus expressed per unit of body weight are considerably greater by infants receiving high intakes of these minerals (e.g., infants fed whole cow milk or evaporated milk) than by infants receiving lesser intakes (e.g., human milk, experimental formula 29B). Although it is possible that deposition of mineral in the body proceeds much more rapidly with relatively high intakes

TABLE 11–2 CALCIUM AND PHOSPHORUS BALANCE STUDIES WITH INFANTS FED MILKS OR VARIOUS COMMERCIAL AND EXPERIMENTAL FORMULAS*

Age Interval (days)	Feeding	Number of Subjects	Number of Studies	Calcium			Phosphorus		
				Intake (mg/kg)	Retention (mg/kg)	Retention (% of intake)	Intake (mg/kg)	Retention (mg/kg)	Retention (% of intake)
8 to 30	Pooled human milk	7	10	82 (22)†	32 (19)	38 (17)	27 (3)	13 (6)	49 (21)
	Whole cow milk	4	4	275 (17)	90 (20)	33 (7)	208 (12)	53 (18)	25 (8)
	Evaporated milk	2	4	285 (51)	107 (48)	36 (10)	225 (55)	79 (54)	33 (15)
	Similac	5	6	141 (28)	36 (18)	25 (8)	109 (18)	27 (11)	25 (7)
	29 B‡	4	8	73 (5)	17§ (26)	23§ (35)	54 (3)	29 (6)	53 (11)
	ProSobee	3	7	157 (21)	35 (9)	22 (5)	134 (18)	33 (7)	24 (5)
	29 A¶	4	10	113 (10)	44 (18)	39 (16)	79 (13)	36 (16)	45 (14)
31 to 60	Pooled human milk	7	13	66 (21)	30 (18)	43 (18)	23 (6)	13 (7)	53 (26)
	Whole cow milk	4	8	326 (58)	122 (47)	37 (11)	247 (48)	64 (41)	25 (13)
	Evaporated milk	2	3	256 (12)	86 (28)	34 (10)	195 (12)	52 (32)	26 (15)
	Similac	5	10	145 (35)	33‖ (51)	23‖ (36)	117 (32)	32‖ (25)	27‖ (18)
	29 B‡	5	10	63 (7)	21 (10)	32 (15)	46 (5)	19 (5)	41 (9)
	ProSobee	3	4	144 (18)	55 (9)	38 (8)	123 (16)	32 (6)	26 (4)
	29 A¶	3	6	109 (9)	56 (11)	52 (12)	77 (6)	37 (10)	49 (14)

61 to 90	Pooled human milk	6	7	50 (7)	24 (10)	47 (17)	18 (3)	12 (4)	63 (22)
	Whole cow milk	3	5	324 (37)	118 (50)	36 (13)	257 (46)	69 (34)	25 (11)
	Evaporated milk	3	5	262 (44)	79 (40)	29 (11)	197 (33)	47 (20)	23 (7)
	Similac	5	7	144 (22)	67 (30)	44 (17)	110 (19)	40 (24)	36 (20)
	29 B‡	4	8	61 (7)	25 (13)	41 (22)	45 (5)	23 (3)	51 (5)
	ProSobee	3	3	133 (7)	49 (15)	36 (10)	112 (9)	18‖ (21)	15‖ (18)
	29 A¶	3	6	100 (9)	45 (25)	43 (22)	70 (6)	29 (15)	40 (19)
91 to 120	Pooled human milk	7	14	55 (11)	30 (13)	54 (15)	19 (3)	12 (5)	55 (20)
	Whole cow milk	3	5	276 (47)	84 (50)	29 (13)	222 (42)	65 (30)	29 (9)
	Evaporated milk	3	6	249 (17)	92 (34)	37 (12)	196 (13)	52 (13)	27 (8)
	Similac	3	6	135 (10)	58 (15)	42 (9)	108 (13)	32 (14)	29 (10)
	29 B‡	3	5	56 (12)	26 (15)	44 (20)	41 (9)	15 (7)	33 (17)
	ProSobee	3	6	141 (10)	44 (12)	31 (8)	118 (10)	24 (7)	21 (5)
	29 A¶	3	5	102 (6)	44 (20)	43 (19)	72 (4)	32 (17)	44 (19)

*Data from Fomon et al. (1963 and unpublished observations).
†Values in parentheses are standard deviations.
‡Experimental milk-based formula.
§Two balances in one infant negative.
¶Experimental soy isolate-based formula.
‖One balance negative.

of calcium and phosphorus than with lower intakes, it is extremely unlikely that the true difference in mineralization could be as great as one might infer from results of metabolic balance studies. In contrast, retention of magnesium (Table 11–3) appears somewhat less dependent on intake.

Feedings of human milk, which provide relatively low mineral intakes, result in retentions of calcium and phosphorus during the early months of life (Table 11–2) that are approximately equal to the estimated requirements for growth (Table 11–1).

Several studies of the relation of fat absorption to absorption of calcium and phosphorus (and, in some cases, magnesium) have been reported in newborn infants receiving various feedings (Widdowson, 1965; Droese and Stolley, 1967; Southgate et al., 1969; Hanna et al., 1970; Williams et al., 1970). Several of these studies appear to demonstrate a positive correlation between excretion of fat and excretion of calcium. Under some circumstances, e.g., when calcium intakes are extremely high, the fecal excretion of calcium soaps may explain loss of fat and calcium in the stool. However, at least in some instances, excretion of calcium is not well correlated with excretion of fat. The data of Filer et al. (1969) have already been discussed in relation to factors affecting absorption of fat (Chapter 7, Fig. 7–4). As may be seen from Figure 11–1, with two feedings identical except for arrangement of fatty acids on the triglyceride molecule, fat excretions were markedly different although excretions of calcium were similar. Moreover, Barltrop and Oppé (1973) found no relation between excretions of fat and calcium among infants fed formulas containing butterfat or olive oil.

Although negative balances of calcium and magnesium may be associated with high fat excretion in the newborn period (Widdowson, 1965), it seems unlikely that transiently negative balances of this sort are of clinical significance for normal infants. When steatorrhea persists (either because a poorly absorbed fat has been included in the diet or because of metabolic abnormality), mineral deficiency may result.

The commonly held belief that the ratio of calcium to phosphorus in human milk is particularly effective in promoting absorption of calcium by the infant is not supported by data from metabolic balance studies. Widdowson et al. (1963) have demonstrated that the addition of moderate amounts of phosphate to the diet of five- to eight-day-old breastfed infants enhanced rather than hindered absorption of calcium and magnesium.

As discussed previously, metabolic balance studies probably do not indicate the rate of deposition of these minerals in the body; nevertheless, they may be of considerable value in assessing the adequacy of the diet. Errors inherent in metabolic balance studies are

TABLE 11–3 MAGNESIUM BALANCE STUDIES IN INFANTS FED VARIOUS COMMERCIAL AND EXPERIMENTAL FORMULAS*

Age Interval (Days)	Feeding	Number of Subjects	Number of Studies	Magnesium Intake (mg/kg)	Magnesium Retention (mg/kg)	Magnesium Retention (% of intake)
8 to 30	PXO†	4	7	14.9 (0.9)‡	2.8 (1.6)	20 (15)
	29 B†	4	8	9.6 (0.4)	4.1 (1.1)	43 (11)
	3215 A†	5	9	10.5 (1.6)	1.8 (1.6)	18 (16)
	ProSobee	3	7	17.5 (2.4)	4.1 (1.3)	23 (9)
	29 A§	4	10	9.9 (0.9)	0.8 (2.4)	6 (25)
31 to 60	PXO†	4	6	14.0 (0.8)	2.6 (1.1)	18 (7)
	29 B†	5	10	8.2 (0.9)	2.6 (0.8)	32 (8)
	3215 A†	5	10	11.3 (2.3)	1.8 (1.3)	16 (12)
	ProSobee	3	4	15.8 (1.6)	4.0 (0.5)	25 (1)
	29 A§	3	6	9.6 (0.8)	2.2 (1.3)	23 (13)
61 to 90	PXO†	2	3	12.3 (0.9)	1.5 (0.8)	13 (6)
	29 B†	4	8	8.0 (0.9)	2.6 (0.6)	33 (6)
	3215 A†	5	10	9.8 (1.3)	2.1 (0.6)	21 (6)
	ProSobee	3	3	14.4 (1.5)	2.7 (1.0)	19 (10)
	29 A§	3	6	8.7 (0.8)	1.2 (1.4)	13 (15)
91 to 120	PXO†	2	4	11.9 (0.6)	2.1 (0.7)	18 (7)
	29 B†	3	5	7.4 (1.6)	2.2 (1.4)	28 (13)
	3215 A†	4	6	9.1 (1.1)	2.1 (0.6)	22 (5)
	ProSobee	3	6	14.6 (1.2)	3.3 (0.8)	22 (5)
	29 A§	3	5	8.9 (0.5)	1.4 (1.3)	15 (16)

*Unpublished data from Pediatric Metabolic Unit, University of Iowa.
†Experimental milk-based formula.
‡Values in parentheses are standard deviations.
§Experimental soy isolate-based formula.

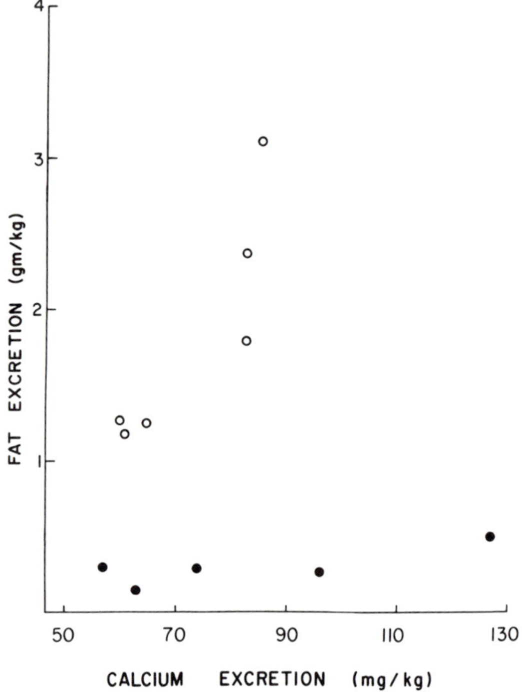

Figure 11–1 Fecal excretion of fat and calcium in 4- to 10-day-old infants fed an experimental formula containing lard *(black dots)* or randomized lard *(open circles).* (Study of Filer et al. (1969); data on calcium excretion not previously reported.)

likely to lead to overestimation of true retention. Therefore, a diet should be considered inadequate if it results in apparent retentions of calcium and phosphorus consistently less than those recorded for infants fed human milk.

CALCIUM, INORGANIC PHOSPHORUS, MAGNESIUM AND ALKALINE PHOSPHATASE IN SERUM

Calcium

In the healthy newborn infant, serum concentration of calcium begins to fall rather precipitously shortly after birth. This fall becomes more pronounced the longer the infant is left unfed and is more marked in infants born prematurely than in fullterm infants (Bruck and Weintraub, 1955; Gittleman et al., 1956). Other factors, such as

TABLE 11–4 CONCENTRATIONS OF CALCIUM AND PHOSPHORUS IN SERA OF NEWBORN INFANTS DURING FIRST THREE WEEKS OF LIFE IN RELATION TO BIRTH WEIGHT*

	Low Birth Weight	Full Size
Calcium		
Number of subjects	51	21
Number of determinations	154	43
Mean (mg/100 ml)	8.3 (1.3)†	9.1 (0.8)
Mean of lowest value of each subject (mg/100 ml)	7.4 (1.2)	8.9 (0.9)
Phosphorus		
Number of subjects	51	20
Number of determinations	145	39
Mean (mg/100 ml)	7.7 (1.7)	7.5 (1.8)
Mean of highest value of each subject (mg/100 ml)	8.7 (1.4)	8.4 (1.7)

*Data of Bruck and Weintraub (1955).
†Values in parentheses are standard deviations.

toxemia of pregnancy, complicated delivery or postnatal illness, are also associated with lower serum concentrations of calcium during the immediate newborn period (see Hypocalcemia of the Newborn). Generally, by 72 hours of age, serum concentration of calcium has passed its lowest point and is rising. Mean concentrations of calcium in sera of newborn low-birth-weight and fullsize infants are presented in Table 11–4.

Although serum concentrations of calcium ordinarily rise during the first weeks of life, these concentrations are dependent, to a large extent, on the type of feeding. Thus, serum concentrations of calcium of breastfed infants are greater than those of infants fed most formulas (Bruck and Weintraub, 1955; Gittleman et al., 1964; Oppé and Redstone, 1968; Barltrop and Oppé, 1970). Figure 11–2 indicates the relation of serum concentration of calcium to the type of feeding on the sixth day of life.

Beyond the newborn period, serum concentrations of calcium are generally somewhat greater than those of older children and adults whether intakes of calcium are relatively low, as in the case of breastfed infants, or high, as in the case of infants fed evaporated milk (Table 11–5). Beyond six months of age, there is a significant age-related decrease of serum concentration of total calcium and of ionized calcium toward adult values (Arnaud et al., 1973). Only concentrations of ionized calcium show a significant correlation with concentrations of immunoreactive parathyroid hormone.

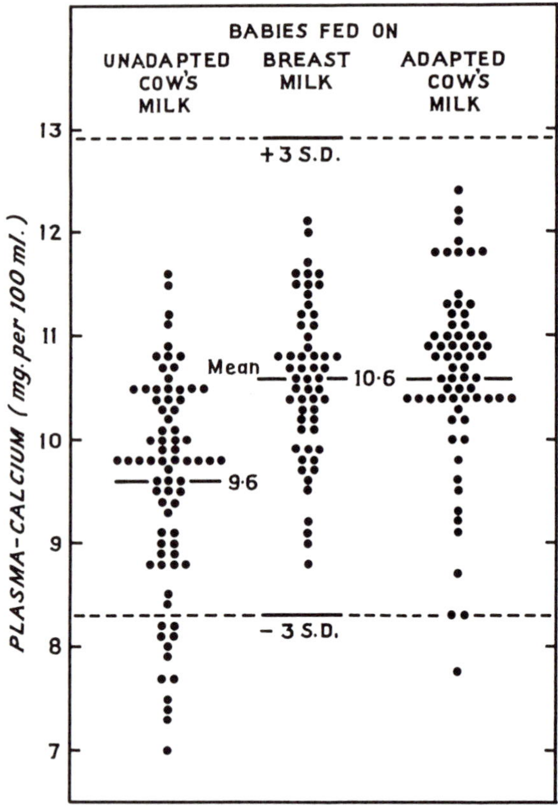

Figure 11–2 Serum concentrations of calcium on the sixth day of life in breastfed infants and infants given feedings providing high ("unadapted cow's milk") or low ("adapted cow's milk") intakes of minerals. Interrupted lines indicate three standard deviations above and below the mean of breastfed infants. (From Oppé, T. E., and Redstone, D.: Calcium and phosphorus levels in healthy newborn infants given various types of milk. Lancet *1*:1045, 1968.)

Inorganic Phosphorus

Serum concentrations of inorganic phosphorus are greater in cord blood than in venous blood of the adult (Bruck and Weintraub, 1955). Although there is a tendency of serum concentration of phosphorus to rise during the immediate neonatal period, this rise is much less than the concomitant decrease in serum concentration of calcium. Furthermore, there is no significant difference between low-birth-weight and fullsize infants, as shown in Table 11–4 (Bruck and Weintraub, 1955).

During the first weeks of life, serum concentrations of phosphorus remain stable or decrease slightly in breastfed infants, whereas there is a significant increase among infants receiving feedings that provide greater intakes of phosphorus (Bruck and Weintraub, 1955; Gittleman et al., 1964; Oppé and Redstone, 1968; Barltrop and Oppé, 1970). Figure 11–3 illustrates this relationship.

In contrast to serum concentrations of calcium, concentrations of inorganic phosphorus of infants beyond the newborn period remain greater than those of older children and adults and appear to be influenced by intake of phosphorus (Table 11–5). Beyond six months of age, serum concentrations of inorganic phosphorus decrease rapidly to age four years and more slowly thereafter (Arnaud et al., 1973).

TABLE 11–5 CONCENTRATIONS OF CALCIUM AND INORGANIC PHOSPHORUS IN SERA OF NORMAL FULLSIZE INFANTS DURING THE FIRST FIVE AND ONE-HALF MONTHS OF LIFE*

	Breastfed			Fed Evaporated Milk and Water		
Age (days)	*Number of Infants*	*Calcium (mg/100 ml)*	*Phosphorus‡ (mg/100 ml)*	*Number of Infants*	*Calcium (mg/100 ml)*	*Phosphorus (mg/100 ml)*
28	24	10.1 (0.6)†	6.8 (0.7)	19	9.9 (0.6)	7.4 (0.7)
56	23	9.8 (0.3)	6.3 (0.7)	17	10.1 (0.5)	7.4 (0.5)
84	23	10.1 (0.6)	6.2 (0.5)	21	10.1 (0.5)	7.1 (0.7)
112	24	10.1 (0.5)	6.2 (0.7)	14	10.0 (0.5)	7.5 (0.5)
140	20	9.9 (0.4)	6.1 (0.6)	20	9.9 (0.6)	7.1 (0.7)
168	18	9.7 (0.5)	6.3 (0.2)	20	9.8 (0.7)	7.0 (0.5)

*Data of Fomon et al. (1966).

†Values in parentheses are standard deviations.

‡For reasons discussed in Chapter 19, concentrations of phosphorus of breastfed infants are less in Table 19–1 than those reported here.

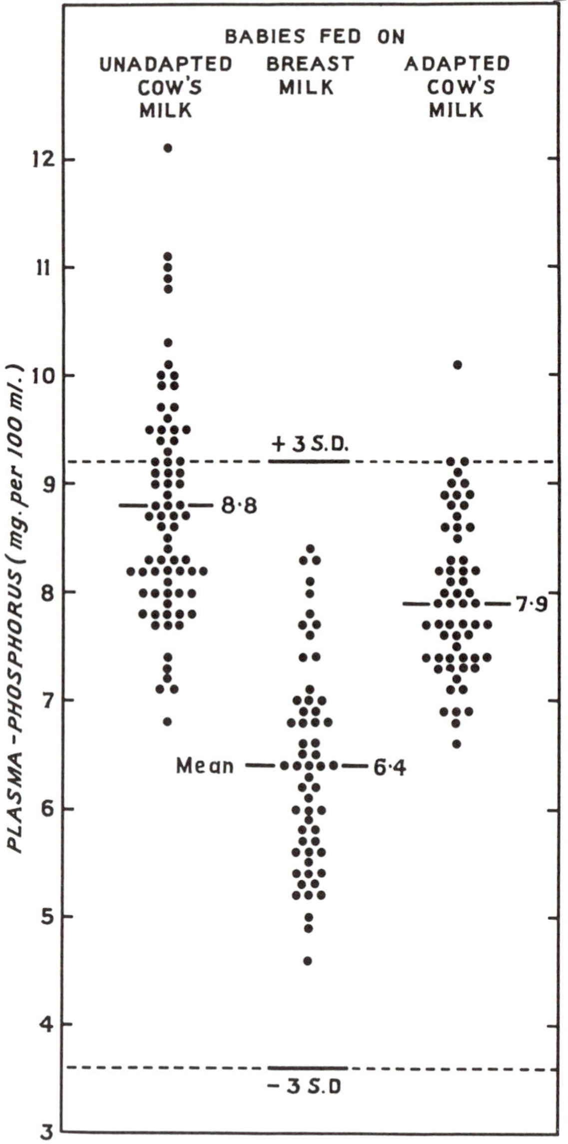

Figure 11–3 Serum concentrations of inorganic phosphorus on the sixth day of life in breastfed infants and infants given feedings providing high ("unadapted cow's milk") or low ("adapted cow's milk") intakes of minerals. Interrupted lines indicate three standard deviations above and below the mean of breastfed infants. (From Oppé, T. E., and Redstone, D.: Calcium and phosphorus levels in healthy newborn infants given various types of milk. Lancet *1*:1045, 1968.)

Magnesium

Serum concentrations of magnesium of normal fullterm infants were found by Jukarainen (1971) to average 2.04 mg/100 ml at the time of delivery, 2.21 mg/100 ml at about 20 hours of age and 1.98 mg/100 ml at around 52 hours of age. During the entire first five days of life, Jukarainen (1971) reported a mean concentration of 2.05 mg/100 ml with standard deviation 0.28 mg/100 ml. These values are in close agreement with values reported by Anast (1964) and by

Gittleman et al. (1964). Serum concentrations of magnesium at three to five days of age are negatively correlated with gestational age and with birth weight (Tsang and Oh, 1970b; Jukarainen, 1971). Concentrations of magnesium in serum are less in infants who are small for gestational age than in those whose size is appropriate for gestational age. Serum concentrations of magnesium of breastfed infants are slightly greater than those of infants fed evaporated milk or commercially prepared formulas (Anast, 1964; Gittleman et al., 1964).

In breastfed infants beyond the newborn period (Chapter 19, Table 19-1) and in older children and adults, serum concentrations of magnesium are quite similar to those of newborn infants (Anast, 1964).

Alkaline Phosphatase

Activity of alkaline phosphatase in serum is known to be elevated in rickets and, for this reason, the test is commonly employed in screening. Although the upper limit of the range of normal has usually been assumed to be 20 to 30 King-Armstrong units (Arneil et al., 1965; Richards et al., 1968a and b; Lapatsanis et al., 1968), it is apparent that greater values are not infrequently observed in apparently normal infants and children. For example, among 583 children one to three years of age in Local Authority Day Nurseries in the London area, Stephen and Stephenson (1971) determined alkaline phosphatase activity after at least 10 weeks of administration of daily supplements of cod liver oil. Values greater than 25 King-Armstrong units were found in 42 children, values above 30 units in 14 children, above 40 units in five children and above 100 units in two children.

The values above 100 units observed by Stephen and Stephenson (1971) decreased without specific treatment. Similarly, Richards et al. (1968a) reported values of 70 and 90 King-Armstrong units in two infants in a Scottish survey. These values decreased to 25 and 32, respectively, without administration of vitamin D. Asanti et al. (1966) had previously reported similar observations. We have observed extremely high alkaline phosphatase activity (159 to 256 autoanalyzer units*) in five infants between 176 and 354 days of age. Signs of illness were not present and, in each instance, there was a return to normal values without therapy. We have speculated that these high values may reflect transient hepatic abnormality associated with clinically unimpressive systemic viral infections.

---

*In normal infants, autoanalyzer units are approximately twice as high as King-Armstrong units.

ABNORMAL SERUM CONCENTRATIONS OF CALCIUM AND MAGNESIUM

Hypocalcemia of the Newborn

From what has been said about concentrations of calcium in serum of the newborn infant, the difficulty in defining a normal range for this age group will be apparent. Various investigators have defined hypocalcemia as serum concentration of calcium less than 9.0 mg/100 ml (Saville and Kretchmer, 1960), less than 8.0 mg/100 ml (Gittleman et al., 1956; Craig and Buchanan, 1958), less than 7.5 mg/100 ml (Keen, 1969) and less than 7.0 mg/100 ml (Tsang and Oh, 1970a). Obviously, the stated incidence of hypocalcemia will depend on the definition of hypocalcemia. Even concentrations less than 7.0 mg/100 ml are not invariably associated with clinical signs. Whether clinical evidences of hypocalcemia are present may be related to the concentration of ionized calcium (Bergman, 1972; Radde et al., 1972) rather than to the concentration of total calcium.

Two types of hypocalcemia may be distinguished in the newborn period. One is the early type, occurring during the first three days of life, and the other is the late type, occurring near the end of the first week of life (Mizrahi et al., 1968; Keen, 1969; Tsang and Oh, 1970a; Cockburn et al., 1973).

The early type, also termed "first day neonatal hypocalcemia," is much more common in premature infants than in infants born at term (Bruck and Weintraub, 1955; Gittleman et al., 1956; Craig and Buchanan, 1958; Tsang and Oh, 1970a). Tsang and Oh (1970a) reported hypocalcemia (serum concentrations of calcium less than 7.0 mg/100 ml) in 30 per cent of low-birth-weight infants at a mean age of 29 hours. As indicated in Table 11–6, at eight hours of age concentrations of calcium were already significantly less and concentrations of phosphorus significantly greater in sera of infants who subsequently became hypocalcemic than in sera of those who remained normocalcemic. Among the factors predisposing to hypocalcemia were a history of previous abortions, one-minute Apgar score of five or less, resuscitation at birth, respiratory distress, septicemia and treatment of acidosis with sodium bicarbonate. The cause or causes of early neonatal hypocalcemia are still poorly understood. Functionally immature or suppressed parathyroid glands may be responsible (Tsang et al., 1973).

The late type of neonatal hypocalcemia occurs on the fifth to eighth day of life (Fig. 11–4), most commonly in otherwise healthy, fullterm infants although rarely in breastfed infants (Keen, 1969). As has already been pointed out, serum concentrations of phosphorus are

TABLE 11–6 SERUM BIOCHEMICAL VALUES IN LOW-BIRTH-WEIGHT INFANTS WITH AND WITHOUT HYPOCALCEMIA*

		With Hypocalcemia			Without Hypocalcemia			
	Age (hours)	*Number of Infants*	*Mean*	*S.E.M.*†	*Number of Infants*	*Mean*	*S.E.M.*	P Value
Calcium								
(mg/100 ml)	8	22	8.9	0.2	55	9.6	0.1	<0.01
	29	37	6.3	0.1	79	9.0	0.1	<0.001
P value			<0.001			<0.01		
Inorganic phosphorus								
(mg/100 ml)	8	22	7.6	0.4	62	6.3	0.2	<0.01
	29	34	8.1	0.3	75	6.7	0.2	<0.001
P value			n.s.‡			n.s.		
Magnesium								
(mg/100 ml)	8	16	2.1	0.1	27	2.1	0.1	n.s.
	29	27	2.2	0.1	68	2.2	0.1	n.s.
P value			n.s.			n.s.		

*Data of Tsang and Oh (1970a).
†Standard error of mean.
‡Not significant.

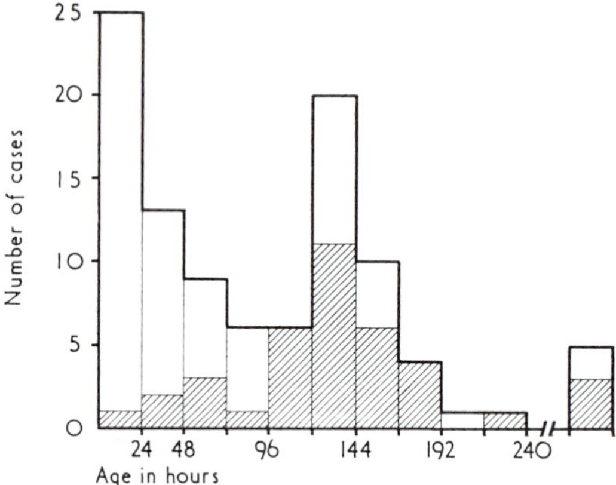

Figure 11–4 Age at first convulsion in 100 cases of neonatal convulsions. Hatching indicates cases with hypocalcemia. (From Keen, J. H.: Significance of hypocalcaemia in neonatal convulsions. Arch. Dis. Child. *44*:356, 1969.)

considerably higher by the end of the first week of life and those of calcium are lower if infants are fed formulas rather than breastfed (Bruck and Weintraub, 1955; Gittleman et al., 1964; Oppé and Redstone, 1968; Barltrop and Oppé, 1970). The data of Barltrop and Oppé (1970) suggest that high serum concentrations of phosphorus and low serum concentrations of calcium occur when the diet provides a high intake of phosphorus as well as a low calcium to phosphorus ratio. It may be concluded that the primary event in late neonatal hypocalcemia is dietary phosphorus intake of such a magnitude that it cannot be adequately excreted by the newborn infant. The resulting hyperphosphatemia is responsible for the hypocalcemia. Hypomagnesemia was present in 47 per cent of infants with hypocalcemia and convulsions (Cockburn et al., 1973).

When serum concentrations of calcium less than 7.5 mg/100 ml are detected (and verified in a second serum sample) in asymptomatic newborn infants, regardless of age, oral treatment with calcium gluconate (0.5 to 1.0 gm/kg/day) is recommended for several days. Symptomatic infants should receive calcium gluconate intravenously with monitoring of the heart rate. Intravenous therapy should be followed by oral therapy for several days. In addition, it seems reasonable, as recommended by Davies et al. (1972), that infants with late hypocalcemia receive reduced dietary intakes of phosphorus.

Hypocalcemia in Older Infants

Hypocalcemia beyond the newborn period occurs in vitamin D-deficiency rickets and in vitamin D-dependency rickets (Smith, 1972), in celiac disease and other forms of malabsorption, in malnutrition (Caddell and Olson, 1973) and in several types of chronic renal disease.

Hypercalcemia

Idiopathic hypercalcemia, a rare disorder of infancy that may represent hypersensitivity to vitamin D, and hypercalcemia caused by overdosage of vitamin D are discussed in Chapter 9.

Hypomagnesemia

Development of atomic absorption spectrophotometry has provided a simple and accurate method for determination of concentration of magnesium in serum and other biologic fluids and has led to greater awareness and more frequent recognition of disturbances of magnesium metabolism, especially in the newborn and young infant (Cockburn et al., 1973).

Hypomagnesemia can be the result either of magnesium deficiency or of disturbed magnesium homeostasis. Although magnesium depletion in the adult almost invariably leads to hypomagnesemia (Shils, 1969), serum concentrations of magnesium in severely malnourished infants are usually normal despite considerable magnesium depletion (Garrow et al., 1968). Hypomagnesemia is usually accompanied by hypocalcemia, which is considered secondary although the involved mechanisms are not clear. Hypomagnesemia is not corrected by intravenous administration of calcium, but administration of magnesium promptly restores concentrations of both minerals to normal. The low serum concentration of ionized calcium characteristic of hypomagnesemia rises rapidly after administration of magnesium (Zimmet et al., 1968). In magnesium deficiency, synthesis or release of parathyroid hormone is markedly impaired but returns to normal after correction of the deficiency (Anast et al., 1972).

Hypomagnesemia may occur in the newborn infant in the absence of any identifiable cause (Clarke and Carré, 1967; Wong and Teh, 1968). Hypocalcemia and tetany or convulsions are usually present (Cockburn et al., 1973), but in some cases infants may be asymptomatic. The condition may be self-correcting or may require treatment with magnesium for a short period of time. Recovery is always complete.

More frequently, hypomagnesemia in the neonate is found to be caused by specific disease in the mother of the infant. Intrauterine growth retardation may be associated with asymptomatic neonatal hypomagnesemia (Tsang and Oh, 1970b). Hypomagnesemia with tetany has been observed in infants born to mothers with hypophosphatemia (Dooling and Stern, 1967), malabsorption due to celiac disease (Davis et al., 1965), diabetes mellitus (Clark and Carré, 1967; Keipert, 1969; Tsang et al., 1972) and hyperparathyroidism (Mizrahi and Gold, 1964; Ertel et al., 1969). Hypoparathyroidism of various etiologies may be present in the infant and cause hypomagnesemia (Tsang, 1972). Transient hypomagnesemia has been documented after exchange transfusions with acid citrate blood, presumably owing to formation of magnesium citrate complexes (Bajpai et al., 1967; Bottini et al., 1968).

Hypomagnesemia has been observed to occur as a consequence of malabsorption in older infants and children who have had extensive intestinal surgical procedures during the newborn period (Atwell, 1966). In untreated celiac disease with hypomagnesemia, Goldman et al. (1962) found loss of magnesium in stools to be as much as four times the intake. Savage and McAdam (1967) observed hypomagnesemia with convulsions in the presence of normal serum concentrations of calcium in an infant with prolonged severe diarrhea.

Magnesium deficiency appears to be a relatively frequent accompaniment of protein-calorie malnutrition, particularly if the latter is associated with gastroenteritis (Montgomery, 1960; Linder et al., 1963; Caddell and Goddard, 1967; Garrow et al., 1968; Caddell and Olson, 1973). Although magnesium content of muscle is decreased in this condition (Montgomery, 1960; Metcoff et al., 1960; Caddell and Goddard, 1967; Caddell and Olson, 1973), serum concentration of magnesium is usually found to be normal to moderately low (Garrow et al., 1968). Urinary magnesium excretion is extremely low and, if given a parenteral loading dose of magnesium, these patients retain a significantly larger proportion of the loading dose than do normal infants (Caddell et al., 1973).

Treatment with magnesium establishes positive balances of magnesium, calcium and nitrogen (Montgomery, 1961; Linder et al., 1963). In a double-blind study by Caddell (1967), treatment with magnesium or a placebo was compared in 26 pairs of Nigerian children critically ill with protein-calorie malnutrition. All of the children received skim milk, vitamins and minerals other than magnesium. One child of each pair received magnesium sulfate intramuscularly and the other received a placebo (isotonic saline). Magnesium therapy was judged to be superior in 15 pairs, placebo in two pairs and there was no apparent difference in nine pairs. Garrow et al. (1968) concluded that administration of supplemental magnesium should be included in the treatment of all severely malnourished infants and children.

A rare congenital disorder which manifests itself with profound hypomagnesemia, hypocalcemia and intractable tetany or convulsions has become known as primary or familial hypomagnesemia (Salet et al., 1966; Friedman et al., 1967; Paunier et al., 1968; Skyberg et al., 1968; Stromme et al., 1969). The mode of inheritance is probably autosomal recessive. Symptoms occur in early infancy, sometimes in the newborn period, and do not respond to administration of calcium. Symptoms subside after parenteral administration of magnesium but recur after a short time. The cause of the disorder is a specific defect in the intestinal absorption of magnesium (Friedman et al., 1967; Paunier et al., 1968; Skyberg et al., 1968; Stromme et al., 1969); with continued oral magnesium supplementation these patients seem to develop entirely normally.

Hypermagnesemia

Newborn infants with neuromuscular depression due to hypermagnesemia have been born to women treated with magnesium sulfate because of toxemia of pregnancy (Lipsitz, 1971). Initial serum concentrations ranged from 3.8 to 9.7 mg/100 ml with most of the values between 5 and 6 mg/100 ml. In some instances, serum concentrations did not return to normal for four or five days. In extreme cases, exchange transfusion may be required to lower excessively high (e.g., 18 mg/100 ml) serum concentrations of magnesium (Brady and Williams, 1967).

INTAKES OF CALCIUM, PHOSPHORUS AND MAGNESIUM DURING THE FIRST THREE YEARS OF LIFE

The magnitude of daily intakes of calcium, phosphorus and magnesium during early infancy depends primarily on the type and quantity of milk or formula consumed (Tables 11–2 and 11–3). Few data on intakes of magnesium by infants more than a few months of age are available. Intakes of calcium and phosphorus by 30 infants from 31 to 300 days of age living in Cincinnati, Ohio were accumulated by Kahn et al. (1969) from mid 1960 to mid 1964. Table 11–7 indicates the mean intakes of calcium and phosphorus by these infants during various age intervals as well as the percentage of the intake derived from various foods. Because beikost was restricted to commercially prepared strained and junior foods, which are generally low in concentrations of calcium and phosphorus (Chapter 16), intakes of calcium and phosphorus were almost certainly less than those of most infants in the United States.

Data on intakes of calcium and phosphorus by 94 infants living in Denver, Colorado were accumulated by Beal (1968) between 1946 and 1966. It is apparent from Table 11–8 that intakes of most infants

TABLE 11–7 DAILY INTAKES OF CALCIUM AND PHOSPHORUS BY NORMAL INFANTS*

	Intake of Calcium			Intake of Phosphorus		
Age (days)	31–120	121–210	211–300	31–120	121–210	211–300
Intake (mg)	474	504	539	404	467	529
Sources (per cent)						
Milk	93	86	83	87	74	68
Water	3	3	3	–	–	–
Fruits, juices, desserts	1	4	6	2	5	6
Vegetables	1	2	2	1	3	3
Mixed meat and vegetables	–	1	2	1	3	6
Meat and eggs	–	2	3	1	7	11
Cereals	1	1	1	7	8	6

*Data of Kahn et al. (1969).

TABLE 11–8 INTAKES OF CALCIUM AND PHOSPHORUS DURING THE SECOND YEAR OF LIFE*

Age (months)	Number of Subjects		Calcium Intake (gm/day) Percentile						Phosphorus Intake (gm/day) Percentile					
			10th		50th		90th		10th		50th		90th	
	M†	*F*†	*M*	*F*	*M*	*F*	*M*	*F*	*M*	*F*	*M*	*F*	*M*	*F*
12–15	47	42	0.67	0.65	0.99	0.91	1.38	1.15	0.68	0.70	0.95	0.90	1.32	1.13
15–18	45	42	0.58	0.60	0.90	0.86	1.36	1.12	0.61	0.66	0.94	0.89	1.35	1.14
18–21	44	42	0.51	0.56	0.82	0.82	1.33	1.10	0.56	0.65	0.92	0.88	1.35	1.15
21–24	43	42	0.47	0.53	0.75	0.79	1.30	1.08	0.50	0.65	0.89	0.87	1.30	1.15

*Data of Beal (1968).
†M = male; F = female.

are several times greater than the advisable intakes suggested in Table 11–1. Generally similar data have been reported by Fox et al. (1971) concerning intakes of calcium and phosphorus by preschool children in the north central region of the United States. The latter authors presented data on 674 males and 512 females between 9 and 36 months of age. The 50th percentile values for intake of calcium by males in the age intervals 9 to 12, 12 to 18, 18 to 24 and 24 to 36 months were 1.10, 1.03, 0.95 and 0.94 gm/day, respectively. Corresponding values for girls were 1.02, 1.02, 0.86 and 0.85 gm/day. The 50th percentile values for intakes of phosphorus in these age intervals were 1.03, 1.07, 1.07 and 1.13 gm/day for males and 0.97, 1.11, 0.99 and 1.02 gm/day for females. Thus, the 50th percentile intakes reported by Fox et al. (1971) appear to be equal to or slightly greater than those reported by Beal (1968). From inspection of figures included in the publication by Fox et al. (1971), 10th percentile values appear to be similar to those reported by Beal (1968).

Table 11–9 presents data on intakes of calcium by children 12 to 36 months of age in three surveys (Center for Disease Control, 1972; Eagles and Steele, 1972; Owen et al., 1974). It is apparent from Table 11–9 that in the United States most toddlers receive generous intakes of calcium and that considerable decrease in intakes of milk and other dairy products would not interfere with adequate intakes of calcium.

POSSIBLE CONSEQUENCES OF HIGH SODIUM INTAKES IN INFANCY

Primarily on the basis of animal studies (Tobian, 1960; Meneely and Dahl, 1961; Dahl et al., 1968), several authors (Dahl et al., 1963; Puyau and Hampton, 1966; Dahl, 1968; Guthrie, 1968; Mayer, 1969) have suggested that the sodium content of the American infant's diet may predispose to hypertension in adult life. Although there is at present no evidence that relatively large intakes of salt by the human infant or toddler predispose to development of hypertension either at the time of receiving the high intakes or later, studies of rats have provided some cause for concern.

When rats of a strain bred for their propensity to develop hypertension are fed a diet high in salt, hypertension develops at a relatively early age and is self-sustaining after withdrawal of salt from the diet (Dahl, 1972). Ease of production of hypertension by addition of salt to the diet is greater with weanling than with older rats.

As indicated in Table 11–1, the estimated requirement for sodium is 2.5 meq/day between birth and four months of age and 2.1 meq/day between 4 and 12 months of age. Human milk provides 0.9 meq of sodium/100 kcal and cow milk provides 3.3 meq/100 kcal (Chapter 16,

TABLE 11–9 INTAKES OF CALCIUM DURING SECOND AND THIRD YEARS OF LIFE REPORTED IN THREE SURVEYS

Age Interval (months)	Survey*	Number of Subjects	Intake of Calcium (mg/day)			
			<300	*300–399*	*400–499*	>499
			Per Cent of Children			
12 to 24	PNS	632	5	6	7	82
	10-State	693	7	3	6	84
	USDA	93	8	2	3	87
24 to 36	PNS	681	6	8	9	77
	10-State	708	12	7	7	74
	USDA	105	8	4	10	78

*PNS is Preschool Nutrition Survey (Owen et al., 1974); 10-State is Ten-State Nutrition Survey, 1968–1970 (Center for Disease Control, 1972); USDA is U.S. Department of Agriculture Survey of low income families (Eagles and Steele, 1972).

Table 16–7). The quantity of sodium per unit of calories in most infant formulas is intermediate between that of human milk and that of cow milk. Infants receiving a major portion of calorie intake from milk or formula therefore receive generous intakes of sodium and one may question the wisdom of parents who add salt to infant foods, presumably in an attempt to improve palatability. As discussed in Chapter 16, certain of the commercially prepared strained and junior foods (especially plain vegetables, soups and dinners) marketed in the United States provide more than 10 meq of sodium/100 kcal. Such concentrations of sodium seem excessive.

Appendix

Requirements of Minerals for Incorporation into Newly Formed Tissues

The requirement of a mineral for growth can be estimated on the basis of rate of growth of fat-free body tissue and an assumed concentration of the mineral in question per unit of gain in fat-free tissue. Estimated chemical composition of the gain in fat-free body weight of the male reference infant has been discussed in Chapter 3 (Table 3–13).

Although normal infants may not be gaining weight during periods of minor illnesses or may actually lose weight (e.g., immediately after birth), it was elected to utilize average rates of gain per day calculated for the entire age interval. Thus, daily gain in fat-free tissue between birth and four months has been calculated from the total gain in four months divided by 365/3.

Sodium

Concentration of sodium per kilogram of fat-free body mass is approximately 85 meq/kg both in the normal newborn and in the adult (Forbes, 1962). Assuming a similar concentration in the tissue gained after birth, the amounts of sodium required for growth during the age intervals specified in Table 11–1 are 173, 241, 198 and 164 meq, respectively. The daily requirements for sodium for growth, therefore, are approximately 1.4, 1.0, 0.5, and 0.5 meq, respectively, for the four age intervals.

Chloride

Chloride concentration is approximately 57 meq/kg of fat-free body mass in the newborn and 50 meq/kg in the adult (Forbes, 1962). It seems reasonable to assume that the concentration of chloride in fat-free body weight gained after birth is approximately 50 meq/kg. On this basis, the requirements for chloride for growth are calculated to be 0.8, 0.6, 0.3 and 0.3 meq/day, respectively, during the four age intervals (Table 11–1).

Potassium

Because concentration of sodium is the same and concentration of chloride is almost the same per unit of fat-free body mass in the newborn infant and in the adult, there is, as already noted, a reasonably satisfactory basis for assumptions concerning concentrations of these minerals per unit of gain in fat-free body mass. In the case of potassium, concentration per unit of fat-free body mass differs appreciably between the newborn (52.1 meq/kg) and the adult (68.6 meq/kg) (Forbes, 1962). We have assumed that fat-free tissue gained between birth and three years contains the concentration of potassium reported for the adult—68.6 meq/kg. Thus, the daily requirement for growth will be approximately 1.2, 0.8, 0.4 and 0.4 meq/day, respectively, in the four age intervals (Table 11–1).

The assumed concentration of potassium in tissue gained between birth and three years of age is slightly greater than that suggested by whole body ^{40}K counting. Recalculation of the data of Burmeister et al. (1970) and Romahn and Burmeister (1970), based on the assumed chemical composition of gains of the reference boy (Chapter 3, Table 3–13), indicates the potassium concentration per unit of fat-free body mass of tissue gained between birth and four months of age to be approximately 65 meq/kg and that in tissue gained between 4 and 12 months of age to be 62 meq/kg. The estimated requirements of potassium for growth (Table 11–1) may therefore be somewhat generous.

Calcium

Concentration of calcium per unit of fat-free body mass is considerably less in the newborn infant than in the adult: 9.5 versus 21.7

gm/kg (Forbes, 1962). Since most of the body calcium is contained in bone, the concentration of calcium in bone may serve as an indicator of calcium concentration in fat-free body mass. The data of Dickerson (1962) indicate that calcium concentration in bone decreases slightly during the early months of life but then increases so that, by one year of age, the concentration is somewhat greater than at birth.

At birth, the concentration of calcium in bone is 89.4 gm/kg (Dickerson, 1962). Thus, weight of bone at birth accounts for approximately 10.7 per cent of fat-free body mass. If one assumes a similar percentage of fat-free body mass to be composed of bone at birth, 4 and 12 months, weight of bone at these ages will be 333, 555 and 855 gm, respectively. If one assumes further, on the basis of the data of Dickerson (1962), that concentration of calcium in bone is 87.8 gm/kg at age four months and 94.0 gm/kg at age 12 months, calcium content of the body of the reference infant at birth, 4 and 12 months will be 29.8, 48.7 and 80.4 gm. Gain between birth and four months will be 18.9 gm (155 mg/day) and, between 4 and 12 months, 31.7 gm (130 mg/day). After one year of age, it was assumed that the increment in body content of calcium may be calculated on the assumption that newly formed fat-free tissue contains the concentration of calcium found in fat-free tissue of the adult—21.7 gm/kg. The increment in body calcium between 12 and 24 months is therefore 139 mg/day and that between 24 and 36 months is 115 mg/day (Table 11–1).

Phosphorus

The ratio of phosphorus to calcium (expressed in grams) is 0.58 at birth and 0.51 in the adult (Forbes, 1962). In the body of one four-and-one-half-year-old child analyzed by Widdowson et al. (1951), this ratio was 0.50. We have assumed that the ratio of phosphorus to calcium in tissue gained during infancy and early childhood is 0.51. On the basis of the calculated tissue increments of calcium, the requirements for phosphorus for growth are 79, 66, 71 and 59 mg/day, respectively, for the four age intervals (Table 11–1).

Magnesium

As is true of phosphorus, magnesium is a component of both hard and soft tissues. The ratio of magnesium to calcium in the body decreases from 0.027 in the newborn to 0.021 in the adult. Assuming that the ratio of magnesium to calcium is 0.021 in tissue gained between birth and age three years, magnesium requirements for tissue increments may be calculated to be 3.3, 2.7, 2.9 and 2.4 mg/day, respectively, for the four age intervals (Table 11–1).

REFERENCES

Anast, C. S.: Serum magnesium levels in the newborn. Pediatrics *33*:969, 1964.

Anast, C. S., Mohs, J. M., Kaplan, S. L., and Burns, T. W.: Evidence for parathyroid failure in magnesium deficiency. Science *177*:606, 1972.

Arnaud, S. B., Goldsmith, R. S., Stickler, G. B., McCall, J. T., and Arnaud, C. D.: Serum parathyroid hormone and blood minerals: interrelationships in normal children. Pediatr. Res. 7:485, 1973.

Arneil, G. C., McKilligin, H. R., and Lobo, E.: Malnutrition in Glasgow children. Scot. Med. J. *10*:480, 1965.

Asanti, R., Hultin, H., and Visakorpi, J. K.: Serum alkaline phosphatase in healthy infants. Occurrence of abnormally high values without known cause. Ann. Paediatr. Fenn. *12*:139, 1966.

Atwell, J. D.: Magnesium deficiency following neonatal surgical procedures. J. Pediatr. Surg. *1*:427, 1966.

Bajpai, P. C., Sugden, D., Stern, L., and Denton, R. L.: Serum ionic magnesium in exchange transfusion. J. Pediatr. *70*:193, 1967.

Barltrop, D., and Oppé, T. E.: Dietary factors in neonatal calcium homoeostasis. Lancet *2*:1333, 1970.

Barltrop, D., and Oppé, T. E.: Absorption of fat and calcium by low birthweight infants from milks containing butterfat and olive oil. Arch. Dis. Child. 48:496, 1973.

Beal, V. A.: Calcium and phosphorus in infancy. J. Amer. Diet. Ass. *53*:450, 1968.

Bergman, L.: Plasma calcium fractions during the first days of life with special reference to neonatal hypocalcaemia. Biol. Neonat. *20*:346, 1972.

Bottini, E., Ventura, G., Cocciante, G., and De Luca-Carapella, E.: Serum magnesium in icteric newborn undergoing exchange-transfusion with donor's blood collected in ACD solution. Biol. Neonat. *12*:102, 1968.

Brady, J. P., and Williams, H. C.: Magnesium intoxication in a premature infant. Pediatrics *40*:100, 1967.

Bruck, E., and Weintraub, D. H.: Serum calcium and phosphorus in premature and full-term infants. Amer. J. Dis. Child. *90*:653, 1955.

Burmeister, W., Romahn, A., and Kunkel, R.: Die Entwicklung des Kalium-Bestandes von 19 einheitlich ernährten Säuglingen. Arch. Kinderheilkd. *180*:218, 1970.

Caddell, J. L.: Studies in protein-calorie malnutrition. II. A double-blind clinical trial to assess magnesium therapy. New. Eng. J. Med. *276*:535, 1967.

Caddell, J. L., and Goddard, D. R.: Studies in protein-calorie malnutrition. I. Chemical evidence for magnesium deficiency. New Eng. J. Med. *276*:533, 1967.

Caddell, J. L., and Olson, R. E.: I. An evaluation of the electrolyte status of malnourished Thai children. J. Pediatr. *83*:124, 1973.

Caddell, J. L., Suskind, R., Sillup, H., and Olson, R. E.: II. Parenteral magnesium load evaluation of malnourished Thai children. J. Pediatr. *83*:129, 1973.

Center for Disease Control: Ten-State Nutrition Survey 1968–70. Vol. V. Dietary. DHEW Publication No. (HSM) 72-8133. Atlanta, Georgia, Center for Disease Control, 1972.

Clarke, P. C. N., and Carré, I. J.: Hypocalcemic, hypomagnesemic convulsions. J. Pediatr. *70*:806, 1967.

Cockburn, F., Brown, J. K., Belton, N. R., and Forfar, J. O.: Neonatal convulsions associated with primary disturbance of calcium, phosphorus, and magnesium metabolism. Arch. Dis. Child. *48*:99, 1973.

Cooke, R. E., Pratt, E. L., and Darrow, D. C.: The metabolic response of infants to heat stress. Yale J. Biol. Med. *22*:227, 1950.

Craig, W. S., and Buchanan, M. F. G.: Hypocalcaemic tetany developing within 36 hours of birth. Arch. Dis. Child. *33*:505, 1958.

Dahl, L. K.: Salt in processed baby foods. Amer. J. Clin. Nutr. *21*:787, 1968.

Dahl, L. K.: Salt and hypertension. Amer. J. Clin. Nutr. *25*:231, 1972.

Dahl, L. K., Heine, M., and Tassinari, L.: High salt content of Western infant's diet: possible relationship to hypertension in the adult. Nature. *198*:1204, 1963.

Dahl, L. K., Knudsen, K. D., Heine, M. A., and Leitl, G. J.: Effects of chronic excess salt ingestion: modification of experimental hypertension in the rat by variations in the diet. Circ. Res. *22*:11, 1968.

Darrow, D. C., Cooke, R. E., and Segar, W. E.: Water and electrolyte metabolism in infants fed cow's milk mixtures during heat stress. Pediatrics *14*:602, 1954.

Davies, P. A., Robinson, R. J., Scopes, J. W., Tizard, J. P. M., and Wigglesworth, J. S.: Medical Care of Newborn Babies. Philadelphia, J. B. Lippincott Co., 1972.

Davis, J. A., Harvey, D. R., and Yu, J. S.: Neonatal fits associated with hypomagnesaemia. Arch. Dis. Child. *40*:286, 1965.

Dickerson, J. W. T.: Changes in the composition of the human femur during growth. Biochem. J. *82*:56, 1962.

Dooling, E. C., and Stern, L.: Hypomagnesemia with convulsions in a newborn infant: report of a case associated with maternal hypophosphatemia. Canad. Med. Ass. J. *97*:827, 1967.

Droese, W., and Stolley, H.: Zur Frage der Calcium-Ausnutzung junger gesunder Säuglinge bei Ernährung mit Kuhmilchmischungen mit unterschiedlichem Fettgehalt. Monatsschr. Kinderheilkd. *115*:238, 1967.

Eagles, J. A., and Steele, P. D.: Food and nutrient intake of children from birth to four years of age. *In* Fomon, S. J., and Anderson, T. A. (eds.): Practices of Low-Income Families in Feeding Infants and Small Children. With Particular Attention to Cultural Subgroups. DHEW Publ. No. (HSM) 72-5605. Washington, D.C., U.S. Government Printing Office, 1972, p. 19.

Ertel, N. H., Reiss, J. S., and Spergel, G.: Hypomagnesemia in neonatal tetany associated with maternal hyperparathyroidism. New Eng. J. Med. *280*:260, 1969.

Filer, L. J., Jr., Mattson, F. H., and Fomon, S. J.: Triglyceride configuration and fat absorption by the human infant. J. Nutr. *99*:293, 1969.

Fomon, S. J., Filer, L. J., Jr., Thomas, L. N., and Rogers, R. R.: Growth and serum chemical values of normal breastfed infants. Acta. Paediatr. Scand. (Suppl. 202), 1970.

Fomon, S. J., and Owen, G. M.: Comment on metabolic balance studies as a method of estimating body composition of infants. With special consideration of nitrogen balance studies. Pediatrics *29*:495, 1962.

Fomon, S. J., Owen, G. M., Jensen, R. L., and Thomas, L. N.: Calcium and phosphorus balance studies with normal full term infants fed pooled human milk or various formulas. Amer. J. Clin. Nutr. *12*:346, 1963.

Fomon, S. J., Younoszai, M. K., and Thomas, L. N.: Influence of vitamin D on linear growth of normal full-term infants. J. Nutr. *88*:345, 1966.

Forbes, G. B.: Methods for determining composition of the human body. With a note on the effect of diet on body composition. (Report of the Committee on Nutrition). Pediatrics *29*:477, 1962.

Fox, H. M., Fryer, B. A., Lamkin, G., Vivian, V. M., and Eppright, E. S.: Diets of preschool children in the north central region. J. Amer. Diet. Ass. *59*:233, 1971.

Friedman, M., Hatcher, G., and Watson, L.: Primary hypomagnesaemia with secondary hypocalcaemia in an infant. Lancet *1*:703, 1967.

Garrow, J. S., Smith, R., and Ward, E. E.: Electrolyte Metabolism in Severe Infantile Malnutrition. Oxford, Pergamon Press, 1968.

Gittleman, I. F., Pinkus, J. B., and Schmertzler, E.: Interrelationship of calcium and magnesium in the mature neonate. Amer. J. Dis. Child. *107*:119, 1964.

Gittleman, I. F., Pincus, J. B., Schmerzler, E., and Saito, M.: Hypocalcemia occurring on the first day of life in mature and premature infants. Pediatrics *18*:721, 1956.

Goldman, A. S., Van Fossan, D. D., and Baird, E. E.: Magnesium deficiency in celiac disease. Pediatrics *29*:948, 1962.

Guthrie, H. A.: Infant feeding practices—a predisposing factor in hypertension? Amer. J. Clin. Nutr. *21*:863, 1968.

Hanna, F. M., Navarrete, D. A., and Hsu, F. A.: Calcium-fatty acid absorption in term infants fed human milk and prepared formulas simulating human milk. Pediatrics *45*:216, 1970.

Horne, R. N., and Nordlie, R. C.: Activation by bicarbonate orthophosphate and sulfate of rat liver microsomal glucose dehydrogenase. Biochim. Biophys. Acta. *242*:1, 1971.

Jukarainen, E.: Plasma magnesium levels during the first five days of life. Acta. Paediatr. Scand. (Suppl. 222), 1971.

Kahn, B., Straub, C. P., Robbins, P. J., Wellman, H. N., Seltzer, R. A., and Telles, N. C.:

Retention of radiostrontium, strontium, calcium, and phosphorus by infants. Pediatrics *43*:651, 1969.

Keen, J. H.: Significance of hypocalcaemia in neonatal convulsions. Arch. Dis. Child. *44*:356, 1969.

Keipert, J. A.: Primary hypomagnesaemia with secondary hypocalcaemia in an infant. Med. J. Aust. *2*:242, 1969.

Lapatsanis, P., Deliyanni, V., and Doxiadis, S.: Vitamin D deficiency rickets in Greece. J. Pediatr. *73*:195, 1968.

Linder, G. C., Hansen, J. D. L., and Karabus, C. D.: The metabolism of magnesium and other inorganic cations and of nitrogen in acute kwashiorkor. Pediatrics *31*:552, 1963.

Lipsitz, P. J.: The clinical and biochemical effects of excess magnesium in the newborn. Pediatrics *47*:501, 1971.

Mayer, J.: Hypertension, salt intake, and the infant. Postgrad. Med. *45*(Jan.):229, 1969.

Meneely, G. R., and Dahl, L. K.: Electrolytes in hypertension: the effects of sodium chloride. The evidence from animal and human studies. Med. Clin. N. Amer. *45*:271, 1961.

Metcoff, J., Frenk, S., Antonowicz, I., Gordillo, G., and Lopez, E.: Relations of intracellular ions to metabolite sequences in kwashiorkor. Pediatrics *26*:960, 1960.

Mizrahi, A., and Gold, A. P.: Neonatal tetany secondary to maternal hyperparathyroidism. J.A.M.A. *190*:155, 1964.

Mizrahi, A., London, R. D., and Gribetz, D.: Neonatal hypocalcemia—its causes and treatment. New Eng. J. Med. *278*:1163, 1968.

Montgomery, R. D.: Magnesium metabolism in infantile protein malnutrition. Lancet *2*:74, 1960.

Montgomery, R. D.: Magnesium balance studies in marasmic kwashiorkor. J. Pediatr. *59*:119, 1961.

Oppé, T. E., and Redstone, D.: Calcium and phosphorus levels in healthy newborn infants given various types of milk. Lancet *1*:1045, 1968.

Owen, G. M., Kram, K. M., Garry, P. J., Lowe, J. E., Jr., and Lubin, A. H.: A study of nutritional status of preschool children in the United States, 1968–1970. Pediatrics *53*:597, 1974.

Paunier, L., Radde, I. C., Kooh, S. W., Conen, P. E., and Fraser, D.: Primary hypomagnesemia with secondary hypocalcemia in an infant. Pediatrics *41*:385, 1968.

Puyau, F. A., and Hampton, L. P.: Infant feeding practices, 1966. Amer. J. Dis. Child. *111*:370, 1966.

Radde, I. C., Parkinson, D. K., Höffken, B., Appiah, K. E., and Hanley, W. B.: Calcium ion activity in the sick neonate: effect of bicarbonate administration and exchange transfusion. Pediatr. Res. *6*:43, 1972.

Richards, I. D. G., Hamilton, F. M. W., Taylor, E. C., Sweet, E. M., Bremner, E., and Price, H.: A search for sub-clinical rickets in Glasgow children. Scot. Med. J. *13*:297, 1968a.

Richards, I. D. G., Sweet, E. M., and Arneil, G. C.: Infantile rickets persists in Glasgow. Lancet *1*:803, 1968b.

Romahn, A., and Burmeister, W.: Gesamtkaliumbestimmung bei Säuglingen und Kleinkindern mit einem Babycounter. Arch. Kinderheilkd. *180*:239, 1970.

Salet, J., Polonovski, C., DeGouyon, F., Pean, G., Melekian, B., and Fournet, J.-P.: Tetanie hypocalcemique recidivante par hypomagnesemie congenitale: une maladie metabolique nouvelle. Arch. Fr. Pediatr. *23*:749, 1966.

Savage, D. C. L., and McAdam, W. A. F.: Convulsions due to hypomagnesaemia in an infant recovering from diarrhoea. Lancet *2*:234, 1967.

Saville, P. D., and Kretchmer, N.: Neonatal tetany: a report of 125 cases and review of the literature. Biol. Neonat. *2*:1, 1960.

Shils, M. E.: Experimental human magnesium depletion. Medicine *48*:61, 1969.

Skyberg, D., Strømme, J. H., Nesbakken, R., and Harnaes, K.: Neonatal hypomagnesemia with selective malabsorption of magnesium—a clinical entity. Scand. J. Clin. Lab. Invest. *21*:355, 1968.

Smith, R.: The pathophysiology and management of rickets. Orthop. Clin. N. Amer. *3*:601, 1972.

Southgate, D. A. T., Widdowson, E. M., Smits, B. J., Cooke, W. T., Walker, C. H. M., and Mathers, N. P.: Absorption and excretion of calcium and fat by young infants. Lancet *1*:487, 1969.
Stephen, J. M. L., and Stephenson, P.: Alkaline phosphatase in normal infants. Arch. Dis. Child. *46*:185, 1971.
Strømme, J. H., Nesbakken, R., Normann, T., Skjørten, F., Skyberg, D., and Johannessen, B.: Familial hypomagnesemia. Acta Paediatr. Scand. *58*:433, 1969.
Tobian, L.: Interrelationship of electrolytes, juxtaglomerular cells and hypertension. Physiol. Rev. *40*:280, 1960.
Tsang, R. C.: Neonatal magnesium disturbances. Amer. J. Dis. Child. *124*:282, 1972.
Tsang, R. C., Kleinman, L. I., Sutherland, J. M., and Light, I. J.: Hypocalcemia in infants of diabetic mothers. Studies in calcium, phosphorus, and magnesium metabolism and parathormone responsiveness. J. Pediatr. *80*:384, 1972.
Tsang, R. C., Light, I. J., Sutherland, J. M., and Kleinman, L. I.: Possible pathogenetic factors in neonatal hypocalcemia of prematurity. J. Pediatr. *82*:423, 1973.
Tsang, R. C., and Oh, W.: Neonatal hypocalcemia in low birth weight infants. Pediatrics *45*:773, 1970a.
Tsang, R. C., and Oh, W.: Serum magnesium levels in low birth weight infants. Amer. J. Dis. Child. *120*:44, 1970b.
Widdowson, E. M.: Absorption and excretion of fat, nitrogen, and minerals from "filled" milks by babies one week old. Lancet *2*:1099, 1965.
Widdowson, E. M., McCance, R. A., Harrison, G. E., and Sutton, A.: Effect of giving phosphate supplements to breast-fed babies on absorption and excretion of calcium, strontium, magnesium, and phosphorus. Lancet *2*:1250, 1963.
Widdowson, E. M., McCance, R. A., and Spray, C. M.: The chemical composition of the human body. Clin. Sci. *10*:113, 1951.
Williams, M. L., Rose, C. S., Morrow, G., III, Sloan, S. E., and Barness, L. A.: Calcium and fat absorption in neonatal period. Amer. J. Clin. Nutr. *23*:1322, 1970.
Wong, H. B., and Teh, Y. F.: An association between serum-magnesium and tremor and convulsions in infants and children. Lancet *2*:18, 1968.
Zimmet, P., Breidahl, H. D., and Nayler, W. G.: Plasma ionized calcium in hypomagnesaemia. Br. Med. J. *1*:622, 1968.

12

IRON

It is well recognized that iron is essential as a component of hemoglobin for transport of oxygen to the tissues and as a component of the cytochromes, which are essential in oxidative mechanisms of all living cells. The body of the adult human contains 4 to 5 gm of iron. Of the trace minerals, only zinc, which is present to the extent of about 1.6 gm (Chapter 13), exists in the body in gram amounts. The next most abundant trace mineral in the human body, copper, contributes only about 0.1 gm to the weight of a 70 kg man.

GENERAL CONSIDERATIONS

In the normal human adult, nearly two-thirds of the iron in the body is in the form of hemoglobin, 3 to 5 per cent in the form of myoglobin, a fraction of 1 per cent in other active iron-containing compounds (transferrin, heme and flavin enzymes), and the remainder in the storage forms of ferritin and hemosiderin (Underwood, 1971).

The body of the human infant contains about 94 mg of iron per kilogram of fat-free tissue (Widdowson and Spray, 1951), and the body of the male reference infant (Chapter 3) at birth may therefore be assumed to contain 293 mg of iron. Most of this iron is in the circulating red cell mass, tissue stores being estimated as no more than 20 mg (Gorten, 1965). During the first six to eight weeks of life, the circulating hemoglobin mass decreases at a rate consistent with that anticipated from the short half-life of fetal red cells (Pearson, 1967). The iron released from the circulation during this time is largely stored in the forms of ferritin and hemosiderin and, although few data are available, one may assume that storage of iron reaches a maximum between 8 and 12 weeks of age. The total content of iron in liver increases from about 30 mg at birth (Widdowson and Spray, 1951) to

100 mg at age three months (Smith et al., 1955). After three months of age, iron content of liver decreases (Smith et al., 1955) as needs for erythropoiesis exceed the quantity absorbed.

Hemoglobin consists of the protein, globin, and four ferroprotoporphyrin or "heme" moieties. Iron in the heme moieties is stabilized in the ferrous state, permitting reversible bonding to oxygen. The molecular weight of hemoglobin is 68,000, of which iron contributes about 0.34 per cent. Iron in plasma is completely bound to transferrin, a β_1-globulin with a molecular weight of 86,000 and two separate binding sites, each capable of binding one atom of ferric iron (Ehrenberg and Laurell, 1955). In normal individuals, only 30 to 40 per cent of the binding sites of transferrin carry iron, the remaining potential for transporting iron in the plasma being referred to as the latent iron-binding capacity. The amount of iron bound to transferrin when all binding sites are saturated is spoken of as the total iron-binding capacity. The quantity of iron in serum is frequently expressed as a percentage of total iron-binding capacity—the per cent saturation of transferrin.

Ferritin and hemosiderin, the nonheme compounds in which iron is predominantly stored, are present in greatest concentrations in liver, spleen and bone marrow. Among the organs and tissues of the body, concentrations of iron are generally 2 to 10 times greater in liver and spleen than in kidney, heart, skeletal muscle, pancreas and brain (Underwood, 1971). Apoferritin, an iron-free globulin with molecular weight of 460,000, is able to combine with iron to the extent that iron may account for 20 per cent of weight of the iron-globulin compound, ferritin (Muir, 1960). An even greater percentage of the weight of hemosiderin may consist of iron (Shoden and Sturgeon, 1960). In the human adult, it appears that more iron is stored in the form of ferritin when iron stores are moderate or low (less than 0.5 gm of iron per kilogram of tissue in liver and spleen) and in the form of hemosiderin when iron stores are high (more than 1 gm of iron per kilogram of tissue in liver and spleen) (Morgan and Walters, 1963).

The ferrous to ferric cycles in iron metabolism have been well reviewed by Frieden (1973).

ABSORPTION AND EXCRETION

Absorption of iron is influenced by age, iron status and state of health of the individual, by conditions within the gastrointestinal tract, by the amount and form of the iron ingested, and by the amounts and proportions of various other components of the diet, both organic and inorganic. Absorption occurs mainly in the duodenum (Brown and Justus, 1958) in the ferrous form. Iron occurs in foods in inorganic forms, in heme compounds as constituents of hemoglobin and myoglobin and in other organic complexes. Gastric juice and other digestive secretions, possibly assisted by organic acids and reducing substances in foods (e.g., ascorbic acid, cysteine), are effective in releasing iron from iron-protein compounds and in reducing iron to the ferrous state. Iron in heme compounds is absorbed directly into mucosal cells of the intestine without the necessity of release from its bound form (Underwood, 1971). Iron appears to be as well absorbed from heme as from ferrous sulfate (Hallberg and Sölvell, 1967).

High intakes of phosphorus, zinc, cadmium, copper and manganese interfere with absorption of iron, presumably by competing for metal-binding sites in the intestinal mucosa. High intakes of zinc may interfere with incorporation of iron into or release from ferritin or may result in decrease in the life span of the erythrocyte (Settlemire and Matrone, 1967a and b).

Absorption from Foods

Food iron is generally less well absorbed than is iron from inorganic iron salts (Layrisse et al., 1969; Underwood, 1971), and iron from vegetable sources is generally less well absorbed than that from animal sources (Hussain et al., 1965; Layrisse et al., 1968). Absorption of iron from vegetable sources may be improved when food of animal origin is included in the diet (Martinez-Torres and Layrisse, 1970). Soy appears to promote better absorption of iron than do other vegetable sources (Layrisse et al., 1969). Absorption of iron from corn has generally been reported, from studies of adults, to be 5 to 10 per cent of intake (Layrisse et al., 1968, 1969; Cook et al., 1972). In studies of Jamaican infants, Ashworth et al. (1973) found that absorption of iron from corn was 4.3 per cent of intake. Absorption of iron from baked soy beans was 9.4 per cent of intake, but lesser absorption was obtained from boiled soy beans.

The iron salt employed for fortification of commercially prepared infant formulas in the United States is ferrous sulfate. This salt has been demonstrated to be well absorbed from a milk-based formula (Marsh et al., 1959; Gorten et al., 1963; Gorten and Cross, 1964; Gorten, 1965; Andelman and Sered, 1966).

Absorption of iron from eggs by human adults appears to be particularly poor (Moore and Dubach, 1951; Chodos et al., 1957; Ministry of Health, 1968; Callender et al., 1970), and the inclusion of eggs in the diet interferes with absorption of iron from other sources (Chodos et al., 1957; Elwood et al., 1968).

Absorption of sodium iron pyrophosphate and metallic iron is of interest, because these forms are currently used for fortification of infant cereals. Fritz et al. (1970) found that the anemic chick and rat absorbed only 2 to 19 per cent as much elemental iron when supplied in the form of sodium iron pyrophosphate as when supplied in the form of ferrous sulfate. The availability of metallic iron appears to depend, to a great extent, on the manufacturing process (Ministry of Health, 1968), larger particles being less well absorbed than smaller ones (Shah and Belonje, 1973).

Losses from Body

Losses of iron from the body of normal infants and toddlers occur from the gastrointestinal tract, primarily in the form of desquamated intestinal epithelial cells, from the skin and in urine. The extent of dermal losses by the adult is estimated to be between 0.6 and 1.0 mg/day (Underwood, 1971), and it may be reasonable to assume that the normal infant, with his lesser surface area of skin and gastrointestinal tract, might lose 0.1 mg/day.

As discussed in Chapter 17, gastrointestinal losses of blood by infants with iron deficiency anemia appear to be greater than those by normal infants. Naiman et al. (1964) demonstrated gastric achlorhydria, steatorrhea and impaired absorption of xylose and vitamin A in the majority of 14 infants and young children with nutritional iron-deficiency anemia. Duodenal biopsies revealed varying degrees of chronic duodenitis and mucosal atrophy. After treatment by oral administration of iron, most of the abnormalities were no longer present. Although feeding of fresh cow milk may provoke gastrointestinal blood loss (Chapter 17), there is a difference of opinion among experts about whether physiologically significant losses of blood from nonanemic infants is a relatively common or very rare event (Lahey and Wilson, 1966; Diamond and Naiman, 1967; Lahey and Wilson, 1967).

Little attention appears to have been given to the possibility that chronic steatorrhea during infancy may be a cause for increased gastrointestinal loss of iron. When small infants receive a high percentage of calories in the form of whole cow milk, steatorrhea is common (Chapter 7). It is possible that such losses of fat are sometimes accompanied by increased desquamation of gastrointestinal mucosal cells. Abnormal fat excretion rather than intolerance to milk protein might therefore account for anemia of infants fed whole cow milk as a major source of calories.

IRON DEFICIENCY AND ANEMIA

Iron Deficiency

The Committee on Nutrition (1969) has summarized the sequence of changes that occur in progressive iron depletion: (1)

Ferritin and hemosiderin can no longer be demonstrated in bone marrow or in other reticuloendothelial tissues. (2) Serum concentration of iron decreases and iron-binding capacity of serum increases. (3) The circulating red cell mass decreases slightly. (4) Changes occur in morphology of red cells, especially microcytosis, hypochromia and poikilocytosis. (5) Progressively severe anemia occurs. (6) Concentrations of intracellular iron-containing enzymes decrease. The Committee concluded that saturation of transferrin less than 15 per cent indicates iron depletion, but points out that the stage of iron depletion at which the concentration of iron-containing enzymes begins to decrease is unknown.

This committee (Committee on Nutrition, 1969) has emphasized the importance of using appropriate standards based on age in evaluating iron nutritional status during the first 18 months of life. Hemosiderin, the form of storage iron most easily identified, is virtually absent from bone marrow of normal infants after six months of age (Smith et al., 1955). Such absence therefore does not appear to have the same significance for the infant as for older individuals.

One may question also the usual interpretation that saturation of transferrin less than 15 per cent indicates that iron is not readily available to the bone marrow for synthesis of hemoglobin (Harris and Kellermeryer, 1970). Active hemoglobin synthesis appears to occur in infants and small children during times when per cent saturation of transferrin in serum is less than 15.

Circumstantial evidence for this supposition is provided by the cross sectional data of Owen et al. (1974) as presented in Table 12–1. Among the lowest income group, per cent saturation of transferrin was less than 15 in 62 per cent of one-year-old children and in 37 per cent of two-year-old children. Concentrations of hemoglobin less than 11.0 gm/100 ml were observed in 27.0 per cent of children between one and two years of age but in only 10.0 per cent of children between two and three years of age. Although both hemoglobin concentration and transferrin saturation were not determined in every individual, it is apparent from Table 12–1 that, in all income groups, a relatively high percentage of children demonstrated transferrin saturations less than 15 per cent at a time when the prevalence of low hemoglobin concentrations appeared to be decreasing.

Definition of Anemia

It has been argued that a moderately decreased concentration of hemoglobin is of little consequence unless it causes decreased capacity for physical work by imposing an increased load on cardiorespira-

TABLE 12–1 CONCENTRATION OF HEMOGLOBIN AND PER CENT SATURATION OF TRANSFERRIN OF ONE- AND TWO-YEAR-OLD CHILDREN SURVEYED IN THE UNITED STATES*

Income Group	Age (years)	Hemoglobin Concentration		Transferrin Saturation	
		Number of Children	*% of Children Hb < 11.0 gm/100 ml*	*Number of Children*	*% of Children Sat. < 15%*
Lowest income	1–2	69	24.6	58	62.0
	2–3	81	10.0	66	37.0
Other income	1–2	280	11.8	201	45.8
	2–3	343	5.1	309	24.7

*Data of Owen et al. (1974).

tory mechanisms (Elwood et al., 1968). As stated by Oski (1973), "Not until physicians begin to think of anemia as a physiologic or biochemical derangement rather than a mere reduction in red cell mass will they be able to answer the seemingly simple question, 'Is this patient anemic?'"

This point of view is reasonable but not currently practical for developing a specific definition of anemia in infants and preschool children. In adults, quantitative measurements of the respiratory gas exchange before, during and after standardized muscular exercise have provided data on the physiologic responses to the reduced oxygen-carrying capacity of the blood associated with anemia (Andersen and Barkve, 1970; Andersen and Stavem, 1972). There is need for study of a larger number of individuals when anemic and after correction of the anemia. It may then be possible to identify some concentration of hemoglobin above which physiologic responses to exercise are similar and below which there is evidence of abnormality. The extent to which such a relationship established for adults would apply to infants and toddlers is unknown.

A second logical approach to establishing a definition of anemia might be the demonstration that some medically significant consequence (e.g., incidence of infections) was directly related to concentration of hemoglobin or to some other index of hematologic status. Data to support use of this approach are not available. In the absence of a satisfactory physiologic or medical basis for defining anemia, an arbitrary definition must be used.

A World Health Organization Scientific Group on Nutritional Anaemias (1968) has recommended that hemoglobin concentrations less than 11.0 gm/100 ml be used to define anemia in children from age six months to six years (but greater concentrations for older individuals), and the Committee on Nutrition (1969) has stated that "hemoglobin levels as low as 11 gm/100 ml, and hematocrits as low as 33% . . . should be considered 'normal'." This arbitrary definition is perhaps as good as any, and it may be a convenience to state that individuals are anemic rather than that hemoglobin concentrations of the individuals are less than 11 gm/100 ml. However, it is important to keep in mind that such a definition is not based on physiologically or medically meaningful data.

The Committee on Nutrition (1969) has recommended that minimum criteria for diagnosing iron-deficiency anemia include microcytosis and hypochromia of the red cells and response to therapy with iron. Because infants with concentrations of hemoglobin between 10.0 and 11.0 gm/100 ml may not demonstrate microcytosis and hypochromia and may yet respond to iron, it may be more reasonable to state that iron-deficiency anemia in infancy is a state in which hemoglobin concentration is less than 11.0 gm/100 ml and responds to administration of iron.

Prevalence of Iron-Deficiency Anemia

In the United States and in most other countries, low concentrations of hemoglobin of infants and preschool children are most commonly an expression of iron deficiency. These low concentrations of hemoglobin are most prevalent among infants of low birth weight and, in the case of fullsize infants, in the age range of 6 to 24 months. In the United States but not in certain other countries, infants in low-income families demonstrate a much greater prevalence of low hemoglobin concentrations. Figure 12–1 presents data of Owen et al. (1974) on percentage of children of various ages with concentrations of hemoglobin less than 11.0 gm/100 ml. The difference in prevalence of low hemoglobin concentrations in relation to age and economic status is evident.

The various studies summarized in Table 12–2 are in general agreement with the pattern of age and socioeconomic status reflected in Figure 12–1.

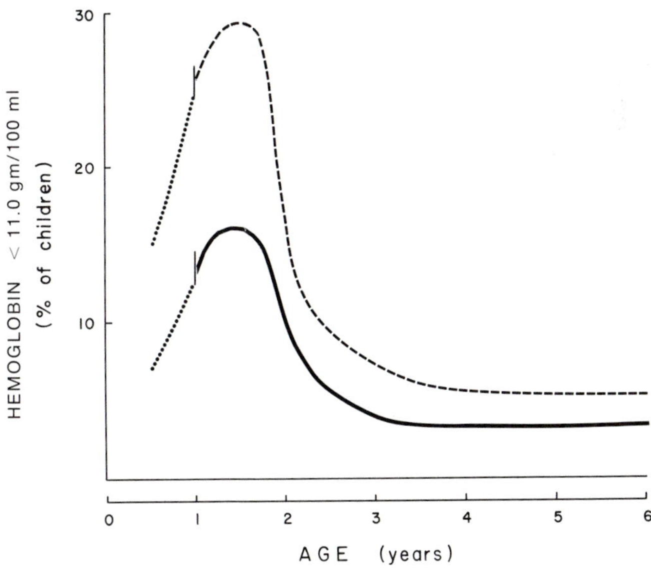

Figure 12–1 Per cent of children with hemoglobin concentrations less than 11.0 gm/100 ml at various ages among the lowest income group (upper curve) and other income groups combined (lower curve). Data concerning one- to six-year-old children are from Owen et al. (1974). Portions of curves for infants less than one year of age are estimated from Table 12–2.

TABLE 12–2 PREVALENCE OF LOW CONCENTRATIONS OF HEMOGLOBIN IN INFANTS AND PRESCHOOL CHILDREN: VARIOUS STUDIES IN THE UNITED STATES

LOCATION	AGE (YEARS)	NUMBER OF CHILDREN	HEMOGLOBIN CONCENTRATION (Per Cent of Children)		REFERENCE	COMMENT
			<10.0 gm/100 ml	*<11.0 gm/100 ml*		
Los Angeles, California	3/4	315	3	14	Fuerth (1971)	
Washington, D.C.	1/2–2	226	46		Gutelius (1969)	
	2–5	189	12			
Washington, D.C.	1/2–1	137	46		Gutelius (1971)	
	1–1 1/2	46	65			
	1 1/2–2	43	26			
	2–3	73	19			
	3–4	48	8			
Gainesville, Florida	3/4–1 1/2	244	15		Pearson et al. (1971)	Hematocrit < 30; hemoglobin not reported
Chicago, Illinois	<2	446	(76)		Andelman and Sered (1966)	Repeated testing of same infant

C & Y Projects						
Fullsize	0–½	1402	12	35	Fomon and Weckwerth (1971)	
	½–1	1005	20	48		
	1–2	1431	27	51		
	2–3	973	10	28		
	3–4	814	3	17		
Low-birth-weight	0–½	261	24	48		
	½–1	232	29	53		
	1–2	268	39	58		
	2–3	181	8	30		
	3–4	131	3	20		
10-State Survey	<2	700	24	44	Center for Disease Control (1972)	
	2–5	3011	6	20		
Preschool Nutrition Survey					Owen et al. (1974)	
Lowest income	1–2	69	14	27		
	2–3	81	4	10		
	3–4	94	2	8		
	4–5	77	0	9		
Other income	1–2	280	5	12		
	2–3	343	<1	4		
	3–4	375	<1	3		
	4–5	366	<1	4		
Iowa	½–3	583	4		Kripke and Sanders (1970)	Rural areas

Beeturia

The urinary excretion of betanin, a red pigment from beetroot, is referred to as beeturia and has often been misinterpreted as hematuria. Tunnessen et al. (1969) studied 41 patients from five months to seven years of age, giving each patient in the fasting state six tablespoons of homogenized beets. Of 19 patients with iron-deficiency anemia, 12 developed marked beeturia. These authors have suggested that the occurrence of beeturia suggests the possibility of iron-deficiency anemia.

INTAKES OF IRON BY CHILDREN IN THE UNITED STATES

Several surveys provide data on intakes of iron by children in the United States. As may be seen from Table 12–3, more than two-thirds of children appear to receive intakes less than 8 mg/day and more than 40 per cent appear to receive intakes less than 6 mg/day. Although these data are based on short-term recall, it seems unlikely that actual intakes by most of these children would average substantially greater than the reported intakes.

REQUIREMENT AND ADVISABLE INTAKE

To the quantity of iron present at birth, an amount must be absorbed that is sufficient to provide for the infant's needs for growth

TABLE 12–3 PERCENTAGE OF CHILDREN RECEIVING INTAKES OF IRON LESS THAN 6 OR 8 MG/DAY

Age Interval (years)	Survey*	Number of Subjects	Intake of Iron <6 mg/day (Per Cent of Children)	<8 mg/day
1–2	PNS	632	–	64
	USDA	93	47	78
	10-State	693	53	70
	NCRS	497	–	>50
2–3	PNS	681	–	61
	USDA	105	41	67
	10-State	708	45	66
	NCRS	551	–	>66

*PNS is Preschool Nutrition Survey (Owen et al., 1974); USDA is U.S. Department of Agriculture Survey of low income families (Eagles and Steele, 1972); 10-State is Ten-State Nutrition Survey, 1968–1970 (Center for Disease Control, 1972); NCRS is North Central Regional Survey (Fox et al., 1971).

(especially expansion of blood volume) and for replacement of inevitable losses.

Iron Endowment at Birth

The data of Widdowson and Spray (1951) indicate the wide variability in iron endowment at birth. Such variability is easy to appreciate when one considers the extent of differences in iron content of the circulating red cell mass at the time of birth. Several hypothetic examples are presented in Table 12–4. One may assume that tissue content of iron also varies from infant to infant.

The extent to which iron nutritional status of the pregnant woman influences iron endowment of the fetus is unknown. The greater prevalence of low hemoglobin concentrations among infants of low socioeconomic status (Fig. 12–1 and Table 12–1) may be attributed, in part, to the greater incidence of low birth weight and lesser intakes of iron in this group. However, a high percentage of infants from upper income families receive low intakes of iron and yet relatively few develop low concentrations of hemoglobin. The possibility that maternal iron status may influence fetal endowment with iron should therefore be further explored.

Requirement for Absorbed Iron

The requirement for *absorbed* iron may be estimated in a number of ways. Table 12–5 indicates the iron content of the body of the reference infant at various ages. The size of the fat-free body mass of the reference infant is the same as that presented in Chapter 3 (Table 3–12). It is assumed that iron content of fat-free body mass is 94 mg/kg at birth and 74 mg/kg in the adult (Widdowson and Spray, 1951). At ages one, two and three years, it is assumed that concentration of iron in fat-free body mass is 80, 90 and 100 per cent, respectively, of the value for the adult. These estimates are almost certainly excessive, because it is

TABLE 12–4 IRON CONTENT OF CIRCULATING RED CELL MASS OF HYPOTHETIC INFANTS AT BIRTH

HEMOGLOBIN CONCENTRATION (GM/100 ML)	RED CELL IRON (MG)	
	Body Weight 2.6 kg	*Body Weight 4.0 kg*
22	136	209
13	80	124

*Assuming blood volume is 70 ml/kg. Iron content is 3.4 mg/gm of hemoglobin.

TABLE 12–5 ESTIMATED IRON CONTENT OF BODY OF REFERENCE BOY AT VARIOUS AGES

AGE (YEARS)	FFBM* (GM)	IRON IN BODY† (mg/kg FFBM)	(mg)
Birth	3115	94	293
1	7991	59	471
2	10,322	67	692
3	12,195	74	902

*Fat-free body mass (Chapter 3, Table 3–12).

†Assuming that iron content of FFBM at birth is as reported by Widdowson and Spray (1951) and at one, two and three years of age is 80, 90 and 100 per cent of the value for the adult.

known that concentrations of hemoglobin in blood equal to those of the adult cannot be achieved at age one year no matter how great the intake of iron, and because little hemosiderin (and probably little ferritin) is present between 6 and 18 months of age.

Utilizing the difference in body content of iron at various ages (Table 12–5) as the requirement for growth and an assumed value for dermal losses, an estimate is made of the total amount of iron needed to be absorbed between birth and age one year, between one and two years and between two and three years of age. These estimates are presented in Table 12–6. The generous nature of the estimate for the first year is suggested by comparison of the estimate of Schulman (1961) of 143 mg of absorbed iron during the first year.

Dietary Requirement

Unfortunately, estimates of the requirement for absorbed iron are of limited value in establishing a recommendation for daily intakes of

TABLE 12–6 ESTIMATED REQUIREMENT FOR ABSORBED IRON AND FOR DIETARY INTAKE OF IRON BY REFERENCE BOY

AGE INTERVAL (YEARS)	REQUIREMENT FOR ABSORBED IRON: For Growth* (mg)	Dermal Losses† (mg)	Total (mg)	ESTIMATED DIETARY REQUIREMENT‡ (mg)	(mg/day)§
0–1	178	36	214	2140	7
1–2	221	73	294	2940	8
2–3	210	73	283	2830	8

*Calculated from Table 12–5.

†Assumed to be 0.1 mg daily during the first year and 0.2 mg daily thereafter.

‡Assuming 10 per cent absorption.

§Calculated on basis of 11 months for absorption in first year, 365 days in second and third years.

iron. The extent of absorption may vary widely and it is difficult to know what value to assign in any calculations that might aid in arriving at an estimate. For example, if 294 mg of iron must be absorbed between one and two years of age (Table 12–6)—approximately 0.8 mg/day—an 8 mg daily intake would be required if 10 per cent of dietary iron were absorbed, but only 5.3 mg daily would be required if 15 per cent of dietary iron were absorbed. Several studies (Schulz and Smith, 1958a and b; Garby and Sjölin, 1959) suggest that more than 10 per cent of dietary iron is absorbed by most infants, but the conservative value of 10 per cent has been utilized in arriving at an estimated requirement for the reference boy (Table 12–6).

Data from several sources may be evaluated in relation to the estimated dietary requirements for iron presented in Table 12–6. Cumulative intakes less than 2140 mg of iron during the first 12 months of life were reported by Beal et al. (1962) for 23 of 59 normal fullsize infants. Three of these infants (with cumulative intakes of 1032, 1613 and 1638 mg in 12 months) demonstrated hemoglobin concentrations less than 11.0 gm/100 ml at age 12 months. Of the infants with cumulative intakes of iron greater than 2140 mg during the first year (median cumulative intake was approximately 2500 mg), only one infant demonstrated a concentration of hemoglobin less than 11.0 gm/100 ml at age 12 months. This infant had a cumulative intake of 2321 mg in 12 months but had received only 647 mg in the first nine months.

In a study by Moe (1963), 75 infants received intakes of iron (from ferrous saccharate in infant cereal) of 0.5 to 1.0 mg daily at age three months, 5.4 to 10.5 mg daily at age six months and 8.6 to 13.5 mg daily between 8 and 12 months of age. If we assume that intakes averaged 0.5 mg daily during the first four months of life, 8.0 mg daily from four to eight months of age and 11.0 mg daily between 8 and 12 months of age, total intakes during the first year of life averaged 2340 mg. Only three infants had concentrations of hemoglobin less than 11.0 gm/100 ml at age 12 months (10.3, 10.7 and 10.8 gm/100 ml) and it is, of course, possible that these infants received amounts of iron considerably less than the average for the group.

Another group of 75 infants received 0.5 to 1.0 mg of iron daily at age three months, 3.2 to 5.9 mg daily at age six months and 3.4 to 7.0 mg daily between 8 and 12 months of age, probably achieving a total intake of iron less than 1500 mg during the first year of life. At age 12 months, 20 of these infants demonstrated concentrations of hemoglobin less than 11.0 gm/100 ml and three infants demonstrated concentrations less than 10.0 gm/100 ml. Thus, intakes of iron of approximately 1500 mg during the first year of life (i.e., less than 5 mg daily) appear inadequate, whereas intakes of approximately 2300 mg during the first year (about 7 mg daily) are probably adequate.

A subsequent follow-up of infants studied by Moe (1963) demonstrated that hemoglobin concentrations of 11.0 gm/100 ml or more at age one year were well maintained between one and three years of age even though supplements of iron were not given after age 12 months (Moe, 1964).

Data from the Preschool Nutrition Survey (Owen et al., 1974) suggest that the daily requirement for iron during the second and third years of life is less than 8 mg daily. Fifty per cent of children between 12 and 24 months of age and approximately 45 per cent of children between 24 and 36 months of age received intakes of iron less than 6.5 mg daily. Yet, a considerably smaller percentage of the 24- to 36-month-old children than of the 12- to 24-month-old children had low concentrations of hemoglobin (Fig. 12–1).

Thus, both calculations and circumstantial evidence from surveys suggest that true requirements for iron during the second and third years of life may be somewhat less than the 8 mg/day estimated in Table 12–6.

Advisable Intake

Reports by Sturgeon (1956, 1958), Moe (1963, 1964, 1965) and others demonstrate that generous supplementation of the diet with iron will result in higher mean concentrations of hemoglobin than are to be found with less vigorous iron supplementation. Whether concentration of 12 gm/100 ml at 12 months of age is evidence of a more satisfactory state of health than 11 gm/100 ml is uncertain. Therefore, it seems unreasonable to set as a goal the achievement of maximal concentrations of hemoglobin in the infant population. Future studies may help to clarify this point.

Fullsize Infants

When infants and preschool children receive a mixed diet supplying iron in a number of different forms, intakes of 7 mg daily during the first year and 8 mg daily during the second and third year are believed to exceed the requirement. The extent to which these intakes exceed the requirement is unknown. There appears to be no reasonable basis for advising an intake greater than 7 mg daily during the first year (8 mg daily between one and three years) *if the infant will receive this intake virtually every day* beginning no later than age four weeks. An intake of 7 mg daily for 11 months would amount to an intake of 2300 mg and would require approximately 9 per cent absorption to supply the 214 mg of absorbed iron estimated for the reference infant (Table 12–6).

It is evident that most infants will not receive a daily intake of 7 mg from age four weeks to age 12 months. To achieve a dietary intake of 2300 mg of iron in six months would require an average daily intake of 12.6 mg. Recommendations for intakes greater than 7 mg daily may therefore be desirable under some circumstances.

Requirement for iron is much less related to body size than to rate of growth, and there would seem to be little justification in a recommendation expressed as milligrams per kilogram of body weight (e.g., Committee on Nutrition, 1969).

Low-Birth-Weight Infants

Greater intakes of iron are probably desirable for low-birth-weight infants than for fullsize infants. Because iron content of the body at birth may be only one-half to two-thirds that of the fullsize infant, greater amounts of iron must be absorbed during the first year of life. Daily intakes of 10 to 15 mg of iron in the form of ferrous aminoacetosulfate (Plesmet) were shown by Grunseit et al. (1971) to achieve hemoglobin concentrations of 10.5 gm/100 ml or more in nearly all low-birth-weight infants by age 12 weeks. Lowest concentrations of hemoglobin were present at age eight weeks (mean of 86 infants, 10.9 gm/100 ml; standard deviation, 1.1 gm/100 ml). At age 12 weeks, mean concentration of hemoglobin of 81 infants was 12.1 (standard deviation, 0.8) gm/100 ml.

MEANS OF ACHIEVING ADVISABLE INTAKES

Human milk and cow milk are poor sources of iron (Table 12–7). Commercially prepared formulas supplemented with iron (generally ferrous sulfate to the extent of 8 to 12 mg/940 ml) will provide a major fraction of the advisable intake of 7 mg of iron daily during the early months of life and more than 7 mg daily by most infants more than three months of age. However, as indicated in Chapter 1 (Fig. 1–4), relatively few infants receive commercially prepared formulas after five months of age. Moreover, many infants who do receive commercially prepared formulas are fed those that are unsupplemented with iron.

In the case of two widely used formulas—Similac (Ross) and Enfamil (Mead)—which are available with or without added iron, unofficial estimates of sales suggest that in January and February 1971 approximately 17 per cent of sales were accounted for by the iron-fortified products. By January and February 1973, it is estimated that 37 per cent of sales of these two products were accounted for by the iron-fortified types. The increase in sales of iron-fortified formula between 1971 and 1973 almost certainly reflects the recommendation

TABLE 12–7 IRON CONTENT OF SELECTED FOODS FED TO INFANTS IN THE UNITED STATES

Food	Elemental Iron (mg/100 gm of food)	Elemental Iron (mg/100 kcal)
Milk or formula		
Human milk*	0.05	0.07
Cow milk*	0.05	0.07
Iron-fortified formula	0.9–1.3	1.2–1.8
Formula unfortified with iron	<0.05	<0.05
Infant cereals		
Iron-fortified (dry) mixed with milk†	7–14	7–14
Wet-packed cereal-fruit	1–6	1.3–7.5
Strained and junior foods		
Meats		
Liver and a few others	4–6	4–6
Most meats	1–2	1–2
Egg yolks	2–3	1.0–1.5
"Dinners"		
High meat	<1	<1
Vegetable-meat	<0.5	<0.5
Vegetables‡	<0.5	<0.5
Fruits‡	<0.5	<0.5

*Data reviewed by Underwood (1971).

†Assuming that one part by weight of dry cereal is mixed with six parts of milk (Chapter 16).

‡A few varieties of vegetables and fruits provide 1 to 2 mg of iron/100 gm (1 to 3 mg/100 kcal).

of the Committee on Nutrition (1971) that infants who are not breast-fed should receive iron-fortified formulas. Whether further increases in use of iron-fortified formulas will occur is unknown.

With the exception of iron-fortified infant formulas, few of the foods commonly fed to infants provide generous amounts of iron. Iron-fortified dry cereals commercially prepared for infants are rich sources of iron and, as discussed in Chapter 16, those currently marketed by Gerber and Heinz in the United States appear to contain a reasonably well absorbed form of iron. Wet-packed cereal-fruit combinations are less highly fortified with iron and contain a rather poorly absorbed form of iron (sodium iron pyrophosphate). However, manufacturing practices relating to infant cereals have changed frequently during the past few years and, in the future, more readily absorbable forms of iron may be used. As may be seen from Table 12–7, most commercially prepared foods for infants are poor sources of iron, providing less than 1 mg of iron/100 gm. It is clear that an infant who consumes several hundred grams of strained foods daily does not necessarily receive an adequate intake of iron.

It is unfortunate that feeding practices in the United States are such that neither iron-fortified formulas nor iron-fortified dry infant cereals are commonly fed after five months of age. If parents and physicians could be educated to the desirability of feeding an iron-fortified food daily until 18 months of age, the prevalence of low hemoglobin concentrations among infants and toddlers might be substantially decreased. Infants who do not receive a regular intake of an iron-fortified food should receive medicinal iron.

Low-Birth-Weight Infants

The great heterogeneity of low-birth-weight infants makes any general recommendation difficult. Use of an iron-fortified formula is desirable during at least the first six months of life. Iron-fortified cereal should be introduced in the diet by three to four months of age, and the importance of giving it regularly should be emphasized to parents. Medicinal iron (e.g., 10 to 15 mg of elemental iron daily as ferrous sulfate) may be utilized instead of an iron-fortified formula or cereal. Concentrations of hemoglobin should be determined at regular intervals, and daily intake of iron increased if concentration of hemoglobin decreases below 11.0 gm/100 ml.

Efficacy and Cost of Medicinal Iron

As stated by Lahey (1972): "There are now excellent studies to show that the soluble, dissociated ferrous salts such as the sulfate, succinate, lactate, fumarate, and gluconate are better absorbed and therefore preferable to other ferrous salts. . . and much preferred to the poorly absorbed ferric salts, particularly the chelated iron compounds such as ferric choline citrate. . . and ferric versenate. The evidence that ferrous salts are better absorbed than ferric salts is so overwhelming that it can be concluded that ferric iron has no place in oral iron therapy. Iron salts complexed with large carbohydrate molecules. . . appear to be poorly absorbed by some children and therefore cannot be recommended for routine use."

Information about preparations of iron available for oral use with infants is presented in Table 12–8.

The method of Afifi et al. (1966) appears to be suitable for determining whether a prescribed dose of iron is being taken (Macdougall, 1970).

ADVERSE EFFECTS OF IRON ADMINISTRATION

A number of adverse effects are attributed to administration of iron. These include constipation, diarrhea, vomiting and a variety of

TABLE 12–8 RELATIVE COSTS OF MEDICINAL IRON*

Name of Product	Formula	Concentration of Iron (mg/ml)	Cost (¢/15 mg)
Feosol elixir	$FeSO_4$	8.8	0.9
Mol-Iron liquid	$FeSO_4$	10	0.9
Fer-in-Sol syrup	$FeSO_4$	6.6	1.3
Ferrolip syrup	Fe choline chelate	10	2.1
Mol-Iron drops	$FeSO_4$; Mo	25	2.2
Chel-Iron liquid	Fe choline chelate	10	2.3
Fer-in-Sol drops	$FeSO_4$	25	2.4
Chel-Iron drops	Fe choline chelate	25	2.8
Stuart hematinic liquid†	Fe gluconate	4.4	3.0
Feostat drops	Fe fumarate	25	3.5
Ferisorb liquid†	Fe pyrophosphate	6	3.8
Zentron†	$FeSO_4$	4	3.9
Feostat suspension	Fe fumarate	6.6	4.0
Troph-Iron†	Fe pyrophosphate	6	5.7
Vi-Sorbin†	Fe pyrophosphate	2.4	8.3
Incremin with Fe†	Fe pyrophosphate	6	9.8
Zymatinic drops†	Fe gluconate	7.5	13.3

*Based on cost to pharmacist as indicated in Drug Topics Red Book 1973 (New York, Topics Publishing Co., 1973), plus 40 per cent pharmacist's markup.

†Also contains vitamins.

other manifestations. In fact, almost any adverse event occurring during administration of iron, whether in infant formula or as medicinal iron, may be attributed to the iron. In this regard, Burman (1972) has reported a study of 217 infants given 10 mg daily of colloidal ferric hydroxide and 217 infants given a placebo between 3 and 24 months of age. Twelve per cent of infants receiving the iron medication were reported to develop constipation, diarrhea, vomiting, refusal of feedings, screaming or skin rash. Similar manifestations were reported in 7 per cent of infants receiving the placebo. Thus, as a rough estimate, perhaps 5 per cent of the infants receiving iron may have developed manifestations caused by the iron medication.

REFERENCES

Afifi, A. M., Banwell, G. S., Bennison, R. J., Boothby, K., Griffiths, P. D., Huntsman, R. G., Jenkins, G. C., Lewin Smith, R. G., McIntosh, J., Qayum, A., Ross Russell, I., and Whittaker, J. N.: Simple test for ingested iron in hospital and domiciliary practice. Br. Med. J. *1*:1021, 1966.

Andelman, M. B., and Sered, B. R.: Utilization of dietary iron by term infants. Amer. J. Dis. Child. *111*:45, 1966.

Andersen, H. T., and Barkve, H.: Iron deficiency and muscular work performance. Scand. J. Clin. Lab. Invest. (Suppl. 114), 1970.

Andersen, H. T., and Stavem, P.: Iron deficiency anaemia and the acid-base variations of exercise. Nutr. Metab. *14*:129, 1972.

Ashworth, A., Milner, P. F., Waterlow, J. C., and Walker, R. B.: Absorption of iron from maize (Zea mays L.) and soya beans (Glycine hispida Max.) in Jamaican infants. Br. J. Nutr. *29*:269, 1973.

Beal, V. A., Meyers, A. J., and McCammon, R. W.: Iron intake, hemoglobin, and physical growth during the first two years of life. Pediatrics *30*:518, 1962.

Brown, E. B., and Justus, B. W.: In vitro absorption of radioiron by everted pouches of rat intestine. Amer. J. Physiol. *194*:319, 1958.

Burman, D.: Haemoglobin levels in normal infants aged 3 to 24 months, and the effect of iron. Arch. Dis. Child. *47*:261, 1972.

Callender, S. T., Marney, S. R., Jr., and Warner, G. T.: Eggs and iron absorption. Br. J. Haematol. *19*:657, 1970.

Center for Disease Control: Ten-State Nutrition Survey, 1968–70. Vol. IV. Biochemical. DHEW Publication No. (HSM) 72-8132. Atlanta, Georgia, Center for Disease Control, 1972.

Chodos, R. B., Ross, J. F., Apt, L., Pollycove, M., and Halkett, J. A. E.: The absorption of radioiron labeled foods and iron salts in normal and iron-deficient subjects and in idiopathic hemochromatosis. J. Clin. Invest. *36*:314, 1957.

Committee on Nutrition, American Academy of Pediatrics: Iron balance and requirements in infancy. Pediatrics *43*:134, 1969.

Committee on Nutrition, American Academy of Pediatrics: Iron-fortified formulas. Pediatrics *47*:786, 1971.

Cook, J. D., Layrisse, M., Martinez-Torres, C., Walker, R., Monsen, E., and Finch, C. A.: Food iron absorption measured by an extrinsic tag. J. Clin. Invest. *51*:805, 1972.

Diamond, L. K., and Naiman, J. L.: Letter to editor. More on iron deficiency anemia. J. Pediatr. *70*:304, 1967.

Eagles, J. A., and Steele, P. D.: Food and nutrient intake of children from birth to four years of age. *In* Fomon, S. J., and Anderson, T. A. (eds.): Practices of Low-Income Families in Feeding Infants and Small Children. With Particular Attention to Cultural Subgroups. DHEW Publ. No. (HSM) 72-5605, Washington, D.C., U.S. Government Printing Office, 1972, p. 19.

Ehrenberg, A., and Laurell, C.-B.: Magnetic measurements on crystallized Fe-transferrin isolated from the blood plasma of swine. Acta Chem. Scand. 9:68, 1955.

Elwood, P. C., Newton, D., Eakins, J. D., and Brown, D. A.: Absorption of iron from bread. Amer. J. Clin. Nutr. *21*:1162, 1968.

Fomon, S. J., and Weckwerth, V. E.: Hemoglobin concentrations of children registered for care in C&Y projects during March and April 1968. *In* Committee on Iron Nutritional Deficiencies, Food and Nutrition Board (eds.): Summary of Proceedings. Workshop on Extent and Meanings of Iron Deficiency in the U.S. Washington, D.C., Food and Nutrition Board, National Academy of Sciences–National Research Council, 1971, p. 30.

Fox, H. M., Fryer, B. A., Lamkin, G., Vivian, V. M., and Eppright, E. S.: Diets of preschool children in the north central region. J. Amer. Diet. Ass. *59*:233, 1971.

Frieden, E.: The ferrous to ferric cycles in iron metabolism. Nutr. Rev. *31*:41, 1973.

Fritz, J. C., Pla, G. W., Roberts, T., Boehne, J. W., and Hove, E. L.: Biological availability in animals of iron from common dietary sources. J. Agric. Food Chem. *18*:647, 1970.

Fuerth, J. H.: Incidence of anemia in full-term infants seen in private practice. J. Pediatr. *79*:560, 1971.

Garby, L., and Sjölin, S.: Absorption of labelled iron in infants less than three months old. Acta Paediatr. Scand. (Suppl. 117), 1959.

Gorten, M. K.: Iron metabolism in premature infants. III. Utilization of iron as related to growth in infants with low birth weight. Amer. J. Clin. Nutr. *17*:322, 1965.

Gorten, M. K., and Cross, E. R.: Iron metabolism in premature infants. II. Prevention of iron deficiency. J. Pediatr. *64*:509, 1964.

Gorten, M. K., Hepner, R., and Workman, J. B.: Iron metabolism in premature infants. I. Absorption and utilization of iron as measured by isotope studies. J. Pediatr. *63*:1063, 1963.

Grunseit, F., Lewis, C. J., and Stevens, L. H.: Haemoglobin levels in the first year of life in low birthweight babies receiving iron supplements. Med. J. Aust. *1*:79, 1971.

Gutelius, M. F.: The problem of iron deficiency anemia in preschool Negro children. Amer. J. Public Health *59*:290, 1969.

Gutelius, M. F.: Iron deficiency anemia in ghetto infants. Clin. Proc. Children's Hosp. Washington, D.C. *27*:1, 1971.

Hallberg, L., and Sölvell, L.: Absorption of hemoglobin iron in man. Acta Med. Scand. *181*:335, 1967.

Harris, J. W., and Kellermeryer, R. W.: Red Cell Production, Metabolism, Destruction, Normal and Abnormal. Rev. ed. Cambridge, Harvard University Press, 1970.

Hussain, R., Walker, R. B., Layrisse, M., Clark, P., and Finch, C. A.: Nutritive value of food iron. Amer. J. Clin. Nutr. *16*:464, 1965.

Kripke, S. S., and Sanders, E.: Prevalence of iron-deficiency anemia among infants and young children seen at rural ambulatory clinics. Amer. J. Clin. Nutr. *23*:716, 1970.

Lahey, M. E.: Anemia due to inadequate erythrocyte or hemoglobin production. *In* Shirkey, H. C.: Pediatric Therapy. 4th ed. St. Louis, C. V. Mosby Co., 1972, p. 665.

Lahey, M. E., and Wilson, J. F.: The etiology of iron deficiency anemia in infants: a reappraisal. J. Pediatr. *69*:339, 1966.

Lahey, M. E., and Wilson, J. F.: Letter to the editor. More on iron deficiency anemia. J. Pediatr. *70*:305, 1967.

Layrisse, M., Cook, J. D., Martinez, C., Roche, M., Kuhn, I. N., Walker, R. B., and Finch, C. A.: Food iron absorption: a comparison of vegetable and animal foods. Blood *33*:430, 1969.

Layrisse, M., Martinez-Torres, C., and Roche, M.: Effect of interaction of various foods on iron absorption. Amer. J. Clin. Nutr. *21*:1175, 1968.

Macdougall, L. G.: A simple test for the detection of iron in stools. J. Pediatr. *76*:764, 1970.

Marsh, A., Long, H., and Stierwalt, E.: Comparative hematologic response to iron fortification of a milk formula for infants. Pediatrics *24*:404, 1959.

Martinez-Torres, C., and Layrisse, M.: Effect of amino acids on iron absorption from a staple vegetable food. Blood *35*:669, 1970.

Ministry of Health: Iron in Flour. Reports on Public Health and Medical Subjects No. 117. London, H. M. Stationery Office, 1968.

Moe, P. J.: Iron requirements in infancy: longitudinal studies of iron requirements during the first year of life. Acta Paediatr. Scand. (Suppl. 150), 1963.

Moe, P. J.: Iron requirements in infancy. II. The influence of iron-fortified cereals given during the first year of life, on red blood picture at 1½–3 years of age. Acta Paediatr. Scand. *53*:423, 1964.

Moe, P. J.: Normal red blood picture during the first three years of life. Acta Paediatr. Scand. *54*:69, 1965.

Moore, C. V., and Dubach, R.: Observations on the absorption of iron from foods tagged with radioiron. Physicians *64*:245, 1951.

Morgan, E. H., and Walters, M. N. I.: Iron shortage in human disease: fractionation of hepatic and splenic iron into ferritin and haemosiderin with histochemical correlations. J. Clin. Path. *16*:101, 1963.

Muir, A. R.: The molecular structure of isolated and intracellular ferritin. J. Exp. Physiol. *45*:192, 1960.

Naiman, J. L., Oski, F. A., Diamond, L. K., Vawter, G. F., and Shwachman, H.: The gastrointestinal effects of iron-deficiency anemia. Pediatrics *33*:83, 1964.

Oski, F. A.: Designation of anemia on a functional basis. J. Pediatr. *83*:353, 1973.

Owen, G. M., Kram, K. M., Garry, P. J., Lowe, J. E., Jr., and Lubin, A. H.: A study of nutritional status of preschool children in the United States, 1968–1970. Pediatrics *53*:597, 1974.

Pearson, H. A.: Life span of the fetal red blood cell. J. Pediatr. *70*:166, 1967.

Pearson, H. A., McLean, F. W., and Brigety, R. E.: Anemia related to age. Study of a community of young black Americans. J.A.M.A. *215*:1982, 1971.

Schulman, I.: Iron requirements in infancy. J.A.M.A. *175*:118, 1961.

Schulz, J., and Smith, N. J.: A quantitative study of the absorption of food iron in infants and children. Amer. J. Dis. Child. *95*:109, 1958a.

Schulz, J., and Smith, N. J.: Quantitative study of the absorption of iron salts in infants and children. Amer. J. Dis. Child. *95*:120, 1958b.

Settlemire, C. T., and Matrone, G.: In vivo interference of zinc with ferritin iron in the rat. J. Nutr. *92*:153, 1967a.

Settlemire, C. T., and Matrone, G.: In vivo effect of zinc on iron turnover in rats and life span of the erythrocyte. J. Nutr. *92*:159, 1967b.

Shah, B. G., and Belonje, B.: Bio-availability of reduced iron. Nutr. Rep. Int. *7*:151, 1973.

Shoden, A., and Sturgeon, P.: Hemosiderin. I. A physico-chemical study. Acta Haemat. *23*:376, 1960.

Smith, N. J., Rosello, S., Say, M. B., and Yeya, K.: Iron storage in the first five years of life. Pediatrics *16*:166, 1955.

Sturgeon, P.: Iron metabolism. A review with special consideration of iron requirements during normal infancy. Pediatrics *18*:267, 1956.

Sturgeon, P.: Studies of iron requirements in infants and children. *In* Wallerstein, R. O., and Mettier, S. R. (eds.): Iron in Clinical Medicine. Berkeley, University of California Press, 1958, p. 183.

Tunnessen, W. W., Smith, C., and Oski, F. A.: Beeturia. A sign of iron deficiency. Amer. J. Dis. Child. *117*:424, 1969.

Underwood, E. J.: Trace Elements in Human and Animal Nutrition. 3rd ed. New York, Academic Press, 1971.

Widdowson, E. M., and Spray, C. M.: Chemical development in utero. Arch. Dis. Child. *26*:205, 1951.

World Health Organization: Nutritional Anaemias. Report of a WHO Scientific Group. Technical Report Series No. 405, Geneva, World Health Organization, 1968.

13

TRACE MINERALS

Karl E. Bergmann
and
Samuel J. Fomon

Major minerals, including sodium, chloride, potassium, calcium, phosphorus, magnesium and sulfur, have been considered in Chapter 11. Iron has been discussed in Chapter 12 and fluoride will be discussed in Chapter 14. In the present chapter, we shall consider other trace minerals of established nutritional importance for the human: chromium, manganese, cobalt, copper, zinc, molybdenum and iodine. Selenium will also be discussed although it has not yet been proved essential for the human. Selenium is an essential nutrient for the chick and eventually may be demonstrated to be essential for many animals, including humans. More than 20 other trace minerals are currently under special consideration with respect to essentiality (Schwarz, 1971) but will not be considered here.

Trace minerals function particularly as components of metalloenzymes or as cofactors for enzymes activated by metal ions. Such diverse compounds as nucleic acids, porphyrins, thyroxin, insulin and vitamin B_{12} require trace minerals for maintaining structural integrity and/or optimal function.

CHROMIUM

Although there has been speculation that chromium deficiency may contribute to development of atherosclerosis (Schroeder et al., 1970), the only manifestation of chromium deficiency thus far documented in human subjects is impaired glucose tolerance. In the rat, chromium deficiency is also characterized by impaired growth and longevity, disturbances of protein and lipid metabolism and by corneal lesions (Underwood, 1971). Trivalent chromium acts as a cofactor for the peripheral action of insulin (Mertz, 1969; Mertz and Roginsky, 1971; Evans et al., 1973), and some human subjects with impaired glucose tolerance respond to chromium supplementation of the diet with normalization of tolerance (Glinsmann and Mertz, 1966; Hopkins et al., 1968; Levine et al., 1968; Gürson and Saner, 1971). Not all subjects respond in this fashion and those who do respond may require weeks of supplementation regardless of the dose. Presumably, only chromium-deficient human subjects respond to supplementation and the lag in response is the result of time required for synthesis within the body of the insulin-potentiating principle (Mertz and Roginski, 1971).

Absorption and Excretion

Great quantitative and qualitative differences in the metabolism and biologic effect of chromium exist, depending on its chemical form. Inorganic chromium is poorly absorbed and in vitro demonstrates only modest potentiation of insulin activity. However, chromium in organically bound form, as it is present in brewer's yeast (and in liver, kidney, wheat, etc.), is better absorbed, has a different tissue distribution and in vitro is much more effective in potentiating the action of insulin. It seems likely that the chromium-containing substance in brewer's yeast and other natural sources is identical to the insulin-potentiating principle, called the "glucose tolerance factor." Semipurified preparations of the glucose tolerance factor are biologically active and this activity parallels chromium content (Mertz, 1969; Mertz and Roginski, 1971; Evans et al., 1973).

Orally administered trivalent chromium appears to be poorly absorbed—1 per cent or less, regardless of dose or chromium nutritional status (Underwood, 1971). Data from several sources (Kirchgessner, 1959; Schroeder et al., 1962; Hambidge, 1971) suggest that concentrations of chromium in cow milk may be in the range of 8 to 13 μg/liter. Most plants provide 100 to 500 μg/kg, but it is not known how much of this is in the form of the relatively well absorbed glucose tolerance factor and how much is in the form of poorly absorbed inorganic chromium. Absorbed or injected chromium is primarily excreted in the urine, with small amounts being lost through the gastrointestinal tract, probably in bile, and through the skin (Underwood, 1971).

Distribution in the Body

Within the cell, chromium is predominantly located in the nucleus, mitochondria and microsomes. Chromium is mobilized in normal subjects in response to administration of glucose, plasma concentration of chromium rising sharply in parallel with the increase in concentration of glucose. The extent of this response seems to reflect chromium nutritional status, whereas baseline concentration of chromium in blood or plasma appears to reflect body stores poorly. Much of the chromium present in the blood is bound to transferrin, probably representing chromium in transport to tissues and thus reflecting recent dietary intake rather than chromium nutritional status (Mertz, 1969). Because transferrin is not excreted in the urine, it is possible that urinary excretion of chromium, which includes chromium in circulating glucose tolerance factor, reflects nutritional status. Unfortunately, the technical difficulties in determining chromium concentration in urine have been sufficiently great to make the method impractical (Hambidge, 1971). Only recently have these difficulties been overcome by the application of flameless atomic absorption spectrometry (Schaller et al., 1972).

Concentration in Hair

Content of chromium in hair after adequate washing is in most instances of endogenous origin (Hambidge and Baum, 1972) and thus may reflect chromium nutritional status. Correlation of chromium concentration of hair to abnormal glucose tolerance and the improvement in glucose tolerance after administration of chromium will be a necessary further step in evaluating the significance of chromium content of hair. However, high concentrations of chromium in hair of newborn infants (Hambidge, 1971) do parallel high tissue concentrations reported from necropsy specimens (Schroeder et al., 1962); chromium concentration in hair increases with gestational age (Hambidge, 1971).

The concentration of chromium at a particular distance from the scalp appears to reflect the quantity of chromium available to the hair follicle at the time of keratinization of that section of hair (Hambidge et al., 1972a). At the time of the first haircut of an 18-month-old female, Hambidge (1971) reported concentrations of chromium in hair to be 940, 576, 330 and 144 μg/kg, respectively, for hair 9 to 18, 5 to 8, 2 to 5 and 0 to 2 cm from the scalp. It was suggested that hair 9 to 18 cm from the scalp had grown before nine months of age.

Protein-Calorie Malnutrition

Impaired glucose tolerance is recognized as a frequent accompaniment of protein-calorie malnutrition. Hopkins et al. (1968), in a study of Jordanian and Nigerian infants with protein-calorie malnutrition, demonstrated significant improvement in glucose tolerance within 18 hours after supplementation of the diet with trivalent chromium. This has been confirmed by Gürson and Saner (1971). The rapidity of this response suggests that malnourished infants may absorb trivalent chromium considerably more readily than do normal or chromium-deficient adults. Carter et al. (1968) failed to demonstrate improvement of the abnormal glucose tolerance after 24 to 72 hours of chromium supplementation of the diet of Egyptian children suffering from protein-calorie malnutrition. It is evident that there are many causes of abnormal glucose tolerance and that improvement with chromium supplementation is to be anticipated only in instances where chromium deficiency is a major cause.

MANGANESE

Although unequivocal evidence of manganese deficiency has not been obtained for human subjects, existence of deficiency has been convincingly demonstrated in poultry, rats, mice, guinea pigs, rabbits, pigs, cattle and sheep (Underwood, 1971). Manifestations of manganese deficiency in animals include growth retardation, reduced fertility, ataxia of the newborn and various abnormalities of bone. Ataxia of the newborn apparently results from faulty development of otoliths (Shrader and Everson, 1967). Abnormalities of bone (nutritional chondrodystrophy), consisting of decreased bone length, density and ash content, are the result of impaired synthesis of the mucopolysaccharides of cartilage (Leach et al., 1969). Impaired glucose tolerance associated with hypoplastic pancreatic islet cells has been reported in guinea pigs (Everson and Shrader, 1968).

Manganese catalyzes formation of glucosamine-serine linkages (Robinson et al., 1966) and is involved in the transcarboxylation part of the pyruvate carboxylase reaction (Mildvan et al., 1966).

The body of the adult human is estimated to contain 12 to 20 mg of manganese (Cotzias, 1958). Liver, pancreas and kidney are rich in manganese (Tipton and Cook, 1963) and within the cell manganese is particularly concentrated in mitochondria. Excretion of manganese occurs mainly in bile. The extent of biliary excretion rather than extent of absorption appears to determine body content.

Because manganese deficiency has not been recognized in human subjects, it is, of course, impossible to estimate the requirement. Intakes by normal one-year-old and three- to five-year-old children have been reported to average 0.8 and 1.4 mg/day, respectively (Belz, 1960; Schlage and Wortberg, 1972a). There appears to be little storage of manganese in the body of the newborn infant (Widdowson et al., 1972). Human milk provides 7 to 15 μg of manganese/liter, and cow milk 20 to 40 μg/liter (Widdowson, 1969; McLeod and Robinson, 1972).

COBALT

Because cobalt forms part of the vitamin B_{12} molecule, it must be considered essential. However, cobalt deficiency has not been produced in a nonruminant animal (Underwood, 1971), and the requirements may therefore be assumed to be minute. Possibly, its only function is as a component of vitamin B_{12} and, if intakes of this vitamin are adequate, no additional cobalt is required. Whether vitamin B_{12} synthesized by intestinal microorganisms can be absorbed by the human is unknown.

Individuals with anemia of various types demonstrate erythropoietic responses after administration of large doses of cobalt (Underwood, 1971). Such effects are probably pharmacologic rather than nutritional in nature.

COPPER

The nutritional essentiality of copper is evident from the fact that copper is necessary for the structure or function of cytochrome oxidase, ceruloplasmin, uricase, amine oxidase and ascorbic acid oxidase (Underwood, 1971; Osaki et al., 1971; Frieden, 1973). Copper-containing enzymes and other copper-containing proteins are required for cellular respiration, normal hematopoiesis, normal bone formation and gastrointestinal function and maintenance of myelin in the nervous system. In addition, in various animals copper has been demonstrated to be necessary for growth, fertility, maintenance of elastin in great blood vessels, keratinization and pigmentation of hair (Dowdy, 1969; Underwood, 1971; Evans, 1973).

Absorption of copper appears to occur predominantly in the duodenum. Excretion occurs mainly with bile rather than in the urine (Cartwright and Wintrobe, 1964a and b). Absorption of copper is adversely affected by the presence of phytate, molybdenum, inorganic sulfate and cadmium in the diet (Underwood, 1971). Under conditions favorable to absorption of copper, it seems possible that as much as one-third of an oral dose can be absorbed (Cartwright and Wintrobe, 1964a and b).

Ceruloplasmin and Plasma Concentration of Copper

Ceruloplasmin, the copper-containing protein synthesized by the liver, catalyzes the oxidation of ferrous iron to ferric iron, making iron available for transport in transferrin (Osaki et al., 1971; Frieden, 1973). More than 90 per cent of copper in plasma is present in ceruloplasmin (Henkin et al., 1973; Evans, 1973). Thus, the deficient synthesis of ceruloplasmin in severe copper deficiency eventually results in hypocupremia. Clinical manifestations of copper deficiency have not been observed in the absence of hypocupremia. That low plasma concentration of copper does not necessarily indicate copper deficiency is suggested by the low serum concentration of the newborn infant in spite of large liver stores of copper (Cartwright and Wintrobe, 1964a). Total copper content of the liver of the fullterm newborn infant is approximately 12 mg, compared with a value of about 8 mg for the adult (Widdowson et al., 1972). Presumably, low serum concentrations of copper at birth are the result of limited ability of the fetus to synthesize ceruloplasmin.

Serum concentrations of copper at birth average approximately 29 μg/100 ml. Concentrations rise gradually and, between 8 and 21 months of age, generally range from 125 to 140 μg/100 ml (Cartwright and Wintrobe, 1964a; Henkin et al., 1973).

Copper Deficiency

For some years it has been recognized that copper deficiency may occur in association with chronic diarrhea, nephrotic syndrome, protein-losing enteropathy, cystic fibrosis of the pancreas and celiac disease (Cartwright and Wintrobe, 1964b). Cordano et al. (1964) have reported that four infants with severe malnutrition developed hypocupremia, anemia, neutropenia and bone changes resembling those of scurvy during treatment with a high calorie diet low in copper content. Two of these infants responded promptly to the administration of copper. Cordano and Graham (1966) have also described a six-and-one-half-year-old child with failure to thrive since early infancy, possibly caused by intestinal lactase deficiency. Hypocupremia, anemia, neutropenia, osteoporosis and pathologic fractures were present. Administration of copper was followed by dramatic clinical improvement.

Additional reports of copper deficiency in protein-calorie malnutrition have appeared (Graham and Cordano, 1969; Lehmann et al., 1971) and copper deficiency has been observed in premature infants (Al-Rashid and Spangler, 1971; Seely et al., 1972; Ashkenazi et al., 1973) and during prolonged parenteral feeding (Karpel and Peden, 1972). A defect in absorption of copper has been identified as the cause of Menkes' kinky hair syndrome (Danks et al., 1972).

Hypocupremia associated with iron-deficiency anemia in infants appears to be restricted to cases in which hypoproteinemia is also present (Sturgeon and Brubaker, 1956; Zipursky et al., 1958; Schubert and Lahey, 1959). In some instances, treatment with iron plus copper has been responsible for more complete correction of the anemia than treatment with iron alone (Zipursky et al., 1958; Schubert and Lahey, 1959).

Possible manifestations of copper deficiency in human subjects include hypocupremia, anemia resistant to iron therapy, neutropenia, retarded growth, bone changes resembling those of scurvy, kinky hair, hypothermia, progressive cerebral degeneration (of gray and white matter) and cardiovascular changes due to fragmentation of the internal elastic lamina. These manifestations are generally similar to those found in copper-deficient animals (Underwood, 1971).

Intake of Copper

Human milk provides approximately 0.4 mg and cow milk 0.3 mg of copper/liter (Chapter 15, Table 15–1)—i.e., approximately 60 and 45 μg/100 kcal, respectively. Many other foods consumed by infants and preschool children provide more generous amounts of copper (Chapter 16, Table 16–2) (Pennington and Calloway, 1973). As appears to be the case with adults (Scheinberg, 1961; Seelig, 1972), intakes of copper by infants and preschool children generally are considerably in excess of requirement.

Requirement

Because of the large hepatic stores of copper acquired in utero, requirement for copper is probably low during early infancy. Wilson and Lahey (1960) restricted copper intake of seven premature infants to 14 μg/kg daily for 60 days without provoking manifestations of deficiency. Presumably, this interval was too short to exhaust hepatic stores.

On the basis of metabolic balance studies, Price et al. (1970) estimated the copper requirement of seven- to nine-year-old girls to be about 60 μg/kg/day, and this value may tentatively be accepted as the requirement for infants and preschool children. For infants and children receiving prolonged intravenous alimentation, Dudrick and Rhoads (1971) recommended an intravenous dose of copper of 22 μg/kg/day, an apparently reasonable recommendation in view of the likelihood that only about one-third of an oral dose may be absorbed.

ZINC

There are at least 18 zinc-containing enzymes and 15 other metal-enzyme complexes activated by zinc (Parisi and Vallee, 1969). Zinc-containing enzymes include carbonic anhydrase, carboxypeptidase, alkaline phosphatase and several pyridine nucleotide dehydrogenases.

The body of the adult human is estimated to contain about 1.6 gm of zinc—i.e., less than half the amount of iron (4.4 gm) and about 16 times the amount of copper (Widdowson et al., 1951; Widdowson and Dickerson, 1964). In the newborn infant, concentrations of iron and copper per unit of body weight exceed those of adult animals, whereas tissue concentration of zinc is somewhat less in the newborn than in the adult. Concentrations of zinc in human milk and cow milk are approximately 3 to 5 mg/liter, and concentrations in colostrum are three to five times this amount (Underwood, 1971). After the first week of life, the breastfed infant probably receives 2 to 5 mg of zinc daily. Intakes of zinc by normal three- to five-year-old children have been reported to average 5 to 7 mg/day (Schlage and Wortberg, 1972b).

Sandstead (1973) has reviewed advances in knowledge of the metabolic role of zinc, factors which influence its availability for intestinal absorption and the effects of zinc deficiency in man.

Concentration of Zinc in Hair

Concentrations of zinc in hair are known to be low in zinc-deficient human subjects (Bradfield et al., 1969; Klevay, 1970a and b). Among Egyptian adolescents, for example, concentrations of zinc less than 70 mg/kg of hair were associated with severe clinical manifestations. For this reason, determination of zinc concentration of hair appears promising as a measure of zinc nutritional status.

Hambidge et al. (1972b) studied zinc concentrations in hair of 338 apparently healthy individuals of upper or middle socioeconomic status in Denver, Colorado. As may be seen from Figure 13–1, concentrations were frequently low in children between three months and four years of age, suggesting low stores of zinc in these subjects. Forty-two of the 93 subjects in this age group demonstrated concentrations of zinc less than 70 mg/kg of hair, and 8 of the 93 demonstrated concentrations less than 30 mg/kg of hair. Six of the eight subjects with these extremely low concentrations of zinc in hair gave a history of poor appetite and demonstrated heights and/or weights at or below the 10th percentile values. Among 4- to 17-year-old children, 7 of 10 with concentrations of zinc less than 70 mg/kg of hair gave a history of poor appetite, and heights of eight were at or below the 10th percentile values. Taste acuity was tested in six of these subjects and hypogeusia was found in five. Supplementation of the diet with small amounts of zinc restored taste acuity.

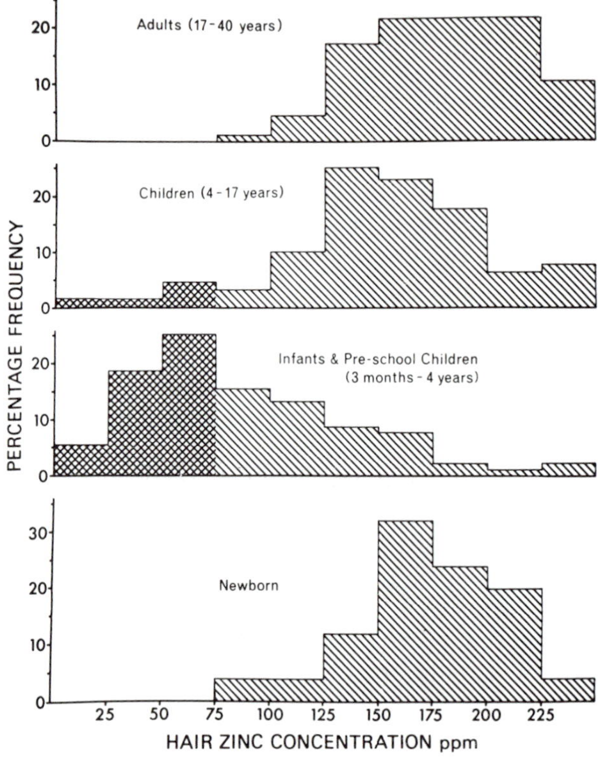

Figure 13–1 Concentrations of zinc in hair (88 adults; 132 children aged 4–17 years; 93 subjects aged three months to four years; and 25 neonates). Checkered area indicates percentage of subjects with levels of zinc in hair less than 75 ppm. (From Hambidge, K. M., et al.: Low levels of zinc in hair, anorexia, poor growth, and hypogeusia in children. Pediatr. Res. *6*:868, 1972.)

Deficiency

Dietary deficiency of zinc in the human is associated with anorexia, hypogeusia, retarded growth, delayed sexual maturation, lymphopenia, impaired wound healing and abnormalities in keratinization (Pories et al., 1967; Sandstead et al., 1970; Greaves and Skillen, 1970; Serjeant et al., 1970). Growth retardation apparently results both from abnormally low food intake and from impaired utilization of nutrients (Prasad et al., 1969; Sandstead et al., 1972). A syndrome of dwarfism, hypogonadism, hepatosplenomegaly and iron deficiency anemia in human subjects has been related to zinc deficiency (Prasad et al., 1961, 1963; Prasad, 1967; Sandstead et al., 1967; Halsted et al., 1972). Decreased alkaline phosphatase activity has been demonstrated in serum of zinc-deficient individuals, and it is possible that activity of this zinc-containing enzyme may be an indication of zinc nutritional status. Zinc deficiency may result from decreased availability (Reinhold et al., 1973) or from insufficient intake of zinc.

Congenital malformations, especially of the central nervous system, have been reported in rat pups born to zinc-deficient dams (Hurley and Swenerton, 1966; Hurley and Mutch, 1973), and it has been suggested (Sever, 1973; Halsted, 1973) that zinc deficiency may be responsible for congenital malformations in human infants. In rats, zinc is necessary to maintain normal concentrations of vitamin A in plasma; in zinc deficiency, mobilization of vitamin A from the liver is impaired (Smith et al., 1973).

Requirement

As has been done in the case of major minerals (Chapter 11), the requirement for zinc for growth may be calculated from the estimated increase in fat-free tissue and an assumed value for zinc concentration in this newly synthesized tissue. Fat-free tissue contains approximately 1.9 mg of zinc/100 gm in the newborn infant and approximately 2.8 mg of zinc/100 gm in the adult (Widdowson, 1969). As indicated in Chapter 3 (Table 3–13), the male reference infant gains 2.04 kg of fat-free tissue between birth and age four months. For this newly synthesized tissue to contain 1.9 mg of zinc/100 gm, it would be necessary for the infant to retain 0.32 mg of zinc daily from the diet.

The data of Widdowson (1969) and our own unpublished data indicate that zinc balance is generally negative during the first week of life. Our unpublished data from balance studies with infants fed a number of commercially prepared formulas suggest that during the first four months of life zinc balance may be slightly negative or slightly positive; however, even when balance is positive, retention is almost invariably less than 0.3 mg/day. Thus, it seems likely that in normal infants body content of zinc decreases (or increases only slightly) during the first few months of life. As already mentioned, zinc content of hair decreases greatly during infancy, possibly reflecting decreased concentration of zinc in fat-free body mass. Zinc balance studies with older infants have not been reported.

At present there appears to be no satisfactory method for estimating the requirement for zinc during infancy or early childhood.

MOLYBDENUM

The flavoprotein enzyme, xanthine oxidase, is a molybdenum-containing metalloenzyme which is dependent for its activity on the presence of this metal (Underwood, 1971). Using highly purified diets, it has been possible to demonstrate that molybdenum is essential for lambs, chicks and turkey poults. Uncomplicated molybdenum deficiency has never been reported in man or in farm animals living under naturally occurring conditions.

Molybdenum is apparently efficiently absorbed from most diets and is excreted predominantly in the urine. Molybdenum metabolism is greatly influenced by dietary intakes of sulfate and copper. Presence of inorganic sulfate in the diet decreases concentration of molybdenum in blood, probably both by interfering with absorption and by increasing urinary excretion. High intakes of molybdenum and sulfate predispose to development of copper deficiency. Concentrations of molybdenum in milk of cows, goats and ewes reflect dietary intakes (Underwood, 1971).

IODINE

The only known role of iodine in animal physiology is that of an essential component of the thyroid hormones—thyroxin and triiodothyronine. The body of the human adult contains 10 to 20 mg of iodine, of which 70 to 80 per cent is concentrated in the thyroid gland (Underwood, 1971). Iodine not concentrated in the thyroid gland is distributed throughout the body in much the same manner as chloride, except for somewhat greater concentration in the salivary glands, the gastric glands and dense connective tissues.

Dietary Sources

The Chilean Iodine Educational Bureau (1952) reported average concentrations of iodine in human milk and cow milk to be 30 and 47 μg/liter, respectively. However, the iodine content of cow milk and, presumably, human milk reflects to a large extent the iodine content of the diet. Several investigators have demonstrated five- to tenfold increases in iodine content of cow milk as the result of iodine supplementation of the cow's diet. A difference in iodine content of cow milk between goitrous and nongoitrous regions of the Netherlands was reported by Binnerts (1954): The mean values were 9.7 and 21.1 μg/liter, respectively, for milk obtained in summer, and 20.6 and 83.5 μg/liter for milk obtained in winter. Seasonal variations in iodine content of cow milk were also noted by Broadhead et al. (1965), who reported a maximum of 200 μg/liter in March and April and a minimum of 10 μg/liter in August and September.

Colostrum is richer in iodine than is mature milk. Lewis and Ralston (1951) reported values of 200 to 350 μg/liter in cow colostrum and 72 to 136 μg/liter in mature cow milk. Similarly, Salter (1950) reported iodine concentrations of 50 to 240 μg/liter in human colostrum and 40 to 80 μg/liter in mature human milk.

As is true of milk, iodine content of many foods varies greatly from sample to sample. Iodine content of plants reflects iodine content of soil and fertilizers, and iodine content of animal products is related to iodine intake of animals. Residents of regions in which the soil is poor in iodine often are unable to obtain adequate intakes of iodine from food grown on that soil, even by judicious choice of foods. Rather, they must rely on iodine-rich marine foods or foods grown in iodine-rich regions or obtain iodine supplements such as iodized salt. As mentioned in Chapter 16, only one U.S. manufacturer (Gerber) adds iodized salt to commercially prepared strained and junior foods. However, many of these foods are grown in areas where adequate quantities of iodine are present in the soil.

Of particular significance as a source of iodine in food is the addition of iodate to commercial bread mix as a "dough conditioner" and as a component of several ingredients added during the "continuous mix process." This process accounted for about 43 per cent of white pan bread consumed in the United States in 1969 (Pittman et al., 1969). A single slice of such bread may provide as much as 150 μg of iodine (London et al., 1965; Pittman et al., 1969).

Requirement

Dietary requirements of iodine are difficult to estimate because of wide individual variability and because of the influence of other dietary components—especially other minerals and goitrogens—on iodine requirement. Elmer (1938) suggested that the requirement of the adult may be 100 to 200 μg/day, and Wayne et al. (1964) have suggested a requirement of 160 μg/day.

However, Malvaux et al. (1969) reported that nongoitrous Belgian children and adolescents consumed only about 32 μg/day. These individuals were in negative iodine balance (mean net loss approximately 24 μg/day), and the investigators hypothesized that occasional high intakes of iodine may have been responsible for the euthyroid state of these subjects. This hypothesis is attractive because North American adolescents with relatively high intakes of iodine (500 μg/day) have also been reported to be in negative iodine balance (Vought et al., 1967). From the data of Malvaux et al. (1969) one might speculate that the requirement for iodine by 8- to 16-year-old children may not be much greater than 56 μg/day (i.e., 32 μg/day intake plus 24 μg/day negative balance).

Presumably, the requirement for iodine for infants and preschool children is slightly less than that of school children. On this basis, one might conclude that the 40 to 80 μg of iodine/liter of mature human milk reported by Salter (1950) would provide an adequate intake of iodine for the fully breastfed infant. Similarly, the soy-isolate formula, ProSobee, which provides 70 μg/liter (65 μg/quart) appears to be nutritionally adequate.

Goitrogens

Many plants are known to contain substances (goitrogens) which produce thyroid enlargement in mammals by interfering with hormone synthesis. In some cases, the effect of the goitrogen can be reversed or at least modified by supplying additional iodine (Underwood, 1971).

Because soy-based foods are widely used for infant feeding in the United States and for feeding of preschool children in a number of other countries, the goitrogenic effects of soy are of particular interest. Results of studies with rats have been summarized by the Committee on Nutrition (1963): Enlargement of the thyroid gland develops when young rats are fed a diet of raw soy beans or of soy flour without additional intake of iodine. The goitrogenic effects of soy flour in rats can be diminished by treatment of the flour with organic solvents (presumably extracting some goitrogenic agent) or by heating, and rats are protected against the goitrogenic effect by supplementation of the diet with iodine.

As discussed in Chapter 15, several reports indicated that goiter sometimes developed in infants fed the soy flour formula, Mull-Soy, when this formula was not supplemented with iodine. The soy-isolate formulas currently marketed in the United States are fortified with iodine – ProSobee providing 70 μg/liter and Isomil and Neo-Mull-Soy providing 158 μg/liter.

SELENIUM

For some years it has been known that administration of selenium will prevent some but not all of the vitamin E deficiency diseases of laboratory and farm animals. These include muscular dystrophy of lambs, calves, foals, rabbits and marsupials; exudative diathesis of chicks; hepatosis dietetica of pigs; and poor growth of sheep and cattle (Underwood, 1971). More recently, Thompson and Scott (1969, 1970) have demonstrated that selenium is essential for normal growth of chicks even when the diet contains abundant quantities of α-tocopherol. One may speculate that the essentiality of selenium for growth of other animals will soon be demonstrated.

In the body, selenium concentrations are greatest in the kidney, particularly the kidney cortex, and in pancreas, pituitary and liver. However, selenium is found in all cells and tissues, the concentrations varying with the selenium content of the diet. In areas in which selenium content of the soil is low, cow milk may provide less than 5 μg of selenium/liter (Hadjimarkos and Bonhorst, 1961; Grant and Wilson, 1968), whereas cow milk in other areas may provide at least 10 times this concentration (Hadjimarkos and Bonhorst, 1961; Allaway et al., 1968). Concentrations of selenium in human milk were reported by Hadjimarkos (1963) and by Hadjimarkos and Shearer (1973) to range from 13 to 50 μg/liter.

Although selenium deficiency has not been demonstrated in human subjects, the suggestion has been made that selenium deficiency may be a complicating feature of kwashiorkor (Majaj and Hopkins, 1966; Burk et al., 1967).

Evidence has been presented by Hadjimarkos (1969) implicating selenium as a caries-enhancing agent. Consumption of selenium during the period of tooth development probably alters the chemical composition of the tooth, primarily in the protein components of enamel, making the tooth more susceptible to caries. Epidemiologic data indicate that caries prevalence in different geographic areas correlates with mean urinary excretion of selenium—the best index of dietary intake of available selenium. Studies of rats (Navia et al., 1968; Büttner, 1969) have demonstrated that inclusion of sodium selenite in drinking water during the time of tooth formation increased dental caries in proportion to the amount of selenium present in the water.

REFERENCES

Allaway, W. H., Kubota, J., Losee, F., and Roth, M.: Selenium, molybdenum, and vanadium in human blood. Arch. Environ. Health *16*:342, 1968.

Al-Rashid, R. A., and Spangler, J.: Neonatal copper deficiency. New Eng. J. Med. *285*:841, 1971.

Ashkenazi, A., Levin, S., Djaldetti, M., Fishel, E., and Benvenisti, D.: The syndrome of neonatal copper deficiency. Pediatrics *52*:525, 1973.

Belz, R.: Ijzer, koper, mangaan en kobalt in gemiddelde dietan van verschillende leeftijdsgroepen in Nederland. Voeding *21*:236, 1960.

Binnerts, W. T.: Goitre and the iodine content of cow's milk. Nature *174*:973, 1954.

Bradfield, R. B., Yee, T., and Baertl, J. M.: Hair zinc levels of Andean Indian children during protein-calorie malnutrition. Amer. J. Clin. Nutr. *22*:1349, 1969.

Broadhead, G. D., Pearson, I. B., and Wilson, G. M.: Seasonal changes in iodine metabolism. 1. Iodine content of cow's milk. Br. Med. J. *1*:343, 1965.

Burk, R. F., Jr., Pearson, W. N., Wood, R. P., II, and Viteri, F.: Blood-selenium levels and in vitro red blood cell uptake of ^{75}Se in kwashiorkor. Amer. J. Clin. Nutr. *20*:723, 1967.

Büttner, W.: Trace elements and dental caries in experiments on animals. Caries Res. *3*:1, 1969.

Carter, J. P., Kattab, A., Abd-El-Hadi, K., Davis, J. T., Gholmy, A. E., and Patwardhan, V. N.: Chromium (III) in hypoglycemia and in impaired glucose utilization in kwashiorkor. Amer. J. Clin. Nutr. *21*:195, 1968.

Cartwright, G. E., and Wintrobe, M. M.: Copper metabolism in normal subjects. Amer. J. Clin. Nutr. *14*:224, 1964a.

Cartwright, G. E., and Wintrobe, M. M.: The question of copper deficiency in man. Amer. J. Clin. Nutr. *15*:94, 1964b.

Chilean Iodine Educational Bureau: Iodine Content of Foods. London, Chilean Iodine Educational Bureau, 1952.

Committee on Nutrition: Appraisal of nutritional adequacy of infant formulas used as cow milk substitutes. Pediatrics *31*:329, 1963.

Cordano, A., Baertl, J. M., and Graham, G. G.: Copper deficiency in infancy. Pediatrics *34*:324, 1964.

Cordano, A., and Graham, G. G.: Copper deficiency complicating severe chronic intestinal malabsorption. Pediatrics *38*:596, 1966.

Cotzias, G. C.: Manganese in health and disease. Physiol Rev. *38*:503, 1958.

Danks, D. M., Campbell, P. E., Stevens, B. J., Mayne, V., and Cartwright, E.: Menkes's kinky hair syndrome: an inherited defect in copper absorption with widespread effects. Pediatrics *50*:188, 1972.

Dowdy, R. P.: Copper metabolism. Amer. J. Clin. Nutr. *22*:887, 1969.

Dudrick, S. J., and Rhoads, J. E.: New horizons for intravenous feeding. J.A.M.A. *215*:939, 1971.

Elmer, A. W.: Iodine Metabolism and Thyroid Function. London, Oxford University Press, 1938.

Evans, G. W.: Copper homeostasis in the mammalian system. Physiol. Rev. *53*:535, 1973.

Evans, G. W., Roginski, E. E., and Mertz, W.: Interaction of the glucose tolerance factor (GTF) with insulin. Biochem. Biophys. Res. Commun. *50*:718, 1973.

Everson, G. J., and Shrader, R. E.: Abnormal glucose tolerance in manganese-deficient guinea pigs. J. Nutr. *94*:89, 1968.

Frieden, E.: The ferrous to ferric cycles in iron metabolism. Nutr. Rev. *31*:41, 1973.

Glinsmann, W. H., and Mertz, W.: Effect of trivalent chromium on glucose tolerance. Metabolism *15*:510, 1966.

Graham, G. G., and Cordano, A.: Copper depletion and deficiency in the malnourished infant. Johns Hopkins Med. J. *124*:139, 1969.

Grant, A. B., and Wilson, G. F.: Selenium content of milk from cows given sodium selenate. New Zeal. J. Agric. Res. *11*:733, 1968.

Greaves, M. W., and Skillen, A. W.: Effects of long-continued ingestion of zinc sulphate in patients with venous leg ulceration. Lancet *2*:889, 1970.

Gürson, C. T., and Saner, G.: Effect of chromium on glucose utilization in marasmic protein-calorie malnutrition. Amer. J. Clin. Nutr. *24*:1313, 1971.

Hadjimarkos, D. M.: Selenium content of human milk: possible effect on dental caries. J. Pediatr. *63*:273, 1963.

Hadjimarkos, D. M.: Selenium: a caries-enhancing trace element. Caries Res. *3*:14, 1969.

Hadjimarkos, D. M., and Bonhorst, C. W.: The selenium content of eggs, milk, and water in relation to dental caries in children. J. Pediatr. *59*:256, 1961.

Hadjimarkos, D. M., and Shearer, T. R.: Selenium in mature human milk. Amer. J. Clin. Nutr. *26*:583, 1973.

Halsted, J. A.: Zinc deficiency and congenital malformations. Lancet *1*:1323, 1973.

Halsted, J. A., Ronaghy, H. A., Abadi, P., Haghshenass, M., Amirhakemi, G. H., Barakat, R. M., and Reinhold, J. G.: Zinc deficiency in man. Amer. J. Med. *53*:277, 1972.

Hambidge, K. M.: Chromium nutrition in the mother and the growing child. *In* Mertz, W., and Cornatzer, W. E. (eds.): Newer Trace Elements in Nutrition. New York, Marcel Dekker, 1971, p. 169.

Hambidge, K. M., and Baum, J. D.: Hair chromium concentrations of human newborn and changes during infancy. Amer. J. Clin. Nutr. *25*:376, 1972.

Hambidge, K. M., Franklin, M. L., and Jacobs, M. A.: Changes in hair chromium concentrations with increasing distances from hair roots. Amer. J. Clin. Nutr. *25*:380, 1972a.

Hambidge, K. M., Hambidge, C., Jacobs, M., and Baum, J. D.: Low levels of zinc in hair, anorexia, poor growth, and hypogeusia in children. Pediatr. Res. *6*:868, 1972b.

Henkin, R. I., Schulman, J. D., Schulman, C. B., and Bronzert, D. A.: Changes in total, nondiffusible, and diffusible plasma zinc and copper during infancy. J. Pediatr. *82*:831, 1973.

Hopkins, L. L., Jr., Ransome-Kuti, O., and Majaj, A. S.: Improvement of impaired carbohydrate metabolism by chromium (III) in malnourished infants. Amer. J. Clin. Nutr. *21*:203, 1968.

Hurley, L. S., and Mutch, P. B.: Prenatal and postnatal development after transitory gestational zinc deficiency in rats. J. Nutr. *103*:649, 1973.

Hurley, L. S., and Swenerton, H.: Congenital malformations resulting from zinc deficiency in rats. Proc. Soc. Exp. Biol. Med. *123*:692, 1966.

Karpel, J. T., and Peden, V. H.: Copper deficiency in long-term parenteral nutrition. J. Pediatr. *80*:32, 1972.

Kirchgessner, M.: Interactions between different elements in colostrum and milk. Z. Tierphysiol. *14*:270, 1959.

Klevay, L. M.: Hair as a biopsy material. I. Assessment of zinc nutriture. Amer. J. Clin. Nutr. *23*:284, 1970a.

Klevay, L. M.: Letter to the Editor. Hair as a biopsy material. Amer. J. Clin. Nutr. *23*:377, 1970b.

Leach, R. M., Jr., Muenster, A.-M., and Wien, E. M.: Studies on the role of manganese in bone formation. II. Effect upon chondroitin sulfate synthesis in chick epiphyseal cartilage. Arch. Biochem. Biophys. *133*:22, 1969.

Lehmann, B. H., Hansen, J. D. L., and Warren, P. J.: The distribution of copper, zinc and manganese in various regions of the brain and in other tissues of children with protein-calorie malnutrition. Br. J. Nutr. *26*:197, 1971.

Levine, R. A., Streeten, D. H. P., and Doisy, R. J.: Effects of oral chromium supplementation on the glucose tolerance of elderly human subjects. Metabolism *17*:114, 1968.

Lewis, R. C., and Ralston, N. P.: Protein-bound iodine levels in dairy cattle plasma. J. Dairy Sci. *36*:33, 1951.

London, W. T., Vought, R. L., and Brown, F. A.: Bread: a dietary source of large quantities of iodine. New Eng. J. Med. *273*:381, 1965.

Majaj, A. S., and Hopkins, L. L., Jr.: (Letter to the Editor.) Selenium and kwashiorkor. Lancet 2:592, 1966.

Malvaux, P., Beckers, C., and DeVisscher, M.: Iodine balance studies in nongoitrous children and in adolescents on low iodine intake. J. Clin. Endocr. Metab. *29*:79, 1969.

McLeod, B. E., and Robinson, M. F.: Dietary intake of manganese by New Zealand infants during the first six months of life. Br. J. Nutr. *27*:229, 1972.

Mertz, W.: Chromium occurrence and function in biological systems. Physiol. Rev. *49*:163, 1969.

Mertz, W., and Roginski, E. E.: Chromium metabolism: the glucose tolerance factor. *In* Mertz, W., and Cornatzer, W. E. (eds.): Newer Trace Elements in Nutrition. New York, Marcel Dekker, 1971, p. 123.

Mildvan, A. S., Scrutton, M. C., and Utter, M. F.: Pyruvate carboxylase. VII. A possible role for tightly bound manganese. J. Biol. Chem. *241*:3488, 1966.

Navia, J. M., Menaker, L., Seltzer, J., and Harris, R. S.: Effect of Na_2SeO_3 supplemented in the diet or the water on dental caries of rats. Fed. Proc. *27*:676, 1968.

Osaki, S., Johnson, D. A., and Frieden, E.: The mobilization of iron from the perfused mammalian liver by a serum copper enzyme, ferroxidase I. J. Biol. Chem. *246*:3018, 1971.

Parisi, A. F., and Vallee, B. L.: Zinc metalloenzymes: characteristics and significance in biology and medicine. Amer. J. Clin. Nutr. *22*:1222, 1969.

Pennington, J. T., and Calloway, D. H.: Copper content of foods. J. Amer. Diet. Ass. *63*:143, 1973.

Pittman, J. A., Jr., Dailey, G. E., III, and Beschi, R. J.: Changing normal values for thyroidal radioiodine uptake. New Eng. J. Med. *280*:1431, 1969.

Pories, W. J., Henzel, J. H., Rob, C. G., and Strain, W. H.: Acceleration of wound healing in man with zinc sulphate given by mouth. Lancet *1*:121, 1967.

Prasad, A. S.: Nutritional metabolic role of zinc. Fed. Proc. *26*:172, 1967.

Prasad, A. S., Halsted, J. A., and Nadimi, M.: Syndrome of iron deficiency anemia, hepatosplenomegaly, hypogonadism, dwarfism, and geophagia. Amer. J. Med. *31*:532, 1961.

Prasad, A. S., Miale, A., Farid, Z., Sandstead, H. H., Schulert, A. R., and Darby, W. J.: Biochemical studies on dwarfism, hypogonadism, and anemia. Arch. Intern. Med. *111*:407, 1963.

Prasad, A. S., Oberleas, D., Wolf, P., Horwitz, J. P., Miller, E. R., and Luecke, R. W.: Changes in trace elements and enzyme activities in tissues of zinc-deficient pigs. Amer. J. Clin. Nutr. *22*:628, 1969.

Price, N. O., Bunce, G. E., and Engel, R. W.: Copper, manganese, and zinc balance in preadolescent girls. Amer. J. Clin. Nutr. *23*:258, 1970.

Reinhold, J. G., Nasr, K., Lahimgarzadeh, A., and Hedayati, H.: Effects of purified phytate and phytate-rich bread upon metabolism of zinc, calcium, phosphorus, and nitrogen in man. Lancet *1*:283, 1973.

Robinson, H. C., Telser, A., and Dorfman, A.: Studies on biosynthesis of the linkage region of chondroitin sulfate-protein complex. Proc. Nat. Acad. Sci. USA *56*:1859, 1966.

Salter, W. T.: The chemistry and physiology of the thyroid hormone. *In* Pincus, G., and Thimann, K. V. (eds.): The Hormones: Physiology, Chemistry and Applications. Vol. 2. New York, Academic Press, 1950, p. 181.

Sandstead, H. H.: Zinc nutrition in the United States. Amer. J. Clin. Nutr. *26*:1251, 1973.

Sandstead, H. H., Gillespie, D. D., and Brady, R. N.: Zinc deficiency: effect on brain of the suckling rat. Pediatr. Res. *6*:119, 1972.

Sandstead, H. H., Lanier, V. C., Shephard, G. H., and Gillespie, D. D.: Zinc and wound healing. Effects of zinc deficiency and zinc supplementation. Amer. J. Clin. Nutr. *23*:514, 1970.

Sandstead, H. H., Prasad, A. S., Schulert, A. R., Farid, Z., Miale, A., Bassilly, S., and Darby, W. J.: Human zinc deficiency, endocrine manifestations and response to treatment. Amer. J. Clin. Nutr. *20*:422, 1967.

Schaller, K.-H., Essing, H.-G., Valentin, H., and Schäcke, G.: Quantitative Chrombestimmung im Harn mit flammenloser Atomabsorptions – Spektrometrie. Z. Klin. Chem. *10*:434, 1972.

Scheinberg, I. H.: Copper metabolism. IV. Applications of chelating agents in medicine. Fed. Proc. *20*(Suppl. 10):179, 1961.

Schlage, C., and Wortberg, B.: Manganese in the diet of healthy preschool and school children. Acta Paediatr. Scand. *61*:648, 1972a.

Schlage, C., and Wortberg, B.: Zinc in the diet of healthy preschool and school children. Acta Paediatr. Scand. *61*:421, 1972b.

Schroeder, H. A., Balassa, J. J., and Tipton, I. H.: Abnormal trace elements in man: chromium. J. Chron. Dis. *15*:941, 1962.

Schroeder, H. A., Nason, A. P., and Tipton, I. H.: Chromium deficiency as a factor in atherosclerosis. J. Chron. Dis. *23*:123, 1970.

Schubert, W. K., and Lahey, M. E.: Copper and protein depletion complicating hypoferric anemia of infancy. Pediatrics *24*:710, 1959.

Schwarz, K.: Tin as an essential growth factor for rats. *In* Mertz, W., and Cornatzer, W. E. (eds.): Newer Trace Elements in Nutrition. New York, Marcel Dekker, 1971, p. 313.

Seelig, M. S.: Review: relationships of copper and molybdenum to iron metabolism. Amer. J. Clin. Nutr. *25*:1022, 1972.

Seely, J. R., Humphrey, G. B., and Matter, B. J.: Copper deficiency in a premature infant fed an iron-fortified formula. New Eng. J. Med. *286*:109, 1972.

Serjeant, G. R., Galloway, R. E., and Gueri, M.: Oral zinc sulphate in sickle-cell ulcers. Lancet *2*:891, 1970.

Sever, L. E.: (Letter to the Editor.) Zinc deficiency in man. Lancet *1*:887, 1973.

Shrader, R. E., and Everson, G. J.: Anomalous development of otoliths associated with postural defects in manganese-deficient guinea pigs. J. Nutr. *91*:453, 1967.

Smith, J. C., Jr., McDaniel, E. G., Fan, F. F., and Halsted, J. A.: Zinc: a trace element essential in vitamin A metabolism. Science *181*:954, 1973.

Sturgeon, P., and Brubaker, C.: Copper deficiency in infants: a syndrome characterized by hypocupremia, iron deficiency anemia, and hypoproteinemia. Amer. J. Dis. Child. 92:254, 1956.

Thompson, J. N., and Scott, M. L.: Role of selenium in the nutrition of the chick. J. Nutr. 97:335, 1969.

Thompson, J. N., and Scott, M. L.: Impaired lipid and vitamin E absorption related to atrophy of the pancreas in selenium-deficient chicks. J. Nutr. *100*:797, 1970.

Tipton, I. H., and Cook, M. J.: Trace elements in human tissue. Part II. Adult subjects from the United States. Health Phys. 9:103, 1963.

Underwood, E. J.: Trace Elements in Human and Animal Nutrition. 3rd ed. New York, Academic Press, 1971.

Vought, R. L., London, W. T., and Stebbing, G. E. T.: Endemic goiter in northern Virginia. J. Clin. Endocr. Metab. 27:1381, 1967.

Wayne, E. J., Koutras, D. A., and Alexander, W. D.: Clinical Aspects of Iodine Metabolism. Oxford, Blackwell, 1964.

Widdowson, E. M.: Trace elements in human development. *In* Barltrop, D., and Burland, W. L. (eds.): Mineral Metabolism in Paediatrics. Oxford, Blackwell, 1969, p. 85.

Widdowson, E. M., Chan, H., Harrison, G. E., and Milner, R. D. G.: Accumulation of Cu, Zn, Mn, Cr and Co in the human liver before birth. Biol. Neonat. *20*:360, 1972.

Widdowson, E. M., and Dickerson, J. W. T.: Chemical composition of the body. *In* Comar, C. L., and Bronner, F. (eds.): Mineral Metabolism. Vol. II, Part A, Chapter 17. New York and London, Academic Press, 1964, p. 1.

Widdowson, E. M., McCance, R. A., and Spray, C. M.: The chemical composition of the human body. Clin. Sci. *10*:113, 1951.

Wilson, J. F., and Lahey, M. E.: Failure to induce dietary deficiency of copper in premature infants. Pediatrics 25:40, 1960.

Zipursky, A., Dempsey, H., Markowitz, H., Cartwright, G., and Wintrobe, M. M.: Studies on copper metabolism. XXIV. Hypocupremia in infancy. Amer. J. Dis. Child. 96:148, 1958.

14

NUTRITIONAL ASPECTS OF DENTAL CARIES

Stephen H. Y. Wei

In most respects, the nutritional needs for maintaining health of the mouth and teeth are similar to those for the remainder of the body. For example, deficiency of vitamin A may interfere with normal tooth development and deficiency of ascorbic acid may adversely affect both the teeth and oral soft tissues. Adequate intake of calcium and phosphorus are clearly necessary for normal tooth development. In addition to those aspects of nutritional health that apply to the entire body, a number of considerations are particularly relevant to nutritional measures aimed at the prevention of dental caries. Pediatricians and nutritionists appear to be increasingly interested in the role of sucrose, other carbohydrates, fluoride and phosphates in the prevention of dental caries. An attempt will be made in this chapter to review information on these topics as they pertain to nutritional management of the infant and young preschool child.

Dental caries consists of localized, progressive decay of the teeth, initiated by demineralization of the outer surface of the tooth due to organic acids produced locally by bacteria that ferment deposits of dietary carbohydrates (Scherp, 1971).

Thus, dental caries is a multifactorial disease requiring the presence of a susceptible tooth, oral environment and diet conducive to enamel demineralization, and the presence of cariogenic microflora. The modern diet is undoubtedly a major factor in the etiology of dental caries; however, genetic and nutritional factors during tooth development may influence the susceptibility of the teeth to dental caries.

STAGES OF TOOTH DEVELOPMENT

Although it is apparent that local factors within the mouth cannot directly affect the tooth until it has erupted, the importance of understanding other aspects of dental development may be less evident. As an example, one may consider the advisability of prescribing fluoride for pregnant women in order to provide fluoride for incorporation in the teeth of the fetus. Although the extent of transmission of fluoride across the placenta is a matter of some controversy (Zipkin and Babeaux, 1965), this controversy is of little importance, since the stage of tooth development in utero has not reached a point at which fluoride could be of much value. Almost all of the most caries-susceptible areas of the primary dentition are calcified after birth (Kraus and Jordan, 1965).

Table 14–1 indicates the gestational age at which hard tissue begins to form in the primary (deciduous) teeth, the amount of enamel present at birth, the age at which enamel formation is completed, the age of eruption of the teeth and the age at which root formation is completed. The areas of the teeth most susceptible to caries – the occlusal fissures, proximal surfaces, gingival buccal and gingival lingual areas – calcify after birth.

An early tooth bud consists of tall, columnar epithelial cells called ameloblasts, which are of ectodermal origin and form the dental enamel. The odontoblasts, on the other hand, are mesodermal in origin and form the bulk of tooth, called dentin. Most of the investing and supporting structures of the tooth, including the dental pulp, are of mesodermal origin (Sicher and Bhaskar, 1972). When teeth first erupt into the mouth, the enamel is relatively immature. Considerable mineralization continues to take place immediately after eruption, modifying surface hardness and mineral density (Shaw, 1970). Saliva possesses physical and chemical properties that promote the post-eruptive maturation of the enamel by a process of remineralization Koulourides, 1966; Wei, 1967; Ericsson, 1968; Briner et al., 1971; Wei and Koulourides, 1972).

That many of the permanent teeth begin to form hard tissue during the early months of life may be seen from Table 14–2. Sound nutrition during this period and throughout childhood is important for development of the permanent dentition. However, nutritional measures to protect the primary teeth against caries must also receive attention.

Primary teeth are equally important for the young child for adequate mastication, formation of correct speech habits, and normal emotional and social development. Furthermore, premature loss of primary teeth, particularly the molars, is a common cause of unnecessary malocclusion of the permanent dentition in later years due to loss of length of the dental arch and faulty alignment of teeth. Severe abscesses in primary teeth due to advanced dental caries may produce

TABLE 14–1 STAGES OF DEVELOPMENT OF PRIMARY TEETH*

Tooth	Gestational Age Hard Tissue Formation Begins (months)	Amount of Enamel Present at Birth	Age Enamel Completed (months)	Age of Eruption (months)	Age Root Completed (years)
Maxillary					
Central incisor	4	Five-sixths	1½	7½	1½
Lateral incisor	4½	Two-thirds	2½	9	2
Cuspid	5	One-third	9	18	3¼
Fist molar	5	Cusps united	6	14	2½
Second molar	6	Cusp tips still isolated	11	24	3
Mandibular					
Central incisor	4½	Three-fifths	2½	6	1½
Lateral incisor	4½	Three-fifths	3	7	1½
Cuspid	5	One-third	9	16	3¼
First molar	5	Cusps united	5½	12	2¼
Second molar	6	Cusp tips still isolated	10	20	3

*Modified from Massler, M., and Schour, I.: Atlas of the Mouth in Health and Disease. 2nd ed. Chicago, American Dental Association, 1958. Copyright by the American Dental Association. Reprinted by permission.

TABLE 14–2 STAGES OF DEVELOPMENT OF PERMANENT TEETH*

TOOTH	HARD TISSUE FORMATION BEGINS†	ENAMEL COMPLETED (YEARS)	ERUPTION (YEARS)	ROOT COMPLETED (YEARS)
Maxillary				
Central incisor	3 – 4mo	4 – 5	7– 8	10
Lateral incisor	10 –12 mo	4 – 5	8– 9	11
Cuspid	4 – 5 mo	6 – 7	11–12	13–15
First bicuspid	1½– 1¾ yr	5 – 6	10–11	12–13
Second bicuspid	2 – 2¼ yr	6 – 7	10–12	12–14
First molar	at birth	2½– 3	7– 7	9–10
Second molar	2½– 3 yr	7 – 8	12–13	14–16
Third molar	7 – 9 yr	12 –16	17–21	18–25
Mandibular				
Central incisor	3 – 4 mo	4 – 5	6– 7	9
Lateral incisor	3 – 4 mo	4 – 5	7– 8	10
Cuspid	4 – 5 mo	6 – 7	9–10	12–14
First bicuspid	1¾– 2 yr	5 – 6	10–12	12–13
Second bicuspid	2¼– 2½ yr	6 – 7	11–12	13–14
First molar	at birth	2½– 3	6– 7	9–10
Second molar	2½– 3 yr	7 – 8	11–13	14–15
Third molar	8 –10 yr	12 –16	17–21	18–25

*Modified from Massler, M., and Schour, I.: Atlas of the Mouth in Health and Disease. 2nd ed. Chicago, American Dental Association, 1958. Copyright by the American Dental Association. Reprinted by permission.

†Enamel formation of the permanent teeth has usually not begun at birth.

localized hypoplastic defects of the enamel in the permanent dentition. The younger the age when abscesses occur, the higher the risk of damage to the permanent dentition. Severe hypoplastic lesions of the enamel of the permanent anterior teeth usually are esthetically objectionable and require costly dental treatment.

PREVALENCE OF DENTAL CARIES

Dental caries is one of the most prevalent diseases of children, and numerous epidemiologic surveys have shown that it affects almost 100 per cent of the population. Army surveys indicate that every 100 inductees require 600 fillings, 112 extractions, 40 bridges, 21 crowns, 18 partial dentures and one full denture (Scherp, 1971).

Nutritional surveys continue to find dental caries to be the most prevalent disease for all age groups beyond infancy (Committee on Nutrition, 1972). By age 10, more than 80 per cent of children have dental caries of permanent teeth (Fulton, 1951; Parfitt, 1954; Barnard, 1956; Downer, 1970; Palmer, 1971). By the time half the number of permanent teeth have erupted, the average child in the United States has 6.2 decayed, missing or filled teeth.

Prevalence of dental caries among infants and young preschool children has been determined in various localities of the United States (Fulton, 1952; Savara and Suher, 1954; Wisan et al., 1957; Hennon et al., 1969), Canada (Gray and Hawk, 1967), Sweden (Nord, 1965), United Kingdom (Timmis, 1971; Beal and James, 1971; Winter et al., 1971), Hungary (Toth and Szabó, 1959), Australia (Halikis, 1963), New Zealand (Hewat et al., 1952; Hollis, 1970) and several other countries. With few exceptions, it appears that at least one-fourth of two-year-old children and approximately two-thirds of three-year-old children have dental caries. In communities in Indiana without fluoridated drinking water, Hennon et al. (1969) reported an average of 4.65 decayed, filled or missing teeth among three-year-old children with dental caries.

CARBOHYDRATES

On the basis of studies with experimental animals (Guggenheim et al., 1966; Guggenheim and Schroeder, 1967; Keyes, 1968; Fitzgerald and Jordan, 1968; Fitzgerald, 1968) and human subjects (Edwardsson, 1968; Krasse, 1968; König, 1968; Keyes, 1969), the cariogenicity of various sugars has been rated as follows (in decreasing order of cariogenicity): sucrose, glucose, maltose, lactose, fructose, sorbitol and xylitol.

Most investigators believe that sucrose is most cariogenic for the human (Newbrun, 1969). However, in some animal studies sucrose was not found to be substantially more cariogenic than other sugars (Keyes and Jordan, 1964; Grenby and Hutchinson, 1969). Although some temporary reduction in the prevalence of dental caries might result from replacement of sucrose by other nutritive sugars, such as glucose or fructose, it is possible that the microorganisms would eventurally adapt metabolically to the new sugars and that the caries attack rate would then increase (Mäkinen, 1972a).

At present, sugarless chewing gum commonly contains sorbitol. A number of other non-nutritive sweetening agents hold promise as replacements for sucrose and considerable research is underway in this area (Newbrun, 1973).

Evidence for Cariogenicity of Sucrose

The cariogenicity of sucrose has been clearly demonstrated in studies of experimental animals (Krasse, 1965; Guggenheim et al., 1966; Bowen and Cornick, 1967). Animal studies also indicate that a local effect of the sugar is necessary and that sucrose is not cariogenic when administered by gavage (Kite et al., 1950; Orland et al., 1954).

A variety of epidemiologic studies have demonstrated the relation between sucrose consumption and dental caries in human subjects. Notable among these is the significant decrease in the dental caries rate among school children in occupied countries during the second half of World War II and the return of the caries rate to prewar levels after the war. These changes in caries rate coincided with the wide availability of sucrose before and after the war and its relative unavailability during the second half of the war (Sognnaes, 1948, 1949; Toverud, 1949; Toverud et al., 1961). Few well controlled clinical studies are available. Gustafsson et al. (1954) demonstrated that consumption of sucrose in sticky form increased the dental caries rate and that the rate fell once such consumption was terminated.

Additional evidence of the cariogenicity of sucrose is provided by observations of patients with the metabolic disorder, hereditary fructose intolerance (Chapter 8). Because sucrose is hydrolyzed to glucose and fructose, and because patients with this metabolic disorder develop vomiting when exposed to fructose, they learn to avoid any food that contains fructose or sucrose. Of 11 patients for whom detailed dental descriptions are available, five were found to be completely free of caries whereas in a random sample of nearly 5000 Navy recruits, only one was found to be caries-free (Newbrun, 1969). Case reports concerning patients with hereditary fructose intolerance have called attention to the excellent condition of the teeth even when detailed dental descriptions were not included.

Mechanism of Cariogenicity of Sucrose

The role of sucrose and other sugars in the development of dental caries has been reviewed by Mäkinen (1972b). Cariogenic streptococci within the mouth anaerobically metabolize sucrose to glucose and fructose, from which long-chain polymers of glucose (dextrans) or fructose (levans) are formed, thereby contributing to formation of plaques on the teeth. These gelatinous, sticky plaques protect the acids produced by cariogenic microbes from the buffering effect of saliva. Fructose enters the bacterial cell and is metabolized and synthesized into glycogen, which is stored intracellularly. Some fructose may also be converted into levans. Demineralization of the enamel is caused by lactic acid, the metabolic byproduct of fructose and levan.

CARIES-INHIBITING FOODS AND FOOD COMPONENTS

In vitro experiments suggest that cow milk is not cariogenic and, in fact, may have a protective effect against the action of sucrose and other cariogenic foods (Jenkins and Ferguson, 1966; Weiss and Bibby, 1966). The addition of cheese to bread has been reported to reduce the cariogenicity of bread fed to experimental animals (König, 1967). The mechanism by which milk or cheese might exert cariostatic effects remains unknown. Jenkins and Ferguson (1966) have suggested that the calcium and phosphate of these foods may suppress enamel demineralization through a common ion effect. The casein in milk may also reduce enamel solubility. A number of possible relationships between foods and dental caries have been suggested (Nikiforuk, 1970; Bibby, 1970). Some fibrous foods (e.g., apple, celery, carrot) have been alleged to have detergent cleansing action and therefore to reduce dental caries by physical and mechanical cleansing actions that remove stagnated soft foods (Caldwell, 1970). This is an important area for future research.

It is possible that antibacterial or other caries-inhibiting factors present in foods may be lost during the refining process (Jenkins, 1966, 1968, 1970). For instance, oat hulls appear to be cariostatic for rats (Taketa and Phillips, 1957; Buttner and Muhler, 1959; McClure, 1964), probably owing to the presence of certain polyphenols. In addition, refining of grains removes some of the phytate. Such removal may have a desirable effect in relation to mineral balance during infancy but, because phytates may be caries-inhibiting (McClure, 1960, 1963; Lilienthal et al., 1966; Grenby, 1967a, b, c; Englander and Keyes, 1970; Magrill, 1973), it may be undesirable with respect to prevention of dental caries. Until we know more about the influence of phytates on mineral balance of infants and young preschool children, it would seem unwise to recommend diets high in phytate content.

Phosphates

It is possible that grains with relatively high phytate content, as well as milk and cheese, may exert a cariostatic effect by virtue of their content of phosphorus. The presence of phosphates in the diet results in a significant decrease in dental caries in rodents (Nizel and Harris, 1964). Most studies have been conducted with inorganic phosphates, and it is evident that these differ in cariostatic activity (McClure, 1963). Sodium trimetaphosphate appears to be most effective (Navia, 1972). The mechanism by which phosphates exert their cariostatic effect is not well understood but presumably is local rather than systemic (Scherp, 1971; Luoma et al., 1972; Larson et al., 1972).

Although the cariostatic effectiveness of inorganic phosphates appears to be established in studies of rodents, it is much less certain that they are effective under the conditions of infant or child feeding.

Favorable effects of clinical trials have been reported by a number of investigators (Strålfors, 1964; Stookey et al., 1967; Carroll et al., 1968; Brewer et al., 1970) but no significant effect has been found by others (Ship and Mickelsen, 1964; Averill and Bibby, 1964; Peterson, 1969).

Some evidence suggests that administration of inorganic phosphates potentiates the cariostatic effect of fluorides (Navia and Harris, 1969; Esposito, 1971; Gonzalez, 1971).

The cariostatic effect of two organic phosphates, in addition to phytate, has been examined. Studies of rats (Lilienthal et al., 1966) and of children 5 to 17 years of age in Australia (Harris et al., 1967, 1968) have suggested that calcium sucrose phosphate is effective in reducing the dental caries rate. The benefit obtained from calcium sucrose phosphate is additive to that of water fluoridation (Rogerson, 1973). Grenby (1973), although unable to confirm in rats the cariostatic effect of calcium sucrose phosphate, demonstrated a positive effect of calcium glycerophosphate.

At present it seems reasonable to conclude that both inorganic and organic phosphates are promising cariostatic agents, but much further study will be required before their usefulness in management of infants and preschool children can be determined.

NURSING BOTTLE SYNDROME

As early as 1862, Jacobi called attention to the association of dental caries with the practice of offering milk or water with sugar at bedtime (Finn, 1969). Several authors have suggested that the lactose of milk might be cariogenic under circumstances of bedtime feeding when sucking and swallowing are infrequent, when milk remains in the mouth for a relatively long time and when salivary flow is minimal (Fass, 1962). Little direct evidence on this point is available. On the other hand, it seems most likely that milk with added carbohydrate or a sugared pacifier at bedtime, after the age of eruption of the teeth, will promote dental caries (Syrrist and Selander, 1953; Winter et al., 1966; Robinson and Naylor, 1963; Kroll and Stone, 1967; Beaver, 1972). One can only assume that the practice of many American families of providing a bottle of Kool-Aid or sweetened fruit juice as a pacifier day and night represents a serious insult to an infant's teeth.

What pedodontists have referred to as "the nursing bottle syndrome" is characterized by the destruction of the maxillary anterior teeth, particularly the interproximal and labial surfaces. The destruction of the teeth is usually extensive and often the entire crowns may be destroyed (Fig. 14–1). Caries may extend to the maxillary and mandibular molars. Most often, the mandibular incisors are free of caries.

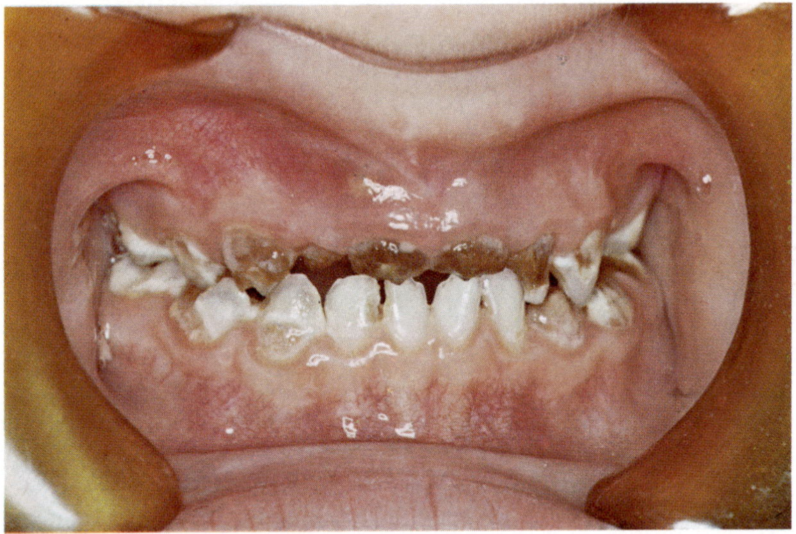

Figure 14–1 Mouth of two-year-old boy with "nursing bottle syndrome," demonstrating extensive carious destruction of the maxillary anterior primary teeth. The mandibular teeth are affected to a lesser extent, probably because of the position of the tongue in relation to the nursing nipple and the protective bathing action of saliva from submandibular and sublingual salivary glands. (Photograph courtesy of Dr. J. R. Pinkham.)

EATING BETWEEN MEALS

As discussed in Chapter 2, not only the diet and the amount of food consumed but the frequency of eating is nutritionally important. In this instance, it appears that frequent small meals may be desirable from the viewpoint of general nutrition, whereas larger, less frequent meals are desirable with respect to prevention of dental caries. Considerable evidence exists that between-meal snacks are conducive to development of dental caries (Zita et al., 1959; Weiss and Trithart, 1960), and one may presume that it is the carbohydrate component of the snacks, especially the sucrose content, that is primarily responsible for the development of caries.

Rather than attempting to eliminate between-meal eating by small children, it seems desirable to offer snacks that are low in content of disaccharides and monosaccharides. Foods to be avoided are sugar, honey, corn syrup, candies, jellies, jams, cookies, cakes, chewing gum and sweetened beverages, including carbonated drinks, Kool-Aid and synthetic orange drinks. In particular, it seems reasonable to avoid consumption of sticky candies. Foods that may be permitted are fresh fruits and vegetables, breads, crackers, peanut butter, cheese, meat, whole and "2 per cent" milk.

It is also probably unrealistic to recommend the total elimination of sweets for all children. Keyes (1969) has suggested that a satisfactory compromise may be to limit intake to "all the sweets you wish *once* a day," but many dentists would restrict such intake of sweets to once a week.

FLUORIDE

There is no doubt that adequate incorporation of fluoride in teeth, particularly in the outer layers of the enamel, increases resistance of teeth to caries (Scherp, 1971). Consumption of fluoridated water (0.7 to 1.2 mg of fluoride per liter of water) throughout life reduces the dental caries attack rate by 50 to 60 per cent in permanent teeth (McClure, 1962; Dunning, 1965; Backer Dirks, 1967; Nizel, 1972) and slightly less in primary teeth (Scherp, 1971). Figure 14–2 indicates the influence of fluoride content of drinking water on prevalence of dental caries. It seems possible that the lesser protection provided for primary than for permanent teeth results from the relatively low intake of

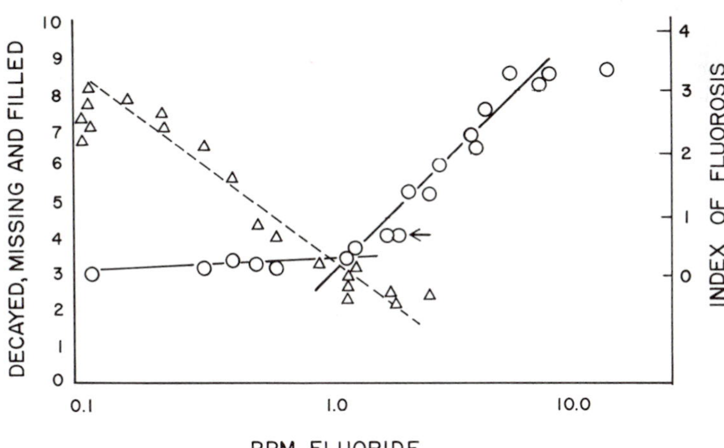

Figure 14–2 The relationship between fluoride content of drinking water, average number of decayed, missing and filled teeth (left-hand ordinate), and index of fluorosis (right-hand ordinate). Each triangle applies to observations concerning decayed, missing and filled teeth in children in one community. Each open circle concerns the index of fluorosis in one community. The arrow indicates the communities of Galesburg (*left*) and Elmhurst (*right*), which are mentioned in the text. (Modified from Hodge, H. C., and Smith, F. A.: Some public health aspects of water fluoridation. *In* Shaw, J. H. (ed.): Fluoridation as a Public Health Measure. Washington, D.C., American Association for the Advancement of Science, 1954, p. 79.)

fluoride by many infants living in communities where drinking water is fluoridated.

In the United States in 1972, 170,000,000 people used public water supplies and about 100,000,000 (60 per cent) of these individuals received water supplies that were fluoridated either naturally (6.5 per cent) or artificially (53.3 per cent) (Small, 1973). Thus, one may assume that less than one-half of the population of the United States received desirable intakes of fluoride from any source. In most other countries, an even smaller percentage of the population receives desirable intakes of fluoride from water. Few foods are rich sources of fluoride (Waldbott, 1963; Bell et al., 1970) and, as has already been suggested, the fluoride content of the water supply may be of relatively little advantage to infants who consume little tap water. Fluoride has been added to milk, table salt and flour as alternate methods of supplementation in several European countries (Held, 1955; Marthaler, 1967, 1972a and b; Toth, 1973). Although these dietary means have been found to be partially successful, they have practical and economic disadvantages compared to the fluoridation of water (Backer Dirks, 1967).

Mechanism of Action of Fluoride

The most widely accepted theory for the effectiveness of fluoride in decreasing dental caries concerns conversion of the enamel mineral, hydroxyapatite, to fluorapatite with a consequent reduction in acid solubility (Newbrun, 1972). However, other mechanisms may also play a part (Jenkins, 1967). The rather modest reduction of solubility in acid of fluorapatite over hydroxyapatite does not seem to explain the large reduction in development of caries (Gray et al., 1962). Other workers have suggested that the presence of fluoride during the formation of hydroxyapatite promoted larger, less soluble and more perfect crystals (Posner et al., 1963). Even in exceedingly small amounts, fluoride enhances the rate of remineralization of enamel (Koulourides, 1966; Wei, 1967; Wei and Koulourides, 1972) and this may be a further factor in caries resistance. Other possible mechanisms include suppression of metabolic activities of the offending oral bacteria (Dawes et al., 1965; Jenkins et al., 1969) or interference with the ability of the microorganisms to form plaque (Sandham and Kleinberg, 1970).

Fluoride may also exert an effect on the morphology of teeth so that the improved morphology (e.g., shallower pits and grooves on molars) may lead to reduction in food stagnation and better cleansing by the toothbrush (Kruger, 1962; Paynter and Grainger, 1956; Cooper and Ludwig, 1965).

Fluoride Intake from Milk or Formula

Although fluoride concentration of human milk was previously believed to be as high as 0.2 mg/liter (Hodge et al., 1970), more recent data suggest that concentrations are less than 0.05 mg/liter (Ericsson, 1969; Armstrong et al., 1970; Ericsson and Ribelius, 1970; Ericsson et al., 1972; Backer Dirks et al., 1974). Fluoride concentration of human milk does not appear to be appreciably greater in areas where water is fluoridated than in areas where it is not fluoridated (Ericcson and Ribelius, 1970).

Fluoride content of cow milk ranges from 0.03 to 0.1 mg/liters (Ericsson and Ribelius, 1970; Backer Dirks et al., 1974). Estimated concentrations of fluoride in milks or formulas in communities with various concentrations of fluoride in water have been summarized by Ericsson and Ribelius (1970). As may be seen from Table 14–3, milk or formula mixed with fluoridated water yielded much greater concentrations of fluoride than did human milk or cow milk.

One may assume that fluoride concentration of a formula made from equal parts of concentrated liquid formula (133 kcal/100 ml) and water will be quite similar to that made with equal parts of cow milk and water (Table 14–3). Ready-to-feed infant formulas (67 kcal/100 ml) will provide fluoride concentrations similar to those of undiluted cow milk. These considerations are important in recommending dosage of fluoride when it is to be administered as a single daily dose.

Fluorosis

Among eight- to nine-year-old children in Uppsala (natural fluoride content of water 1.2 mg/liter), the extent of fluorosis was not

TABLE 14–3 ESTIMATED AVERAGE FLUORIDE CONTENT OF MILKS AND FORMULAS USED IN SWEDEN*

	Fluoride Concentration (mg/liter)	
Food	*Water*	*Feeding*
Human milk		0.025
Cow milk		0.03
Cow milk and water (1:1)†	0.1	0.06
	1.0	0.52
	5.0	2.52
Powdered formula‡ and water (1:6)†	0.1	0.17
	1.0	1.07
	5.0	5.07

*Modified from Ericsson, Y., and Ribelius, U.: Increased fluoride ingestion by bottle-fed infants and its effect. Acta Paediatr. Scand. 59:424, 1970.

†Proportions by weight.

‡Fluoride content 0.40 mg/kg.

found to be significantly different for 131 children who had been fully breastfed for five months than for 129 children who had received powdered formulas. Intakes of fluoride during the first five months may be estimated to have been at least 50 times greater by the formula-fed infants. However, the portion of exfoliated primary teeth formed while infants were fed the powdered formulas contained only two to three times the concentration of fluoride present in enamel formed before birth or that in the teeth of infants who had been breastfed (Ericsson, 1973). Examination of 10 children who had received powdered formulas in Billesholm (natural fluoride content of water 5 mg/liter) demonstrated dental fluorosis in only two, and these had limited fluorosis of the enamel of deciduous second molars (Ericsson and Ribelius, 1971).

These observations suggest that a considerable margin of safety exists with respect to fluoride ingestion during infancy. Nevertheless, until more extensive data are available pertaining to longer periods of observation, it seems desirable to restrict fluoride intakes during infancy to approximately 0.5 mg daily.

The effect of high fluoride content of drinking water on development of fluorosis with long-term exposure is well recognized. Dean (1942) developed a numerical index for rating the degree of fluorosis in permanent teeth. This index was based on examinations of 5824 white children in 22 cities in 10 states. An indication of the relation of the fluorosis index to clinical observations concerning mottled enamel is provided by several examples.

In Lubbock, Texas, where fluoride concentration of the drinking water was 4.4 ppm, examination of 189 9- to 12-year-old children demonstrated that 46.0 per cent had moderate and 17.9 per cent had severe dental fluorosis; the fluorosis index was 2.7. In the communities of Galesburg and Elmhurst, Illinois, with natural fluoride content of drinking water 1.9 and 1.8 ppm, respectively, the indices of fluorosis were 0.69 and 0.68, respectively. More than 1 per cent of the 443 children in these communities had moderate fluorosis. Dean stated, "For public health administrative guidance an index of dental fluorosis of 0.4 or less is of no concern from the standpoint of mottled enamel *per se*; when, however, the index rises above 0.6 it begins to constitute a public health problem warranting increasing consideration." Small (1973) has concluded that communities where fluoride concentration of drinking water is 1.6 ppm or less may be expected to demonstrate fluorosis indices of 0.6 or less.

Figure 14–2 is modified from Hodge and Smith (1954). This figure indicates the number of decayed, missing and filled teeth in various communities in relation to the fluoride concentration of drinking water in those communities. In addition, the data of Dean (1942) on index of fluorosis in relation to the fluoride concentration of drinking water are included.

Single Daily Dose of Fluoride

That single daily dosage of fluoride in drop or tablet form reduces the caries attack rate has been adequately demonstrated (O'Meara, 1968; Stookey, 1970). However, it is unlikely that fluoride administered once daily will be as effective as the same quantity of fluoride obtained in small amounts from water throughout the day. The reduced benefit is related to the rapid excretion of fluoride by the body mostly in the urine during the first two hours after ingestion (McClure, 1946; Smith and Hodge, 1959; Muhler et al., 1966; Hodge et al., 1970). Furthermore, the fluoride ingested in a single dose in tablet form (except chewable tablets) can impart little local contact benefit to erupted teeth. The topical beneficial effect of fluoridated water and of topical applications of fluoride solutions to teeth by the dentist is now well established (Lemke et al., 1970; Stookey, 1970).

Desirable fluoride supplementation of the diets of infants and small children will depend on the fluoride content of the community water supply and upon the extent to which such water is consumed by the infant. Suggestions for fluoride supplementation of the diet are provided in Table 14–4 for the first year of life and in Table 14–5 for children from one to three years of age. It may be noted that no fluoride supplementation is recommended in communities in which concentration of the drinking water is more than 1 mg/liter. Although intakes of fluoride from human milk and cow milk in such areas will be low, the possibility of excessive fluoride intake after the early months of life is sufficiently high to warrant caution at all ages.

Preparations of fluoride for infants and small children generally contain 0.1 mg of fluoride per drop, and it is therefore convenient to

TABLE 14–4 RECOMMENDED FLUORIDE SUPPLEMENTATION DURING FIRST YEAR OF LIFE*

	DESIRABLE FLUORIDE SUPPLEMENTATION (MG/DAY)			
	When Fluoride Concentration of Water Supply (ppm) is			
MILK OR FORMULA	*<0.3*	*0.3–0.7*	*0.8–1.1*	*>1.1*
Human milk	0.5	0.5	0.5	0
Cow milk	0.5	0.5	0.5	0
Commercially prepared formula				
Ready-to-use	0.5	0.5	0.5	0
Concentrated liquid	0.5	0.25	0	0
Powder	0.5	0	0	0†
Evaporated milk formula	0.5	0.25	0	0

*From Fomon, S. J.: Personal communication, 1973. Recommendations are aimed at providing approximately 0.5 mg of fluoride daily.

†In reconstituting commercially prepared powdered formulas, it is desirable to avoid use of water containing more than 1.1 ppm of fluoride.

TABLE 14–5 RECOMMENDED FLUORIDE SUPPLEMENTATION FOR ONE- TO THREE-YEAR-OLD CHILDREN

Fluoride Concentration of Water Supply (ppm)	Desirable Fluoride Supplementation (mg/day)
<0.3	0.5
0.3–0.7	0.25
>0.7	0

adjust the dosage as necessary. Parents must be cautioned about the desirability of restricting dosage to the prescribed amount.

Combined fluoride-vitamin preparations (drop or chewable tablets) are widely used and appear to be clinically effective (Margolis et al., 1967; Hennon et al., 1966, 1967, 1972). These supplements have considerably greater acceptance than fluoride preparations free of vitamins (Arnold et al., 1960; Richardson, 1967). However, the adjustment of fluoride dosage to a desirable quantity without adversely adjusting the vitamin intake represents a major problem. This is probably the main reason why fluoride-vitamin supplements have not received endorsement from the Council on Dental Therapeutics of the American Dental Association (American Dental Association, 1973).

In communities with fluoride concentration of water less than 0.3 mg/liter, administration of vitamin-fluoride drop preparations or chewable tablets represents a nutritionally sound approach. Such preparations commonly provide advisable intakes of two or more vitamins in association with 0.5 mg of fluoride.

ESTABLISHING HABITS

Eating habits are established in infancy and early childhood. Although frequent feedings are probably desirable in early infancy, the constant presence of a bottle within the infant's reach should be avoided. Once the teeth have erupted, sweetened beverages, including milk with added sugar, should be avoided. Many parents use as a pacifier a bottle of sweetened fruit juice, Kool-Aid or milk formula. This practice is highly threatening to the teeth and should be prohibited.

For reasons already mentioned, it does not seem desirable to restrict food intake of one- to three-year-old children to three meals daily. Rather, the choice of foods eaten between meals should be supervised, and these foods should contribute to an adequate intake of all desired nutrients. Intake of sucrose and other nutritive sugars should be restricted between meals and sticky candies should be avoided.

Traditionally, children have not been examined by a dentist before about two years of age. By this time, nursing bottle syndrome may already have developed and unsatisfactory eating habits may be rather firmly established. Counseling of parents regarding dental care of infants should be a part of prenatal indoctrination and the first visit to a dentist, preferably a pedodontist, should be made no later than nine months of age. During early infancy, when other preventive measures are being undertaken (e.g., immunizations against communicable diseases), parents may be particularly receptive to measures aimed at prevention of dental caries. Periodic examinations and counseling by the dentist should be repeated at six-month intervals until adolescence.

Parents should be taught proper techniques of cleaning the child's teeth (brushing is not synonymous with cleaning); proper cleaning should be initiated during the second year of life, always under parental supervision. Young preschool children are unable to brush their teeth adequately without supervision (McClure, 1966).

REFERENCES

American Dental Association: Accepted Dental Therapeutics. 35th ed. Chicago, American Dental Association, 1973, p. 241.

Armstrong, W. D., Gedalia, I., Singer, L., Weatherell, J. A., and Weidmann, S. M.: Distribution of fluorides. *In* World Health Organization: Fluorides and Human Health. WHO Monographs Ser. No. 59. Geneva, World Health Organization, 1970, p. 93.

Arnold, F. A., Jr., McClure, F. J., and White, C. L.: Sodium fluoride tablets for children. Dent. Progr. *1*:8, 1960.

Averill, H. M., and Bibby, B. G.: A clinical test of additions of phosphate to the diet of children. J. Dent. Res. *43*:1150, 1964.

Backer Dirks, O.: The relation between the fluoridation of water and dental caries experience. Int. Dent. J. *17*:582, 1967.

Backer Dirks, O., Jongeling-Eijndhoven, J. M. P. A., Flissebaalje, T. D., and Gedalia, I.: Total and free ionic fluoride in human and cow's milk as determined by gas-liquid chromatography and the fluoride electrode. Caries Res. *8*:181, 1974.

Barnard, P. D.: Dental Survey of State School Children in New South Wales. January, 1954–June, 1955. Canberra, National Health and Medical Research Council, Special Report Ser. No. 8, 1956.

Beal, J. F., and James, P. M. C.: Dental caries prevalence in 5-year-old children following five and a half years of water fluoridation in Birmingham. Br. Dent. J. *130*:284, 1971.

Beaver, H. A.: The effect of a nursing bottle on the teeth of a young child. Mich. Med. *71*:113, 1972.

Bell, M. E., Largent, E. J., Ludwig, T. G., Muhler, J. C., and Stookey, G. K.: The supply of fluorine to man. *In* World Health Organization: Fluorides and Human Health. WHO Monographs Ser. No. 59. Geneva, World Health Organization, 1970, p. 17.

Bibby, B. G.: Methods for comparing the cariogenicity of foodstuffs. J. Dent. Res. *49*:1334, 1970.

Bowen, W. H., and Cornick, D. E.: Effects of carbohydrate restriction in monkeys (M. irus) with active caries. Helv. Odont. Acta *11*:27, 1967.

Brewer, H. E., Stookey, G. K., and Muhler, J. C.: A clinical study concerning the anticariogenic effects of NaH_2PO_4-enriched breakfast cereals in institutionalized subjects: results after two years. J. Amer. Dent. Ass. *80*:121, 1970.

Briner, W. W., Francis, M. D., and Widder, J. S.: Factors affecting the rate of post-eruptive maturation of dental enamel. Calcif. Tissue Res. *7*:249, 1971.

Buttner, W., and Muhler, J. C.: The effect of oat hulls on the dental caries experience in rats. J. Dent. Res. *38*:823, 1959.

Caldwell, R. C.: Physical properties of foods and their caries-producing potential. J. Dent. Res. *49*:1293, 1970.

Carroll, R. A., Stookey, G. K., and Muhler, J. C.: The clinical effectiveness of phosphate-enriched breakfast cereals on the incidence of dental caries in adults: results after one year. J. Amer. Dent. Ass. *76*:564, 1968.

Committee on Nutrition, American Academy of Pediatrics: Fluoride as a nutrient. Pediatrics *49*:456, 1972.

Cooper, V. K., and Ludwig, T. G.: Effect of fluoride and of soil trace elements on the morphology of the permanent molars in man. New Zeal. Dent. J. *61*:33, 1965.

Dawes, C., Jenkins, G. N., Hardwick, J. L., and Leach, S. A.: The relation between the fluoride concentrations in the dental plaque and in drinking water. Br. Dent. J. *119*:164, 1965.

Dean, H. T.: The investigation of physiological effects by the epidemiological method. *In* Moulton, F. R. (ed.): Fluorine and Dental Health. American Association for Advancement of Science, Publ. No. 19. Washington, D.C., 1942, p. 23.

Downer, M. C.: Dental caries and periodontal disease in girls of different ethnic groups. A comparison in a London secondary school. Br. Dent. J. *128*:379, 1970.

Dunning, J. M.: Current status of fluoridation. New Eng. J. Med. *272*:30, 1965.

Edwardsson, S.: Characteristics of caries-inducing human streptococci resembling Streptococcus mutans. Arch. Oral Biol. *13*:637, 1968.

Englander, H. R., and Keyes, P. H.: Effect of phosphate supplements on cavitation in hamsters infected with caries-conducive streptococci. J. Dent. Res. *49*:140, 1970.

Ericsson, Y.: The chemistry of the enamel-saliva interface. Alabama J. Med. Sci. *5*:256, 1968.

Ericsson, Y.: Fluoride excretion in human saliva and milk. Caries Res. *3*:159, 1969.

Ericsson, Y.: Effect of infant diets with widely different fluoride contents on the fluoride concentrations of deciduous teeth. Caries Res. *7*:56, 1973.

Ericsson, Y., Hellström, I., and Hofvander, Y.: Pilot studies on the fluoride metabolism in infants on different feedings. Acta Paediatr. Scand. *61*:459, 1972.

Ericsson, Y., and Ribelius, U.: Increased fluoride ingestion by bottle-fed infants and its effect. Acta Paediatr. Scand. *59*:424, 1970.

Ericsson, Y., and Ribelius, U.: Wide variations of fluoride supply to infants and their effect. Caries. Res. *5*:78, 1971.

Esposito, E. J.: Effects of sodium chloride and sucrose on caries activity in rats. J. Dent. Res. *50*:850, 1971.

Fass, E. N.: Is bottle feeding of milk a factor in dental caries? J. Dent. Child. *29*:245, 1962.

Finn, S. B.: Dental caries in infants. Curr. Dent. Comment *1*:35, 1969.

Fitzgerald, R. J.: Plaque microbiology and caries. Alabama J. Med. Sci. *5*:256, 1968.

Fitzgerald, R. J., and Jordan, H. V.: Polysaccharide-producing bacteria and caries. *In* Harris, R. S. (ed.): Art and Science of Dental Caries Research. New York, Academic Press, 1968, p. 79.

Fulton, J. T.: Experiment in Dental Care. Results of New Zealand's Use of School Dental Nurses. Monographs Ser. No. 4. Geneva, World Health Organization, 1951.

Fulton, J. T.: Dental caries experience in primary teeth. J. Dent. Res. *31*:839, 1952.

Gonzalez, M.: Effect of trimetaphosphate ions on the process of mineralization. J. Dent. Res. *50*:1056, 1971.

Gray, A. S., and Hawk, D. R.: Significance of caries experience in preschool children aged 3 to 5. J. Canad. Dent. Ass. *33*:87, 1967.

Gray, J. A., Francis, M. D., and Griebstein, W. J.: Chemistry of enamel dissolution. *In* Sognnaes, R. F.: Chemistry and Prevention of Dental Caries. Springfield, Ill., Charles C Thomas, 1962, p. 164.

Grenby, T. H.: Flour, bread and wheat grain fractions in decalcification tests. Arch. Oral Biol. *12*:513, 1967a.

Grenby, T. H.: Wheat bran factors in decalcification tests. Arch. Oral Biol. *12*:523, 1967b.

Grenby, T. H.: Phytates in decalcification tests *in vitro*. Arch. Oral Biol. *12*:531, 1967c.

Grenby, T. H.: Trials of three organic phosphorus-containing compounds as protective agents against dental caries in rats. J. Dent. Res. *52*:454, 1973.

Grenby, T. H., and Hutchinson, J. B.: The effects of diets containing sucrose, glucose or fructose on experimental dental caries in two strains of rats. Arch. Oral Biol. *14*:373, 1969.

Guggenheim, B., König, K. G., Herzog, E., and Mühlemann, H. R.: The cariogenicity of different dietary carbohydrates tested on rats in relative gnotobiosis with a streptococcus producing extracellular polysaccharide. Helv. Odont. Acta *10*:101, 1966.

Guggenheim, B., and Schroeder, H. E.: Biochemical and morphological aspects of extracellular polysaccharides produced by cariogenic streptococci. Helv. Odont. Acta *11*:131, 1967.

Gustafsson, B. E., Quensel, C.-E., Lanke, L. S., Lundqvist, C., Grahnén, H., Bonow, B. E., and Krasse, B.: The Vipeholm dental caries study. The effect of different levels of carbohydrate intake on caries activity in 436 individuals observed for five years. Acta Odont. Scand. *11*:232, 1954.

Halikis, S. E.: A study of dental caries in a group of Western Australian children. Part II. The incidence of dental caries in children aged 2–6 years. Aust. Dent. J. *8*:114, 1963.

Harris, R., Schamschula, R. G., Beveridge, J., and Gregory, G.: The cariostatic effect of calcium sucrose phosphate in a group of children aged 5–17 years. Aust. Dent. J. *13*:32, 1968.

Harris, R., Schamschula, R. G., Gregory, G., Roots, M., and Beveridge, J.: Observations on the cariostatic effect of calcium sucrose phosphate in a group of children aged 5–17 years. Aust. Dent. J. *12*:105, 1967.

Held, H. R.: Kariesprophylaxe durch endogene Fluorzufuhr. Praxis *44*:875, 1955.

Hennon, D. K., Stookey, G. K., and Muhler, J. C.: The clinical anticariogenic effectiveness of supplementary fluoride-vitamin preparations. Results at the end of three years. J. Dent. Child. *33*:3, 1966.

Hennon, D. K., Stookey, G. K., and Muhler, J. C.: The clinical anticariogenic effectiveness of supplementary fluoride-vitamin preparations – results at the end of four years. J. Dent. Child. *34*:439, 1967.

Hennon, D. K., Stookey, G. K., and Muhler, J. C.: Prevalence and distribution of dental caries in preschool children. J. Amer. Dent. Ass. *79*:1405, 1969.

Hennon, D. K., Stookey, G. K., and Muhler, J. C.: Prophylaxis of dental caries: relative effectiveness of chewable fluoride preparations with and without added vitamins. J. Pediatr. *80*:1018, 1972.

Hewat, R. E. T., Eastcott, D. F., and Bibby, J. B.: The prevalence of caries in deciduous teeth of N.Z. children. New Zeal. Dent. J. *48*:160, 1952.

Hodge, H. C., and Smith, F. A.: Some public health aspects of water fluoridation. *In* Shaw, J. H. (ed.): Fluoridation as a Public Health Measure. Washington, D. C., American Association for the Advancement of Science, 1954, p. 79.

Hodge, H. C., Smith, F. A., and Gedalia, I.: Excretion of fluorides. *In* World Health Organization: Fluorides and Human Health. WHO Monographs Ser. No. 59. Geneva, World Health Organization, 1970, p. 141.

Hollis, M. J.: Dental caries experience of New Zealand children over a twenty-year period. New Zeal. Dent. J. *66*:167, 1970.

Jenkins, G. N.: The refinement of foods in relation to dental caries. *In* Staple, P. H. (ed.): Advances in Oral Biology. New York, Academic Press, 1966, p. 67.

Jenkins, G. N.: The mechanism of action of fluoride in reducing caries incidence. Int. Dent. J. *17*:552, 1967.

Jenkins, G. N.: Diet and caries: protective factors. Alabama J. Med. Sci. *5*:276, 1968.

Jenkins, G. N.: Enamel protective factors in food. J. Dent. Res. *49*:1318, 1970.

Jenkins, G. N., Edgar, W. M., and Ferguson, D. B.: The distribution and metabolic effects of human plaque fluorine. Arch. Oral Biol. *14*:105, 1969.

Jenkins, G. N., and Ferguson, D. B.: Milk and dental caries. Br. Dent. J. *120*:472, 1966.

Keyes, P. H.: Research in dental caries. J. Amer. Dent. Ass. *76*:1357, 1968.

Keyes, P. H.: Present and future measures for dental caries control. J. Amer. Dent. Ass. *79*:1395, 1969.

Keyes, P. H., and Jordan, H. V.: Periodontal lesions in the Syrian hamster. III. Findings related to an infectious and transmissible component. Arch. Oral Biol. *9*:377, 1964.

Kite, O. W., Shaw, J. H., and Sognnaes, R. F.: The prevention of experimental tooth decay by tube-feeding. J. Nutr. *42*:89, 1950.

König, K. G.: Caries induced in laboratory rats. Post-eruptive effect of sucrose and of bread of different degrees of refinement. Br. Dent. J. *123*:585, 1967.

König, K. G.: Diet and caries: cariogenic factors. Alabama J. Med. Sci. *5*:269, 1968.

Koulourides, T.: Dynamics of tooth surface-oral fluid equilibrium. *In* Staple, P. H. (ed.): Advances in Oral Biology. Vol. 2. New York, Academic Press, 1966, p. 149.

Krasse, B.: The effect of caries-inducing streptococci in hamsters fed diets with sucrose or glucose. Arch. Oral Biol. *10*:223, 1965.

Krasse, B.: Effects of dietaries on oral microbiology. *In* Harris, R. S. (ed.): Art and Science of Dental Caries Research. New York, Academic Press, 1968, p. 111.

Kraus, B. S., and Jordan, R. E.: The Human Dentition Before Birth. Philadelphia, Lea & Febiger, 1965.

Kroll, R. G., and Stone, J. H.: Nocturnal bottle-feeding as a contributory cause of rampant dental caries in the infant and young child. J. Dent. Child. *34*:454, 1967.

Kruger, B. J.: Influence of boron, fluorine, and molybdenum on the morphology of the rat molar. J. Dent. Res. *41*:215, 1962.

Larson, R. H., Clemmer, B., and Scherp, H. W.: Reduction of rat caries by trimetaphosphate on different tooth surfaces: variations produced by diet and oral flora. Arch. Oral Biol. *17*:883, 1972.

Lemke, C. W., Doherty, J. M., and Arra, M. C.: Controlled fluoridation: the dental effects of discontinuation in Antigo, Wisconsin. J. Amer. Dent. Ass. *80*:782, 1970.

Lilienthal, B., Bush, E., Buckmaster, M., Gregory, G., Gagolski, J., Smythe, B. M., Curtin, J. H., and Napper, D. H.: The cariostatic effect of carbohydrate phosphates in the diet. Aust. Dent. J. *11*:388, 1966.

Ling, E. R., Kon, S. K., and Porter, J. W. G.: The composition of milk and the nutritive value of its components. *In* Kon, S. K., and Cowie, A. T. (eds.): Milk: The Mammary Gland and Its Secretion. Vol. II. New York, Academic Press, 1961, p. 195.

Luoma, H., Meurman, J. H., Helminen, S. K. J., Koskinen, K., and Ranta, H.: Modification of dental caries and calculus in rats by fluoride and bicarbonate-phosphate-fluoride additions to dietary sugar. Arch. Oral Biol. *17*:821, 1972.

Magrill, D. S.: The reduction of the solubility of hydroxyapatite in acid by adsorption of phytate from solution. Arch. Oral Biol. *18*:591, 1973.

Mäkinen, K. K.: Enzyme dynamics of a cariogenic streptococcus: the effect of xylitol and sorbitol. J. Dent. Res. *51*:403, 1972a.

Mäkinen, K. K.: The role of sucrose and other sugars in the development of dental caries: a review. Int. Dent. J. *22*:363, 1972b.

Margolis, F. J., Macauley, J., and Freshman, E.: The effects of measured doses of fluoride on deciduous dentition: a five-year preliminary report. Amer. J. Dis. Child. *113*:670, 1967.

Marthaler, T. M.: The value in caries prevention of other methods of increasing fluoride ingestion, apart from fluoridated water. Int. Dent. J. *17*:606, 1967.

Marthaler, T. M.: Decrease of DMF-levels 4 years after the introduction of a caries-preventive program, observations in 5819 schoolchildren of 20 communities. Helv. Odont. Acta *16*:45, 1972a.

Marthaler, T. M.: Reduction of caries, gingivitis and calculus after eight years of preventive measures: observations in seven communities. Helv. Odont. Acta *16*:69, 1972b.

Massler, M., and Schour, I.: Atlas of the Mouth in Health and Disease. 2nd ed. Chicago, American Dental Association, 1958.

McClure, D. B.: A comparison of toothbrushing technics for the preschool child. J. Dent. Child. *33*:205, 1966.

McClure, F. J.: Nondental physiological effects of trace quantities of fluorine. *In* Moulton, F. R. (ed.): Dental Caries and Fluorine. Washington, D.C., American Association for the Advancement of Science, 1946, p. 74.

McClure, F. J.: The cariostatic effect in white rats of phosphorus and calcium supplements added to the flour of bread formulas and to bread diets. J. Nutr. *72*:131, 1960.

McClure, F. J. (ed.): Fluoride drinking waters. U.S. Public Health Service Publ. No. 825. Washington, D.C., U.S. Government Printing Office, 1962.

McClure, F. J.: Further studies on the cariostatic effect of organic and inorganic phosphates. J. Dent. Res. *42*:693, 1963.

McClure, F. J.: Inhibition of experimental caries by oat hulls. Arch. Oral Biol. 9:219, 1964.

Muhler, J. C., Stookey, G. K., Spear, L. B., and Bixler, D.: Blood and urinary fluoride studies following the ingestion of single dosages of fluoride. J. Oral Ther. Pharm. *2*:241, 1966.

Navia, J. M.: Prevention of dental caries: agents which increase tooth resistance to dental caries. Int. Dent. J. *22*:427, 1972.

Navia, J. M., and Harris, R. S.: Longitudinal study of cariostatic effects of sodium trimetaphosphate and sodium fluoride when fed separately and together in diets of rats. J. Dent. Res. *48*:183, 1969.

Newbrun, E.: Sucrose, the arch criminal of dental caries. J. Dent. Child. *36*:239, 1969.

Newbrun, E. (ed.): Fluorides and Dental Caries, Springfield Ill., Charles C Thomas, 1972.

Newbrun, E.: Sugar, sugar substitutes and noncaloric sweetening agents. Int. Dent. J. *23*:344, 1973.

Nikiforuk, G.: Posteruptive effects of nutrition on teeth. J. Dent. Res. *49*:1252, 1970.

Nizel, A. E.: Nutrition in Preventive Dentistry: Science and Practice. Philadelphia, W. B. Saunders Co., 1972.

Nizel, A. E., and Harris, R. S.: The effects of phosphates on experimental dental caries: a literature review. J. Dent. Res. *43*:1123, 1964.

Nord, C.-E.: En undersökning över kariessituationen hos barn i åldern 2–5 år, vilka sökt behandling vid pedodontiavdelningen. Odont. Foren. T. *29*:291, 1965.

O'Meara, W. F.: Fluoride administration in single daily dose: a survey of its value in prevention of dental caries. Clin. Pediatr. *7*:177, 1968.

Orland, F. J., Blayney, J. R., Harrison, R. W., Reyniers, J. A., Trexler, P. C., Wagner, M., Gordon, H. A., and Luckey, T. D.: Use of the germfree animal technic in the study of experimental dental caries. I. Basic observations on rats reared free of all microorganisms. J. Dent. Res. *33*:147, 1954.

Palmer, J. D.: Dietary habits at bedtime in relation to dental caries in children. Br. Dent. J. *130*:288, 1971.

Parfitt, G. J.: Report on the condition of the teeth of children in a London school from 1950 to 1953. Br. Dent. J. *96*:33, 1954.

Paynter, K. J., and Grainger, R. M.: The relation of nutrition to the morphology and size of rat molar teeth. J. Canad. Dent. Ass. *22*:519, 1956.

Peterson, J. K.: North Dakota field test of cariostatic effect of 1% sodium dihydrogen phosphate and disodium hydrogen phosphate added to presweetened breakfast cereals. J. Dent. Res. *48*:1308, 1969.

Posner, A. S., Eanes, E. D., Harper, R. A., and Zipkin, I.: X-ray diffraction analysis of the effect of fluoride on human bone apatite. Arch. Oral Biol. *8*:549, 1963.

Richardson, A. S.: Parental participation in the administration of fluoride supplements. Canad. J. Public Health *58*:508, 1967.

Robinson, S., and Naylor, S. R.: The effects of late weaning on the deciduous incisor teeth. A pilot survey. Br. Dent. J. *115*:250, 1963.

Rogerson, M. J.: The role of a calcium sucrose phosphate-calcium orthophosphate complex in the reduction of dental caries. Aust. Dent. J. *18*:160, 1973.

Sandham, H. J., and Kleinberg, I.: Contribution of lactic and other acids to the pH of a human salivary sediment system during glucose catabolism. Arch. Oral Biol. *15*:1263, 1970.

Savara, B. S., and Suher, T.: Incidence of dental caries in children 1 to 6 years of age. J. Dent. Res. *33*:808, 1954.

Scherp, H. W.: Dental caries: prospects for prevention. Science *173*:1199, 1971.

Shaw, J. H.: Preventive nutrition. *In* Bernier, J. L., and Muhler, J. C. (eds.): Improving Dental Practice Through Preventive Measures. 2nd ed. St. Louis, C. V. Mosby Co., 1970, p. 30.

Ship, I. I., and Mickelsen, O.: The effects of calcium acid phosphate on dental caries in children: a controlled clinical trial. J. Dent. Res. *43*:1144, 1964.

Sicher, H., and Bhaskar, S. N., (eds.): Orban's Oral Histology and Embryology. 7th ed. St. Louis, C. V. Mosby Co., 1972, p. 17.

Small, J.: Preventive Practices Branch, Division of Dental Health, Bureau of Health. Manpower Education, National Institutes of Health, Bethesda, Maryland. Personal communication, 1973.

Smith, F. A., and Hodge, H. C.: Fluoride toxicity. *In* Muhler, J. C., and Hine, M. K. (eds.): Fluorine and Dental Health. Port Washington, N.Y., Kennikat Press, 1959, p. 11.

Sognnaes, R. F.: Analysis of wartime reduction of dental caries in European children. Amer. J. Dis. Child. *75*:792, 1948.

Sognnaes, R. F.: Further analysis of wartime caries observations: an opportunity and a responsibility. Br. Dent. J. *87*:291, 1949.

Stookey, G. K.: Fluoride therapy. *In* Bernier, J. L., and Muhler, J. C. (eds.): Improving Dental Practice Through Preventive Measures. 2nd ed. St. Louis, C. V. Mosby Co., 1970, p. 92.

Stookey, G. K., Carroll, R. A., and Muhler, J. C.: The clinical effectiveness of phosphate-enriched breakfast cereals on the incidence of dental caries in children: results after 2 years. J. Amer. Dent. Ass. *74*:752, 1967.

Strålfors, A.: The effect of calcium phosphate on dental caries in school children. J. Dent. Res. *43*:1137, 1964.

Syrrist, A., and Selander, P.: Some aspects on comforters and dental caries. Odont. T. *61*:237, 1953.

Taketa, F., and Phillips, P. H.: Oat hull fractions and the development of dental caries. J. Amer. Diet. Ass. *33*:575, 1957.

Timmis, J. C.: Caries experience of 5-year-old children living in fluoride and non-fluoride areas of Essex. Br. Dent. J. *130*:278, 1971.

Toth, K.: Caries prevention in deciduous dentition using table salt fluoridation. J. Dent. Res. *52*:533, 1973.

Toth, K., and Szabó, I.: Dental conditions of preschool children (one to six years of age) in Szeged, Hungary. J. Dent. Res. *38*:451, 1959.

Toverud, G.: Decrease in caries frequency in Norwegian children during World War II. J. Amer. Dent. Ass. *39*:127, 1949.

Toverud, G., Rubal, L., and Wiehl, D. G.: The influence of war and postwar conditions on the teeth of Norwegian school children. IV. Caries in specific surfaces of the permanent teeth. Milbank Mem. Fund Quart. *39*:489, 1961.

Waldbott, G. L.: Fluoride in food. Amer. J. Clin. Nutr. *12*:455, 1963.

Wei, S. H. Y.: Remineralization of enamel and dentine: a review. J. Dent. Child. *34*:444, 1967.

Wei, S. H. Y., and Koulourides, T.: Electron microprobe and microhardness studies of enamel remineralization. J. Dent. Res. *51*:648, 1972.

Weiss, M. E., and Bibby, B. G.: Effects of milk on enamel solubility. Arch. Oral Biol. *11*:49, 1966.

Weiss, R. L., and Trithart, A. H.: Between-meal eating habits and dental caries experience in preschool children. Amer. J. Public Health *50*:1097, 1960.

Winter, G. B.: Sucrose and cariogenesis. Br. Dent. J. *124*:407, 1968.

Winter, G. B., Hamilton, M. C., and James, P. M. C.: Role of the comforter as an aetiological factor in rampant caries of the deciduous dentition. Arch. Dis. Child. *41*:207, 1966.

Winter, G. B., Rule, D. C., Mailer, G. P., James, P. M. C., and Gordon, P. H.: The prevalence of dental caries in pre-school children aged 1 to 4 years. Br. Dent. J. *130*:271, 1971.

Wisan, J. M., and Lavell, M., and Colwell, F. H.: Dental survey of Philadelphia preschool children by income, age and treatment status. J. Amer. Dent. Ass. *55*:1, 1957.

Zipkin, I., and Babeaux, W. L.: Maternal transfer of fluoride. J. Oral Ther. Pharm. *1*:652, 1965.

Zita, A. C., McDonald, R. E., and Andrews, A. L.: Dietary habits and the dental caries experience in 200 children. J. Dent. Res. *38*:860, 1959.

15

MILKS AND FORMULAS

Samuel J. Fomon
and
L. J. Filer, Jr.

Most infants are dependent on human milk or formulas based on animal milk for nearly all of their nutritional needs during the early weeks or months of life. Even after the introduction of other foods into the diet, milk generally continues to supply a large percentage of caloric intake and is the major source of most of the essential nutrients. Knowledge of the composition of human milk, other milks and various formulas is therefore essential to adequate management of infant feeding.

As pointed out by Kon (1959), "It stands to reason that milk, which only for a limited time and with certain reservations is the ideal food for the young of any one species, is further restricted in value when used by another species, and the limitations of milks of domesticated animals in human nutrition must be frankly accepted and understood." In this respect, it is worth noting that growth rates of the human infant and the calf are quite different, the human infant requiring about twice as long as the calf to double his birth weight (100 versus 50 days). Thus, the ratio of nutrient requirement for growth to that for maintenance will be greater for the calf than for the human infant. Furthermore, protein and minerals account for smaller percentages of weight gain in the human infant than in the calf. It is, therefore, not surprising that cow milk is richer in protein and minerals than is human milk.

The extent of variability in composition of milk secreted by different women or by different animals of the same species is not generally appreciated. It would appear from the chemical analyses of 24-hour samples of human milk reported by Morrison (1952) that approximately one-sixth of women secreted milk with protein concentration less than 0.95 gm/100 ml and another one-sixth secreted milk with protein concentration greater than 1.47 gm/100 ml. Similar ranges for minus and plus one standard deviation for fat and lactose in these samples were 2.76 to 3.90 and 6.56 to 7.90 gm/100 ml, respectively.

Evaporated milk and commercially prepared infant formulas are standardized with respect to concentrations of protein, fat, carbohydrate and major minerals. Tabular data concerning chemical composition of these products are therefore extremely useful. Much less revealing are tabular data concerning composition of cow milk, since breed of cow may determine to a large extent the chemical composition of the milk. An example is the study by Reinart and Nesbitt (1956, cited by Ling et al., 1961) concerning 75 samples from holstein and 72 samples from jersey cows. Concentrations of total solids, protein and calcium averaged 20 to 23 per cent greater for the jersey than for the holstein cows and concentration of fat averaged 40 per cent greater for the jerseys.

When milk is obtained from a single cow (or goat) rather than from the pool of milk from the entire herd, the composition may be even less likely to agree with averages published in the literature.

COMPOSITION OF HUMAN MILK

Colostrum and Transitional Milk

The mean energy value of human milk is less during the first five days after parturition (67 kcal/100 ml) than later (75 kcal/100 ml) (Macy and Kelly, 1961). Ash content of human colostrum is relatively high, and concentrations of sodium, potassium and chloride are greater in colostrum than in mature human milk. Major changes in composition of human milk in transition from colostrum to mature milk are completed by the tenth day (Committee on Nutrition, 1960).

As discussed subsequently in this chapter (see Resistance to Infection), human colostrum is a rich source of antibodies which may provide protection against various enteric infections.

Hytten (1954b) demonstrated that the total fat output on the seventh day of nursing was predictive of later success in breast feeding. Ninety per cent of the women whose milk contained at least 20 gm of fat on the seventh day were still breast feeding three months later as compared with only 20 per cent of the women who secreted from 4.9 to 10 gm of fat on the seventh day.

Mature Human Milk

A voluminous literature exists with respect to proximate composition and mineral content of human milk, including reports from India (Gopalan, 1958), New Guinea (Bailey, 1965), West Pakistan (Underwood et al., 1970) and a number of other developing countries. Among the developed countries, few data are available concerning analyses carried out during the past 20 years. Data most commonly utilized in the United States are those published by Macy et al. (1953) and by Macy and Kelly (1961). Table 15–1 summarizes data from a number of sources.

Major Components

It is unfortunate that recent data are not available on composition of human milk of women in developed countries. Unpublished data from the Pediatric Metabolic Unit of the University of Iowa (Jensen et al., 1972) concerning milk of 17 women sampled serially between 14 and 84 days of lactation and milk of 12 women at 112 days of lactation demonstrated remarkable decreases in concentrations of protein (34 per cent decrease between 14 and 84 days of lactation) as duration of lactation increased (Table 15–2). The relatively low concentration of fat in these samples may reflect the fact that many of the samples were expressed when the breasts were full rather than at the end of nursing. The large standard deviation in concentration of fat at each stage of lactation (Table 15–2) indicates the great variability in fat content from one woman to another.

An even greater variability (mean 4.1, standard deviation 1.8 gm/100 ml) in concentrations of fat from 52 samples of human milk collected from women in Pennsylvania at various stages of lactation has been reported by Kroger (1972). In this instance, the relatively high concentration of fat in a number of the samples was attributed to collection of the sample after the infant had nursed—i.e., with the breast nearly empty. Hytten (1954a) showed that during a single feeding or emptying by pump, the milk from the two breasts might differ in fat content by 1 to 2 gm/100 ml. Furthermore, a diurnal rhythm in total yield and fat content of the milk could be demonstrated. The amount of milk obtainable was greatest at 6 AM and least at 10 PM.

Because of the variability in fat content of samples of human milk and the evidence of major changes in milk composition with duration of lactation (Table 15–2), it is apparent that more extensive data than currently available are needed on composition of human milk. Samples equivalent to an entire breast feeding must be analyzed and these must be considered in relation to time of day and stage of lactation. Until such data are available, many of our calculations relating to

TABLE 15–1 COMPOSITION OF MATURE HUMAN MILK AND COW MILK*

Composition	Human Milk	Cow Milk
Water (ml/100 ml)	87.1	87.2
Energy (kcal/100 ml)	75	66
Total solids (gm/100 ml)	12.9	12.8
Protein (gm/100 ml)	1.1	3.5
Fat (gm/100 ml)	4.5	3.7
Lactose (gm/100 ml)	6.8	4.9
Ash (gm/100 ml)	0.2	0.7
Proteins (% of total protein)		
Casein	40	82
Whey proteins	60	18
Nonprotein nitrogen (mg/100 ml)	32	32
(% of total nitrogen)	15	6
Amino acids (mg/100 ml)		
Essential		
Histidine	22	95
Isoleucine	68	228
Leucine	100	350
Lysine	73	277
Methionine	25	88
Phenylalanine	48	172
Threonine	50	164
Tryptophan	18	49
Valine	70	245
Nonessential		
Arginine	45	129
Alanine	35	75
Aspartic acid	116	166
Cystine	22	32
Glutamic acid	230	680
Glycine	0	11
Proline	80	250
Serine	69	160
Tyrosine	61	179

*Data on proximate composition are from Macy and Kelly (1961) for human milk, and from Watt and Merrill (1963) for cow milk; per cent of proteins from casein and whey and content of nonprotein nitrogen are from Macy and Kelly (1961); concentrations of amino acids are from Food and Nutrition Board (1963) except for alanine, aspartic acid, glutamic acid, glycine, proline and serine, which are from Macy and Kelly (1961); concentrations of calcium, phosphorus, sodium and potassium in cow milk are from Watt and Merrill (1963), whereas concentrations of other major minerals are from Macy and Kelly (1961); iron and trace minerals are from sources identified in Chapters 12 and 13; concentrations of vitamins are from Hartman and Dryden (1965) except for those of folacin and vitamins E and K, which are from sources identified in Chapter 9.

(Table continued on opposite page.)

TABLE 15–1 COMPOSITION OF MATURE HUMAN MILK AND COW MILK *(Continued)*

Composition	Human Milk	Cow Milk
Fatty acids (see Chapter 7, Table 7–1)		
Major minerals per liter		
Calcium (mg)	340	1170
Phosphorus (mg)	140	920
Sodium (meq)	7	22
Potassium (meq)	13	35
Chloride (meq)	11	29
Magnesium (mg)	40	120
Sulfur (mg)	140	300
Trace minerals per liter		
Chromium (μg)	–	8–13
Manganese (μg)	7–15	20–40
Copper (μg)	400	300
Zinc (mg)	3–5	3–5
Iodine (μg)	30	47†
Selenium (μg)	13–50	5–50
Iron (mg)	0.5	0.5
Vitamins per liter		
Vitamin A (I.U.)	1898	1025‡
Thiamin (μg)	160	440
Riboflavin (μg)	360	1750
Niacin (μg)	1470	940
Pyridoxine (μg)	100	640
Pantothenate (mg)	1.84	3.46
Folacin (μg)	52	55
B_{12} (μg)	0.3	4
Vitamin C (mg)	43	11§
Vitamin D (I.U.)	22	14¶
Vitamin E (mg)	1.8	0.4
Vitamin K (μg)	15	60

†Range 10 to 200 μg/liter.
‡Average value for winter milk; value for summer milk, 1690 I.U./liter.
§As marketed; value for fresh cow milk 21 mg/liter.
¶Average value for winter milk; value for summer milk, 33 I.U.

TABLE 15–2 COMPOSITION OF HUMAN MILK AT VARIOUS STAGES OF LACTATION*

Stage of Lactation	Proximate Analysis (gm/liter)					Non-protein Nitrogen (gm/liter)
	Total Solids	*Protein (N × 6.25)*	*Fat*	*Carbo-hydrate*	*Ash*	
14th day						
Mean	126.5	15.4	26.3	83.2	2.32	0.49
S.D.	12.2	1.8	9.1	9.0	0.28	0.13
28th day						
Mean	127.6	13.8	29.4	82.3	2.18	0.40
S.D.	14.6	1.8	12.3	11.1	0.47	0.13
42nd day						
Mean	122.7	12.6	26.8	81.3	1.81	0.41
S.D.	17.3	1.4	15.9	12.0	0.52	0.12
56th day						
Mean	116.1	10.9	22.3	80.7	2.15	0.46
S.D.	16.8	1.8	11.9	12.5	0.60	0.16
84th day						
Mean	116.6	10.2	21.0	88.4	2.22	0.38
S.D.	17.0	2.6	13.3	14.5	0.54	0.11
112th day						
Mean	127.7	8.7	28.4	88.6	1.84	0.32
S.D.	25.5	2.6	12.5	18.5	0.83	0.09

*Data of Jensen et al. (1972). Seventeen healthy women at each stage except 112 days; 12 women at stage 112 days.

mean concentrations of nutrients in human milk will be likely to be misleading.

Vitamins and Minerals

Human milk from a well nourished woman, if taken in adequate quantity by the infant, may be expected to satisfy advisable intakes for vitamin A, thiamin, riboflavin, niacin, vitamin B_6, vitamin B_{12}, folacin, vitamin C and vitamin E. Although human milk is not a particularly rich source of preformed niacin, it is a good source of tryptophan, so that total intake of niacin (preformed plus nicotinamide equivalents) is more than adequate (see Chapter 9). Human milk provides little vitamin D; supplementation of the infant's diet with this vitamin in a dosage of 400 I.U. daily is therefore advisable.

As may be seen from Table 15–2, concentrations of phosphorus, sodium, potassium and zinc have been noted to decrease as duration of lactation increases. Neither iron nor fluoride is present in human milk in sufficient concentration to provide the advisable intake of these minerals, and supplementation of the diet is recommended as discussed in Chapters 12 and 14.

ABLE 15–2 COMPOSITION OF HUMAN MILK AT VARIOUS STAGES OF LACTATION (*Continued*)

Minerals (mg/liter)						
Calcium	*Phosphorus*	*Magnesium*	*Sodium*	*Potassium*	*Chloride*	*Zinc*
278	188	30	204	421	410	3.7
45	33	3	58	90	119	1.2
261	169	28	161	347	441	2.6
64	45	5	62	121	193	1.1
255	151	28	151	367	427	2.2
78	30	4	64	129	137	0.9
266	150	31	135	374	378	2.0
56	28	6	79	66	98	0.7
247	130	30	125	343	406	2.0
56	33	6	52	90	165	1.2
236	132	32	120	296	399	1.1
38	26	5	48	129	147	0.5

Maternal Diet and Composition of Milk

Although differences in diet may affect total volume of milk secreted, moderate changes in dietary intake of protein, fat and calcium do not correlate well with changes in concentrations of these nutrients in human milk (Morrison, 1952). When a woman is poorly nourished, the volume of secreted milk is likely to decrease, but the percentage of protein, fat and carbohydrate will be relatively little affected (Committee on Nutrition, 1960). On the other hand, fatty acid composition and vitamin content generally do reflect maternal intake.

Enzymes in Milk

A large number of enzymes are known to be present in human milk and cow milk (Heyndrickx, 1962, 1963). However, it seems probable that these enzymes are nearly all destroyed in passage through the stomach and are of little nutritional significance.

Some Consequences of Feeding Human Milk

Bacterial Flora

Although the mechanisms are poorly explained, it is evident that feeding of human milk promotes establishment of a gastrointestinal bifidobacterial flora (Mata and Wyatt, 1971; Goldman and Smith, 1973). Presumably, the difference between human milk and cow milk in this respect is related to the presence, in human milk, of a group of nitrogen-containing polysaccharides, the "bifidus factor," not present in appreciable concentrations in cow milk (György, 1971). The pH of stools of breastfed infants is generally somewhat less than that of infants receiving other milks, apparently because of production of acetic and lactic acid by the lactobacillus. The acid environment inhibits in vitro the growth of *E. coli*, yeast and shigella (Hentges, 1967). Possibly, similar inhibition occurs in vivo.

Resistance to Infection

It has been known for some time that bacterial and viral antibodies are present in human milk and that substances in human milk inhibit the growth of a number of viruses (Schubert and Grünberg, 1949; Vahlquist, 1958; Arnon et al., 1959; Schmidt, 1960; Sussman, 1961; Sabin and Fieldsteel, 1962; Hodes, 1964; Michaels, 1965; Adinolfi et al., 1966; Kenny et al., 1967). Because little absorption of these antibodies occurs when they are fed to the human infant (Nordbring, 1957; Ammann and Stiehm, 1966), there is no reason to believe that they are important in resistance to infections by organisms other than those that enter the body through the gastrointestinal tract—poliomyelitis, coxsackie, enteropathogenic strains of *E. coli*, salmonella, shigella and other enteric organisms. Against infections with these organisms, human milk may offer considerable protection.

Human colostrum is relatively rich in secretory IgA (Ammann and Stiehm, 1966; Hanson et al., 1971; Mata and Wyatt, 1971) and in IgE (Bennich and Johansson, 1971). Concentrations of IgG, IgM and C′3 component of complement are less in a woman's milk than in her serum (Ammann and Stiehm, 1966; Mata and Wyatt, 1971). Colostral IgA appears to be resistant to tryptic digestion (Shim et al., 1969), therefore explaining the failure of digestion of these antibodies and their appearance in feces.

Antibodies to salmonella H agglutinins have been found in stools of breastfed infants whose mothers had been immunized with the antigen (Schubert and Grünberg, 1949). Several investigators (Kenny et al., 1967; Michael et al., 1971; Gindrat et al., 1972) have reported antibodies to *E. coli* in stools of infants fed human milk containing high titers of *E. coli* antibodies. Michael et al. (1971) demonstrated a correlation between number of coliforms in stools of breastfed infants and presence of high agglutinating and bactericidal titers against specific serotypes of *E. coli* in the stools of these infants. Infections with enteropathogenic strains of *E. coli* have been reported to be relatively uncommon in breastfed infants (Hinton and MacGregor, 1958; Neter,

1959) and feeding of human milk appeared to aid in controlling an outbreak of *E. coli* 0:111 enteritis in premature infants (Svirsky-Gross, 1958). The hazard of septicemia by bacteria of enteric origin may be reduced by feeding of human milk (Winberg and Wessner, 1971).

Infants breastfed by women with high serum titers of antibodies to poliomyelitis are relatively resistant to infection with orally administered poliovaccine (Lepow et al., 1961; Holguin et al., 1962; Sabin et al., 1963; Warren et al., 1964). Similar protection is afforded by cow milk containing poliovirus antibody (Gonzaga et al., 1963).

Human milk is a rich source of lysozymes (Braun, 1960; Jollès and Jollès, 1961; Chandan et al., 1964) and there is some suggestion that lysozyme may interact with other components in milk to achieve a bactericidal effect (Adinolfi et al., 1966; Miller, 1969).

Lactoferrin, an iron-binding protein of external secretions, is present in relatively high concentration in human milk (Johansson, 1960). Staphylococci and *E. coli* are inhibited by lactoferrin, apparently because lactoferrin robs them of iron (Masson et al., 1966; Masson and Heremans, 1966; Oram and Reiter, 1968; Bullen et al., 1972). Lactoferrin in cow milk (and presumably in human milk) is largely unsaturated (Gordon et al., 1962) and therefore might inhibit growth of microorganisms in the gastrointestinal tract of the breastfed infant. In this respect, unsaturated lactoferrin from human milk has been shown to inhibit growth of *Candida albicans* (Kirkpatrick et al., 1971).

Gastrointestinal Passage Time

During the first 45 days of life, carmine passage time generally ranges from 3 to 10 hours regardless of diet. After 45 days of age, as may be seen from Figure 15–1, gastrointestinal passage time is longer in infants receiving fresh human milk (fed from the breast or by bottle) than in those fed processed human milk (pasteurized, frozen, stored, thawed), cow milk or a formula with protein from cow milk and fat supplied as a mixture of corn and coconut oils. When an infant's diet was changed from fresh to processed or from processed to fresh human milk, gastrointestinal passage time was immediately characteristic of the new feeding, suggesting that alteration in intestinal flora is probably not an important determinant of carmine passage time. The significance of the longer gastrointestinal passage time in the breastfed infant than in the infant fed cow milk is unknown.

Hyperbilirubinemia

In the first four days of life, hyperbilirubinemia is not detected more frequently in breastfed than in bottle-fed infants (Dahms et al.,

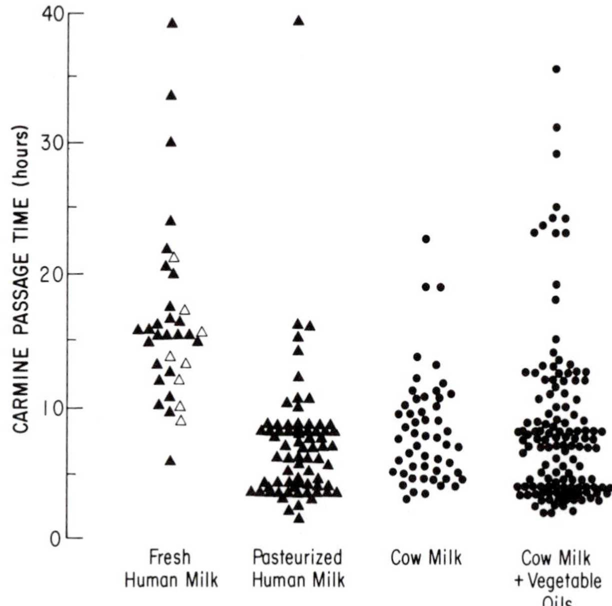

Figure 15–1 Gastrointestinal passage time, as determined by use of a carmine marker, in normal infants between 45 and 180 days of age. Solid triangles refer to observations of infants fed human milk by bottle; open triangles refer to observations of breastfed infants. (Unpublished data of Fomon et al., 1966.)

1973). However, prolonged severe unconjugated hyperbilirubinemia occurs in some breastfed infants (Newman and Gross, 1963; Arias et al., 1964; Stiehm and Ryan, 1965; Gartner and Arias, 1966) and may be related to inhibition of the hepatic glucuronide conjugating mechanism that is essential for excretion of bilirubin.

Arias et al. (1964) reported that milk from women nursing jaundiced infants contained $3\alpha,20\beta$-pregnanediol, which inhibited glucuronide conjugation in rat liver slices and glucuronide synthesis in liver homogenates or microsome preparations. Subsequently, Arias and Gartner (1964) reported that two healthy one-week-old infants developed hyperbilirubinemia after administration of $3\alpha,20\beta$-pregnanediol. However, Adlard and Lathe (1970) were unable to demonstrate that either $3\alpha,20\beta$-pregnanediol or $3\alpha,20\alpha$-pregnanediol inhibited conjugation of bilirubin by human liver slices or by solubilized human liver microsomes. Hargreaves and Piper (1971) found that $3\alpha,20\beta$-pregnanediol inhibited the secretion of bilirubin glucuronide from rat liver slices, whereas human milk inhibited the activity of glucuronyl transferase. They therefore concluded that the steroid was probably not the sole inhibitory factor. Free fatty acids have been shown to inhibit conjugation of bilirubin in rat liver slices (Bevan and Holton,

1972), but the practical significance of this observation remains uncertain.

As stated by Arias and Gartner (1970), many questions about "breast milk jaundice" remain unanswered; the syndrome is probably of multiple etiology. It is generally agreed (Stiehm and Ryan, 1965; Gartner and Arias, 1966) that the condition is relatively harmless and ordinarily is not a contraindication to continued breast feeding.

Breast Cancer

The Bittner virus, an RNA tumor virus of mice, is transmitted in milk of mice and can be responsible for mouse mammary carcinoma. Several studies have raised the possibility that at least some forms of mammary carcinoma in the human may be similar. A virus particle with structure similar or identical to that of the Bittner virus is known to be present in certain human milks and in human mammary carcinomas (Feller and Chopra, 1969; Moore et al., 1969, 1971). In a survey of American woman (Moore et al., 1971), such particles were detected in the milk of 60 per cent of those with a familial history of breast cancer and in only 5 per cent of those with no familial history of breast cancer.

A number of studies (Schlom et al., 1971, 1973; Axel et al., 1972) have now provided convincing evidence of the chemical similarity (or, possibly, identity) of the human milk RNA particle and known oncogenic RNA viruses.

The significance of RNA tumor viruses in human milk is not yet known. Although there is the implication that RNA molecules appear in cancer cells because human milk virus is replicating in these cells, the findings by no means prove that human breast cancer virus causes breast cancer. It is possible that the virus replicates in the cancer cells because they are cancerous, rather than the converse. It is also possible that human milk virus may be transmitted in ovum and sperm as well as in milk. Avoidance of breast feeding by women with a family history of breast cancer might then have little effect on the likelihood of occurrence of breast cancer in their offspring.

Epidemiologic data generally fail to support the hypothesis that breast feeding is the major mode of transmitting breast cancer in the human (Miller and Fraumeni, 1972). If breast feeding were a major factor in transmission of breast cancer, the decreasing frequency of breast feeding between 1900 and 1950 should have been associated with decreasing rates of breast cancer in the 1950s and 1960s. In fact, breast cancer rates increased (Feinleib and Garrison, 1969). In countries where breast feeding is common, rates of breast cancer are generally low (MacMahon et al., 1970). Family histories of women with breast cancer indicate that cases of breast cancer occur equally in female antecedants on both sides of the family (Macklin, 1959)—not predominantly on the maternal side as would be anticipated if breast feeding were the major mode of transmission. Finally, in the single study of mother-daughter occurrences of breast cancer in regard to infant feeding, no relation to breast feeding was found (Tokuhata, 1969).

Thus, there is at present some basis for concern that human breast cancer virus may be transmitted from mother to infant by breast feeding. However, from the evidence currently available it seems unlikely that total elimination of all breast feeding in the United States would substantially alter breast cancer rates. Additional studies of mother-daughter occurrences of breast cancer in relation to infant feeding are urgently needed. Meanwhile, the possibility of transmission of breast cancer does not appear to be sufficient reason for advising women to avoid breast feeding.

COW MILK

Protein, Fat and Carbohydrate

As previously mentioned, differences in composition of milk from one cow to another are of relatively little significance in infant nutrition, since most infants receive milk pooled from many cows.

Data on composition of cow milk are included in Table 15–1. Major differences are the greater concentrations of protein and minerals and lower concentrations of lactose in cow milk than in human milk. As discussed in Chapter 6, the higher ratio of whey proteins (lactalbumin and lactoglobulins) to casein in human milk than in cow milk has not been demonstrated to be of nutritional advantage for the human infant. Both casein and whey proteins are of exceptionally high quality. Because the content of sulfur-containing amino acids in casein appears to be adequate when requirements for protein are met, the fact that whey proteins contain more of these amino acids than does casein is probably not relevant for the human. However, the high casein content of whole cow milk is responsible for formation of a large and relatively poorly digested mass of curds in the stomach if the milk is not properly treated (e.g., by homogenization, acidification, heating) to reduce curd tension.

Although nonprotein nitrogen comprises a lower percentage of total nitrogen in cow milk (6 per cent) than in human milk (15 per cent), little significance is attributed to this difference. When a protein of high quality is fed, at least some of the nonprotein nitrogen can be utilized by the infant (Snyderman et al., 1962; Picou and Phillips, 1972). It seems likely that the nitrogen of human milk and cow milk can be fully utilized by the infant.

As discussed in Chapter 7, the fat of cow milk is less well digested by infants than is the fat of human milk.

Vitamins and Minerals

The cow, as is true of all ruminants, has a rumen in which food undergoes extensive fermentation and microbial digestion before it reaches the true stomach. For this reason, the nutritional requirements of the cow differ sharply from those of single-stomached omnivorous animals, such as man. Microorganisms in the rumen break down food proteins and, from this source as well as from simple nitrogenous compounds such as ammonia and urea, synthesize proteins, vitamins and other nutrients. It is, to a large extent, this bacterially synthesized protein that the ruminant digests and uses, so that the nutritional quality of food proteins matters much less to ruminant than to nonruminant animals. All vitamins of the B group are synthesized in the rumen through microbial activity, and concentrations of these vitamins in milk of ruminants are therefore less influenced by diet than by factors such as breed and stage of lactation.

Although seasonal variation in content of protein, fat and carbohydrate is not great, amounts of vitamins A* and D are somewhat greater in summer than in winter (Table 15–1). But winter or summer, cow milk is a rich source of vitamin A and a poor source of vitamin D.

Thiamin, riboflavin, vitamin B_6, vitamin B_{12} and folacin are present in greater amounts in cow milk than in human milk. Cow milk contains less preformed niacin than does human milk, but the content of tryptophan in cow milk is greater and total niacin is similar in the two milks.

A major difference in the feeding of human milk and cow milk is that the former is ordinarily consumed directly from the breast and all vitamins originally present in the milk are transferred to the infant; on the other hand, losses of vitamins from cow milk occur during collection, processing, transportation, delivery and storage. In the case of most of the B vitamins, the initial content in cow milk is sufficiently high that moderate losses are of little nutritional significance. As it is expressed from the udder, the vitamin C content of cow milk averages approximately 21 mg/liter, numerous reports giving average values of 16.5 to 27.5 mg/liter (Hartman and Dryden, 1965). Concentrations of vitamin C decrease with processing and storage and, at the time of purchase, have been reported by various authors to range from 2.4 to 20.5 mg/liter with a mean of approximately 11 mg/liter (Hartman and

*That is, vitamin A equivalents calculated from content of vitamin A and carotene.

Dryden, 1965). Further decreases in concentration of vitamin C will occur during storage after purchase. As is true of human milk, the amounts of iron and fluoride in cow milk are too low to make it possible to obtain advisable dietary intakes from this source (Chapters 12 and 14).

Available Forms of Cow Milk

The terms "whole," "pasteurized," "homogenized," "skim," "2 per cent," "evaporated," "condensed," "freeze-dried," "roller-dried," and "spray-dried," as applied to milk, are discussed in the Chapter Appendix. Composition of various forms of cow milk—evaporated, 2 per cent and skim—is indicated in Table 15–3.

TABLE 15–3 COMPOSITION OF SEVERAL FORMS OF COW MILK AND OF FRESH FLUID GOAT MILK*

	Cow Milk			Goat Milk (Fresh Fluid)
	Evaporated Diluted 1:1 With Water	*Fresh Fluid Skim Milk*	*"2 Per Cent"*	
Energy (kcal/100 ml)	68.5	36	59	67
Major constituents (gm/100 ml)				
Protein	3.5	3.6	4.2	3.2
Fat	3.8	0.1	2.0	4.0
Carbohydrate	4.8	5.1	6.0	4.6
Caloric distribution (% of calories)				
Protein	19	40	28	19
Fat	50	3	31	53
Carbohydrate	31	57	41	28
Minerals per liter				
Calcium (mg)	1260	1210	1430	1290
Phosphorus (mg)	1025	950	1120	1060
Sodium (meq)	26	23	27	15
Potassium (meq)	39	37	45	46
Iron (mg)	0.5	trace	1	1
Vitamins per liter				
Vitamin A (I.U.)	1850	90	800	2074
Thiamin (μg)	280	400	400	400
Riboflavin (μg)	1900	1700	2100	1840
Niacin (mg)	1.0	0.9	1.0	1.9
Pyridoxine (μg)	370	450	–	70
Pantothenate (mg)	3.5	3.6	–	3.4
Folacin (μg)	55	55	55	6
Vitamin C (mg)	5.5	19	10	15
Vitamin D (I.U.)	400	–	400	24
Vitamin E (I.U.)	1.3	–	–	–

*Major constituents and minerals from Watt and Merrill (1963); vitamins in "2 per cent" milk from Watt and Merrill (1963); other vitamins from Hartman and Dryden (1965) except folacin. Concentration of folacin in the various types of cow milk is assumed equal to concentration in whole cow milk (Table 15–1); concentration in goat milk is from Ford and Scott (1968).

GOAT MILK

Surprisingly little information has been published concerning nutritional evaluations of goat milk. However, wide clinical experience with this milk as a food for infants and children in many parts of the world suggests that it is nutritionally adequate in most respects. Information about its composition is included in Table 15–3. Its energy value (67 kcal/100 ml) is similar to that of cow milk. Concentrations of chloride, potassium, phosphorus and magnesium are greater in goat milk than in cow milk, and concentrations of sodium and sulfur are less. Goat milk is especially rich in niacin.

Fat of goat milk differs from that of cow milk in that it contains more of the essential fatty acids, linoleic and arachidonic, than does cow milk (4.1 versus 2.6 gm/100 gm of milk fat), and it has a greater percentage of medium- and short-chain fatty acids and a somewhat smaller percentage of long-chain, saturated fatty acids (Chapter 7, Table 7–1). These differences suggest that the fat of goat milk may be more readily digested than that of cow milk.

As discussed in Chapter 9, goat milk is a relatively poor source of folacin. Ford and Scott (1968) have reported a mean value of 6 μg folacin/liter for goat milk (range 2 to 11 μg/liter) compared with mean values of 52 and 55 μg/liter, respectively, for human milk and pasteurized cow milk. The values for goat milk and cow milk reported by Ford and Scott (1968) are similar to values reported by Becroft and Holland (1966). Because it is recognized that infants receiving goat milk as a major source of calories are likely to develop megaloblastic anemia as an expression of folate deficiency, it is recommended that a supplement of 50 μg of folacin be given daily to such infants.

FOREIGN SUBSTANCES IN MILK

Drugs

As pointed out by Knowles (1965), nearly all agents received by the lactating woman will be found in her milk. The distribution of a drug across the membrane between plasma and milk will be influenced by its solubility in lipid and water, by its pKa or degree of ionization and by poorly understood transport mechanisms. In some instances, the amount of drug excreted in milk is considerable. Catz and Giacoia (1972) and Rasmussen (1973) have reviewed various aspects of the passage of drugs from blood plasma to milk, and Rasmussen (1973) has discussed the distribution of drugs in the water, fat and protein phases of milk. Catz and Giacoia (1973) have recommended that the following drugs not be given to nursing women: antimetabolites, most cathartics, radioactive drugs, anticoagulants, tetracycline, iodides, ergot, atropine, metronidazole (Flagyl, Searle), dehydrotachysterol and thiouracil. They suggest that the following be given only under supervision: oral contraceptives, lithium carbonate, sulfonamides, reserpine, steroids, diazepam, diuretics, nalidixic acid, barbiturates, diphenylhydantoin and cough medicines with codeine.

Pesticides

Pesticides are needed to achieve maximum production of acceptable foodstuffs, and adequate control of pests is not possible without some of the pesticide remaining on the plant at harvest. Organochlorine pesticides, including DDT, are now ubiquitous pollutants and can be detected in virtually all animal tissues, even those sampled in remote parts of the world far from areas of large scale pesticide use (Woodwell, 1967).

A Joint FAO/WHO Meeting (1971) has suggested 0.005 mg of DDT per kilogram of body weight as the maximum admissible daily intake for human subjects and has set a practical residue limit for total DDT in cow milk at 0.05 ppm (approximately 50 μg/liter). An alternate method of expressing the practical residue limit is in terms of dietary fat: 1.25 mg of total DDT per kilogram of fat (assuming approximately 40 gm fat per liter of cow milk). Concentrations of DDT in cow milk have generally been maintained within the limits specified by FAO/WHO, at least with respect to milk shipped in interstate commerce in the United States.

That human milk contains higher concentrations of pesticides than does cow milk is not surprising, since pesticides tend to become more concentrated as one samples successively up the food chain; that is, meat-eaters store more DDT than do herbivores (Woodwell, 1967, Woodwell et al., 1967). Concentrations of DDT in human milk have generally been reported to be well above 50 μg/liter (Quinby et al., 1965; Egan et al., 1965; Curley and Kimbrough, 1969; Ritcey et al., 1972; Kroger, 1972; Wilson et al., 1973). Wilson et al. (1973) reported that the concentration of DDT in human milk averaged 100 μg/liter in one city in the United States and 150 to 220 μg/liter in the other six cities in which samples were obtained, with an average concentration in all samples of 170 μg/liter. Similarly, Kroger (1972) reported that only 8 of 53 samples of human milk collected in Pennsylvania had total DDT concentrations less than the tolerance set for cow milk. Reports reviewed by Ritcey et al. (1972) – seven published in the USSR and 12 in European countries – suggest that the situation in the United States is not unlike that elsewhere.

Lead

Utilizing atomic absorption spectroscopy, Murthy and Rhea (1971) reported the average concentration of lead in samples of human milk collected in Cincinnati in April and May of 1968 to be 1.2 μg/100 ml. An average lead concentration of 2.0 μg/100 gm was reported by Lamm et al. (1973) in samples of milk collected in Connecticut in 1971 and 1972. Mitchell and Aldous (cited by Mitchell, 1974) reported an average concentration of 4 μg of lead/100 ml in 270 samples of bulk, pasteurized, homogenized milk collected in New York State. Employing a method of analysis (flameless atomic absorption spectroscopy) that they believed to be superior to the method (conventional atomic absorption spectroscopy) used previously, Lamm and Rosen (1974) reported inability to detect lead in samples of human milk collected in 1972 and 1973 in New York City. The limit of detection by the method was 0.5 μg/100 ml. The average lead content of whole cow milk was reported by Lamm et al. (1973) to be 4.0 μg/100 ml and by Lamm and Rosen (1974) to be less than 0.5 μg/100 ml. On the basis of these observations, it seems likely that the lesser concentration of lead in human milk and cow milk reported by Lamm and Rosen in 1974 than by Lamm et al. (1973) and by other investigators reflects either difference in methods or geographic differences in lead content of human milk and cow milk. The topic is one of lively debate (Sarett, 1974; Rosen and Lamm, 1974; Committee on Nutrition, 1974).

Although the data of Lamm and Rosen (1974) suggest that concentrations of lead in human milk and whole cow milk may be quite low, greater concentrations are present in evaporated milk and infant formulas (Table 15–4). The medical significance of these concentra-

TABLE 15–4 CONCENTRATION OF LEAD IN MILKS AND FORMULAS*

Product	Source	Number of Samples	Lead (μg/100 ml)
Evaporated milk	3 brands	15	11.0 (4–22)†
Infant formulas			
Concentrated	2 brands	6	8.3 (4–12)
Ready-to-feed	2 brands	30	3.3 (0–8)
Homogenized cow milk	3 brands	19	<0.5‡
Human milk	10 women	10	<0.5‡

*Modified from Lamm, S. H., and Rosen, J. F.: Lead contamination in milks fed to infants, 1972–1973. Pediatrics 53:137, 1974.

†Values in parentheses indicate range.

‡Detection limit.

tions of lead in milks and of the lead content of other foods consumed by infants and preschool children is difficult to evaluate (Chapter 19).

FILLED AND IMITATION MILKS

Two distinct types of milks, "filled milk" and "imitation milk," are promoted as substitutes for fresh fluid milk (Chapter Appendix). Filled milk of high nutritional quality can be produced; in fact, except for a specific exemption under the provisions of the Filled Milk Act (1923), most commercially prepared infant formulas would be classified as filled milks.

Filled and imitation milks are usually less expensive than is fresh fluid cow milk. However, as a group, they cannot be recommended for feeding of infants or small children. Prolonged use of most of the imitation milks and of at least some of the filled milks is likely to lead to development of nutritional deficiency disorders.

INFANT FORMULAS – GENERAL CONSIDERATIONS*

With the exception of formulas prepared for use in specific disorders, it seems desirable that a formula provide 7 to 16 per cent of the calories from protein, 30 to 55 per cent of the calories from fat and the remainder of the calories from carbohydrate (Chapter 19). Linoleic acid should account for at least 1 per cent of calories. Minimum desirable concentrations of minerals and vitamins recommended by the Committee on Nutrition (1967) are indicated in Table 15–5. These suggestions have been accepted by the U. S. Food and Drug Administration (Federal Register, 1971). When formulas do not supply these quantities of essential nutrients, supplementation should be provided either as a vitamin-mineral supplement or as a component of other foods. Examples of milk-based formulas are included in Tables 15–6, 15–7 and 15–8, and examples of soy-based formulas, in Table 15–9. Compositions of several special formulas are presented in Table 15–10.

---

*The first edition of this book (in 1967) included specific data on composition of infant formulas marketed in the United States. By 1970, several of the formulas had been modified by the manufacturers, some were no longer marketed at all and a number of new formulas had appeared. The tables were therefore likely to be somewhat misleading. The present edition includes a more general treatment. A reliable source of current information about composition of specific infant formulas marketed in the United States is the annual publication of the Physicians' Desk Reference (e.g., 1974).

TABLE 15–5 MINIMUM VITAMIN AND MINERAL LEVELS/100 KCAL OF FORMULA*

VITAMINS	MINIMUM AMOUNT†
Vitamin A (U.S.P. units)	250
Vitamin D (U.S.P. units)	40
Vitamin E (I.U.)	0.3
Ascorbic acid	8
Thiamin	0.025
Riboflavin	0.06
Niacin	0.25
Vitamin B_6	0.035
Folic acid (μg)	4
Pantothenic acid	0.3
Vitamin B_{12} (μg)	0.15
MINERALS	
Calcium	50
Phosphorus	25
Magnesium	6
Iron	1
Iodine (μg)	5
Copper	0.06

*From Committee on Nutrition, American Academy of Pediatrics: Proposed changes in food and drug administration regulations concerning formula products and vitamin-mineral dietary supplements for infants. Pediatrics *40*:916, 1967.

†Values in milligrams except as noted.

FORMULAS BASED ON COW MILK

Cow Milk With or Without Added Carbohydrate

As mentioned in Chapter 1, formulas made of evaporated milk and added carbohydrate came into widespread use late in the 1920s and, in the United States, accounted for most formula feeding until the 1950s. Similar formulas can be made with fresh fluid whole cow milk and added carbohydrate. These formulas, still occasionally utilized in the United States and commonly used in other countries, supply approximately four-fifths of the calories from cow milk and one-fifth from added carbohydrate, thus providing 14 to 16 per cent of the calories from protein, 36 to 38 per cent from fat and 46 to 50 per cent from carbohydrate. Content of vitamin A and of B vitamins is generous and content of vitamins C and D will depend on whether the milk has been fortified with these vitamins.

In many countries, formulas from powdered whole cow milk with or without added carbohydrate, vitamins and iron are widely used. Examples of such products are presented in the first two columns of Table 15–6. Golden Ostermilk (Glaxo), Ostermilk Two (Glaxo),

TABLE 15–6 EXAMPLES OF COMMERCIALLY PREPARED MILK-BASED FORMULAS MARKETED IN WESTERN EUROPE*

Components						
Protein	Cow milk	Cow milk	Cow milk		Whey and cow milk	
Fat	Butterfat	Butterfat	Butterfat and/or vegetable oils		Vegetable oils†	
Added carbohydrate	None	Variable	Variable		Variable	
Examples	Golden Ostermilk (Glaxo)	Pelargon‡ (Nestlé)	Nidina (Nestlé)	Bebiron (Nutricia)	NAN (Nestlé)	Almiron M2 (Nutricia)
	Ostermilk Two (Glaxo)	Nido ler age (Nestlé)	Nektarmil 1 (Milupa)	Multival§ (Von Heyden)	Baby Semp (Semper)	Humana 1 (Humana)
	Utilac 26 (Glaxo)	Milumil (Milupa)	Tillägg (Findus; Semper)	Trufood¶ (Cow & Gate)	Aptamil (Milupa)	Pomila (Maizena)
	Babymilk 2 (Cow & Gate)		Lemiel 1 (Glaxo)			
Major Constituents (gm/100 ml)						
Protein	3.3–3.6	2.4–3.5	1.8–2.4		1.5–1.8	
Fat	3.4–3.7	2.1–2.8	2.3–3.7		3.5–3.7	
Carbohydrate	4.7–5.3	8.1–10.4	6.6–10.0		7.0–8.3	
Caloric Distribution (% of calories)						
Protein	20–22	14–19	10–14		9–10	
Fat	48–52	25–38	30–45		42–47	
Carbohydrate	28–30	47–57	42–57		43–48	

*A number of formulas are marketed under the same name in different countries although the composition differs; therefore, the classification given here may not apply in some countries. See also Table 15–7 for formulas marketed in the United States and, in some cases, also in Western Europe.

†Several formulas contain some butterfat.

‡Acidified formula; also contains corn oil.

§This product is identical to Similac (Table 15–7).

¶Contains added whey.

TABLE 15–7 EXAMPLES OF COMMERCIALLY PREPARED MILK-BASED FORMULAS MARKETED IN THE UNITED STATES*

Components			
Protein	Nonfat cow milk	Demineralized whey and nonfat cow milk	Nonfat cow milk and soy-protein isolate
Fat	Vegetable oils	Vegetable oils and oleo oil	Corn oil
Added carbohydrate	Lactose or corn syrup solids	Lactose	Sucrose
Examples	Enfamil† (Mead) Similac‡ (Ross)	SMA§ (Wyeth)	Similac Advance (Ross)
Major constituents (gm/100 ml)			
Protein	1.5–1.6	1.5	3.6
Fat	3.6–3.7	3.6	1.6
Carbohydrate	7.0–7.1	7.2	6.6
Minerals	0.3–0.4	0.3	0.7
Caloric distribution (% of calories)			
Protein	9	9	26
Fat	48–50	48	27
Carbohydrate	41–43	43	47
Minerals per liter			
Calcium (mg)	550–600	445	1000
Phosphorus (mg)	440–455	330	800
Sodium (meq)	11–17	7	17
Potassium (meq)	16–28	14	32
Chloride (meq)	12–14	10	29
Magnesium (mg)	40–48	53	85
Sulfur (mg)	130–160	145	310
Copper (mg)	0.4–0.6	0.4	1
Zinc (mg)	2.0–4.2	3.2	4.0
Iodine (μg)	40–69	69	100
Iron (mg)	trace–1.5‖	12.7	18
Vitamins per liter			
Vitamin A (I.U.)	1700–2500	2650	3000
Thiamin (μg)	400–650	710	750
Riboflavin (μg)	600–1000	1060	900
Niacin (mg)	7–8.5	7	10
Pyridoxine (μg)	320–400	423	700
Pantothenate (mg)	2.1–3.2	2.1	5
Folacin (μg)	50–100	32	100
Vitamin B_{12} (μg)	1.5–2.0	1.1	2.5
Vitamin C (mg)	55	58	50
Vitamin D (I.U.)	400–423	423	400
Vitamin E (I.U.)	8.5–12.7	9.5	6.3

*Some are marketed in other countries as well.
†Enfalac in Canada.
‡Multival in some European countries.
§S-26 in other countries. Product marketed as SMA in other countries has different composition.
‖Products also available with 12 to 13 mg iron per liter.

TABLE 15–8 EXAMPLES OF WESTERN EUROPEAN FORMULAS RECOMMENDED FOR YOUNGER AND OLDER INFANTS

			Caloric Distribution (% of Calories)		
Formula	Age* (months)	Energy (kcal/100 ml)	*Protein*	*Fat*	*Carbohydrate*
Nido 1er age		72	19	25	56
Nido 2e age	5	85	16	38	46
Nektarmil 1		72	10	33	57
Nektarmil 2	4–5	92	14	31	55
Humana 1		69	10	46	44
Humana 2	1–2	75	8	52	40

*Youngest age suggested for use of second formula.

Utilac 26 (Glaxo) and Babymilk 2 (Cow and Gate) are generally prepared in the home by addition of water and sucrose. Babymilks and Utilac are marketed as the full-cream products (the examples included in Table 15–6) and as half-cream products (half-cream Utilac and Babymilk 1).

Examples of formulas made from cow milk and added carbohydrate are presented in the second column of Table 15–6. The added carbohydrate is sucrose, corn syrup solids, starch, glucose, fructose or some combination of these. Protein supplies 14 to 19 per cent of calories, fat 25 to 38 per cent of calories and carbohydrate 47 to 57 per cent of calories. Pelargon (Nestlé) is acidified by the action of *Streptococcus lactis.* These products may be marketed in several countries and the composition sometimes differs for the same product in various countries. For example, in some countries vegetable oils may be included as well as butterfat. Vitamin D may not be added and amounts of other vitamins may differ.

As discussed in Chapter 7, fat excretion will generally be somewhat greater when butterfat is fed than when an equal amount of fat is consumed in the form of certain combinations of vegetable oils. The difference in fat absorption will rarely be clinically significant in full-size infants except during the first two weeks of life, but mild to moderate steatorrhea may occur when these formulas are fed to infants of low birth weight. This possibility should be considered when an infant with adequate caloric intake fails to gain weight normally.

Serum concentrations of cholesterol of infants receiving formulas in which the fat is supplied in the form of butterfat are more similar to those of breastfed infants than is true of infants receiving formulas containing various mixtures of vegetable oils (Chapter 7).

A practical consideration in the use of formulas containing butter-

TABLE 15–9 EXAMPLES OF COMMERCIALLY PREPARED FORMULAS WITH PROTEIN FROM SOY ISOLATE OR SOY FLOUR

Components		
Protein	Soy isolate	Soy flour
Fat	Vegetable oils	Vegetable oils
Carbohydrate	Corn syrup solids and/or sucrose	Corn syrup solids and/or sucrose
Examples		
	Isomil (Ross) Neo-Mull-Soy (Syntex) ProSobee (Mead) Nursoy (Wyeth)	Sobee (Bristol Myers)* Mull-Soy (Syntex)
Major constituents (gm/100 ml)		
Protein	1.8–2.5	3.1–3.2
Fat	3.0–3.6	2.6–3.6
Carbohydrate	6.4–6.8	5.2–7.7
Minerals	0.4–0.5	0.5–0.8
Caloric distribution (% of calories)		
Protein	12–15	19
Fat	45–48	35–49
Carbohydrate	39–40	32–46
Minerals per liter		
Calcium (mg)	700–950	1060–1200
Phosphorus (mg)	500–690	530–800
Sodium (meq)	9–24	16–22
Potassium (meq)	15–28	33–41
Chloride (meq)	7–15	14–16
Magnesium (mg)	50–80	75
Copper (mg)	0.4–0.6	0.4
Zinc (mg)	2.0–5.3	3.0
Iodine (μg)	70–160	70–160
Iron (mg)	8.5–12.7	5.0–8.5
Vitamins per liter		
Vitamin A (I.U.)	2100–2500	1590–2110
Thiamin (μg)	400–700	530
Riboflavin (μg)	600–1060	850–1060
Niacin (mg)	5.0–8.4	7.4–9.5
Pyridoxine (μg)	400–530	420–430
Pantothenate (mg)	2.6–5.0	1.0–2.6
Folacin (μg)	50–100	70
Vitamin B_{12} (μg)	2.0–3.0	2.1
Vitamin C (mg)	50–55	42–53
Vitamin D (I.U.)	400–423	423
Vitamin E (I.U.)	9–11	5–11
Vitamin K (mg)	0.09–0.15	0.09

*Not marketed in the United States.

TABLE 15–10 SELECTED SPECIAL FORMULAS

	NUTRAMIGEN (MEAD)	LOFENALAC (MEAD)	PORTAGEN (MEAD)	PREGESTIMIL (MEAD)
Components				
Protein	Casein hydrolysate	Casein hydrolysate	Sodium caseinate	Casein hydrolysate
Fat	Corn oil	Corn oil	MCT and corn oil	MCT and corn oil
Carbohydrate	Sucrose and tapioca starch	Tapioca starch and corn syrup solids	Corn syrup solids and sucrose	Glucose and tapioca starch
Major constituents (gm/100 ml)				
Protein	2.2	2.2	2.3	2.2
Fat	2.6	2.7	3.2	2.8
Carbohydrate	8.6	8.7	7.7	8.8
Caloric distribution (% of calories)				
Protein	13	13	14	13
Fat	35	35	42	36
Carbohydrate	52	52	44	51
Minerals per liter				
Calcium (mg)	950	950	710	950
Phosphorus (mg)	660	660	560	740
Sodium (meq)	14	21	18	14
Potassium (meq)	27	27	27	24
Chloride (meq)	24	23	18	23
Magnesium (mg)	80	80	138	80
Manganese (mg)	2.1	2.1	2.1	2.1
Copper (mg)	0.64	0.64	1.06	0.64
Zinc (mg)	4.2	4.2	4.2	4.2
Iodine (μg)	70	69	106	69
Iron (mg)	12.7	12.7	12.7	12.7
Vitamins per liter				
Vitamin A (I.U.)	2120	2120	2820	2120
Thiamin (μg)	635	635	1060	635
Riboflavin (μg)	1060	1060	1270	1060
Niacin (mg)	8.5	8.5	12.7	8.5
Pyridoxine (μg)	530	530	1370	530
Pantothenate (mg)	3.2	3.2	7.4	3.2
Folacin (μg)	50	50	70	50
Vitamin B_{12} (μg)	2.6	2.6	3.5	2.6
Vitamin C (mg)	55	55	56	55
Vitamin D (I.U.)	423	423	282	423
Vitamin E (I.U.)	10.6	10.6	10.6	10.6
Vitamin K (mg)	0.11	0.11	0.04	0.11

fat is the sour odor of the vomitus. This odor arises from presence of free volatile fatty acids (e.g., butyric acid) and is thus absent when butterfat has been replaced by vegetable oils.

Formulas of Whole Cow Milk, Vegetable Oils and Added Carbohydrate

Formulas made from whole cow milk, vegetable oils and added carbohydrate are little used in the United States but are commonly fed in many other countries. Examples of such products are included in the third column of Table 15–6. These products are generally marketed as powders, but some are also available as concentrated liquid products. They are fortified with vitamins and, in many instances, with iron. The added carbohydrate is sucrose, corn syrup solids, starch, glucose, fructose or some combination of these. Protein supplies 10 to 14 per cent of calories, fat 30 to 45 per cent, and carbohydrate 42 to 57 per cent.

Formulas of Nonfat Cow Milk, Vegetable Oils and Carbohydrate

A number of commercially available formulas are prepared from nonfat cow milk, vegetable oils and added carbohydrate—generally lactose or corn syrup solids. Two examples (Enfamil and Similac) are included in Table 15–7. Protein provides about 10 per cent of calories and fat generally provides about 48 to 50 per cent of calories. The most widely used vegetable oils are corn, coconut and soy—all well absorbed fats (Chapter 7). Approximately one-half of the carbohydrate is lactose, introduced as a component of the fat-free milk solids, and the added carbohydrate may also be lactose. However, since about 1970 a trend toward increased use of corn syrup solids has been evident. Replacement of the added lactose with corn syrup solids appears to be of little nutritional consequence and is economically advantageous.

Formulas in this category provide generous intakes of vitamins (Table 15–7). In the United States, formulas are available either unfortified with iron or fortified to the extent of 12 mg/liter. As discussed in Chapter 12, in spite of recommendations to the contrary (Committee on Nutrition, 1971a), formulas unfortified with iron are still commonly used in the United States. In several countries, iron-fortified formulas are not available.

Commercially prepared milk-based formulas in the United States are generally available in the form of powder, concentrated liquid (133 kcal/100 ml) or ready-to-feed liquid (67 kcal/100 ml). Powdered product is now rarely fed in the United States (Chapter 1, Table 1–6) but remains the most widely used form in other countries and, in some countries, is the only form available.

Formulas with Added Whey Proteins

By combining whey with nonfat cow milk, it is possible to achieve a ratio of whey proteins to casein resembling that of human milk—i.e., approximately 60 per cent of protein from whey and 40 per cent from casein. This differs considerably from cow milk, in which casein accounts for approximately 80 per cent of the protein and whey for only about 20 per cent. Through electrodialysis or ion exchange processes, it is technologically feasible to remove the substantial quantities of minerals present in whey. Minerals can then be added to the formula in any amounts desired and it is therefore possible to produce a formula based on cow milk in which concentrations of individual minerals are similar to average concentrations in human milk. Composition of such formulas, referred to in a number of countries as "humanized" or "adapted" formulas, is presented in Tables 15–6 and 15–7.

SMA (Wyeth) (Table 15–7) contains electrodialyzed whey, nonfat cow milk, lactose, oleo (Chapter 7, Table 7–1) and vegetable oils—coconut, high oleic safflower (Table 7–1) and soy oils—minerals (including iron) and vitamins. The product PM 60/40 (Ross) is generally similar to SMA, except that the fat consists of corn and coconut oils. Concentration of phosphorus is somewhat less in PM 60/40 than in SMA. Several "humanized" formulas marketed in countries other than the United States contain a variable amount of butterfat as well as vegetable oils. Although "humanized" formulas are generally considered to contain no carbohydrate except lactose, similar formulas may contain starch, sucrose or corn syrup solids.

As discussed in Chapter 6, it was at one time generally believed that lactalbumin, the predominant protein of human milk, was nutritionally superior to casein for feeding of infants. This belief was based in part on the historically better growth and lower incidence of disease in breastfed infants than in those fed formulas of cow milk, and in part on the demonstrated nutritional superiority of lactalbumin over casein in studies with various hair-bearing animals. However, it now seems clear that the difficulties once encountered with formula feeding were due at least partially to bacterial contamination and to the relatively high curd tension of many of the formulas.

Although formulas containing partially demineralized whey proteins have not been demonstrated to be nutritionally superior to other milk-based formulas for the normal infant, they appear to be of high nutritional quality and are likely to be preferable in certain instances. The relatively low renal solute load is an asset in management of the infant with inability to concentrate the urine because of renal disease or diabetes insipidus. It may also be an asset in management of infants with severe congenital heart disease and other conditions in which difficulty is encountered in achieving an adequate caloric intake (Chapter 10). Because renal solute load in relation to caloric concentration is less than that of other formulas, a greater margin of safety is provided when high caloric feedings (i.e., 100 kcal/100 ml or greater) are indicated. In addition, because the advisable daily intake of sodium is supplied but is not greatly exceeded when caloric requirements are met, these formulas are useful in long-term management of infants with congestive cardiac failure.

Milk-Based Formulas for Older Infants

As discussed previously (Chapter 1, Fig. 1–5), most parents discontinue formula feeding of their infants between four and five months of age and thereafter feed whole, skim or "2 per cent" cow milk. For the infant who has been receiving an iron-fortified formula, the substitution of fresh milk for formula will almost certainly be associated with a decreased intake of iron. If "2 per cent" milk or, especially, if skim milk is fed, the diet will usually be unbalanced with respect to percentage of calories supplied from protein, fat and carbohydrate (Chapter 19). When skim milk is fed, calorie intake may be inadequate (Chapter 3).

Thus, the concept of a formula specifically designed for the older infant seems sound, if for no other reason than to ensure continued feeding of a nutritionally adequate product after infants are graduated from "infant formula." In Western Europe, there is a long tradition in use of such formulas which originated in the concept of maturation of absorptive functions, particularly with regard to fat. From the examples presented in Table 15–8, one cannot easily determine the nutritional rationale in these pairs of formulas. At least in one instance (Humana), only the formula for the older infant is fortified with iron. In formulas for the older infant, caloric density is higher and usually a higher percentage of calories is provided by fat. The age suggested for change-over varies from six weeks to five months. In the United States, on the other hand, the product, Similac Advance (Ross), promoted for feeding of older infants, is of relatively low caloric concentration and provides a small percentage of calories in the form of fat (Table 15–7). Percentage of calories from protein is even greater than that of the European formulas for older infants (Table 15–8).

Similac Advance is certainly preferable to skim milk for infant feeding and, on the basis of its content of ascorbic acid and iron, is probably preferable to "2 per cent" milk. Nevertheless, there appears to be little sound rationale for feeding four- to six-month-old infants in the United States a formula relatively high in content of protein and carbohydrate and low in content of fat. As discussed in Chapter 19, an infant's diet should provide 7 to 16 per cent of calories from protein, 30 to 55 per cent of calories from fat and the remainder from carbohydrate.

A formula fed to older infants should be designed to complement the other dietary components. In the United States, where beikost generally contributes substantially to intakes of carbohydrate and protein but not to intakes of fat (Chapter 16), a formula rich in protein and carbohydrate and poor in fat does not appear to be the most logical choice. Nevertheless, many physicians and parents in the United States believe that use of such a formula will aid in preventing or correcting obesity. Evidence to support this belief is not available and further studies regarding factors controlling food intake and obesity of infants are needed. Similarly, the desirability of the formulas high in caloric density and in protein content fed to older infants in Europe must be questioned. Conflicting opinions concerning nutritional management of older infants in developed countries will not be resolved without well designed feeding studies.

MILK-FREE FORMULAS AND SPECIAL FORMULAS

Milk-free diets are utilized most commonly in management of infants who are allergic to milk or are suspected of milk allergy (Chapter 17). They have been recommended for management of "the potentially allergic infant" (Glaser and Johnstone, 1953; Johnstone and Dutton, 1966) and are essential in management of infants with galactosemia and congenital or secondary lactase deficiency (Chapter 8). They may also be of value in management of certain infants with inborn errors of amino acid metabolism. In addition, milk-free or specially prepared formulas based on milk or on components of milk are utilized for management of infants with a variety of illnesses. It is evident that management of the allergic infant, the infant with lactase deficiency, an inborn error of metabolism or other serious disease, is likely to include extensive dietary restriction in addition to avoidance of milk. A milk-free or special formula thus often becomes the major or even sole source of most essential nutrients for many months.

Published reports of deficiency diseases developing in infants receiving various milk-free formulas indicate the importance of an awareness of the composition and the nutritional properties of these diets. As will be discussed, deficiencies of vitamins A, K and thiamin have been reported in infants receiving soy-based formulas unsupplemented with these vitamins. Deficiencies of riboflavin, folic acid and vitamin E have been reported in infants receiving a protein hydrolysate formula produced in England for treatment of phenylketonuria (Wilson and Clayton, 1962), and vitamin K deficiency has been reported in infants receiving a protein-hydrolysate formula (Goldman and Desposito, 1966).

Milk-free formulas currently marketed in the United States appear to provide adequate amounts of vitamin K (Schneider et al., 1974).

Soy-Based Formulas

In the United States in the 1950s and 1960s, formulas with protein contributed from soy flour were utilized as milk substitutes. Although more satisfactory than most other milk substitutes available at the time, parents complained that the formulas produced loose, somewhat malodorous stools that stained the diapers and not infrequently resulted in excoriation of the diaper area. The formulas were pale tan in color and had a slightly nutty odor.

Formulas based on soy flour are rarely used in the United States at present. However, a great deal of information is available from animal studies and clinical experience with such formulas as Mull-Soy and Sobee (Table 15–9). Bebenago (Nago) and Lactopriv (Töpfer) are soy flour-based formulas marketed in Europe.

In the mid 1960s, formulas with protein from water-soluble soy isolates rather than from soy flour became popular in the United States, and early in the 1970s these formulas almost completely replaced soy flour formulas. Soy-isolate formulas* are white in color, nearly odorless and are rarely reported to cause loose or malodorous stools. Unofficial estimates by manufacturers of infant formulas suggest that, in 1973, about 10 per cent of infants in the United States were fed soy-isolate formulas. Examples of soy-isolate formulas are included in Table 15–9.

General Considerations

Howard et al. (1956) reported that reproduction and lactation were adequately supported in several generations of rats fed a soy-flour formula (Mull-Soy). Similar studies of other soy-based formulas have not been reported.

The influence of processing on protein quality appears to be much greater in the case of soy than in the case of milk. For various commercially available soy-based formulas, György et al. (1961) reported PER values from 1.39 to 2.20 (skim milk control 2.63), and the Committee on Nutrition (1963) reported values from 1.3 to 2.0 (casein control 2.5). As discussed in Chapter 6, results of PER studies applying, as they do, to rats fed protein-deficient diets, may not be predictive of nutritionally important differences when generous amounts of these proteins are fed to infants. However, when soy protein is fed at intakes approaching the requirement, the quality of the protein may be critical. A well processed soy-isolate protein supplemented with

*For convenience, we have referred to soy protein isolate-based formulas as "soy isolate formulas" or "soy isolate-based formulas."

small amounts of L-methionine and fed in amounts that provide 1.6 gm of protein/100 kcal appears to be nutritionally equivalent to cow milk or human milk protein fed at the same percentage of calories (Fomon et al., 1973). Omans et al. (1963) reported that food efficiency in premature infants fed soy-based formulas correlated reasonably well with PER values.

Heat-labile, physiologically active substances, including a trypsin inhibitor, are present in raw soybean meal and are presumably the cause of adverse reactions (e.g., poor growth, low protein efficiency ratios and pancreatic hypertrophy) when raw soybeans are fed to nonruminant animals. Theuer and Sarett (1970) have reported that 100 mg of unheated soy-protein isolate inhibited 3.9 mg of trypsin. After heat treatment in processing of three commercially available soy-isolate formulas, amounts of trypsin inhibited were 0.05, 0.3 and 0.8 mg/100 mg of protein. Whether this 16-fold difference in residual concentration of trypsin inhibitor is of nutritional significance is unknown. Longenecker et al. (1964) demonstrated that properly heat-treated soy-protein isolates supplemented with methionine gave PER values nearly equivalent to those with casein. Earlier studies with formulas containing soy flour gave PER values 62 to 80 per cent those of casein (Omans et al., 1963; Committee on Nutrition, 1963; Harkins and Sarett, 1967). An experimental soy-isolate formula with lactose as the carbohydrate promoted growth of infant pigs at about 85 per cent that found with a similar milk-based formula (Schneider and Sarett, 1969).

As discussed in Chapter 7, fats appear to be somewhat less well absorbed from some soy-based than from milk-based formulas. Soy-based formulas contain hemicelluloses and α-galactosides (raffinose and stachyose), which are undigestible. However, the amount of these sugars in soy flour formulas is only about 130 mg/gm of protein and therefore represents only a small percentage of total carbohydrate in the formula (Gitzelmann, 1965; Gitzelmann and Auricchio, 1965). Even smaller amounts of these undigestible sugars are present in soy-isolate formulas. As discussed in Chapter 8, the fact that stachyose and raffinose contain galactose is not a contraindication to use of these formulas in patients with galactosemia.

Percentage absorption of minerals from soy-based formulas is less than from milk-based formulas. The absence of lactose in soy-based formulas may explain, at least in part, the relatively poor absorption of minerals. Theuer et al. (1971) have reported that processing of soy isolate-based formulas may increase the bioavailability of iron salts from these products.

Enlargement of the thyroid gland develops when young rats are fed a diet of raw soybeans or soy flour without additional intake of iodine. The goitrogenic effects of soy flour in rats can be diminished by treatment with organic solvents (presumably extracting some goitrogenic agent) or by heating, and rats are protected against the goitrogenic effects by supplementation of the diet with iodine (Sarett, 1955; Committee on Nutrition, 1963). Several investigators reported development of goiter in infants fed Mull-Soy before this formula was supplemented with iodine (Van Wyk et al., 1959; Shepard et al., 1960; Hydovitz, 1960; Ripp, 1961). Soy formulas are now commonly fortified with iodine, and studies of weanling rats demonstrate no thyroid enlargement when such formulas are fed.

When organic solvents are employed for the extraction of fat from soy flour, the fat-soluble vitamins native to the bean are lost (Committee on Nutrition, 1963). Deficiencies of vitamin A (Cornfield and Cooke, 1952; Bass and Caplan, 1955; Wolf, 1958) and vitamin K (Goldman and Desposito, 1966; Williams et al., 1970, Committee on Nutrition, 1971b) have been reported in infants receiving soy formulas not supplemented with vitamins A or K. Vitamins of the B complex may also be lost during processing of soy (Committee on Nutrition, 1963) and thiamin deficiency has been reported in infants receiving soy formulas not supplemented with thiamin (Davis and Wolf, 1958; Cochrane et al., 1961.)

Clinical Studies With Soy-Based Formulas

Glaser and Johnstone (1952) reported generally satisfactory growth of 42 infants fed the soy flour-based formula, Mull-Soy, during the first five to nine months of life. Experimental formulas based on soy meal supplemented with DL-methionine were found to promote retention of nitrogen by normal infants to the same extent as human milk (Fomon, 1959; Fomon et al., 1964). Kay et al. (1960) reported that gains in weight and length were similar for 12 infants fed Mull-Soy and 12 infants fed an evaporated milk formula during the first three months of life. Hemoglobin concentration, hematocrit and serum concentration of albumin were also reported to be similar for the two groups.

Omans et al. (1963) reported comparative studies of two soy-based formulas fed to low-birth-weight infants. Sobee, a full-fat soy flour formula, promoted weight gain to nearly the same extent as did the control, milk-based formula. However, because the fat of the milk-based formula was butterfat, one might question its suitability as a control for studies of low-birth-weight infants. The other formula, Soyalac (Loma Linda), was a soy isolate-based product that did not promote satisfactory weight gain.

The most satisfactory report of clinical evaluation of a soy flour formula is that published by Bates et al. (1968) with 20 normal infants fed Mull-Soy between 8 and 112 days of age. Growth in weight and length was similar to that of infants fed milk-based formulas, and serum concentrations of albumin were similar to those of normal breastfed infants.

Formulas based on soy isolates fortified with DL- or with L-methionine have been studied by a number of investigators. Cherry et al. (1968) have reported a comparative study of female infants fed a milk-based formula or an experimental soy-isolate formula during the first six months of life. Weight gain and bone development (as judged by roentgenographic evidence of tibial width) were considerably less rapid by infants fed the soy-isolate formula. It seems likely that the formula was deficient in magnesium and zinc and, possibly, in methionine. Bates et al. (1968) demonstrated normal growth in weight and length by 19 normal infants fed Neo-Mull-Soy (Syntex) between 8 and 112 days of age. Serum concentrations of albumin at age 112 days were similar to those of normal breastfed infants. Graham et al. (1970) have demonstrated similar rates of gain in weight and increase in serum concentration of albumin by malnourished infants fed ProSobee (Mead) as by those fed milk-based formulas. The relation between retention and intake of nitrogen with the two feedings was also similar. A study comparing growth and acceptability of two soy-isolate formulas – Neo-Mull-Soy (Syntex) and Nursoy (Wyeth) – has been reported by Wiseman (1971). However, only 170 of the 239 infants completed the planned two months of feeding. Because of this and because of the variable ages at time of enrollment, it is difficult to evaluate the results.

The study of an experimental soy-isolate formula with concentration of protein similar to that of human milk (Fomon et al., 1973) is discussed in Chapter 6. This formula was judged to be completely satisfactory so far as could be determined by growth, serum chemical determinations and metabolic balance studies.

From the human studies just mentioned as well as from a number of animal studies (e.g., Committee on Nutrition, 1963; Sarett, 1973), it is apparent that nutritional adequacy may vary considerably from one product to another. Extensive clinical testing of new products is desirable before they are marketed.

Special Formulas

A number of milk-free, soy-free formulas and special milk-based formulas are utilized for feeding infants with particular problems. The composition of four such formulas is presented in Table 15–10.

Nutramigen (Mead). This product consists of enzymatic hydrolysate of casein with added sucrose, tapioca starch, corn oil, minerals and vitamins. Approximately 65 per cent of the amino acids are present in the free form and the remainder are present as polypeptides. The pattern of essential amino acids is the same as that of casein. Nitrogen retention of children receiving Nutramigen was reported by Hartmann et al. (1942) to be similar to that of infants receiving milk, meat and eggs, but the conditions of testing were not sufficiently rigorous to provide an adequate evaluation. Nevertheless, PER studies suggest excellent nutritional quality (Committee on Nutrition, 1963; Sarett, 1973). Long-term growth studies of normal infants receiving this formula have not been reported; however, our unpublished observations of 14 normal female infants between 8 and 112 days of age demonstrated normal growth and serum biochemical values.

Acidosis and failure to thrive have been reported in five infants fed Nutramigen (Healy, 1972) and it was suggested that some infants may be unable to compensate metabolically for the acid load supplied by the formula. The formula is buffered to pH 6.5 because of its amino acid content. As suggested by Kildeberg and Winters (1972), further study of acid-base balance of infants receiving various feedings is desirable.

Nutramigen contains a trace of lactose (approximately 16 mg/67 kcal) believed to represent a contaminant of the casein from which it is prepared (Committee on Nutrition, 1963). However, it has been used successfully by Isselbacher (1959) and Donnell et al. (1961) in the management of patients with galactosemia.

Lofenalac (Mead). In the preparation of Lofenalac by the manufacturer, various aromatic amino acids, including phenylalanine, are absorbed by charcoal from an enzymatic digest of casein similar to that used in Nutramigen. The product is then supplemented with L-methionine, L-tyrosine, L-tryptophan and L-histidine. Corn oil, corn syrup solids, tapioca starch, vitamins and minerals are added. Concentrations of vitamins and minerals are, in most instances, the same in Lofenalac as in Nutramigen (Table 15–10).

Lofenalac supplemented with phenylalanine appears to be nutritionally equivalent to Nutramigen when fed to growing rats (Sarett, 1973). Normal rhesus monkeys fed Lofenalac supplemented with phenylalanine between 30 and 75 days of age grew at rates similar to those of monkeys fed Similac, but demonstrated dermatitis and abnormal serum concentrations of several amino acids (Kerr et al., 1969).

A preliminary estimate of requirement for phenylalanine by normal infants during the first few months of life is 57 mg/100 kcal (Chapter 6), and the data of Kennedy et al. (1967) suggest that the requirement for infants with phenylketonuria may be in the same general range. Thus, Lofenalac, which provides approximately 18 mg of phenylalanine/100 kcal is almost certainly inadequate as a sole source of this amino acid. It is therefore not surprising that a number of complications of treatment have been reported in patients receiving little phenylalanine other than that supplied by Lofenalac. Such complications include retarded growth, dermatitis, abnormal bone development, megaloblastic anemia and hypoproteinemia (Hanley et al., 1970). Few investigators now attempt to maintain serum concentrations of phenylalanine in the range described for normal individuals. Hunt and Sutherland (1971) reported that normal growth and mental development could be achieved when serum concentrations of phenylalanine were maintained between 5 and 10 mg/100 ml. By careful proportioning of the amounts of Lofenalac or other semi-synthetic products low in phenylalanine and of another source of protein of known phenylalanine content, it is usually possible to maintain serum concentrations within the desired range.

Because of the lesser concentration of phenylalanine in whey proteins than in casein, formulas with a predominance of whey proteins (i.e., "humanized" formulas) seem preferable to cow milk as a supplementary source of phenylalanine. Hambraeus et al. (1970) reported satisfactory results in management of two infants fed the greater part of their caloric intake in the form of the humanized formula, Milkotal, and a smaller part of their intake in the form of the phenylalanine-poor formula, Minafen (Trufood).

Portagen (Mead). Some properties of medium-chain triglycerides (i.e., triglycerides of fatty acids with C-8 or C-10 chain length) have been discussed in Chapter 7. Portagen has been formulated to take advantage of these properties. It is prepared from sodium caseinate, medium-chain triglycerides (from coconut oil), corn oil (to provide essential fatty acids), sucrose, corn syrup solids, vitamins and minerals. The product is supplied as a powder.

It is useful in management of patients with chyluria, intestinal lymphangiectasia and various steatorrheas. Feeding studies with normal infants have not been reported but Graham et al. (1973) have reported success in management of four infants with kwashiorkor and three infants with persistent hypoalbuminemia. It was the impression of these investigators that Portagen was at least as satisfactory as the casein-sucrose-cottonseed oil mixture they had used in other studies. They consider that the vitamin and mineral content is particularly favorable, stating that with locally formulated feeding mixtures they had encountered evidences of magnesium deficiency, inadequate niacin intake, probable zinc deficiency and probable zinc toxicity.

Pregestimil (Mead). This product, with nitrogen supplied in the form of casein hydrolysate, fat predominantly in the form of medium-chain triglycerides (MCT) and carbohydrate primarily in the form of glucose, has been found useful in management of infants with short bowel syndrome and other severe gastrointestinal abnormalities in which absorption of a number of nutrients is impaired. Favorable results with this product have been reported by Graham et al. (1973) in management of patients with marasmus and, in some instances, associated severe diarrhea and infection.

Because of the presence of glucose and amino acids, which would give rise to the Maillard reaction (Chapter 6) if the product were heated after addition of glucose, it is available only in powdered form. The tapioca starch, which provides 15 per cent of calories, may not be fully digested by the young infant (Chapter 8).

Lonalac (Mead). Designed as an aid in the management of adults and children with congestive cardiac failure, Lonalac is a product extremely low in sodium (approximately 1 meq/liter or /667 kcal). It is prepared from casein, coconut oil, lactose, minerals and vitamins and provides a caloric distribution similar to that of whole milk. Because it is nearly free of an essential nutrient (sodium), it is clearly not designed for long-term management in the absence of an additional source of sodium. Lonalac is the only formula marketed in the United States in which fat is derived exclusively from coconut oil. Whether difficulties reported with other formulas containing coconut oil as the sole fat (Ballabriga et al., 1962) apply to Lonalac is not known. Renal solute load is relatively high and there is some question about whether the formula, Lonalac, should be used under any circumstances. Feedings that may be more suitable for management of infants with severe congenital heart disease are discussed in Chapters 10 and 19.

Cho-Free Formula Base (Syntex). With the exception that it is free of carbohydrate, this product is similar to the formula, Neo-Mull-Soy (Table 15–9). It consists of soy-isolate protein, soy oil, vitamins and minerals. In cases of suspected disaccharidase deficiency or monosaccharide intolerance, Cho-Free Formula Base is a highly useful aid in diagnosis because it permits comparison of the effects of feeding diets which are identical except for carbohydrate content. Mixed with glucose, the product is useful in treating patients with combined deficiency of lactase, maltase and sucrase. Use of this product without addition of carbohydrate should be avoided because of the danger of ketosis and hypoglycemia (Lifshitz et al., 1970).

Meat-Based Formulas. Meat Base Formula (M.B.F., Gerber) is prepared from beef heart with added fat and carbohydrate. Approximately 50 per cent of fat in the formula is derived from meat, the remainder from sesame oil. The carbohydrate is supplied from sucrose and modified tapioca starch. Since Meat Base Formula is relatively high in protein and fat, but relatively low in carbohydrate, additional carbohydrate is ordinarily added before feeding.

Several studies of growth and nitrogen balance in infants receiving meat as the sole source of protein have been reported (Committee on Nutrition, 1963), but studies with commercially available products have not been published. The protein efficiency ratio of Meat Base Formula was found to be 80 per cent that of casein.

Although a trace of galactose is present, presumably arising from a galactoside in heart muscle (Committee on Nutrition, 1963), it seems unlikely that the amounts present would be harmful to patients with galactosemia.

RADIOACTIVITY OF INFANT FOODS*

"We live in a sea of radiation. As far as is known, man always has and always will live in an environment filled with radiation. There are radioactive materials present naturally in the ground, the sea, and the air. Cosmic rays bombard us from outerspace" (Dunning, 1962). To consider radioactivity of foods in proper perspective, it is desirable to compare the estimated whole body radiation doses from natural sources, from medical sources, from fallout (including contamination of food) and from miscellaneous sources. As may be seen from Table 15–11, radiation from natural sources contributes an estimated 130 mrem/year; medical sources contribute an estimated 98 mrem/year, whereas fallout contributes only about 4 mrem/year. Although radioactive contamination of foods constitutes some hazard for the infant and small child, these hazards are almost certainly exceedingly small.

Since the advent of nuclear weapons testing, radioactive fallout has been attributable in large measure to such testing. However, peacetime operations are becoming increasingly important as possi-

---

*The authors gratefully acknowledge the aid of Dr. Gilbert B. Forbes in preparation of this section.

TABLE 15–11 ESTIMATED WHOLE BODY RADIATION DOSE TO UNITED STATES POPULATION IN 1970*

Source of Radiation	Dosage (mrem/person/year)
Natural sources (cosmic rays, terrestrial, internal emitters)	130
Medical (diagnostic radiology, therapy)	98
Fallout (including contamination of food)	4
Miscellaneous (television, other consumer products†, air transport)	3

*Adapted by Forbes (1973) from Special Studies Group, Environmental Protection Agency, 1972. It should be noted that these are average figures. Certain groups such as physicians, radiology personnel, laboratory workers, airplane pilots, atomic plant personnel, etc., receive considerably more radiation.

†Including luminous watch dials, fire detection devices, gauges, etc.

ble sources of radioactive contamination of the environment. Reactor installations in power plants, submarines and ships contribute radioactivity to the environment both through normal operation and through accidents; radioisotope applications in medicine, industry and agriculture are also a source of contamination. In addition to physical half-life and the amount of the fission products released into the environment, the relative hazard from a specified radioactive material is governed by the efficiency of transfer through the food chain to the human diet, the degree of absorption by the body, and the length of time retained in the body. By these criteria, the radioisotopes of greatest concern are iodine-131, barium-140, strontium-89, strontium-90 and cesium-137. Strontium-90 and cesium-137 are long-lived isotopes and constitute the major contaminants of food from fallout during peacetime and in the absence of atomic testing.

Iodine-131, Barium-140 and Strontium-89

Iodine-131, with a half-life of approximately eight days, is present in the infant's diet primarily in cow milk, since fallout of this isotope on grass results in a relatively high intake by the cow. Concentrations of iodine-131 in cow milk are greatest during the summer months that follow detonation of a nuclear device (Fig. 15–2). The concentration

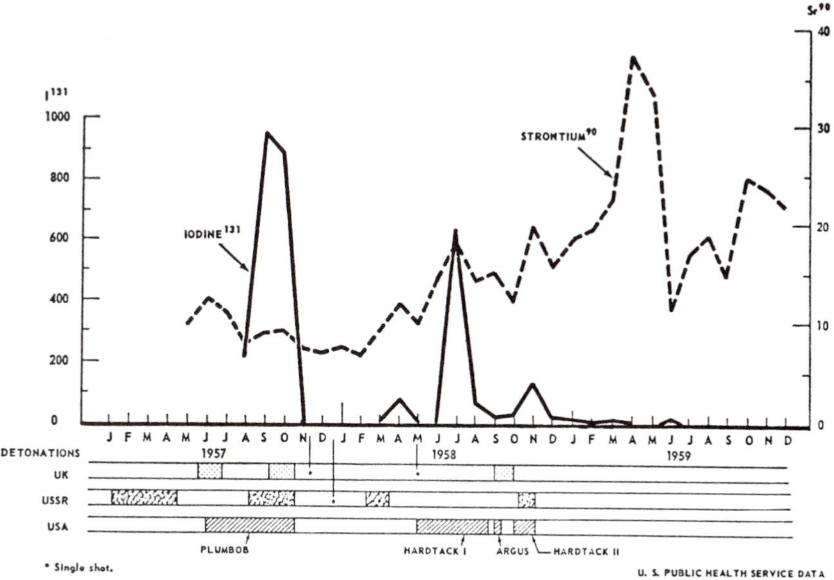

Figure 15–2 Concentrations of iodine-131 and strontium-90 in cow milk in St. Louis, Missouri, from 1957 through 1959. (From Dunning, G. M.: Foods and fallout. Borden's Rev. Nutr. Res. *23*:1, 1962.)

of iodine-131 in human milk is only about one-tenth that in cow milk. Iodine-131 is concentrated in the thyroid gland and, because of the relatively large intake of milk by the infant and the relatively small size of the thyroid gland, resulting thyroid radiation will be greater for the infant than for the adult. Because of the short half-life, storing the milk or milk product for a time before it is consumed will result in loss of the isotope. In the case of iodine-131, storage for one month will reduce the concentration to 7 per cent of its original value (Forbes, 1962). After two months, only 0.6 per cent of the original amount remains. Thus, any powdered or evaporated milk product will be nearly free of iodine-131. In addition, it is possible to block uptake of iodine-131, to some extent, by daily intake of a few milligrams of stable iodine in the form of potassium iodide (Forbes, 1962).

Barium-140, with a half-life of 13 days, and strontium-89, with a half-life of 53 days, are relatively short-lived radioisotopes whose metabolism is somewhat similar to that of calcium. These materials are deposited primarily in bone, as is true of strontium-90. Because of the short half-lives of these radionuclides, they will continue to be present in the diet for only a limited time after atmospheric detonation of a nuclear device and are therefore of less biologic significance than strontium-90.

Strontium-90

Strontium-90, with a half-life of 20 years, is a major radionuclide of fallout responsible for radiation of bone. Because it is handled by the body in much the same fashion as calcium, the ratio of strontium-90 to calcium in food is of more medical significance than the absolute amount of strontium-90 in the diet. Intake of strontium-90 is therefore frequently considered in terms of the "strontium unit," defined as one picocurie (2.2 disintegrations per minute) of strontium-90 per gram of calcium. Proportionately less strontium than calcium is absorbed by the intestine, passed from mother to fetus across the placenta and secreted in milk. Proportionately more strontium than calcium is excreted in urine. Human milk contains only about one-tenth as much strontium-90 per gram of calcium as does the woman's diet (Lough et al., 1960).

Commercially prepared liquid and powdered formulas based on cow milk contain approximately the same ratio of strontium-90 to calcium as does cow milk. Formulas based on demineralized whey, casein hydrolysate or soy protein contain calcium predominantly added from sources uncontaminated with strontium-90 and therefore the strontium to calcium ratio in these products is low.

Figure 15–3 indicates the strontium-90 intake from the average diets consumed by inhabitants of New York City and San Francisco

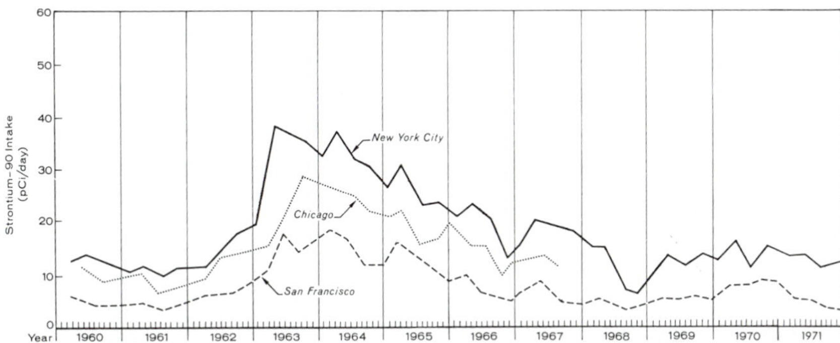

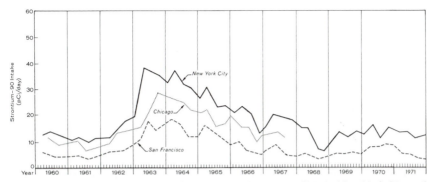

Figure 15–3 Concentrations of strontium-90 in average diets in New York City and San Francisco from 1960 to 1971, and in Chicago from 1960 to 1967. (From U. S. Environmental Protection Agency, Office of Radiation Programs: Radiation Data and Reports. Vol. 13. Washington, D.C., U.S. Government Printing office, 1972, p. 683.)

from 1960 through 1971 and in Chicago from 1960 to 1967. It may be seen that appreciable increases in concentration occurred in 1963 and 1964, reflecting atomic weapons testing in 1961. Of the total strontium intake of the U.S. population in 1968, it is estimated that 38 per cent was contributed by dairy products, 22 per cent by vegetables, 22 per cent by fruits and 11 per cent by cereals and bakery products (Committee on Food Protection, 1973).

Intakes and excretions of strontium-90 by infants in Cincinnati from 1960 through 1964 have been reported by Kahn et al. (1969). One may speculate that intakes in 1972 and 1973 were only one-third to one-fourth the intakes in 1962 and 1963.

Cesium-137

Cesium-137, with a half-life of 30 years, is distributed through the fat-free body tissues in a manner similar to potassium. The body burden of cesium-137 is contributed primarily by milk, meat and grain. The body does not discriminate against cesium-137 in favor of potassium, and the ratio of cesium-137 to potassium in the body eventually becomes about threefold greater than that in the diet. Although the physical half-life is long, the biologic half-life is short, the average value being about 100 days. For the infant, biologic half-life may be as short as 20 days. Data on the cesium-137 content of infant formulas in the 1970s are not available. However, in 1971 in New York City, Chicago and San Francisco, the cesium-137 content of the average diet of adults was extremely low—near the limit of detectability (U.S. Environmental Protection Agency, 1972) and it may be assumed that infant diets were also low in this radionuclide.

Appendix

Whole Milk

In the United States, standards for the composition of whole milk have been set by individual states. Many states define whole milk as milk that contains not less than 3.25 per cent fat and not less than 8.25 per cent fat-free milk solids. Most of the milk marketed in the United States is pasteurized and homogenized. Milk that receives no heat treatment is spoken of as raw milk. Most whole milk sold by dairies is fortified with 400 I.U. of vitamin D per quart.

Pasteurized Milk

Milk is heated to at least 63° C (145° F) and held at or above this temperature continuously for at least 30 minutes, or (as is now more commonly done) heated to at least 72° C (161° F) and held at or above this temperature continuously for at least 15 seconds, then cooled promptly.

Homogenized Milk

Heated milk is forced under high pressure through small openings to disperse the fat into smaller globules which then remain for days as a fine emulsion throughout the milk.

Skim Milk

Milk from which fat has been removed by centrifugation is referred to as skim milk and generally contains 0.1 per cent fat. In the United States, the product is pasteurized and contains a minimum of 8.0 to 9.25 per cent total solids, depending on the laws of the various states. Skim milk may be fortified with vitamins A and D, usually to the extent of 2000 and 400 I.U., respectively, per quart. Additional fat-free milk solids are sometimes added. Fresh fluid, evaporated and dry skim milk are available.

Two Per Cent Milk

The designation "2 per cent milk" is applied to a product made from fresh whole and skim milk combined to contain 2 per cent fat.

The milk is pasteurized and homogenized. Fat-free milk solids, vitamins and minerals may be added.

Evaporated Milk

In older methods, milk was preheated to about 95° C (203° F) for 10 minutes and then concentrated in vacuum pans at a temperature of 50 to 55° C (122 to 131° F). The product was next homogenized and run into cans which were sterilized in a steam autoclave at about 115° C (239° F) for not less than 15 minutes. In modern methods of processing, preheating is done at much higher temperatures for a much shorter time. For example, preheating may be at 120° C (248° F) for three minutes, or the concentrated product may be sterilized in a continuous flow and then run aseptically into cans. Such a product has a lower viscosity, whiter color and fresher flavor than the double-heated product. The ratio of fat to nonfatty solids in the original milk is usually standardized so that proportions in the final product remain constant.

Condensed Milk

In the preparation of condensed milk, sugar is added to the milk before the evaporation process is initiated. This milk contains not less than 28.0 per cent milk solids and 8.3 per cent milk fat. Sugar accounts for 40 to 45 per cent of weight of the product, acting as a preservative. The ratio of calories to water is high (321 kcal/100 ml compared to 146 kcal/100 ml in evaporated milk, 67 kcal/100 ml in fresh fluid milk). Condensed milk is not recommended for infant feeding.

Freeze-Dried Milk

Milk is produced by a process in which water is removed by sublimation of the ice crystals from the deep-frozen product at low temperature in a relatively high vacuum.

Roller-Dried Milk

Preheated, and sometimes homogenized, milk is delivered in a thin film on the smooth surface of a single or of twin steam-heated rotating drums; the film of dried milk is scraped off as it forms and is then ground to powder. A refinement of this process includes prior removal of some of the water by enclosing the drums in a vacuum chamber. In its most modern form, the roller process gives a high quality product of relatively good solubility. The process is little used in the United States.

Spray-Dried Milk

Concentrated milk, usually preheated, is "atomized" to a foglike mist into a current of heated air. The minute milk particles give off their moisture almost instantaneously and drop to the bottom of the drying chamber as small grains of dried milk. Solubility and flavor of the product are good.

Filled Milk

A filled milk is a combination of skim milk and vegetable oil, usually coconut, partially hydrogenated soy or corn oil (Council on Foods and Nutrition, 1969). Two types of filled milk are sold. One is a combination of fluid skim milk and vegetable oil, sometimes with the addition of skim milk solids. The other consists of water, nonfat dry milk, vegetable oil, corn syrup solids and soy protein or sodium caseinate (Committee on Nutrition, 1972).

Imitation Milk

Imitation milks consist of water, protein (usually sodium caseinate or soy isolate), corn syrup solids, sucrose and vegetable oil. Many such products are nutritionally inferior to milk, and some contain as little as 1.0 gm protein/100 ml (Committee on Nutrition, 1972).

REFERENCES

Adinolfi, M., Glynn, A. A., Lindsay, M., and Milne, C. M.: Serological properties of γA antibodies to *Escherichia coli* present in human colostrum. Immunology *10*:517, 1966.

Adlard, B. P. F., and Lathe, G. H.: Breast milk jaundice: effect of 3-α 20-β-pregnanediol on bilirubin conjugation by human liver. Arch. Dis. Child. *45*:186, 1970.

Ammann, A. J., and Stiehm, E. R.: Immune globulin levels in colostrum and breast milk, and serum from formula- and breast-fed newborns. Proc. Soc. Exp. Biol. Med. *122*:1098, 1966.

Arias, I. M., and Gartner, L. M.: Production of unconjugated hyperbilirubinaemia in full-term newborn infants following administration of pregnane 3α, 20β-diol. Nature *203*:1292, 1964.

Arias, I. M., and Gartner, L. M.: Breast-milk jaundice. Br. Med. J. *4*:177, 1970.

Arias, I. M., Gartner, L. M., Seifter, S., and Furman, M.: Prolonged neonatal unconjugated hyperbilirubinemia associated with breast feeding and a steroid, pregnane 3 (alpha) 20 (beta)-diol, in maternal milk that inhibits glucuronide formation *in vitro*. J. Clin. Invest. *43*:2037, 1964.

Arnon, H., Salzberg, M., and Olitzk, A. L.: The appearance of antibacterial and antitoxic antibodies in maternal sera, umbilical-cord blood and milk. Observations on the specificity of antibacterial antibodies in human sera. Pediatrics *23*:86, 1959.

Axel, R., Schlom, J., and Spiegelman, S.: Presence in human breast cancer of RNA homologous to mouse mammary tumour virus RNA. Nature *235*:32, 1972.

Bailey, K. V.: Quantity and composition of breast milk in some New Guinean populations. J. Trop. Pediatr. *11*:35, 1965.

Ballabriga, A., Sanz, S., and Escriu, J. M.: Coconut-oil-filled milk in infant feeding. Helv. Pediatr. Acta *17*:103, 1962.

Bass, M. H., and Caplan, J.: Vitamin A deficiency in infancy. J. Pediatr. *47*:690, 1955.

Bates, R. D., Barrett, W. W., Anderson, D. W., Jr., and Saperstein, S.: Milk and soy formulas: a comparative growth study. Ann. Allergy *26*:577, 1968.

Becroft, D. M. O., and Holland, J. T.: Goat's milk and megaloblastic anaemia of infancy: a report of three cases and a survey of the folic acid activity of some New Zealand milks. New Zeal. Med. J. *65*:303, 1966.

Bennich, H., and Johansson, S. G. O.: Structure and function of human immunoglobulin E. Advances Immunol. *13*:1, 1971.

Bevan, B. R., and Holton, J. B.: Inhibition of bilirubin conjugation in rat liver slices by free fatty acids, with relevance to the problem of breast milk jaundice. Clin. Chim. Acta *41*:101, 1972.

Braun, O. H.: Der Einfluss der Ernährung auf die fäkale Lysozymausscheidung bei darmgesunden Säuglingen. Z. Kinderheilkd. *83*:690, 1960.

Bullen, J. J., Rogers, H. J., and Leigh, L.: Iron-binding proteins in milk and resistance to *Escherichia coli* infection in infants. Br. Med. J. *1*:69, 1972.

Catz, C. S., and Giacoia, G. P.: Drugs and breast milk. Pediatr. Clin. N. Amer. *19*:151, 1972.

Catz, C. S., and Giacoia, G. P.: Drugs and metabolites in human milk. *In* Galli, C., Jacini, G., and Pecile, A. (eds.): Dietary Lipids and Postnatal Development. New York, Raven Press, 1973, p. 247.

Chandan, R. C., Shahani, K. M., and Holly, R. G.: Lysozyme content of human milk. Nature *204*:76, 1964.

Cherry, F. F., Cooper, M. D., Stewart, R. A., and Platou, R. V.: Cow versus soy formulas. Amer. J. Dis. Child. *115*:677, 1968.

Cochrane, W. A., Collins-Williams, C., and Donohue, W. L.: Superior hemorrhagic polioencephalitis (Wernicke's disease) occurring in an infant—probably due to thiamine deficiency from use of a soya bean product. Pediatrics *28*:771, 1961.

Committee on Food Protection, Food and Nutrition Board: Radionuclides in Foods. Washington, D. C., National Academy of Sciences, 1973.

Committee on Nutrition, American Academy of Pediatrics: Composition of milks. Pediatrics *26*:1039, 1960.

Committee on Nutrition, American Academy of Pediatrics: Appraisal of nutritional adequacy of infant formulas used as cow milk substitutes. Pediatrics *31*:329, 1963.

Committee on Nutrition, American Academy of Pediatrics: Proposed changes in food and drug administration regulations concerning formula products and vitamin-mineral dietary supplements for infants. Pediatrics *40*:916, 1967.

Committee on Nutrition, American Academy of Pediatrics: Iron-fortified formulas. Pediatrics *47*:786, 1971a.

Committee on Nutrition, American Academy of Pediatrics: Vitamin K supplementation for infants receiving milk substitute infant formulas and for those with fat malabsorption. Pediatrics *48*:483, 1971b.

Committee on Nutrition, American Academy of Pediatrics: Filled milks, imitation milks, and coffee whiteners. Pediatrics *49*:770, 1972.

Committee on Nutrition, American Academy of Pediatrics: Review by Committee on Nutrition. Lead contamination in milks fed to infants: 1972–1973. Pediatrics 53: 146, 1974.

Cornfield, D., and Cooke, R. E.: Vitamin A deficiency: unusual manifestations in a 5½ month old baby. Case report. Pediatrics *10*:33, 1952.

Council on Foods and Nutrition: Substitutes for whole milk. J.A.M.A. *208*:1686, 1969.

Curley, A., and Kimbrough, R.: Chlorinated hydrocarbon insecticides in plasma and milk of pregnant and lactating women. Arch. Environ. Health *18*:156, 1969.

Dahms, B. B., Krauss, A. N., Gartner, L. M., Klain, D. B., Soodalter, J., and Auld, P. A. M.: Breast feeding and serum bilirubin values during the first 4 days of life. J. Pediatr. *83*:1049, 1973.

Davis, R. A., and Wolf, A.: Infantile beriberi associated with Wernicke's encephalopathy. Pediatrics *21*:409, 1958.

Donnell, G. N., Collado, M., and Koch, R.: Growth and development of children with galactosemia. J. Pediatr. *58*:836, 1961.

Dunning, G. M.: Foods and fallout. Borden's Rev. Nutr. Res. *23*:1, 1962.

Egan, H., Goulding, R., Roburn, J., and Tatton, J. O'G.: Organochlorine pesticide residues in human fat and human milk. Br. Med. J. *2*:66, 1965.

Federal Register *36*:23553, 1971.

Feinleib, M., and Garrison, R. J.: Interpretation of the vital statistics of breast cancer. Cancer *24*:1109, 1969.

Feller, W. F., and Chopra, M. C.: Studies of human milk in relation to the possible viral etiology of breast cancer. Cancer *24*:1250, 1969.

Filled Milk Act: An Act to prohibit the shipment of filled milk in interstate or foreign commerce. Public Law No. 513.21. U. S. Code, Sec. 61-64, March 4, 1923.

Fomon, S. J.: Comparative study of human milk and a soya bean formula in promoting growth and nitrogen retention by infants. Pediatrics *24*:577, 1959.

Fomon, S. J., Owen, G. M., and Thomas, L. N.: Methionine, valine and isoleucine. Requirements during infancy: growth and nitrogen balance studies with normal fullterm infants receiving soybean protein. Amer. J. Dis. Child. *108*:487, 1964.

Fomon, S. J., Thomas, L. N., Filer, L. J., Jr., Anderson, T. A., and Bergmann, K. E.: Requirements for protein and essential amino acids in early infancy. Studies with a soy-isolate formula. Acta Paediatr. Scand. *62*:33, 1973.

Fomon, S. J., Younoszai, M. K., and Thomas, L. N.: Gastrointestinal passage time of normal infants in relation to feeding. Unpublished data, 1966.

Food and Nutrition Board: Evaluation of Protein Quality. Washington, D. C., National Academy of Science–National Research Council, Publ. No. 1100, 1963.

Forbes, G. B.: Nutrition in relation to problems of radioactivity. Pediatr. Clin. N. Amer. *9*:1009, 1962.

Forbes, G. B.: Personal communication, 1973.

Ford, J. E., and Scott, K. J.: The folic acid activity of some milk foods for babies. J. Dairy Res. *35*:85, 1968.

Gartner, L. M., and Arias, I. M.: Studies of prolonged neonatal jaundice in the breast fed infant. J. Pediatr. *68*:54, 1966.

Gindrat, J.-J., Gothefors, L., Hanson, L. Å., and Winberg, J.: Antibodies in human milk against *E. coli* of the serogroups most commonly found in neonatal infections. Acta Paediatr. Scand. *61*:587, 1972.

Gitzelmann, R.: (Letter to the Editor.) Soya alpha-galactosides (continued). Pediatrics *36*:806, 1965.

Gitzelmann, R., and Auricchio, S.: The handling of soya alpha-galactosides by a normal and a galactosemic child. Pediatrics *36*:231, 1965.

Glaser, J., and Johnstone, D. E.: Soy bean milk as a substitute for mammalian milk in early infancy. Ann. Allergy *10*:433, 1952.

Glaser, J., and Johnstone, D. E.: Prophylaxis of allergic disease in the newborn. J.A.M.A. *153*:620, 1953.

Goldman, A. S., and Smith, C. W.: Host resistance factors in human milk. J. Pediatr. *82*:1082, 1973.

Goldman, H. I., and Desposito, F.: Hypoprothrombinemic bleeding in young infants. Association with diarrhea, antibiotics and milk substitutes. Amer. J. Dis. Child. *111*:430, 1966.

Gonzaga, A. J., Warren, R. J., and Robbins, F. C.: Attenuated poliovirus infection in infants fed colostrum from poliomyelitis immune cows. Pediatrics *32*:1039, 1963.

Gopalan, C.: Studies on lactation in poor Indian communities. J. Trop. Pediatr. *4*:87, 1958.
Gordon, W. G., Ziegler, J., and Basch, J. J.: Isolation of an iron-binding protein from cow's milk. Biochim. Biophys. Acta *60*:410, 1962.
Graham, G. G., Baertl, J. M., Cordano, A., and Morales, E.: Lactose-free, medium-chain triglyceride formulas in severe malnutrition. Amer. J. Dis. Child. *126*:330, 1973.
Graham, G. G., Placko, R. P., Morales, E., Acevedo, G., and Cordano, A.: Dietary protein quality in infants and children. VI. Isolated soy protein milk. Amer. J. Dis. Child. *120*:419, 1970.
György, P.: Biochemical aspects. Amer. J. Clin. Nutr. *24*:970, 1971.
György, P., Omans, W. B., and Hau, E. W.-S.: Feeding value of soy milks for premature infants. Proceedings of Conference on Soybean Products for Protein in Human Foods. Washington, D. C., U. S. Department of Agriculture, Agricultural Research Service, 1961, p. 179.
Hambraeus, L., Wranne, L., and Lorentsson, R.: Whey protein formulas in the treatment of phenylketonuria in infants. Nutr. Metab. *12*:152, 1970.
Hanley, W. B., Linsao, L., Davidson, W., and Moes, C. A. F.: Malnutrition with early treatment of phenylketonuria. Pediatr. Res. *4*:318, 1970.
Hanson, L. Å., Borssen, R., Holmgren, J., Jodal, U., Johansson, B. G., and Kaijser, B.: Secretory IgA. *In* Kagan, B. M., and Stiehm, E. R. (eds.): Immunologic Incompetence. Chicago, Year Book Medical Publishers, 1971, p. 39.
Hargreaves, T., and Piper, R. F.: Breast milk jaundice. Effect of inhibitory breast milk and 3α, 20β-pregnanediol on glucuronyl transferase. Arch. Dis. Child. *46*:195, 1971.
Harkins, R. W., and Sarett, H. P.: Methods of comparing protein quality of soybean infant formulas in the rat. J. Nutr. *91*:213, 1967.
Hartman, A. M., and Dryden, L. P.: Vitamins in Milk and Milk Products. American Dairy Science Association, 1965.
Hartmann, A. F., Meeker, C. S., Perley, A. M., and McGinnis, H. G.: Studies of amino acid administration. I. Utilization of an enzymatic digest of casein. J. Pediatr. *20*:308, 1942.
Healy, C. E.: Acidosis and failure to thrive in infants fed Nutramigen. Pediatrics *49*:910, 1972.
Hentges, D. J.: Influence of pH on the inhibitory activity of formic and acetic acids for *shigella*. J. Bacteriol. *93*:2029, 1967.
Heyndrickx, G. V.: Investigations on the enzymes in human milk. Ann. Paediatr. *198*:356, 1962.
Heyndrickx, G. V.: Further investigations on the enzymes in human milk. Pediatrics *31*:1019, 1963.
Hinton, N. A., and MacGregor, R. R.: A study of infections due to pathogenic serogroups of *Escherichia coli*. Canad. Med. Ass. J. *79*:359, 1958.
Hodes, H.: (Letter to the Editor.) Poliomyelitis antibodies in human colostrum and milk. J. Pediatr. *65*:319, 1964.
Holguin, A. H., Reeves, J. S., and Gelfand, H. M.: Immunization of infants with the Sabin oral poliovirus vaccine. Amer. J. Public Health *52*:600, 1962.
Howard, H. W., Block, R. J., Anderson, D. W., and Bauer, C. D.: The effect of long time feeding of a soybean infant food diet to white rats. Ann. Allergy *14*:166, 1956.
Hunt, M., Sutherland, B. S., and Berry, H. K.: Nutritional management in phenylketonuria. Amer. J. Dis. Child. *122*:1, 1971.
Hydovitz, J. D.: Occurrence of goiter in an infant on a soy diet. New Eng. J. Med. *262*:351, 1960.
Hytten, F. E.: Clinical and chemical studies in human lactation. II. Variation in major constituents during a feeding. Br. Med. J. *1*:176, 1954a.
Hytten, F. E.: Clinical and chemical studies in human lactation. VII. The effect of differences in yield and composition of milk on the infant's weight gain and the duration of breast-feeding. Br. Med. J. *1*:1410, 1954b.
Isselbacher, K. J.: Galactose metabolism and galactosemia. Amer. J. Med. *26*:715, 1959.
Jensen, R. L., Thomas, L. N., Bergmann, K. E., Filer, L. J., Jr., and Fomon, S. J.: Composition of milk of Iowa City women. Unpublished data, 1972.
Johansson, B. G.: Isolation of an iron-containing red protein from human milk. Acta Chem. Scand. *14*:510, 1960.

Johnstone, D. E., and Dutton, A. M.: Dietary prophylaxis of allergic disease in children. New Eng. J. Med. *274*:715, 1966.

Joint FAO/WHO Meeting: Pesticide residues in food. WHO Techn. Rep. Ser. No. 474, Geneva, FAO/WHO, 1971.

Jollès, P., and Jollès, J.: Lysozyme from human milk. Nature *192*:1187, 1961.

Kahn, B., Straub, C. P., Robbins, P. J., Wellman, H. N., Seltzer, R. A., and Telles, N. C.: Retention of radiostrontium, strontium, calcium and phosphorus by infants. Pediatrics *43*:651, 1969.

Kay, J. L., Daeschner, C. W., and Desmond, M. M.: Evaluation of infants fed soybean and evaporated milk formulae from birth to three months. Amer. J. Dis. Child. *100*:264, 1960.

Kennedy, J. L., Jr., Wertelecki, W., Gates, L., Sperry, B. P., and Cass, V. M.: The early treatment of phenylketonuria. Amer. J. Dis. Child. *113*:16, 1967.

Kenny, J. F., Boesman, M. I., and Michaels, R. H.: Bacterial and viral coproantibodies in breast-fed infants. Pediatrics *39*:202, 1967.

Kerr, G. R., Chamove, A. S., Harlow, H. F., and Waisman, H. A.: The development of infant monkeys fed low phenylalanine diets. Pediatr. Res. *3*:305, 1969.

Kildeberg, P., and Winters, R.: Infant feeding and blood acid-base balance. Pediatrics *49*:801, 1972.

Kirkpatrick, C. H., Green, I., Rich, R. R., and Schade, A. L.: Inhibition of growth of *Candida albicans* by iron-unsaturated lactoferrin: relation to host defense mechanisms in chronic mucocutaneous candidiasis. J. Infect. Dis. *124*:539, 1971.

Knowles, J. A.: Excretion of drugs in milk—a review. J. Pediatr. *66*:1068, 1965.

Kon, S. K.: Milk and Milk Products in Human Nutrition. FAO Nutritional Studies No. 17, Rome, Food and Agriculture Organization, 1959.

Kroger, M.: Insecticide residues in human milk. J. Pediatr. *80*:401, 1972.

Lamm, S., Cole, B., Glynn, K., and Ullmann, W.: Lead content of milks fed to infants—1971–1972. New Eng. J. Med. *289*:574, 1973.

Lamm, S. H., and Rosen, J. F.: Lead contamination in milks fed to infants: 1972–1973. Pediatrics *53*:137, 1974.

Lepow, M. L., Warren, R. J., Guay, N., Ingram, V. G., and Robbins, F. C.: Effects of Sabin Type I poliomyelitis vaccine administered by mouth to newborn infants. New Eng. J. Med. *264*:1071, 1961.

Lifshitz, F., Coello-Ramírez, P., and Gutiérrez-Topete, G.: Monosaccharide intolerance and hypoglycemia in infants with diarrhea. I. Clinical course of 23 infants. J. Pediatr. *77*:595, 1970.

Ling, E. R., Kon, S. K., and Porter, J. W. G.: The composition of milk and the nutritive value of its components. *In* Kon, S. K., and Cowie, A. T. (eds.): Milk: The Mammary Gland and Its Secretion. Vol. II. Chap. 17. New York, Academic Press, 1961, p. 195.

Longenecker, J. B., Martin, W. H., and Sarett, H. P.: Improvement in the protein efficiency of soybean concentrates and isolates by heat treatment. J. Agr. Food Chem. *12*:411, 1964.

Lough, S. A., Hamada, G. H., and Comar, C. L.: Secretion of dietary strontium 90 and calcium in human milk. Proc. Soc. Exp. Biol. Med. *104*:194, 1960.

Macklin, M. T.: Comparison of the number of breast-cancer deaths observed in relatives of breast-cancer patients and the number expected on the basis of mortality rates. J. Nat. Cancer Inst. *22*:927, 1959.

MacMahon, B., Lin, T. M., Lowe, C. R., Mirra, A. P., Ravnihar, B., Salber, E. J., Trichopoulos, D., Valaoras, V. G., and Yuasa, S.: Lactation and cancer of the breast. A summary of an international study. Bull. W.H.O. *42*:185, 1970.

Macy, I. G., and Kelly, H. J.: Human milk and cow's milk in infant nutrition. *In* Kon, S. K., and Cowie, A. T. (eds.): Milk: The Mammary Gland and Its Secretion. Vol. II. Chap. 18. New York, Academic Press, 1961, p. 265.

Macy, I. G., Kelly, H. J., and Sloan, R. E.: The Composition of Milks: A Compilation of the Comparative Composition and Properties of Human, Cow, and Goat Milk, Colostrum, and Transitional Milk. Publ. No. 254, Washington, D.C., National Academy of Sciences—National Research Council, 1953.

Masson, P. L., and Heremans, J. F.: Studies on lactoferrin, the iron-binding protein of secretions. Protides Biol. Fluids *14*:115, 1966.

Masson, P. L., Heremans, J. F., and Dive, C.: An iron-binding protein common to many external secretions. Clin. Chim. Acta *14*:735, 1966.

Mata, L. J., and Wyatt, R. G.: Host resistance to infection. Amer. J. Clin. Nutr. *24*:976, 1971.

Michael, J. G., Ringenback, R., and Hottenstein, S.: The antimicrobial activity of human colostral antibody in the newborn. J. Infect. Dis. *124*:445, 1971.

Michaels, R. H.: Studies of antiviral factors in human milk and serum. J. Immunol. *94*:262, 1965.

Miller, R. W., and Fraumeni, J. F., Jr.: Does breast-feeding increase the child's risk of breast cancer? Pediatrics *49*:645, 1972.

Miller, T. E.: Killing and lysis of gram-negative bacteria through the synergistic effect of hydrogen peroxide, ascorbic acid, and lysozyme. J. Bacteriol. *98*:949, 1969.

Mitchell, D. G.: Increased lead absorption: paint is not the only problem. Pediatrics *53*:142, 1974.

Moore, D. H., Charney, J., Kramarsky, B., Lasfargues, E. Y., Sarkar, N. H., Brennan, M. J., Burrows, J. H., Sirsat, S. M., Paymaster, J. C., and Vaidya, A. B.: Search for a human breast cancer virus. Nature *229*:611, 1971.

Moore, D. H., Sarkar, N. H., Kelly, C. E., Pillsbury, N., and Charney, J.: Type B particles in human milk. Texas Rep. Biol. Med. *27*:1027, 1969.

Morrison, S. D.: Human Milk: Yield, Proximate Principles and Inorganic Constituents. Commonwealth Agricultural Bureaux, Farnham Royal, Slough Bucks, England, 1952.

Murthy, G. K., and Rhea, U. S.: Cadmium, copper, iron, lead, manganese, and zinc in evaporated milk, infant products, and human milk. J. Dairy Sci. *54*:1001, 1971.

Neter, E.: Enteritis due to *Escherichia coli*: present-day status and unsolved problems. J. Pediatr. *55*:223, 1959.

Newman, A. J., and Gross, S.: Hyperbilirubinemia in breast-fed infants. Pediatrics *32*:995, 1963.

Nordbring, F.: The failure of newborn premature infants to absorb antibodies from heterologous colostrum. Acta Paediatr. Scand. *46*:569, 1957.

Omans, W. B., Leuterer, W., and György, P.: Feeding value of soy milks for premature infants. J. Pediatr. *62*:98, 1963.

Oram, J. D., and Reiter, B.: Inhibition of bacteria by lactoferrin and other iron-chelating agents. Biochim. Biophys. Acta *170*:351, 1968.

Physicians Desk Reference. 28th ed. Oradell, N. J., Medical Economics Co., 1974.

Picou, D., and Phillips, M.: Urea metabolism in malnourished and recovered children receiving a high or low protein diet. Amer. J. Clin. Nutr. *25*:1261, 1972.

Quinby, G. E., Armstrong, J. F., and Durham, W. F.: DDT in human milk. Nature *207*:726, 1965.

Rasmussen, F.: The mechanism of drug secretion into milk. *In* Galli, C., Jacini, G., and Pecile, A. (eds.): Dietary Lipids and Postnatal Development. New York, Raven Press, 1973, p. 231.

Ripp, J. A.: Soybean-induced goiter. Amer. J. Dis. Child. *102*:106, 1961.

Ritcey, W. R., Savary, G., and McCully, K. A.: Organochlorine insecticide residues in human milk, evaporated milk and some milk substitutes in Canada. Canad. J. Public Health *63*:125, 1972.

Rosen, J. F., and Lamm, S. H.: Further comments. Lead contamination in milks fed to infants: 1972–1973. Pediatrics *53*:143, 1974.

Sabin, A. B., and Fieldsteel, A. H.: Antipoliomyelitic activity of human and bovine colostrum and milk. Pediatrics *29*:105, 1962.

Sabin, A. B., Michaels, R. H., Krugman, S., Eiger, M. E., Berman, P. H., and Warren, J.: Effect of oral poliovirus vaccine in newborn children. I. Excretion of virus after ingestion of large doses of type 1 or of mixture of all three types, in relation to level of placentally transmitted antibody. Pediatrics *31*:623, 1963.

Sarett, H. P.: (Letter to the Editor.) Feeding of soybean product and development of goiter. Pediatrics *24*:855, 1955.

Sarett, H. P.: Nutritional value of commercially produced foods for infants. Bibl. Nutr. Diet. *18*:246, 1973.

Sarett, H. P.: Comments. Lead contamination in milks fed to infants: 1972–1973. Pediatrics *53*:143, 1974.

Schlom, J., Colcher, D., Spiegelman, S., Gillespie, S., and Gillespie, D.: Quantitation of RNA tumor viruses and viruslike particles in human milk by hybridization to polyadenylic acid sequences. Science *179*:696, 1973.

Schlom, J., Spiegelman, S., and Moore, D.: RNA-dependent DNA polymerase activity in virus-like particles isolated from human milk. Nature *231*:97, 1971.

Schmidt, E.: Grippevirushemmstoffe in Frauenmilch und Kuhmilch. I. Vergleichende Untersuchungen über Neuraminsäuregehalt und die Höhe des Hemmtiters im Hämagglutinationstest. Z. Kinderheilkd. *84*:339, 1960.

Schneider, D. L., Fluckiger, H. B., and Manes, J. D.: Vitamin K_1 content of infant formula products. Pediatrics *53*:273, 1974.

Schneider, D. L., and Sarett, H. P.: Growth of baby pigs fed infant soybean formulas. J. Nutr. *98*:279, 1969.

Schubert, J., and Grünberg, A.: Zur Frage der Uebertragung von Immun-Antikörpern von der Mutter auf das Kind. Schweiz. Med. Wschr. *79*:1007, 1949.

Shepard, T. H., Pyne, G. E., Kirschvink, J. F., and McLean, M.: Soybean goiter: report of three cases. New Eng. J. Med. *262*:1099, 1960.

Shim, B.-S., Kang, Y.-S., Kim, W.-J., Cho, S.-H., and Lee, D.-B.: Self-protective activity of colostral IgA against tryptic digestion. Nature *222*:787, 1969.

Snyderman, S. E., Holt, L. E., Jr., Dancis, J., Roitman, E., Boyer, A., and Balis, M. E.: "Unessential" nitrogen: a limiting factor for human growth. J. Nutr. *78*:57, 1962.

Special Studies Group, Environmental Protection Agency: Estimates of Ionizing Radiation Doses in the United States, 1960–2000. Rockville, Maryland, Division of Criteria and Standards, Office of Radiation Programs, Environmental Protection Agency, 1972.

Stiehm, E. R., and Ryan, J.: Breast-milk jaundice. Amer. J. Dis. Child. *109*:212, 1965.

Sussman, S.: The passive transfer of antibodies to *Escherichia coli* 0111: B_4 from mother to offspring. Pediatrics *27*:308, 1961.

Svirsky-Gross, S.: Pathogenic strains of *E. coli* (0,111) among prematures and the use of human milk in controlling the outbreak of diarrhea. Ann. Paediatr. *190*:109, 1958.

Theuer, R. C., Kemmerer, K. S., Martin, W. H., Zoumas, B. L., and Sarett, H. P.: Effect of processing on availability of iron salts in liquid infant formula products. Experimental soy isolate formulas. J. Agr. Food Chem. *19*:555, 1971.

Theuer, R. C., and Sarett, H. P.: Nutritional adequacy of soy isolate infant formulas in rats: choline. J. Agr. Food Chem. *18*:913, 1970.

Tokuhata, G. K.: Morbidity and mortality among offspring of breast cancer mothers. Amer. J. Epidemiol *89*:139, 1969.

Underwood, B. A., Hepner, R., and Abdullah, H.: Protein, lipid and fatty acids of human milk from Pakistani women during prolonged periods of lactation. Amer. J. Clin. Nutr. *23*:400, 1970.

U. S. Environmental Protection Agency, Office of Radiation Programs: Radiation Data and Reports. Vol. 13. Washington, D.C., U.S. Government Printing Office, 1972, p. 683.

Vahlquist, B.: The transfer of antibodies from mother to offspring. Advances Pediatr. *10*:305, 1958.

Van Wyk, J. J., Arnold, M. B., Wynn, J., and Pepper, F.: The effects of a soybean product on thyroid function in humans. Pediatrics *24*:752, 1959.

Warren, R. J., Lepow, M. L., Bartsch, G. E., and Robbins, F. C.: The relationship of maternal antibody, breast feeding, and age to the susceptibility of newborn infants to infection with attenuated polioviruses. Pediatrics *34*:4, 1964.

Watt, B. K., and Merrill, A. L.: Composition of Foods—Raw, Processed, Prepared. Agriculture Handbook No. 8, Revised. Washington, D.C., Agricultural Research Service, 1963.

Williams, T. E., Arango, L., Donaldson, M. H., and Shepard, F. M.: Vitamin K requirement of normal infants on soy protein formula. Clin. Pediatr. *9*:79, 1970.

Wilson, K. M., and Clayton, B. E.: Importance of choline during growth, with particular reference to synthetic diets in phenylketonuria. Arch. Dis. Child. *37*:565, 1962.

Wilson, D. J., Locker, D. J., Ritzen, C. A., Watson, J. T., and Schaffner, W.: DDT concentrations in human milk. Amer. J. Dis. Child. *125*:814, 1973.

Winberg, J., and Wessner, G.: Does breast milk protect against septicaemia in the newborn? Lancet *1*:1091, 1971.

Wiseman, H. J.: Comparison of two soy-protein isolate infant formulas. Ann. Allergy *29*:209, 1971.

Wolf, I. J.: Vitamin A deficiency in an infant. J.A.M.A. *166*:1859, 1958.

Woodwell, G. M.: Toxic substances and ecological cycles. Sci. Amer. *216* (No. 3):24, 1967.

Woodwell, G. M., Wurster, C. F., Jr., and Isaacson, P. A.: DDT residues in an east coast estuary: a case of biological concentration of a persistent insecticide. Science *156*:821, 1967.

16

BEIKOST

Thomas A. Anderson
and
Samuel J. Fomon

Because no equivalent word is available in the English language it seems appropriate to introduce the German word "Beikost": foods other than milk or formula.

The secular trend toward increasingly early introduction of beikost in the infant's diet in the United States has been discussed in Chapter 1. Most infants currently receive commercially prepared strained foods before the end of the first month. Verbal reports from pediatricians and infant food manufacturers in countries other than the United States suggest that introduction of beikost is generally begun between 6 and 10 weeks of age. More satisfactory documentation of feeding practices during early infancy both in the United States and in other countries would be desirable.

The data of Filer and Martinez (1963) suggest that at that time six-month-old infants received approximately two-thirds of calorie intake from milk and one-third from beikost. At present, many infants may receive considerably larger percentages of calorie intake from beikost at age six months, particularly because of the recent practice of feeding skim milk, "2 per cent milk" or commercially prepared formula (e.g., Similac Advance, Ross) with reduced caloric content. The volume of milk consumed by infants appears to decrease progressively from age 6 to 24 months (Eppright et al., 1969).

Because an adequate intake of all essential nutrients can be provided without beikost, there appears to be no advantage in introducing such foods during the first six months of life. Nevertheless, it is apparent that social customs at present favor much earlier introduction of beikost. Mothers not uncommonly state that they believe feeding of cereals encourages the infant to sleep through the night. Many pediatricians suspect that feeding of beikost at an early age is looked upon by parents as a sign of achievement by the infant. If there is a major objection other than cost (Chapter 1) to early introduction of beikost, it may be that the practice is likely to encourage overfeeding and establishment of unsound food habits. This possibility has been discussed in Chapter 2.

During the first six months of life, most of the beikost fed in the United States consists of commercially prepared strained and junior foods. The three major manufacturers (Gerber Products Co., H. J. Heinz Co. and Beech-Nut, Inc.*) produce more than 400 varieties of strained and junior foods, accounting in 1971 for 386 million dollars in sales (Ringler, 1972). A summary of composition of the various foods as classified by the manufacturers is presented in Tables 16–1 and 16–2.

COMPOSITION OF CEREALS

In the United States, cereals are usually the first beikost. Discussion of nutritional considerations of the various commercially prepared cereals for infants seems particularly important because the content of a specified essential nutrient may be 10 times greater in one cereal than in another, and because the increasingly popular strained cereals with fruit differ as a group in nutritional properties from the dry cereals after the latter have been diluted with milk or water and are ready to feed.

Dry Cereals

In the United States, precooked dry cereals commercially prepared for infants are marketed in 28, 227 and 454 gm (1, 8 and 16 oz) boxes. Rice, mixed, oatmeal, high-protein and barley cereals are produced. Mixed cereals are made from wheat, oats, and corn, sometimes with the addition of barley and soy. High-protein cereals are made with soy, wheat and oat flours.

Label declarations on the boxes of dry cereal marketed in the United States indicate proximate composition and vitamin and mineral content.

As may be seen from Table 16–1, high-protein cereal provides

---

*Subsequently, these companies will be referred to as Gerber, Heinz and Beech-Nut, respectively.

(*Text continued on page 416.*)

TABLE 16–1 AVERAGE PROXIMATE, MINERAL AND VITAMIN COMPOSITION OF INFANT CEREAL PRODUCTS* (CONSTITUENTS/100 gm)

Product Category	Number of Products	Energy kcal	Proximate Analysis (gm) Water	Protein	Fat	Carbohydrate Total	Carbohydrate Fiber	Ash
				Strained				
Cereal								
Dry								
High protein	3	360 (349–372)†	6.8 (6.4–7.0)	35.2 (35.0–35.5)	4.6 (2.7–6.2)	44.3 (43.2–45.7)	2.4 (2.3–2.5)	6.7 (5.5–7.3)
Barley, mixed, oatmeal	8	374 (356–393)	6.9 (6.5–7.2)	13.2 (11.3–15.4)	4.6 (1.6–8.0)	69.9 (65.2–73.7)	1.1 (1.0–1.4)	4.3 (2.7–5.8)
Rice	3	370 (362–376)	7.3 (6.6–7.5)	7.0 (5.5–8.9)	4.2 (2.1–5.6)	75.9 (74.6–76.8)	1.2 (0.7–2.0)	4.4 (3.8–4.7)
With fruit‡								
High protein	1	98	74.7	4.3	0.5	19.2	0.4	0.9
Mixed, oatmeal	5	81 (73–89)	79.8 (77.3–82.2)	1.4 (1.2–1.6)	0.6 (0.1–0.9)	17.5 (15.6–20.4)	0.3 (0.2–0.8)	0.4 (0.4–0.7)
Rice	1	69	82.9	0.3	0.6	15.7	0.2	0.3
				Junior				
Cereal with fruit								
Mixed, oatmeal	2	78 (76–81)	80.3 (79.5–81.1)	1.5 (1.4–1.6)	0.5 (0.3–0.7)	17.1 (15.8–18.2)	0.2 (0.2–0.3)	0.4 (0.4–0.5)

Product Category	Number of Products	Minerals (mg) Calcium	Phosphorus	Potassium	Sodium	Iron	Copper
			Strained				
Cereal							
Dry							
High protein	3	811 (660–972)	849 (751–900)	1492	68 (10–141)	80 (50–100)	0.10
Barley, mixed, oatmeal	8	914 (660–1570)	788 (698–881)	317 (281–362)	66 (10–196)	73 (53–100)	0.28 (0.04–0.47)

Rice	3	883 (660–1190)	722 (600–829)	316	97 (10–175)	72 (53–100)	0.34
With fruit							
High protein	1	45	85	123	15	5.3	0.2
Mixed, oatmeal	5	8 (4–16)	48 (24–74)	34 (20–67)	111 (6–152)	2.7 (0.4–5.2)	0.01
Rice	1	8	12	10	122	0.2	–
Junior							
Cereal with fruit							
Mixed, oatmeal	2	6 (4–8)	54 (46–62)	44 (41–48)	114 (89–139)	3.9	–

Product Category	Number of Products	Vitamins					
		Vitamin A IU	Thiamin μg	Riboflavin μg	Niacin mg	B_6 μg	Vitamin C mg
Strained							
Cereal							
Dry							
High protein	3	–	3220 (1620–5220)	1850 (2120–3200)	21.0 (3.5–45.5)	560	–
Barley, mixed, oatmeal	8	–	3699 (2800–5540)	2552 (2120–3200)	26.4 (14.1–55.1)	313 (240–460)	–
Rice	3	–	3343 (2800–4410)	1851 (233–3200)	23.9 (14.1–39.9)	550	–
With fruit							
High protein	1	–	244	431	3.0	–	–
Mixed, oatmeal	5	38 (0–119)	191 (187–200)	444 (425–450)	3.3 (2.8–3.7)	190	5.9 (4.3–7.5)
Rice	1	2	187	448	3.0	190	20.0
Junior							
Cereal with fruit							
Mixed, oatmeal	2	8 (2–13)	195	469	3.1	21 (20–22)	1.8 (1.2–2.4)

*Nutritive Values and Ingredients of Beech-Nut Baby Foods, January 1972, Professional & Consumer Services, Beech-Nut Baby Foods, Beech-Nut, Inc., 460 Park Ave., New York, N.Y. 10022; Nutrient Values of Gerber Baby Foods, 1972, Professional Communications Department, Gerber Products Company, Fremont, Mich. 49412; Heinz Nutritional Data, Sixth edition, 1972, Heinz International Research Center, H. J. Heinz Company, P.O. Box 57, Pittsburgh, Pa. 15230.

†Values in parentheses indicate range. Where range is not given, only one value was available.

‡With one exception, all cereals with fruit contain applesauce and bananas; rice cereal with applesauce and pineapple is mentioned in text.

TABLE 16–2 PROXIMATE, MINERAL AND VITAMIN COMPOSITION OF COMMERCIALLY PREPARED STRAINED AND JUNIOR BABY FOODS (CONSTITUENTS/100 gm)

A. Strained Foods

Category	Number of Products	Energy kcal	Proximate Analysis (gm)					
			Water	Protein	Fat	Carbohydrate Total	Carbohydrate Fiber	Ash
Juices	32	65 (45–98)*	83.6 (75.7–88.4)	0.3 (0.0–0.7)	0.2 (0.0–0.4)	15.6 (10.9–22.8)	0.0 (0.0–0.1)	0.3 (0.1–0.4)
Fruits	33	85 (69–125)	78.2 (68.4–81.4)	0.4 (0.1–1.9)	0.2 (0.1–0.7)	20.4 (16.4–29.7)	0.5 (0.1–1.5)	0.3 (0.1–0.4)
Vegetables								
Plain	24	45 (27–78)	87.7 (80.5–91.8)	1.5 (0.7–4.3)	0.3 (0.1–1.3)	9.0 (5.0–15.5)	0.7 (0.4–1.2)	0.8 (0.5–1.1)
Creamed	6	63 (42–94)	84.0 (76.5–88.8)	1.8 (0.9–2.7)	0.8 (0.2–1.8)	12.2 (6.0–20.4)	0.3 (0.2–0.5)	0.9 (0.5–1.3)
Meats	25	106 (80–194)	79.2 (71.6–82.1)	13.6 (9.9–16.4)	5.6 (2.8–17.1)	0.4 (0.0–2.2)	0.1 (0.0–0.2)	1.1 (0.8–1.4)
Egg yolks	4	192 (184–199)	70.8 (70.3–71.2)	10.0 (9.6–10.7)	16.1 (14.1–17.8)	1.7 (0.0–3.5)	0.1 (0.0–0.1)	1.3 (1.2–1.5)
High-meat dinners	15	84 (62–106)	82.8 (80.6–85.1)	6.0 (5.3–6.6)	4.0 (1.4–6.6)	6.0 (4.4–8.3)	0.2 (0.1–0.3)	1.0 (0.7–1.4)
Soups and dinners	42	58 (39–94)	86.9 (79.8–89.5)	2.2 (1.1–4.4)	2.0 (0.1–5.7)	7.8 (5.8–11.4)	0.2 (0.1–0.4)	0.9 (0.4–1.4)
Desserts	37	96 (70–136)	76.6 (70.0–81.7)	1.0 (0.1–6.2)	0.8 (0.0–4.7)	21.1 (16.9–28.6)	0.2 (0.0–0.9)	0.4 (0.1–0.9)

Category	Number of Products	Minerals (mg)					
		Calcium	Phosphorus	Potassium	Sodium	Iron	Copper
Juices	32	8 (3–13)	10 (4–27)	104 (33–207)	2 (0–5)	0.46 (0.10–0.95)	0.10 (0.03–0.18)
Fruits	33	8 (1–24)	12 (4–45)	79 (16–200)	17 (1–71)	0.36 (0.10–0.90)	0.06 (0.02–0.22)

Vegetables							
Plain	24	26 (12–46)	34 (13–75)	153 (75–236)	117 (30–174)	0.66 (0.29–1.32)	0.12 (0.02–0.23)
Creamed	6	41 (10–96)	36 (24–53)	105 (26–202)	106 (81–128)	0.56 (0.24–0.88)	0.03 (0.01–0.04)
Meats	25	16 (4–59)	128 (60–250)	168 (60–288)	173 (99–332)	1.57 (0.70–4.43)	0.46 (0.05–4.70)
Egg yolks	4	66 (38–87)	281 (262–292)	86 (68–122)	153 (100–219)	3.12 (3.02–3.20)	0.13 (0.06–0.22)
High-meat dinners	15	20 (6–66)	63 (42–98)	113 (58–184)	146 (99–206)	0.76 (0.47–1.71)	0.04 (0.00–0.16)
Soups and dinners	42	18 (5–46)	34 (15–68)	70 (17–175)	144 (90–324)	0.51 (0.12–2.13)	0.05 (0.00–0.30)
Desserts	37	23 (4–67)	23 (3–91)	56 (6–179)	55 (4–153)	0.30 (0.10–0.71)	0.02 (0.00–0.06)

		Vitamins							
Category	Number of Products	*Vitamin A* IU	*Thiamin* μg	*Riboflavin* μg	*Niacin* mg	B_6 μg	B_{12} mμg	*Folacin* μg	*Vitamin C* mg
Juices	32	81 (0–590)	27 (5–65)	13 (2–70)	0.17 (0.06–0.34)	33 (12–80)	0 (0–0)	0.6 (0.2–1.3)	45.8 (40.0–76.0)
Fruits	33	119 (0–681)	15 (5–40)	23 (7–80)	0.22 (0.00–0.92)	46 (8–180)	61 (44–100)	0.4 (0.1–0.8)	6.8 (0.9–30.9)
Vegetables									
Plain	24	3803 (0–13,600)	43 (8–113)	49 (17–150)	0.50 (0.10–1.38)	75 (30–130)	67 (30–100)	0.7 (0.5–0.9)	7.5 (1.7–14.0)
Creamed	6	751 (21–2578)	35 (10–101)	64 (29–110)	0.44 (0.20–0.80)	45 (20–70)	69 (53–80)	1.1 (0.3–2.6)	6.8 (2.4–11.0)
Meats	25	3570 (0–25,655)	85 (10–306)	372 (80–2530)	3.17 (0.69–8.42)	297 (46–810)	17132 (660–130,000)	23.7 (0.2–180.0)	5.1 (2.7–19.2)
Egg yolks	4	1974 (450–3613)	88 (40–182)	344 (300–397)	0.28 (0.00–1.10)	102 (30–175)	1680 (1680–1680)	9.6 (9.6–9.6)	3.8 3.8–3.8)
High-meat dinners	15	540 (22–1273)	64 (9–222)	90 (50–205)	1.91 (0.98–3.40)	179 (63–630)	691 (280–914)	2.5 (1.4–3.8)	3.1 (2.3–5.1)
Soups and dinners	42	882 (0–2700)	45 (9–202)	772 (10–30,000)	0.57 (0.08–1.55)	54 (20–130)	912 (60–13,500)	1.4 (0.5–7.6)	2.3 (0.8–8.1)
Desserts	37	90 (0–520)	17 (4–55)	42 (6–202)	0.14 (0.00–0.50)	23 (0–73)	67 (0–140)	0.6 (0.1–1.6)	6.0 (0.2–54.9)

(Table continued on following page.)

TABLE 16–2 PROXIMATE, MINERAL AND VITAMIN COMPOSITION OF COMMERCIALLY PREPARED STRAINED AND JUNIOR BABY FOODS (CONSTITUENTS/100 gm) (*Continued*)

B. Junior Foods

Category	Number of Products	Energy kcal	Proximate Analysis (gm)					
			Water	Protein	Fat	Carbohydrate Total	Carbohydrate Fiber	Ash
Fruits	30	85 (69–116)	78.1 (70.2–81.5)	0.4 (0.1–2.2)	0.2 (0.0–0.5)	20.4 (16.5–28.3)	0.6 (0.1–1.3)	0.3 (0.1–1.1)
Vegetables								
Plain	16	46 (27–71)	87.5 (81.2–91.8)	1.3 (0.7–3.6)	0.4 (0.1–1.2)	9.3 (5.3–15.7)	0.6 (0.3–1.3)	0.8 (0.5–1.3)
Creamed	5	64 (45–72)	84.5 (81.7–88.1)	1.9 (0.9–2.7)	1.2 (0.2–2.8)	11.2 (6.2–16.1)	0.3 (0.2–0.5)	0.9 (0.3–1.5)
Meats	17	103 (88–135)	79.4 (75.6–81.6)	14.3 (13.0–15.7)	4.9 (3.7–8.3)	0.3 (0.0–1.1)	0.1 (0.0–0.2)	1.1 (0.9–1.4)
Meat sticks	6	168 (112–204)	71.3 (67.0–78.6)	13.5 (9.8–15.9)	12.0 (6.5–15.6)	1.5 (0.4–3.4)	0.2 (0.1–0.2)	1.5 (1.2–1.7)
High-meat dinners	15	85 (64–110)	82.6 (77.7–85.1)	6.2 (5.1–7.1)	4.1 (1.2–6.4)	5.9 (3.9–9.3)	0.2 (0.1–0.3)	1.0 (0.6–1.4)
Soups and dinners	45	61 (39–100)	86.2 (78.7–89.9)	2.2 (1.1–4.4)	2.0 (0.1–5.8)	8.4 (6.6–12.5)	0.2 (0.1–0.5)	0.9 (0.4–1.6)
Desserts	32	93 (73–112)	77.0 (72.1–81.4)	0.8 (0.1–3.1)	0.7 (0.0–2.7)	21.0 (16.3–26.8)	0.2 (0.0–0.6)	0.3 (0.1–0.7)

Category	Number of Products	Minerals (mg)					
		Calcium	Phosphorus	Potassium	Sodium	Iron	Copper
Fruits	30	7 (3–18)	12 (2–42)	81 (14–174)	17 (1–97)	0.38 (0.10–1.50)	0.02 (0.00–0.05)
Vegetables							
Plain	16	25 (13–41)	32 (18–87)	152 (60–251)	118 (95–149)	0.64 (0.17–1.35)	0.12 (0.01–0.28)

Creamed	5	36 (16–86)	39 (22–57)	118 (68–244)	153 (96–308)	0.50 (0.20–0.80)	0.06 (0.05–0.06)
Meats	17	15 (6–49)	124 (109–150)	163 (73–296)	179 (135–243)	1.36 (0.70–1.97)	0.16 (0.04–0.39)
Meat sticks	6	66 (35–112)	108 (86–140)	116 (61–188)	490 (315–600)	1.49 (0.90–2.00)	0.12 (0.08–0.24)
High-meat dinners	15	21 (8–68)	71 (50–101)	112 (55–190)	167 (97–252)	0.71 (0.30–1.00)	0.09 (0.03–0.16)
Soups and dinners	45	18 (6–52)	35 (17–73)	68 (9–180)	136 (62–410)	0.50 (0.20–1.66)	0.06 (0.02–0.18)
Desserts	32	17 (4–57)	20 (4–61)	46 (8–94)	59 (5–147)	0.31 (0.10–1.12)	0.06 (0.01–0.24)

		Vitamins							
Category	Number of Products	Vitamin A IU	Thiamin μg	Riboflavin μg	Niacin mg	B_6 μg	B_{12} $m\mu g$	Folacin μg	Vitamin C mg
Fruits	30	98 (0–467)	17 (6–40)	27 (6–80)	0.20 (0.00–0.67)	31 (5–80)	52 (0–103)	0.4 (0.1–1.0)	6.2 (0.0–32.3)
Vegetables									
Plain	16	4695 (406–13,061)	38 (20–80)	55 (26–170)	0.53 (0.28–1.30)	72 (45–110)	80 (80–80)	0.7 (0.6–0.8)	7.1 (1.8–14.0)
Creamed	5	514 (21–2281)	34 (9–86)	62 (64–100)	0.43 (0.25–0.80)	62 (26–130)	105 (80–130)	0.4 (0.3–0.5)	5.3 (2.1–12.3)
Meats	17	–	46 (9–193)	188 (100–350)	3.08 (2.30–3.86)	256 (42–490)	1802 (1070–2500)	0.9 (0.4–1.5)	3.6 (2.6–4.3)
Meat sticks	6	126 (0–378)	58 (10–149)	198 (145–240)	1.85 (1.45–2.10)	176 (75–370)	1550 (1200–1900)	1.4 (0.6–2.3)	7.7 (2.9–16.4)
High-meat dinners	15	610 (56–1273)	63 (10–201)	90 (60–211)	1.86 (0.97–3.60)	169 (46–600)	778 (500–1100)	2.4 (1.3–4.0)	3.0 (2.1–5.7)
Soups and dinners	45	756 (0–460)	43 (7–112)	58 (10–230)	0.63 (0.17–1.80)	50 (16–100)	109 (0–213)	0.9 (0.2–1.6)	2.3 (1.2–3.8)
Desserts	32	77 (0–460)	14 (4–33)	38 (7–195)	0.12 (0.02–0.31)	24 (0–90)	61 (0–200)	0.3 (0.1–0.7)	5.8 (0.0–39.5)

*Values in parentheses indicate ranges.

more than five times the protein content of rice cereal and approximately twice that of other varieties of dry cereals. In the manufacturing process, granulated or brown sugar may be added. All dry cereals are supplemented with calcium and phosphorus in the form of dicalcium or tricalcium phosphate and, sometimes, calcium carbonate. They are also fortified with thiamin, riboflavin and niacin.

All of the Gerber dry cereals are fortified with electrolytic iron powder whereas those manufactured by Beech-Nut are fortified with sodium iron pyrophosphate. Of the cereals marketed by Heinz, high-protein, mixed and oatmeal cereals contain "iron" (presumably electrolytic iron); rice cereal contains sodium iron pyrophosphate and barley cereal contains both sodium iron pyrophosphate and "iron." Comments about the probable availability of these iron salts will be presented later in this chapter.

Phytate, a component of soy and oat flours, is known to interfere with absorption of minerals (Miller et al. 1965; Mickelsen, 1968) in at least some circumstances. However, the quantity of phytate provided by a serving of cereal is quite small and it seems unlikely that it would be of nutritional significance. Much larger intakes of phytate are consumed by infants fed soy-isolate formulas (see Chapter 15).

Dilution of Dry Cereal

Because little information is available concerning composition of dry infant cereals after dilution with milk or water, 34 women visiting the Well Child Clinic at the University of Iowa were asked to mix cereal and diluent as they would at home (Anderson and Fomon, 1971a). Weights of dry cereal and diluent may be seen from Figure 16–1. Average ratios of dry cereal to diluent were 1:7.1 for infants less than six months of age, 1:5.5 for infants 5 to 10 months of age and 1:5.6 for infants 11 to 14 months of age. The average weight of the cereal-milk (or cereal-formula) mixture prepared for the 34 infants was 58 gm, and the average proportions were 1 part of cereal to 6.2 parts of diluent. Almost all of the mothers whose infants were less than five months of age used formula as the diluent; mothers of older infants used either whole milk or skim milk. Water was not used.

On the basis of this limited sample, it would appear that 5 to 15 gm of dry cereal was used to prepare approximately 30 to 90 gm of the cereal-milk (or cereal-formula) mixture fed to these infants. The label declaration concerning vitamin and mineral content is based on a serving containing 28 gm (1 oz) of dry cereal—a considerably larger amount than an infant is likely to receive at a single feeding.

When 1 part of dry cereal is diluted with approximately 6 parts of milk or formula, it is evident that both the cereal and the diluent will

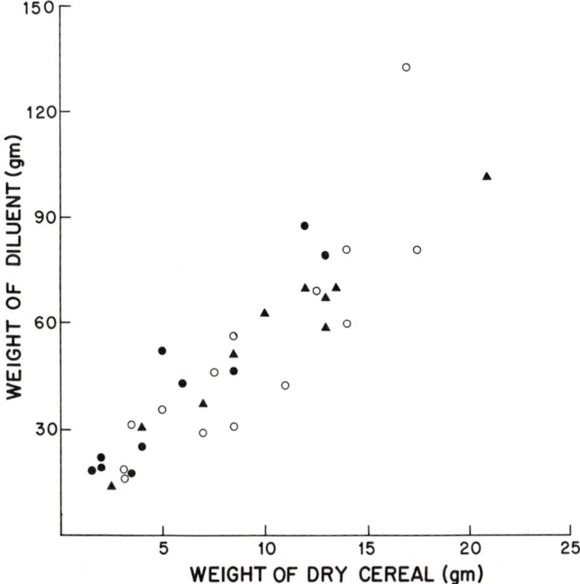

Figure 16–1 Amounts of dry cereal and diluent used in preparation for infant feeding. Each symbol indicates the quantities of dry cereal and diluent used by one mother. The age of the infant for whom the cereal was prepared is indicated by the symbol: ● = less than five months; ○ = 5 to 10 months; ▲ = 10 to 14 months.

contribute calories and essential nutrients. Calorie and protein content of cereal diluted with whole cow milk or water may be seen in Table 16–3. The vitamin and mineral content of cereal-milk or cereal-water mixtures have been discussed elsewhere (Anderson and Fomon, 1971a and c).

TABLE 16–3 EFFECT OF VARIETY OF INFANT CEREAL AND CHOICE OF DILUENT ON CALORIE AND PROTEIN CONTENT OF CEREAL-DILUENT MIXTURE*†

Cereal	Energy (kcal/100 gm)		Protein (gm/100 gm)	
	Dry Cereal Mixed With		*Dry Cereal Mixed With*	
	Milk‡	*Water*	*Milk*	*Water*
High protein	107	52	8.1	5.1
Barley, mixed, oatmeal	109	53	5.2	2.2
Rice	108	52	3.9	0.9

*Adapted from Anderson, T. A. and Fomon, S. J.: Commercially prepared infant cereals: nutritional considerations. J. Pediatr. 78:788, 1971.

†Mixed 1 part cereal, 6 parts diluent by weight; data presented are averages of Gerber, Beech-Nut and Heinz nutritional data.

‡Values presented are based on the assumption that whole milk provides 67 kcal and 3.5 gm protein in 100 gm.

Cereals with Fruit

As may be seen from a comparison of data presented in Tables 16–1 and 16–3, calorie content of strained cereal with fruit is intermediate between that of dry cereal diluted with milk and dry cereal diluted with water. Protein content varies widely among the various types of cereals (Table 16–1). With the exception of the high protein product, cereals with fruit provide little calcium (Table 16–1). Iron is not added to cereals with fruit marketed by Beech-Nut or to rice cereal with applesauce and bananas marketed by Gerber. With one exception, the other cereals with fruit are fortified with sodium iron pyrophosphate. Junior rice cereal with applesauce and pineapple is fortified with ferrous sulfate. Cereals with fruit provide between 0.2 and 5.3 mg of iron/100 gm (Table 16–1). Thus, although several of the cereals with fruit are better sources of iron than are most other varieties of strained or junior foods, some are relatively poor sources of iron and none provides as much iron as do the dry cereals after usual dilution. For example, the iron content of Gerber rice cereal diluted with water or milk is approximately 80 times as great as that of a similar-sized portion of strained rice cereal with applesauce and bananas.

Cereals with fruit are fortified by all manufacturers with niacin, riboflavin and thiamin to provide amounts of these vitamins approximately equivalent to those provided by dry cereals diluted with milk. Cereals with fruit may also be fortified with ascorbic acid and vitamin B_6.

COMPOSITION OF STRAINED AND JUNIOR FOODS

The many varieties of strained and junior foods offer a wide range in caloric density and individual essential nutrients. Appropriate foods can be found for almost any specific dietary requirement; however, poor choice of these foods may, under certain circumstances, result in inadequate diets. Data presented in Table 16–2 demonstrate few differences in nutrient composition between strained and junior foods. The differences are mostly organoleptic—certain junior foods having a slightly larger particle size and coarser texture. The following discussion of nutrient composition of infant foods therefore applies to both the strained and junior varieties.

In the United States, fruit juices are packed in cans containing 126 ml (4.2 fl. oz), whereas all other infant foods are marketed in glass jars. With the exception of strained meats and strained egg yolks, which are marketed in 100 gm (3 1/2 oz) jars, all strained foods are sold either in 128 gm (4 1/2 oz) or 134 gm (4 3/4 oz) jars. Junior meats are marketed in 100 gm jars, junior high-meat dinners in 128 or 134 gm jars, and all other junior foods in 212 mg (7 1/2 oz) or 220 gm (7 3/4 oz) jars.

Strained and junior foods are marketed in 128 gm (4 1/2 oz) and 227 gm (8 oz) cans (England, Australia) and in jars of various sizes (Canada, Scandinavia, France, Germany, Italy). In some countries (e.g., England, France, Italy), infant foods are available in precooked dried form.

Fruit Juices

With the exception of orange juice and apple juice, which are prepared from single fruits, all of the strained fruit juices are prepared from two or three fruits. All contain additional sucrose or dextrose. For this reason, total solids and caloric density of most varieties are higher than those of freshly squeezed or canned fruit juices not specifically prepared for infants. Gerber products are generally lower in carbohydrate content than are those of other manufacturers.

Strained fruit juices are fortified with ascorbic acid to the extent that one can (126 ml) supplies 50 mg of ascorbic acid.

Fruits

Among the various categories of infant foods, fruits account for a high percentage of sales (Table 16–4). Sugar is added to all strained and junior fruits. Approximately one-third of all fruits contain modi-

TABLE 16–4 SALES OF STRAINED AND JUNIOR BABY FOODS BY PRODUCT CATEGORY FOR 1971*

Variety	Per Cent of Sales
Cereals	
Dry	2.9
With fruit	3.1
Juices	9.7
Fruits	18.9
Vegetables	8.3
Meats	9.7
High-meat dinners	4.4
Soups and dinners	23.3
Desserts	17.1
Other	2.6

*Adapted from Chain Store Age, July 1972, p. 76.

fied tapioca starch and in each instance the variety name of the food includes "tapioca" (e.g., plums with tapioca). Although cornstarch is not included in variety names, labels indicate that this starch is sometimes included in fruits. For example, the label on a jar of Heinz "strained bananas" lists the following ingredients: water, fully ripened bananas, sugar, food starch modified (from corn), concentrated orange juice, citric acid and vitamin C. Less than 30 per cent of the total solids in the jar are supplied in the form of "strained bananas." There is actually little difference in recipe formulation between starch-containing fruits and some of the fruit-containing desserts. In fact, nutritional information published by the manufacturers is not entirely consistent in assigning products between these categories. Salt is added to most of the fruits that contain tapioca or "food starch modified."

Ascorbic acid, usually 10 mg in a 134 gm jar, is added to most of the strained and junior fruits marketed by Heinz and Gerber but only to strained banana products marketed by Beech-Nut. Citric acid may be added to lower pH to less than 4, thus reducing the heat required in processing. The ratio of sugar to acid is closely adjusted by each manufacturer. With the addition of acidity in the form of citric acid, fruits may require proportionally more sugar than would be needed if only the natural acidity of the fruit were present.

Desserts and Puddings

All desserts and puddings contain sugar and modified corn and/or tapioca starch. Carbohydrate content is relatively high, while protein content is variable (Table 16–2). The number of items in this product category has increased substantially in recent years.

Vegetables

Two types of vegetables are marketed—plain and creamed. The creamed products include whole milk solids, modified cornstarch and, in some instances, sucrose. Consequently, total solids and caloric density of the creamed vegetables are usually greater than those of plain vegetables (Table 16–2). Sucrose is added to almost all plain vegetables produced by Heinz and Beech-Nut but not to those produced by Gerber.

Soups and Dinners, High-Meat Dinners

Products of this category account for a substantial percentage of sales (Table 16–4). With the exception of plain (i.e., noncreamed) vegetables, the total solids content and caloric density of soups and dinners are generally less than those of products in other categories, including fruit juices.

Meat appears first in the variety name of the high-meat dinners – e.g., chicken with vegetables – indicating that meat is the principal ingredient. Protein concentration is about half that of strained or junior meats but about three times that of products simply classified as "dinners."

Meats

Water is added to strained meats and egg yolks during processing, resulting in lower concentrations of total solids and protein than would be found in pureed products prepared in the home; nevertheless, meats are a good source of protein (Table 16–2). Fat content is generally less than that of meats not formulated especially for infants. Meat sticks – a junior food item – are low in water and quite high in protein, fat and caloric content (Table 16–2).

Strained meats with considerably greater concentrations of fat and lower concentrations of protein than indicated in Table 16–2 are marketed in Canada.* Concentrations of fat in samples of strained lamb and liver purchased in Canada and analyzed in our laboratory were three to four times as great as those of corresponding products sold by the same manufacturer in the United States. Because strained meats are relatively expensive and presumably are useful primarily in contributing protein, iron and B vitamins to the diet, an increase in fat content, with corresponding decrease in content of protein and other essential nutrients, would seem undesirable.

NUTRITIONAL CONSIDERATIONS

Accuracy of Nutritional Information

Frequent recipe changes are made in the formulation of infant foods, reflecting advances in food technology and, presumably, also aiding in controlling production costs. In view of such recipe changes, it is apparent that published data on chemical composition of these foods will be only approximations.

Because commercially prepared strained and junior foods are classified as foods for special dietary uses, the law (Federal Register, 1970) requires that "the label shall bear, if such food is fabricated from

*H. J. Heinz Co., Ltd., Leamington, Ontario, Canada.

two or more ingredients, the common or usual name of each ingredient, including spices, flavoring and coloring." In addition to the label declaration, each manufacturer publishes lists of products containing common allergens, such as those present in wheat, milk, eggs and citrus fruits. Approximately one-half of the strained and junior foods included in Tables 16–1 and 16–2 are free of these allergens. However, because of frequent recipe changes, published lists of foods free of specific allergens are likely to become outdated. Careful reading of the list of ingredients on the label is thus recommended.

Water and Total Solids

Relatively large amounts of water must be added in the preparation of most infant foods because many of the ingredients are obtained in dehydrated form and are rehydrated during preparation. In addition, the slurry made up of the various ingredients must be sufficiently fluid to be pumped through the steam injection and pureeing equipment and, finally, through the pipes leading to the filling lines. The generally high water content of soups and dinners, in spite of their semi-solid appearance, may be noted in Table 16–2. The solids content of fruit juices is relatively high because of the added sugar.

One important reason for the difference in nutrient content between a specified commercially prepared strained or junior food and a home-prepared food with the same name relates to the higher water content of commercially prepared infant foods. In the case of chicken and noodles (Tables 16–5), water accounts for 71.1 per cent of the home-prepared product and for 88.5 per cent of the infant food. Thus, the total solids content of the infant food is 11.5 per cent whereas that of the home-prepared product is 28.9 per cent—two and one-half times greater in the home-prepared product not specifically designed for infant feeding.

Similarly, in the case of junior spaghetti, tomato sauce and meat (Table 16–5), total solids are substantially less than those of the home-prepared product.

Calories

Not only is water content of commercially prepared infant foods relatively high but fat content is generally low. The combination of these two characteristics results, in most instances, in a caloric density considerably less than that of the corresponding home-prepared product. In the case of strained chicken noodle dinner (Table 16–5), for ex-

TABLE 16–5 PROXIMATE COMPOSITION AND SODIUM CONTENT OF SELECTED COMMERCIALLY PREPARED BABY FOODS AND HOME-PREPARED FOODS OF THE SAME NAME*

Product	Energy kcal/100 gm	Proximate Analysis (gm/100 gm)						Sodium (meq/100 kcal)
		Water	*Protein*	*Fat*	*Carbohydrate Total*	*Carbohydrate Fiber*	*Ash*	
Chicken and noodles, cooked from home recipe†	153	71.1	9.3	7.7	10.7	trace	1.2	7.1
Strained chicken noodle dinner‡	46	88.5	2.0	1.0	7.1	0.3	1.1	28.0
Spaghetti with meatballs in tomato sauce cooked from home recipe§	134	70.0	7.5	4.7	15.3	0.3	2.2	13.2
Junior spaghetti, tomato sauce, and meat‡	70	82.9	2.7	1.7	11.0	0.3	1.4	29.3

*From Anderson, T. A., and Fomon, S. J.: Commercially prepared strained and junior foods for infants. J. Amer. Diet. Ass. 58:520, 1971.

†From Watt and Merrill, 1963, item 752.

‡Mean calculated from data in Table 16–2.

§From Watt and Merrill, 1963, item 2165.

ample, the infant food provides only 46 kcal/100 gm, while the home-prepared product yields 153 kcal/100 gm.

Although comparisons between nutritional properties of commercially prepared infant foods and home-prepared foods are of interest, we believe that other frames of reference are more meaningful in relation to infant nutrition. Because commercially prepared strained and junior foods may be thought of as replacing some of the milk (or formula) that might otherwise comprise the entire caloric intake, it is important to compare the caloric density of various infant foods with that of milk.

Insufficient data are available to determine whether strained or junior foods are substituted for milk or formula predominantly on a caloric basis (e.g., 100 kcal of strained food replacing 100 kcal of formula); predominantly on a quantity basis (e.g., 100 ml or 100 gm of strained food replacing 100 ml or 100 gm of formula); or on some other basis. Studies in which groups of infants received formulas similar except for caloric density suggested that food intake of infants fed ad libitum was determined partly on a quantity basis during the first six weeks of life but predominantly on a caloric basis thereafter (Chapter 2). Consideration of caloric density of commercially prepared infant foods in relation to the caloric density of milk or formula is therefore of interest.

Milk or formula generally provides approximately 67 kcal/100 gm. Most plain vegetables, soups and dinners and some creamed vegetables provide less than 67 kcal/100 gm whereas the caloric density of fruit juices, fruits, high-meat dinners and meats is generally greater (Table 16–6). Foods of low caloric density should be avoided in management of infants with caloric undernutrition—e.g., those with neuromuscular disease or congenital heart disease (Chapter 19). For such infants to achieve an adequate caloric intake is often difficult, and it is desirable to restrict the selection of commercially prepared infant foods to those of relatively high caloric density.

Fat

Strained egg yolks provide approximately 76 per cent of calories from fat, meat sticks about 63 per cent, strained and junior meats about 45 per cent, high-meat dinners about 40 per cent, and soups and dinners about 28 per cent (Table 16–6). Fat content of fruits and vegetables is low, while that of desserts and puddings is variable but generally low. Thus, in comparison with milk or formula, those infant foods accounting for the great majority of sales (fruits, soups and dinners, desserts and puddings) provide relatively low percentages of calories from fat.

Consideration of the list of ingredients included in strained and

TABLE 16–6 CALORIC DISTRIBUTION OF STRAINED AND JUNIOR FOODS*

Category	Number of Products	Energy kcal/100 gm	Per Cent of Calories		
			Protein	*Fat*	*Carbohydrate*
Strained					
Juices	32	65† (45–98)	2 (0–5)	2 (0–7)	96 (89–100)
Fruits	33	85 (79–125)	2 (0–10)	2 (1–7)	96 (87–99)
Vegetables					
Plain	24	45 (27–78)	14 (5–32)	6 (1–19)	80 (62–92)
Creamed	6	63 (42–94)	13 (5–26)	13 (3–25)	74 (57–90)
Meats	25	106 (86–194)	53 (20–72)	46 (28–80)	1 (0–8)
Egg yolks	4	192 (184–199)	21 (20–23)	76 (69–80)	3 (0–8)
High-meat dinners	15	84 (63–106)	29 (20–42)	47 (20–57)	29 (19–40)
Soups and dinners	42	58 (39–94)	16 (7–33)	28 (2–54)	56 (34–86)
Desserts	37	96 (71–136)	4 (0–18)	7 (0–31)	89 (51–99)
Junior					
Fruits	30	85 (69–116)	2 (0–11)	2 (0–5)	96 (86–98)
Vegetables					
Plain	16	46 (27–71)	12 (6–24)	7 (1–19)	81 (65–92)
Creamed	5	64 (45–72)	13 (5–24)	17 (3–38)	70 (51–90)
Meats	17	103 (88–135)	56 (43–64)	43 (36–55)	1 (0–4)
Meat sticks	6	168 (112–204)	32 (27–38)	63 (52–70)	5 (1–12)
High-meat dinners	15	85 (64–110)	30 (22–39)	42 (17–57)	28 (16–44)
Soups and dinners	45	61 (39–100)	15 (6–21)	27 (2–55)	58 (34–86)
Desserts	32	93 (73–112)	4 (0–14)	6 (0–25)	90 (68–99)

*Calculated from averages presented in Table 16–2.
†Mean with range in parentheses.

junior foods suggests that the essential fatty acid content is low. This is the case because total fat content is relatively low and the fats are not highly unsaturated.

Vegetable oil is used as an ingredient in 16 Heinz strained and junior soups, dinners and creamed vegetables. Gerber and Beech-Nut do not add vegetable oils to products in these categories. Assuming that vegetable oil provides half of the lipid content of these products (average lipid content 2 per cent) and that the vegetable oil (presumably soybean oil) is approximately 50 per cent linoleic acid, the essential fatty acid content would be about 0.5 per cent. Because creamed vegetables and dinners generally provide about 60 kcal/100 gm, linoleic acid might contribute approximately 8 per cent of calories of these foods. Obviously, the percentage of unsaturated fatty acids in these products may be greater than in products containing fat derived mainly from whole milk solids, egg yolk or meat.

Protein

As already mentioned, a specified number of calories consumed in the form of commercially prepared strained or junior foods is likely to substitute for a similar caloric intake the infant would otherwise receive from milk or formula. From this point of view, it may be noted that protein accounts for approximately 7 per cent of the calories supplied by human milk, 9 to 14 per cent of calories supplied by most commercially prepared infant formulas, and 20 per cent of of calories supplied by whole cow milk. Data in Table 16–6 indicate that meats, egg yolks and most high-meat dinners supply more than 20 per cent of calories from protein. On the other hand, fruits and most desserts and puddings supply less than 7 per cent of calories from protein. Vegetables, soups and dinners provide variable amounts of protein; generally they provide more protein per unit of calories than human milk but less than cow milk. Considering the lesser biologic value of most vegetable proteins than of milk proteins, it seems unsound to rely on commercially prepared strained or junior vegetables and soups and dinners in circumstances in which intake of protein may be limiting.

Because most infants will receive from milk or formula more than enough protein to fulfill their needs, it will usually not be necessary to rely on strained or junior foods for this purpose. As discussed in Chapter 6 (Table 6–9), the breastfed infant may be an exception. Infants receiving adequate caloric intakes from human milk will also receive adequate intakes of protein; however, the breastfed infant who receives only half of his calories from human milk and the remainder from strained foods could become protein deficient if his mother consistently selected fruits, puddings and desserts and those vegetables, soups and dinners with particularly low protein content. Breastfed infants who receive substantial intakes of calories, e.g., more than 25 per cent, from sources other than human milk should receive a significant portion of these calories in the form of cow milk, an infant formula or protein-rich infant foods.

Carbohydrate

With the exception of egg yolks, meats and high-meat dinners, all categories of infant foods are rich in carbohydrate. Because whole cow milk supplies only about 30 per cent of calories from carbohydrate, infant foods supplying a high percentage of calories from carbohydrate are a reasonable addition to the diet of infants fed whole cow milk. As discussed in Chapter 19, we recommend that the change in an infant's diet from formula to whole cow milk be deferred at least until the infant is eating the equivalent of at least one and one-half jars of strained food daily. Under these circumstances, the diet is likely to be reasonably well balanced with respect to percentage of calories derived from protein, fat and carbohydrate.

Sucrose and Dextrose. All fruit juices, fruits, creamed vegetables, desserts and puddings include added sucrose or dextrose. Although Nisbett and Gurwitz (1970) in study of newborn infants found that heavy infants consumed more of a sweetened formula than did lighter infants (Chapter 2), no published reports document the preference of infants for highly sweetened strained foods. It is possible that widespread use of highly sweetened foods during the early months of life may predispose to a taste preference for sweet foods subsequently, with consequent increased severity of dental caries.

Lactose. More than 40 per cent of the soups, dinners and desserts and all creamed vegetables contain lactose in the form of whole milk solids or nonfat dry milk. Juices, fruits, plain vegetables, meats and egg yolks do not contain lactose.

Starches. It has been known for many years that pancreatic amylase activity in the human infant is low, particularly in the early months of life (Chapters 4 and 8), but few studies of ability to digest food starches have been carried out with the human infant. A number of starch-containing ingredients are included in dinners, desserts and creamed vegetables—wheat, oat, rice and potato flours; wheat starch; durum granular flour; farina; macaroni; noodles; spaghetti; and "baked" flour. In addition, approximately 65 per cent of commercially prepared infant foods currently contain one or more of six or eight different modified corn, milo or tapioca starches. Modification consists of chemical cross-linking between branches of the starch polymers as discussed in Chapter 8. Such modified food starches are included in infant foods because they impart texture, consistency and "mouth-feel" believed by manufacturers to be desirable. These starches are cold-stable and resist syneresis (separation of water from the starch)—important properties, particularly when an unused portion of the food is refrigerated.

Many of the soups and dinners contain 3 to 5 per cent modified cornstarch. In view of the relatively low (10 to 20 per cent) total solids of most soups and dinners (Table 16–2), it is apparent that modified cornstarch may account for a relatively high percentage of total solids and calories.

Modified food starches are classified by the Food and Drug Administration as food additives (Federal Food, Drug and Cosmetic Act, 1965). In labeling food for special dietary uses, including infant foods, the law (Federal Register, 1970) requires that the plant source from which the starch is derived be designated, e.g., corn, tapioca. Results of digestibility studies in weanling rats must receive favorable review by the Food and Drug Administration before a modified food starch is approved for human use; however, with respect to digestibility of starch, one wonders whether performance by the weanling rat, a relatively mature animal, is likely to reflect performance by the relatively immature human infant.

Satisfactory carbohydrate tolerance tests cannot be performed with infants fed those modified food starches included in strained and junior foods. The quantity of starch required results in a solution that is either too voluminous or too viscous to be fed. The same problem exists in the case of unmodified food starches. When modified or unmodified food starches have been reduced in viscosity by acid treatment, they are referred to as thin-boiling starches. As discussed in Chapter 8, glucose concentration of the blood increases only slightly after administration of thin-boiling starch to human infants. These findings are compatible with either poor or delayed absorption of starches by the infant.

Minerals

Iron. Although iron-fortified formulas are unquestionably useful in preventing iron deficiency, formulas of any type are not commonly fed beyond the age of about five months (Chapter 1, Fig. 1–5). It is therefore important to consider the iron content of other commercially prepared infant foods. We have previously called attention to the relative generous fortification of infant cereals with iron (Fomon, 1970; Anderson and Fomon, 1971a) and to our lack of information concerning the availability of the forms of iron included in these cereals (Anderson et al., 1972).

As discussed in Chapter 12, little is known about the extent to which human infants absorb iron in the form of sodium iron pyrophosphate, electrolytic iron or reduced iron.

Data concerning availability to human infants of electrolytic iron from infant cereals have not been published. Label declarations referring to "available iron" are therefore meaningless. Levels of iron fortification in most dry cereal products marketed in Australia and Canada are similar to those used in the United States; however, dry cereals marketed in France, Germany, Italy and Scandinavia are supplemented with much less iron—generally 1 to 15 mg/100 gm dry product. A recent directive by the Food and Drug Administration (Federal Register, 1973) limits added iron in infant cereals to <50 per cent of the 15 mg infant U.S. RDA ("recommended daily allowance") for iron (0.5×15 mg $= 7.5$ mg) per 0.5 oz serving, unless the product is labeled as a dietary supplement. If the manufacturer does not choose to so designate an infant cereal product, the level of iron fortification cannot exceed 50 mg/100 gm—one-half the amount of iron currently added to cereals produced by the major U.S. manufacturer of baby food.

Because of the higher water content of commercially prepared infant foods, concentrations of iron in these foods (except cereals) are less than those in corresponding fresh or home-prepared foods. Strained and junior meats, with the exception of liver and egg yolks, generally provide less than 2 mg elemental iron/100 gm food, whereas vegetables, soups, dinners and fruits generally provide less than 1 mg/100 gm food (Table 16–2).

Sodium. As discussed in Chapter 11, several authors have suggested that amounts of sodium chloride previously present (i.e., until 1971) in certain commercially available strained and junior foods might predispose susceptible infants to development of hypertension in later life. Salt appears to be added to these foods solely, or at least primarily, for improvement of palatability and not on the basis of nutritional considerations. Strained foods with added salt are stated by the manufacturer to be preferred by mothers,* although a study of normal four- and seven-month-old infants failed to demonstrate that consumption of strained foods was influenced by the presence or absence of added sodium chloride (Fomon et al., 1970).

In 1970, an ad hoc committee appointed by the National Academy of Science–National Research Council, at the request of the Food and Drug Administration, recommended that the level of salt added to strained and junior foods not exceed 0.25 per cent (Filer, 1971) and the manufacturers agreed to abide by this recommendation. The val-

*With respect to commercially prepared strained and junior foods, the mother appears to be looked upon as the "consumer."

TABLE 16–7 AVERAGE SODIUM CONTENT (MEQ/100 KCAL) OF INFANT FOODS

Milk	
Human	0.9
Cow	3.3
Strained Foods*	
Juices	0.1
Fruits	0.9
Vegetables	
Plain	11.3
Creamed	7.4
Meats	7.0
High-meat dinners	7.6
Soups and dinners	10.8
Desserts	2.5

*Calculated from averages presented in Table 16–2.

ues for sodium content of strained foods shown in Table 16–7 reflect this reduced level.

Because normal infants beyond six weeks of age appear to regulate food intake largely on the basis of caloric needs (Chapter 2), it is reasonable to consider sodium content of infant foods in relation to caloric density (Table 16–7). Human milk provides approximately 0.9 meq of sodium/100 kcal—a ratio of sodium to calories that is presumably adequate (Chapter 11). Cow milk provides more than three times the sodium to calorie ratio of human milk (Table 16–7), and commercially prepared formulas generally provide ratios intermediate between that of human milk and that of cow milk. As previously mentioned, calorie intake from commercially prepared strained or junior foods probably substitutes for an equivalent calorie intake from milk or formula. From this point of view, concentrations of sodium greater than 3.3 meq/100 kcal may be considered excessive. Nearly all commercially prepared strained and junior foods with caloric densities less than 50 kcal/100 gm provide 8 meq or more of sodium/100 kcal.

Other Minerals. The ash content of most strained and junior foods is relatively low, reflecting the low total solids content. A significant proportion of the ash in many products is contributed by the added sodium chloride.

Tabular data on concentrations of various minerals are available from all three manufacturers.

Vitamins

All three manufacturers provide data on content of vitamin A, thiamin, riboflavin, niacin and ascorbic acid. Data on vitamin B_6, vitamin B_{12} and folacin may also be available (Table 16–2).

The addition of ascorbic acid to fruit juices and to some strained and junior fruits has been mentioned previously. Dry cereals and cereals with fruit are the only other infant foods to which vitamins are added in processing. By comparison with the estimated requirements or advisable intakes for niacin, riboflavin and thiamin (Chapter 9), it will be apparent in Table 16–1 that dry cereals are good sources of these vitamins. When milk is used as a diluent for dry cereal, the riboflavin content will be substantially augmented (Anderson and Fomon, 1971a and c).

Modern methods of food processing result in minimum destruction of vitamins in the ingredients. However, because of the low total solids content of most strained and junior foods and the addition of sugar or starch to many, concentrations of vitamins are likely to be considerably less than those of corresponding foods prepared in the home.

Renal Solute Load

As discussed in Chapter 10, solutes that must be excreted in the urine are spoken of collectively as renal solute load. Relatively high renal solute loads result from feeding strained meats, egg yolk and high-meat dinners, whereas low renal solute loads result from feeding fruit juices, fruits, puddings and desserts. The other classifications of infant foods yield intermediate renal solute loads (Chapter 10, Table 10–3).

FEEDING THE TODDLER

Surprisingly few data exist regarding the nutrient composition and quantities of foods consumed by the toddler. Between one and three years of age growth rate is markedly less than that during the first year of life (Chapter 3) and appetite usually decreases accordingly. Parents may often overestimate the amount of food required for normal growth and development during the toddler years. The comparative disinterest by the toddler in foods served in the formal meal time setting is often of concern to parents and, if the child is forced to eat, unpleasant associations with certain foods may develop.

In summarizing the results of the Preschool Nutrition Survey, Kram and Owen (1972) have presented frequency distributions of nutrient intakes for three age ranges: 12 to 23, 24 to 35 and 36 to 47 months. In addition, data were presented on feeding practices. Permissiveness toward the child's choices of foods appeared to be related to income—parents with lower incomes being more permissive than

TABLE 16–8 EATING BEHAVIOR OF PRESCHOOL CHILDREN—CONCERNS OF MOTHERS*

Age Group	0–3 mo	3–6 mo	6–9 mo	9–12 mo	1–1½ yr	1½–2 yr	2–3 yr
				(Per Cent)			
1. Chooses limited variety	2.6	8.7	12.0	24.6	34.1	37.6	40.3
2. Dawdles with food	10.3	3.1	15.5	14.6	34.1	25.7	36.8
3. Eats too little fruits and vegetables	0.0	2.4	12.9	14.5	15.8	29.4	27.2
4. Eats too many sweets	0.0	0.0	0.0	1.4	4.7	7.8	26.3
5. Eats too little meat	0.9	4.7	7.2	22.5	22.6	30.3	22.3
6. Eats too little food	8.5	2.4	8.2	10.1	14.7	13.8	21.6
7. Drinks too little milk	0.0	3.9	4.8	10.9	10.8	16.5	20.1
8. Drinks too much milk	9.4	7.9	7.1	5.1	10.0	13.8	10.0
9. Eats too much food	7.7	4.7	8.2	8.7	5.1	3.7	2.7
10. Eats too much meat	0.0	0.0	0.0	0.0	1.4	5.0	3.5
Number of subjects	117	127	84	138	279	218	551

*Adapted from Eppright, E. S., et al.: Eating behavior of preschool children. J. Nutr. Educ. *1*:16, 1969.

those with higher incomes. Poorer families also were more apt to punish or reward the child by withholding or offering food.

Eagles and Steele (1972) have reanalyzed data collected during the USDA Diet Survey (U.S. Department of Agriculture, 1965). These data include 24-hour food intakes of 719 children less than four years of age living in low-income households. Geographic differences in feeding practices were evident. For example, in the south, children consumed less milk and more carbonated drinks and Kool-Aid than did children in families of similar income in the north. Consumption of foods high in sucrose was somewhat greater in one-year-old children living in the north but in the second and third year consumption of such foods was greater among children living in the south.

Eppright et al. (1969) surveyed 2000 households regarding the eating behavior of 3444 infants and children ranging in age from birth to six years. Table 16–8 indicates the concerns of mothers about eating behavior of children between birth and three years of age. Mothers seemed most concerned about limited choices of foods and dawdling over food. Frequent consumption of sweets is of major concern to mothers by the second year of life. Interestingly, preferences of the toddler for certain foods were found by Eppright et al. (1969) to be more closely correlated with those of older siblings than of either parent (Table 16–9).

A useful guide to the proper nutrition and feeding of infants and children under three years of age in the group day care setting has been published by Maternal and Child Health Service (1971); a sample daily food plan and suggested daily meal plans suitable for the toddler are included.

TABLE 16–9 ATTITUDE OF FAMILY MEMBERS TO VEGETABLE DISLIKED BY CHILD*

	LIKES	DISLIKES		NUMBER OF CHILDREN
		Will Not Eat	*Will Eat*	
Father	76.4	17.1	6.5	170
Mother	82.5	12.2	5.3	183
Older brother	49.3	44.3	6.4	79
Older sister	60.9	34.5	4.6	87

*From Eppright, E. S., et al.: Eating behavior of preschool children. J. Nutr. Educ. *1*:16, 1969.

REFERENCES

Anderson, T. A., and Fomon, S. J.: Commercially prepared infant cereals: nutritional considerations. J. Pediatr. *78*:788, 1971a.

Anderson, T. A., and Fomon, S. J.: Commercially prepared strained and junior foods for infants. J. Amer. Diet. Ass. *58*:520, 1971b.

Anderson, T. A., and Fomon, S. J.: (Letter to the Editor.) Commercially prepared infant cereals. J. Pediatr. *79*:512, 1971c.

Anderson, T. A., Kim, I., and Fomon, S. J.: Iron status of anemic rats fed iron-fortified cereal-milk diets. Nutr. Metab. *14*:355, 1972.

Chain Store Age, July 1972, p. 76.

Eagles, J. A., and Steele, P. D.: Food and nutrient intake of children from birth to four years of age. *In* Fomon, S. J., and Anderson, T. A. (eds.): Practices of Low-Income Families in Feeding Infants and Small Children. With Particular Attention to Cultural Subgroups. DHEW Publ. No. (HSM) 72-5605. Washington, D. C., U.S. Government Printing Office, 1972, p. 19.

Eppright, E. S., Fox, H. M., Fryer, B. A., Lamkin, G. H., and Vivian, V. M.: Eating behavior of preschool children. J. Nutr. Educ. *1*:16, 1969.

Federal Food, Drug and Cosmetic Act, As Amended. Title 21 U.S. Code, Section 409 (348), Food Additives, 121.1031, 1965.

Federal Register *35*:16737, 1970.

Federal Register *38*:20702, 1973.

Filer, L. J., Jr.: Subcommittee on Safety and Suitability of MSG and Other Substances in Baby Foods. Food Protection Committee, Food and Nutrition Board, NAS-NRC: Salt in infant foods. Nutr. Rev. *29*:27, 1971.

Filer, L. J., Jr., and Martinez, G. A.: Caloric and iron intake by infants in the United States: an evaluation of 4,000 representative six-month-olds. Clin. Pediatr. *2*:470, 1963.

Fomon, S. J.: Prevention of iron-deficiency anemia in infants and children of preschool age. Public Health Service Publ. No. 2085, 1970.

Fomon, S. J., Thomas, L. N., and Filer, L. J., Jr.: Acceptance of unsalted strained foods by normal infants. J. Pediatr. *76*:242, 1970.

Kram, K. M., and Owen, G. M.: Nutritional studies on United States preschool children: dietary intakes and practices of food procurement, preparation and consumption. *In* Fomon, S. J., and Anderson, T. A. (eds.): Practices of Low-Income Families in Feeding Infants and Small Children. With Particular Attention to Cultural Subgroups. DHEW Publ. No. (HSM) 72-5605. Washington, D.C., U.S. Government Printing Office, 1972, p. 3.

Maternal and Child Health Service and Committee on Infant and Preschool Child, American Academy of Pediatrics: Nutrition and Feeding of Infants and Children Under Three in Group Day Care. DHEW Publ. No. (HSM) 72-5606. Washington, D.C., U.S. Government Printing Office, 1971.

Mickelsen, O.: Present knowledge of naturally occurring toxicants in foods. Nutr. Rev. *26*:129, 1968.

Miller, E. R., Ullrey, D. E., Zutaut, C. L., Hoefer, J. A., and Luecke, R. L.: Comparisons of casein and soy proteins upon mineral balance and vitamin D_2 requirement of the baby pig. J. Nutr. *85*:347, 1965.

Nisbett, R. E., and Gurwitz, S. B.: Weight, sex, and the eating behavior of human newborns. J. Comp. Physiol. Psychol. *73*:245, 1970.

Ringler, W. M. (ed.): Annual consumer expenditures study, 1971. Supermarketing *27*:31, 1972.

U.S. Department of Agriculture: Food intake and nutritive value of diets of men, women, and children in the United States, spring 1965. Agricultural Research Service, Beltsville, Maryland, U.S. Department of Agriculture Publications ARS 62–18, 1965.

Watt, B. K., and Merrill, A. L.: Composition of Foods—Raw, Processed, Prepared, Revised. USDA Agricultural Handbook No. 8, Revised. Washington, D.C., Agricultural Research Service, 1963.

17

FOOD ALLERGY

Charles D. May

Fanatics and faddists inevitably flourish in areas so intimately interwoven with human foibles and enshrouded with mystery as food and allergy. Some of the beliefs and practices imposed upon victims of ill-defined complaints under the guise of food allergy bear as little relation to scientific knowledge as astrology does to astronomy. There are cults which hold themselves aloof from documentation of their opinions and so communication is impossible with adherents to modern objective methods of acquisition of knowledge. The darkness will be scattered only by more light, just as alchemy gave way before advances in chemistry.

Good practice in infant nutrition requires familiarity with current understanding of allergic reactions to foods. The commonly expressed opinion that disorders due to food allergy are so poorly understood that rational management is impossible does not reflect the current state of knowledge. Actually, comprehension of food allergy compares favorably with knowledge of other allergic disorders such as hay fever. Progress in the past decade has brought the content of allergy abreast of other fields of scientific medicine, and the applications to practice are now being realized (Coombs and Gell, 1968; Ellis, 1969; Goldstein and Heiner, 1970; Bluemink, 1970; Becker, 1971).

An attempt will be made here to place allergic reactions to food in proper perspective among the various causes of reactions to food. Relevant aspects of immunology will be presented as the basis for consideration of clinical manifestations of food allergy and for rational diagnosis and treatment. An easily grasped set of concepts and facts from immunology can ease the feeling of chaos and frustration arising from efforts to deal with food allergy, which is inevitable without this advantage.

Allergy to food is generally believed to be an important cause of symptoms (according to various estimates, from 0.3 to 7 per cent of children are sensitive to cow milk) (Goldstein and Heiner, 1970), but the actual prevalence has not been settled. Lack of simple, dependable, objective means for verification of a clinical diagnosis of allergy to a food has hindered clarification of the symptoms that may be properly ascribed to food allergy and, consequently, determination of the true prevalence. As the symptoms may range from pallor and altered behavior to life-threatening shock, little wonder that confusion and quackery are widespread. Unjustified elimination of staple foods from the diet or use of expensive substitutes does not serve to promote optimal nutrition.

Clinical Manifestations of Adverse Reactions to Foods

An astonishing array of manifestations have been observed as reactions to foods, these having been confirmed by repeated elimination and reintroduction of the suspected food (Crook et al., 1961; Morishima and Kessler, 1962; Goldman et al., 1963a; Wilson et al., 1964). These are listed in Table 17–1, where grouping into systemic, gastrointestinal, respiratory, cutaneous and nervous categories is easily discerned, as are the symptoms most often accepted as consistent with, but not necessarily due to, allergy such as rhinitis, asthma and eczema. As these reactions are contrary to the goal of optimal nutrition, they may be viewed as adverse reactions. One cannot hastily assume that an adverse reaction is due to allergy because other disorders give

TABLE 17–1 SYMPTOMS AND SIGNS ATTRIBUTABLE TO ADVERSE REACTIONS TO FOOD

Vascular	*Dermatologic*
Shock	Urticaria
	Eczema
Gastrointestinal	Miscellaneous ("rash")
Vomiting	
Abdominal pain	*Central Nervous*
Diarrhea	Headache
Malabsorption	Apathy
Enteropathy	Irritability
	Moodiness
Respiratory	Miscellaneous ("behavioral changes")
Rhinitis	
Cough	*General*
Wheezing	Pallor
	Retarded growth

TABLE 17–2 MECHANISMS RESPONSIBLE FOR ADVERSE REACTIONS TO FOODS

Enzymatic
- Enzyme deficiency
  - Example – disaccharidase (especially lactase) deficiency

Immunologic
- Humoral
  - Antigen-antibody reaction
  - Example – dysgammaglobulinemia
- Cellular
  - Lymphocyte
  - Example – thymic dysplasia

Psychologic or Behavioral

Unknown
- Contaminants
  - Antibiotics
    - Example – penicillin
  - Drugs
  - Microorganisms and their byproducts
    - Examples – bacteria, fungi, protozoa
- Additives
- β-Lactoglobulin
- Milk-induced gastrointestinal loss of erythrocytes and proteins

rise to the same assortment of symptoms through the different mechanisms listed in Table 17–2 (Davidson et al., 1965; Townley, 1966; Chafee and Settipane, 1967; Dubois et al., 1970).

There has been a tendency to consider any adverse reaction to food as allergic, but the term allergy was originally introduced by Von Pirquet (1906) to designate development of a change in reactivity of the individual from an original unreactive state associated with appearance of antibodies after exposure to antigenic substances. Allergy should be reserved for adverse reactions for which an immunologic basis can be demonstrated.

The examples of the different mechanisms provided in Table 17–2 indicate the diversity of conditions having symptomatology resembling allergic reactions and the need for caution if serious diagnostic error is to be avoided. The mechanisms have not been determined for the sometimes violent reactions to β-lactoglobulin from cow milk (Davidson et al., 1965), soybean extract (Ament and Rubin, 1972b) and dyes commonly used to color foods, drugs and cosmetics (such as Yellow No. 5 or Tartrazine) (Chafee and Settipane, 1967); particularly, no immunologic basis has been identified.

Not only may the symptoms be similar in the various adverse reactions to foods given as examples in Table 17–2, but all the disorders may become manifest as early as the first month of life. Diarrheal stools may sometimes be bloody or abdominal pain severe enough for confusion with surgical conditions. Alterations in behavior or signs of nervous system disturbance due to adverse reaction to food unaccompanied by other manifestations may be difficult to distinguish from functional neurosis or organic neurologic disease. Malabsorption and protein-losing enteropathy have attracted special interest with respect to an immunologic pathogenesis, and the evidence for this will be considered. Some cases of sudden death in infancy (cot death) may be due to anaphylactic allergic reactions (Bluemink, 1970), but the cause is more often undetermined (Valdes-Dapena and Felipe, 1971).

Immunologic Basis of Adverse Reaction to Food

Several recent reviews (Coombs and Gell, 1968; Ellis, 1969; Becker, 1971) concern the immunologic basis of allergic manifestations. Antibodies to antigenic substances in food are derived in part from passage of intact protein or antigenic products of digestion through the intestinal wall into the circulation to reach antibody-forming cells and tissues throughout the body (Ratner and Gruehl, 1934). Also, the intestinal mucosa contains many antibody-forming cells which can respond locally (Walker and Hong, 1973).

Each distinct antigenic substance stimulates production of not just one type but heterogeneous classes of specific antibodies or immunoglobulins. Each class of immunoglobulin (Ig) has characteristic physical and chemical properties which facilitate separation into the classes termed IgA, IgE, IgG, IgM, etc. When an antigen (Ag) combines with its specific antibodies (Ab), complexes of the type $Ag_x\ Ab_y$ or aggregates of the type $(AgAb)_n$ are formed, which may or may not act on serum or cells to give biologic effects. Antibodies may attach to cells or remain free in the circulation, and the biologic effects of combination with antibody may be influenced accordingly. Action on serum may initiate complement reactions or produce biologically active substances like anaphylatoxin or kinins. Cells may respond with release of mediators of allergic reactions or enzymes or undergo proliferation (Fig. 17–1). Substances active as mediators of allergic reactions or in inflammation or proliferation, which are derived from the various cell types, are listed in Table 17–3.

Whether an antigen elicits these reactions from serum or cells and thereby evokes symptoms depends on a dynamic interplay with its corresponding specific antibodies of different combining powers and their participation in the reaction as freely circulating or cell-bound antibodies. A biologically inactive combination may prevail over combinations which would produce biologic disturbances. For example,

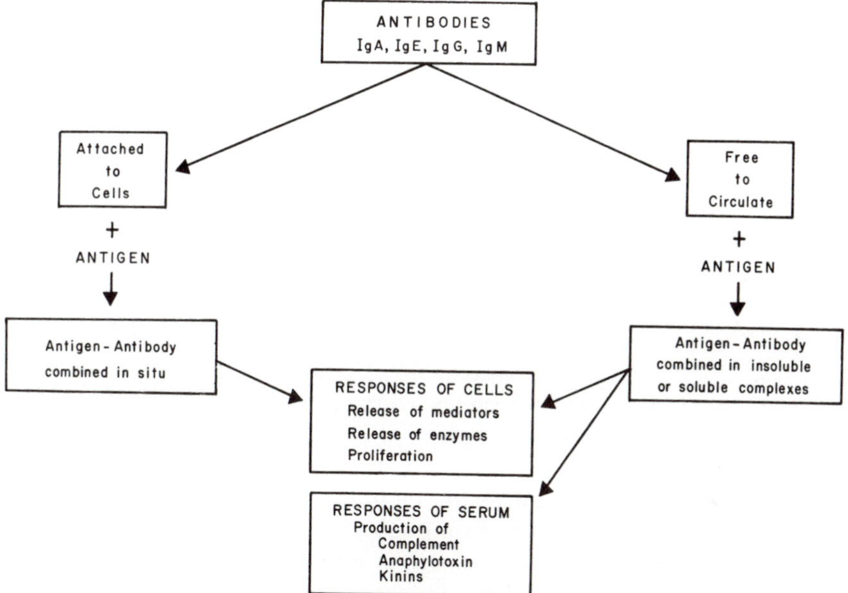

Figure 17–1 A schematic view of antigen-antibody interactions.

Ag + IgE might release histamine but Ag + IgG could be a benign combination. If the latter predominates, the antigen could be neutralized without symptoms. Finally, the end organs affected by the products of the interactions of antigen, antibody and cells or serum will differ in reactivity among individuals and on various occasions.

Thus, whereas antibodies are necessary for an allergic reaction, they are not alone sufficient to insure symptoms. Simple quantitative measurement of any one class of specific antibody is unlikely to aid either in prediction of occurrence of symptoms upon exposure to an-

TABLE 17–3 CELLULAR RESPONSES*

Basophils, Mast Cells
Release histamine; slow-reacting substance; kinins

Neutrophils
Release β-glucuronidase; lactate dehydrogenase; muramidase

Lymphocytes
Blast transformation yields active factors (migration inhibiting, cytotoxic, mitogenic, skin-reactive, chemotactic)

*For elaboration, see Becker (1971).

TABLE 17–4 RELATION OF IMMUNOLOGIC FACTORS TO SYMPTOMS OR SIGNS

ANTIBODIES	SYMPTOMS OR SIGNS	TIMING
IgE	Rhinitis, asthma, urticaria, abdominal pain, "rash"	Immediate (minutes)
IgG, IgM	Urticaria, inflammation, edema, eczema, asthma	Early (hours)
IgA	Malabsorption, enteropathy	Intermediate (days)
IgG, IgM	Nephritis, arthritis, fever, "rash"	Late (weeks)
Cellular	Unknown effects	

tigen or in confirmation of a suspicion that symptoms of an adverse reaction to a food were on an immunologic basis; antibodies may be merely coincidental or their reactions with antigen entirely benign (Barrick and Farr, 1965).

When the interaction of antigen, antibody and cells or serum does produce symptoms, the nature of the clinical manifestations will be influenced by the class of antibody and the type of cells involved. Table 17–4 indicates the usual types of clinical manifestations and their time of appearance in relation to the class of antibodies which may combine with the antigen in allergic reactions to foods.

The amount and combining power of antibody stimulated by exposure to antigen in food may change with age, so that a person allergic in early life may not react to the food at a later date, as histories frequently reveal (Hartley, 1942; Rothberg and Farr, 1965; Korenblat et al., 1968; Kletter et al., 1971b).

Thus far, circulating or humoral antibodies have been under consideration. Another major type of immunologic phenomena depends on a cellular type of immunity independent of humoral antibodies. This is sometimes referred to as delayed hypersensitivity after the characteristic delayed skin reaction to tuberculin, a form of cellular immunity developing in tuberculosis. A role of cellular immune reactions in food allergy has not been demonstrated.

Finally, considering that all the processes under discussion are subject to genetic influences, the heterogeneity of human beings adds further obstacles to finding simple universal means of ascertaining by immunologic methods whether an adverse reaction to a food is due to allergy.

These few facts and concepts enable one to have some insight into the complex, and what otherwise may seem chaotic, events in persons demonstrating adverse reactions to food.

Identification of Immunologic Factors

The physicochemical properties of the different classes of immunoglobulins and the biologic activity of their combinations with antigen form the basis of the methods for quantitative determination (Minden et al., 1966). Some of the procedures devised for each class are listed in Table 17–5. While each has been eagerly applied in an effort to find a correlation with symptoms, none has been found to serve the purpose of clinical diagnosis (Goldstein and Heiner, 1970). The reasons have already been presented: (1) A single antigen stimulates production of a complex array of heterogeneous specific antibodies; (2) difficulty in identifying which of the many antigenic materials in a food or its digestive products are associated with symptoms through combination with one or more classes of the antibodies evoked; (3) the added complication of sensitivity of an individual to multiple foods; (4) uncertainty as to preference for measurement of circulating or bound antibodies; (5) the methods usually measure amounts of antibody when determination of the functional consequences is what is needed—e.g., ability to release mediators or combining power for antigen; and (6) the vagaries introduced by genetic heterogeneity.

To gain a high correlation between antibody measurements and symptoms, quantitative information about all major antigen-antibody interactions contributing to symptoms would be necessary (Voss et al., 1966). This is too formidable in food allergy to be practical even if it were possible. Success with any one method and a single antigen and class of specific antibody would be rare good fortune, not yet experienced. The implications for a diagnostic approach to food allergy will be considered below.

The foregoing gloomy view does not apply to the extensive use of tools of immunology in comprehensive study of the mechanism of allergic reactions to foods, and delineation of various types of reactions. The progress in elucidation of food allergy may be illustrated by the following examples of allergy to cow milk and wheat. The role of

TABLE 17–5 IDENTIFICATION OF IMMUNOLOGIC FACTORS

Antibodies
- IgE
  - Skin tests, Prausnitz-Kustner tests, histamine release
- IgA, IgG, IgM
  - Precipitins, hemagglutinins, antigen-binding
  - Antigen-antibody complexes (complement fixation, fluorescence, radioisotope)
  - Lymphocyte stimulation

Cellular
- Delayed skin reaction, lymphocyte stimulation and production of lymphokines

these foods in the malabsorption syndrome will be given consideration in a following section.

Allergy to Milk as an Example

Goldman and associates collected considerable clinical experience and laboratory data in a collaborative study of what was termed milk allergy (Goldman et al., 1963a and b; Saperstein et al., 1963). Actually what was studied were adverse reactions to cow milk, but the findings are no less interesting and valuable, and illustrate a number of points. The symptoms reported in the histories (Goldman et al., 1963a) are compared with the symptoms observed after challenge with cow milk in Figure 17–2. The array of symptoms is the same as given in Table 17–1 for adverse reactions to foods in general, and the agreement between symptoms by history and after challenge is impressive. Some of the adverse reactions to cow milk may not have been due to allergy but to other conditions indistinguishable by symptoms, as indicated in Table 17–2.

The age at onset of symptoms is shown in Figure 17–3. The largest portion had onset under one month, which points out the need to

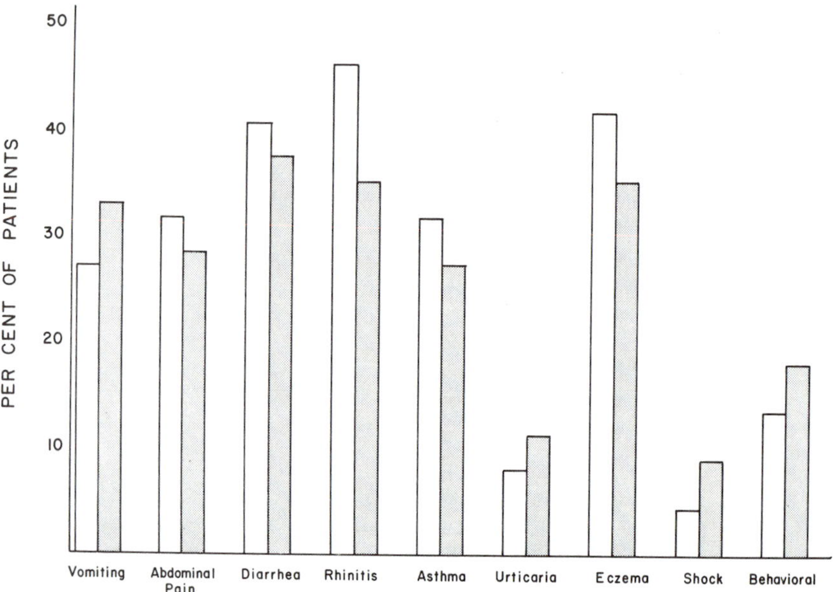

Figure 17–2 Clinical symptoms (*open columns*) presented in histories of 89 children manifesting adverse reaction to cow milk compared to symptoms appearing in response to feeding cow milk under observation (*shaded columns*). Behavioral manifestations include lethargy, irritability, restlessness and moodiness. (Data of Goldman et al., 1963a.)

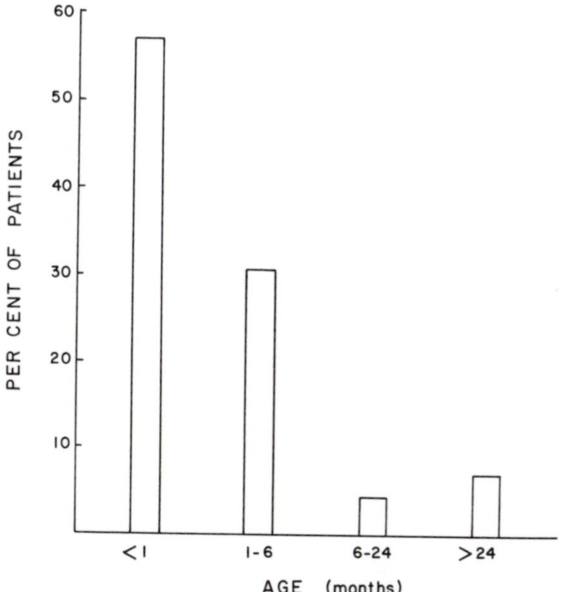

Figure 17–3 Age at onset of 89 children manifesting adverse reactions to cow milk. (Data of Goldman et al., 1963a.)

know if these were all adverse reactions to cow milk on an immunologic basis or if some may have been due to other mechanisms in Table 17–2. Even if all the infants had been fed cow milk from birth, the peak immunologic response would be more than a month after institution of cow-milk feeding (Kletter et al., 1971b). The intervals to onset of symptoms after challenge with cow milk are shown in Figure 17–4. The grouping by minutes, hours and days corresponds to the types of reactions associated with the different classes of antibodies (Table 17–4).

Immunologic factors pertinent to allergic adverse reactions to cow milk identified by various authors (Gunther et al., 1962; Saperstein et al., 1963; Goldstein and Heiner, 1970; Kletter et al., 1971b and c) are listed in Table 17–6. The four major antigenic proteins are indicated; of these, β-lactoglobulin and α-lactalbumin are most antigenic even though casein is present in much higher concentration. There are many more antigenic milk proteins and digestive derivatives (Spies et al., 1970), any of which could be the most important in certain individuals. Antibodies stimulated by antigens in milk fall into the many heterogeneous classes. Methods of identification are those shown in Table 17–5.

Wheal formation in response to intradermal injection of milk proteins is the most sensitive means of detection of IgE; use of an extract

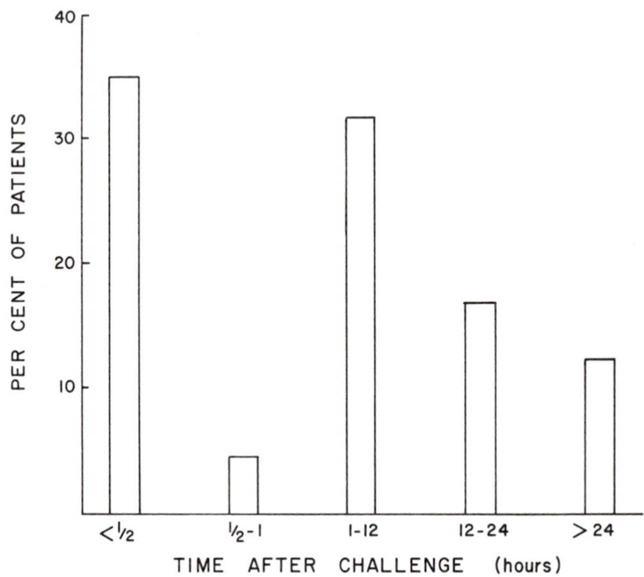

Figure 17–4 Interval to onset of symptoms provoked by challenge with cow milk in 89 children manifesting adverse reactions to cow milk. (Data of Goldman et al., 1963a.)

of skim milk containing 100 μg protein nitrogen/ml yielded the results shown in Table 17–7 in the study by Goldman et al. (1963b). The findings shown convey one of the simplest and most important but widely ignored lessons in allergy. Failure to learn it accounts for loose and misleading statements frequently encountered: "Skin tests don't mean anything in food allergy" and "False positive skin tests are frequent with extracts of food."

When extracts are correctly prepared and used properly, wheal response to intracutaneous injection is an exquisitely sensitive and re-

TABLE 17–6 IMMUNOLOGIC FACTORS IN COW MILK ALLERGY

Antigens
Major proteins in skim milk (Goldman et al., 1963a)
Casein – 28 mg/ml
β-Lactoglobulin – 4.2 mg/ml
α-Lactalbumin – 0.7 mg/ml
Bovine serum albumin – 0.2 mg/ml
Digestive products
Antibodies
IgA, IgE, IgG, IgM
Cellular Immunity
Not demonstrated

TABLE 17–7 INTRADERMAL SKIN TESTS WITH MILK PROTEINS (100 μg protein nitrogen/ml)*

Patient Category	Number of Subjects	Wheal No.	Reaction† %
Not allergic	102	6	6
Allergic, but not to milk	31	21	68
Allergic to milk	85	50	59

*Data of Goldman et al. (1963b).
†2 mm greater than any bleb remaining from the injection.

liable indicator of reaginic (usually IgE) antibody. Correct preparation entails making an extract which, at the concentration required to evoke a wheal reaction upon intradermal injection into specifically hypersensitive persons, will not evoke a wheal in persons with no evidence of allergic disorders. The proper concentration is found by trial, taking pains that the "normals" are truly nonallergic (ascertained by careful history and testing with some other commonly allergenic substances, such as pollen, house dust, molds, egg). If the nonallergic group is carefully selected, and an extract of a substance at a certain concentration does not evoke a wheal by intracutaneous injection, and then when this concentration evokes a wheal in persons suspected of allergy to the substance, the evidence for presence of specific IgE or reaginic antibody is strong and the person is very probably hypersensitive to the substance. Lack of response (a negative test) means no specific reaginic antibody or insufficient to cause a wheal response (or, rarely, the person's skin does not respond to mediators released by the allergic reaction).

A few foods actually contain histamine—e.g., spinach (Doeglas and Nater, 1968)—or other irritants and give wheal or erythema reactions in nearly everyone. These are eliminated by the correct procedure outlined. Otherwise, wheal reactions are not "false," but the significance of a wheal reaction is only that specific IgE or reaginic antibody is present in an amount to justify considering the person hypersensitive or allergic, and not that he will have symptoms upon ingestion of the food. The reasons for this were set forth in the review of immunologic principles in an earlier section.

Returning to Table 17–7, the 6 per cent of significant wheal reactions in nonallergic children to what appears to be a correctly prepared extract of milk proteins should lead one to suspect that more thorough examination would prove these to be allergic children. The group of children designated allergic, but not having symptoms from consuming milk, understandably showed an incidence of 68 per cent of wheal reactions to milk, because allergic individuals are prone to develop IgE antibodies in response to antigens. The mere presence of antibodies is not sufficient to cause symptoms. That only 59 per cent of the group of children considered by the authors to have had "allergic" symptoms to cow milk exhibited a wheal reaction to intracutaneous extract of milk proteins is not surprising; this means either that the symptoms were not due to allergy but to some other adverse reaction to milk or that the symptoms were due to interaction of milk proteins with a class of antibodies other than IgE.

As already mentioned, antigenic protein from food passes through the wall of the intestinal tract. This apparently occurs in all persons alike, nonallergic or allergic. Therefore, antibody formation is stimulated in all immunologically competent persons. The so-called atopic type of allergic person has a propensity to respond with production of IgE antibodies, which are involved in the immediate types of reactions like rhinitis and shock (Table 17–4). Both atopic and nonatopic persons respond with production of IgG and IgM classes of antibodies, and in about the same amounts. This is seen in Table 17–8, where titers of antibovine serum albumin antibodies are shown to be present in nearly the same percentage and in similar titer in the allergic and nonallergic groups.

All this illustrates the fundamental point: Measurement of a single class of antibody is not likely to suffice for high correlation between a positive test and symptoms, but the positive test is not without meaning or thereby "false."

The same kind of considerations apply to the findings in determination of histamine release from cells by milk proteins and to stimulation of lymphocytes to blast transformation upon addition of milk proteins to cultures in vitro (May and Alberto, 1972).

TABLE 17–8 ANTIBODY TO MILK PROTEIN IN INFANTS AND CHILDREN THROUGH 15 YEARS OF AGE
(Antibody = ^{131}I BSA*-Binding Capacity)†

Patient Category	Number of Subjects	Anti-BSA Activity Present (%)	Average Per Cent IBSA Bound
Well	158	69	53
Various disorders	221	79	64
Allergic disorders	31	84	56

*BSA = bovine serum albumin.
†Data of Rothberg and Farr (1965).

The reader who took the trouble to understand the facts and concepts in the section on immunologic basis of adverse reactions to foods would have been prepared to find that to confirm or predict allergic symptoms from ingestion of cow milk (or any food) by immunologic methods with a high degree of accuracy is a formidable task. At least the state of knowledge of the immunologic basis of reactions to food accounts for the inadequacy of the diagnostic procedures tested to date. The reader must persevere to the end to find a way out of the difficulties.

Incidentally, the same difficulties face the allergist in use of skin tests in diagnosis of disorders caused by inhalation of allergens, such as hay fever and asthma. Why anyone should be more comfortable about these limitations with allergy from inhalants than from ingestants is a mystery, or perhaps just the influence of tradition.

Allergy to Wheat as an Example

Although less extensively studied, adverse reactions to wheat appear to be governed by the same principles as those to cow milk. Allergists generally consider wheat to be a major cause of allergic reactions. There are many antigenic proteins in wheat and so a complex array of specific antibodies can be anticipated (Beckwith and Heiner, 1966; Heiner et al., 1970). Immediate types of reactions based on IgE are relatively easily recognized (Goldstein et al., 1969). Antibodies of the IgG and IgM classes are found in sera of allergic and nonallergic persons but at a much higher frequency in allergic subjects and in higher titer in malabsorption disorders (Alarcón-Segovia et al., 1964; Heiner et al., 1970). Antibodies which might be associated with more subtle adverse reactions clearly attributable to wheat have not been identified, as is the case with cow milk. All that has been presented regarding allergy to cow milk in the preceding section seems to apply to wheat, and probably to other foods as well.

Complexities mount when an individual is allergic to more than one food, as is frequently the case with cow milk and wheat. Combined effects of allergic or other adverse reactions to more than one food may give rise to symptoms when reaction to any one of the guilty foods would not suffice. Sometimes customary intake of a food does not produce obvious reactions but larger amounts will.

Immunologic Aspects of Malabsorption and Protein-Losing Enteropathy

Celiac disease in children and nontropical sprue in adults have fascinated physicians for nearly a century. The identity of the syndromes is now generally accepted and the designation "intestinal malabsorption" is preferable (Rubin, 1961; Ament, 1972). A great advance in elucidation and management came from the discovery that the malabsorption was provoked by wheat (Dicke et al., 1953) and sometimes by milk (Davidson et al., 1965; Fällström et al., 1965; Liu et al., 1967; Visakorpi and Immonen, 1967).

The protein fractions were soon incriminated, especially α-gliadin in wheat (Beckwith and Heiner, 1966) and possibly β-lactoglobulin in milk (Davidson et al., 1965). Inevitably, allergy was entertained as the mechanism of pathogenesis. As the onset of malabsorption was gradual and there were often no accompanying symptoms commonly ascribed to allergy (rhinitis, asthma, eczema), the immediate type of allergic reaction based on IgE was considered unlikely, and results of intracutaneous injection of wheat and milk extracts were inconsistent with immediate-type allergy (Collins-Williams and Ebbs, 1954).

Through measurement of titers in serum of antibodies to wheat and milk of the IgG and IgM classes, it became apparent that these antibodies were not only found in normal persons who consume wheat and milk, but that even the higher titers frequently found in cases of malabsorption were probably a secondary consequence of permeability of the injured gut and not the primary agents in pathogenesis of malabsorption (Alarcón-Segovia et al., 1964; Kivel et al., 1964; Beckwith and Heiner, 1966; Heiner et al., 1970).

Simultaneously, studies by jejunal biopsy revealed characteristic damage to intestinal villi (Fig. 17–5), which could be produced or relieved by the administration and withdrawal of wheat in persons susceptible to malabsorption from wheat ingestion (Rubin et al., 1962). Enzymes which degrade gliadin are normally present in the villi. If these were lacking, gliadin might damage the villi through a toxic effect and cause malabsorption. Such a mechanism would place the disorder among errors of metabolism due to congenital or acquired deficiency of enzyme activity. Intestinal disaccharidases and peptidases were found to be absent or greatly reduced in malabsorption, but it was soon learned that activity of these enzymes was restored to normal upon withdrawal of wheat and return of biopsy specimens of villi to normal appearance (Plotkin and Isselbacher, 1964; Lindberg et al., 1968; Heizer and Laster, 1969). These enzymes are located near the surface of the villi and therefore vulnerable to the injury induced by gliadin.

Meanwhile, knowledge about IgA began to accumulate and this immunoglobulin was found to be produced in cells in the mucosa lining the respiratory tract and intestine (Walker and Hong, 1973).

Measurement of specific antibody to gliadin secreted into the lumen of the gut in response to gliadin administration revealed IgA to

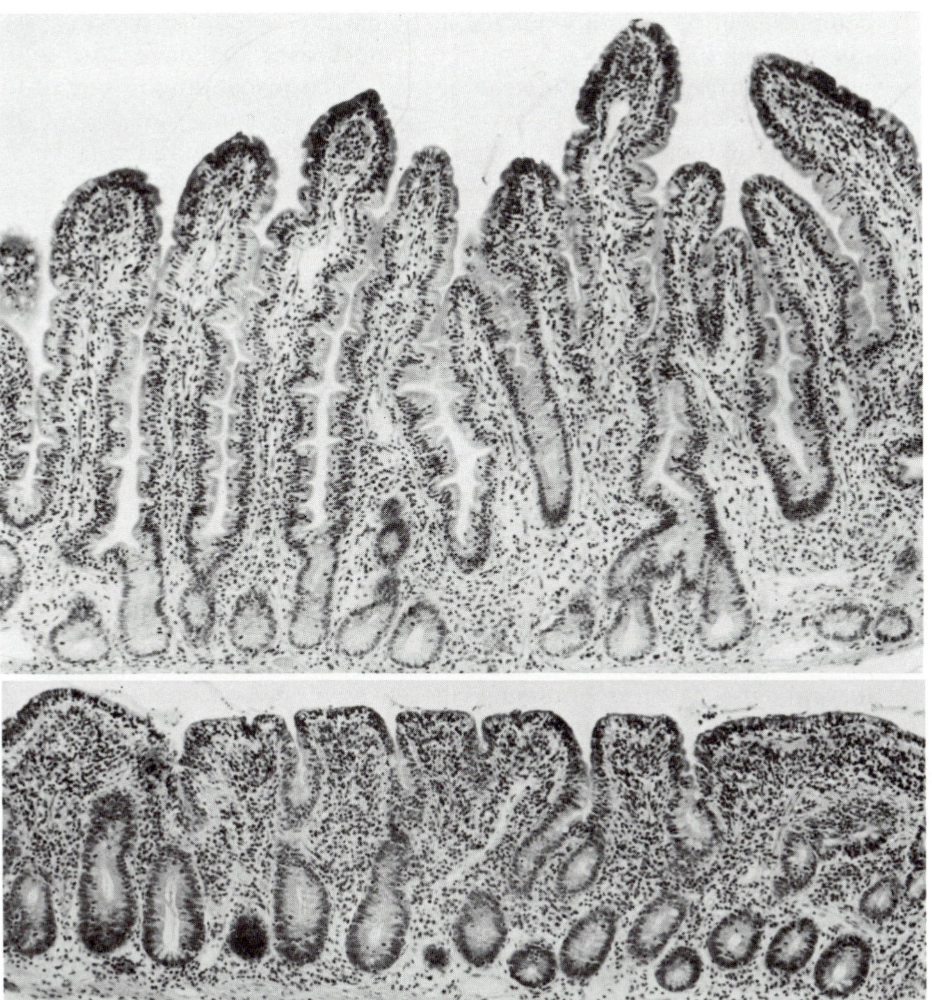

Figure 17–5 (*Above*) Biopsy from jejunoileal junction from patient with malabsorption, after wheat-free diet just before wheat instillation—near normal appearance (× 100). (*Below*) Biopsy from jejunoileal junction of same patient immediately after 9 days of wheat instillation to site by tube—severe abnormality (× 100). (From Rubin, C. E., et al.: Studies of celiac sprue. III. The effect of repeated wheat instillation into the proximal ileum of patients on a gluten free diet. Gastroenterology *43*:621, 1962.)

be the most prominent class of antibodies in persons suffering from malabsorption due to wheat (Immonen, 1967; Katz et al., 1968; Kletter et al., 1971a). Gliadin was found to be bound to cells in the villi (Rubin et al., 1965). Immune-complexes containing IgA appeared in the villi in response to ingested wheat protein in cases of malabsorption (Shiner and Ballard, 1972). In addition to atrophy, infiltration of the villi by eosinophils and other histologic alterations characteristic of an allergic response are seen in biopsy material. The immune-complexes appeared in a matter of hours after exposure to wheat (Shiner and Ballard, 1972), and the characteristic pathology in the villi, within nine days (Rubin et al., 1962), corresponding to recurrence of malabsorption.

Many of these features have been observed in some individuals who develop malabsorption after ingestion of cow milk protein (Liu et al., 1967; Visakorpi and Immonen, 1967); sometimes intolerance to wheat develops as a complication (Fällström et al., 1965; Visakorpi and Immonen, 1967). Specific IgA antibodies to wheat and cow milk proteins have been found elevated in the serum only in patients exhibiting malabsorption (Kletter et al., 1971a), and increase in total IgA occurs especially in this disorder (Immonen, 1967). A protein-losing enteropathy has been described in which allergy, especially to milk, was involved (Waldmann et al., 1967).

All this evidence points to IgA antibodies to wheat and cow milk proteins playing a role in pathogenesis of malabsorption comparable to the role played by IgE antibodies to pollens in the pathogenesis of hay fever (Table 17–9). Cell-bound IgE in the nasal mucosa reacts with antigen in pollen to release histamine and thus produce rhinitis, in certain genetically predisposed persons. By analogy, in certain people, IgA (or IgG) produced in the intestinal mucosa in response to ingestion of wheat forms immune-complexes with wheat (and perhaps the same with milk proteins). The complexes are injurious to the mucosa, and malabsorption or protein-losing enteropathy ensues. The evidence for an allergic pathogenesis of malabsorption is of the same nature as the evidence we accept as proof of the allergic nature of hay fever, albeit considerably less abundant, and IgA (or IgG) is incriminated in place of IgE antibodies in the pathogenesis. Some individu-

TABLE 17–9 MALABSORPTION AND ENTEROPATHY

Etiologic Factors
- Proteins in cow milk, wheat, etc.
  - Examples – β-lactoglobulin, α-gliadin

Secondary (Complicating) Factors
- Disaccharidase deficiency
- Peptidase deficiency

Features
- Gradual onset, chronic nature, reversible
- Specific IgA in serum and gut uniquely increased
- Differs from IgE-mediated allergy

Basic Lesion (in Intestinal Mucosa)
- Offending food stimulates IgA production and complex formation in hours and histologic change in days.

als have a propensity to produce both IgE and IgA specific antibodies, which have the potential of forming injurious combinations with antigen and causing allergic disorders of respiratory and gastrointestinal and even cutaneous systems concomitantly.

Malabsorption associated with wheat ingestion occurs frequently but not regularly in persons with selective deficiency of IgA (Mawhinney and Tomkin, 1971; Nell et al., 1972). Most patients with malabsorption do not have deficiency of IgA. Lack of IgA may make the gut more susceptible to injury by foreign proteins or infection (Ament and Rubin, 1972a) and to increased production of IgG and IgM antibodies. These in turn may form complexes with antigen in the mucosa and play a role in pathogenesis of malabsorption in the manner described for IgA.

Milk-Induced Gastrointestinal Loss of Blood Cells and Protein

More than a decade ago, Rasch et al. (1960) and Hoag et al. (1961) independently called attention to increased occult loss of blood from the gastrointestinal tract in infants who had developed iron-deficiency anemia. In addition to abnormal loss of blood cells, there is increased protein exudation from the gastrointestinal tract. Subsequent findings (Wilson et al., 1962, 1964; Gross, 1968; Woodruff and Clark, 1972; Woodruff et al., 1972; Wilson et al., 1974) concerning this phenomenon exemplify particularly well the need to demonstrate an immunologic basis for an adverse reaction to a food before designating it an allergic reaction.

The increased gastrointestinal loss of blood and protein in infancy has been found to be associated with relatively high intake of pasteurized cow milk (a liter or more per day) which has not been further heated as are commercially prepared formulas. Abnormal enteric loss of blood and protein may be decreased when the intake of pasteurized cow milk is lowered or is replaced by heat-treated cow milk, and the losses are reduced to normal levels with soybean formula. This suggests that heat-labile milk proteins may be responsible. Bovine serum albumin alone will induce the loss of blood and protein but lactose will not.

The phenomenon seems to be common, as it has been found in 50 per cent of unselected groups of infants from the general population who had developed iron-deficiency anemia. The affected infants did not manifest symptoms associated with allergic disorders, but titers of precipitating antibodies to heat-labile cow milk proteins may be higher in the serum and feces of affected infants. Therapy with iron will correct the anemia but not the abnormal enteric loss of blood cells and protein, i.e., the pathology in the gut is not secondary to iron deficiency. It is not certain whether the milk protein-induced injury to the gut is due to an antigen-antibody reaction or to a direct damage of cells by some heat-labile constituent among the milk proteins. After the first 18 to 24 months of life, as the intake of milk decreases, the excessive occult loss of blood and protein usually subsides, but milk-induced gastroenteropathy has been reported in later life (Waldmann et al., 1967).

Diagnostic Procedures to Distinguish Allergic From Other Adverse Reactions to Food

The first obligation is to consider whether an adverse reaction after ingestion of a food is actually due to allergy or to another condition. Unless an allergic basis is demonstrated, it is improper to use the term "allergy" for an adverse reaction to food. Immediate reactions exhibiting the most characteristic manifestations of allergy (shock, rhinitis, asthma, urticaria) are usually unequivocal. Chronic disturbance of the gastrointestional or respiratory tracts, nondescript neurologic and behavioral symptoms and vague systemic signs can arise from any of the disorders listed in Table 17–2 at any time during infancy and childhood, and care must be taken to identify which is responsible for an adverse reaction to food.

When some of the manifestations strongly suggest an allergic reaction, direct confirmation may be attempted with prompt removal and later reintroduction of suspected foods. If relief of symptoms is not prompt and lasting or if unequivocal symptoms of allergy are lacking, a more extensive, thorough and systematic investigation is indicated.

A distinguishing feature of congenital and acquired deficiencies of the immune system is unusual frequency and persistence of infections. A warning of disaccharidase deficiency is irritation of the buttocks due to acid feces.

History and Physical Examination. As part of a complete history and physical examination, particular attention to the following may expedite accurate diagnosis: age of onset, familial or epidemic occurrence, continuous or intermittent, diet, suspicions regarding foods, character of feces, infections, general appearance, nutritional status, eczema and irritation of buttocks.

Immunologic Investigation. Immunoglobulins A, G and M in serum should always be determined quantitatively and, if indicated by history and course, a complete study of competency of the immune system should be undertaken. To learn whether a patient is atopic, or prone to allergy based on IgE, a few skin tests may be done with extracts of ragweed, alternaria, house dust, cow milk, chicken egg or other allergens common in the patient's environment, using precautions and technique customary in clinical allergy and proper extracts (see p. 445). In addition, skin tests with a few suspected foods may be of interest. In two previous sections (see Immunologic Basis of Adverse Reactions to Food; and Allergy to Milk as an Example), it was explained why skin tests are not done with the expectation that the foods causing an allergic reaction can be identified, but only to find evidence of an allergic constitution. Routine skin testing with numerous food extracts is not only useless and misleading but outmoded and inconsiderate.

There is not much to be gained for practical diagnosis and management from measuring titers of specific antibodies in serum by any of the current methods, such as precipitins, hemagglutinins, etc., for reasons already given.

The comprehensive, quantitative measurements of specific antibodies and their interactions with antigens and cells required for characterization of the fundamental processes in pathogenesis of allergic reactions are necessary in a research project, but not for practical diagnosis and management.

Other Procedures. To distinguish allergic reactions from other disorders, some of the following procedures may be needed: (1) culture and parasitologic examination of feces (infections); (2) roentgenograms of lungs, gastrointestinal tract (infection, malformation); (3) intestinal absorption—xylose, fat; (4) jejunal biopsy—enzymes, histology; and (5) chloride content of sweat (cystic fibrosis).

Diagnostic Procedures to Identify Causative Foods in Allergic Reactions

For the present and foreseeable future, the identification of the food or foods responsible for symptoms in allergic reactions by immunologic means alone is too cumbersome and inadequate for practical purposes. Profligate, arbitrary and empirical use of procedures like skin tests and determination of titers of a few specific antibodies in serum is irrational in view of lack of close correlation of any one or a combination with production of symptoms, and such practice ignores the complexity of immunochemical processes involved in allergic reactions to foods.

Under the circumstances, the rational approach to diagnosis and management of food allergy calls for intelligent use of the history, judicious elimination of suspected foods from the diet and subsequent systematic challenge with any believed to have contributed to symptoms. Of course, foods which have clearly caused shock should not be tested and, when in doubt, tested most cautiously. To be truly rational, elimination and challenge must be carried out skillfully and critically. A major pitfall is that other adverse reactions will respond equally well to elimination and exhibit exacerbations upon reintroduction of the offending food substance—e.g., lactose in disaccharidase deficiency. Results of dietary manipulation must be weighed with the other findings already discussed in order to conclude that the adverse reaction is due to allergy to a food in question. When no clues are obtained as to which food may be responsible for reactions, a diet composed of foods seldom causing allergic reactions may be employed (Sheldon et al., 1967).

How long foods should be eliminated to be sure no deleterious effects persist, and how long to continue a food challenge to judge its effect, and what the interval between challenges should be are questions without answers at present. At least a week of elimination before challenge, and challenge long enough to reach a usual portion of a food by gradual increases, and a week of observation afterward seems a sensible program. The common dictum that challenge should be repeated three times with positive results to incriminate a food may be fallacious as, after the first reaction, the individual may be in a changed or refractory immunologic status. As a safeguard, repeated elimination and challenge with a given food should be weeks apart. It would be preferable for the patient not to know when a suspected food is being offered as a challenge to avoid psychologic influences. This is possible if capsule amounts suffice to evoke a reaction, but larger quantities may be required which would be difficult to mask.

Most male physicians are neither interested nor proficient in dietetics, and yet clear and helpful instructions are essential to success. A diet which cannot be followed, or failure to exclude a suspected ingredient in every form and item, will not provide a valid test. The physician will have to take serious interest in the dietary manipulation or get someone who can. Details are available in various sources (Sheldon et al., 1967; Ralston Purina Company; U. S. Dept. of Agriculture).

Optimal nutrition is not vital during a single episode of elimination and challenge but must be given appropriate attention if the procedure is prolonged.

Treatment

Once allergic reactions to food have been demonstrated by elimination and challenge, strict avoidance is at present the only rational treatment. An optimal diet can be contrived without dependence on many foods, and adequate substitutes are available for such items as milk in infant feeding. Optimal nutrition is as much a goal as relief from symptoms. Neither goal will be reached by casual management. The diet must be properly designed and strictly followed. Only after complete relief of symptoms has been achieved for weeks should any of the incriminated foods be tried cautiously.

The possibility of cross-reactivity between antigenic substances in foods, particularly within related groups, must be taken into account (Sheldon et al., 1967). Exact knowledge does not exist in this area and so the possibility must simply be kept in mind. The complexity of modern food technology introduces many items into processing and preservation of foods and creates numerous mixtures of foods. Studious attention to lists of ingredients on labels affords some protection. Education of mothers and patients regarding sources and avoidance of unwanted items is mandatory.

With regard to cow milk allergy, heating or substitution of milk of other animal species is not enough to avoid all cross-reactive antigenic milk proteins. Formulas in which protein is derived from soybean or meat are successful substitutes but, as protein is still present, an occasional individual may become allergic or have other adverse reactions to these products (Hill, 1942; Mortimer, 1961; Ament and Rubin, 1972b). Chapter 15 includes consideration of milk-free formulas.

Since dietetics is not the forte of most physicians, the availability of acceptable diets and recipes composed to eliminate such common ingredients as cow milk, egg and wheat and other major allergens will be welcomed (Sheldon et al., 1967; Ralston Purina Company; U. S. Dept. of Agriculture).

Prevention of Allergy to Food

The utopian goal of physicians is to prevent the occurrence of allergic disorders due to food as well as to pollens, animal danders, etc. Injections of extracts of these substances in an effort to immunize have been of dubious value with pollens and never gained popularity with foods. Glaser and Johnstone have advocated the notion that withholding the more allergenic foods such as milk, egg and wheat from the diet in the first six to nine months of life would prevent or lessen development of allergy to these and other substances (Glaser and Johnstone, 1952; Glaser, 1966; Johnstone and Dutton, 1966). IgA antibody secreted from the intestinal mucosa upon stimulation by a food protein is specifically directed against that particular food protein. This antibody could conceivably neutralize undigested protein of the food and prevent this antigenic material from passing through the mucosa. In infancy, production of IgA antibody is low in the neonate and does not reach a peak until about seven months of age. Perhaps these considerations provide an argument for breast feeding or use of the least allergenic foods for the first six months of infancy, especially in infants with allergic heritage (Taylor et al., 1973). While the rationale is appealing, the prophylactic dietary programs involving mother and infant have not yielded results which justify routine utilization of this approach.

Once breast feeding is abandoned or supplemented, a foreign protein will inevitably be introduced through the prepared formula. Whether additional foreign protein is to be added in the form of solid foods at one or six months of age, or any arbitrary time, is beyond current knowledge as far as allergy is concerned. It is generally believed that rice cereal is the least allergenic cereal for inauguration of feeding solid food.

REFERENCES

Alarcón-Segovia, D., Herskovic, T., Wakim, K. G., Green, P. A., and Scudamore, H. H.: Presence of circulating antibodies to gluten and milk fractions in patients with nontropical sprue. Amer. J. Med. *36*:485, 1964.

Ament, M. E.: Malabsorption syndromes in infancy and childhood. J. Pediatr. *81*:685, 867, 1972.

Ament, M. E., and Rubin, C. E.: Relation of giardiasis to abnormal intestinal structure and function in gastrointestinal immunodeficiency syndromes. Gastroenterology *62*:216, 1972a.

Ament, M. E., and Rubin, C. E.: Soy protein: another cause of the flat intestinal lesion. Gastroenterology *62*:227, 1972b.

Barrick, R. H., and Farr, R. S.: The increased incidence of circulating anti-beef albumin in the sera of allergic persons and some comments regarding the possible significance of this occurrence. J. Allergy *36*:374, 1965.

Becker, E. L.: Nature and classification of immediate-type allergic reactions. Advances Immunol. *13*:267, 1971.

Beckwith, A. C., and Heiner, D. C.: An immunological study of wheat gluten proteins and derivatives. Arch. Biochem. Biophys. *117*:239, 1966.

Bluemink, E.: Food allergy. World Rev. Nutr. Diet. *12*:505, 1970.

Chafee, F. H., and Settipane, G. A.: Asthma caused by FD&C approved dyes. J. Allergy *40*:65, 1967.

Collins-Williams, C., and Ebbs, J. H.: The use of protein skin tests in the celiac syndrome. Ann. Allergy *12*:237, 1954.

Coombs, R. R. A., and Gell, P. G. H.: Clinical Aspects of Immunology. 2nd ed. Oxford, Blackwell, 1968.

Crook, W. G., Harrison, W. W., Crawford, S. E., and Emerson, B. S.: Systemic manifestations due to allergy. Report of fifty patients and a review of the literature on the subject (sometimes referred to as allergic toxemia and the allergic tension fatigue syndrome). Pediatrics *27*:790, 1961.

Davidson, M., Burnstine, R. C., Kugler, M. M., and Bauer, C. H.: Malabsorption defect induced by ingestion of beta lactoglobulin. J. Pediatr. *66*:545, 1965.

Dicke, W. K., Weijers, H. A., and v. d. Kamer, J. H.: Coeliac disease. II. The presence in wheat of a factor having a deleterious effect in cases of caeliac disease. Acta Paediatr. Scand. *42*:34, 1953.

Doeglas, H. M. G., and Nater, J. P.: Histamine in foods causing false positive scratch tests. J. Allergy *42*:164, 1968.

Dubois, R. S., Roy, C. C., Fulginiti, V. A., Merrill, D. A., and Murray, R. L.: Disaccharidase deficiency in children with immunologic deficits. J. Pediatr. *76*:377, 1970.

Ellis, E. F.: Immunologic basis of atopic disease. Advances Pediatr. *16*:65, 1969.

Fällström, S. P., Winberg, J., and Andersen, H. J.: Cow's milk induced malabsorption as a precursor of gluten intolerance. Acta Paediatr. Scand. *54*:101, 1965.

Glaser, J.: The dietary prophylaxis of allergic disease in infancy. J. Asthma Res. *3*:199, 1966.

Glaser, J., and Johnstone, D. E.: Soy bean milk as a substitute for mammalian milk in early infancy, with special reference to prevention of allergy to cow's milk. Ann. Allergy *10*:433, 1952.

Goldman, A. S., Anderson, D. W., Jr., Sellars, W. A., Saperstein, S., Kniker, W. T., Halpern, S. R., and collaborators: Milk allergy. I. Oral challenge with milk and isolated milk proteins in allergic children. Pediatrics *32*:425, 1963a.

Goldman, A. S., Sellars, W. A., Halpern, S. R., Anderson, D. W., Furlow, T. E., Johnson, C. H., et al.: Milk allergy. II. Skin testing of allergic and normal children with purified milk proteins. Pediatrics *32*:572, 1963b.

Goldstein, G. B., and Heiner, D. C.: Clinical and immunological perspectives in food sensitivity. J. Allergy *46*:270, 1970.

Goldstein, G. B., Heiner, D. C., and Rose, B.: Studies of reagins to α-gliadin in a patient with wheat hypersensitivity. J. Allergy *44*:37, 1969.

Gross, S.: The relationship between milk protein and iron content on hematologic values in infancy. J. Pediatr. *73*:521, 1968.

Gunther, M., Cheek, E., Matthews, R. H., and Coombs, R. R. A.: Immune responses in infants to cow's milk proteins taken by mouth. Int. Arch. Allergy *21*:257, 1962.

Hartley, G.: The permeability of the gastro-intestinal mucosa of guinea pigs to crystalline egg-albumin. J. Immunol. *43*:297, 1942.

Heiner, D. C., Goldstein, G., and Rose, B.: Immunochemical studies of selected subjects with wheat intolerance. J. Allergy *45*:333, 1970.

Heizer, W. D., and Laster, L.: Peptide hydrolase activities of mucosa of human small intestine. J. Clin. Invest. *48*:210, 1969.

Hill, L. W.: The production of nonetiological skin hypersensitivity to foods by natural means in atopic persons. J. Allergy *13*:366, 1942.

Hoag, M. S., Wallerstein, R. O., and Pollycove, M.: Occult blood loss in iron deficiency anemia of infancy. Pediatrics *27*:199, 1961.

Immonen, P.: Levels of the serum immunoglobulins IgA, IgG, and IgM in the malabsorption syndrome in children. Ann. Paediatr. Fenn. *13*:115, 1967.

Johnstone, D. E., and Dutton, A. M.: Dietary prophylaxis of allergic disease in children. New Eng. J. Med. *274*:715, 1966.

Katz, J., Kantor, F. S., and Herskovic, T.: Intestinal antibodies to wheat fractions in celiac disease. Ann. Intern. Med. *69*:1149, 1968.

Kivel, R., Kearns, D. H., and Liebowitz, D.: Significance of antibodies to dietary proteins in the serums of patients with nontropical sprue. New Eng. J. Med. *271*:769, 1964.

Kletter, B., Freier, S., Davies, A. M., and Gery, I.: The significance of coproantibodies to cow's milk proteins. Acta Paediatr. Scand. *60*:173, 1971a.

Kletter, B., Gery, I., Freier, S., and Davies, A. M.: Immune responses of normal infants to cow milk. I. Antibody type and kinetics of production. Int. Arch. Allergy *40*:656, 1971b.

Kletter, B., Gery, I., Freier, S., Noah, Z., and Davies, A. M.: Immunoglobulin E antibodies to milk proteins. Clin. Allergy *1*:249, 1971c.

Korenblat, P. E., Rothberg, R. M., Minden, P., and Farr, R. S.: Immune responses of human adults after oral and parenteral exposure to bovine serum albumin. J. Allergy *41*:226, 1968.

Lindberg, T., Norden, A., and Josefsson, L.: Intestinal dipeptidases. Dipeptidase activities in small intestinal biopsy specimens from a clinical material. Scand. J. Gastroent. *3*:177, 1968.

Liu, H. Y., Tsao, M. U., Moore, B., and Giday, Z.: Bovine milk protein-induced intestinal malabsorption of lactose and fat in infants. Gastroenterology *54*:27, 1967.

Mawhinney, H., and Tomkin, G. H.: Gluten enteropathy associated with selective IgA deficiency. Lancet *2*:121, 1971.

May, C. D., and Alberto, R.: In-vitro responses of leucocytes to food proteins in allergic and normal children: lymphocyte stimulation and histamine release. Clin. Allergy *2*:335, 1972.

Minden, P., Reid, R. T., and Farr, R. S.: A comparison of some commonly used methods for detecting antibodies to bovine albumin in human serum. J. Immunol. *96*:180, 1966.

Morishima, A., and Kessler, W. R.: Food hypersensitiveness? Report of two cases with acute constitutional reactions. Pediatrics *29*:129, 1962.

Mortimer, E. Z.: Anaphylaxis following ingestion of soybean. J. Pediatr. *58*:90, 1961.

Nell, P. A., Ammann, A. J., Hong, R., and Stiehm, E. R.: Familial selective IgA deficiency. Pediatrics *49*:71, 1972.

Plotkin, G. R., and Isselbacher, K. J.: Secondary disaccharidase deficiency in adult celiac disease (nontropical sprue) and other malabsorption states. New Eng. J. Med. *271*:1033, 1964.

Ralston Purina Company, 1 Checkerboard Square, St. Louis, Mo.: Milk-free, egg-free, wheat-free, milk-egg-wheat-free diets. (Consumers Services.)

Rasch, C. A., Cotton, E. K., Harris, J. W., and Griggs, R. C.: Blood loss as a contributing factor in the etiology of iron-lack anemia of infancy. (Abstract) Amer. J. Dis. Child. *100*:627, 1960.

Ratner, B., and Gruehl, H. L.: Passage of native proteins through the normal gastro-intestinal wall. J. Clin. Invest. *13*:517, 1934.

Rothberg, R. M., and Farr, R. S.: Anti-bovine serum albumin and anti-alpha lactalbumin in the serum of children and adults. Pediatrics *35*:571, 1965.

Rubin, C. E.: Malabsorption: celiac sprue. Ann. Rev. Med. *12*:39, 1961.

Rubin, C. E., Brandborg, L. L., Flick, A. L., Phelps, P., Parmentier, C., and van Niel, S.: Studies of celiac sprue. III. The effect of repeated wheat instillation into the proximal ileum of patients on a gluten free diet. Gastroenterology *43*:621, 1962.

Rubin, W., Fauci, A. S., Sleisenger, M. H., and Jeffries, G. H.: Immunofluorescent studies in adult celiac disease. J. Clin. Invest. *44*:475, 1965.

Saperstein, S., Anderson, D. W., Goldman, A. S., and Kniker, W. T.: Milk allergy. III. Immunological studies with sera from allergic and normal children. Pediatrics *32*:580, 1963.

Sheldon, J. M., Lovell, R. G., and Mathews, K. P.: A Manual of Clinical Allergy. 2nd ed. Philadelphia, W. B. Saunders Co., 1967, p. 196.

Shiner, M., and Ballard, J.: Antigen-antibody reactions in jejunal mucosa in childhood celiac disease after gluten challenge. Lancet *1*:1202, 1972.

Spies, J. R., Stevan, M. A., Stein, W. J., and Coulson, E. J.: The chemistry of allergens. XX. New antigens generated by pepsin hydrolysis of bovine milk proteins. J. Allergy *45*:208, 1970.

Taylor, B., Norman, A. P., Orgel, H. A., Stokes, C. R., Turner, M. W., and Soothill, J. F.: Transient IgA deficiency and pathogenesis of infantile atopy. Lancet *2*:111, 1973.

Townley, R. R. W.: Disaccharidase deficiency in infancy and childhood. Pediatrics *38*:127, 1966.

United States Department of Agriculture, Agricultural Research Service, Consumer Food Economics Institute, Beltsville, Maryland 20705: List of publications on Allergy Recipes.

Valdes-Dapena, M. A., and Felipe, R. P.: Immunofluorescent studies in crib deaths: absence of evidence of hypersensitivity to cow's milk. Amer. J. Clin. Path. *56*:412, 1971.

Visakorpi, J. K., and Immonen, P.: Intolerance to cow's milk and wheat gluten in the primary malabsorption syndrome in infancy. Acta Paediatr. Scand. *56*:49, 1967.

Von Pirquet, C.: Allergie. München. Med. Wschr. *53*:1457, 1906.

Voss, H. E., Redmond, A. P., and Levine, B. B.: Clinical detection of the potential allergic reactor to penicillin by immunological tests. J. Allergy *37*:99, 1966.

Waldmann, T. A., Wochner, R. D., Laster, L., and Gordon, R. S.: Allergic gastroenteropathy. A cause of excessive gastrointestinal protein loss. New Eng. J. Med. *276*:761, 1967.

Walker, W. A., and Hong, R.: Immunology of the gastrointestinal tract. J. Pediatr. *83*:517, 1973.

Wilson, J. F., Heiner, D. C., and Lahey, M. E.: Studies on iron metabolism: evidence of gastrointestinal dysfunction in infants with iron deficiency anemia. A preliminary report. J. Pediatr. *60*:787, 1962.

Wilson, J. F., Heiner, D. C., and Lahey, M. E.: Milk-induced gastrointestinal bleeding in infants with hypochromic microcytic anemia. J.A.M.A. *189*:568, 1964.

Wilson, J. F., Lahey, M. E., and Heiner, D. C.: Studies on iron metabolism. V. Further observations on cow's milk-induced gastrointestinal bleeding in infants with iron deficiency anemia. J. Pediatr. *84*:335, 1974.

Woodruff, C. W., and Clark, J. L.: The role of fresh cow's milk in iron deficiency. I. Albumin turnover in infants with iron deficiency anemia. Amer. J. Dis. Child. *124*:18, 1972.

Woodruff, C. W., Wright, S. W., and Wright, R. P.: The role of fresh cow's milk in iron deficiency. II. Comparison of fresh cow's milk with a prepared formula. Amer. J. Dis. Child. *124*:26, 1972.

18

NUTRITIONAL STATUS

The other chapters of this book deal primarily with nutritional considerations relevant to the individual. In contrast, the present chapter focuses on groups of individuals. A knowledge of the nature and extent of common health problems, including nutritional problems, is important in planning community health programs for children. Even a minimal screening program will require knowledge of the community and of food intakes and physical findings of the children. Some laboratory analyses will also be necessary. Much of the material that follows has been modified from that presented in a publication by Maternal and Child Health Service (1971).

INFORMATION ABOUT THE COMMUNITY

Planning a nutritional screening program suitable for a specific community will be greatly aided by knowledge of the demographic characteristics of the community and by certain information about the food and water supply. Feeding practices and choices of foods frequently differ from one ethnic group to another, and therefore knowledge of the racial and ethnic composition of the community and of the customs of each group will be of considerable value.

In addition, the economic and educational status of the community is likely to be correlated with the prevalence of nutritional disorders. Information about the presence of specific nutrients in various foods and about local customs concerning food and feeding will be readily available in most communities. Such information will frequently provide clues regarding nutritional problems likely to be met in that locality and may suggest approaches to prevention.

Although fluid whole milk sold by dairies in the United States is generally fortified with vitamin D, fluid whole milk not fortified with vitamin D is available in rural areas and in many cities, often at a slightly reduced price. Whether or not such milk is readily available within a community should be determined, and an estimate should be made of the extent of its use. Although fluid low-fat and skim milks are commonly fortified with vitamins A and D, powdered skim milk is usually not so fortified.

Similarly, most states have laws requiring enrichment of commercially prepared breads and rolls with iron, riboflavin, thiamin and niacin.* Enrichment of these foods with calcium and vitamin D is optional. In communities where rice or grits is a dietary staple, it is important to determine whether products fortified with iron and vitamins are available.

Particularly in areas in which goiter is found in children, knowledge of the availability and usage of iodized salt is valuable. Information on this topic can ordinarily be obtained from retail grocers.

The major source or sources of drinking water (e.g., community water supply, individual wells) should be determined. Information about fluoride content of water from these sources is usually available from state or local health authorities.

INFORMATION ABOUT THE FAMILY AND THE CHILD

The frequency of nutritional deficiency disorders is highly correlated with the economic status of the family and with the educational level of the parents, especially the mother. Suggestions regarding useful items of information about the family may be found in the previously mentioned publication (Maternal and Child Health Service, 1971).

Information relating to a child's past medical history and current state of health will generally be available in the child's health records and will not need to be obtained separately in relation to screening for nutritional status. Among the various items that may be useful to record are birth weight, past history of serious or chronic illness and presence of any current illness.

FOOD INTAKE

Information about food intake is mandatory in screening for nutritional status. If knowledge of food intake of the group to be

---

*Information about laws relating to flours and grains in individual states is readily available from the American Institute of Baking, 400 East Ontario Street, Chicago, Ill. 60611.

screened is lacking, it will generally be desirable to accumulate data on food intake before laboratory aspects of screening are undertaken. This sequential approach is particularly desirable when laboratory facilities are limited.

No single method of collecting dietary intake information will be satisfactory for all purposes. Intake of food on a single day may not be typical of usual or long-term intake and cannot be expected on an individual basis to be correlated with physical or biochemical findings. Nevertheless, for the purpose of screening *groups* of children of similar age, sex, income level, etc., information about one day's intake can be of great value in alerting health workers to the *possibility* that a particular nutritional problem is present in some groups of children in the community. Appropriate further action can then be initiated. For example, if a substantial percentage of one- to two-year-old children in the community were found by 24-hour recall to have extremely low intakes of ascorbic acid, it would seem important to introduce biochemical screening with respect to ascorbic acid nutritional status of the children in that age group. Obviously, nutrition counseling in the community might also be altered.

The 24-hour recall has the great advantage of simplicity. It can be completed in 15 or 20 minutes by personnel with relatively little technical nutrition training. A method for machine analysis of the data has been reported (U.S. Department of Agriculture, 1964). Shortcuts aimed at obtaining dietary information in less than 15 minutes usually provide data of little value. It is preferable to spend 20 minutes obtaining relatively reliable information from one-fourth of the children than to spend five minutes with every child obtaining information of questionable value.

Suggestions for interviewers and a form for obtaining additional information on dietary patterns and food practices are readily available (Maternal and Child Health Service, 1971).

ANTHROPOMETRIC MEASURES

Stature and Weight

Stature and weight are among the most important indices of nutritional status and should be determined accurately as discussed in Chapter 3. Deficiency of total calorie intake, of protein or of any other essential nutrient may result in decreased rate of growth and, ultimately, in abnormally low stature or weight.

Use in Screening

In developing countries it has been suggested (Falkner et al., 1972) that data concerning socioeconomically favored children of the same ethnic background and from the same general geographic area be utilized as references for weight and stature. This approach clearly has much appeal. In affluent nations, one must consider the possibility that in children, as in adults, there may be a high prevalence of obesity. Lesser weight or lesser weight and stature of a surveyed population does not necessarily indicate an unsatisfactory state of health. Nevertheless, nutritional deficiency, whether of calories or of a specific essential nutrient, is likely to interfere with normal growth. Therefore, among infants and children in a community, those of least weight and stature may be most likely to demonstrate evidence of nutritional deficiency. Any of the commonly employed reference data will be suitable for identifying those individuals in the surveyed population who are smallest in relation to age and sex. In general, it may be desirable to identify the 10 per cent of children of least weight or stature and to focus particularly (although not exclusively) on this group in intensive nutritional screening efforts.

Although satisfactory definitions of obesity in childhood have not yet been developed (Chapter 3), it seems reasonable to single out also those individuals in the surveyed population who demonstrate the greatest weight or weight to height ratio for age. Careful measurements of skinfolds (Chapter 3) may be desirable in this group as a means of identifying those individuals who are large for their age but do not demonstrate excessive amounts of subcutaneous fat.

Interpretation

Problems involved in interpretation of data on stature and weight are considerable. If one accepts any specified set of reference data, it is theoretically possible to compare the lower percentiles for size of those presumably normal children with size of children in the surveyed population. Thus, if 25 per cent of the children in the surveyed population demonstrate stature for age less than the 10th percentile value of the reference population, one might conclude that 15 per cent were abnormally short—i.e., 10 per cent *expected* below the reference value and 25 per cent *observed* below the reference value—therefore, an excess of 15 per cent.

Considerable caution is necessary in this type of interpretation. It is evident that in the past erroneous conclusions have often been drawn. An example is presented in Figure 18–1, which compares data from the Ten-State Nutrition Survey (Center for Disease Control, 1972) with the data of Stuart as summarized in Nelson's Textbook of Pediatrics (Nelson et al., 1969). The six-month-old infants stud-

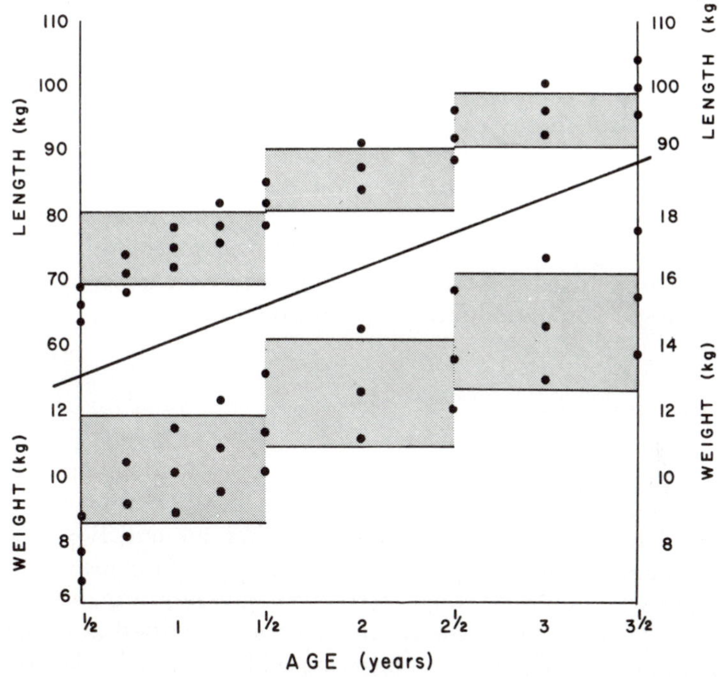

Figure 18–1 Illustration of misinterpretation of size data. Each vertical set of three dots indicates the 10th, 50th and 90th percentile values for length (or weight) at the stated age for white male infants studied by Stuart (Nelson et al., 1969). Each shaded area indicates the 15th to 85th percentile range for white male infants in the Ten-State Nutrition Survey (Center for Disease Control, 1972), ranging in age from 1/2 to 1 1/2, 1 1/2 to 2 1/2 or 2 1/2 to 3 1/2 years.

ied by Stuart were measured at five and one-half to six and one-half months of age, the one-year-old infants at 11 to 13 months of age and the one and one-half-year-old infants at 17 to 19 months of age. It may be seen that the 90th percentile value for length at six months of age is less than the 10th percentile value at age one year. The 90th percentile value for length at age one year is nearly identical to the 10th percentile value at age one and one-half years. In analyzing the Ten-State Survey data, a one-year-old infant was defined as a child who had passed his six-month birthday and not yet reached his 18-month birthday. Data from this group of individuals were analyzed against the data of Stuart for 12-month-old infants, with the conclusion that 27 per cent of infants in the Ten-State Survey had lengths less than the 10th percentile value for normal infants. Such a conclusion is clearly unwarranted.

In order to avoid the misinterpretation of data presented in the previous example, it is necessary either to utilize reference data concerning the identical age intervals employed in the survey or to analyze data of the surveyed population by plotting the value for each individual at his or her exact age in relation to percentile curves plotted from the reference data.

Reference data will ordinarily pertain to fullsize infants without chronic disease. In any case, the incidence of low-birth-weight will be greater among low-income than among higher income groups. Therefore, in attempting to interpret data on size of low-income infants or small children, it may be advantageous to evaluate separately the group of individuals of normal birth weight believed to be free of chronic disease. Such a group may more clearly reflect the influence of environmental factors, including diet.

Head Circumference

When intake of calories or protein has been inadequate during at least several months of the first year of life, head circumference may be diminished (Stoch and Smythe, 1968; Winick and Rosso, 1969). Measurement of head circumference may therefore provide clues regarding whether nutritional status was severely impaired during early life. Measurements should be made as described in Chapter 3. Although the data of Nellhaus (1968) are widely used, the data of Karlberg et al. (1968) seem preferable because increments as well as distance measurements are included (Chapter 3).

PHYSICAL FINDINGS

Although physical examinations are essential in nutritional screening of groups of children, these examinations will ordinarily be performed routinely in programs for delivering health care; therefore, the need for this information in nutritional screening will not constitute an added burden. Special attention should be paid to such general features as pallor, apathy and irritability. The skin should be examined for petechiae, ecchymoses or dermatitis, and the skeletal system for cranial bossing, enlarged joints or costochondral beading. The lower extremities should be examined for edema; the condition of gingiva and teeth should be noted and visible thyroid enlargement recorded. The presence of heart murmurs or of enlargement of liver or spleen may suggest presence of a chronic disease responsible for growth retardation.

Physical findings will be of value primarily in identifying diseases that may interfere with growth and general health. While such disorders (e.g., congenital heart disease, chronic liver disease) may lead to unsatisfactory nutritional status, they must be distinguished from nutritional deficiencies resulting primarily from failure to *provide* an individual with food of adequate quantity and nutritional quality. Personnel with the degree of training necessary for detection of clinical signs of nutritional deficiencies in the hair, eyes, tongue, skin and nails will not usually be available.

Interpretation

A physical finding suggesting nutritional abnormality should be looked upon as a clue rather than as a diagnosis. Costochondral beading should not be interpreted as evidence of rickets without roentgenographic confirmation. Thyroid enlargement should not be interpreted as evidence of iodine deficiency without appropriate laboratory confirmation.

McGanity (1970) has offered some insight into the reliability of specific physical signs of nutritional deficiency. In the Ten-State Nutrition Survey, among examinations of adults in Texas three presumably highly trained examiners found remarkably different prevalences of various physical signs (Table 18–1). For example, filiform papillary atrophy was found by examiner No. 2 in 1.1 per cent of individuals and by examiner No. 3 in 11.2 per cent of individuals. Although the same patients were not examined by the three examiners, it seems unlikely that a ten-fold difference in filiform papillary atrophy would be present in low-income groups examined in the same general geographic area. Of greater interest are results of 895 duplicate examina-

TABLE 18–1 CLINICAL FINDINGS REPORTED BY THREE EXAMINERS IN TEXAS NUTRITIONAL SURVEY, 1968–69*

Examiner	No. 1	No. 2	No. 3
Number of examinations	1123	1127	589
Identification of physical finding (% of examinations)			
Filiform papillary atrophy	4.1	1.1	11.2
Follicular hyperkeratosis	4.0	0.6	6.8
Swollen red gums	2.8	3.7	4.1
Angular lesions	0.4	0.4	1.2
Glossitis	0.6	0.4	0.5
Goiter	3.6	0.6	3.6

*From McGanity, W. J.: Problems of assessment of nutritional status: an overview of clinical methodologies. *In* Hansen, R. G., and Munro, H. N. (eds.): Problems of Assessment and Alleviation of Malnutrition of the United States. Proceedings of a workshop (Nashville, Tenn., January 13–14, 1970). Bethesda, Md., The Nutrition Study Section, Division of Research Grants, National Institutes of Health, 1972.

TABLE 18–2 RESULTS OF 895 DUPLICATE EXAMINATIONS OF ADULTS IN PANAMA SURVEY, 1967*

PHYSICAL FINDING	EXAMINER AGREEMENT (PER CENT)†
Abnormal hair	31
Filiform papillary atrophy	50
Follicular hyperkeratosis	50
Swollen red gums	33
Angular lesions	75
Glossitis	0
Goiter	63

*From McGanity, W. J.: Problems of assessment of nutritional status: an overview of clinical methodologies. *In* Hansen, R. G., and Munro, H. N. (eds.): Problems of Assessment and Alleviation of Malnutrition in the United States. Proceedings of a workshop (Nashville, Tenn., January 13–14, 1970). Bethesda, Md., The Nutrition Study Section, Division of Research Grants, National Institutes of Health, 1972.

†The number of individuals in which the physical finding was detected by both examiners expressed as a percentage of the number of individuals in which the physical finding was detected by either or both examiners.

tions of adults carried out in Panama in 1967 (McGanity, 1970). The extent of agreement between two examiners is indicated in Table 18–2. With respect to subjects classified as having abnormal hair, agreement between the two examiners occurred in only 31 per cent. Among individuals identified by one of the examiners as having filiform papillary atrophy, agreement occurred in only 50 per cent and—not indicated in the table—agreement was still only 50 per cent among individuals classified as having *severe* filiform papillary atrophy. Agreement between examiners with respect to other physical signs was generally not much better.

LABORATORY AND ROENTGENOGRAPHIC STUDIES

Laboratory studies are of great assistance in screening children for nutritional disorders. Seldom will it be feasible to perform the full range of determinations listed in Table 18–3. In most instances, it will be desirable to select a few laboratory studies to be carried out routinely and to do other studies based on clues provided by knowledge of the environment and by clinical examinations.

As a minimum, it is suggested that hemoglobin concentration or hematocrit be determined. The feasibility of performing other laboratory studies on a routine basis will depend, in part, on the level of laboratory competency available locally or on the ease with which arrangements can be made for laboratory studies to be performed at a more distant site.

Certain laboratory determinations are likely to be of greatest value in one community, while other determinations may be more valuable in another community. Within the same community, priorities may vary from year to year or even within a period of several months. In general, specific analyses will be selected on the basis of clues provided by knowledge of the community, by information about food intake or by physical findings. For example, in a cloudy city where unfortified milk is widely available, screening for rickets might receive highest priority. For at least several months, preferably including late winter, alkaline phosphatase activity might be determined in sera of all children less than three years of age; roentgenograms of the wrist might be made of all children with elevated alkaline phosphatase activity or with the slightest clinical suggestion of rickets. When several hundred children had been screened in this manner, it would ordinarily be possible to draw a conclusion about whether or not intensive preventive measures needed to be instituted. If rickets did not appear to be a problem of major importance in the community, routine screening would probably be discontinued.

If food intake data or physical findings suggested the possibilities of ascorbic acid deficiency and protein deficiency, high priority among laboratory studies would be given (at least for several months) to determining concentrations of ascorbic acid and albumin in sera. Thus, the laboratory can be used most effectively if analyses to be performed routinely are selected on the basis of information obtained by other screening efforts.

In most instances, it will be desirable to obtain a small sample of venous blood from the antecubital or external jugular vein (the femoral vein is not recommended). However, several of the determinations listed can be performed on an amount of capillary blood readily obtained from fingertip or heel. Blood should be placed immediately into plain tubes (for serum) or into dry, heparinized tubes (for plasma).

Microhematocrit and concentration of hemoglobin should be determined with blood obtained directly from the fingertip or heel or from the heparinized tube. Heparinized blood should then be centrifuged immediately, whereas blood in plain tubes should be centrifuged as soon as it has clotted. If concentration of ascorbic acid is to be determined, it should be performed immediately or the plasma should be mixed with metaphosphoric acid and frozen (without separating the supernatant from the protein precipitate) until the determination can be performed. Other determinations should be performed within eight hours or the serum or plasma should be frozen

TABLE 18–3 BIOCHEMICAL METHODS AND REMARKS REGARDING INTERPRETATION

Substance	Method	Quantity Required	Comment
Hemoglobin (blood)	Cyanomethemoglobin (O'Brien et al., 1968a)	20 μl	Concentration of hemoglobin (Hb) less than 11.0 gm/100 ml or hematocrit less than 34 is assumed to indicate anemia (see Chapter 12). Mean corpuscular Hb concentration less than 30 gm/100 ml of packed RBCs indicates hypochromia and is strong presumptive evidence of iron deficiency.
Hematocrit (blood)	Capillary tube (O'Brien et al., 1968b)	40 μl	
Total protein (serum)	Microbiuret manually (O'Brien et al., 1968c) or automated (Failing et al., 1961)	50 μl	With manual method, a serum blank is desirable (see Chap. 6).
Albumin (serum)	Electrophoresis on cellulose acetate (Fomon et al., 1970)	10 μl	Concentration of albumin less than 2.9 gm/100 ml suggests poor protein nutritional status.
Ascorbic acid (plasma)	2,4-DNP reaction manually (O'Brien et al., 1968d) or automated (Garry et al., 1974)	20 μl	Concentration less than 0.3 mg/100 ml suggests that recent dietary intake has been low (see Chapter 9).
Vitamin A (plasma or serum)	Fluorometry (Thompson et al., 1971)	200 μl	Concentration less than 10 μg/100 ml suggests deficiency and concentration less than 20 μg/100 ml indicates low stores (see Chapter 9).
Alkaline phosphatase (serum)	Liberation of p-nitrophenol manually (O'Brien et al., 1968e) or automated (Morgenstern et al., 1965)	100 μl	Activity greater than 25 Bodansky units/100 ml is suggestive of rickets (see Chapter 11).

Inorganic phosphorus (serum or plasma)	Modification of method of Fiske and Subba Row manually (O'Brien et al., 1968f) or automated (Kraml, 1966)	50 μl	Concentration less than 4.0 mg/100 ml is abnormal and suggestive of rickets. However, normal concentration does not rule out the presence of rickets.
Urea nitrogen (serum)	Urease manually (O'Brien et al., 1968g) or diacetyl monoxime manually or automated (Marsh et al., 1965)	100 μl 50 μl	Concentration less than 8 mg/100 ml suggests low recent dietary intake of protein. However, concentrations as low as 3.5 mg/100 ml are sometimes found in breastfed infants (see Chapter 6).
Cholesterol (serum)	Manually by method of Carr and Drekter (1956) or automated (Levine and Zak, 1964)	100 μl	Concentration greater than 200 mg/100 ml during the first two years of life or greater than 230 mg/100 ml after age two years indicates hypercholesterolemia (see Chapter 7).
Iron and iron-binding capacity (serum)	Manually by method of Fischer and Price (1964) or automated (Garry and Owen, 1968)	200 μl	Concentration of iron, iron-binding capacity and per cent saturation of transferrin may require different interpretation in infants than in older individuals (see Chapter 12).
Creatinine (urine)	Alkaline picrate manually (O'Brien et al., 1968h) or automated (Zender and Falbriard, 1965)	100 μl	Serves as reference for other urine determinations.
Riboflavin (urine)	Fluorometry (Horwitz, 1970a)	2 ml	Excretion less than 250 μg/gm of creatinine suggests low recent dietary intake (see Chapter 9).
Thiamin (urine)	Thiochrome fluorometry (Horwitz, 1970b)	10 ml	Excretion of less than 125 μg/gm of creatinine suggests that dietary intake has been low for weeks or months.
Iodine (urine)	Automated ceric ion-arsenious acid system (Garry et al., 1973)	5 ml	Excretion of less than 50 μg/gm of creatinine suggests low recent dietary intake.

and maintained in the frozen state until the analyses can be performed.

Urine should be acidified with hydrochloric acid to a final pH less than 3.0. If analyses cannot be carried out within eight hours, the samples should be stored in the frozen state. The significance of urinary excretion of creatinine and hydroxyproline is discussed in Chapter 3.

ROENTGENOGRAMS

Whenever clinical or biochemical evidence suggests rickets or scurvy, it is desirable to confirm the finding by roentgenograms of the wrist. It is not recommended that roentgenograms of the wrist be made routinely in screening unless (1) a roentgenologist experienced in interpreting early evidences of rickets and scurvy is available; and (2) biochemical studies of plasma routinely include determinations of ascorbic acid, inorganic phosphorus and alkaline phosphatase.

REFERENCES

Carr, J. J., and Drekter, I. J.: Simplified rapid technic for the extraction and determination of serum cholesterol without saponification. Clin. Chem. *2*:353, 1956.

Center for Disease Control: Ten-State Nutrition Survey 1968–1970. Vol. III. Clinical, Anthropometry, Dental. Atlanta, Georgia, Center for Disease Control, DHEW Publ. No. (HSM) 72-8131, 1972.

Failing, J. F., Jr., Buckley, M. W., and Zak, B.: A study on an ultramicro and automated procedure for serum proteins. Amer. J. Med. Technol. *27*:177, 1961.

Falkner, F., Buzina, R., Chopra, J., György, P., Jelliffe, D. B., McKigney, J., Read, M. S., and Roche, A. F.: The creation of growth standards: a committee report. Amer. J. Clin. Nutr. *25*:218, 1972.

Fischer, D. S., and Price, D. C.: A simple serum iron method using the new sensitive chromogen tripyridyl-s-triazine. Clin. Chem. *10*:21, 1964.

Fomon, S. J., Filer, L. J., Jr., Thomas, L. N., and Rogers, R. R.: Growth and serum chemical values of normal breastfed infants. Acta Paediatr. Scand. (Suppl. 202), 1970.

Garry, P. J., Lashley, D. W., and Owen, G. M.: Automated measurement of urinary iodine. Clin. Chem. *19*:950, 1973.

Garry, P. J., and Owen, G. M.: Automated micro determination (100μl) of serum iron and total iron binding capacity. Technicon Symposium, Automation in Analytical Chemistry. Vol. I. New York, Mediad, Inc., 1968.

Garry, P. J., Owen, G. M., Lashley, D. W., and Ford, P. C.: Automated determination of plasma and whole blood ascorbic acid. Canad. J. Biochem. *7* (June), 1974.

Horwitz, W. (ed.): Official Methods of Analysis of the Association of Official Analytical Chemists. 11th ed. Washington, D.C., Association of Official Analytical Chemists, 1970a, p. 774; 1970b, p. 771.

Karlberg, P., Engström, I., Lichtenstein, H., and Svennberg, I.: The development of children in a Swedish urban community. A prospective longitudinal study. III. Physical growth during the first three years of life. Acta Paediatr. Scand. (Suppl. 187):48, 1968.

Kraml, M.: A semi-automated determination of phospholipids. Clin. Chim. Acta *13*: 442, 1966.

Levine, J. B., and Zak, B.: Automated determination of serum total cholesterol. Clin. Chim. Acta *10*:381, 1964.

Marsh, W. H., Fingerhut, B., and Miller, H.: Automated and manual direct methods for the determination of blood urea. Clin. Chem. *11*:624, 1965.

Maternal and Child Health Service: Screening Children for Nutritional Status: Suggestions for Child Health Programs. DHEW Publ. No. (HSM) 2158. Washington, D.C., U.S. Government Printing Office, 1971.

McGanity, W. J.: Problems of assessment of nutritional status: an overview of clinical methodologies. *In* Hansen, R. G., and Munro, H. N. (eds.): Problems of Assessment and Alleviation of Malnutrition in the United States. Proceedings of a workshop (Nashville, Tenn., January 13–14, 1970). Bethesda, Md., The Nutrition Study Section, Division of Research Grants, National Institutes of Health. (Publication date not listed, 1970 assumed.)

Morgenstern, S., Kessler, G., Auerbach, J., Flor, R. V., and Klein, B.: An automated p-nitrophenylphosphate serum alkaline phosphatase procedure for the autoanalyzer. Clin. Chem. *11*:876, 1965.

Nellhaus, G.: Head circumference from birth to eighteen years. Practical composite international and interracial graphs. Pediatrics *41*:106, 1968.

Nelson, W. E., Vaughan, V. C., and McKay, R. J.: Textbook of Pediatrics. 9th ed. Philadelphia, W. B. Saunders Co., 1969.

O'Brien, D., Ibbott, F. A., and Rodgerson, D. O.: Laboratory Manual of Pediatric Micro Biochemical Techniques. 4th ed. New York, Harper & Row, 1968a, p. 167; 1968b, p. 187; 1968c, p. 279; 1968d, p. 47; 1968e, p. 248; 1968f, p. 252; 1968g, p. 347; 1968h, p. 114.

Stoch, M. B., and Smythe, P. M.: Does undernutrition during infancy inhibit brain growth and subsequent intellectual development? Arch. Dis. Child. *38*:546, 1968.

Thompson, J. N., Erdody, P., Brien, R., and Murray, T. K.: Fluorometric determination of vitamin A in human blood and liver. Biochem. Med. *5*:67, 1971.

U.S. Department of Agriculture: Calculating the Nutritive Value of Diets. A Manual of Instruction for the Use of Punch Cards for Machine Tabulation. USDA Publ. No. ARS 62-10. Washington, D.C., U.S. Government Printing Office, 1964.

Winick, M., and Rosso, P.: Head circumference and cellular growth of the brain in normal and marasmic children. J. Pediatr. *74*:774, 1969.

Zender, R., and Falbriard, A.: Analyse automatique de la créatinine dans le sérum et dans l'urine. Valeurs "normales" chez l'homme de la créatininemie et de la clearance. Clin. Chim. Acta *12*:183, 1965.

19

INFANT FEEDING IN HEALTH AND DISEASE

Samuel J. Fomon,
Ekhard E. Ziegler
and
Alejandro M. O'Donnell

NUTRITIONAL PRINCIPLES

Although most infants appear to grow normally and to maintain a satisfactory state of health in spite of wide variations in nutritional management, several nutritional principles should be kept in mind.

1. The diet should be adequate but not excessive in water, calories and all essential nutrients.
2. The diet and the manner in which it is fed should be conducive to development of sound eating habits.
3. The diet should be readily digestible.
4. A reasonable distribution of calories should be derived from protein, fat and carbohydrate.

A large proportion of the first 13 chapters of this book has been concerned with the discussion of adequate but not excessive intakes of calories and various nutrients. The importance of establishing sound eating habits early in infancy—especially the avoidance of overeating—has been mentioned in Chapter 2, and feeding habits likely to minimize dental caries have been discussed in Chapter 14. Digestibility of the infant's diet has been discussed in relation to feeding of butterfat (Chapter 7), starch (Chapter 8) and fiber, as in diets based on soy flour (Chapter 15). Unfortunately, there is little experimental evidence for determining what percentages of calories in the infant's diet should be derived from protein, fat and carbohydrate. Further research on this point is needed.

Tentatively, it seems reasonable to recommend for fullsize infants that 7 to 16 per cent of calories be derived from protein, 30 to 55 per cent from fat and the remainder from carbohydrate. Human milk provides approximately 7, 55 and 38 per cent of calories from protein, fat and carbohydrate, respectively (Chapter 15), and most commercially prepared formulas fed in the United States supply 9 to 15 per cent of calories from protein, 45 to 50 per cent of calories from fat and the remainder from carbohydrate (Tables 15–7 and 15–9). When intakes of protein account for less than 6 per cent of caloric intake, protein deficiency is likely to result. Intakes of protein accounting for more than 16 per cent of calories may not be harmful but certainly constitute a metabolically and economically inefficient manner of providing the infant with calories. When percentage of calories supplied by fat is extremely high, ketosis will result. Little evidence is available to define "extremely high" in this respect. Diets supplying less than 30 per cent of calories from fat or more than 65 per cent of calories from carbohydrate may possibly be of low satiety value but, once again, little evidence is available.

EARLY NUTRITIONAL MANAGEMENT OF NORMAL FULLSIZE INFANTS

A water-miscible preparation of vitamin K should be administered parenterally in a single dose of 1 mg soon after birth. At four to six hours of age, a feeding of distilled water should be offered. If at least 15 ml of water are taken and retained, breast or formula feeding may be instituted. If less than 15 ml of distilled water are accepted or if 15 ml are accepted and regurgitated, a second feeding of distilled water should be offered four hours after the first. If 15 ml of the distilled water are not accepted and retained at the second feeding, a soft rubber or plastic catheter should be inserted into the stomach, the stomach contents aspirated and 15 ml of water instilled into the stomach. If this amount is not retained, additional diagnostic studies should be undertaken before breast or formula feedings are instituted.

Breast or formula feeding should be offered at approximately three- to four-hour intervals. There is little point in offering formula less concentrated than 67 kcal/100 ml. As pointed out in Chapter 2, no attempt should be made to encourage the infant to accept greater amounts of food than seem to satisfy him. Bottle-fed infants should not be encouraged to drain the last drop from the bottle. During the first four months of life, there is no medical or nutritional advantage in reducing the number of feedings to less than five daily.

Although it is common practice in the United States to introduce beikost before six weeks of age (often before three weeks of age), there is no evidence that such early introduction of beikost is advantageous. As will be discussed subsequently, feeding of beikost is relatively expensive and such feeding during the first few months of life is likely to be wasteful of food and of the energy of the person doing the feeding. Early introduction of beikost might contribute to establishing habits of overeating and, in that case, would be medically and nutritionally objectionable. Concern over this possibility arises from the observation of physicians and nutritionists that parents appear to have a strong inclination to encourage the infant to finish the last spoonful of food in the dish.

BREAST FEEDING

In developing countries, mortality is much less among breastfed than among bottle-fed infants. Although mortality in developed countries appears to be similar for breastfed and bottle-fed infants, human milk has certain advantages over other milks and formulas for infant feeding (Chapter 15), and breast feeding may be an important mode of promoting sound feeding habits (Chapter 2). One may therefore question the infrequency of breast feeding in the United States and other developed countries.

Among the many reasons for infrequency of breast feeding in the United States, several can be identified as likely to be most important. Because only about 30 per cent of women breast feed their infants even for one week and only 15 per cent for as long as two months (Chapter 1, Figs. 1–2 and 1–3), it is evident that women who breast feed are in the minority and this, in itself, discourages some. Perhaps more importantly, in the absence of widespread breast feeding in a country, the women generally are inept at offering advice and encouragement to their sisters or daughters who may wish to breast feed. Without support from family and friends, the woman who encounters difficulty in breast feeding will generally turn for advice and support to a physician. Unfortunately, most physicians have had little experience in providing such advice and encouragement and may recommend discontinuation of breast feeding rather than attempting to deal with the problem presented by the mother.

Many women in developed countries work outside the home. It may be necessary for such women to be separated from their infants for 9 or 10 hours at a time and breast feeding may therefore not be feasible. In addition, oral contraceptives seriously interfere with the success of breast feeding (Kora, 1969; Kamal et al., 1969; Abdel Kader et al., 1969; Miller and Hughes, 1970; Barsivala and Virkar, 1973) by diminishing the flow of milk and/or decreasing the concentrations of major nutrients. Whether newer low dosage preparations will prove to be more compatible with continuation of breast feeding remains to be established. Injected progestogens in the absence of administration of estrogens seem to have no adverse effect on milk flow or on duration of lactation (Karim et al., 1971).

Serum Chemical Values of Normal Breastfed Infants

Serum chemical values of normal infants may vary with age and type of feeding. In addition, in some instances, a sex-related difference may be demonstrated. Table 19–1 presents data on serum chemical values of normal breastfed infants in the nonfasting state. Several comments may be made about the various serum values: Concentrations of urea nitrogen vary with recent dietary intake of protein and are generally greater in formula-fed than in breastfed infants, reflecting the greater protein intakes of formula-fed infants (Chapter 6). Concentrations of calcium of breastfed infants are similar to those of formula-fed infants, whereas concentrations of inorganic phosphorus are generally less for breastfed than for formula-fed infants (Chapter 11, Figs. 11–2 and 11–3). Concentrations of inorganic phosphorus are greater during infancy than during childhood or adulthood. Concentrations of magnesium appear to be similar in infants, children and adults.

Alkaline phosphatase activity was found previously to be significantly greater in serum of breastfed male than of breastfed female infants (Fomon et al., 1970). Although the data in Table 19–1 do not demonstrate a statistically significant sex-related difference in alkaline phosphatase activity, the mean value at each age is greater for males than for females. At each age, mean concentration of cholesterol was found to be greater in serum of females than of males and, at 84 and 112 days of age, the difference was statistically significant ($p < 0.05$). Concentrations of cholesterol vary with diet, being less when infants are fed formulas in which vegetable oils supply the fat than when they are breastfed or fed butterfat-containing formulas (Chapter 7, Tables 7–6 and 7–7). As indicated by the large standard deviations, concentrations of triglycerides are highly variable, probably reflecting to some extent the known postprandial increases and the random nature of the samples with respect to the time of the last feeding.

TABLE 19–1 SERUM CHEMICAL VALUES OF NORMAL BREASTFED INFANTS*

Concentration/ 100 ml of Serum	Sex	Age 28 Days			Age 56 Days			Age 84 Days			Age 112 Days		
		N	*Mean*	*S.D.*	*N*	*Mean*	*S.D.*	*N*	*Mean*	*S.D.*	*N*	*Mean*	*S.D.*
Urea nitrogen (mg)	M + F	66	7.7	2.2	64	6.7	2.0	70	6.5	1.7	69	6.6	3.5
Calcium (mg)	M + F	65	10.4	0.6	68	10.4	0.6	73	10.3	0.7	69	10.2	0.8
Phosphorus (mg)	M + F	62	5.7	0.9	67	5.6	0.9	72	5.4	0.8	67	5.4	1.2
Magnesium (mg)	M + F	64	2.1	0.2	68	2.2	0.2	73	2.2	0.2	68	2.2	0.2
Alkaline phosphatase†	M	22	42	16	21	42	15	23	37	12	22	35	9
	F	22	40	12	25	35	11	30	35	11	25	32	11
Cholesterol (mg)	M	25	137	26	24	125	20	22	127	25	23	133	26
	F	37	139	30	36	136	40	39	145	32	42	145	43
Triglycerides (mg)	M	25	204	80	22	171	70	23	184	96	21	238	131
	F	36	165	75	39	165	87	40	217	113	42	209	117

*Unpublished data from the Pediatric Metabolic Unit, University of Iowa. Serum concentrations of proteins of breastfed infants are presented in Chapter 6 (Table 6–3).

†Autoanalyzer units.

VITAMIN AND MINERAL SUPPLEMENTATION OF THE DIETS OF FULLSIZE INFANTS

Table 19–2 presents a summary of vitamin and mineral supplementation considered desirable for normal fullsize infants. Vitamin C may be given in the form of a vitamin concentrate or fruit juice. Means of providing iron have been discussed in Chapter 12. Because milks and formulas as marketed are uniformly low in content of fluoride, the desirability of supplementing the diet with fluoride will depend on the amount of water, if any, subsequently added to the milk or formula or consumed alone, and the concentration of fluoride in the water (Chapter 14, Table 14–4).

When goat milk is a major source of calories, the diet should be fortified with 50 μg of folacin daily.

FORMULA PREPARATION

Although physicians, hospital personnel and public health workers in the United States generally recommend that infant formulas prepared in the home be terminally sterilized or prepared aseptically according to a single-feeding method, verbal reports from public health workers, nutritionists and physicians suggest that the in-

TABLE 19–2 VITAMIN AND MINERAL SUPPLEMENTATION OF THE DIET OF FULLSIZE INFANTS

	Desirable Supplementation*			
Major Source of Energy	*Vitamin A*	*Vitamin D*	*Vitamin C*	*Iron*
Human milk		+		+
Cow milk				
whole, fresh fluid		±	+	+
whole, powdered		±	+	+
2 per cent	±	±	+	+
skim, fresh fluid	±	±	+	+
skim, powdered	±	±	+	+
evaporated			+	+
Goat milk, fresh fluid†		±	+	+
Commercially prepared formulas				±

*The designation + indicates that supplementation is desirable; the designation ± indicates that supplementation is desirable if the milk or formula has not been fortified with the nutrient in question. Recommendations regarding cow milk and commercially prepared formulas apply to the United States; fortification differs in several countries. Desirable fluoride supplementation is indicated in Chapter 14 (Table 14–4).

†Folacin, 50 μg daily, should be given.

structions are generally ignored or poorly carried out. The infrequency with which gastrointestinal disorders of infants are traced to bacterial contamination of formulas probably reflects the infrequent occurrence of enteric pathogens in the environment. Bacterial contamination with other organisms is the rule rather than the exception in the United States (Fischer and Whitman, 1959; Fomon et al., 1959; Vaughan et al., 1962), England (Gatherer and Wood, 1966; Anderson and Gatherer, 1970) and Sweden (Söderhjelm, 1972).

Because obvious adverse consequences are not apparent from convenient methods of formula preparation in widespread use at present, it is unlikely that parents will be motivated to adopt more complicated and less convenient methods. An attempt should therefore be made to promote convenient methods that minimize the likelihood of contamination of the formula with enteric pathogens and that minimize the likelihood of multiplication of such organisms if they are introduced.

When water supplies are uncontaminated and the environment is relatively free of carriers of enteric pathogens, the most important measures for control of bacterial growth in formulas are effective cleaning of bottles and nipples and avoidance of storage of formula at temperatures above 10°C. If bottles and nipples are thoroughly washed with soap or detergent, rinsed and dried, few bacteria will remain and sterilization is probably not necessary. Soaking in a weak solution of sodium hypochlorite as an additional precaution in eliminating microorganisms is considered by many mothers to be convenient (Söderhjelm, 1972). The need for thorough rinsing of bottles after soaking in sodium hypochlorite solution should be stressed to parents.

When a powdered formula is used, preparation of a single bottle at the time of each feeding is probably the safest method. An appropriate amount of water is introduced into the clean bottle and the powder added. Lumpiness can be avoided by allowing the powder to settle for a minute or two before being shaken into suspension. When a single bottle is prepared from commercially available concentrated liquid formula, it is merely necessary to utilize equal volumes of concentrated formula and water. An evaporated milk formula may be prepared by combining 60 ml of the milk, 90 ml of water and 10 ml (two teaspoonfuls) of corn syrup. It is desirable to keep the can of concentrated liquid formula or evaporated milk in the refrigerator or the coolest available place in which it will not freeze. In using the single bottle method, it is preferable to prepare only the amount that the infant is likely to consume at that time and to discard any residual. If a bottle must be prepared some hours before it is fed, it should be prepared with cold ingredients and stored in the refrigerator or other cool place.

When bottles are to be made for an entire 24-hour period, it is desirable that bottles be boiled or soaked in a weak solution of sodium hypochlorite. However, the hazard from use of clean but not sterilized bottles is small. To the desired amount of cool water in each bottle is added the appropriate amount of formula powder, of commercially prepared concentrated liquid formula or of evaporated milk and corn syrup, in each case proceeding much as in preparing a single bottle. With most municipal water supplies, it will not be necessary to boil the water. If boiled water is used, it should be cooled before use; as soon as the formulas are made, they should be placed in the refrigerator.

In the absence of refrigeration, bacterial growth may be retarded by acidification of the formula. Cool water (or, for an evaporated milk formula, water and corn syrup) in sufficient quantity for the 24-hour period is placed in a clean receptacle and 10 ml of vinegar (acetic acid) is added. The evaporated milk or concentrated formula is then added slowly with stirring.

DISTRIBUTION OF CALORIES IN DIET

When a high percentage of calorie intake is derived from a single source, such as milk or formula, it is simple to estimate the approximate percentage of dietary calories derived from protein, fat and carbohydrate. As discussed in Chapter 16, beikost is generally a rich source of carbohydrate, a moderate source of protein and a poor source of fat. Our unpublished observations indicate that, when parents are permitted to feed three-and-one-half- to six-and-one-half-month-old infants an unrestricted selection of strained foods, the mixture of strained foods provides approximately 7 per cent of calories from protein, 10 per cent from fat and 83 per cent from carbohydrate. As indicated in Chapter 2 (Table 2–4), during ad libitum feeding of a 67 kcal/100 ml formula to normal infants between three and one-half and five and one-half months of age, approximately 76 per cent of calories were derived from formula and 24 per cent from beikost. At ages four, five and six months, beikost accounted for 22, 26 and 31 per cent, respectively, of calorie intake (Table 19–3). When skim milk was fed, beikost accounted for 34 and 40 per cent of calorie intake at ages four and five months, respectively—the low caloric density of skim milk presumably accounting for the greater percentage of calorie intake from beikost.

Utilizing these observations on caloric intake from formula or skim milk and from beikost, together with the percentages of protein, fat and carbohydrate from each source, the caloric distribution of the entire diet has been calculated (Table 19–3). The caloric distribution of

TABLE 19–3 ESTIMATED CALORIC DISTRIBUTION OF VARIOUS DIETS FED TO FOUR-, FIVE- AND SIX-MONTH-OLD INFANTS*

	MILK OR FORMULA											
	Similac			*Whole Cow Milk*			*2 Per Cent Milk*			*Skim Milk*		
Age (months)	4	5	6	4	5	6	4	5	6	4	5	6
Calories from beikost (%)	22	26	31	22	26	31	28	33	–	34	40	–
Caloric distribution of total diet (% of calories)												
Protein	9	8	8	18	17	17	22	21	–	29	27	–
Fat	40	39	37	41	40	37	25	24	–	5	6	–
Carbohydrate	51	53	55	41	43	46	53	55	–	66	67	–

*Data on Similac and skim milk are unpublished observations of Pediatric Metabolic Unit, University of Iowa (see text).

the diet has also been estimated for infants fed whole cow milk and 2 per cent milk—assuming the same percentage of beikost with whole cow milk as with 67 kcal/100 ml formula and assuming that the percentage of calories from beikost by infants fed 2 per cent milk would fall midway between the percentage observed in infants fed 67 kcal/100 ml formula and that observed in infants fed skim milk.

It is evident from Table 19–3 that, when a commercially prepared formula such as Similac, Enfamil or SMA is fed to four- to six-month-old infants, the total diet (formula plus beikost) is likely to provide a distribution of calories well within the recommended range. It may be noted that the distribution of calories would be within the recommended range even under circumstances in which two-thirds of the calories were supplied by whole milk and one-third from beikost—a circumstance that would likely occur between 9 and 12 months of age. Thus, on the basis of considerations of caloric distribution, there is little reason to discontinue formula feeding before about nine months of age.

When infants are fed whole cow milk and receive at least 22 per cent of calories from beikost (Table 19–3), intakes of protein will be rather high but distribution of calories will otherwise fall within the desirable range. Percentage of calories from fat will be less than that commonly associated with steatorrhea (Chapter 7). In relation to digestibility of the diet and distribution of calories from protein, fat and carbohydrate, there is therefore no major objection to substituting whole cow milk for commercially prepared formula when at least 22 per cent of calories is supplied from beikost. In practical terms, this means an intake of approximately 215 gm of commercially prepared strained foods daily—slightly more than one and one-half jars of strained foods daily.

When 2 per cent milk is fed, it seems likely that percentage of calories from protein will be substantially above the desirable range and percentage of calories from fat will be below the desirable range (Table 19–3). Intake of essential fatty acids will probably be less than the advisable intake. Although feeding of 2 per cent milk will probably result in a caloric distribution outside the desirable ranges for protein and fat, there is at present no reason to assume that this is harmful to the infant. Neither has any advantage been established for feeding a diet so high in protein and low in fat. The product, Similac Advance (Chapter 15, Table 15–7), is not remarkably different in caloric distribution from 2 per cent milk.

When skim milk is fed, the diet will provide a high intake of protein (more than four times the estimated requirement), an exceedingly low intake of fat and a high intake of carbohydrate. Dietary intake of essential fatty acids will almost certainly be less than the estimated requirement (Chapter 7). Although skim milk is probably preferable to whole milk in the diets of most children over two years of age, it is not recommended for infants.

COST OF INFANT FEEDING

Because infants appear to eat largely for calories (Chapter 2), it is of some interest to consider the cost of various infant foods per unit of calories. Data presented in Chapter 1 (Table 1–1) demonstrate that the cost per unit of calories is relatively high for commercially prepared strained foods. To feed a four-month-old infant 650 kcal/day would cost approximately 44¢/day if the total calorie intake were derived solely from a commercially prepared formula purchased as a concentrated liquid. If 24 per cent of this calorie intake were derived from beikost (assuming an average cost of 14.5¢/100 kcal) and the remainder from formula purchased as concentrated liquid, the cost of feeding would likely be between 55 and 60¢/day.

LEAD

As stated in Chapter 15, Lamm and Rosen (1974) reported concentrations of lead in human and fresh fluid cow milk to be less than 0.5 μg/100 ml (i.e., not detectable by the method used). Such low concentrations are somewhat difficult to interpret in view of the earlier reports of Lamm et al. (1973) and of other workers (Murthy and Rhea, 1971; Mitchell and Aldous, cited by Mitchell, 1974). However, it is evident that concentrations of lead in evaporated milk and in commercially prepared infant formulas are greater than those in fresh human or cow milk (Chapter 15, Table 15–4). Still greater concentrations of lead appear to be present in fruit juices and beverages. Mitchell and Aldous (cited by Mitchell, 1974) found that 20 per cent of 155 fruit juices or beverages in leaded-seam cans contained more than 40 μg of lead/100 ml. This is in agreement with another study in which 7 of 15 products in this category were found to contain, on the average, more than 30 μg/100 gm (Somers, 1973).

A survey of 333 infants by the National Canners Association (Somers, 1973) has suggested that the average dietary intake of lead during the first year of life is 93 μg/day, with less than 2 per cent of infants receiving more than 200 μg/day. However, the medical significance of these data is difficult to evaluate because of uncertainty regarding the metabolism of lead in infants and children. In the adult, absorbed lead is rapidly stored and retained in bone. Concentrations of lead in blood and soft tissue do not rise until bone is overloaded with lead (Browder et al., 1973). Little quantitative information regarding these aspects of lead metabolism in infants and children is available (Mitchell, 1974).

Basing their conclusions on data from study of adult subjects, an ad hoc committee of the Bureau of Community Environmental Management (King, 1971) concluded that intakes of lead greater than 300 μg/day from all sources would permit accumulation of lead within the bodies of children. Thus, in a sense, 300 μg/day could be considered the maximal permissible intake. Barltrop (cited by Lamm et al., 1973; Lin-Fu, 1973; Mitchell, 1974), using a similar approach, suggested daily permissible intakes of 59, 104 and 133 μg/day, respectively, for newborn infants and one- and two-year-old children.

As pointed out by Lin-Fu (1973), lead intake by infants and toddlers from nondietary sources is likely to be substantial even if frank pica is absent. In view of the uncertainty regarding permissible intakes of lead and the additive effects of dietary and nondietary intakes of lead, it cannot be concluded that lead content of current diets of infants and children in the United States is regularly within the limits of safety. In fact, dietary lead may contribute significantly to the lead intake in this age group (Mitchell, 1974).

NITRATES, NITRITES AND METHEMOGLOBINEMIA

The nitrite ion oxidizes ferrous iron of hemoglobin to the ferric state. Because the resulting compound, methemoglobin, is incapable of binding molecular oxygen, a sufficient concentration of methemoglobin in the blood will result in cyanosis. Although methemoglobin accounts for only about 1 per cent of total hemoglobin in the normal adult, it may account for as much as 5 per cent of total hemoglobin in the premature infant and for as much as 2.8 per cent of the total hemoglobin in the fullterm newborn and older infant (Kravitz et al., 1956). Infants and children with normal concentrations of hemoglobin may be free of cyanosis when 5 to 8 per cent of hemoglobin is in the form of methemoglobin (Committee on Nutrition, 1970). Death from asphyxia is likely to occur when the proportion of methemoglobin exceeds 70 per cent of total hemoglobin (Knotek and Schmidt, 1964). Infants are known to be more susceptible to development of methemoglobinemia than are older children and adults.

The occurrence of methemoglobinemia in infants who have consumed well water with high nitrate content is extensively documented (Comly, 1945; Walton, 1951; Committee on Nutrition, 1970). Conditions for reducing ingested nitrate to nitrite must exist or nitrate will be metabolized and excreted without adverse consequence. The necessary conditions for reducing nitrate to nitrite within the gastrointestinal tract of the human infant appear to be pH of gastric juice greater than 4 and the presence of nitrate-reducing bacteria in the upper portion of the gastrointestinal tract (Cornblath and Hartmann, 1948).

The consumption of nitrate in foods has not been demonstrated to result in methemoglobinemia, possibly because (1) naturally occurring protective agents (e.g., ascorbic acid, vitamin K) are present in foods; (2) plant nitrates may occur in chemical combinations that are less readily reduced to nitrites in the gastrointestinal tract than is the case with nitrates in water; and/or (3) the chronicity of water ingestion compared with the intermittency of ingestion of nitrates from plant sources (Committee on Nutrition, 1970).

However, under some conditions plant nitrates may be converted to nitrites before consumption by the infant and thereby lead to serious and even fatal disease. Methemoglobinemia from nitrites of plant origin has been reported from consumption of home-prepared spinach puree (Sinios, 1964; Hölscher and Natzschka, 1964; Sinios and Wodsak, 1965; Schuphan, 1965; Simon et al., 1966), carrot soup (L'Hirondel et al., 1971) and carrot juice (Keating et al., 1973). Although methemoglobinemia has not been reported after consumption of beets, the nitrate content of beets is often high and this food is not recommended for infants.

Commercially prepared strained and junior foods tested under a variety of conditions have been found to contain only traces of nitrite (Wilson, 1949; Kamm et al., 1965). Nitrite does not appear to accumulate in these foods when opened and stored in a refrigerator for periods as long as 35 days (Phillips, 1968, 1969). Methemoglobinemia has, in fact, not been observed following consumption of commercially prepared strained foods.

The potential hazard of feeding infants spinach, carrots or beets pureed in the home may outweigh any advantage of home preparation. However, it may be noted that methemoglobinemia has rarely been reported in infants fed carrot soup, in spite of the widespread custom in Western Europe of feeding home-prepared carrot soup to infants with diarrhea.

ACUTE DIARRHEA

Variability in fecal excretion is great from one infant to another and, in the same infant, from one period to another during infancy. It is well recognized that the normal breastfed infant at 10 days of age is likely to pass 8 to 10 stools per day; on the other hand, a two-month-old breastfed infant not receiving beikost may pass only one stool in two or three days. Furthermore, the consistency of the feces varies with the nature of the diet and from one infant to another with the same diet. It is therefore not surprising that diarrhea is loosely defined as the passage of frequent, unformed or watery stools. Use of the term generally implies fecal excretion of abnormally great amounts of water and electrolytes and, except in chronic forms of diarrhea, a change from the previously observed stool pattern for the particular infant.

Acute diarrhea caused by bacteria (enteropathogenic *E. coli*, salmonella, shigella, etc.) requires appropriate treatment with antibiotics, but in the developed countries, such diarrhea is more commonly caused by viruses (most commonly, however, no known pathogens are identifiable), and administration of antibiotics is of no value.

Infants with acute diarrhea demonstrate impaired intestinal absorption of all major nutrients including water. Unabsorbed nutrients, particularly carbohydrate, and bacterial overgrowth give rise to increased fermentation in the intestinal tract, with production of large amounts of organic acids (Torres-Pinedo et al., 1966a, 1968). These acids increase the osmolality of intestinal contents and lead to increased fluid loss. Absorption of fat and nitrogen is impaired to a certain extent, although the relative significance of the various involved mechanisms is not very clear. Absorption of glucose is impaired, with a consequent decrease in net absorption of water and sodium (Torres-Pinedo et al., 1966b). As will be discussed, hydrolysis and absorption of disaccharides are frequently impaired.

Treatment of acute diarrhea frequently requires temporary reduction or withholding of food, with close attention to maintenance of fluid and electrolyte balance. Excessive fluid loss may necessitate parenteral fluid therapy, but many infants and children with mild to moderate diarrhea do not require parenteral fluid therapy. As pointed out by Cooke (1969), the decision to employ oral rather than parenteral fluid therapy rests on clinical appraisal of the patient. If there are signs of circulatory insufficiency, lethargy, vomiting, abdominal distention or continuing weight loss, intravenous therapy is necessary. In the absence of these findings, oral therapy may be employed.

Mild or Moderate Diarrhea of Short Duration

Diarrhea frequently is of only one to four days' duration and thus presents a problem primarily with respect to water and electrolyte balance, with little need for attention to intake of calories, protein and other essential nutrients. Withholding of food is seldom necessary for more than 24 hours.

There is little agreement between authorities with respect to methods of providing water and electrolytes for short-term management of acute diarrhea. Davidson (1973) suggests use of skim milk diluted with an equal quantity of water, a mixture which, although somewhat low in content of sodium and potassium, has the advantage of offering little likelihood of serious error in home preparation. The objections to use of undiluted skim milk because of the high renal solute load (Chapter 10) do not apply, and the dilution results in a lesser intake of lactose than would otherwise be the case. Cooke (1969) has suggested a solution of 50 gm sucrose, 1.7 gm (30 mmoles) sodium chloride and 2.0 gm (20 mmoles) potassium bicarbonate in 1 liter of water. The commercially available powder, Lytren (Mead), when properly diluted, and the commercially available liquid, Pedialyte (Ross), yield concentrations of sodium, chloride and potassium similar to those recommended by Cooke (1969).

The greater concentrations of electrolytes utilized by some investigators (e.g., Hirschhorn et al., 1973) cannot be recommended except when fed under close medical supervision to assure that fluid intakes are relatively high. Great care is required in the mixing of any electrolyte-containing powder with water. Because of the possibility of errors in dilution, parents should generally not be given the responsibility of preparing such a mixture for their infant.

Other mixtures sometimes used in treatment of mild or moderate diarrhea include bouillon, weak tea sweetened with sugar, Kool-Aid (General Foods), sweetened and flavored gelatin and, especially in parts of Western Europe, carrot soup. Bouillon cannot be recommended for treatment of diarrhea. Bouillon cubes (and, presumably, bouillon granules) are approximately 24 per cent sodium (Watt and Merrill, 1963) and nearly free of carbohydrate. Bouillon contributes a substantial renal solute load from the sodium, chloride and protein and is quite low in potassium. Edema has been reported in infants given bouillon for treatment of diarrhea (Nomura, 1966).

Sweetened tea and Kool-Aid are good sources of water and sugar but cannot replace fecal losses of electrolytes and therefore should not be used. Commercially available flavored gelatins, if diluted sufficiently to be fed by bottle, will provide sugar and modest amounts of sodium but very little potassium. As in the case of sweetened tea or Kool-Aid, a gelatin solution is not recommended.

Carrots are a rich source of potassium. Carrot soup made according to a recipe that provides an appropriate quantity of sodium chloride is likely to be a suitable mixture for management of infants with diarrhea. Stalder (1972) recommends that 500 gm of cleaned carrots and 3.0 gm of sodium chloride be cooked for two hours, then passed through a fine sieve and made up to 1 liter with water. The resulting 1-liter mixture will probably provide approximately 50 meq of sodium and 40 meq of potassium. Usually, additional water is given, 1 part of water being fed for each 4 parts of carrot soup (Stalder, 1972). A somewhat similar mixture made from strained carrots commercially available in the United States by dilution with an equal volume of water would provide approximately 25 meq of sodium, 22 meq of potassium and approximately 60 gm of carbohydrate per liter, and is preferable to the more concentrated mixture suggested by Stalder (1972); furthermore, the use of the commercially prepared product would largely eliminate the danger of methemoglobinemia.

Although it has been suggested (Cooke, 1969) that large feedings be given infrequently to avoid stimulating gastrointestinal motility, there is no evidence to indicate that total fecal loss of fluid is less with such management. Large feedings given to ill infants may predispose to vomiting and are therefore undesirable.

Regardless of the composition of the fluid offered to the infant, fluid intake should be carefully recorded. With any of the mixtures mentioned, fluid intake of 120 ml/kg/day plus an amount of fluid equal to that lost in feces will provide sufficient water to maintain water balance unless insensible water losses are excessive because of fever or elevated environmental temperature. If fluid intake is less than 120 ml/kg during the first 24 hours of therapy, the infant should be again evaluated clinically and, if possible, the osmolality of the urine should be determined. Urine concentration greater than 400 mosmol/liter will generally indicate the desirability of initiating parenteral fluid therapy. When environmental temperature is high or the infant has fever, intakes of 150 ml/kg/day for maintenance are desirable. As diarrhea subsides, increasing amounts of formula may be given.

Mild or Moderate Diarrhea of Longer Duration

When diarrhea persists for more than four days, attention should be directed at providing adequate or nearly adequate intakes of calories and all essential nutrients. Goals of management should be focused more on maintenance of water balance and on provision of maintenance amounts of nutrients than on decreasing the number or size of the stools.

Although the excretion of various nutrients in the stools is greater during feeding than during fasting, absorption of nutrients is also greater (Chung, 1948). Butterfat and other poorly absorbed fats should be avoided. It seems likely that in at least some categories of patients, bacterial production of significant amounts of hydroxy fatty acids from dietary unsaturated long-chain fatty acids may occur (Soong et al., 1972) and may perpetuate the diarrhea because of the cathartic action of these acids. Reduced intakes of fat and/or use of medium-chain triglycerides may therefore be desirable. Lactose should be temporarily eliminated from the diet and it may be necessary to eliminate other disaccharides. Soy-isolate formulas or Nutramigen (Mead) (Chapter

15, Tables 15–9 and 15–10) are satisfactory lactose-free formulas. The commercially available powdered product, Portagen (Mead) (Table 15–10), may be useful, but extreme care is necessary to assure correct dilution.

Management During Recovery from Severe Diarrhea

Parenteral fluid therapy of severe diarrhea will not be discussed here. Nevertheless, it seems desirable to comment on nutritional aspects of management during recovery from severe diarrhea. Both during the course of diarrhea and during recovery, intolerance to carbohydrate is common. Most often, the infant is intolerant to lactose but may be intolerant to other carbohydrates as well. A temporary deficiency of intestinal disaccharidases has been described in diarrheal disease of infancy (Weijers et al., 1962; Lifshitz and Holman, 1964; Sunshine and Kretchmer, 1964) and could be responsible, at least in part, for temporary intolerance to disaccharides after recovery from severe diarrhea. Several investigators (Lifshitz et al., 1970a and b) have reported that the majority of infants recovering from severe diarrhea are intolerant to lactose. By four months after cessation of diarrhea, all infants were able to tolerate lactose normally (Lifshitz et al., 1971a).

When carbohydrates are fed during the course of severe diarrhea, Lifshitz et al. (1971b) have suggested that two or three liquid stools be examined daily to determine fecal pH and content of reducing substances. The stools must be examined immediately after passage. Carbohydrate intolerance is diagnosed when reducing substances are excreted in stools in concentrations of 0.25 per cent or more (as judged by Clinitest tablet method, Kerry and Anderson, 1964) and/or pH is less than 6. Repeated stool testing is necessary because a high percentage of stools of carbohydrate-intolerant infants have pH greater than 6 and demonstrate relatively low concentrations of reducing substances.

Infants identified as lactose intolerant on the basis of such repeated stool testing should be managed with a lactose-free diet such as a soy-isolate or casein hydrolysate (Chapter 15, Tables 15–9 and 15–10) for several weeks or months until recovery is well advanced. Similarly, infants demonstrated in this way to be intolerant to other carbohydrates should be managed with diets free of those carbohydrates—e.g., Cho-Free Formula Base (Syntex) with added carbohydrates or Pregestimil (Mead) (Chapter 15, Table 15–10). In some instances, monosaccharide intolerance may also be present (Torres-Pinedo et al., 1966b; Lifshitz et al., 1970a and b; Rodriguez-de-Curet et al., 1970) and it will then be necessary for a time to provide a carbohydrate-free diet while administering glucose intravenously. Diets completely free of carbohydrate should not be fed because of danger of hypoglycemia (Lifshitz et al., 1970a). In diarrheal disease of infancy, the absorption of fructose is impaired to a greater extent and for longer periods of time than that of glucose (Rodriguez-de-Curet et al., 1970; Lifshitz et al., 1970a and b). Thus, the administration of formulas with fructose as the only carbohydrate should be restricted to treatment of patients with glucose-galactose malabsorption.

CYSTIC FIBROSIS OF THE PANCREAS

Almost all patients with cystic fibrosis of the pancreas suffer from malabsorption due to exocrine pancreatic insufficiency. It has been stated that as many as 80 per cent of patients may have pancreatic insufficiency at birth and that an additional 10 per cent will develop pancreatic insufficiency during the first year of life (Silverman et al., 1971). Replacement therapy for pancreatic insufficiency seems to be more important for the infant and young child than for older patients (di Sant-Agnese, 1973). Adequate replacement therapy improves intestinal absorption, thus contributing to the general well-being of the patient and avoiding such consequences of malabsorption as deficiencies of fat-soluble vitamins.

Replacement therapy consists of the administration of pancreatic extracts—e.g., Cotazym (Organon) or Viokase (Viobin)—with each meal. Constipation occasionally presents a problem in management and can usually be solved by reducing the dosage of pancreatic extract or by administration of the surface-wetting agent, dioctyl sodium sulfosuccinate (Colace, Mead). The practice of administering mineral oil to prevent or alleviate constipation of patients with cystic fibrosis of the pancreas is unsound because it leads to increased loss of fat-soluble vitamins, thereby complicating management.

Because of increased fecal losses of fat and nitrogen, intakes of food will generally be greater than those by normal infants and children, even during therapy with pancreatic enzymes. Because of the deficiency in pancreatic enzymes, diets high in content of protein and carbohydrate and low or moderate in content of fat have generally been recommended. However, commercially prepared formulas that supply approximately 50 per cent of calories from a readily digestible mixture of vegetable oils, together with an adequate intake of pancreatic extract, will prove satisfactory for many infants and, if well tolerated, should be continued until at least one year of age. Butterfat should be avoided because of its poor digestibility, and a daily supplement of fat-soluble vitamins should be given because of the possibility of their poor absorption from the diet. In the case of infants who receive as much as 4 gm of pancreatic extract at each feeding and continue to pass large, foul stools, the percentage of calories from fat may be reduced by adding 2 or 3 gm of skim milk powder to each 100 ml of formula. Parents should be cautioned against adding greater amounts of skim milk powder because of danger from excessive renal solute load.

When stools remain excessively large and foul with the management just outlined, it may be desirable to feed Portagen (Mead) as the major source of calories or to utilize Portagen for approximately one-half the caloric intake and a conventional formula to supply most of the remainder. Medium-chain triglycerides, the fat of Portagen, are known to reduce the extent of steatorrhea and to improve the character of the stools in patients with cystic fibrosis of the pancreas (Kuo and Huang, 1965). Increased rates of gain in weight and height have been observed after introduction of diets containing medium-chain triglycerides (Allan et al., 1973).

Regular administration of pancreatic extract and relatively simple modifications of the diet will often be sufficient to control steatorrhea and promote normal growth. In such instances, there is probably little need for regular monitoring with respect to nutritional status. However, in infants with steatorrhea, it is important to evaluate nutritional status at regular intervals. Among the most important measures are weight and length, prothrombin time, serum concentration of albumin and activity of alkaline phosphatase. During the first year of life, roentgenograms of the wrist should be made at approximately four-month intervals.

Infants more than one year of age should be fed diets providing 10 to 20 per cent of calories from protein and approximately 40 per cent of calories from fat. The greater part of the fat should be readily digestible. Intake of butterfat and other animal fats should be limited.

Vitamin Supplementation

Supplementation of the diet with the fat-soluble vitamins A, D, E and K is desirable. Although there may be malabsorption of vitamin B_{12}, pancreatic extract restores absorption of this vitamin to normal and supplementation seems to be unnecessary (Toskes et al., 1971).

Vitamin A. Supplementation with vitamin A is recommended at a daily dosage of 5000 to 10,000 I. U. of an oily preparation or, preferably, 2000 I.U. of a water-miscible preparation. Although concentration of vitamin A in serum is often low even with continuous supplementation, concentration of vitamin A in liver may be elevated (Underwood and Denning, 1972), probably because of reduced serum concentrations of retinol-binding protein (Smith et al., 1972), although impaired release from the liver may also be involved. Therefore, low serum concentrations of vitamin A are not necessarily an indication for increasing the level of fortification of the diet.

Vitamin D. Vitamin D is recommended at a daily dosage of 1000 I.U. Adjustment of dosage of vitamin D can be made on the basis of serum concentrations of calcium and phosphorus, activity of alkaline phosphatase and roentgenograms of the wrist.

Vitamin E. As discussed in Chapter 9, vitamin E deficiency is common in patients with cystic fibrosis of the pancreas. It may lead to histologic and biochemical abnormalities which respond to administration of vitamin E. A daily supplement of 1 mg of a water-miscible preparation of vitamin E per kilogram body weight will correct deficiency and prevent recurrence (Harries and Muller, 1971).

Vitamin K. Hemorrhagic disease due to deficiency of vitamin K is not uncommon in patients with cystic fibrosis of the pancreas who receive no supplementary vitamin K (Chapter 9). Hemorrhage may sometimes be the initial manifestation of the previously unsuspected disease in infants (Torstenson et al., 1970; Walters and Koch, 1972). It is suggested that during the first month of life a water-miscible preparation of vitamin K_1 be given daily by mouth or that 1 to 2 mg be given intramuscularly at one and two months of age. After two months of age, 1 mg of a water-soluble analogue of menadione should be given daily. One-stage prothrombin time should be determined at intervals of two months or less and dosage adjusted as necessary.

CELIAC DISEASE

As discussed in Chapter 17, celiac disease (gluten-induced enteropathy) is a malabsorption syndrome in which damage to the intestinal mucosa results from abnormal sensitivity to dietary gluten. The protein, gluten, comprises about 10 per cent by weight of flour made from wheat and rye and somewhat less in that made from barley and oats. On the basis of solubility in alcohol, wheat gluten may be separated into two fractions — glutenin and gliadin — of which only gliadin causes mucosal damage in susceptible individuals.

The immunologic mechanisms through which gliadin presumably exerts its damaging effects upon the mucosa, as well as the significance of circulating antibodies against gliadin and cow milk proteins, have been discussed in Chapter 17. Although the hypothesis that mucosal damage results from an inborn deficiency of intestinal peptidase(s) (Frazer, 1956) has long been discounted, evidence now available suggests that the hypothesis may deserve reconsideration (Cornell and Townley, 1973).

Although rare in the United States, the disease is relatively common in many other countries. Clinical picture, age at onset of symptoms and pathologic findings have been well described (Hamilton et al., 1969; Visakorpi et al., 1970a; Rubin, 1971; Shmerling and Zimmerli-Häring, 1971). Diagnosis requires biopsy of the small intestine. One biopsy should be obtained before initiation of dietary treatment and a second biopsy is desirable about six months later. If the diagnosis is correct and the gluten-free diet has been adhered to, the mucosa will at that time have become normal or at least will show marked improvement. Many authors require a gluten challenge with relapse of the intestinal mucosa as final proof of celiac disease.

Dietary management requires elimination of wheat and rye from the diet. Whether barley and oats must be eliminated remains controversial (Anderson et al., 1972). Initial management may require more extensive dietary restriction, especially in the case of severely malnourished patients. Temporary intolerance to lactose is common and temporary intolerance to fat is sometimes observed. Intolerance to cow milk may coexist with intolerance to wheat (Visakorpi and Immonen, 1967). The recommended diet should therefore be free of wheat and rye, probably free of barley and oats and should initially contain milk only if it is well tolerated. Because unabsorbed long-chain fatty acids may be converted to hydroxy fatty acids (Soong et al., 1972), which may produce diarrhea, dietary content of fat should be modest. Initially, this diet might consist primarily of a soy-based formula or a formula containing casein or a hydrolysate of casein (Chapter 15). Information regarding gluten content of beikost may be obtained from the manufacturer. Water-miscible preparations of fat-soluble vitamins should be given to correct deficiencies frequently present.

With abatement of symptoms after weeks or months of this restricted dietary regimen, milk and milk products may be cautiously introduced. However, gluten must continue to be excluded; even small amounts of gluten may cause relapse in susceptible individuals (Hamilton and McNeill, 1972). Although there is no consensus regarding the age at which gluten can be safely permitted (Visakorpi, 1970), it seems that restriction should continue at least during the preschool years, even if gluten does not cause symptoms. Several authors (Shmerling, 1969; Visakorpi et al., 1970b; Hamilton and McNeill, 1972) have shown that after prolonged treatment with a gluten-free diet, many patients will remain asymptomatic when receiving an unrestricted or partially restricted diet; however, in such patients mucosal damage frequently recurs.

PROTEIN-LOSING ENTEROPATHY

Proteins are normally secreted from plasma into the gastrointestinal tract where they are rapidly broken down by proteolytic enzymes, the component amino acids then being reabsorbed. In normal individuals, this process accounts for less than 10 per cent of the degradation of albumin (Kerr et al., 1967). If the amount of protein secreted into the intestinal tract is excessive and catabolism of serum proteins exceeds the synthetic capacity of the body, hypoproteinemia will result. Excessive secretion of proteins into the intestinal tract, known as protein-losing enteropathy, occurs in a wide variety of disease entities (Waldmann, 1966; Schussheim, 1972; Colon and Sandberg, 1973). Diagnosis of protein-losing enteropathy is based upon demonstration of excessive leakage into the gastrointestinal tract of parenterally administered proteins or synthetic macromolecules. Iodine-131-labeled polyvinylpyrrolidone (Gordon, 1959), chromium-51-labeled albumin (Waldmann, 1961) and copper-67-labeled ceruloplasmin have all been used for the diagnosis of gastrointestinal protein loss (Waldmann, 1966).

Symptomatic treatment—e.g., high-protein diet—will rarely, if ever, meet with success. Protein-losing enteropathy caused by celiac disease or milk allergy responds to specific dietary therapy. Protein-losing enteropathy associated with constrictive pericarditis (Plauth et al., 1964), Hirschsprung's disease, regional enteritis, Whipple's disease and a number of less frequently occurring conditions generally responds to appropriate surgical or medical treatment and does not require dietary intervention. The protein-losing enteropathy associated with intestinal lymphangiectasia responds to treatment with a diet low in long-chain fatty acids in which the greater part of fat consists of medium-chain triglycerides (Holt, 1964; Jeffries et al., 1964; Amirhakimi et al., 1969; Leyland et al., 1969).

EXTENSIVE BOWEL RESECTION

Survival of infants who have had major segments of bowel removed depends, to a considerable extent, on postoperative management. Nutritional support must be provided during a period in which the intestinal tract undergoes adaptive changes (Weser, 1971). It may take weeks to months before the bowel attains the absorptive capacity necessary to support growth. If this period is survived, a number of patients will eventually demonstrate normal growth and development with little evidence of absorptive defects (Lawler and Bernard, 1962; Benson et al., 1967; Wilmore et al., 1969).

Postoperative nutritional management requires provision of parenteral fluids, calories and electrolytes and, if the period exceeds a few days, of all other essential nutrients until such time as oral feedings will be tolerated. The introduction of total intravenous alimentation (Wilmore and Dudrick, 1968; Filler et al., 1969) has markedly improved chances of survival in patients in whom oral feeding cannot be instituted for prolonged periods of time. Reviews of this technique have been presented by Filler and Eraklis (1970) and by Heird et al. (1972). Administration of all nutrients parenterally has been carried out for periods as long as 400 days (Wilmore et al., 1969), although, in general, oral alimentation can be instituted much earlier.

Introduction of oral feedings is often followed by increased fecal loss of fluid and electrolytes. Therefore, the ratio of water to nutrients should initially be high and be reduced stepwise. Because disaccharides are usually absorbed poorly, most dietary carbohydrate should be provided as monosaccharides, e.g., glucose and/or fructose. In adult patients with massive bowel resections, replacement of dietary long-chain triglycerides by medium-chain triglycerides leads to marked diminution of steatorrhea and increased nitrogen retention (Winawer et al., 1966; Zurier et al., 1966; French, 1968; Pinter et al., 1969; Tandon et al., 1972); for infants, it also seems reasonable to provide the major portion of dietary fat in the form of medium-chain triglycerides. The formula, Pregestimil (Chapter 15, Table 15–10) may be useful. Whether feedings containing protein hydrolysates offer any advantage over those with intact proteins is unknown. As consistency of feces improves and satisfactory weight gain occurs, disaccharides and polysaccharides may gradually be introduced. Metabolic balance studies are useful as a guide to nutritional management.

Supplements of all vitamins must be given regularly and, if necessary, parenterally. In infants with ileal resection, particular attention must be paid to vitamin B_{12}. Supplemental iron should be given. Infants with bowel resections seem to be prone to development of magnesium deficiency (Booth et al., 1963; Atwell, 1966) and may require supplements of magnesium. Metabolic balance studies are of value in providing information regarding absorption of water, electrolytes, nitrogen, fat and other nutrients, thereby permitting adjustments to be made before deficiencies result in recognizable disturbances.

CONGENITAL HEART DISEASE

Infants with severe, chronic disease often present particularly difficult problems in nutritional management. Many of these problems may be illustrated by consideration of infants with congenital heart disease. One major difficulty—that of maintaining water balance in the face of necessity to utilize calorically concentrated feedings—has been discussed in Chapter 10. A more general discussion of nutritional management is presented here.

Basis of the Nutritional Problem

That retardation of growth is a common feature in infants with severe congenital heart disease has been amply documented in the literature (Mehrizi and Drash, 1962; Linde et al., 1967; Bayer and Robinson, 1969; Feldt et al., 1969); its anatomic features have been well described (Naeye, 1965, 1967). Growth retardation is observed both in acyanotic heart disease, especially in the presence of congestive failure, and in cyanotic heart disease. The ultimate cause of growth retardation must be sought in the hemodynamic alterations present in severe heart disease, with chronic hypoxia as at least one of the important pathogenetic factors (Pittman and Cohen, 1964); however, abnormally low food intake is frequently present.

Many affected infants seem unwilling or unable to accept volumes of feeding equal to those consumed by normal infants of similar size. Severe congenital heart disease is associated with tachypnea, and this breathlessness interferes with ability to suck. It has been demonstrated that forced feeding may lead to increased rates of growth (Krieger, 1970).

In addition to decreased food intake, patients with severe cardiac disease, especially those with congestive failure, may exhibit gastrointestinal absorptive defects (Pittman and Cohen, 1964; Puyau, 1969). In children and adults with hypoxemia due to pulmonary or cardiac disease, abnormal absorption of xylose was found to be correlated with degree of hypoxemia, and reverted to normal when normoxemia was restored (Milledge, 1972). In addition, patients with severe congenital heart disease are hypermetabolic – i.e., caloric expenditures per unit of body weight are greater than those of normal subjects (Lees et al., 1965; Levison et al., 1965; Krieger, 1970; Stocker et al., 1972). The degree of hypermetabolism is related to the extent of congestive failure, probably because of increased energy expenditures associated with tachypnea, and to the extent of growth retardation. Infants with growth retardation due to other causes also demonstrate increased energy expenditures per unit of body weight (Montgomery, 1962; Sinclair and Silverman, 1964; Krieger and Whitten, 1969).

Thus, while normal rates of growth may not be achieved even with unusually high caloric intakes, it is desirable to make every effort to provide adequate food intake. For these reasons, it is frequently necessary to utilize a diet of relatively high caloric density. Attention must then be paid to maintenance of water balance – a consideration of particular importance because water losses through the skin and lungs are often greater in patients with congenital heart disease than in normal subjects (Morgan and Nadas, 1963; Elliott and Cooke, 1968;

Puyau, 1969). In addition, gastrostomy feeding may be helpful in overcoming the infant's inability to take adequate amounts of food by mouth.

Characteristics of a Satisfactory Diet

Although it may not be possible to achieve a fully adequate intake of calories, an attempt should be made to achieve calorie intakes equal to the 50th percentile value for normal infants of similar size. All essential nutrients should be provided. Water balance must be maintained and this aspect of management will require particular attention during illness. To attain an adequate intake of protein without incurring an unnecessarily high renal solute load, 8 to 10 per cent of dietary calories should be supplied from protein, 35 to 50 per cent of calories from fat, and 35 to 65 per cent of calories from carbohydrate. All dietary components should be of high digestibility and sodium intake should not be excessive.

In the face of relatively low volumes of intake, it will not be possible to achieve a satisfactory calorie intake by feeding the 67 kcal/100 ml formulas commonly fed to normal infants. With good nutritional supervision, formulas supplying 100 kcal/100 ml can be safely fed. Commercially prepared strained foods of high caloric density are also available, but must be selected with care in order to avoid foods yielding a high renal solute load.

Foods other than formula will generally present a higher renal solute load per unit of protein intake than will formulas. It is therefore recommended that most of the dietary protein be derived from formula.

Two major types of formulas with approximately 9 per cent of calories from protein are commercially available. In one, nonfat milk solids provide the protein (e.g., Enfamil, Similac—Chapter 15, Table 15–7); in the other, most of the protein is supplied as partially demineralized whey (e.g., SMA, NAN—Chapter 15, Tables 15–6 and 15–7). The mineral content and, consequently, the renal solute load are somewhat less in formulas of the latter type (Chapter 10).

Digestibility of Diet. Although the renal solute load should be one major consideration in the choice of formula for feeding infants with congenital heart disease, other factors must also be considered. When a fat of relatively low digestibility is fed ad libitum to a normal infant, the infant will merely increase his intake to compensate for the fecal loss of fat (Chapter 7). In the case of the infant with congenital heart disease, an increased volume of intake may not be possible, and excessive fecal losses of fat will then be responsible for reduction in available calories. As discussed in Chapter 3, the greater part of calorie intake is used for maintenance; fecal loss of 10 per cent of calorie intake could amount to a relatively high percentage of residual calories not required for maintenance and therefore potentially available for growth. For this reason, formulas providing all or most of the fat in the form of butterfat are not recommended. Similarly, because of uncertainty regarding the ability of the infant to digest starch (Chapter 8), it seems desirable to avoid feeding cereals and starch-containing strained foods.

Sodium Content of Diet. The requirement of normal infants for sodium has been estimated to be slightly more than 2.5 meq/day during the first four months of life and slightly more than 2.1 meq/day between 4 and 12 months of age (Chapter 11). Corresponding advisable intakes of 8 and 6 meq/day have been suggested. In the case of the infant with congestive heart failure, intakes of sodium more than a few milliequivalents per day above the "advisable intake" (i.e., 7 to 8 meq/day) seem undesirable. Because the sodium content of cow milk is approximately 25 meq/liter and because many commercially prepared strained foods contribute substantial amounts of sodium (Chapter 16), it is apparent that unsupervised feeding may result in rather generous intakes of sodium. On the other hand, sodium is an essential nutrient and it is clearly necessary to include adequate amounts of it in the diet. Formulas such as Lonalac (Mead) and S-29 (Wyeth), which at normal dilution provide only about 1 meq of sodium per liter, are not recommended because of the hazards of sodium depletion.

Beikost. There would appear to be many more disadvantages than advantages in inclusion of beikost in the diet of the infant with congenital heart disease. Formula feeding alone will generally be more satisfactory than the combination of formula and beikost in providing calories and essential nutrients in adequate amounts and in highly digestible form with a minimum of renal solute load. Most commercially prepared strained foods are undesirable for the infant with congenital heart disease because of their content of starch or sodium or because they provide a relatively large renal solute load per unit of calories. Home-prepared foods commonly fed to infants may also be undesirable for the same reasons. There is, however, no objection to feeding modest amounts of applesauce or pureed pears, peaches or other fruits prepared in the home or commercially prepared without the addition of starch.

Evaluation of Nutritional Adequacy of Diet

Suggestions for assuring the maintenance of adequate water balance during management of infants with congenital heart disease have been presented in Chapter 10. The comments that follow concern other aspects of nutritional management and evaluation of growth.

Body weight should be recorded at frequent intervals. Because overhydration or even clinical evidence of edema will frequently be present, growth progress should be assessed at monthly intervals by measurements of length. The measurements should be made in a standardized fashion by trained personnel using proper equipment and techniques (Chapter 3). Two examiners are required for such measurements.

When gain in weight is less than the 25th percentile value for normal infants of similar sex and size (Chapter 3; Appendix II, p. 535), modification of the caloric concentration and/or composition of the formula will be desirable. The desirable nature of the modification may be indicated by the urinary concentration. When the concentration of the urine is less than 300 mosmol/liter (average concentration of two or three consecutively voided specimens), the concentration of the formula may be increased merely by increasing the proportion of commercially prepared concentrated liquid (133 kcal/100 ml) to water. When the concentration of the urine is greater than 300 mosmol/liter, the caloric density of the formula should be increased by the addition of fat and/or carbohydrate.

When caloric intake of an infant with congenital heart disease is greater than the 25th percentile for normal infants of similar size (Chapter 2, Tables 2–1 and 2–2) and the infant gains weight at less than the 25th percentile value (Chapter 3, Tables 3–4 and 3–5), it is desirable to carry out a three-day metabolic balance study. If it is found that excretion of fat is greater than 1 gm/kg/day, it may be desirable to replace a portion of the dietary fat with carbohydrate or medium-chain triglycerides. In a hospital setting, Portagen (Chapter 15, Table 15–10) may be employed as a source of medium-chain triglycerides, a satisfactory formula consisting of 60 per cent of the calories from a commercially prepared concentrated liquid (e.g., SMA – Chapter 15, Table 15–7), 30 per cent of the calories from Portagen and 10 per cent of the calories from corn syrup solids. However, for use in the home, formulas proposed for feeding at 100 kcal/100 ml or greater should not include powders that provide protein and electrolytes (as is true of Portagen) because of the danger of errors in formula preparation.

When infants are fed formulas that supply less than 8 per cent of calories from protein, serum concentration of albumin should be determined at intervals of one to two months.

NUTRITIONAL MANAGEMENT OF THE LOW-BIRTH-WEIGHT INFANT

As discussed in Chapter 3, weight gain from about the thirtieth through the thirty-sixth week of fetal life averages approximately 32 gm/day (Fig. 3–6). Gain in weight after about the thirty-sixth week of fetal life is less rapid, presumably because of relative inadequacy in placental transport of nutrients. Once the immediate adjustments to extrauterine life have been made during the first few days after birth, the normal fullterm infant demonstrates remarkably rapid gain in weight—e.g., the 50th percentile gain by males between 8 and 42 days of age is 38 gm/day (Table 3–4)—possibly representing catch-up growth. It therefore seems reasonable to speculate that the growth potential of the premature infant is sufficient to attain a rate of growth equal to that of the healthy fetus of similar gestational age. Low-birth-weight infants who have suffered intrauterine growth retardation may exhibit catch-up growth postnatally and gain more rapidly than 32 gm/day.

One goal in the nutritional management of low-birth-weight infants is the provision of nutrient intakes that will permit the infant to achieve a rate of growth approaching his potential.

For purposes of the discussion that follows, low birth weight is defined as birth weight less than 2500 gm.

Management During the First Week of Life

Parenteral administration of 1 mg of vitamin K (phytylmenaquinone) soon after birth is more important for the low-birth-weight than for the fullsize infant. Attention should then be directed toward satisfying the infant's needs for water and energy. Provision of other nutrients is somewhat less urgent.

It is evident that nutritional needs of the infant must be considered in the context of the extensive cardiorespiratory, renal and gastrointestinal adaptive changes that occur after birth. In addition, the infant may have experienced insults at birth, such as trauma or exposure to infection, and the effects of these insults are likely to complicate nutritional management. Provision of nutrients must therefore be individualized with particular attention to the size, maturity and state of health of the infant.

The feeding plans presented by Babson (1971) have been modified in several respects but form the basis for much of the following discussion. With respect to management during the first few days of life, three groups of infants may be distinguished, with body weights indicated merely as broad general guides: (1) Infants weighing more than 2000 gm at birth, and without evidence of respiratory distress or other disease; (2) infants weighing between 1500 and 2000 gm at birth, without evidence of respiratory distress or other disease, and able to suck; and (3) infants weighing less than 1500 gm at birth and larger infants with respiratory distress or other disease, or unable to suck.

During the first week (sometimes the first two or three weeks of life), volumes of food consumed will generally be relatively small and renal solute load must be a primary consideration in choice of formula. As discussed in Chapter 10, renal solute load is particularly likely to cause problems in water balance when the volume of intake is relatively low. For this reason, formula concentration will need to be adjusted in relation to the volume of intake.

Infants Weighing More Than 2000 gm at Birth and Without Evidence of Respiratory Distress or Other Disease. Such infants may generally be fed by bottle in about the same manner employed with fullsize infants. With certain precautions to be described, breast feeding is permissible. For reasons to be discussed, breast feeding is not recommended for infants with birth weights less than 2000 gm.

Infants Weighing Between 1500 and 2000 gm at Birth, Without Evidence of Respiratory Distress or Other Disease, and Able to Suck. At age four to six hours, 5 to 15 ml of distilled water are offered by nipple to test the feeding behavior. If this fluid is taken and retained, 5 to 15 ml of a 10 per cent solution of glucose are offered at three-hour intervals for two feedings. Thereafter, equal parts of a 10 per cent solution of glucose and 100 kcal/100 ml formula are offered at three-hour intervals, the size of the feeding being increased by 3 to 5 ml each day. Amounts of the glucose solution are replaced by formula in a stepwise fashion while monitoring urine osmolality, and attempting to maintain urine solute concentration between 300 and 400 mosmol/liter. By the fourth to sixth day, 140 ml/kg/day may often be fed and, at this intake, even with the relatively high concentration of protein suggested (see Formula Composition), 80 kcal/100 ml is unlikely to result in urine concentration greater than 400 mosmol/liter.

Infants Weighing Less Than 1500 gm at Birth and Larger Infants With Respiratory Distress or Other Disease, or Unable to Suck. Intravenous administration of fluids is begun on the first day of life to provide approximately 60 ml/kg/day, increasing by 10 or 20 ml/kg/day until a total intake of 120 ml/kg/day is reached. When gavage feedings are begun, the amount of fluid administered intravenously is decreased (Fig. 19–1). Each 100 ml of fluid administered intravenously should contain 10 gm of glucose, 2 meq of sodium, and 2 meq of potassium. Gavage feedings should be delivered by soft rubber or plastic tubing (size Fr. 8) at two- or three-hour intervals, beginning as early as the infant's condition permits.

Initially, distilled water, 2 or 3 ml/kg at a feeding, should be introduced after careful aspiration of the stomach contents. If the aspirate is less than 2 ml three hours after the second or third gastric instillation of distilled water, formula should be substituted for the distilled water in subsequent feedings. Formula concentration should be 100 kcal/100 ml. A discussion of some desirable characteristics of

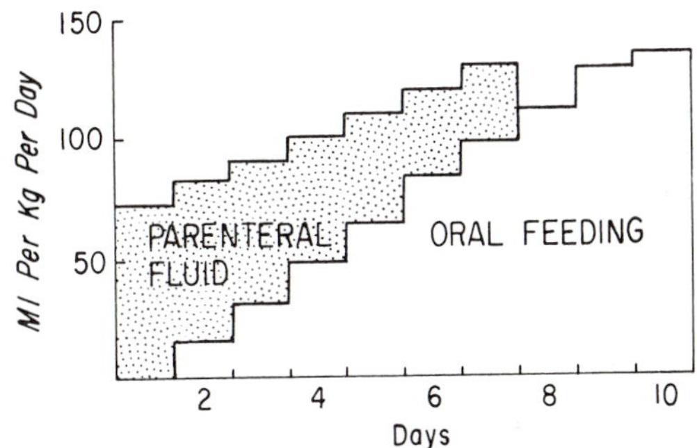

Figure 19–1 Schema of combined parenteral and oral feeding for a newborn infant weighing less than 1500 gm at birth and with poor ability to suck. As the quantity delivered orally is increased, the amount delivered parenterally may be decreased. Individualization of management is necessary. (From Babson, S. G.: Feeding the low-birth-weight infant. J. Pediatr. *79*:694, 1971.)

the formula will be presented subsequently. The volume of gavage feedings should be increased each day by 1 to 2 ml/kg (i.e., with eight feedings, an increase of 8 to 16 ml/kg/day). Feedings should be temporarily discontinued if the gastric residual is greater than 2 to 4 ml, depending on the size of the infant, or if distention, regurgitation, diarrhea or cyanotic episodes are noted.

When gavage feedings reach 100 ml/kg/day, urine osmolality should be monitored as the volume of intravenously administered fluid is decreased. Urine osmolality should be maintained below 400 mosmol/liter (Chapter 10). When administration of fluids intravenously is discontinued, formula concentration should be reduced to 80 kcal/100 ml if oral intakes are less than 140 ml/kg/day.

Need for Individualization of Management. As already mentioned, the weight ranges utilized in the classification just presented are meant only as rough guides. Some infants weighing 1800 gm will be vigorous, demonstrate good suck and may be managed in a manner quite similar to that of the fullsize infant except that breast feeding is not recommended. Depending on vigor, the infants small for gestational age may be managed either according to size as previously described or, more commonly, as the large premature infants in good condition. Because of the frequency of hypoglycemia in these infants, it is desirable to monitor the concentration of glucose in the blood; such monitoring can be done with Dextrostix (Ames). If hypoglycemia is detected, intravenous administration of a glucose solution is indicated.

Supplementation With Vitamins and Iron. Vitamin supplementation should ordinarily be initiated by the third day of life. Commercially prepared formulas that supply adequate intakes of vitamins for the fullsize infant may supply inadequate amounts for the low-birth-weight infant because of the small quantity of formula consumed. In the absence of specific information on the vitamin requirements of low-birth-weight infants, it seems reasonable to offer the same amounts of vitamins recommended for fullsize infants (Chapter 9, Table 9–2).

By the time the infant begins to gain weight, the diet should be supplemented with iron. When gain in weight is less than 20 gm/day, an intake of 5 to 10 mg/day of iron from ferrous sulfate or from another well-absorbed iron salt (Chapter 12) is adequate. When weight gain exceeds 20 gm/day, a daily intake of 15 mg of iron is advised.

Management After the First Week of Life

In the case of infants with particularly limited stomach capacity, lack of vigor, respiratory distress or other neonatal difficulty, the management outlined for the first week of life may extend well into the second or third week of life.

From the discussion in Chapter 6, it is evident that the infant who is growing slowly will have a relatively low requirement for protein per unit of calorie intake. The greater the rate of growth in relation to body size, the greater will be the protein requirement per unit of calorie intake. Somewhat similar relations apply to various other nutrients. Thus, the infants of lowest birth weight who demonstrate the least evidences of neonatal difficulty and gain weight rapidly are likely to be the ones presenting the greatest quantitative differences from fullsize infants with respect to nutritional requirements. As discussed in Chapter 10, protein and minerals contribute most of the renal solute load. Requirements for these nutrients are likely to be high, and a satisfactory formula must provide adequate intakes of all nutrients without providing an unnecessarily high renal solute load.

Requirements for Protein and Minerals. Because a relatively large proportion of the requirements of the low-birth-weight infant for protein and for various minerals is accounted for by the requirements for growth, it is necessary to obtain some estimate of the chemical composition of weight gain by low-birth-weight infants. If one assumes that growth of the prematurely born infant is qualitatively and quantitatively similar to that of the fetus, data on the chemical composition of weight gained in utero may be useful in estimating nutrient needs for growth. Utilizing the data of Widdowson and Dickerson (1964) from whole body chemical analyses of stillborn infants, we have calculated the chemical composition of the gain in weight of a hypothetic fetus, the "reference fetus." As may be seen in Table 19–4, fat accounts for an estimated 3, 14 and 35 per cent, respectively, of the 500, 1000 and 1000 gm increments in body weight between 1000 and 1500, 1500 and 2500, and 2500 and 3500 gm. These percentages are less than the estimated 41.6 per cent of gain accounted for by fat in the fullsize infant between birth and four months of age (Chapter 3, Fig. 3–9 and Table 3–13).

TABLE 19–4 COMPOSITION OF GAIN OF REFERENCE FETUS

Body Weight (gm)	Gestational Age (weeks)	Estimated Content/100 gm of Gain*						Caloric Cost† (kcal/100 gm)
		Protein (gm)	*Fat (gm)*	*Water (gm)*	*Sodium (meq)*	*Potassium (meq)*	*Calcium (gm)*	
1000–1500	27–30	15.0	3	80	6.8	4.4	0.96	150
1500–2500	30–35	12.6	14	71	6.6	4.4	0.88	260
2500–3500	35–40	11.4	35	51	4.3	4.2	0.98	490

*Calculated from data of Widdowson and Dickerson (1964).
†Assuming that 7.5 kcal is required for deposition of each gram of protein and 11.6 kcal for deposition of each gram of fat (Chapter 3).

Requirement for Protein

As discussed in Chapter Six, in the fullsize infant the portion of the protein requirement that cannot be accounted for by the increment in body protein amounts to approximately 0.95 gm/kg/day. Assuming that this value also applies to the low-birth-weight infant, the protein requirement of a hypothetic 1250 gm infant gaining 20 gm/day may be calculated. The increment in body protein is approximately 3.0 gm/day (20 gm/day times 15 per cent protein), and the remainder of the protein requirement would be approximately 1.2 gm/day (0.95 gm/kg/day times 1.25 kg). Assuming absorption of nitrogen to be 95 per cent of intake, the total protein requirement of this hypothetic infant may be estimated to be 4.4 gm/day (Table 19–5). Assuming that the total calorie intake which will permit a gain in weight of 20 gm/day is 155 kcal/day (Table 19–5), the protein requirement may be estimated to be 2.8 gm/100 kcal.

In this regard, the data of Davidson et al. (1967) concerning low-birth-weight infants fed 120 kcal/kg/day and various concentrations of protein are of interest. In several studies of infants weighing 1000 to 1499 gm, those fed 2 gm of protein per kilogram per day (1.7 gm/100 kcal) generally exhibited mean gains in weight of 15 to 17 gm/day, whereas those fed 4 gm of protein per kilogram per day (3.3 gm/100 kcal) generally exhibited mean gains of approximately 23 gm/day. When these infants had attained body weights of approximately 2300 gm, serum concentration of total protein averaged 6.6 gm/100 ml for 31 infants fed 3.3 gm protein/100 kcal and 5.8 gm/100 ml for 22 infants fed 1.7 gm protein/100 kcal. These data suggest that an intake of protein of 1.7 gm/100 kcal is inadequate for infants with birth weights of 1000 to 1499 gm.

Table 19–5 also includes estimates of protein requirements of 2000 and 3000 gm infants. It may be seen that the protein requirement is estimated to be 2.2 gm/100 kcal for the 2000 gm infant and 1.6 gm/100 kcal for the 3000 gm infant. Because of the uncertainty of such estimates of requirements, it is generally desirable to set a value for advisable intake somewhat above the estimated requirement. In the case of the fullsize infant, the advisable intake has been set at a value 20 per cent greater than the estimated requirement (Chapter 6), and we suggest that the advisable intake for low-birth-weight infants weighing more than 1500 gm be set at approximately 30 per cent above the estimated requirement: 2.8 gm/100 kcal for infants with weights between 1500 and 2500 gm and 2.1 gm/100 kcal for infants with weights between 2500 and 3500 gm. For infants weighing less than 1500 gm, we suggest that the advisable intake be the same as the estimated requirement, a compromise that we believe desirable because of considerations of renal solute load. Thus, an advisable intake

TABLE 19–5 ESTIMATED DAILY REQUIREMENTS OF HYPOTHETIC PREMATURE INFANTS OF VARIOUS WEIGHTS

		Estimated Daily Requirements*									
		Protein				*Calcium*			*Energy*		
				Total			*Total*				
Body Weight	Assumed Gain in Weight (gm/day)	*Growth (gm)*	*Non-growth (gm)*	*(gm)*	*(gm/100 kcal)*	*Growth (mg)*	*(mg)*	*(mg/100 kcal)*	*Growth (kcal)*	*Non-growth (kcal)*	*Total (kcal)*
1250	20	3.0	1.2	4.4	2.8	192	480	310	30	110	155
2000	30	3.8	1.9	6.0	2.2	264	660	246	78	163	268
3000	30	3.4	2.8	6.6	1.6	294	734	176	147	228	417

*Requirements for protein and calcium for growth are based on the assumption that weight gained is of the composition indicated in Table 19–4. Energy requirements per unit of weight gain are assumed to be as indicated in Table 19–4. For needs other than those for growth ("nongrowth"), requirements for protein are assumed to be 0.95 gm/kg/day, requirements for calcium are assumed to be insignificant in relation to requirements for growth, and requirements for energy are assumed to be 88, 82 and 76 kcal/kg/day, respectively, for infants weighing 1000 to 1500 gm, 1500 to 2500 gm and for those weighing more than 2500 gm. In estimating total requirements for protein, calcium and energy, it is assumed that 95 per cent of nitrogen, 40 per cent of calcium and 90 per cent of calories are absorbed.

of protein of 2.8 gm/100 kcal is suggested for all infants weighing less than 2500 gm, and 2.1 gm/100 kcal is suggested for these infants during their later management from the time they reach a weight of 2500 gm until they achieve a weight of 3500 gm.

At the same ratio of protein to calorie intake, it is evident that infants with birth weights between 2000 and 2500 gm are at less risk of developing protein deficiency than are smaller infants. Although human milk is inadequate in content of protein and various minerals for the needs of the 2000 to 2500 gm infant and may provide a somewhat excessive lactose load, other advantages of breast feeding may outweigh the disadvantages. When infants with birth weights between 2000 and 2500 gm are breastfed, it is recommended that one or two bottle feedings be given each day to supplement the intake of protein and minerals. For this purpose, it is reasonable to utilize a soy-isolate formula (Chapter 15, Table 15–9) or Nutramigen (Table 15–10). Either of these types of formulas may be supplemented with skim milk powder to yield a final concentration of 100 kcal/100 ml and 4.0 to 4.5 gm protein/100 ml.

Requirement for Calcium

The difficulties likely to be encountered in achieving adequate intakes of minerals may be illustrated by consideration of requirement for calcium. Utilizing the data in Table 19–4 on calcium content of gain in weight and assuming that 40 per cent of dietary calcium is absorbed, an estimate of the daily requirement for calcium may be made (Table 19–5). Thus, for a gain of 20 gm/day, a 1.25 kg infant would require 310 mg of calcium/100 kcal, and a 2.0 kg infant gaining 30 gm/day would require 246 mg of calcium/100 kcal. Whether a satisfactory formula with this ratio of calcium to calories could be made is unknown.

Fat-free milk solids provide approximately 33 mg of calcium per gram of protein and a formula with protein content of 2.8 gm/100 kcal supplied from fat-free milk solids would provide 94 mg of calcium/100 kcal. The formula would therefore need to be supplemented with 204 mg of calcium/100 kcal in order to achieve the estimated requirement. Supplementation to this extent might prove technologically impossible. Thus, some undermineralization of the skeleton might be inevitable. Unquestionably, provision of an adequate intake of readily absorbable calcium (and other minerals) is one of the major nutritional problems in management of the low-birth-weight infant.

From what has been said, it is evident that human milk (calcium content, 45 mg/100 kcal) and such formulas as Similac, Enfamil (calcium content, 88 mg/100 kcal) and SMA (calcium content, 66 mg/100 kcal) provide only a fraction of the estimated calcium requirement of the low-birth-weight infant.

Formula Composition. No commercially available formula is completely satisfactory for management of the low-birth-weight infant. It may be appreciated that the smaller the infant and the more rapid the rate of growth, the greater will be the need for a formula specifically designed to meet the needs of the low-birth-weight infant. The discussion that follows will consider some of the characteristics of a satisfactory formula for infants with birth weights less than 2500 gm. These are offered in the hope that they may be considered by manufacturers and may be of some value to physicians who wish to modify commercially available formulas to make them more suitable for management of low-birth-weight infants.

The formula should be relatively generous in content of protein and minerals and modest in content of lactose. Formula concentration should be 80 to 100 kcal/100 ml. Fat, calcium and phosphorus should all be readily absorbable. Such a formula might be prepared from fat-free milk solids, corn syrup solids and vegetable oils or a mixture of lard and vegetable oils with or without medium-chain triglycerides. It seems desirable to supply approximately 11 per cent of calories from protein (i.e., 2.8 gm/100 kcal). Utilizing readily absorbable fats, it should be possible to provide 50 per cent of calories from fat without provoking steatorrhea. To avoid an excessive intake of lactose, it is suggested that one-half to two-thirds of the carbohydrate be lactose, and the remainder, corn syrup solids. As already mentioned, such a formula would supply only 94 mg of calcium/100 kcal unless additional calcium were included.

Monitoring for Safety. Because a formula of sufficient caloric concentration and one that provides an adequate intake of all nutrients may provide an excessive renal solute load for some infants, thoughtful individualization of management and careful monitoring of clinical progress and urinary osmolality are necessary.

Although a formula made to the general specifications will be safe for most infants receiving 140 kcal/kg/day, lesser intakes of the formula are likely to provide an excessive renal solute load in relation to water available for excretion. Monitoring of the urine osmolality and serum concentration of urea will be necessary. If the concentration of the urine is consistently greater than 400 mosmol/liter, the volume of intake should be increased or the caloric concentration of the formula should be reduced. If the serum concentration of urea is greater than 30 mg/100 ml but the urine concentration is less than 400 mosmol/liter, the formula should be diluted with carbohydrate (glucose, sucrose or corn syrup solids rather than lactose) and/or medium-chain triglycerides.

MALNUTRITION DURING INFANCY AND LATER INTELLECTUAL CAPABILITY

Throughout the world, a large proportion of individuals suffer during at least some period of infancy or childhood from calorie undernutrition and/or from deficiency of one or more essential nutrients, especially protein. Subsequently, many of these individuals demonstrate subnormal mental function which persists throughout life. However, as stated by Frisch (1970), there is at present no conclusive evidence that malnutrition in infancy per se *causes* permanent mental retardation.

Subnormal mental function has multiple causes, including genetic endowment, non-genetic prenatal factors and postnatal factors. The difficulty in determining whether postnatal malnutrition interferes with attainment of maximum intellectual potential will be evident from study of Figure 19–2. The box in the center of this figure is meant to suggest that abnormal behavior and abnormal brain development are inseparable. Presumably, abnormal behavior can come about only through structural, biochemical or neurophysiologic abnormalities of the brain, abnormalities that may be too subtle to be detected by current methods of investigation. As indicated in the lower portion

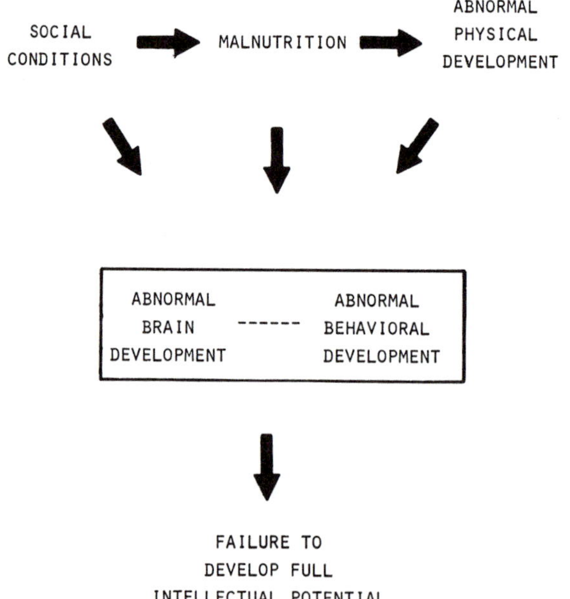

Figure 19–2 Schematic diagram indicating the relation of social conditions and malnutrition to mental development. For discussion, see text.

of the figure, the complex of abnormal brain development-abnormal behavior may be responsible for failure of an individual to achieve his full intellectual potential.

Although malnutrition is frequently the result of social conditions, social conditions alone in the absence of malnutrition may lead to the complex of abnormal brain development-abnormal behavior with consequent failure to achieve full intellectual potential. In most instances, it will therefore be impossible to determine whether failure to achieve full intellectual potential is the result of adverse social conditions alone, of malnutrition alone or of a combination of adverse social conditions and malnutrition.

Complexity of Problem Illustrated by Animal Studies

Because malnutrition and adverse social conditions nearly always coincide in human subjects, investigations of experimental animals have great appeal. Nevertheless, it should not be imagined that use of experimental animals affords clear distinction between the effects of malnutrition and of other environmental factors. Various interactions between factors influencing early development and later behavior of rats have been discussed by Fraňková (1972):

> *. . . the animal grows in a specific psychological and social situation, conditioned by mother, composition of a family, by the individuality of litter-mates and nearest environment. From the beginning, it receives a scale of stimuli, it enters into relations with litter-mates, earns first experiences, which are preconditions of further attitudes, motivations and ways of responding to adverse stimuli in the future. The time from birth to weaning is considered as the most relevant period. In rats, the first 2 weeks of postnatal life are critical developmental periods, in which the organism is most sensitive to external stimuli. During this period the young rat is highly dependent upon mother and littermates. The nest, its thermal and tactual conditions, and the close environment become the sources of its first experience. Variables such as nutrition, mother and external environment make an intricate complex of early influences. To understand better the role of nutrition in development and later behaviour, interactions among all these factors need to be taken into account.*

A schema (Fig. 19–3) indicates the probable relation between a number of these factors.

The complexity of the problem may be appreciated from results of an experiment combining variations in litter size in rats with the presence or absence of early stimulation in the form of daily handling. It has been known for a number of years (Kennedy, 1957) that rats nursed in small litters are relatively large at weaning, whereas those

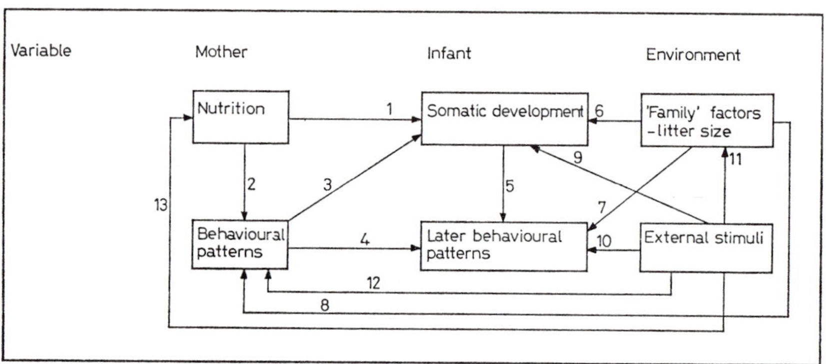

Figure 19–3 Interactions between factors determining the early development and later behavior of rats. (From Fraňková, S.: Influence of nutrition and early experience on behaviour of rats. A review. Bibl. Nutr. Diet. No. 17, pp. 96–110 [Karger, Basel 1972].)

nursed in large litters are relatively small at weaning. These observations have been confirmed and extended by numerous investigators, and it is now known that (1) with ad libitum feeding of identical diets after weaning, the difference in size between rats that have been nursed in large or small litters persists and, in fact, increases; (2) increase in cell number (as reflected by DNA content) and myelination (reflected by content of myelin lipids) proceed more rapidly in brains of the more rapidly growing animals (those nursed in small litters); (3) exploratory behavior is greater among the more rapidly growing rats nursed in small litters (Lát et al., 1960).

These findings have generally been attributed to the greater milk supply available to the animals nursed in small litters; however, it is apparent that from several points of view the environment of a rat pup in a small litter differs from that in a large litter. Other studies have demonstrated that rats which were handled each day during infancy perform differently as adults in various physiologic and behavioral tests than do rats which were not handled or were handled only after weaning (Altman, 1970). Rats handled before weaning have been found subsequently to be more resistant to deprivation of food and water, to be "less emotional" and to respond better to learning tasks than is true of unhandled animals. Handled animals could also be distinguished from unhandled controls on the basis of various endocrinologic tests.

The study of Fraňková (1972) concerning effects of handling on modification of the effects of litter size is of particular interest. Rats were reared in litters of 4, 9, 13 or 17. Each day from soon after birth until weaning at 28 days of age, the pups from one-half of the litters were weighed and handled. Pups from the other litters were not handled and were not intentionally stimulated; however, inadvertent stimulation resulted from such disturbances as feeding the animals and cleaning the cages. After weaning, the animals were all fed the same diet ad libitum. From 91 to 110 days of age, the mean number of standing-up reactions (one index of activity) of rats in the various groups was determined.

As may be seen in Figure 19–4, among the rats that had not been handled during infancy, the number of standing-up reactions decreased as litter size increased. The mean number of standing-up reactions of the rats that had been handled during infancy was greater for each litter size than that of rats not handled during infancy. Among rats that had not been handled during infancy, the mean number of standing-up reactions was greater for those raised in litters of 4 than for those raised in litters of 13. However, among rats that had been handled during infancy, the mean number of standing-up reactions was greater for those raised in litters of 13. Thus, the experiment dem-

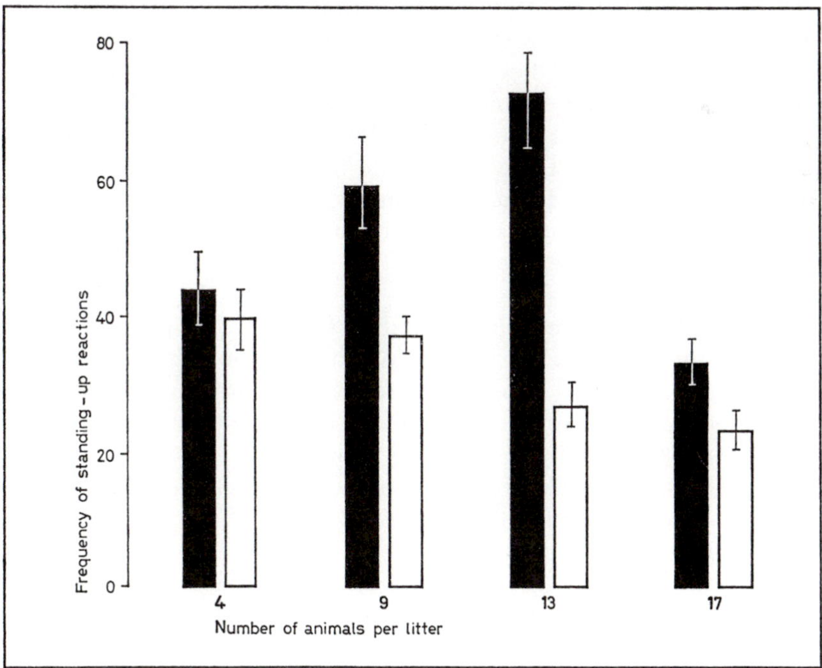

Figure 19–4 Exploratory activity of 91- to 110-day-old rats that were stimulated *(black columns)* or unstimulated *(white columns)* during the preweaning period. Plus and minus one standard error of the mean are indicated. (From Fraňková, S.: Influence of nutrition and early experience on behaviour of rats. A review. Bibl. Nutr. Diet. No. 17, pp. 96–110 [Karger, Basel 1972].)

onstrated that stimulation during infancy was sufficient to reverse the effect of litter size with respect to at least one behavioral measurement.

Whether the effect of litter size on difference in later performance of unhandled rat pups was primarily the result of differences in nutritional status during infancy is, of course, unknown. If one assumes that undernutrition of rats raised in large litters and not handled was primarily responsible for their lesser exploratory activity as adults, it is apparent that stimulation in the form of handling during infancy was more than able to compensate for the early difference in nutritional status.

Behavioral Abnormalities Versus Learning Ability. That behavioral abnormalities can be demonstrated in adult animals which were malnourished during infancy does not necessarily imply decreased learning ability of these animals. The behavioral abnormalities of both rats and pigs after recovery from malnutrition appear to be fear of a new environment, elevated level of excitement under conditions of stress ("greater emotionality") and inability to inhibit responses once they have been established (Barnes et al., 1970). However, in pigs that had been undernourished during infancy and demonstrated these behavioral abnormalities as adults, performance in a shock avoidance task was found by Barnes et al. (1970) to be similar to that of control animals which had not been malnourished. Similarly, in studies of adult mice that had been malnourished during infancy, Howard and Granoff (1968) were able to demonstrate no lasting impairment in learning a maze. In fact, males that had been undernourished during infancy performed better than did control males in learning a delayed response test. Such animal studies indicate the complexity of the area of investigation and the need for caution in interpreting observations of human subjects.

Difficulty in Developing Suitable Controls. In attempting to employ animal models for gaining insight into the relation between early malnutrition and subsequent mental performance, it must be recognized that the experimental design employed for production of malnutrition will usually, if not always, alter other environmental factors as well as food intake. In addition, we must consider both the relevance of the animal model and the suitability of the test chosen to evaluate performance.

Production of malnutrition in rats between birth and weaning has generally been accomplished by nursing in large litters, by infrequent feeding of the young or by utilizing malnourished dams or malnourished foster dams to nurse the young. Each of these approaches results in important changes in the environment. Apart from availability of food, the rat pup in a small litter is in a different environment from the one in a larger litter. Similarly, rat pups constantly with the dam are in a different environment from that of pups separated from the dam except at times of feeding. Widely spaced meals produce nutritional results that differ remarkably from results of feeding the same diet more frequently (Fábry and Tepperman, 1970). Finally, it has been shown that a malnourished dam may behave differently toward her pups than does a well nourished dam (Fraňková, 1971).

Of particular importance is consideration of the relevance of the animal model to each question that is asked. It is well recognized that the brain is morphologically and functionally heterogeneous and, within it, growth sequences take place at different times and different rates in various tracts and regions (Winick et al., 1972a and b; Dobbing and Sands, 1973). Each species differs in the timing of these growth sequences. Thus, a postnatal nutritional insult may have an effect in one species that cannot be produced in another.

Speculation Relative to the Human

By analogy with animal studies, we may assume that when malnutrition of sufficient severity is induced sufficiently early in life, permanent decreases in cellularity and myelination of the brain and long-lasting behavioral abnormalities, including decrease in learning ability, result (Barnes, 1972). It is therefore inviting to speculate that severe malnutrition during early infancy may result in subnormal mental development. However, as pointed out by Barnes (1972), even though instances exist in which biochemical changes in brains of experimental animals seem to correlate with functional changes, as manifested by altered behavior and learning, this is not proof of a causal relation between the two. Similarly, a number of studies have demonstrated that children who had been severely malnourished during infancy exhibit inferior levels of cognitive performance that seem to limit their ability to profit from school exposure (Cravioto, 1971). The inferior performance of previously malnourished children is evident even in comparison with performance of siblings but, as emphasized by Cravioto (1971), "the use of siblings as a comparison group does not prove a causal relationship between malnutrition and mental competence."

Thus, there is considerable reason to *suspect* that severe and long-lasting malnutrition during early infancy may have permanent effects on mental capability, but there is as yet no proof. The Subcommittee on Nutrition, Brain Development and Behavior, Food and Nutrition Board (1973), has stated: "At present, it is impossible to say whether malnutrition, *per se*, contributes more or less to the depressed cognitive development of previously malnourished children than do unfortunate social and environmental conditions." One might state further, as has Frisch (1970), that, in fact, there is no conclusive evidence that malnutrition causes permanent mental retardation.

REFERENCES

Abdel Kader, M. M., Abdel Hay, A., El-Safouri, S., Abdel Aziz, M. T., Saad El-Din, J., Kamal, I., Hefnawi, F., Ghoneim, M., Talaat, M., Younis, N., Tagui, A., and Abdalla, M.: Clinical, biochemical, and experimental studies on lactation. III. Biochemical changes induced in human milk by gestagens. Amer. J. Obstet. Gynec. *105*:978, 1969.

Allan, J. D., Mason, A., and Moss, A. D.: Nutritional supplementation in treatment of cystic fibrosis of the pancreas. Amer. J. Dis. Child. *126*:22, 1973.

Altman, J.: Postnatal neurogenesis and the problem of neural plasticity. *In* Himwich, W. E. (ed.): Developmental Neurobiology. Springfield, Ill., Charles C Thomas, 1970, p. 197.

Amirhakimi, G.-H., Samloff, I. M., Bryson, M. F., and Forbes, G. B.: Intestinal lymphangiectasia. Metabolic studies. Amer. J. Dis. Child. *117*:178, 1969.

Anderson, C. M., Gracey, M., and Burke, V.: Coeliac disease. Some still controversial aspects. Arch. Dis. Child. *47*:292, 1972.

Anderson, J. A. D., and Gatherer, A.: Hygiene of infant-feeding utensils. Practices and standards in the home. Br. Med. J. *2*:20, 1970.

Atwell, J. D.: Magnesium deficiency following neonatal surgical procedures. J. Pediatr. Surg. *1*:427, 1966.

Babson, S. G.: Feeding the low-birth-weight infant. J. Pediatr. *79*:694, 1971.

Barnes, R. H.: Introductory remarks. Points of concern with current interpretations of the effects of early malnutrition on mental development. Bibl. Nutr. Diet. *17*:1, 1972.

Barnes, R. H., Moore, A. U., and Pond, W. G.: Behavioral abnormalities in young adult pigs caused by malnutrition in early life. J. Nutr. *100*:149, 1970.

Barsivala, V. M., and Virkar, K. D.: The effect of oral contraceptives on concentrations of various components of human milk. Contraception *7*:307, 1973.

Bayer, L. M., and Robinson, S. J.: Growth history of children with congenital heart defects. Amer. J. Dis. Child. *117*:564, 1969.

Benson, C. D., Lloyd, J. R., and Krabbenhoft, K. L.: The surgical and metabolic aspects of massive small bowel resection in the newborn. J. Pediatr. Surg. *2*:227, 1967.

Booth, C. C., Babouris, N., Hanna, S., and MacIntyre, I.: Incidence of hypomagnesaemia in intestinal malabsorption. Br. Med. J. *2*:141, 1963.

Browder, A. A., Joselow, M. M., and Louria, D. B.: The problem of lead poisoning. Medicine *52*:121, 1973.

Chung, A. W.: The effect of oral feeding at different levels on the absorption of foodstuffs in infantile diarrhea. J. Pediatr. *33*:1, 1948.

Colon, A. R., and Sandberg, D. H.: Protein-losing enteropathy in children. Southern Med. J. *66*:641, 1973.

Comly, H. H.: Cyanosis in infants caused by nitrates in well water. J.A.M.A. *129*:112, 1945.

Committee on Nutrition, American Academy of Pediatrics: Infant methemoglobinemia. The role of dietary nitrate. Pediatrics *46*:475, 1970.

Cooke, R. E.: Parenteral fluid therapy. *In* Nelson, W. E., Vaughan, V. C., III, and McKay, R. J. (eds.): Textbook of Pediatrics. 9th ed. Philadelphia, W. B. Saunders Co., 1969, p. 217.

Cornblath, M., and Hartmann, A. F.: Methemoglobinemia in young infants. J. Pediatr. *33*:421, 1948.

Cornell, H. J., and Townley, R. R. W.: Investigation of possible intestinal peptidase deficiency in coeliac disease. Clin. Chim. Acta *43*:113, 1973.

Cravioto, J.: Infant malnutrition and later learning. *In* Margen, S. (ed.): Progress in Human Nutrition. Vol. 1. Westport, Conn., Avi Publishing Co., 1971, p. 80.

Davidson, M.: Intractable diarrhea. *In* Gellis, S. S., and Kagan, B. M. (eds.): Current Pediatric Therapy. 6th ed. Philadelphia, W. B. Saunders Co., 1973, p. 194.

Davidson, M., Levine, S. Z., Bauer, C. H., and Dann, M.: Feeding studies in low-birth-weight infants. I. Relationships of dietary protein, fat, and electrolyte to rates of weight gain, clinical courses, and serum chemical concentrations. J. Pediatr. *70*:695, 1967.

di Sant' Agnese, P. A.: Cystic fibrosis. *In* Gellis, S. S., and Kagan, B. M. (eds.): Current Pediatric Therapy. 6th ed. Philadelphia, W. B. Saunders Co., 1973, p. 229.

Dobbing, J., and Sands, J.: Quantitative growth and development of human brain. Arch. Dis. Child. *48*:757, 1973.

Elliott, D. A., and Cooke, R. E.: Insensible weight loss in normal children and cardiacs. *In* Cheek, D. B.: Human Growth. Philadelphia, Lea & Febiger, 1968, p. 494.

Fábry, P., and Tepperman, J.: Meal frequency—a possible factor in human pathology. Amer. J. Clin. Nutr. *23*:1059, 1970.

Feldt, R. H., Stickler, G. B., and Weidman, W. H.: Growth of children with congenital heart disease. Amer. J. Dis. Child. *117*:573, 1969.

Filler, R. M., and Eraklis, A. J.: Care of the critically ill child: intravenous alimentation. Pediatrics *46*:456, 1970.

Filler, R. M., Eraklis, A. J., Rubin, V. G., and Das, J. B.: Long-term total parenteral nutrition in infants. New Eng. J. Med. *281*:589, 1969.

Fischer, C. C., and Whitman, M. A.: Simplified method of infant feeding: bacteriologic and clinical study. J. Pediatr. *55*:116, 1959.

Fomon, S. J., Filer, L. J., Jr., Thomas, L. N., and Rogers, R. R.: Growth and serum chemical values of normal breastfed infants. Acta Paediatr. Scand. (Suppl. 202), 1970.

Fomon, S. J., Thomas, L. N., Cerny, J., and Morris, R. L.: (Letter to the Editor.) Bacterial counts of formulas prepared by mothers. J. Pediatr. *55*:122, 1959.

Fraňková, S.: Relationship between nutrition during lactation and maternal behaviour of rats. Activ. Nerv. Sup. *13*:1, 1971.

Fraňková, S.: Influence of nutrition and early experience on behaviour of rats. Bibl. Nutr. Diet. *17*:96, 1972.

Frazer, A. C.: On the growth defect in coeliac disease. Proc. Roy. Soc. Med. *49*:1009, 1956.

French, A. B.: Effects of graded increments of medium chain triglycerides on nutrient balance in subjects with intestinal resection. *In* Senior, J. B. (ed): Medium Chain Triglycerides. Philadelphia, University of Pennsylvania Press, 1968, p. 109.

Frisch, R. E.: Present status of the supposition that malnutrition causes permanent mental retardation. Amer. J. Clin. Nutr. *23*:189, 1970.

Gatherer, A., and Wood, N.: Home standards of sterilization of infant feeding bottles and teats. Monthly Bull. Minist. Health *25*:126, 1966.

Gordon, R. S., Jr.: Exudative enteropathy. Abnormal permeability of the gastrointestinal tract demonstrable with labelled polyvinylpyrrolidone. Lancet *1*:325, 1959.

Hamilton, J. R., Lynch, M. J., and Reilly, B. J.: Active coeliac disease in childhood. Quart. J. Med. *38*:135, 1969.

Hamilton, J. R., and McNeill, L. K.: Childhood celiac disease: response of treated patients to a small uniform daily dose of wheat gluten. J. Pediatr *81*:885, 1972.

Harries, J. T., and Muller, D. P. R.: Absorption of different doses of fat soluble and water miscible preparations of vitamin E in children with cystic fibrosis. Arch. Dis. Child. *46*:341, 1971.

Heird, W. C., Driscoll, J. M., Jr., Schullinger, J. N., Grebin, B., and Winters, R. W.: Intravenous alimentation in pediatric patients. J. Pediatr. *80*:351, 1972.

Hirschhorn, N., McCarthy, B. J., Ranney, B., Hirschhorn, M. A., Woodward, S. T., Lacapa, A., Cash, R. A., and Woodward, W. E.: Ad libitum oral glucose-electrolyte therapy for acute diarrhea in Apache children. J. Pediatr. *83*:562, 1973.

Hölscher, P. M., and Natzschka, J.: Methämoglobinämie bei jungen Säuglingen durch nitrithaltigen Spinat. Dtsch. Med. Wschr. *89*:1751, 1964.

Holt, P. R.: Dietary treatment of protein loss in intestinal lymphangiectasia. The effect of eliminating dietary long chain triglycerides on albumin metabolism in this condition. Pediatrics *34*:629, 1964.

Howard, E., and Granoff, D. M.: Effect of neonatal food restriction in mice on brain growth, DNA and cholesterol, and on adult delayed response learning. J. Nutr. *95*:111, 1968.

Jeffries, G.H., Chapman, A., and Sleisenger, M. H.: Low-fat diet in intestinal lymphangiectasia. Its effect on albumin metabolism. New Eng. J. Med. *270*:761, 1964.

Kamal, I., Hefnawi, F., Ghoneim, M., Talaat, M., Younis, N., Tagui, A., and Abdalla, M.: Clinical, biochemical and experimental studies on lactation. II. Clinical effects of gestagens on lactation. Amer. J. Obstet. Gynec. *105*:324, 1969.

Kamm, L., McKeown, G. G., and Smith, D. M.: Food additives: new colorimetric method for the determination of the nitrate and nitrite content of baby foods. J. Ass. Official Agr. Chem. *48*:892, 1965.

Karim, M., Ammar, R., El Mahgoub, S., El Ganzoury, B., Fikri, F., and Abdou, I.: Injected progestogen and lactation. Br. Med. J. *1*:200, 1971.

Keating, J. P., Lell, M. E., Strauss, A. W., Zarkowsky, H. and Smith, G. E.: Infantile methemoglobinemia caused by carrot juice. New Eng. J. Med. *288*:824, 1973.

Kennedy, G. C.: The development with age of hypothalamic restraint upon the appetite of the rat. J. Endocr. *16*:9, 1957.

Kerr, R. M., Du Bois, J. J., and Holt, P. R.: Use of ^{125}I- and ^{51}Cr-labeled albumin for the measurement of gastrointestinal and total albumin catabolism. J. Clin. Invest. *46*:2064, 1967.

Kerry, K. R., and Anderson, C. M.: (Letter to the Editor.) A ward test for sugar in faeces. Lancet *1*:981, 1964.

King, B. G.: Maximum daily intake of lead without excessive body lead-burden in children. Amer. J. Dis. Child. *122*:337, 1971.

Knotek, Z., and Schmidt, P.: Pathogenesis, incidence, and possibilities of preventing alimentary nitrate methemoglobinemia in infants. Pediatrics *34*:78, 1964.

Kora, S. J.: Effect of oral contraceptives on lactation. Fertil. Steril. *20*:419, 1969.

Kravitz, H., Elegant, L. D., Kaiser, E., and Kagan, B. M.: Methemoglobin values in premature and mature infants and children. Amer. J. Dis. Child. *91*:1, 1956.

Krieger, I.: Growth failure and congenital heart disease. Amer. J. Dis. Child. *120*:497, 1970.

Krieger, I., and Whitten, C. F.: Energy metabolism in infants with growth failure due to maternal deprivation, undernutrition, or causes unknown. II. Relationship between nitrogen balance, weight gain, and postprandial excess heat production. J. Pediatr. *75*:374, 1969.

Kuo, P. T., and Huang, N. N.: Effect of medium chain triglyceride upon fat absorption and plasma lipid and depot fat of children with cystic fibrosis of the pancreas. J. Clin. Invest. *44*:1924, 1965.

Lamm, S., Cole, B., Glynn, K., and Ullmann, W.: Lead content of milks fed to infants, 1971–1972. New Eng. J. Med. *289*:574, 1973.

Lamm, S. H., and Rosen, J. F.: Lead contamination in milks fed to infants, 1972–1973. Pediatrics *53*:137, 1974.

Lát, J., Widdowson, E. M., and McCance, R. A.: Some effects of accelerating growth. III. Behaviour and nervous activity. Proc. Roy. Soc. Lond. (Biol.) *153*:347, 1960/61.

Lawler, W. H., Jr., and Bernard H. R.: Survival of an infant following massive resection of the small intestine. Ann. Surg. *155*:204, 1962.

Lees, M. H., Bristow, J. D., Griswold, H. E., and Olmsted, R. W.: Relative hypermetabolism in infants with congenital heart disease and undernutrition. Pediatrics *36*:183, 1965.

Levison, H., Delivoria-Papadopoulos, M., and Swyer, P. R.: Variations in oxygen consumption in the infant with hypoxaemia due to cardiopulmonary disease. Acta Paediatr. Scand. *54*:369, 1965.

Leyland, F. C., Fosbrooke, A. S., Lloyd, J. K., Segall, M. M., Tamir, I., Tomkins, R., and Wolff, O. H.: Use of medium-chain triglyceride diets in children with malabsorption. Arch. Dis. Child. *44*:170, 1969.

L'Hirondel, J., Guihard, J., Morel, C., Freymuth, F., Signoret, N., and Signoret, C.: Une cause nouvelle de méthémoglobinémie due nourrisson: la soupe de carottes. Ann. Pediatr. (Paris) *18*:625, 1971.

Lifshitz, F., Coello-Ramírez, P., and Contreras-Gutiérrez, M. L.: The response of infants to carbohydrate oral loads after recovery from diarrhea. J. Pediatr. *79*:612, 1971a.

Lifshitz, F., Coello-Ramírez, P., and Gutiérrez-Topete, G.: Monosaccharide intolerance and hypoglycemia in infants with diarrhea. I. Clinical course of 23 infants. J. Pediatr. *77*:595, 1970a.

Lifshitz, F., Coello-Ramírez, P., and Gutiérrez-Topete, G.: Monosaccharide intolerance and hypoglycemia in infants with diarrhea. II. Metabolic studies in 23 infants. J. Pediatr. *77*:604, 1970b.

Lifshitz, F., Coello-Ramirez, P., Gutiérrez-Topete, G., and Cornado-Cornet, M. C.: Carbohydrate intolerance in infants with diarrhea. J. Pediatr. 79:760, 1971b.

Lifshitz, F., and Holman, G. H.: Disaccharidase deficiencies with steatorrhea. J. Pediatr. *64*:34, 1964.

Linde, L. M., Dunn, O. J., Schireson, R., and Rasof, B.: Growth in children with congenital heart disease. J. Pediatr. *70*:413, 1967.

Lin-Fu, J. S.: Vulnerability of children to lead exposure and toxicity. New Eng. J. Med. *289*:1229, 1289, 1973.

Mehrizi, A., and Drash, A.: Growth disturbance in congenital heart disease. J. Pediatr. *61*:418, 1962.

Milledge, I. S.: Arterial oxygen desaturation and intestinal absorption of xylose. Br. Med. J. *3*:557, 1972.

Miller, G. H., and Hughes, L. R.: Lactation and genital involution. Effects of a new low-dose oral contraceptive on breast-feeding mothers and their infants. Obstet. Gynec. *35*:44, 1970.

Mitchell, D. G.: Increased lead absorption: paint is not the only problem. Pediatrics *53*:142, 1974.

Montgomery, R. D.: Changes in the basal metabolic rate of the malnourished infant and their relation to body composition. J. Clin. Invest. *41*:1653, 1962.

Morgan, C. L., and Nadas, A. S.: Sweating and congestive heart failure. New Eng. J. Med. *268*:580, 1963.

Murthy, G. K., and Rhea, U. S.: Cadmium, copper, iron, lead, manganese, and zinc in evaporated milk, infant products, and human milk. J. Dairy Sci. *54*:1001, 1971.

Naeye, R. L.: Organ and cellular development in congenital heart disease and in alimentary malnutrition. J. Pediatr. *67*:447, 1965.

Naeye, R. L.: Anatomic features of growth failure in congenital heart disease. Pediatrics *39*:433, 1967.

Nomura, F. M.: Broth edema in infants. New Eng. J. Med. *274*:1077, 1966.

Phillips, W. E. J.: Changes in the nitrate and nitrite contents of fresh and processed spinach during storage. J. Agr. Food Chem. *16*:88, 1968.

Phillips, W. E. J.: Lack of nitrate accumulation in partially consumed jars of baby food. Canad. Inst. Food Technol. J. *2*:160, 1969.

Pinter, K. G., Hyman, H., III, and Bolanos, O.: Fat and nitrogen balance with medium-chain triglycerides after massive intestinal resection. Amer. J. Clin. Nutr. *22*:14, 1969.

Pittman, J. G., and Cohen, P.: The pathogenesis of cardiac cachexia. New Eng. J. Med. *271*:403, 453, 1964.

Plauth, W. H., Waldmann, T. A., Wochner, R. D., Braunwald, N. S., and Braunwald, E.: Protein-losing enteropathy secondary to constrictive pericarditis in childhood. Pediatrics *34*:636, 1964.

Puyau, F. A.: Evaporative heat losses of infants with congenital heart disease. Amer. J. Clin. Nutr. *22*:1435, 1969.

Rodriguez-de-Curet, H., Lugo-de-Rivera, C., and Torres-Pinedo, R.: Studies on infant diarrhea. IV. Sugar transit and absorption in small intestine after a feeding. Gastroenterology *59*:396, 1970.

Rubin, W.: Celiac disease. Amer. J. Clin. Nutr. *24*:91, 1971.

Schuphan, W.: Der Nitratgehalt von Spinat (Spinacia oleraces L.) in Beziehung zur Methämoglobinämie. Z. Ernährungswiss. *5*:207, 1965.

Schussheim, A.: Protein-losing enteropathies in children. Amer. J. Gastroent. *58*:124, 1972.

Shmerling, D. H.: An analysis of controlled relapses in gluten-induced coeliac disease. (Abstract) Acta Paediatr. Scand. *58*:311, 1969.

Shmerling, D. H., and Zimmerli-Häring, S. M.: Die floride Zöliakie, Untersuchungsergebnisse bei 88 Patienten zwischen 1963 und 1969. Helv. Paediatr. Acta *26*:565, 1971.

Silverman, A., Roy, C. C., and Cozzetto, F. J.: Pediatric Clinical Gastroenterology. St. Louis, C. V. Mosby Co., 1971, p. 449.

Simon, C., Kay, H., and Mrowetz, G.: Über den Gehalt an Nitrat, Nitrit und Eisen von Spinat und anderen Gemüsearten und die damit verbundene Gefahr einer Methämoglobinämie für Säuglinge. Arch. Kinderheilkd. *175*:42, 1966/67.

Sinclair, J. C., and Silverman, W. A.: (Letter to the Editor.) Relative hypermetabolism in undergrown human neonates. Lancet *2*:49, 1964.

Sinios, A.: Methämoglobinämie durch nitrithaltigen Spinat. Münch. Med. Wschr. *106*:1180, 1964.

Sinios, A., and Wodsak, W.: Die Spinatvergiftung des Säuglings. Dtsch. Med. Wschr. *90*:1856, 1965.

Smith, F. R., Underwood, B. A., Denning, C. R., Varma, A., and Goodman, D. S.: Depressed plasma retinol-binding protein levels in cystic fibrosis. J. Lab. Clin. Med. *80*:423, 1972.

Söderhjelm, L.: Infant feeding hygiene in Sweden. A survey of bottle and teat hygiene. Acta Paediatr. Scand. *61*:565, 1972.

Somers, I.: National Canners Association. Personal communication, 1973.

Soong, C. S., Thompson, J. B., Poley, J. R., and Hess, D. R.: Hydroxy fatty acids in human diarrhea. Gastroenterology *63*:748, 1972.

Stalder, G.: Die Ernährungsstörungen des Säuglings. *In* Fanconi, G., and Wallgren, A.: Lehrbuch der Pädiatrie, Basel/Stuttgart, Schwabe, 1972, p. 111.

Stocker, F. P., Wilkoff, W., Miettinen, O. S., and Nadas, A. S.: Oxygen consumption in infants with heart disease. Relationship of severity of congestive failure, relative weight, and caloric intake. J. Pediatr. *80*:43, 1972.

Subcommittee on Nutrition, Brain Development and Behavior of the Committee on International Nutrition Programs: The Relationship of Nutrition to Brain Development and Behavior. Washington, D.C., National Academy of Sciences–National Research Council, 1973.

Sunshine, P., and Kretchmer, N.: Studies of small intestine during development. III. Infantile diarrhea associated with intolerance to disaccharides. Pediatrics *34*:38, 1964.

Tandon, R. K., Rodgers, J. B., and Balint, J. A.: The effects of medium-chain triglycerides in the short bowel syndrome. Increased glucose and water transport. Amer. J. Dig. Dis. *17*:233, 1972.

Torres-Pinedo, R., Conde, E., Robillard, G., and Maldonado, M.: Studies on infant diarrhea. III. Changes in composition of saline and glucose-saline solutions instilled into the colon. Pediatrics *42*:303, 1968.

Torres-Pinedo, R., Lavastida, M., Rivera, C. L., Rodriguez, H., and Ortiz, A.: Studies on infant diarrhea. I. A comparison of the effects of milk feeding and intravenous therapy upon the composition and volume of the stool and urine. J. Clin. Invest. *45*:469, 1966a.

Torres-Pinedo, R., Rivera, C. L., and Fernández, S.: Studies on infant diarrhea. II. Absorption of glucose and net fluxes of water and sodium chloride in a segment of the jejunum. J. Clin. Invest. *45*:1916, 1966b.

Torstenson, O. L., Humphrey, G. B., Edson, J. R., and Warwick, W. J.: Cystic fibrosis presenting with severe hemorrhage due to vitamin K malabsorption: a report of three cases. Pediatrics *45*:857, 1970.

Toskes, P. P., Hansell, J., Cerda, J., and Deren, J. J.: Vitamin B_{12} malabsorption in chronic pancreatic insufficiency. Studies suggesting the presence of a pancreatic "intrinsic factor". New Eng. J. Med. *284*:627, 1971.

Underwood, B. A., and Denning, C. R.: Blood and liver concentrations of vitamins A and E in children with cystic fibrosis of the pancreas. Pediatr. Res. *6*:26, 1972.

Vaughan, V. C., Dienst, R. B., Sheffield, C. R., and Roberts, R. W.: A study of techniques of preparation of formulas for infant feeding. J. Pediatr. *61*:547, 1962.

Visakorpi, J. K.: An international inquiry concerning the diagnostic criteria of coeliac disease. Acta Paediatr. Scand. *59*:463, 1970.

Visakorpi, J. K., and Immonen, P.: Intolerance to cow's milk and wheat gluten in the primary malabsorption syndrome in infancy. Acta Paediatr. Scand. *56*:49, 1967.

Visakorpi, J. K., Kuitunen, P., and Pelkonen, P.: Intestinal malabsorption: a clinical study of 22 children over 2 years of age. Acta Paediatr. Scand. *59*:273, 1970a.

Visakorpi, J. K., Kuitunen, P., and Savilahti, E.: Frequency and nature of relapses in children suffering from the malabsorption syndrome with gluten intolerance. Acta Paediatr. Scand. *59*:481, 1970b.

Waldmann, T. A.: Gastrointestinal protein loss demonstrated by ^{51}Cr-labelled albumin. Lancet *2*:121, 1961.

Waldmann, T. A.: Protein-losing enteropathy. Gastroenterology *50*:422, 1966.

Walters, T. R., and Koch, H. F.: Hemorrhagic diathesis and cystic fibrosis in infancy. Amer. J. Dis. Child. *124*:641, 1972.

Walton, G.: Survey of literature relating to infant methemoglobinemia due to nitrate-contaminated water. Amer. J. Public Health *41*:986, 1951.

Watt, B. K., and Merrill, A. L.: Composition of Foods—Raw, Processed, Prepared. Agriculture Handbook No. 8, Revised. Washington, D. C., Agricultural Research Service, 1963.

Weijers, H. A., Van de Kamer, J. H., Dicke, W. K., and Ijsseling, J.: Diarrhoea caused by deficiency of sugar splitting enzymes. I. Acta Paediatr. Scand. *50*:55, 1961.

Weser, E.: Intestinal adaptation to small bowel resection. Amer. J. Clin. Nutr. *24*:133, 1971.

Widdowson, E. M., and Dickerson, J. W. T.: Chemical composition of the body. *In* Comar, C. L., and Bronner, F. (eds): Mineral Metabolism. Vol. II. Part A. New York, Academic Press, 1964, p. 1.

Wilmore, D. W., and Dudrick, S. J.: Growth and development of an infant receiving all nutrients exclusively by vein. J.A.M.A. *203*:860, 1968.

Wilmore, D. W., Groff, D. B., Bishop, H. C., and Dudrick, S. J.: Total parenteral nutrition in infants with catastrophic gastrointestinal anomalies. J. Pediatr. Surg. *4*:181, 1969.

Wilson, J. K.: Nitrate in foods and its relation to health. Agronomy J. *41*:20, 1949.

Winawer, S. J., Broitman, S. A., Wolochow, D. A., Osborne, M. P., and Zamcheck, N.: Successful management of massive small-bowel resection based on assessment of absorption defects and nutritional needs. New Eng. J. Med. *274*:72, 1966.

Winick, M., Brasel, J. A., and Rosso, P.: Nutrition and cell growth. *In* Winick, M. (ed.): Nutrition and Development. New York, J. Wiley & Sons, 1972a, p. 49.

Winick, M., Rosso, P., and Brasel, J. A.: Malnutrition and cellular growth in the brain. Bibl. Nutr. Diet. *17*:60, 1972b.

Zurier, R. B., Campbell, R. G., Hashim, S. A., and Van Itallie, T. B.: Use of medium-chain triglyceride in management of patients with massive resection of the small intestine. New Eng. J. Med. *274*:490, 1966.

APPENDICES

Appendix I

VOLUME OF INTAKE AND INTAKE OF CALORIES BY NORMAL FULLSIZE INFANTS

Data concerning volume of intake and intake of calories by normal fullsize infants fed various milk-based formulas are summarized in relation to body weight in Table I–1 and in Figures I–1 to I–12. These data have been published in detail elsewhere (Fomon et al., 1971). Each figure includes the regression and the 90 per cent confidence interval. Additional data on food consumption by normal infants and by children less than three years of age are presented in Chapter 2 (especially Tables 2–1 and 2–2).

TABLE I–1 RELATION OF VOLUME OF INTAKE AND CALORIE INTAKE TO BODY WEIGHT DURING SIX CONSECUTIVE AGE INTERVALS*

Age Interval (days)	Regression† Equation	Correlation Coefficient	Residual Variance	Regression† Equation	Correlation Coefficient	Residual Variance
	Volume of Intake (ml/day)			*Calorie Intake (kcal/day)*		
Males						
8–13	$Y = 128x + 134$	.33	131	$Y = 86x + 90$	.33	88
14–27	$Y = 161x + 78$	.42	132	$Y = 108x + 52$	.42	89
28–41	$Y = 160x + 65$	.43	141	$Y = 107x + 48$	.42	97
42–55	$Y = 132x + 167$	.44	124	$Y = 89x + 114$	.44	84
56–83	$Y = 150x - 6$	.60	108	$Y = 103x - 14$	.60	74
84–111	$Y = 108x + 192$	.62	91	$Y = 75x + 128$	.61	63
Females						
8–13	$Y = 38x + 435$	.13	120	$Y = 25x + 291$	.13	80
14–27	$Y = 36x + 503$	.14	96	$Y = 24x + 337$	.14	65
28–41	$Y = 65x + 422$	.22	114	$Y = 42x + 292$	.21	77
42–55	$Y = 103x + 227$	.36	108	$Y = 70x + 151$	.37	73
56–83	$Y = 103x + 210$	.49	81	$Y = 69x + 147$	.48	55
84–111	$Y = 104x + 184$	.47	97	$Y = 66x + 158$	.44	67

*From Fomon, S. J., et al.: Food consumption and growth of normal infants fed milk-based formulas. Acta Paediatr. Scand. (Suppl. 223), 1971.

†Y is volume of intake (ml/day) or calorie intake (kcal/day) and x is body weight (kg).

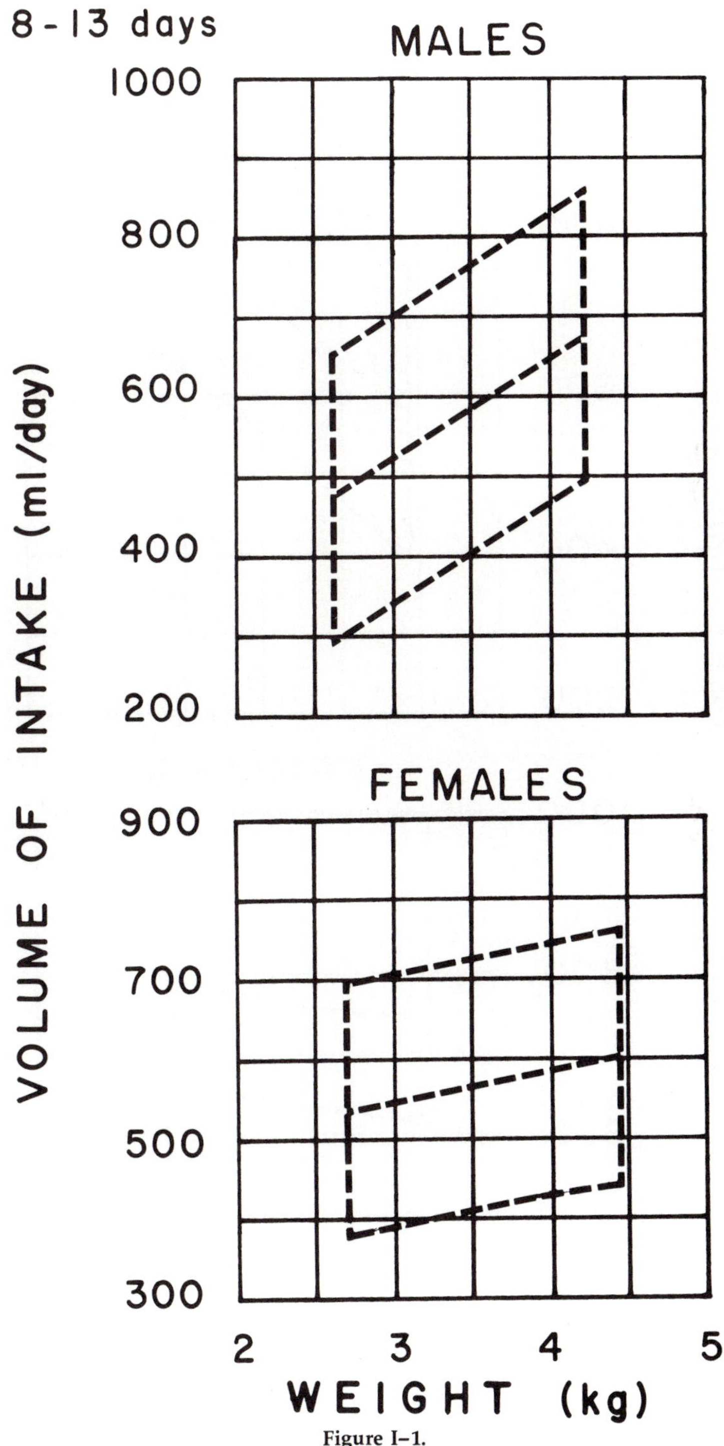

8-13 days
MALES
FEMALES
1000
800
600
400
200
900
700
500
300
2
3
4
5
VOLUME OF INTAKE (ml/day)
WEIGHT (kg)

Figure I–1.

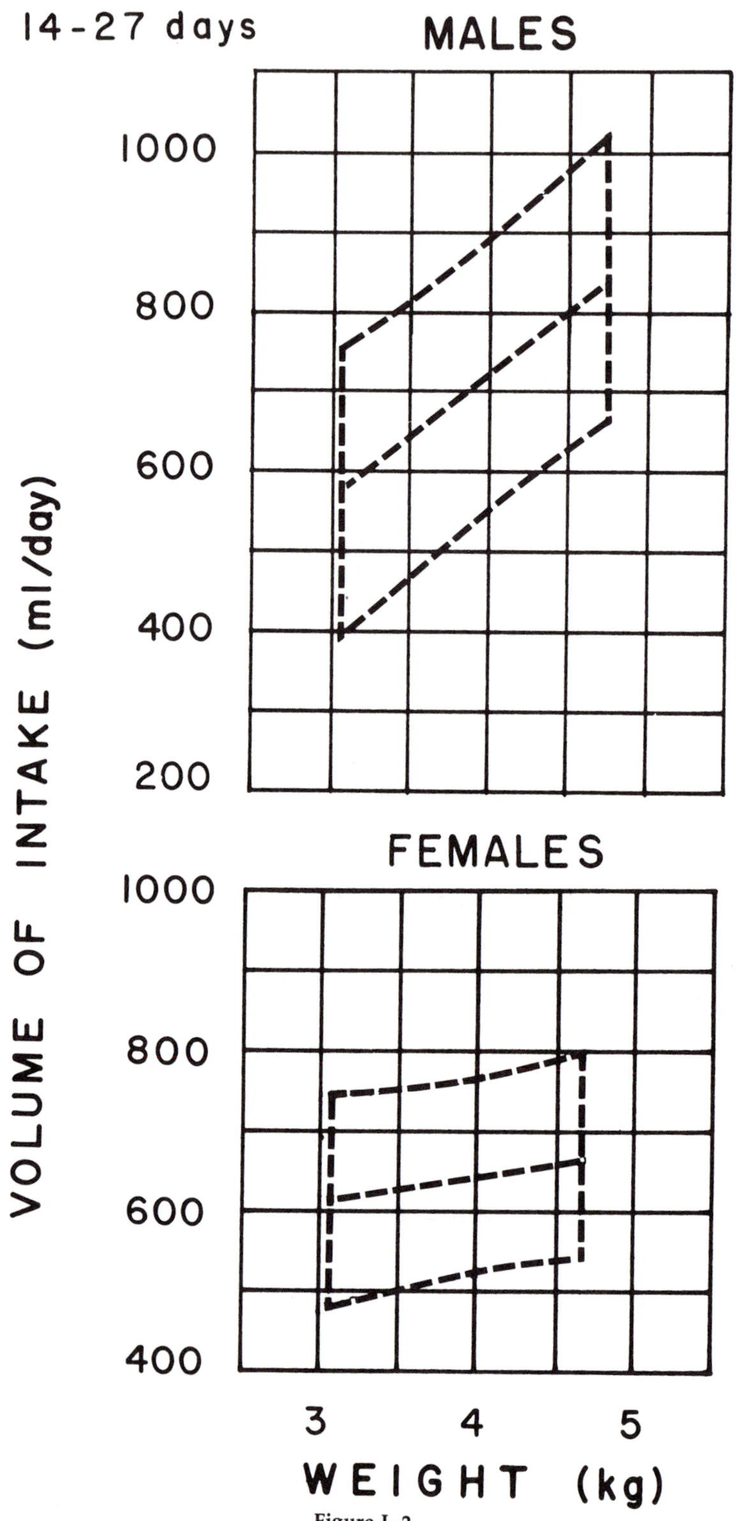

14-27 days
MALES
1000
800
600
400
200
VOLUME OF INTAKE (ml/day)
FEMALES
1000
800
600
400
3
4
5
WEIGHT (kg)

Figure I–2.

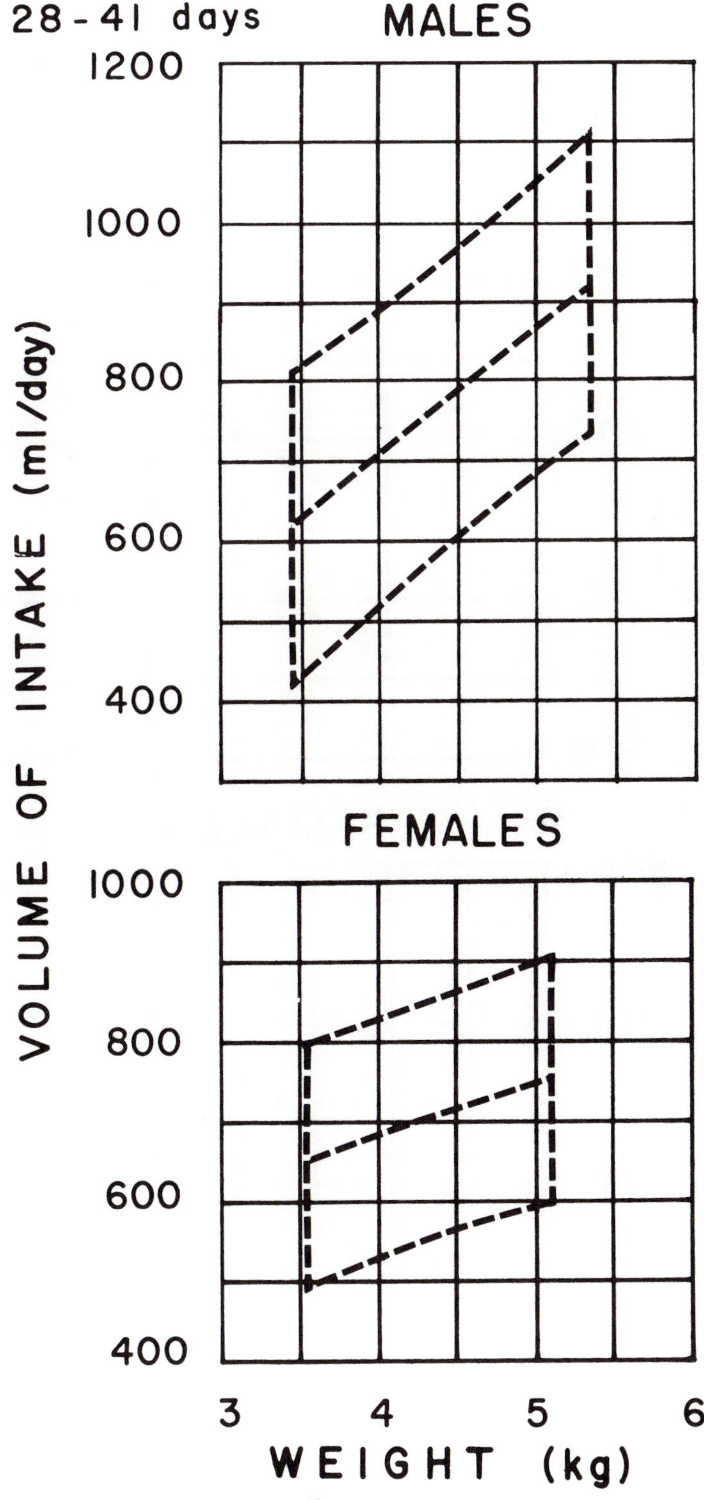
28 - 41 days
MALES
1200
1000
800
600
400
VOLUME OF INTAKE (ml/day)
FEMALES
1000
800
600
400
3
4
5
6
WEIGHT (kg)
Figure I–3.

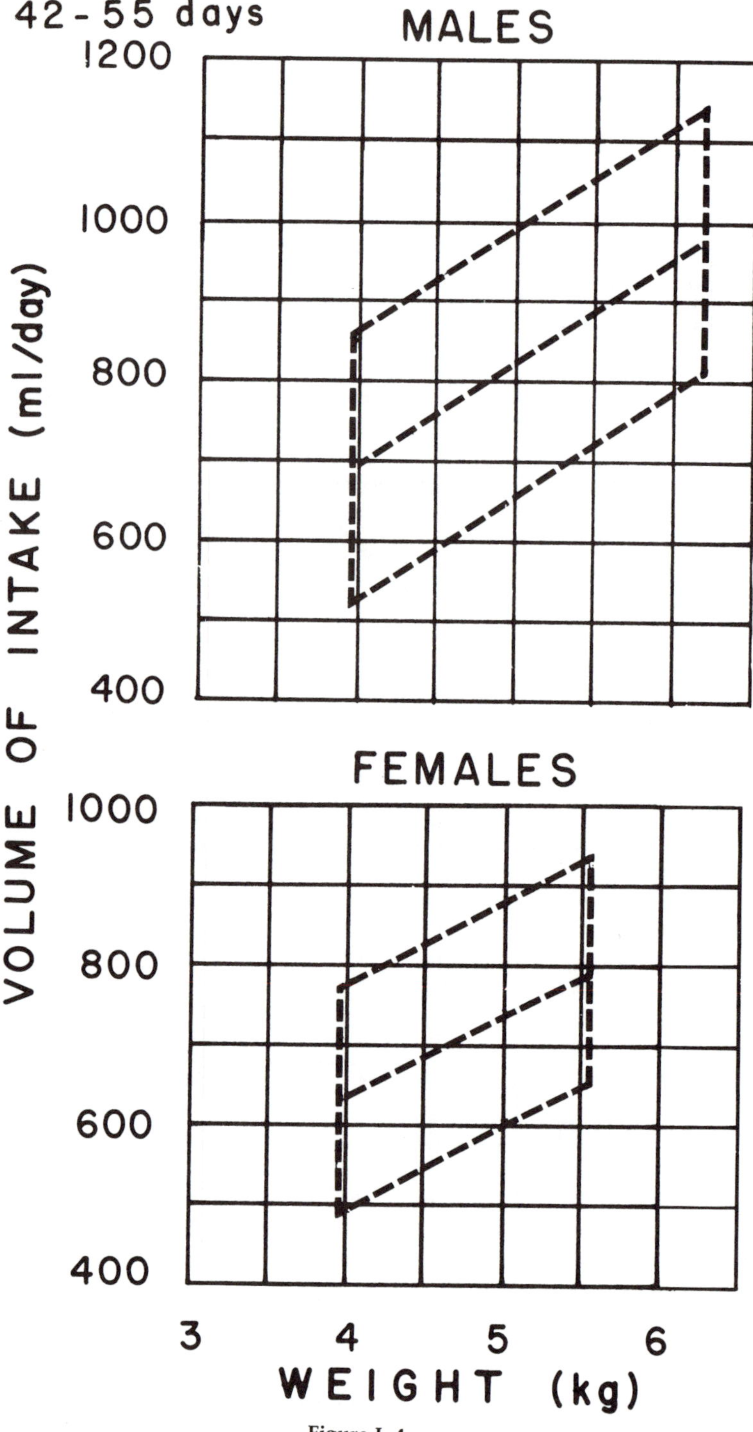
42-55 days
MALES
1200
1000
800
600
400
VOLUME OF INTAKE (ml/day)
FEMALES
1000
800
600
400
3
4
5
6
WEIGHT (kg)

Figure I–4.

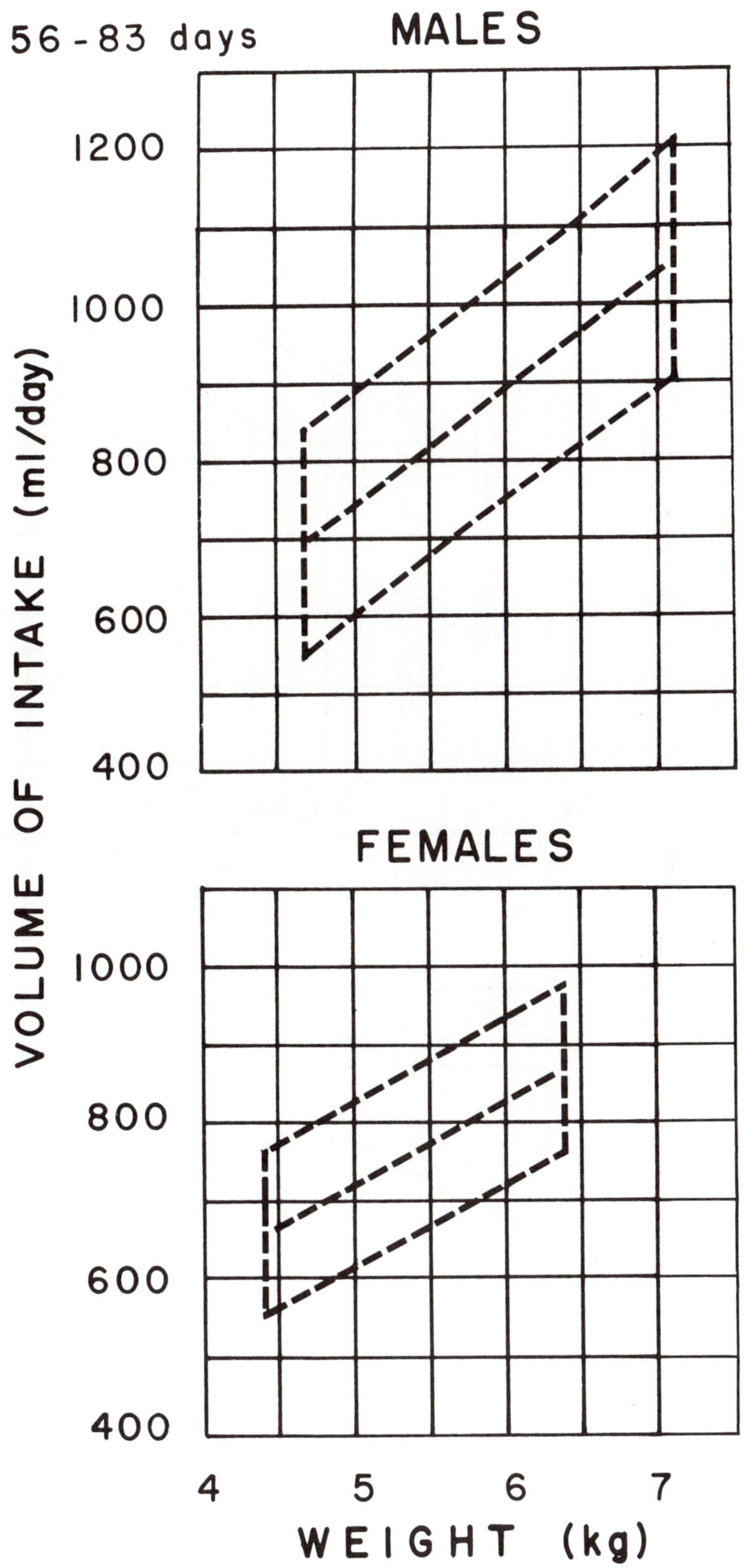

56 - 83 days
MALES
1200
1000
800
600
400
VOLUME OF INTAKE (ml/day)
FEMALES
1000
800
600
400
4
5
6
7
WEIGHT (kg)

Figure I–5.

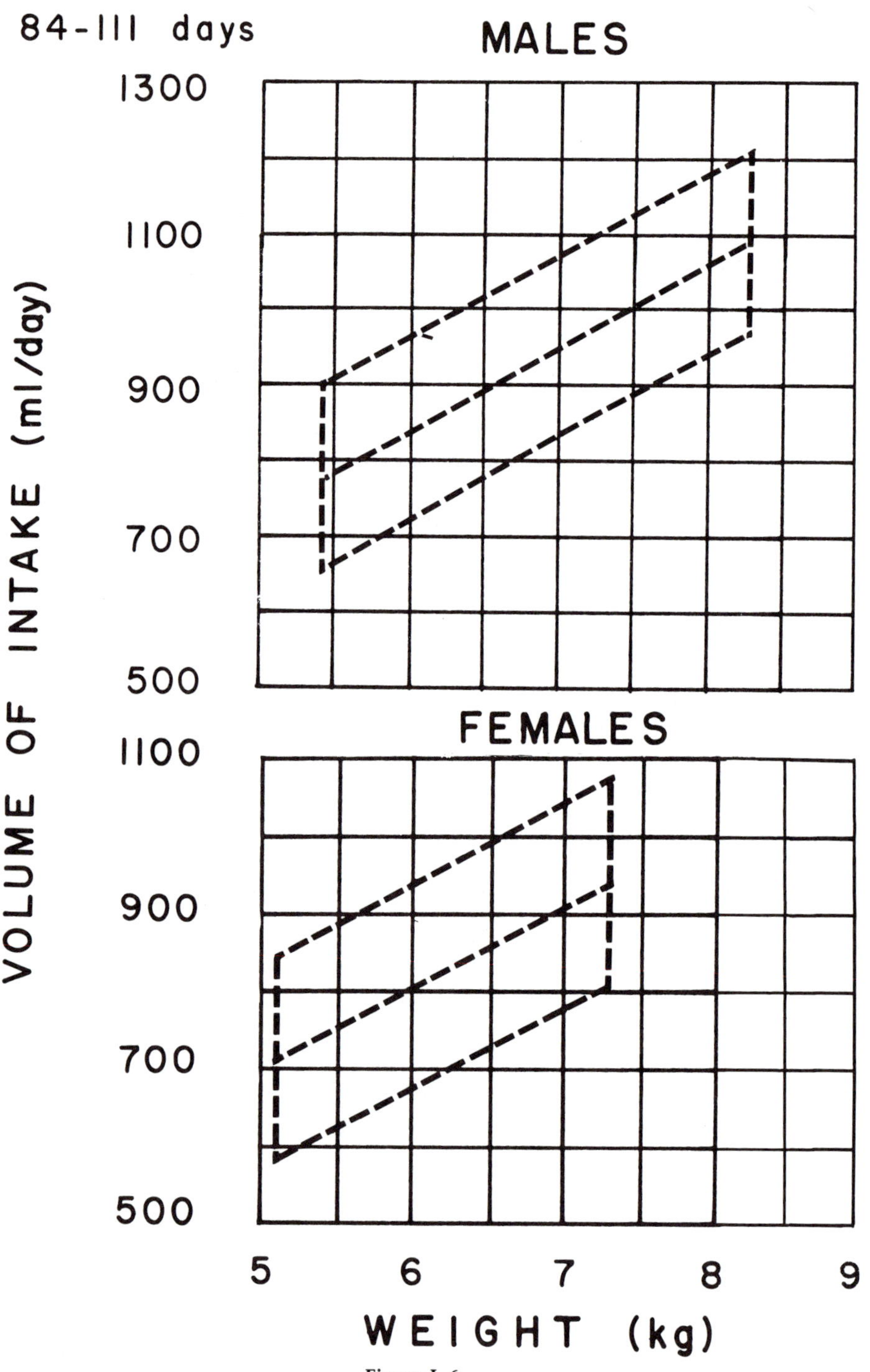
84-111 days
MALES
1300
1100
900
700
500
FEMALES
1100
900
700
500
VOLUME OF INTAKE (ml/day)
5
6
7
8
9
WEIGHT (kg)

Figure I–6.

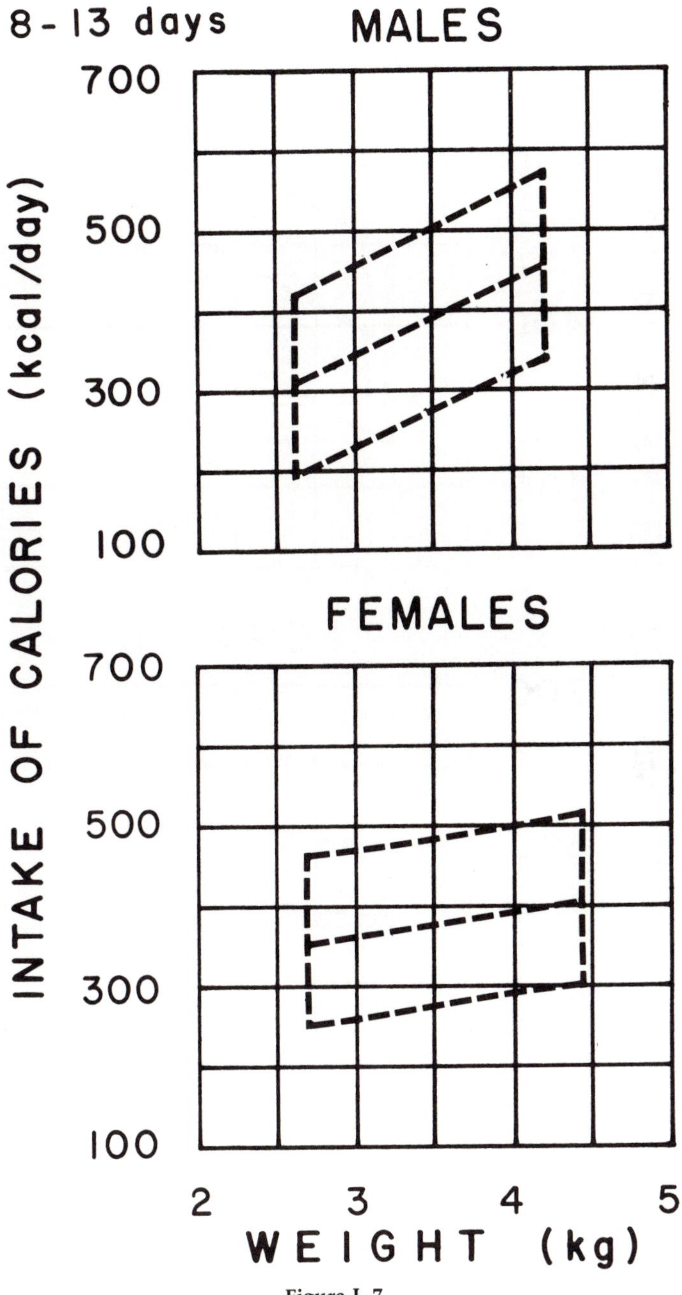
8-13 days
MALES
700
500
300
100
FEMALES
700
500
300
100
INTAKE OF CALORIES (kcal/day)
2
3
4
5
WEIGHT (kg)

Figure I–7.

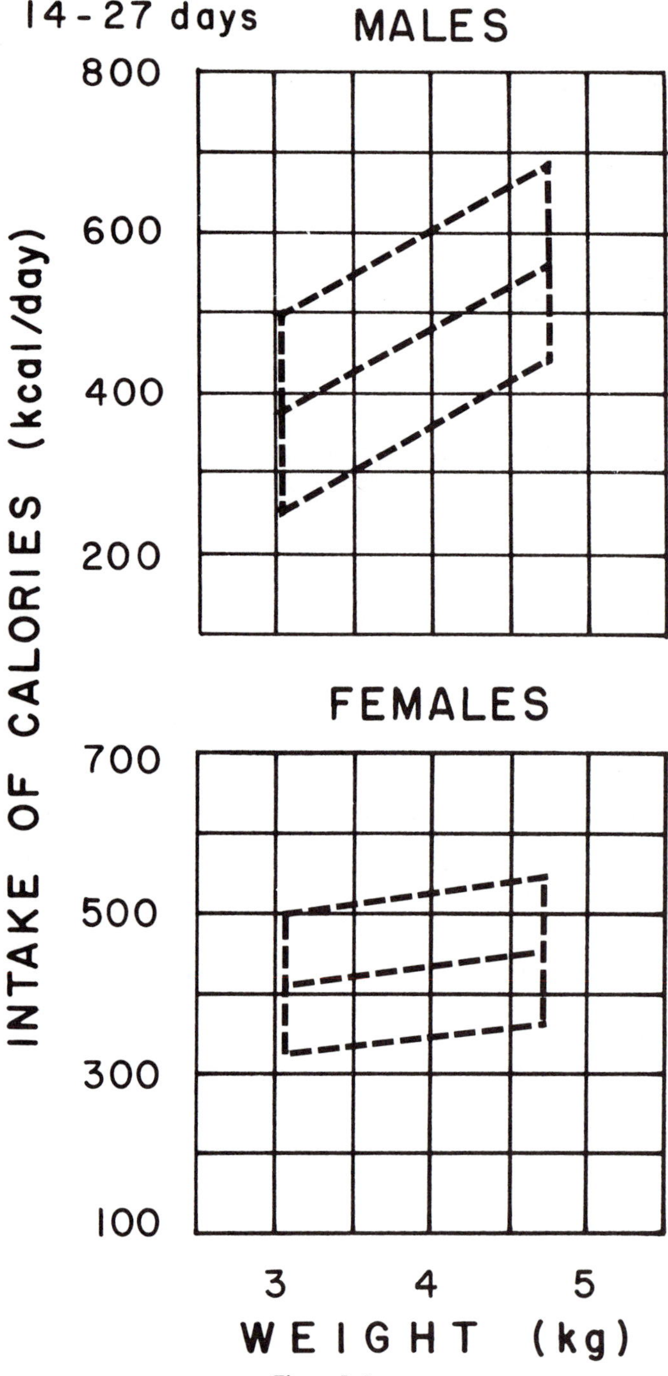
14 - 27 days
MALES
800
600
400
200
INTAKE OF CALORIES (kcal/day)
FEMALES
700
500
300
100
3
4
5
WEIGHT (kg)

Figure I–8.

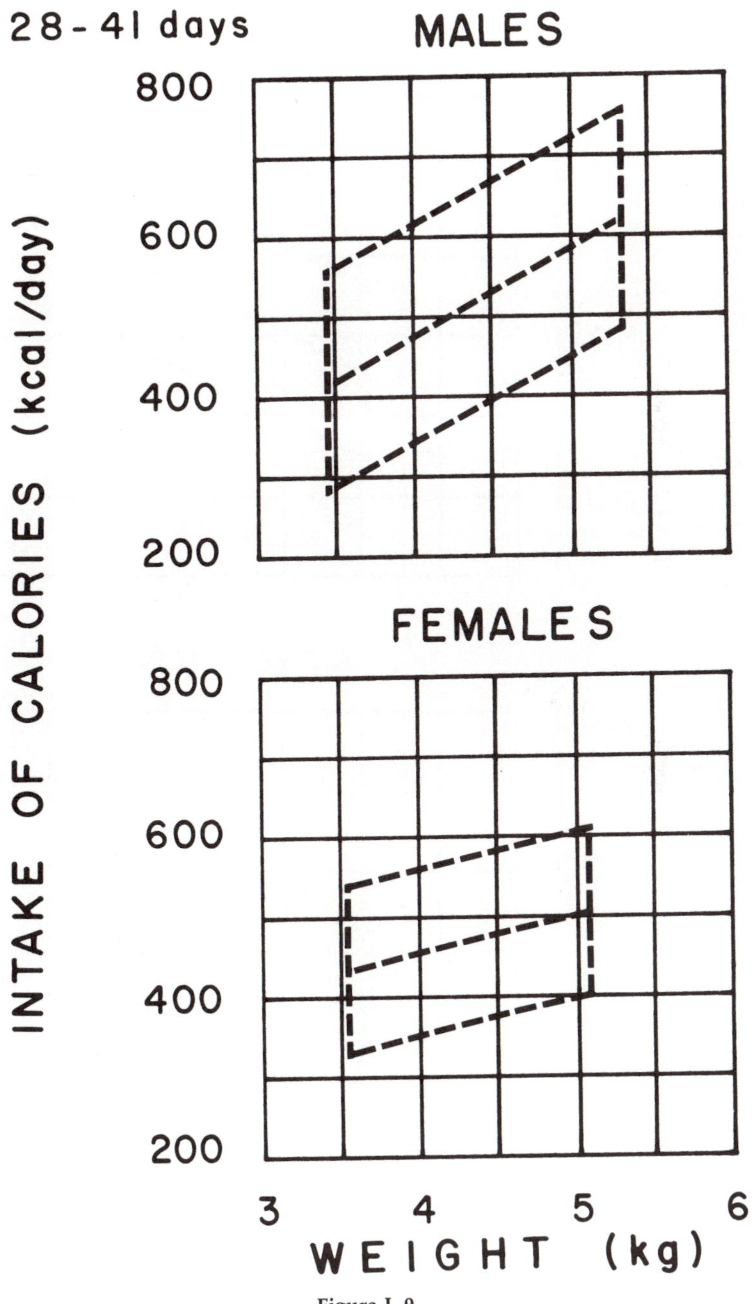

28-41 days
MALES
800
600
400
200
FEMALES
800
600
400
200
INTAKE OF CALORIES (kcal/day)
3
4
5
6
WEIGHT (kg)

Figure I–9.

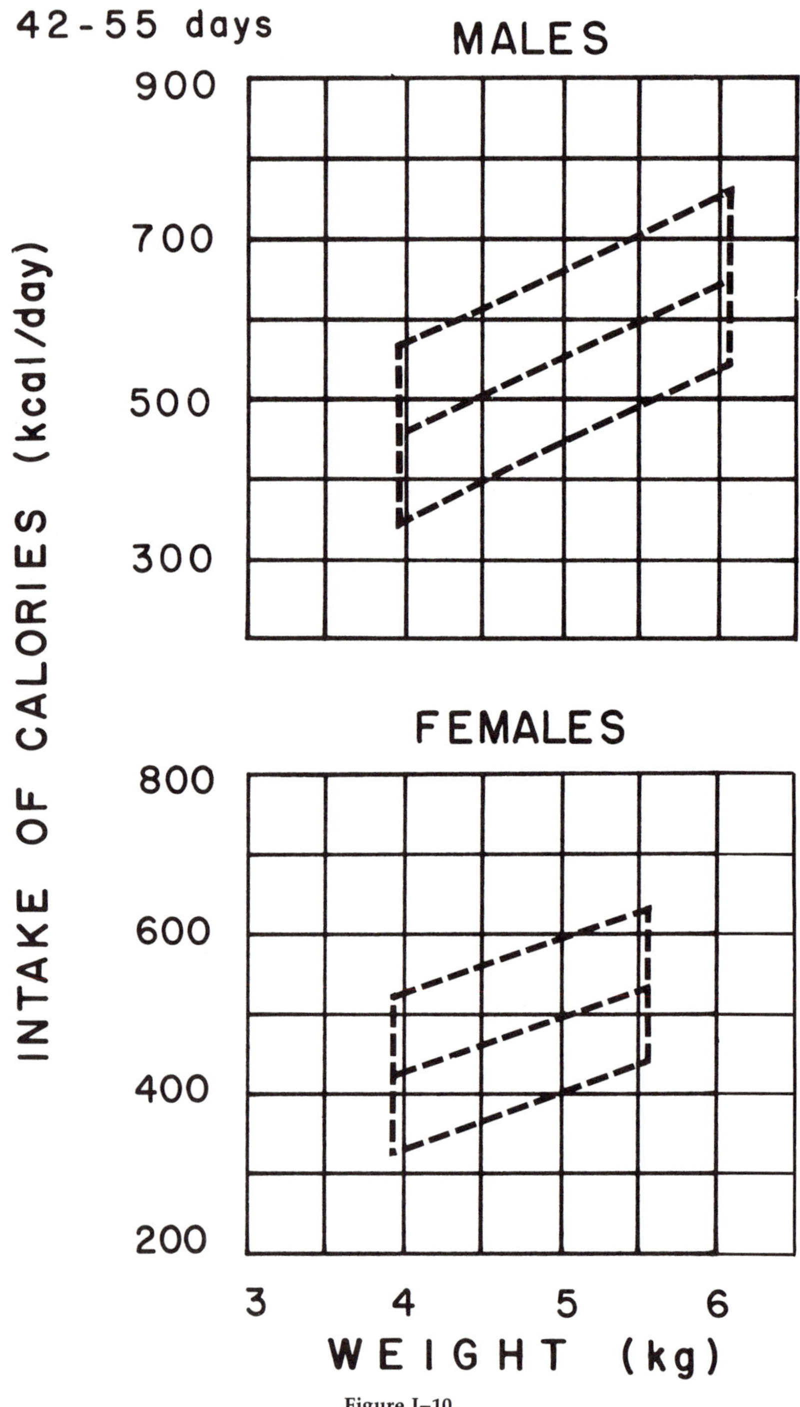
42-55 days
MALES
900
700
500
300
INTAKE OF CALORIES (kcal/day)
FEMALES
800
600
400
200
3
4
5
6
WEIGHT (kg)

Figure I–10.

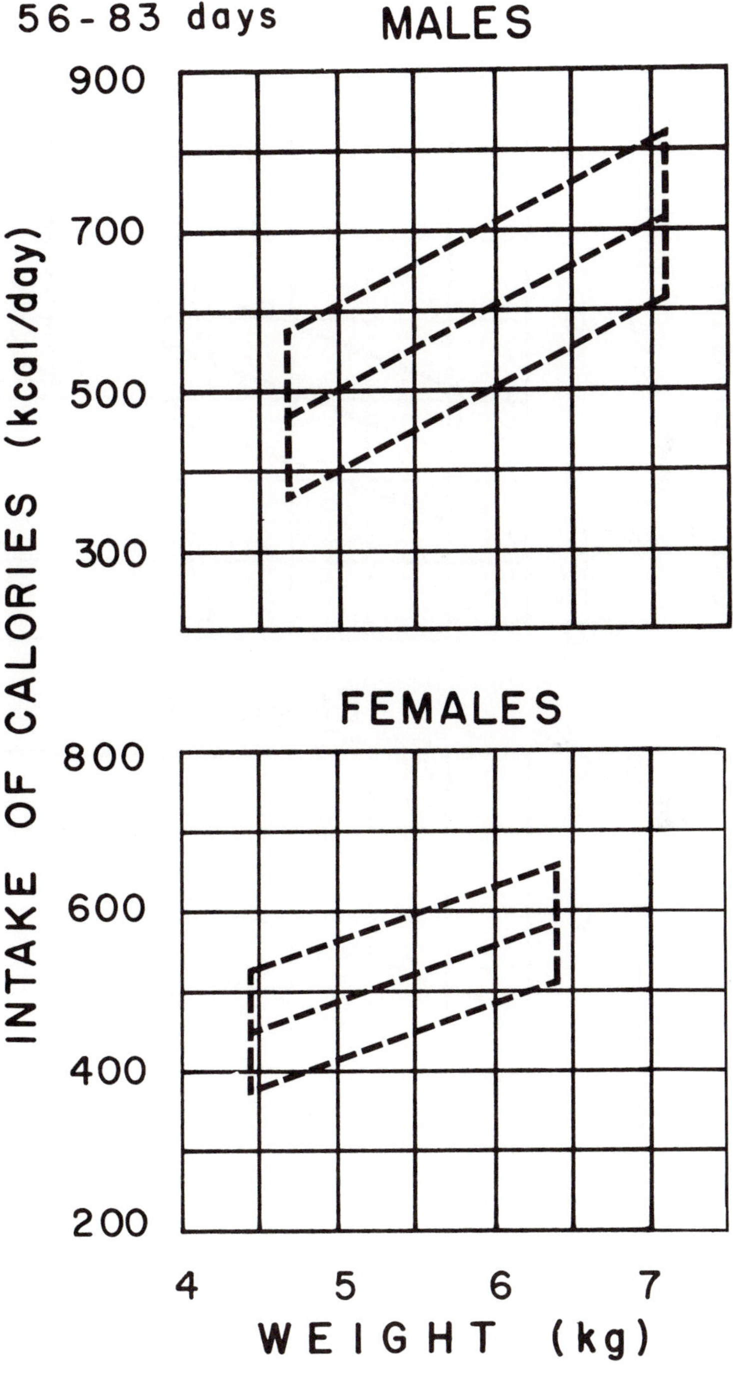
56-83 days
MALES
900
700
500
300
INTAKE OF CALORIES (kcal/day)
FEMALES
800
600
400
200
4
5
6
7
WEIGHT (kg)

Figure I–11.

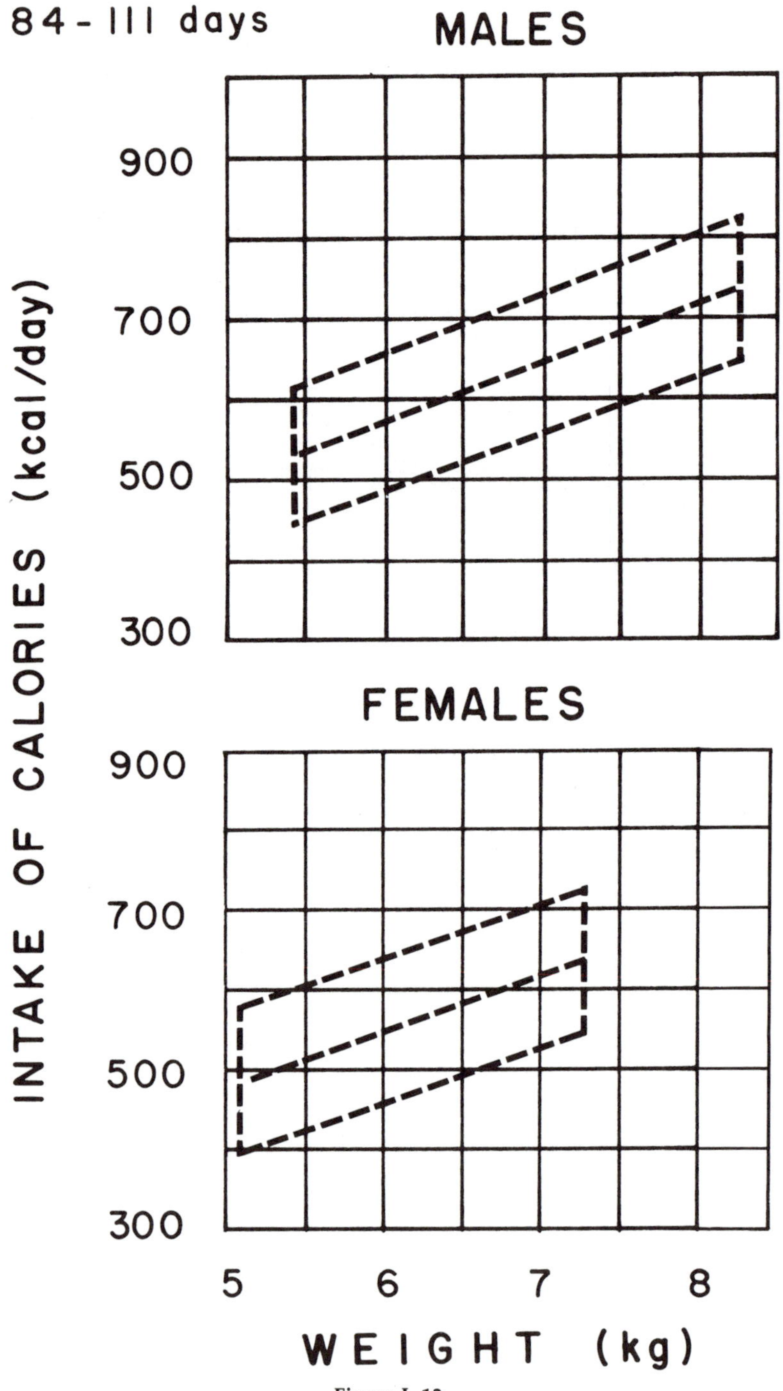
84-111 days
MALES
900
700
500
300
INTAKE OF CALORIES (kcal/day)
FEMALES
900
700
500
300
5
6
7
8
WEIGHT (kg)

Figure I–12.

Appendix II

GAIN IN WEIGHT IN RELATION TO INTAKE OF CALORIES BY NORMAL FULLSIZE INFANTS

Data on relation of gain in weight to intake of calories by normal fullsize infants fed 67 kcal/100 ml milk-based formulas are summarized in Table II–1 and in Figures II–1 to II–6. Each figure includes the regression and 90 per cent confidence interval. Additional data on the relation of gain in weight to intake of calories are presented in Chapters 2 (especially Tables 2–3 and 2–4) and 3 (especially Table 3–9).

TABLE II–1 RELATION OF WEIGHT GAIN TO CALORIE INTAKE DURING VARIOUS AGE INTERVALS*

AGE INTERVAL (DAYS)	REGRESSION† EQUATION	CORRELATION COEFFICIENT	RESIDUAL VARIANCE
Males			
8– 13	$Y = .058x + 8$	.36	190
14– 27	$Y = .067x + 10$	.66	55
28– 41	$Y = .046x + 15$	.51	70
42– 55	$Y = .079x - 9$	.61	91
56– 83	$Y = .062x - 6$	.70	35
84–111	$Y = .044x - 1$	.49	39
8– 55	$Y = .069x + 4$	.74	27
56–111	$Y = .054x - 4$	.67	24
8–111	$Y = .064x - 3$	.77	17
Females			
8– 13	$Y = .008x + 28$	.06	142
14– 27	$Y = .065x + 8$	.48	59
28– 41	$Y = .051x + 6$	.49	51
42– 55	$Y = .062x - .7$	.60	43
56– 83	$Y = .056x - 3$	.57	25
84–111	$Y = .039x + .7$	.39	48
8– 55	$Y = .069x + .3$	.67	21
56–111	$Y = .051x - 4$	.56	22
8–111	$Y = .064x - 4$	.66	15

*From Fomon, S. J., et al.: Food consumption and growth of normal infants fed milk-based formulas. Acta Paediatr. Scand. (Suppl. 223), 1971.

†Y is gain in weight (gm/day) and x is calorie intake (kcal/day).

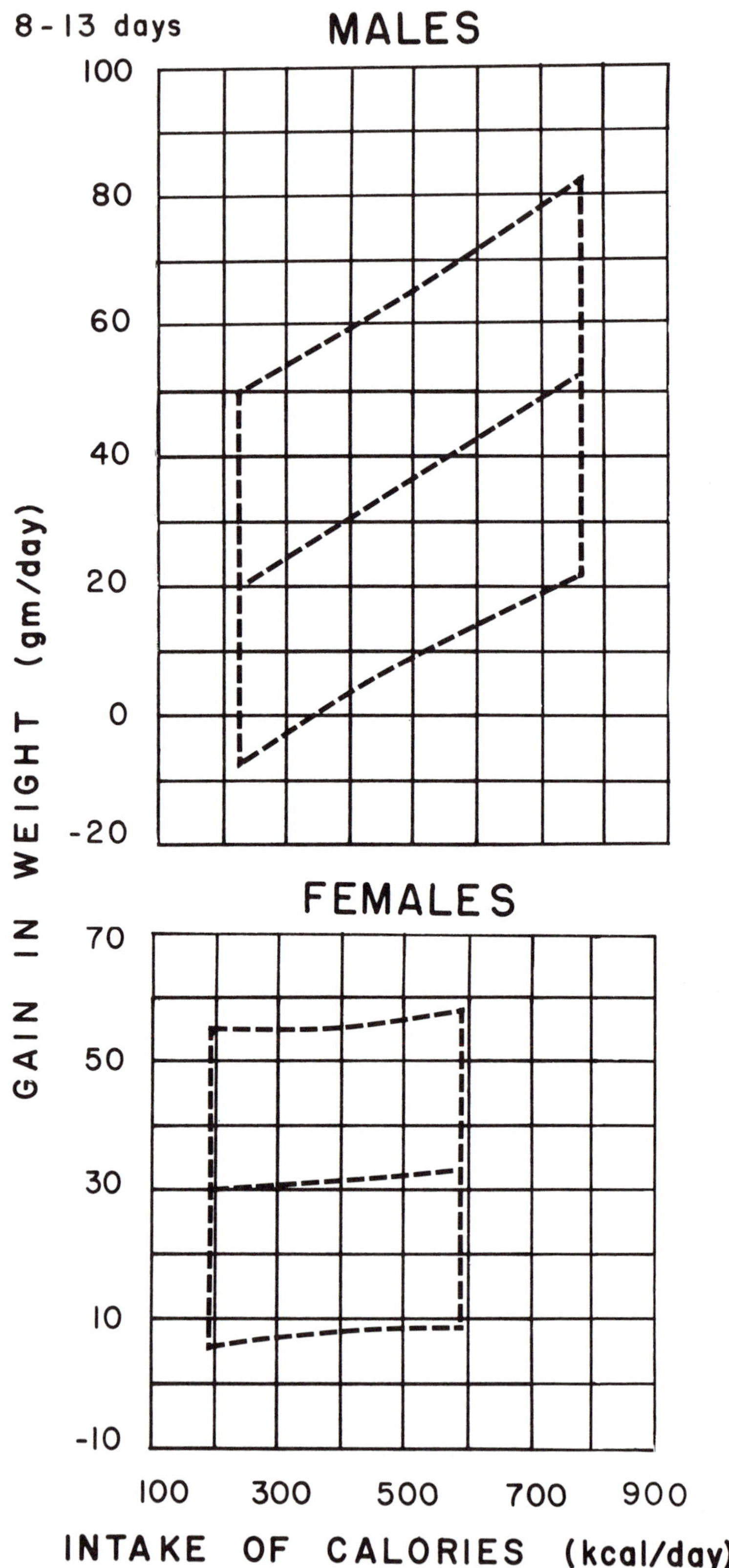
8 - 13 days
MALES
100
80
60
40
20
0
-20
GAIN IN WEIGHT (gm/day)
FEMALES
70
50
30
10
-10
100
300
500
700
900
INTAKE OF CALORIES (kcal/day)

Figure II–1.

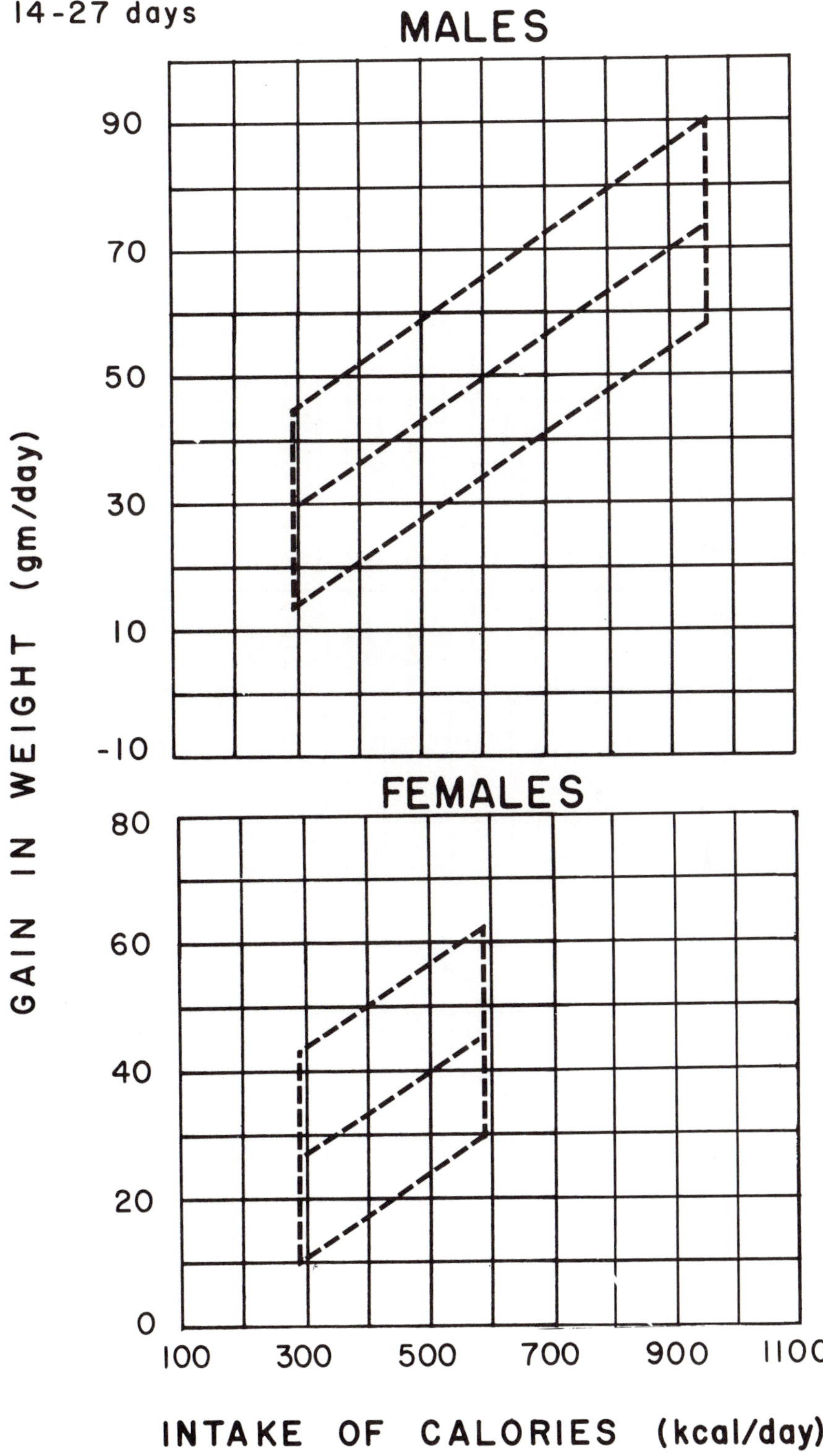
14-27 days
MALES
90
70
50
30
10
-10
GAIN IN WEIGHT (gm/day)
FEMALES
80
60
40
20
0
100
300
500
700
900
1100
INTAKE OF CALORIES (kcal/day)

Figure II–2.

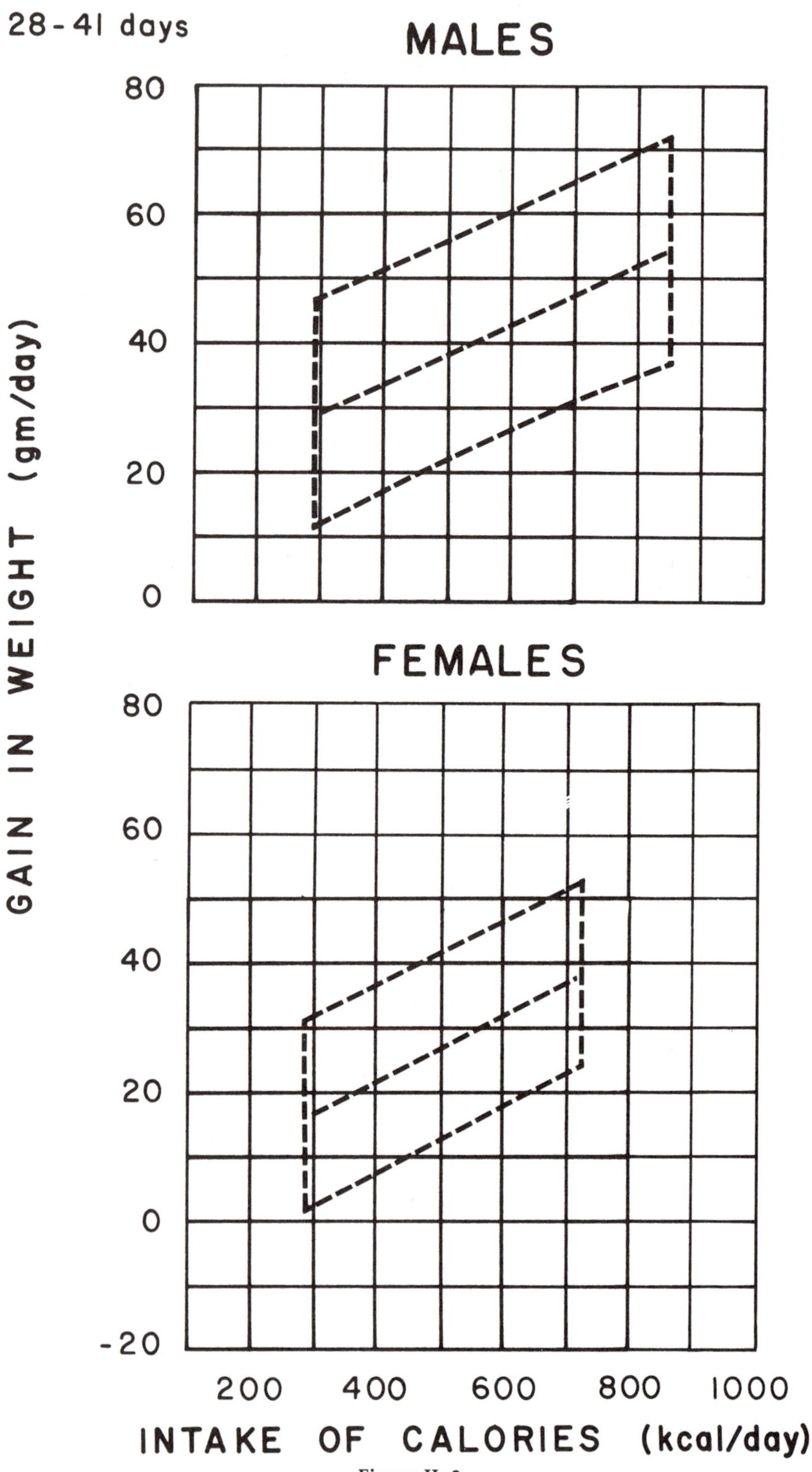
28-41 days
MALES
FEMALES
GAIN IN WEIGHT (gm/day)
80
60
40
20
0
-20
200
400
600
800
1000
INTAKE OF CALORIES (kcal/day)

Figure II–3.

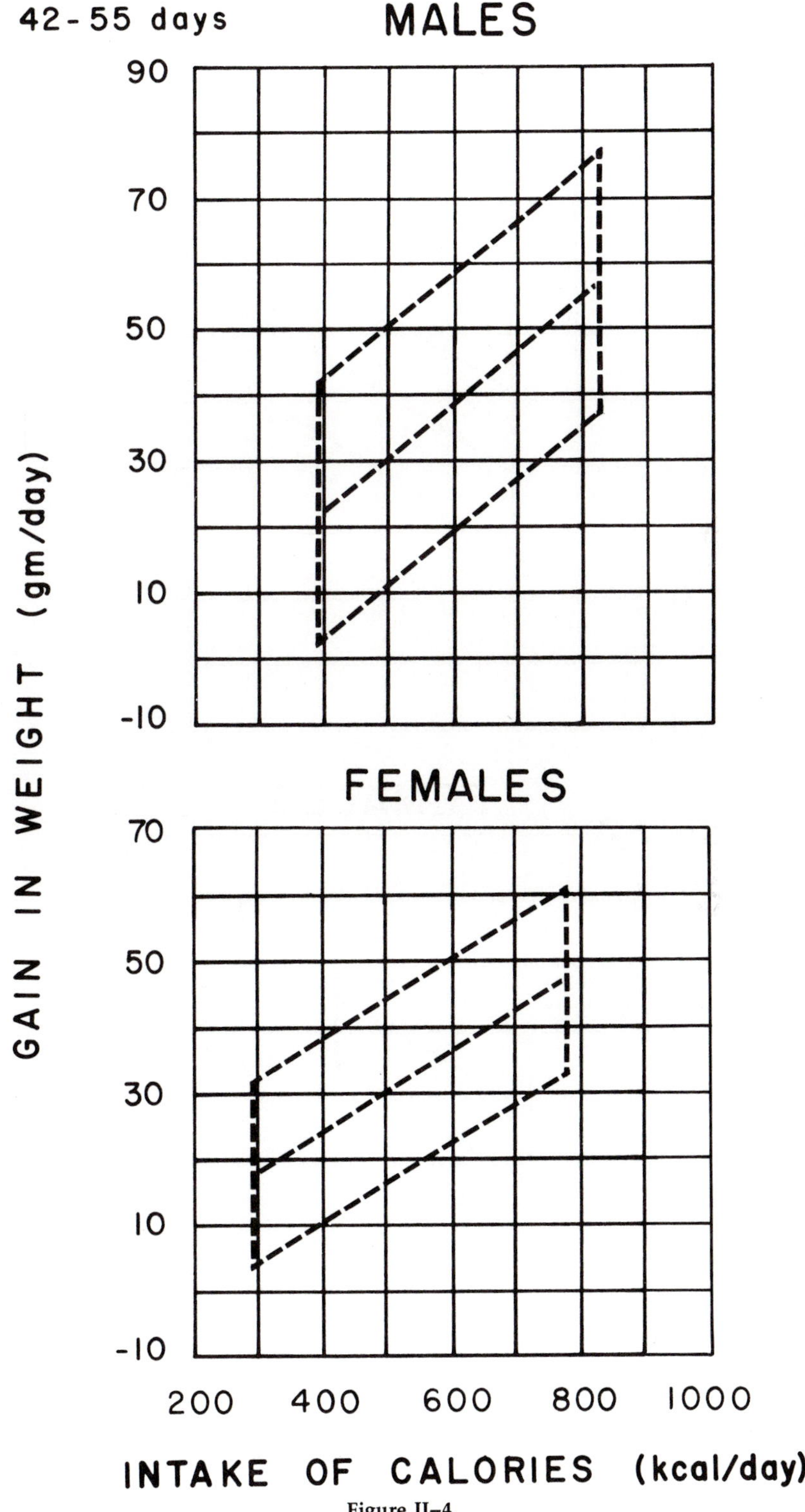
42-55 days
MALES
90
70
50
30
10
-10
FEMALES
70
50
30
10
-10
200
400
600
800
1000
GAIN IN WEIGHT (gm/day)
INTAKE OF CALORIES (kcal/day)

Figure II–4.

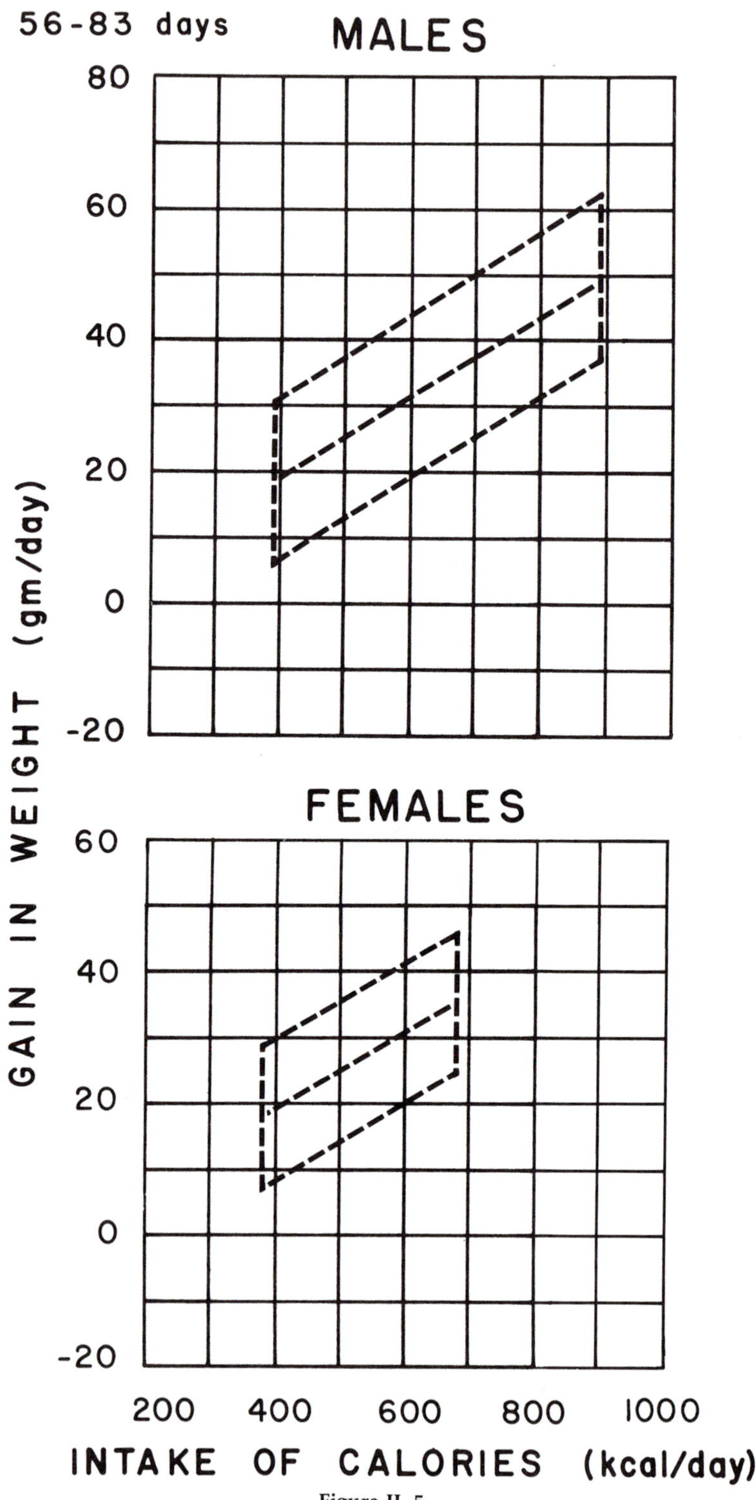
56-83 days
MALES
80
60
40
20
0
-20
GAIN IN WEIGHT (gm/day)
FEMALES
60
40
20
0
-20
200
400
600
800
1000
INTAKE OF CALORIES (kcal/day)

Figure II–5.

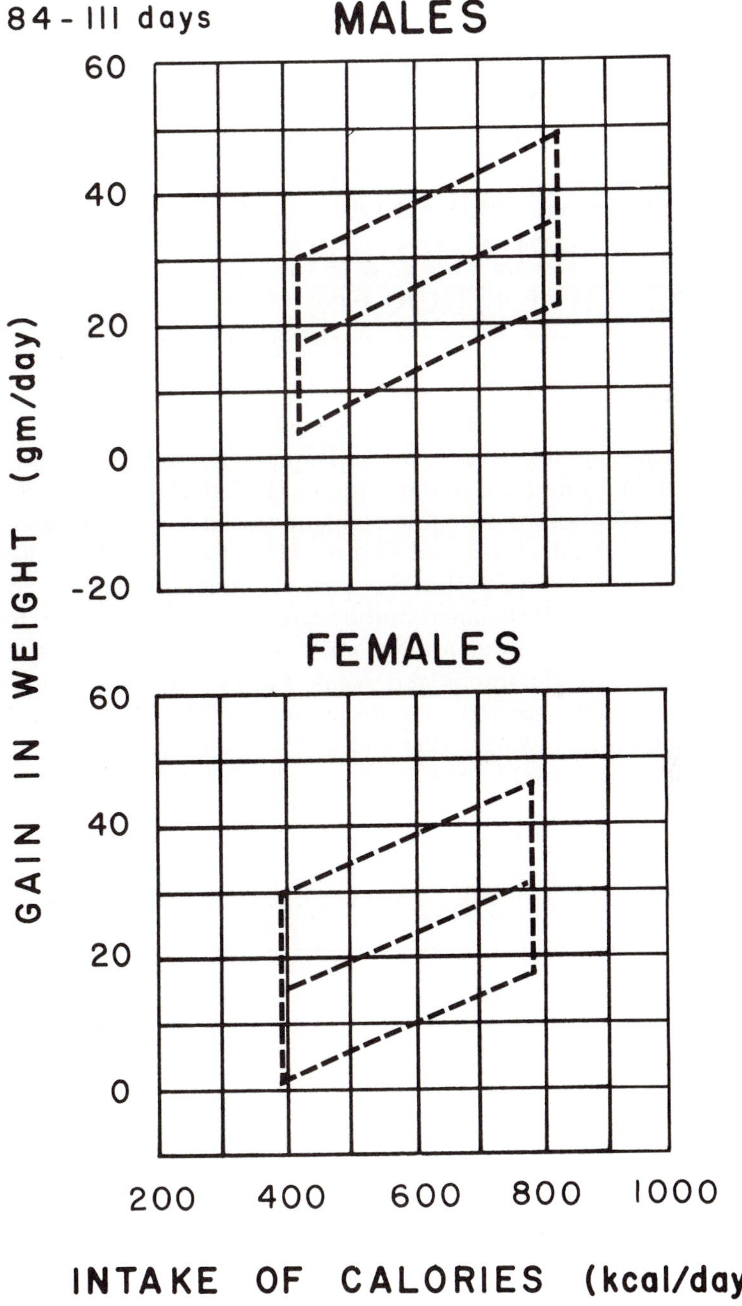
84 - 111 days
MALES
FEMALES
60
40
20
0
-20
60
40
20
0
GAIN IN WEIGHT (gm/day)
200
400
600
800
1000
INTAKE OF CALORIES (kcal/day)

Figure II–6.

Appendix III

URINARY EXCRETION OF NITROGEN AND RETENTION OF NITROGEN BY NORMAL FULLSIZE INFANTS: RELATION TO INTAKE OF NITROGEN

Data on urinary excretion of nitrogen in relation to intake of nitrogen by normal fullsize infants fed milks or milk-based formulas are summarized in Table III–1 and in Figures III–1 to III–5. Corresponding data on retention of nitrogen in relation to intake of nitrogen are summarized in Table III–2 and Figures III–6 to III–10. Each figure includes the regression and the 95 per cent confidence interval. These data concern metabolic balance studies carried out at the University of Iowa with infants fed human milk, milk-based formulas or formulas based on partially demineralized whey and nonfat cow milk. Both published and unpublished data are included. Published data are as follows: Fomon and May, 1958a and b; Fomon et al., 1958; Fomon, 1960; Fomon and Owen, 1962; Fomon and Filer, 1967. Studies with two other milk-based formulas (Formulas 5024A and 3215A) have

TABLE III–1 RELATION OF URINARY EXCRETION OF NITROGEN TO NITROGEN INTAKE

N*	Age Interval (days)	Regression† Equation	Correlation Coefficient	Residual Variance
76	8–30	$Y = .397x - 12.7$	.66	1881
84	31–60	$Y = .427x - 2.5$	.76	1206
78	61–90	$Y = .426x + 8.6$	.72	1642
79	91–120	$Y = .417x + 24.9$	.71	1468
63	121–180	$Y = .651x - 28.4$	.91	555

*Number of balance studies.

†Y is urinary excretion of nitrogen (mg/kg/day) and x is intake of nitrogen (mg/kg/day).

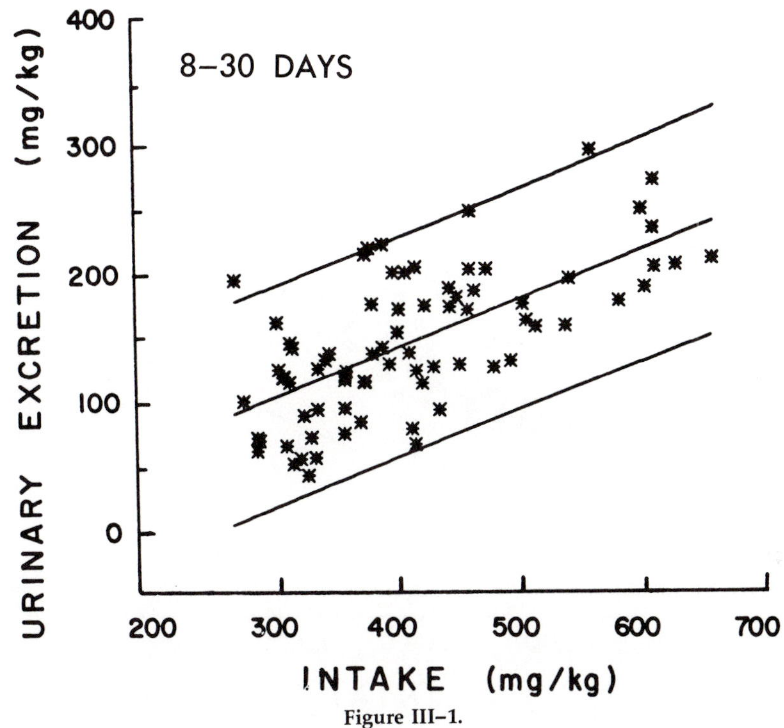

Figure III–1.

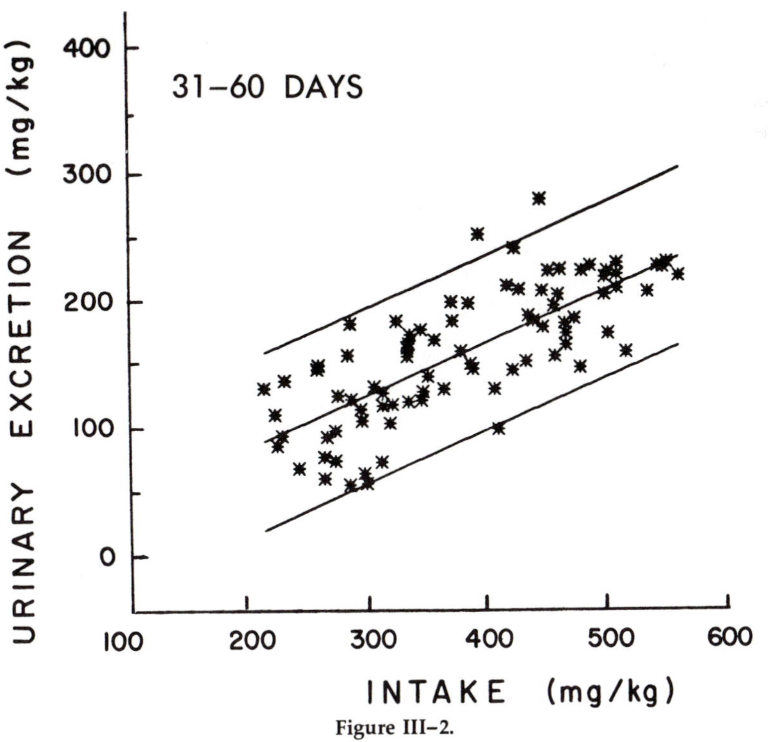

Figure III–2.

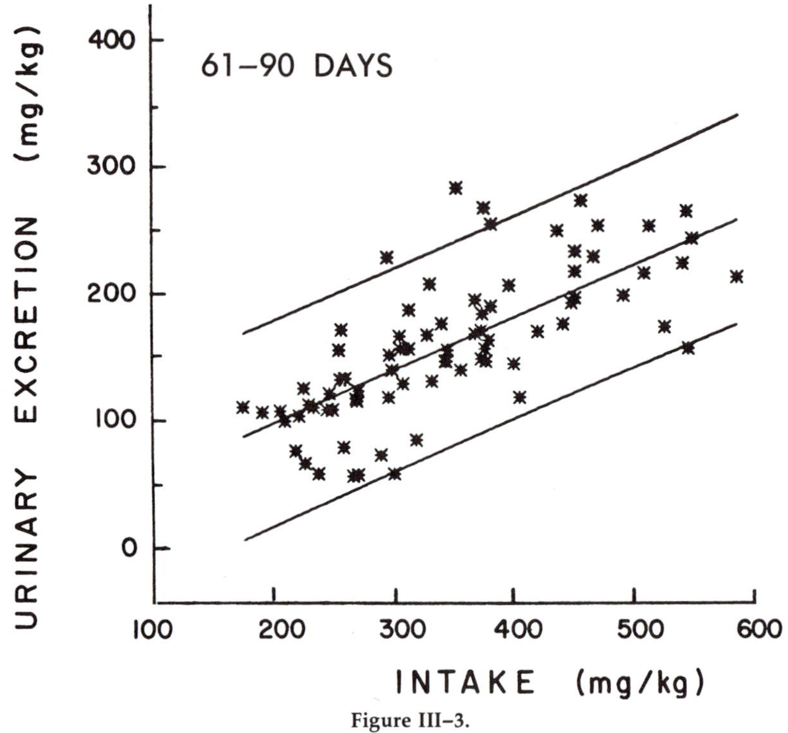

Figure III–3.

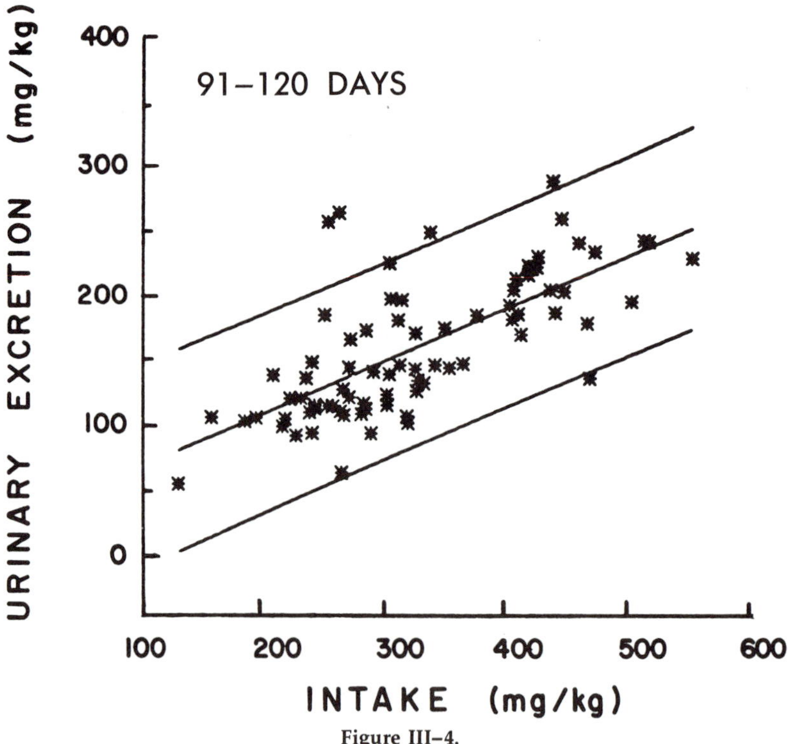

Figure III–4.

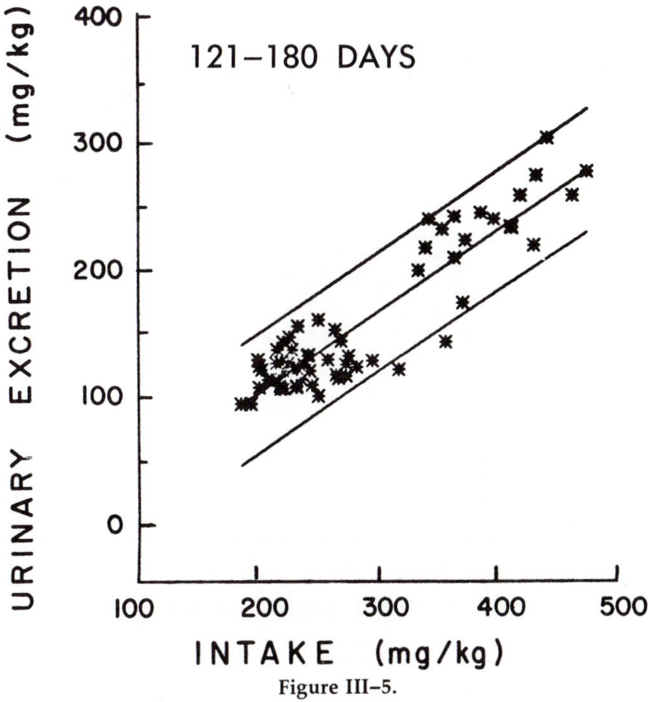

Figure III–5.

been described in detail (Fomon et al., 1971), but results of metabolic balance studies by infants receiving these formulas have not been published. Also unpublished are data from study of infants fed a formulation of Similac (Ross) containing a mixture of soy, coconut and corn oils (40–40–20), SMA (Wyeth) and NAN (Nestlé).

TABLE III–2 RELATION OF NITROGEN RETENTION TO NITROGEN INTAKE

N*	Age Interval (days)	Regression† Equation	Correlation Coefficient	Residual Variance
83	8–30	$Y = .482x - 5.2$	.70	2261
93	31–60	$Y = .412x + 1.0$	.71	1701
87	61–90	$Y = .403x - 4.7$	.73	1456
87	91–120	$Y = .379x - 5.1$	.70	1233
83	121–180	$Y = .436x - 69.0$	.86	427

*Number of balance studies.
†Y is retention of nitrogen (mg/kg/day) and x is intake of nitrogen (mg/kg/day).

8–30 DAYS
RETENTION (mg/kg)
INTAKE (mg/kg)
0
100
200
300
400
200
300
400
500
600
700

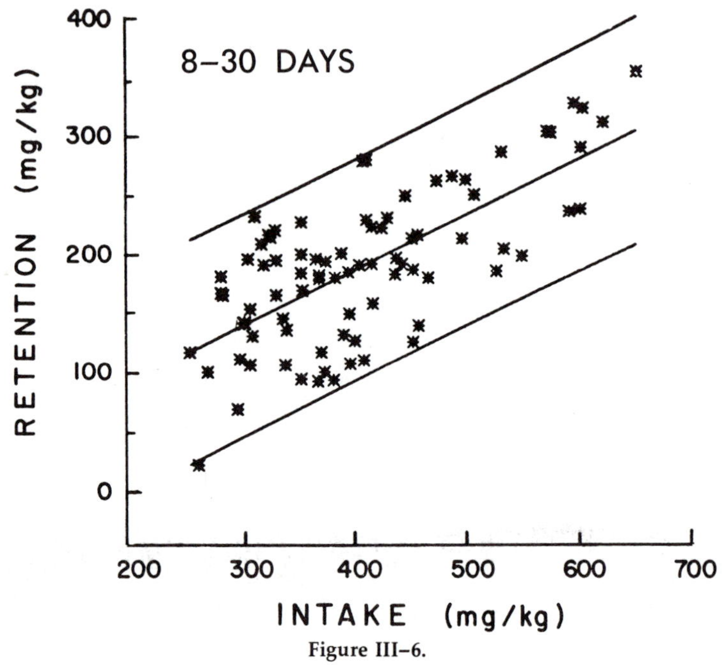

Figure III–6.

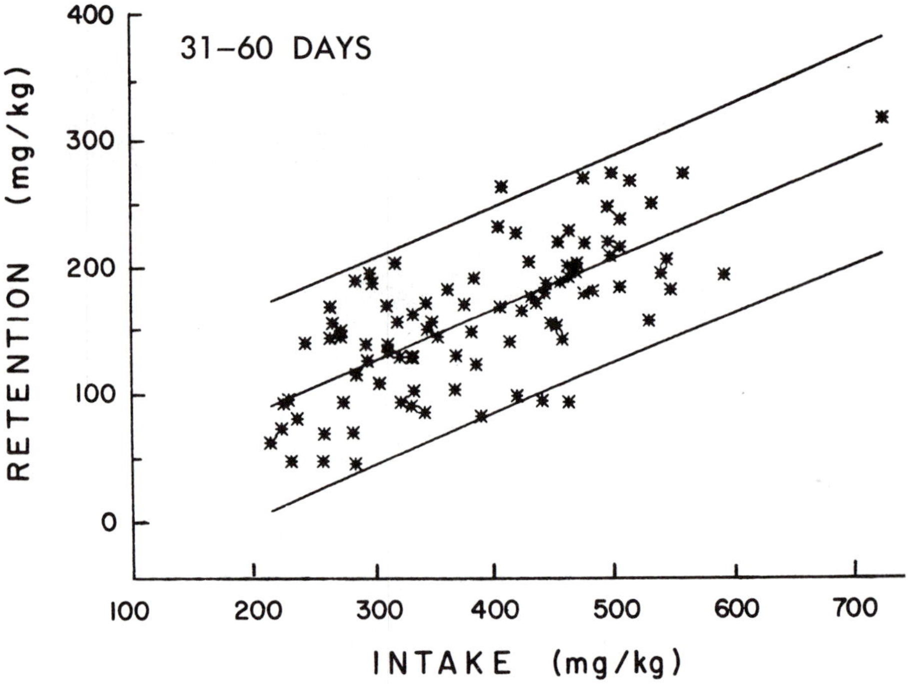

31–60 DAYS
RETENTION (mg/kg)
INTAKE (mg/kg)
0
100
200
300
400
100
200
300
400
500
600
700

Figure III–7.

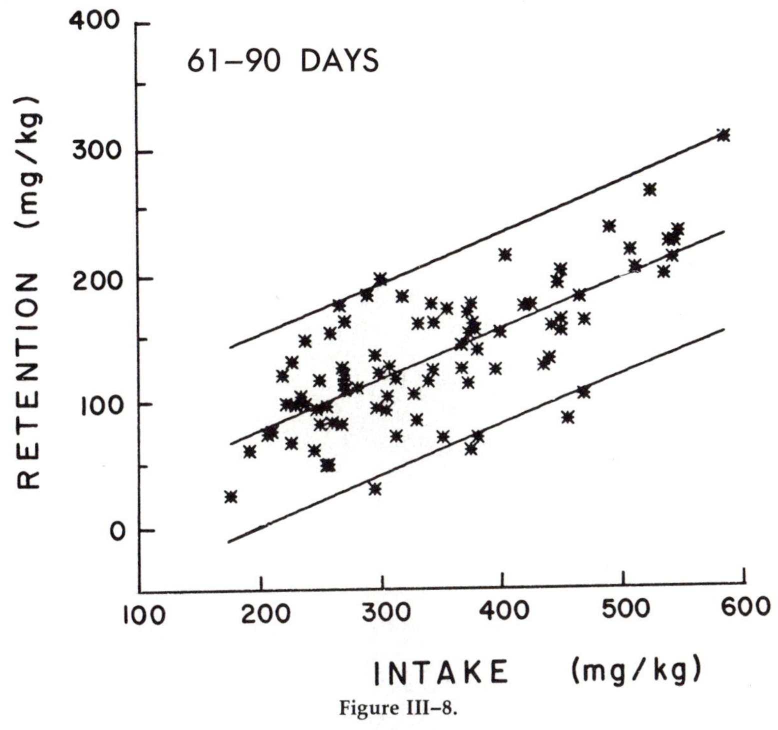

Figure III–8.

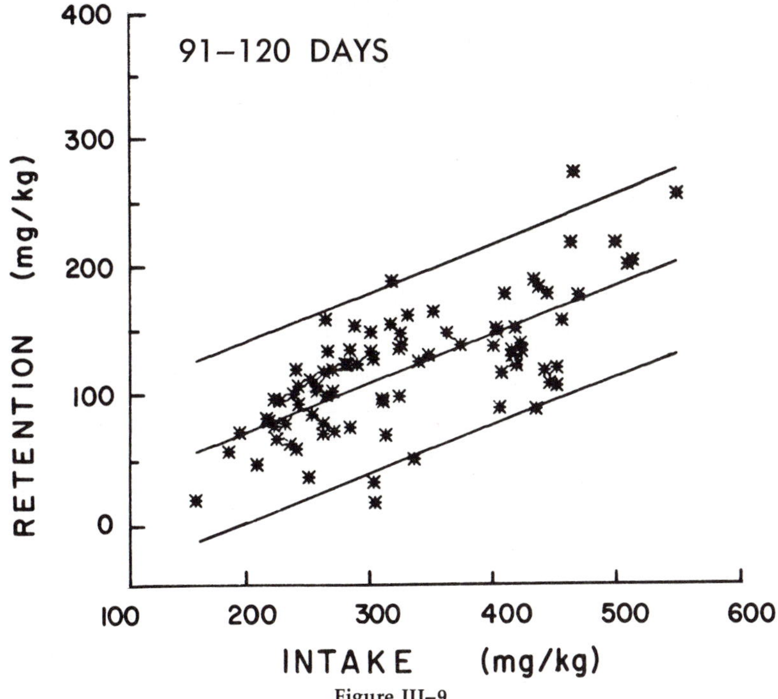

Figure III–9.

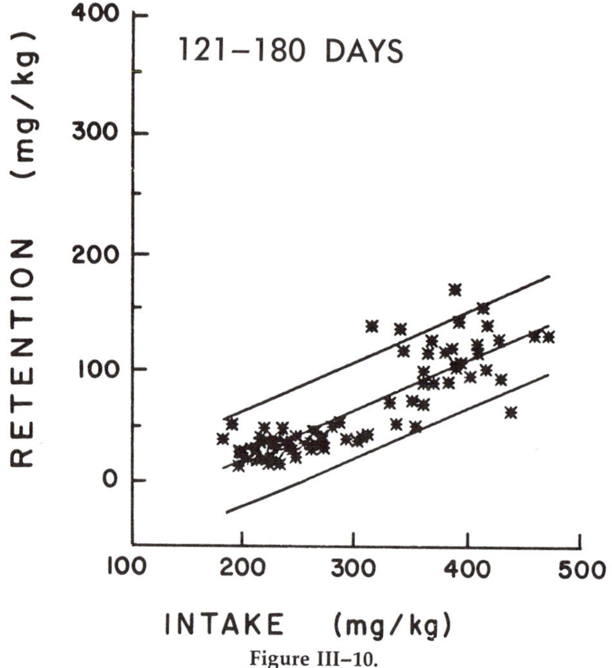

Figure III–10.

REFERENCES

Fomon, S. J.: Comparative study of adequacy of protein from human milk and cow's milk in promoting nitrogen retention by normal full-term infants. Pediatrics *26*:51, 1960.

Fomon, S. J., and Filer, L. J., Jr.: Amino acid requirements for normal growth. *In* Nyhan, W. L. (ed.): Amino Acid Metabolism and Genetic Variation. New York, McGraw-Hill Book Co., 1967, p. 391.

Fomon, S. J., and May, C. D.: Metabolic balance studies of normal full-term infants fed pasteurized human milk. Pediatrics *22*:101, 1958a.

Fomon, S. J., and May, C. D.: Metabolic balance studies of normal full-term infants fed a prepared formula providing intermediate amounts of protein. Pediatrics *22*:1134, 1958b.

Fomon, S. J., and Owen, G. M.: Retention of nitrogen by normal full-term infants receiving an autoclaved formula. Pediatrics *29*:1005, 1962.

Fomon, S. J., Thomas, L. N., Filer, L. J., Jr., Ziegler, E. E., and Leonard, M. T.: Food consumption and growth of normal infants fed milk-based formulas. Acta Paediatr. Scand. (Suppl. 223), 1971.

Fomon, S. J., Thomas, L. N., and May, C. D.: Equivalence of pasteurized and fresh human milk in promoting nitrogen retention by normal full-term infants. Pediatrics *22*:935, 1958.

Appendix IV

COLLECTION OF URINE AND FECES AND METABOLIC BALANCE STUDIES

Nutritional evaluation of infants may require quantitative collection of specimens of urine and/or feces for periods of 24 to 72 hours. Occasionally, a 72-hour metabolic balance study with accurate analysis of intake as well as urinary and fecal excretion will be helpful. It should be noted that intakes of infants receiving milk or formula as exclusive or major source of calories can be measured with much greater accuracy than can mixed diets of older children or adults. Methods previously described by the author and his associates (Fomon et al., 1958; Fomon, 1960) will therefore be reviewed in some detail. Alternate procedures for collecting urine or for carrying out metabolic balance studies with infants have been described by Newberry and Van Wyk (1955), Geist (1960), Hepner and Lubchenco (1960) and Winter et al. (1967).

Quantitative collections of urine from infants are necessary not only in metabolic balance studies but in determining urinary excretion of endogenous creatinine and hydroxyproline, in certain loading tests employed to detect nutritional and metabolic abnormalities, and in investigation or management of a variety of disorders unrelated to nutrition. Quantitative determination of fecal excretion of fat is often of great value even when a metabolic balance study is not performed. The method of Van de Kamer et al. (1949) is useful for this purpose, although it may lead to an overestimation of fat excretion when a large percentage of dietary fat is in the form of medium-chain triglycerides.

Many reports published during the past 60 years indicate the usefulness of metabolic balance studies in at least three areas of investigation: (1) comparison of nutritional properties of foods fed to comparable groups of human subjects or experimental animals under standardized conditions, (2) comparison of performance of normal subjects or experimental animals with those having certain metabolic abnormalities, and (3) comparison of the effects of two regimens of management with a single subject.

PROCEDURE

Metabolic Bed and Accessories

Metabolic beds of the design employed by the author and his associates (Fomon et al., 1958, 1962) are not commercially available but may be constructed from wood in almost any carpentry shop. A drawing indicating dimensions is presented in Figure IV–1 and a photograph appears in Figure IV–2.

Lacing the canvas to the frame of the metabolic bed, as shown in Figure IV–2, requires some practice, since the comfort of the infant is dependent upon having this canvas quite taut.

The restraining jacket used for maintaining the infant's position on the metabolic bed is shown in Figures IV–3 and IV–4.

Apparatus for Boys. Apparatus employed in urine collection from boys is prepared from a finger cot or finger of a rubber glove, adhesive tape, a glass adapter and a length of rubber tubing. A stellate perforation, large enough to accommodate the finger cot, is made toward one end of an 20-cm length of 7- to 10-cm-wide adhesive tape. The other end of the adhesive tape is cut down the center to make two tails that are 2.5 cm wide and at least 20 cm long (Fig. IV–5). Narrow strips of adhesive are cut diagonally to provide reinforcement pieces. The finger cot is fringed at the open end by making 6-mm cuts into

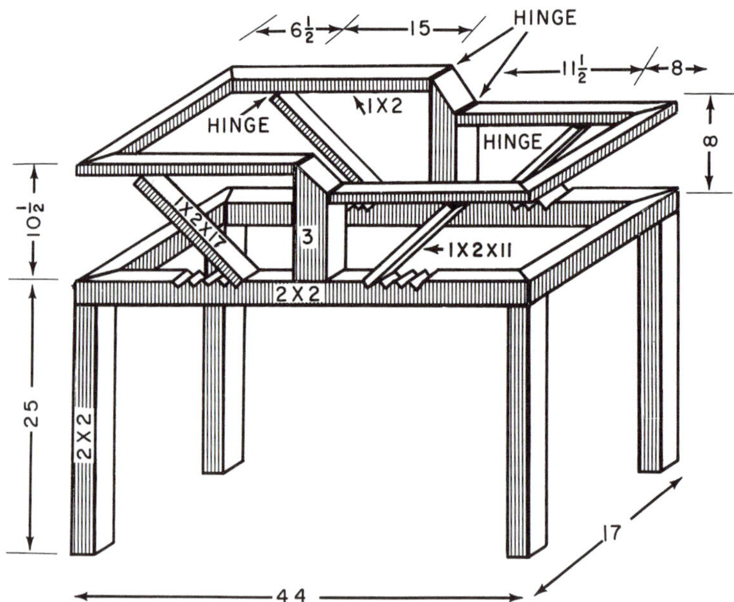

Figure IV–1 Dimensions (in inches) of frame for metabolic bed. (From Fomon, S. J., Thomas, L. N., Jensen, R. L., and Owen, G. M.: (Letter to Editor.) Metabolic bed. Pediatrics *29*:330, 1962.)

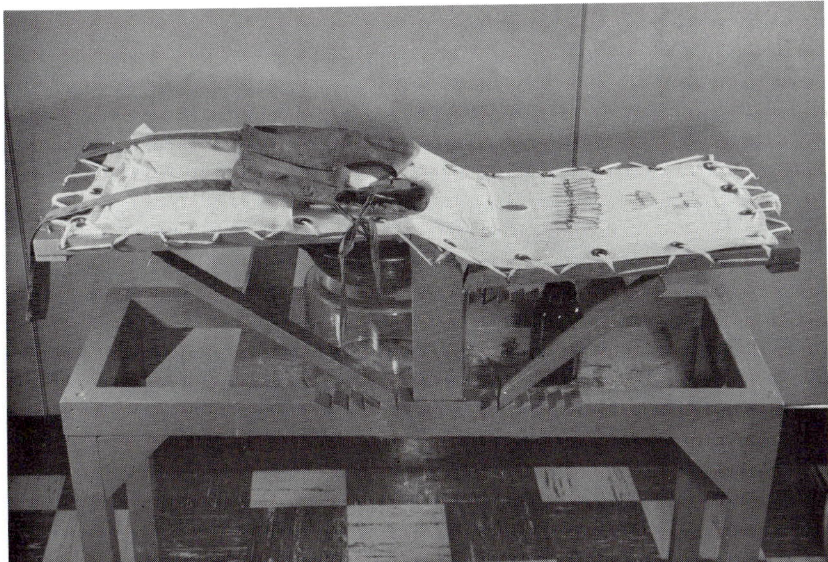

Figure IV–2 Metabolic bed. Canvas has been laced tightly to frame and jacket is in place. Foam rubber has been placed around the larger circular hole in the canvas and covered with plastic sheeting held in place with safety pins. The metal pan for collection of feces (urine plus feces from a girl) may be seen. A smaller circular hole in the canvas permits the rubber tubing of the apparatus for collection of urine from boys to be led directly to the collection jar.

A piece of plastic sheeting is attached as an apron across the abdomen of a girl and pinned to the lower portion of the restraining jacket to direct urine into the metal pan. (From Fomon, S. J., Thomas, L. N., Jensen, R. L., and May, C. D.: Determination of nitrogen balance of infants less than 6 months of age. Pediatrics *22*:94, 1958.)

it. The cot is then pushed through the stellate perforation from the adhesive side of the tape. The fringed end of the cot is pressed to the adhesive tape and anchored with the reinforcement pieces as shown in Figure IV–6.

The distal end of the finger cot is then cut off and the apparatus is placed on the infant so that the penis projects into the finger cot. The adhesive tails are brought around the upper posterior part of the thighs, leaving the anus exposed; tincture of benzoin applied to the appropriate area of skin affords some protection against excoriation that might otherwise arise from the tape. The free end of the finger cot is slipped over the glass adapter (made from a test tube) and secured with adhesive tape. The tapered end of the adapter is inserted into rubber tubing which leads to a urine collection bottle. Some practice is required in preparing this adapter for collection of urine. Leakage of urine will occur unless it is well constructed.

Apparatus for Girls. In metabolic balance studies with girls, an adapter for separate urine collection is not employed. A piece of polyethylene sheeting attached to the abdomen of the infant is

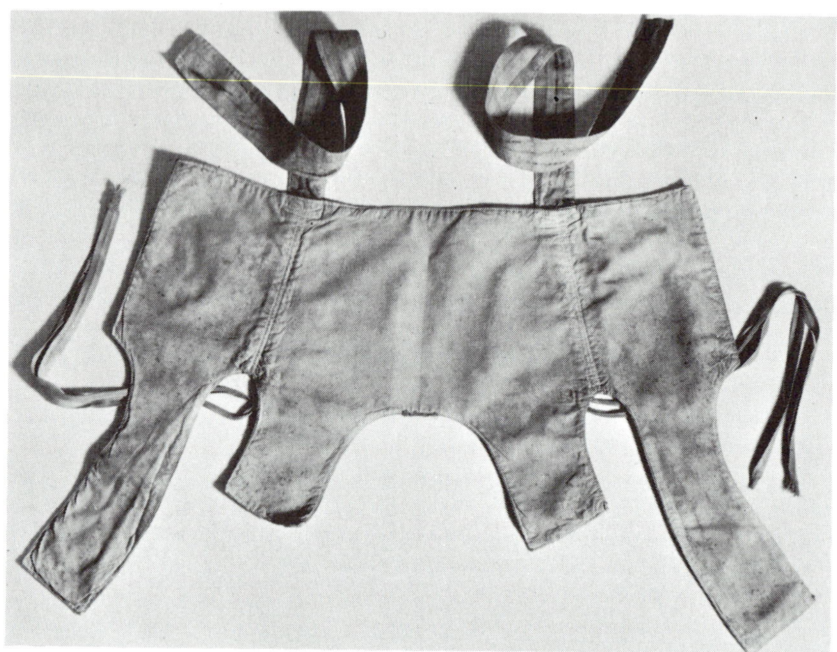

Figure IV–3 Jacket for maintaining infant in position on the metabolic bed. The wide upper ribbons are attached to the head of the metabolic bed and the narrow lower ribbons are attached to the sides of the bed (Fig. IV–2). The central panel of the jacket is pinned to the canvas of the bed. With the infant lying supine on the jacket, the side panels are folded toward the center (Fig. IV–4) and pinned about the thighs of the infant. (From Fomon, S. J., Thomas, L. N., Jensen, R. L., and May, C. D.: Determination of nitrogen balance of infants less than 6 months of age. Pediatrics *22*:94, 1958.)

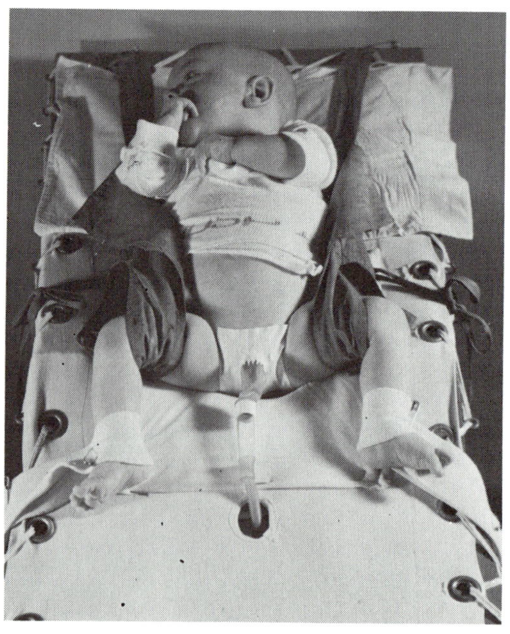

Figure IV–4 Infant positioned on metabolic bed. (From Fomon, S. J., Thomas, L. N., Jensen, R. L., and May, C. D.: Determination of nitrogen balance of infants less than 6 months of age. Pediatrics *22*: 94, 1958.)

Figure IV–5 Steps in preparation of apparatus for collection of urine from boys. *Front view. Left,* Adhesive tape has been cut in the proper shape with two long strips of the tape arising from a square central portion. The adhesive tape is mounted on a piece of cloth. A stellate incision for insertion of the finger cot has been made. *Center,* The finger cot has been inserted from the rear. *Right,* Additional small strips of adhesive tape have been placed around the base of the finger cot. The end of the finger cot is then cut off and the finger cot attached to a glass adapter from which rubber tubing leads to the collection bottle.

When the adapter has been removed from the cloth and the central portion of the adhesive surface placed against the pubis with the infant's penis projecting into the finger cot, the long strips of adhesive tape are made to encircle the posterior aspect of the upper portion of the thigh. (From Fomon, S. J., Thomas, L. N., Jensen, R. L., and May, C. D.: Determination of nitrogen balance of infants less than 6 months of age. Pediatrics *22*:94, 1958.)

directed through the larger opening of the canvas on which the infant lies. This sheeting extends into a metal pan so constructed that the central portion is elevated 0.25 to 0.5 cm above the remaining portion. The elevated portion of this pan is placed beneath the infant in such a fashion that feces will fall onto the central elevated area while urine will flow by gravity into the shallow depression around the periphery. The method employed in obtaining an estimate of separate urinary and fecal excretion from girls will be described.

The infant is restrained on the metabolic bed as indicated in Figure IV–4.

Feeding

Metabolic balance studies with infants are greatly facilitated if the sole food given during the balance study consists of formula

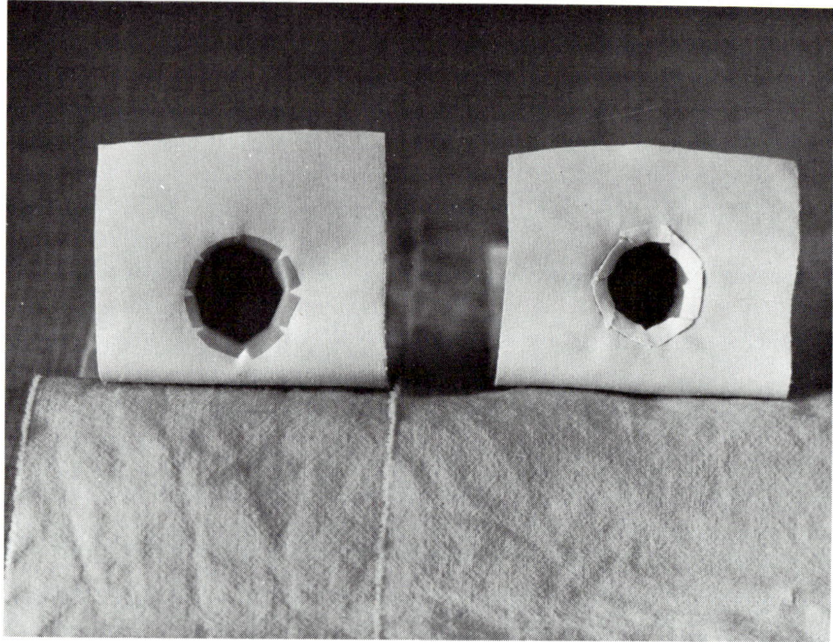

Figure IV–6 Steps in preparation of apparatus for collection of urine from boys. *Rear view. Left,* The finger cot has been inserted through the stellate incision in the adhesive tape. *Right,* Small strips of adhesive tape have been put in place. (From Fomon, S. J., Thomas, L. N., Jensen, R. L., and May, C. D.: Determination of nitrogen balance of infants less than 6 months of age. Pediatrics *22*:94, 1958.)

supplied by a manufacturer in ready-to-feed disposable units. It is then probable that composition of any one bottle of formula will be representative of that of all food consumed. However, several bottles of formula should be selected at random for analysis.

At 8 A.M. on the day the metabolic balance period is to begin, sufficient carmine is added to the milk or formula to contribute a definite pink color. The infant is placed on the metabolic bed at about 8:20 A.M., and the time of the first voiding of urine thereafter is noted. This specimen and all urine voided during the ensuing 72 hours is saved. Later in the day when the first stool containing carmine is passed, the carmine-containing portion is saved as the first aliquot of the 72-hour collection of feces. Seventy-two hours after the initial administration of carmine, another bottle of milk or formula with carmine is given. When the stool containing this second dose of carmine is passed, that portion of the stool not containing carmine is saved as the last aliquot of feces to be included in the 72-hour collection. The infant is then removed from the metabolic bed.

Collection of Urine and Feces

Urine and feces are collected separately from boys with the aid of the apparatus shown and described in Figures IV–2 to IV–6.

Two containers are used for storage of urine from each girl, one for "uncontaminated urine" and one for urine contaminated with feces. By close observation of the infants and by transferring urine to the storage container in the refrigerator soon after each voiding, it is usually possible to obtain the greater portion of the 72-hour specimen of urine uncontaminated with feces. The volumes of uncontaminated and contaminated urine are then measured and the contaminated specimen added to the fecal collection.

The *total excretion* of nitrogen (or mineral) is determined by multiplying the value for volume of urine with that for concentration of nitrogen in uncontaminated urine and adding to this result the volume times concentration of nitrogen in the fecal homogenate to which urine contaminated with feces was added.

The *urinary excretion* of nitrogen is estimated from the total volume of urine (contaminated with feces and uncontaminated) and the concentration of nitrogen in the uncontaminated urine. Fecal excretion of nitrogen is obtained by subtracting the estimated urinary excretion from the total.

MISUSE OF METABOLIC BALANCE STUDIES

Successful use of metabolic balance studies in nutritional evaluation of two foods under satisfactorily controlled circumstances or in comparison of performance of normal subjects with subjects having certain metabolic abnormalities has sometimes led individuals to conclude that results of metabolic balance studies are precisely quantitative. Were this true, it would be possible on the basis of continuously or serially performed balance studies between two specified ages, to make an accurate calculation of the change in one or another aspect of body composition. For example, the change in nitrogen or calcium content of the body could be calculated; from the change in nitrogen content, the change in protein content could be estimated, and from the change in calcium content, the change in skeletal mass could be estimated.

As an example, one might consider a normal infant with a birth weight of 3500 gm. If protein comprised 11 per cent of body weight, protein content of the body at birth (assuming that nitrogen accounts for 16 per cent by weight of protein) would be 61 gm. The mean retention of nitrogen in three-day metabolic balance studies, performed biweekly from birth until six months of age, with the infant receiving a high-protein formula (3.5 gm protein in 100 ml), might be 1.25 gm/day

(Fomon, 1961) or 228 gm in 182 days. The total content of nitrogen in the body at six months of age would be 228 gm + 61 gm = 289 gm. With an estimated body weight of 8.28 kg at six months of age, protein would account for 21.8 per cent of the body weight.

Because a protein content of the body equal to 21.8 per cent of body weight is far more than has been found by direct chemical analysis of the human body (Chapter 3), it is clear that the calculations given above are not justified.

It seems probable that several factors must be considered jointly in explaining the falsely high body content of protein calculated on the basis of nitrogen balance studies. Of these, the most important are cumulative errors inherent in balance techniques, nitrogen loss in sweat and desquamated epithelium and, especially, differences in retention of nitrogen during balance studies and in intervals between balance studies. Confirmation or refutation of the conclusion based on metabolic balance studies – that feeding of high-protein diets results in accumulation of relatively large amounts of protein in the body – must certainly come from assessments of body composition of normal infants made with techniques other than metabolic balance studies (Fomon and Owen, 1962).

Similar errors are inherent in calculating body content of calcium, phosphorus, sodium and other minerals from results of metabolic balance studies. With some substances, e.g., sodium and potassium, failure to measure losses from skin will introduce a much greater error than is the case with nitrogen or calcium.

REFERENCES

Fomon, S. J.: Comparative study of adequacy of protein from human milk and cow's milk in promoting nitrogen retention by normal full-term infants. Pediatrics *26*:51, 1960.

Fomon, S. J.: Nitrogen balance studies with normal full-term infants receiving high intakes of protein. Comparisons with previous studies employing lower intakes of protein. Pediatrics *28*:347, 1961.

Fomon, S. J., and Owen, G. M.: Comment on metabolic balance studies as a method of estimating body composition of infants. With special consideration of nitrogen balance studies. Pediatrics *29*:495, 1962.

Fomon, S. J., Thomas, L. N., Jensen, R. L., and May, C. D.: Determination of nitrogen balance of infants less than 6 months of age. Pediatrics *22*:94, 1958.

Fomon, S. J., Thomas, L. N., Jensen, R. L., and Owen, G. M.: (Letter to Editor.) Metabolic bed. Pediatrics *29*:330, 1962.

Geist, D. I.: Round-the-clock specimens. Amer. J. Nursing *60*:1300, 1960.

Hepner, R., and Lubchenco, L. O.: A method for continuous urine and stool collection in young infants. Pediatrics *26*:828, 1960.

Newberry, E., and Van Wyk, J. J.: A technique for quantitative urine collection in the metabolic study of infants and young children. Pediatrics *16*:667, 1955.

Van de Kamer, J. H., Ten Bokkel Huinink, H., and Weijers, H. A.: Rapid method of determining fat in feces. J. Biol. Chem. *177*:347, 1949.

Winter, J. S. D., Baker, L., and Eberlein, W. R.: A mobile metabolic crib for infants. Amer. J. Dis. Child. *114*:150, 1967.

INDEX

Page numbers in *italics* indicate figures; those followed by a T signify a table.